RACING POST · RACING & FOOTBALL · OUTLO

FOOTBALL/ANNUAL
17/18

PRESENTED WITH THE COMPLIMENTS OF

Editor *Dan Sait*

Contributors *Joe Champion, Paul Charlton, Dan Childs, Michael Cox, Steve Davies, Alex Deacon, Danny Hayes, Glenn Jeffreys, Mark Langdon, James Milton, Kevin Pullein, Dan Sait*

Data editor *Chris Mann*

Cover design *Jay Vincent*

Published in 2017 by Racing Post Books,

27 Kingfisher Court, Hambridge Road, Newbury, Berkshire, RG14 5SJ

Copyright © 2017 Racing Post Books

A catalogue record for this book is available from the British Library.

ISBN 978-1-910497-12-8

ISSN 977-1753-334-506

Printed and bound in Great Britain by Buxton Press

CONTENTS

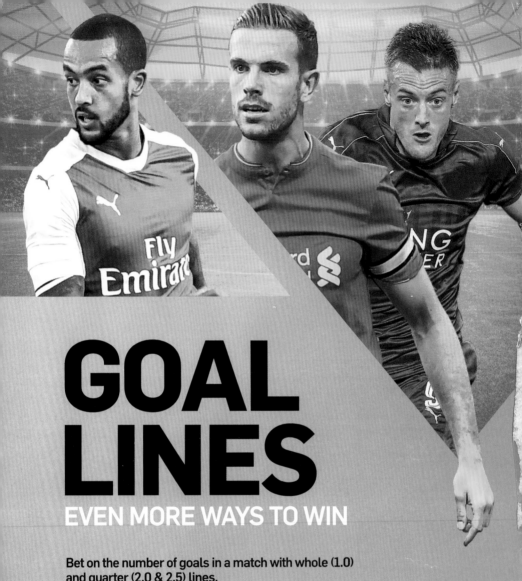

GOAL LINES

EVEN MORE WAYS TO WIN

Bet on the number of goals in a match with whole (1.0) and quarter (2.0 & 2.5) lines.

betfair EXCHANGE

EDITOR'S INTRODUCTION

If it really is the hope that kills you, we could be in trouble. England's youth teams have been disconcertingly impressive over the summer of 2017, winning the under-20 World Cup and Toulon Tournament, reaching the under-17 and under-19 European Championship finals – the latter kicked off as we went to press – and only departing the under-21 European Championships at the semi-final stage. Albeit in that all-too familiar style of a penalty shootout defeat to Germany.

False dawns are as much an English speciality as afternoon tea and, well, losing to Germany on penalties, but there really are green shoots of progress emerging. A structured, concerted attempt to improve England at youth level is bearing fruit, even if it will take time to filter through to the seniors.

Of course the real test lies in the next stage – getting playing time for the kids. The early summer transfer market has been a frenzy of manic spending, with the value of money seemingly utterly lost among the broadcasting riches bestowed upon clubs. Average players will soon cost more than new stadiums and with cash so freely available it seems less likely than ever that fresh-faced hopefuls will be able to break into the top teams.

However, steps are being made in the right direction and those youngsters who do prove themselves too good to ignore on this pitfall-laden path can surely look forward to a bright future for club and country.

Of course, more money doesn't always mean greater quality, and the fact that Leicester were the last English side standing in the Champions League says much about the Premier League – plucky, lucky, but not a patch on the true heavyweights of Europe.

Maybe this season will be different. Manchester United's Europa League success means England have five Champions League representatives this term, while clubs of the stature of Arsenal and Everton should surely be able to make a serious impact in Uefa's second-tier club competition.

Glory might still be too much to hope for, but with a World Cup to follow the domestic season we certainly shouldn't be starved of entertainment in 2017-18. And with the Racing & Football Outlook guiding you through the campaign and the Racing Post delivering your daily hit of punting expertise, readers can look forward to a season as profitable as it will be action-packed.

Dan Sait

Once in a lifetime event likely to prove just that

1 Foxes fairy tale was a one-season wonder

This time last year all the bookmakers were sending out press releases telling us football punting habits had changed. Inspired by Leicester's stunning 5,000-1 title success in 2015-16, the likes of Middlesbrough were being backed to win the Premier League.

What followed was total domination by the big six of Chelsea, Tottenham, Man City, Liverpool, Arsenal and Man United to see normal service resume.

Seventh-place Everton finished eight points behind a Manchester United team who concentrated on the Europa League and 32 points off champions Chelsea, while Southampton finished eighth on 46 points which was only six better than 17th-place Watford.

Given the financial power of the big boys that gap is unlikely to close any time soon and Leicester's success was nothing more than a glorious fluke.

2 White Hart pain as Tottenham head to Wembley

How Tottenham cope with their one-season switch to Wembley as they wait for their new stadium to be built will determine whether they can launch another title bid, but the omens don't look good judging by their 2016-17 performances.

Spurs were sensational at White Hart Lane, finishing with a record of 17 wins and two draws from their 19 games with a goal difference in those fixtures of plus 38.

However, they fell apart when switching to Wembley for their European outings, losing in the Champions League to Monaco and Bayer Leverkusen, and drawing 2-2 with Gent in the Europa League.

The only victory came against a poor CSKA Moscow side and Mauricio Pochettino needs to find a solution to the Wembley hoodoo.

3 Saints left praying for a goalscorer

Southampton averaged 14.5 shots per game in the Premier League and Arsenal averaged 14.9 but Saints scored just 41 goals compared to the Gunners' 77.

Saints notched a woeful 17 league goals at St Mary's, with Nathan Redmond top-scoring with seven. January arrival Manolo Gabbiadini looked the answer initially but fired blanks in his last eight appearances and injury-prone Charlie Austin can't be relied upon to last the pace.

Interestingly, Austin scored in seven matches last season and all of them were the first goal.

4 Liverpool were the team to follow in big matches

Consistency was not Liverpool's strong point and they came up short against the lesser lights, but Jurgen Klopp's men are well worth following in the crunch clashes.

Liverpool won at Arsenal and Chelsea, drew at Tottenham, Manchester United and Manchester City, and none of the top teams were able to win away at Anfield.

The Reds also beat both north London clubs easily at home and downed the Citizens 1-0 on Merseyside.

5 New stadium brings problems for Hammers

The switch to Stratford proved a shocker for West Ham, who won only seven league games at the London Stadium after leaving Upton Park.

It may take a few more years for home advantage to again become a decisive a factor for the unhappy Hammers with the fans unable to recreate the intimidating Boleyn Ground atmosphere.

Normal service resumes as Blues capture title – but logic dictates another shock

After the seismic shock of Leicester's 5,000-1 Premier League triumph in 2015-16, last season was more about gentle ripples. Summer gambles on the Manchester clubs went astray as Antonio Conte's Chelsea (11-2) left Pep Guardiola and Jose Mourinho trailing in their wake while Tottenham finished above Arsenal for the first occasion during Alex Iwobi's lifetime.

The ante-post relegation betting suggested promoted trio Middlesbrough, Burnley and Hull were as doomed as a relationship between two Love Island contestants.

Hull and Boro duly obliged but Sean Dyche's Clarets stayed up, even managing to record an away win – at the 18th attempt – against Crystal Palace at the end of April.

Two of the top flight's most reliable trends – Arsenal being crap but always finishing in the top four and Sunderland being crap but always avoiding relegation – came to an end and there can't have been many more depressing experiences than watching the Black Cats under David Moyes.

Selling goal minutes in Swansea versus Crystal Palace wouldn't have been much fun either. It finished 5-4 to Swansea, having been 1-1 after 66 minutes – and, ludicrously, Palace were 4-3 up at the start of injury time.

On the subject of costly spread trades, hands up who sold goalscorers' shirt numbers in Borussia Dortmund's Champions League clash with Legia Warsaw? Not only did the Germans win 8-4 but two of Legia's goals came from striker Aleksandar Prijovic, who wears number 99.

Back in the Prem, Tottenham's Harry Kane retained the Golden Boot despite having only two goals at the start of November.

Kane finished in style, scoring seven times in his last two games and proving that, when it comes to being top goalscorer, it's not how

you start that matters but how you finish.

That was also true in the Football League as ante-post jollies Newcastle (15-8), Sheffield United (6-1) and Portsmouth (9-2) claimed their respective titles – just about.

Blades backers had an early sweat with the League One side taking just one point from their first four matches but they soon hit their stride, finishing with 100 points.

Newcastle and Portsmouth were both given Jamie Spencer-style hold-up rides before getting up in the shadow of the winning post.

Aston Villa fans will have hoped their club would play a pivotal role in the Championship title race and so it proved as Jack Grealish's 89th-minute equaliser against Brighton on the final day handed top spot to Rafa Benitez's Magpies.

Portsmouth's triumph was even more of a smash-and-grab raid. Doncaster topped League Two for 129 days, Plymouth for 102 days, and Pompey for just 33 minutes but boss Paul Cook – with his tongue slightly in his cheek – gleefully declared that the league table never lies.

'Don't back the Champions League holders' is one of the cast-iron rules of football betting but Real Madrid ruined that system, becoming the first club to retain Europe's top prize since Milan in 1990.

Real also won La Liga, meaning Zinedine Zidane has claimed a league title and two

The moment Cristiano Ronaldo realised he forgot to back himself to win the Golden Boot at 25-1

Champions League medals in his first 18 months as coach. Zizou may not have been much of a player but he seems to have got the hang of this management lark.

Zidane had a bit of help from Cristiano Ronaldo, who ended the Champions League campaign with hat-tricks against Bayern Munich and Atletico Madrid before a brace in the final against Juventus.

Fans of missed opportunities may be interested to learn that Ronny drifted to 25-1 for the Golden Boot having scored only twice in six group games. Mind you, those odds weren't overly generous given that he was eight goals behind some bloke called Messi at that stage.

Manchester United's habit of flopping as short-priced favourites in Premier League matches forced Jose Mourinho to chuck all his eggs in the Europa League basket.

Indeed, Jose became so obsessed with the competition that Uefa considered taking out a restraining order but the Portuguese gaffer had the last laugh.

United were hot favourites at 5-1 before the last-32 stage and who can forget their magnificent wins over St-Etienne, Rostov, Anderlecht, Celta Vigo and Ajax? Or perhaps that should be 'who can remember?' …

But which team are we backing to win this season's Premier League? The last two champions, Leicester and Chelsea, finished 14th and 10th in the campaigns preceding their triumphs – an average position of 12th.

By the rock-solid logic of that small sample size, the 2017-18 champions will be last term's 12th-placed team … flipping heck – it's Leicester again. Get on!

Stats matter but it's how we use them that affects our success

Yes, but what do they mean? When I started writing about football there very few stats. Scorers, results, appearances. I do not remember any more.

That was 30 years ago. Today there are loads of stats. Every pundit supports their argument with figures. But how often do their numbers really prove their point?

For bettors there is an even more important question. Stats tell us what happened before. We want to know what will happen next. Which stats from the past, if any, are good predictors of the future?

Michael J. Mauboussin is managing director and head of global financial strategies at Credit Suisse. In a book called The Success Equation he wrote: "Statistics are widely used in a range of fields. But rarely do the people who use statistics stop and ask how useful they really are."

We should try to discover if and when statistics tell us something about what will happen next.

A few years ago analysts at Manchester City detected a link in football between winning and line breaks. Line breaks was a concept borrowed from rugby. In football it meant getting the ball to one of your players behind a line of the opposition's defence. The more often you broke lines of the opposition's defence the more likely you were to win.

Line break stats, though, are not released to you and me.

The first stats packaged for the public, about 20 years ago, were simple ones – shots, corners, free kicks and possession. But they are the sort of things we probably have in mind when we talk about the run of play. And, pleasingly, they are reliable indicators of what will happen in other games.

When watching a match you will sometimes feel that a goal is coming. Why? One team, you might say, look like they will score. Why? They have had a lot

Tottenham had the most shots and scored the most goals in the Premier League last season

in the next match and a variety of stats from previous matches. I did this for many seasons and many competitions, including the Premier League, La Liga, Bundesliga, Serie A and Ligue 1.

The stats from previous matches were goals, shots, corners, free kicks and possession. In every competition I found the same thing. There was a correlation between goals in the next match and each stat from previous matches. It was weaker for free kicks than the others, but for all the others it was strong and similar.

Yes, similar. Some of the things a team did in previous games when trying to score told us as much about the goals they would score in the next game as the goals they scored in previous games.

Now there are more sophisticated stats, such as expected goals – a calculation that takes into account the position of a shot and how frequently goals have been scored from there. But older, simpler stats can tell us a lot. Shots on target are good predictors but, interestingly, no better than shots in total.

Academic researchers have suggested something even more startling – that the best predictor of how many goals a striker will score in a season is not how many goals they scored last season, or even the accuracy of past shots, but the number of past shots, irrespective of whether those went high, wide or handsome. I do not go that far. What I say is that some basic stats reveal a lot, and about the same amount.

Sometimes all stats send the same message, which should reassure us that the team have been getting the results they deserved. Other times stats contradict each other. Maybe a team have had a lot of shots but not scored many goals.

Do not trust one stat and dismiss the others. Assume instead that each stat has captured a different fragment of the truth. If that is so, you will get closer to the whole truth if you put the stats together. That is what I found in my studies. Each stat on its own tells you something. Together they tell you more.

of the ball, won free-kicks, forced corners and fired shots.

Sometimes a goal does not come. Still, we should think better of a team who do not score from, say, 20 shots than a team who do not score from, say, ten shots. Neither scored today but if both do the same things next time the first team are more likely to score than the second.

Any description must be incomplete, and therefore inaccurate, even when the statements it contains are not plain wrong. We can get a better understanding if we have more than one description, different sources of information.

I studied the relationship between goals

Contrasting styles of leading contenders should provide a thrilling title race

The Premier League markets itself as the most unpredictable league around and a quick glance at the title odds from across Europe proves the point nicely. In Spain, Germany and France there are only two sides below 20-1 to win the title. In Italy it's a healthier five, but in England, there are six – in fact, all six are generally priced 12-1 or shorter.

Indeed, it's about time the Premier League featured a proper title race. The last three league campaigns turned into a procession, and while neither of the last two winners were predictable at the start of the campaign – Leicester in particular – not since 2013-14 has there been a genuinely nailbiting title fight going into the final few games.

This season's title race is unusual because there are no new managers at the top of the Premier League. Whereas this time last season Jose Mourinho, Pep Guardiola and Antonio Conte had all recently taken charge of their clubs, now there can be no excuses about 'transition seasons' this time around.

Intriguingly, the top six all feature managers of different nationalities and each club has a distinct playing style, which means the tactical battles between the top sides this season should be thoroughly interesting.

Guardiola's Manchester City start as favourites, and clearly a huge improvement is expected at the Etihad – but last season's experiences were hardly convincing.

Guardiola seemed genuinely surprised by the fast-paced, scrappy nature of English football, complaining about the number of long balls and the extent to which winning 'second balls' was important in midfield.

Whereas he started with an exciting, flexible 4-3-3 system with the full-backs drifting inside, technical players deployed out of position at centre-back and Kevin De Bruyne and David Silva together in the engine room, by the end of the campaign Guardiola had switched to a much more rigid 4-2-3-1 system, which felt little different to the way Roberto Mancini and Manuel Pellegrini set out their sides. Are City any closer to title winners after a year under Guardiola?

Defending champions Chelsea will surely suffer from the added pressures of European football this season and it's notable that the last two title winners haven't been forced to juggle continental competition and the Premier League. Although often considered in terms of fitness and recovery times, extra time on the training ground is also essential in terms of tactical planning as it allows a manager to spend multiple days working on his gameplan for the upcoming opposition.

Conte drilled his players strictly in a tactical sense last season, working on team shape almost every day, but his amount of time on the training ground will be significantly reduced. Besides, teams eventually found a way to nullify Chelsea's 3-4-3 last season and Conte may look to find a new shape.

Mourinho's Manchester United weren't truly part of last season's title race but demonstrated their ability to clinch trophies by winning both the League Cup and Europa League, and it feels like there will be a significant improvement this season.

Their defence has looked solid since the Louis van Gaal days, and with Paul Pogba

Antonio Conte and Pep Guardiola head a stellar cast of managerial talent in the Premier League

likely to benefit from a proper pre-season and Romelu Lukaku arriving upfront to provide runs into the channels, United pack more attacking punch. Their problem last season was the number of home draws against poor sides, but Lukaku is the type of striker who will bully inferior opponents.

Tottenham look the most underrated side coming into the new campaign. Although their transfer business hasn't been as eye-catching as other sides, Mauricio Pochettino's young team have improved steadily under the Argentine – 64, 70 and 86 points in his three campaigns – because of their increased levels of tactical cohesion and because individuals are getting better. Playing at Wembley will be a notable handicap, but 86 points again could well clinch the title.

Arsenal have slipped back to being outsiders once again and now have to face the Europa League, with Thursday matches and potentially extra travel to far-flung destinations. It's difficult to see a significant improvement upon last season.

Finally, Jurgen Klopp's Liverpool are another team who have strengthened well, but questions persist about whether Klopp's favoured style of high-intensity football is workable over the entire course of a Premier League campaign, especially with the added pressures of the Champions League.

Excellent against top sides but toothless when attempting to break down deep defences last season, it's difficult to see what will have changed for 2017-18 to make them potential champions.

But this a genuine six-way title fight, between six very different sides coached by six very different managers. The Premier League can't boast the favourites for the Champions League any more, but its title fight should be the best in Europe.

ASK THE JURY

Mark Langdon
RP Football Editor

Last season's best bet?
Chelsea to win the Premier League. It looked unwise after those early defeats to Liverpool and Arsenal but Antonio Conte is one of the world's best coaches and came good in the end.

And what was your head-in-hands betting moment?
Plymouth losing the League Two title on the final day having been odds-on. I put them up in last year's Annual and the professional pride took a blow, but not as much as my pocket!

How will the Premier League title race shape up?
Manchester City can take the title. Pep Guardiola has had a year to suss everything out and they are signing well.

And who wins the other three English leagues?
Sheffield Wednesday, Blackburn and Luton.

A dark horse for 2017-18...
Tammy Abraham. The England Under-21 international scored 23 times in 41 Championship appearances on loan at Bristol City last term and is ready for the step up to the Premier League.

Your betting golden rule...
Price is all that matters. Bet value long-term and you stand a better chance of profiting.

Best bet for 2017-18?
Liverpool to finish above Arsenal in a match bet. The Gunners were poor for much of last season and I reckon Arsene Wenger may go for the Europa League as he has never won a European trophy with Arsenal.

Dan Childs
Racing Post tipster

Last season's best bet?
Lincoln to win the National League at 16-1. I had heard great things about their new manager, Danny Cowley, and he didn't disappoint.

And what was your head-in-hands betting moment?
I was on Bournemouth to finish above Southampton at 7-2. They led 1-0 at Leicester on the final day of the season and drew 1-1, meaning they finished below Saints on goal difference.

How will the Premier League title race shape up?
Chelsea to retain the league title and I fancy Man City, Spurs and Arsenal for the top four. Bournemouth look overrated and may struggle. Palace can do better than expected and may finish in the top half.

And who wins the other three English leagues?
Norwich, Wigan, Mansfield.

A dark horse for 2017-18...
Watch out for Ben Brereton at Nottingham Forest. This kid had bundles of ability and will only get better under an astute manager like Mark Warburton.

Your betting golden rule...
Try not to get too positive or negative about certain teams. Football is a fast-moving sport and fortunes can change in a very short space of time.

Best bet for 2017-18?
Manchester United to finish outside the top four at 11-4. It looks like being hugely competitive at the top end and United, without Zlatan Ibrahimovic, look vulnerable.

Steve Davies
Scotland expert

Last season's best bet?
A couple of Europa League group-stage corkers – a lay of Inter and Genk to win Group F – were second best to Livingston at 11-2 to win Scottish League One.

And what was your head-in-hands betting moment?
Being seduced by Wolves and Villa at several points of the Championship season only for neither to get anywhere close.

How will the Premier League title race shape up?
It's Man City for me. Spurs will eclipse Arsenal and finish in the top four.

And who wins the other three English leagues?
Aston Villa, Oxford and Carlisle.

A dark horse for 2017-18...
The market says Huddersfield are doomed but I disagree. Progressive boss David Wagner can guide the Terriers to safety, and I love some of his signings, none more so than Matias Jorgensen, a top-class centre-back with Champions League clean sheets to his name.

Your betting golden rule...
Don't overly fret about team news. Newspapers might regard the absence of three or four players as a crisis but on closer inspection it usually isn't. All teams start with 11.

Best bet for 2017-18?
West Ham to go down. The loyalty towards Slaven Bilic looks misplaced. They never replaced Payet and look a bits-and-pieces team unhappy with themselves and where they play.

Joe Champion
European expert

Last season's best bet?
It wasn't a massive price but Real Madrid looked in control of La Liga from start to finish. The El Clasico defeat at the end of April did make me sweat but they closed out the title race in dominant fashion.

And what was your head-in-hands betting moment?
I was keen on Juventus in the Champions League and they did absolutely nothing wrong until the final. Made worse by the fact that I'd backed them win only...

How will the Premier League title race shape up?
Chelsea looked overpriced before Eden Hazard got injured but I still expect the bulk of the battle to be fought between them and Manchester City. Tottenham have to prove themselves at Wembley.

And who wins the other three English leagues?
Norwich, Blackburn, Lincoln.

A dark horse for 2017-18...
Juventus youngster Moise Kean became the first player born this century to score a goal in Europe's big five leagues and this big, bustling striker could get more game time this term.

Your betting golden rule...
Avoid getting caught up in last year's results. They provide a guide as to what might happen next time but teams can often undergo summer makeovers.

Best bet for 2017-18?
Real Madrid were deserving winners of La Liga last season and they look overpriced to retain the title.

Dan Sait
Annual Editor

Last season's best bet?
Four of five Championship tips landed so I ended up a happy punter. Wigan and Blackburn dropping at 9-1 and 11-2 was particularly pleasing, but I rode my luck with the Newcastle-Brighton one-two.

And what was your head-in-hands betting moment?
If Sheffield Wednesday had won promotion it would have completed the Championship clean sweep, so I was gutted to see them lose their playoff semi-final penalty shootout.

How will the Premier League title race shape up?
The Manchester clubs should feature but look far too short, while Chelsea and Liverpool will find life tougher with European commitments. The Wembley factor seems overstated and I would rather back Tottenham at 10-1 than Man City at 19-10

And who wins the other three English leagues?
Fulham, Blackburn, Luton.

A dark horse for 2017-18...
A bunch of England youngsters impressed over the summer with Josh Onomah, Ademola Lookman and Rob Holding all knocking on the door. And Will Hughes finally gets a shot the top flight with Watford.

Your betting golden rule...
Understand luck. Don't blame poor judgement on it, but do accept it can turn a good bet into a loser. Learn to recognise when you were wrong but lucky or right but unfortunate.

Best bet for 2017-18?
Blackburn to win League One.

Ian Griffin
Betfair trader

Best result for Betfair last season?
Man City not winning the league. With a lot of favourites winning in the UK and Europe, City would of let down a lot of accas, saving us a fortune!

And what was the worst?
Real beating Juventus in the Champions League final with Ronaldo scoring first. With the scoreline ending 4-1 we lost on multiple markets; WDW & BTTS and the handicaps where we felt the brunt of the goals spree.

How will the Premier League title race shape up?
Pep Guardiola has bolstered the Man City squad and can justify favouritism this time. Man Utd look far too short at 100-30 for the title and Spurs may find it difficult playing at Wembley. So Man City, Chelsea second, Liverpool third, Man Utd fourth.

And who wins the other three English leagues?
Boro, Blackburn, Coventry.

A dark horse for 2017-18...
Sandro Ramirez could prove a steal for Everton at £5m. And Mo Salah was involved in 26 Serie A goals last term, so adds even more potency to Liverpool.

Your betting golden rule...
Don't go telling people you've backed a winner after the result is known! And don't bet for the sake of it – stay disciplined.

Best bet for 2017-18?
Wolves have a decent manager, are spending big by bringing in the likes of Ruben Neves and have links to super agent Jorge Mendes. They could take the Championship by surprise.

Premier League winner

	bet365	Betfair	Betfred	Hills	Lads	Skybet
Man City	15-8	19-10	7-4	7-4	9-5	15-8
Man Utd	10-3	7-2	3	10-3	10-3	10-3
Chelsea	7-2	7-2	7-2	7-2	3	7-2
Tottenham	9	8	10	8	8	8
Arsenal	11	12	12	12	11	11
Liverpool	12	11	12	10	11	10
Everton	80	80	66	80	80	80
Leicester	200	250	200	200	200	250
Southampton	250	250	200	150	200	250
Stoke	500	750	750	500	750	750
Newcastle	500	750	500	500	500	500
West Ham	350	500	500	500	750	500
Bournemouth	750	750	1000	750	750	750
West Brom	500	1000	1000	750	750	1000
Brighton	1500	1500	1500	1000	750	1500
Crystal Palace	500	750	1000	750	750	750
Swansea	750	750	1000	1000	750	
Watford	1000	1000	1500	1000	1000	1500
Burnley	1000	1000	1500	1000	1000	1500
Huddersfield	2000	2000	1500	1000	1500	2000

Win or each-way

Premier League relegation

	bet365	Betfair	Betfred	Hills	Lads	Skybet
Huddersfield	4-6	8-13	4-7	4-7	4-7	2-3
Burnley	5-4	13-10	5-4	5-4	5-4	5-4
Brighton	6-5	5-4	5-4	6-5	6-5	6-5
Watford	6-4	13-8	13-8	7-4	13-8	3-2
Swansea	9-4	9-4	9-4	7-4	9-4	9-4
Newcastle	7-2	10-3	4	4	4	10-3
Crystal Palace	9-2	9-2	9-2	7-2	9-2	9-2
West Brom	6	6	11-2	4	11-2	5
Bournemouth	6	11-2	6	4	11-2	13-2
Stoke	7	6	13-2	7	13-2	13-2
West Ham	9	8	9	8	8	7
Leicester	14	14	12	16	14	14
Southampton	25	22	22	20	25	20
Everton	100	90	80	50	80	66
Tottenham	1000	500	1000	750	1000	1000
Arsenal	1000	500	1000	500	1000	1000
Liverpool	1000	500	1000	500	1000	1000
Man Utd	2500	500	1000	1000	1500	2500
Chelsea	2500	500	1000	1000	1500	2500
Man City	2500	500	1000	1000	2000	2500

Win only

Premier League top-four finish

	bet365	Betfair	Betfred	Hills	Lads	Skybet
Man City	1-5	1-6	1-6	1-6	1-6	1-6
Chelsea	3-10	2-7	4-11	2-7	2-7	4-11
Man Utd	1-3	3-10	3-10	4-11	1-3	2-7
Tottenham	8-11	4-6	4-5	4-6	8-11	4-5
Arsenal	1	10-11	10-11	10-11	10-11	5-6
Liverpool	1	5-6	10-11	10-11	10-11	1
Everton	10	9	15-2	8	8	13-2
Southampton	20	20	20	16	18	20
Leicester	25	20	20	20	20	22
Stoke	80	80	66	66	66	66
West Ham	50	50	50	66	50	50
Bournemouth	80	150	80	100	100	50
Newcastle	80	100	50	66	100	150
West Brom	66	100	80	125	80	100
Crystal Palace	66	100	80	100	100	100
Swansea	250	150	100	200	200	250
Watford	200	200	200	200	200	250
Brighton	200	200	200	200	250	250
Huddersfield	500	300	250	200	400	500
Burnley	250	250	200	200	250	250

Win only

Premier League top-half finish

	bet365	Betfair	Betfred	Hills	Lads	Skybet
Chelsea	1-200	-	1-200	1-100	-	-
Man City	1-200	-	1-200	1-100	-	-
Man Utd	1-200	-	1-200	1-100	-	-
Arsenal	1-66	-	1-66	1-66	-	-
Liverpool	1-66	-	1-66	1-66	-	-
Tottenham	1-100	-	1-100	1-100	-	-
Everton	1-5	1-7	1-8	1-7	-	-
Southampton	8-15	4-7	8-15	1-2	-	-
Leicester	4-5	5-6	5-6	5-6	-	-
West Ham	11-8	6-4	6-4	13-8	-	-
Bournemouth	9-4	23-10	9-4	9-4	-	-
Stoke	9-4	21-10	9-4	5-2	-	-
West Brom	9-4	11-5	5-2	11-4	-	-
Newcastle	11-4	11-4	5-2	3	-	-
Crystal Palace	3	3	3	7-2	-	-
Swansea	13-2	5	11-2	5	-	-
Watford	8	6	15-2	7	-	-
Burnley	9	15-2	15-2	8	-	-
Brighton	10	17-2	10	10	-	-
Huddersfield	16	11	16	16	-	-

Win only

Championship winner

	bet365	Betfair	Betfred	Hills	Lads	Skybet
Aston Villa	7	13-2	7	7	13-2	7
Fulham	9	8	9	7	9	9
Middlesbrough	15-2	7	8	9	8	7
Norwich	10	10	8	9	9	10
Sheffield Wed	10	10	10	10	9	10
Wolves	10	12	12	10	10	11
Derby	14	14	12	11	11	12
Sunderland	16	14	16	14	14	16
Hull	16	14	12	14	14	14
Leeds	16	14	14	16	16	16
Reading	20	14	20	16	18	25
Birmingham	20	22	25	16	25	25
Brentford	20	25	20	20	20	28
Sheffield Utd	33	22	25	25	25	28
Cardiff	25	22	25	25	20	25
Bristol City	40	30	40	33	40	28
Nottm Forest	40	33	33	33	33	33
Preston	50	40	50	50	50	50
QPR	50	40	50	66	66	66
Ipswich	66	100	66	80	66	80
Millwall	100	75	80	80	80	100
Barnsley	100	100	100	100	100	100
Bolton	100	80	100	100	80	150
Burton	150	175	100	150	150	150

Win or each-way

Championship relegation

	bet365	Betfair	Betfred	Hills	Lads	Skybet
Burton	6-4	17-10	13-8	11-8	6-4	13-8
Barnsley	15-8	15-8	7-4	7-4	7-4	2
Bolton	9-4	13-5	2	2	12-5	7-4
Millwall	9-4	12-5	2	9-4	12-5	9-4
Ipswich	10-3	23-10	11-4	11-4	3	11-4
QPR	7-2	4	4	9-2	7-2	7-2
Preston	4	9-2	4	5	4	9-2
Nottm Forest	11-2	13-2	5	11-2	11-2	5
Bristol City	9-2	11-2	5	11-2	11-2	8
Sheffield Utd	11-2	6	7	7	6	8
Cardiff City	8	8	7	7	8	9
Brentford	12	9	12	9	8	9
Birmingham	12	17-2	7	10	7	15-2
Reading	14	14	10	10	12	9
Sunderland	14	14	12	12	14	12
Hull	12	18	16	12	14	12
Leeds	14	11	14	10	12	14
Wolves	20	12	14	16	12	18
Derby	25	14	16	33	20	20
Norwich	40	20	40	40	25	25
Sheffield Wed	40	22	20	33	25	33
Fulham	33	22	33	40	25	25
Middlesbrough	50	33	40	33	40	40
Aston Villa	50	33	50	40	40	50

Win only

League One winner

	bet365	Betfair	Betfred	Hills	Lads	Skybet
Blackburn	9-2	9-2	9-2	9-2	9-2	9-2
Wigan	8	7	7	7	7	7
Portsmouth	9	9	9	9	9	9
Bradford	12	9	10	11	11	12
MK Dons	12	14	12	12	12	16
Charlton	14	14	16	12	16	16
Scunthorpe	20	20	20	16	16	18
Oxford	16	14	16	14	16	14
Peterborough	20	20	20	20	18	22
Southend	25	20	20	25	20	20
Bristol Rovers	20	20	20	20	20	20
Fleetwood	25	22	25	25	25	18
Bury	20	20	20	16	22	25
Doncaster	33	28	33	25	25	22
Rochdale	33	28	33	25	28	28
Northampton	20	28	28	25	25	28
Plymouth	33	28	25	25	33	33
Rotherham	20	25	25	25	25	25
Wimbledon	40	40	40	40	40	33
Walsall	66	66	40	40	50	50
Gillingham	66	70	50	66	66	80
Blackpool	100	80	50	40	66	80
Oldham	100	66	66	66	80	100
Shrewsbury	100	80	66	80	66	100

Win or each-way

League One relegation

	bet365	Betfair	Betfred	Hills	Lads	Skybet
Blackpool	11-8	11-8	13-8	13-8	13-8	3-2
Shrewsbury	11-8	11-8	6-4	11-8	13-8	6-5
Oldham	5-4	7-4	6-4	5-4	11-8	11-8
Gillingham	11-8	13-8	13-8	6-4	6-4	13-8
Walsall	2	5-2	3	7-4	12-5	11-4
Wimbledon	10-3	11-4	3	5-2	3	4
Plymouth	10-3	4	9-2	4	10-3	4
Northampton	6	5-2	9-2	5-2	4	4
Doncaster	4	6	6	6	9-2	6
Bury	6	4	11-2	6	5	5
Rochdale	9-2	5	4	4	5	5
Fleetwood	11-2	13-2	7	5	5	7
Southend	6	6	8	5	6	7
Scunthorpe	7	8	9	8	8	7
Rotherham	9	6	5	6	5	9-2
Bristol Rovers	9	7	8	6	7	7
Peterborough	9	7	9	10	7	11-2
Charlton	14	10	11	14	9	15-2
MK Dons	11	11	11	16	12	8
Oxford	12	9	14	20	14	10
Bradford	25	16	16	20	16	12
Portsmouth	33	25	25	33	16	14
Wigan	25	20	25	33	25	18
Blackburn	33	33	33	33	33	33

Win only

League Two winner

	bet365	Betfair	Betfred	Hills	Lads	Skybet
Mansfield	5	9-2	5	5	5	9-2
Luton	7	8	7	8	7	7
Coventry	9	9	8	8	9	8
Swindon	14	12	12	12	12	14
Lincoln	14	10	12	10	10	10
Exeter	16	16	16	16	14	16
Cambridge U	16	16	16	16	16	16
Notts County	14	16	14	12	14	12
Chesterfield	16	14	18	16	18	16
Carlisle	16	16	18	16	16	18
Forest Green	25	22	25	20	20	25
Accrington	25	20	25	20	25	22
Stevenage	33	25	28	25	25	25
Colchester	20	20	20	20	22	20
Port Vale	20	20	28	20	25	25
Wycombe	25	16	25	20	22	28
Crewe	40	40	33	40	33	40
Grimsby	40	33	40	33	33	40
Cheltenham	40	28	40	40	40	40
Barnet	50	40	33	40	50	66
Yeovil	66	66	40	66	66	66
Crawley	100	80	66	66	80	100
Newport Co	100	66	50	50	80	66
Morecambe	150	100	66	100	125	150

Win or each-way

League Two relegation

	bet365	Betfair	Betfred	Hills	Lads	Skybet
Morecambe	2	2	9-4	2	11-5	15-8
Crawley	4	7-2	5-2	7-2	10-3	3
Newport Co	7-2	7-2	3	7-2	7-2	9-2
Yeovil	4	4	9-2	11-2	9-2	9-2
Cheltenham	8	15-2	7	8	7	13-2
Crewe	8	8	9	8	8	15-2
Grimsby	8	15-2	7	8	7	15-2
Barnet	9	13-2	7	7	7	13-2
Forest Green	12	12	12	12	12	12
Stevenage	11	12	11	9	12	12
Wycombe	14	14	12	12	12	14
Port Vale	16	12	10	9	10	10
Accrington	12	18	14	14	12	14
Chesterfield	14	18	16	12	16	18
Carlisle	20	20	16	20	16	16
Colchester	16	14	14	14	14	16
Exeter	16	18	16	25	20	20
Notts County	20	18	20	25	20	25
Swindon	20	22	25	25	25	22
Cambridge	20	18	20	25	20	22
Lincoln	16	22	25	16	25	40
Coventry	33	33	33	33	40	40
Luton	40	33	40	50	50	50
Mansfield	50	50	50	50	66	80

Win only

National League winner

	bet365	Betfair	Betfred	Hills	Lads	Skybet
Tranmere	3	-	-	5-2	10-3	3
Dagenham	10	-	-	10	9	10
Eastleigh	11	-	-	10	10	8
Hartlepool	12	-	-	10	11	12
Wrexham	14	-	-	12	12	12
Aldershot	16	-	-	9	14	12
Fylde	16	-	-	10	14	14
Leyton Orient	12	-	-	16	12	16
Sutton Utd	16	-	-	25	20	25
Ebbsfleet	20	-	-	20	18	16
Barrow	20	-	-	16	18	25
Gateshead	25	-	-	20	20	20
Macclesfield	25	-	-	20	28	25
Dover	33	-	-	25	33	28
Maidstone	33	-	-	25	33	33
Halifax	40	-	-	40	33	33
Woking	50	-	-	50	50	40
Boreham Wood	50	-	-	40	40	40
Bromley	50	-	-	40	33	40
Chester	66	-	-	66	50	50
Torquay	66	-	-	40	50	50
Maidenhead	66	-	-	66	50	66
Guiseley	80	-	-	66	66	66
Solihull Moors	100	-	-	100	100	100

Win or each-way

FA Cup winner

	bet365	Betfair	Betfred	Hills	Lads	Skybet
Chelsea	6	-	11-2	6	5	5
Man City	5	-	5	6	5	5
Man Utd	13-2	-	7	7	6	5
Arsenal	8	-	8	10	8	8
Tottenham	9	-	10	9	8	7
Liverpool	9	-	10	9	9	10
Everton	16	-	20	14	14	20
Southampton	25	-	25	25	20	25
Leicester	33	-	33	33	25	28
Stoke	40	-	40	40	33	40
West Ham	33	-	33	33	33	33
Bournemouth	50	-	50	40	40	40
Crystal Palace	40	-	33	40	40	33
Newcastle	40	-	40	40	50	40
Burnley	66	-	50	50	50	66
West Brom	50	-	50	40	50	40
Swansea	66	-	50	50	50	40
Watford	66	-	66	66	50	50
Brighton	80	-	80	66	50	66
Aston Villa	100	-	100	100	66	80
Huddersfield	125	-	100	66	66	80
Middlesbrough	100	-	100	80	66	80
Sunderland	100	-	100	100	66	100
Hull	150	-	150	100	66	100

Others available. Win or each-way. See bookmakers for details

Scottish Premiership winner

	bet365	Betfair	Betfred	Hills	Lads	Skybet
Celtic	1-20	1-9	1-12	1-10	1-10	1-12
Rangers	12	17-2	9	8	8	8
Aberdeen	20	15-2	20	12	16	12
Hibernian	250	100	250	250	150	150
Hearts	200	80	250	100	100	80
St Johnstone	500	500	500	250	250	500
Dundee	1000	500	1000	500	500	500
Ross County	1000	500	1000	500	500	500
Partick	1500	500	1500	500	750	500
Hamilton	2000	500	2000	500	1000	500
Kilmarnock	1000	500	1000	500	500	500
Motherwell	1000	500	1000	500	500	500

Win or each-way

Scottish Championship winner

	bet365	Betfair	Betfred	Hills	Lads	Skybet
Dundee Utd	15-8	2	2	2	2	2
St Mirren	7-2	7-2	4	4	10-3	10-3
Falkirk	5	7-2	7-2	7-2	4	5
Inverness	5	6	9-2	4	9-2	9-2
Dunfermline	9	10	10	9	10	10
Morton	14	16	12	10	16	14
Queen of Sth	16	16	14	16	16	16
Livingston	20	14	20	25	16	20
Dumbarton	50	50	33	50	40	40
Brechin	100	150	100	100	125	100

Win or each-way

Scottish League One winner

	bet365	Betfair	Betfred	Hills	Lads	Skybet
Raith	5-4	5-4	6-5	11-10	6-5	6-5
Ayr	11-4	11-4	5-2	5-2	5-2	5-2
Alloa	11-2	11-2	6	4	5	6
Airdrie	10	12	10	14	12	12
East Fife	16	16	12	14	14	16
Queens Park	20	20	20	20	18	18
Arbroath	16	16	14	20	16	18
Stranraer	25	16	20	14	18	25
Forfar	33	20	25	33	25	28
Albion	66	66	40	50	50	50

Win or each-way

Scottish League Two winner

	bet365	Betfair	Betfred	Hills	Lads	Skybet
Peterhead	6-4	6-4	9-4	9-4	7-4	2
Stenhousemuir	7-2	7-2	9-2	10-3	4	4
Clyde	6	9-2	7-2	4	4	9-2
Elgin	14	12	15-2	11	9	11
Annan Athletic	14	12	11	12	12	14
Montrose	10	14	11	9	10	10
Stirling Albion	10	14	10	7	12	12
Edinburgh City	12	16	16		18	16
Cowdenbeath	16	22	10	14	12	11
Berwick	25	20	20	25	25	25

Win or each-way

Champions League winner

	bet365	Betfair	Betfred	Hills	Lads	Skybet
Barcelona	5	4	5	5	9-2	5
Bayern Munich	11-2	9-2	11-2	11-2	11-2	11-2
Real Madrid	5	11-2	5	5	5	9-2
Juventus	9	8	10	10	10	9
Man City	12	12	12	10	11	12
Chelsea	12	14	14	14	12	14
Man Utd	16	16	16	14	14	14
Atl Madrid	14	12	12	16	12	14
PSG	16	20	20	16	16	18
Dortmund	22	18	20	20	20	25
Liverpool	25	25	20	20	25	25
Tottenham	25	25	25	20	25	22
Monaco	33	40	50	40	33	40
Napoli	40	40	66	66	66	80
RB Leipzig	50	33	50	40	66	50
Sevilla	50	50	40	40	50	50
Roma	50	40	80	50	66	66
Benfica	66	80	100	66	80	80
Porto	66	90	80	66	80	80
Hoffenheim	100	125	150	66	150	150
Besiktas	100	100	100	100	100	100
Shak. Donetsk	150	100	100	150	150	200
Ajax	200	250	150	125	200	200
Sporting	150	225	125	150	125	250
Nice	100	175	200	150	150	150
CSKA Moscow	200	125	150	200	200	200
Feyenoord	200	275	200	200	200	500
Spartak Moscow	200	125	200	200	200	500
Celtic	500	100	500	250	500	1000

Others available. Win or each-way. See bookmakers for details

Europa League winner

	bet365	Betfair	Betfred	Hills	Lads	Skybet
Arsenal	9	7	8	7	8	8
AC Milan	12	10	9	8	10	12
Villarreal	25	14	20	16	20	18
Everton	20	16	20	20	20	20
Athletic Bilbao	25	16	25	20	20	-
Lazio	25	14	20	16	20	20
Lyon	25	20	25	25	20	28
Real Sociedad	33	25	25	25	25	28
Marseille	25	25	33	33	33	33
FC Koln	40	25	33	33	33	33
Zenit	33	50	40	-	40	50
Hertha Berlin	40	33	40	40	40	50
Atalanta	50	50	50	50	50	50
Bordeaux	50	50	50	50	-	-
Fenerbahce	66	66	66	-	50	-
PSV	50	50	50	40	50	66
Panathinaikos	80	-	50	-	66	-
Freiburg	66	50	66	-	66	-
Braga	66	50	66	80	66	66
Guimaraes	100	100	100	100	100	100

Others available. Win or each-way. See bookmakers for details

June 2017

Tuesday 27-28	Champions League first qualifying round, first leg
Thursday 29	Europa League first qualifying round, first leg

July 2017

Tuesday 4-5	Champions League first qualifying round, second leg
Thursday 6	Europa League first qualifying round, second leg
Tue-Wed 11-12	Champions League second qualifying round, first leg
Thursday 13	Europa League second qualifying round, first leg
Friday 14	Champions League third qualifying round draw
	Europa League third qualifying round draw
	Scottish League Cup group stage, matchday one
Tue-Wed 18-19	Champions League second qualifying round, second leg
	Scottish League Cup group stage, matchday two
Thursday 20	Europa League second qualifying round, second leg
Friday 21-23	Scottish League Cup group stage, matchday three
Tue-Wed 25-26	Champions League third qualifying round, first leg
	Scottish League Cup group stage, matchday four
Thursday 27	Europa League third qualifying round, first leg
Sat-Sun 29-30	Scottish League Cup group stage, matchday five

August 2017

Tue-Wed 1-2	Champions League third qualifying round, second leg
Thursday 3	Europa League third qualifying round, second leg
Friday 4	Champions League playoff round draw
	Europa League playoff round draw
Saturday 5	Start of Football League season
	Start of National League season
	FA Cup extra preliminary round
	Start of Scottish Football League season
	Start of French Ligue 1 season
Sunday 6	FA Community Shield
	Arsenal v Chelsea
Tuesday 8	Uefa Super Cup, Skopje
	Real Madrid v Manchester United
	Scottish League Cup last 16
Wednesday 9	League Cup first round
	Start of Portuguese Primeira Liga season
Friday 11	Start of Premier League season
	Start of Spanish La Liga season
	Start of Dutch Eredivisie season
Saturday 12	Scottish Cup first preliminary round
Tue-Wed 15-16	Champions League playoff round, first leg
	Scottish Challenge Cup first round
Thursday 17	Europa League playoff round, first leg
Friday 18	Start of German Bundesliga season
Saturday 19	FA Cup preliminary round
	Start of Italian Serie A season
Tue-Wed 22-23	Champions League playoff round, second leg
	League Cup second round
Thursday 24	Champions League group stage draw
	Europa League playoff round, second leg
Friday 25	Europa League group stage draw
Wednesday 30	EFL Trophy group stage, matchday one

September 2017

Friday 1	World Cup qualifiers
	Lithuania v Scotland
	Malta v England
	San Marino v Northern Ireland
Saturday 2	World Cup qualifiers
	Georgia v Ireland
	Wales v Austria
	FA Cup first qualifying round
	Scottish Cup second preliminary round
	Scottish Challenge Cup second round
Monday 4	World Cup qualifiers
	England v Slovakia
	Northern Ireland v Czech Republic
	Scotland v Malta
Tuesday 5	World Cup qualifiers
	Ireland v Serbia
	Moldova v Wales
Saturday 9	FA Vase first qualifying round
Tue-Wed 12-13	Champions League group stage, matchday one
Thursday 14	Europa League group stage, matchday one
Saturday 16	FA Cup second qualifying round
Tue-Wed 19-20	League Cup third round
	Scottish League Cup quarter-finals
Saturday 23	FA Vase second qualifying round
	Scottish Cup first round
Tue-Wed 26-27	Champions League group stage, matchday two
Thursday 28	Europa League group stage, matchday two
Saturday 30	FA Cup third qualifying round

October 2017

Wednesday 4	EFL Trophy group stage, matchday two
Thursday 5	World Cup qualifiers
	England v Slovenia
	Northern Ireland v Germany
	Scotland v Slovakia
Friday 6	World Cup qualifiers
	Georgia v Wales
	Ireland v Moldova
Saturday 7	FA Trophy preliminary round
	Scottish Challenge Cup third round
Sunday 8	World Cup qualifiers
	Lithuania v England
	Norway v Northern Ireland
	Slovenia v Scotland
Monday 9	World Cup qualifiers
	Wales v Ireland
Saturday 14	FA Cup fourth qualifying round
	Scottish Cup second round
Tue-Wed 17-18	Champions League group stage, matchday three
Thursday 19	Europa League group stage, matchday three
Saturday 21	FA Vase first round
	Scottish League Cup semi-finals
Wednesday 25	League Cup fourth round
Saturday 28	FA Trophy first qualifying round
Tuesday 31	Champions League group stage, matchday four

November 2017

Wednesday 1	Champions League group stage, matchday four
Thursday 2	Europa League group stage, matchday four
Saturday 4	FA Cup first round
Wednesday 8	EFL Trophy group stage, matchday three
Thu-Sat 9-11	World Cup qualifying playoff (Uefa), first leg
Saturday 11	FA Trophy second qualifying round
	FA Vase second round
	Scottish Challenge Cup quarter-final
Sun-Tues 12-14	World Cup qualifying playoff (Uefa), second leg
Saturday 18	Scottish Cup third round
Tue-Wed 21-22	Champions League group stage, matchday five
Thursday 23	Europa League group stage, matchday five
Saturday 25	FA Trophy third qualifying round
Sunday 26	Scottish League Cup final

December 2017

Friday 1	World Cup finals draw
Saturday 2	FA Cup second round
	FA Vase third round
Tue-Wed 5-6	Champions League group stage, matchday six
	EFL Trophy last 32
Wednesday 6	Fifa Club World Cup begins, United Arab Emirates
Thursday 7	Europa League group stage, matchday six
Monday 11	Champions League last 16 draw
	Europa League last 32 draw
Saturday 16	Fifa Club World Cup final, Abu Dhabi
	FA Trophy first round
Wednesday 20	League Cup fifth round

January 2018

Saturday 6	FA Cup third round
	FA Vase fourth round
Wednesday 10	League Cup semi-final, first leg
	EFL Trophy last 16
Saturday 13	FA Trophy second round
Saturday 20	Scottish Cup fourth round
Wednesday 24	League Cup semi-final, second leg
	EFL Trophy quarter-final
Saturday 27	FA Cup fourth round

February 2018

Saturday 3	FA Trophy third round
	FA Vase fifth round
Saturday 10	Scottish Cup fifth round
Tue-Wed 13-14	Champions League last 16, first leg
Thursday 15	Europa League last 32, first leg
Saturday 17	FA Cup fifth round
	Scottish Challenge Cup semi-final
Tue-Wed 20-21	Champions League last 16, first leg
Thursday 22	Europa League last 32, second leg
Friday 23	Europa League last 16 draw
Saturday 24	FA Trophy fourth round
	FA Vase sixth round
Sunday 25	League Cup final
Wednesday 28	EFL Trophy semi-final

March 2018

Saturday 3	Scottish Cup quarter-finals
Tue-Wed 6-7	Champions League last 16, second leg
Thursday 8	Europa League last 16, first leg
Tue-Wed 13-14	Champions League last 16, second leg
Thursday 15	Europa League last 16, second leg
Friday 16	Champions League quarter-final draw
	Europa League quarter-final draw
Saturday 17	FA Cup quarter-final
	FA Trophy semi-final, first leg
	FA Vase semi-final, first leg
Friday 23	International friendlies
Saturday 24	FA Trophy semi-final, second leg
	FA Vase semi-final, second leg
	Scottish Challenge Cup final
Tuesday 27	International friendlies

April 2018

Tue-Wed 3-4	Champions League quarter-final, first leg
Thursday 5	Europa League quarter-final, first leg
Sunday 8	EFL Trophy final
Tue-Wed 10-11	Champions League quarter-final, second leg
Thursday 12	Europa League quarter-final, second leg
Friday 13	Champions League semi-final draw
	Europa League semi-final draw
SatSun 14-15	Scottish Cup semi-finals
Sat-Sun 21-22	FA Cup semi-finals
	Scottish Premiership splits
Tuesday 24-25	Champions League semi-final, first leg
Thursday 26	Europa League semi-final, first leg
Saturday 28	National League season ends
	Scottish Championship, League One, League Two seasons end

May 2018

Tue-Wed 1-2	Champions League semi-final, second leg
Thursday 3	Europa League semi-final, second leg
Saturday 5	Football League season ends
Saturday 12	National League Premier playoff final
	National League North & South playoff finals
Sunday 13	Premier League season ends
	Scottish Premiership season ends
Wednesday 16	Europa League final, Lyon
Thursday 17	Scottish Premiership playoff final, first leg
Saturday 19	FA Cup final
	Scottish Cup final
Sunday 20	FA Trophy final
	FA Vase final
	Scottish Premiership playoff final, second leg
Saturday 26	Champions League final, Kiev
	Championship playoff final
Sunday 27	League One playoff final
Monday 28	League Two playoff final

June 2018

Thursday 14	World Cup finals begins, Russia

July 2018

Sunday 15	World Cup final, Moscow

Chelsea have the quality to fight on several fronts and retain their league crown

The Premier League title race is arguably the most competitive of any major league in Europe, boasting six genuine contenders, writes Dan Childs. But there may be no change at the top with Chelsea able to stage the first successful title defence since Manchester United in 2008-09, even though the Blues have the extra workload of Champions League football and start without Eden Hazard, who is recovering from an ankle operation.

Any team would miss their best players but Chelsea excelled in the 2017 FA Cup semi-final against Tottenham despite starting without Hazard and Diego Costa.

The biggest challenge to the Blues may come from Manchester City.

Pep Guardiola was regarded to have underperformed last season, but City posted 78 points which was 12 more than the campaign before. Add another 12 in 2017-18 and they will be very difficult to stop.

Sergio Aguero and Gabriel Jesus are two of the most dangerous front men in the country and the supply line is top class with Kevin De Bruyne, David Silva and new signing Bernardo Silva providing creative impetus.

However, doubts remain over the City defence with John Stones still learning his trade and Vincent Kompany injury-prone.

Tottenham will be impacted by the move to Wembley. There will almost certainly be a reduction in the points won at home (53 from 57 last term) but they are a young, improving side and can finish in the top three again.

The battle for fourth looks a scrap between Arsenal, Manchester United and Liverpool.

Arsenal are out of the Champions League for the first time in 20 years and hungry to get back. They may not be as distracted by the Europa League as Liverpool and United will be by Champions League campaigns.

Liverpool's lack of squad depth may be exposed and United – outside the top four in three of the last four seasons – are going to miss Zlatan Ibrahimovic.

Crystal Palace have scope for improvement if they sort out their home form and adjust to new manager Frank De Boer. Only the top six won more away games than Palace, who have every chance of a top-half finish.

Newcastle's promotion adds greater depth to the league and makes it unlikely that all three new boys will go straight back down.

Bournemouth are among the clubs at risk. There were goals in the side even before the arrival of Jermain Defoe, but the Cherries are suspect defensively and finished only six points clear of 17th place last season.

Burnley could be in trouble if their home form deteriorates. They have won only one of their last six matches at Turf Moor and that is a huge worry for a side who picked up 33 of their 40 points at home.

Huddersfield look the most vulnerable of the promoted clubs. Their high-pressing style may leave them exposed against the superior pace and movement of top-flight strikers.

Recommendations

Chelsea to win Premier League, 15-4
Tottenham top-four finish, 5-6
Arsenal top-four finish, Evens
Crystal Palace top-ten finish, 3-1
Huddersfield to be relegated, 4-6
Burnley to be relegated, 11-8
Bournemouth to be relegated, 13-2

Key to the data

The table next to every team profile shows head-to-head data for every side they will have to play in the league this season.

1 Every team the club will play in the league in the order they finished last season

2 Results of last season's league meetings **W** win **D** draw **L** loss. Where there was more than one league meeting, the latest is at the right. Regular season only

3 Head-to-head results over the last six seasons at the club's own ground. **P** games played **W** wins **D** draws **L** losses **OV** games with over 2.5 total goals **UN** games with under 2.5 total

goals **BS** games in which both teams scored **CS** number of clean sheets for the home side

4 Promoted and relegated teams shown in fawn in the order in which they finished last season

5 League finishes over the last three seasons

6 Over and under 2.5 and both sides to score stats, including rank in club's division last season. The bar chart shows, horizontally, from top to bottom and rounded to the nearest 5 per cent, the division high, the profiled club and the division low

Leading scorers Numbers in brackets show first goals then 'any-time' goals

	2016-17		Last six seasons at home							
	H	A	P	W	D	L	OV	UN	BS	CS
1 Chelsea										
2 Tottenham				0	1	1	1	1	1	
Man City	L	L	2	0	0	2	1	1	0	0
Liverpool	W	D	2	1	0	1	2	0	2	0
Arsenal			2	1	0	1	1	1	1	0
Man United	L	L	2	1	0	1	2	0	2	0
Everton	W		2	1	1	0	1	1	1	1
Southampton			2	1	0	1	1	1	1	1
Bournemouth										
West Brom			2	1	1	0	0	2	1	1
West Ham	W		2	1	0	1	2	0	2	0
Leicester	W		3	1	1	0	3	1	1	1
Stoke	W		2	0	1	1	2	0	2	0
Crystal Palace	L	W	2	0	1	1	0	2	0	1
Swansea	W		2	2	0	0	1	1	1	1
Burnley	W		2	1	1	0	1	1	1	0
Watford			4	1	3	0	1	3	3	1
4 Newcastle			1	0	0	1	0	1	0	0
Brighton			2	1	1	0	1	1	2	0
Huddersfield			3	2	1	0	1	2	2	1

5

Season	Division	Pos	P	W	D	L	F	A	GD	Pts
2016-17	Premier League	9	38	12	10	16	55	67	-12	46
2015-16	Premier League	16	38	11	9	18	45	67	-22	42
2014-15	Championship	1	46	26	12	8	98	45	+53	90

6 Over/Under 61%/39% 6th   Both score 55%/45% 4th

ARSENAL

Nickname: The Gunners
Colours: Red and white
Ground: Emirates Stadium
Tel: 0207-619-5000

Capacity: 60,432
arsenal.com

Arsenal's run of 19 successive Champions League campaigns has come to an end but they can ensure an immediate return to Europe's top table by finishing in the top four in 2017-18.

The mood around the club was lifted by the FA Cup final triumph over Chelsea, allowing Arsene Wenger to bask in the glory of winning the famous old trophy for a seventh time.

However, the announcement of a new two-year contract for Wenger was met with dismay by a section of the club's support and the mood could turn ugly unless Arsenal can feature prominently in the title race.

Wenger's top priority will be to mount a title challenge but Arsenal were some way off last term and could be distracted by a lengthy run in the Europa League.

Longest run without a loss: 14
Longest run without a win: 3
Highest/lowest league position: 2/7
Clean sheets: 13
Yellow cards: 68 **Red cards:** 3
Avg attendance: 59,956
Players used: 29
Leading scorer: A Sanchez 24 (9,17)

| | 2016-17 | | Last six seasons at home | | | | | | | |
	H	A	P	W	D	L	OV	UN	BS	CS
Chelsea	W	L	6	1	3	2	2	4	1	4
Tottenham	D	L	6	3	3	0	2	4	5	1
Man City	D	L	6	2	3	1	3	3	4	1
Liverpool	L	L	6	2	2	2	3	3	3	2
Arsenal										
Man United	W	D	6	2	2	2	3	3	3	3
Everton	W	W	6	4	2	0	2	4	3	3
Southampton	W	W	5	4	1	0	2	3	2	3
Bournemouth	W	D	2	2	0	0	1	1	1	1
West Brom	W	L	6	6	0	0	2	4	1	5
West Ham	W	W	5	4	0	1	4	1	2	2
Leicester	W	D	3	3	0	0	2	1	2	1
Stoke	W	W	6	6	0	0	4	2	3	3
Crystal Palace	W	L	4	3	1	0	1	3	2	2
Swansea	W	W	6	2	1	3	3	3	3	1
Burnley	W	W	2	2	0	0	2	0	1	1
Watford	L	W	2	1	0	1	2	0	1	1
Newcastle			5	5	0	0	4	1	3	2
Brighton			-	-	-	-	-	-	-	-
Huddersfield			-	-	-	-	-	-	-	-

Season	Division	Pos	P	W	D	L	F	A	GD	Pts
2016-17	Premier League	5	38	23	6	9	77	44	+33	75
2015-16	Premier League	2	38	20	11	7	65	36	+29	71
2014-15	Premier League	3	38	22	9	7	71	36	+35	75

Over/Under 66%/34% 3rd

Both score 61%/39% 2nd

Key stat: Arsenal scored 17 headed goals in the league last season – the highest in the division

2016-17 Premier League appearances

	P	G		Y	R
H Bellerin	27 (6)	1	▌	4	-
S Cazorla	7 (1)	2	▌▌	2	-
P Cech	35	-		2	-
C Chambers	1	1	▌	-	-
F Coquelin	22 (7)	-		5	-
M Debuchy	1	-		-	-
M Elneny	8 (6)	-		1	-
Gabriel Paulista	15 (4)	-		6	-
K Gibbs	8 (3)	-		3	-
O Giroud	11 (18)	12	▌▌▌▌▌▌▌▌▌▌▌▌	2	-
R Holding	9	-		3	-
A Iwobi	18 (8)	3	▌▌▌	1	-
C Jenkinson	1	-		-	-
L Koscielny	33	2	▌▌	4	1
L Perez	2 (9)	1	▌	-	-
A Maitland-Niles	0 (1)	-		-	-
D Martinez	2	-		-	-
P Mertesacker	0 (1)	-		-	-
N Monreal	35 (1)	-		5	-
S Mustafi	26	2	▌▌	11	-
D Ospina	1 (1)	-		-	-

	P	G		Y	R
A Ox-Chamberlain	16 (13)	2	▌▌	1	-
M Ozil	32 (1)	8	▌▌▌▌▌▌▌▌	2	-
A Ramsey	13 (10)	1	▌	3	-
A Sanchez	36 (2)	24	▌▌▌▌▌▌▌▌▌▌▌▌▌▌▌▌▌▌▌▌▌▌▌▌	6	-
T Walcott	23 (5)	10	▌▌▌▌▌▌▌▌▌▌	1	-
D Welbeck	8 (8)	2	▌▌	-	-
J Wilshere	0 (2)	-		1	-
G Xhaka	28 (4)	2	▌▌	5	2

Arsene Wenger is staying put at the Emirates

BOURNEMOUTH

Nickname: The Cherries
Colours: Red and black
Ground: Dean Court
Tel: 0344-576-1910

Capacity: 11,464
afcb.co.uk

Bournemouth's preference for attacking football has won them many friends but it may put their top-flight status at risk in a season which promises to be much tougher than the 2016-17 campaign.

The league looks stronger after Newcastle's promotion and Bournemouth could be dragged into trouble if they fail to address defensive shortcomings.

The arrival of England striker Jermain Defoe has excited supporters. But Defoe will want to play through the middle and his signing may upset the attacking balance of a team who scored 55 goals last term – the highest among the teams finishing outside the top seven.

Bournemouth need to maintain their attacking threat because they conceded 67 league goals last season – the fourth-worst defensive record in the division.

Longest run without a loss: 5
Longest run without a win: 8
Highest/lowest league position: 9/16
Clean sheets: 10
Yellow cards: 54 **Red cards:** 3
Avg attendance: 11,182
Players used: 27
Leading scorer: J King 16 (4,13)

	2016-17		Last six seasons at home							
	H	A	P	W	D	L	OV	UN	BS	CS
Chelsea	L	L	2	0	0	2	2	0	2	0
Tottenham	D	L	2	0	1	1	1	1	1	1
Man City	L	L	2	0	0	2	1	1	0	0
Liverpool	W	D	2	1	0	1	2	0	2	0
Arsenal	D	L	2	0	1	1	1	1	1	0
Man United	L	D	2	1	0	1	2	0	2	0
Everton	W	L	2	1	1	0	1	1	1	1
Southampton	L	D	2	1	0	1	1	1	1	1
Bournemouth										
West Brom	W	L	2	1	1	0	0	2	1	1
West Ham	W	L	2	1	0	1	2	0	2	0
Leicester	W	D	3	1	1	1	0	3	1	1
Stoke	D	W	2	0	1	1	2	0	2	0
Crystal Palace	L	D	2	0	1	1	0	2	0	1
Swansea	W	W	2	2	0	0	1	1	1	1
Burnley	W	L	2	1	1	0	1	1	2	0
Watford	D	D	4	1	3	0	1	3	3	1
Newcastle			1	0	0	1	0	1	0	0
Brighton			2	1	1	0	1	1	2	0
Huddersfield			3	2	1	0	1	2	2	1

Season	Division	Pos	P	W	D	L	F	A	GD	Pts
2016-17	Premier League	9	38	12	10	16	55	67	-12	46
2015-16	Premier League	16	38	11	9	18	45	67	-22	42
2014-15	Championship	1	46	26	12	8	98	45	+53	90

Over/Under 61%/39% 6th

Both score 55%/45% 4th

Key stat: Bournemouth matches featured 122 goals last season at an average of 3.21 per game – the highest in the division

2016-17 Premier League appearances

	P G	Y	R
B Afobe	14 (17) 6	1	-
N Ake	8 (2) 3	-	-
R Allsop	1	-	-
H Arter	33 (2) 1	12	1
A Boruc	35	2	-
B Cargill	0 (1)	-	-
S Cook	38 2	5	-
L Cook	4 (2)	1	-
C Daniels	34 4	1	-
A Federici	2	1	-
S Francis	34	4	1
R Fraser	19 (9) 3	3	-
D Gosling	14 (13) 2	6	-
L Grabban	0 (3)	-	-
M Gradel	0 (11)	3	-
J Ibe	13 (12)	-	-
J King	31 (5) 16	1	-
M Worthington	0 (1)	-	-
T Mings	5 (2)	-	-
L Mousset	3 (8)	-	-
M Pugh	16 (5) 2	1	-

	P G	Y	R
B Smith	3 (2)	1	-
A Smith	34 (2) 1	6	-
J Stanislas	18 (3) 7	1	-
A Surman	21 (1)	2	1
J Wilshere	22 (5)	3	-
C Wilson	16 (4) 6	-	-

Josh King impressed in attack for Bournemouth

BRIGHTON

Nickname: The Seagulls
Colours: Blue and white
Ground: Amex Stadium
Tel: 0344-324-6282

Capacity: 30,750
seagulls.co.uk

Brighton are back in the top flight for the first time since 1983 but they face a battle to stay there.

Glenn Murray starred in the promotion push, scoring 23 goals, but lacks pace and scored just three goals in 22 appearances during his 2015-16 top-flight campaign.

Enhancements to the squad must be made but Brighton have the right manager. Chris Hughton has won two promotions to the Premier League and his teams are usually very well organised.

Brighton conceded 40 goals last term – the joint-fewest in the Championship – but will be mindful of the fate of Middlesbrough, who relied too much on defence last season and paid the price.

Anthony Knockaert was their star man in 2016-17, scoring 15 goals, and his creative play will again be crucial.

Longest run without a loss: 18
Longest run without a win: 3
Highest/lowest league position: 1/7
Clean sheets: 21
Yellow cards: 80 **Red cards:** 5
Avg attendance: 27,995
Players used: 28
Leading scorer: G Murray 23 (9,19)

	2016-17 H	A	Last six seasons at home P	W	D	L	OV	UN	BS	CS
Chelsea			-	-	-	-	-	-	-	-
Tottenham			-	-	-	-	-	-	-	-
Man City			-	-	-	-	-	-	-	-
Liverpool			-	-	-	-	-	-	-	-
Arsenal			-	-	-	-	-	-	-	-
Man United			-	-	-	-	-	-	-	-
Everton			-	-	-	-	-	-	-	-
Southampton			1	1	0	0	1	0	0	1
Bournemouth			2	0	1	1	0	2	1	0
West Brom			-	-	-	-	-	-	-	-
West Ham			1	0	0	1	0	1	0	0
Leicester			3	2	1	0	1	2	2	1
Stoke			-	-	-	-	-	-	-	-
Crystal Palace			2	1	0	1	2	0	1	1
Swansea			-	-	-	-	-	-	-	-
Burnley			4	2	1	1	1	3	1	2
Watford			4	0	2	2	2	2	3	0
Newcastle	L	L	1	0	0	1	1	0	1	0
Brighton										
Huddersfield	W	L	5	3	2	0	2	3	2	3

Season	Division	Pos	P	W	D	L	F	A	GD	Pts
2016-17	Championship	2	46	28	9	9	74	40	+34	93
2015-16	Championship	3	46	24	17	5	72	42	+30	89
2014-15	Championship	20	46	10	17	19	44	54	-10	47

Over/Under 48%/52% 13th   **Both score** 39%/61% 23rd

Key stat: Brighton conceded just 14 goals at home last term – the fewest of any team in the Football League

2016-17 Championship appearances

	P	G		Y	R
S Adekugbe	1	-		-	-
C Akpom	1 (9)	-		-	-
S Baldock	27 (4)	11		5	1
G Bong	24	-		6	1
Bruno	42	-		7	-
S Duffy	31	2		5	-
L Dunk	43	2		13	1
C Goldson	4 (1)	-		-	-
T Hemed	20 (17)	11		2	-
U Hunemeier	11	1		-	-
R Hunt	0 (1)	-		-	-
B Kayal	17 (3)	-		1	-
A Knockaert	44 (1)	15		10	-
K Lua Lua	0 (3)	-		-	-
N Maenpaa	1	-		-	-
E Manu	0 (2)	-		1	-
S March	9 (16)	3		-	-
J Murphy	20 (15)	2		1	-
G Murray	39 (6)	23		6	1
O Norwood	16 (17)	-		3	-
S Pocognoli	17 (3)	1		3	-

	P	G		Y	R
L Rosenior	9 (1)	-		2	-
S Sidwell	26 (8)	1		4	-
J Skalak	24 (7)	-		2	-
D Stephens	33 (6)	2		7	1
D Stockdale	45	-		1	-
F Tomori	2 (7)	-		-	-
R Towell	0 (1)	-		-	-

Brighton will make their Premier League debut

BURNLEY

Nickname: The Clarets
Colours: Claret and blue
Ground: Turf Moor
Tel: 01282-446800

Capacity: 21,401
burnleyfootballclub.com

Burnley are looking forward to a second successive Premier League season for the first time but are at risk of being dragged into the relegation scrap in 2017-18.

Home results were crucial to survival last term, with 33 of their 40 points coming from matches at Turf Moor.

However, performances tailed off at the end of the season with Burnley winning just one of their final six home league games of the campaign.

If that deterioration continues it will prove costly, unless Burnley can improve significantly on their away form.

The Clarets won once on the road and scored just 13 away goals – the fewest among teams outside the drop zone.

Sam Vokes and Andre Gray were the key men, scoring ten and nine of Burnley's 39-goal tally.

Longest run without a loss: 3
Longest run without a win: 7
Highest/lowest league position: 9/16
Clean sheets: 10
Yellow cards: 66 **Red cards:** 2
Avg attendance: 20,558
Players used: 27
Leading scorer: S Vokes 10 (6,9)

	2016-17		Last six seasons at home							
	H	A	P	W	D	L	OV	UN	BS	CS
Chelsea	D	L	2	0	1	1	1	1	2	0
Tottenham	L	L	2	0	1	1	0	2	0	1
Man City	L	L	2	1	0	1	1	1	1	1
Liverpool	W	L	2	1	0	1	0	2	0	1
Arsenal	L	L	2	0	0	2	0	2	0	0
Man United	L	D	2	0	1	1	0	2	0	1
Everton	W	L	2	1	0	1	2	0	2	0
Southampton	W	L	3	2	1	0	0	3	1	2
Bournemouth	W	L	2	1	1	0	1	1	2	0
West Brom	D	L	2	0	2	0	2	0	2	0
West Ham	L	L	3	0	1	2	3	0	3	0
Leicester	W	L	5	1	0	4	1	4	1	1
Stoke	W	L	2	1	1	0	0	2	0	2
Crystal Palace	W	W	4	2	1	1	2	2	3	1
Swansea	L	L	2	0	0	2	0	2	0	0
Burnley										
Watford	W	L	4	1	3	0	1	3	2	2
Newcastle			1	0	1	0	0	1	1	0
Brighton			4	1	2	1	1	3	2	2
Huddersfield			3	2	0	1	2	1	2	0

Season	Division	Pos	P	W	D	L	F	A	GD	Pts
2016-17	Premier League	16	38	11	7	20	39	55	-16	40
2015-16	Championship	1	46	26	15	5	72	35	+37	93
2014-15	Premier League	19	38	7	12	19	28	53	-25	33

Over/Under 50%/50% 12th   **Both score** 50%/50% 8th

Key stat: Burnley had the second worst away record in the top flight last term. They have won one of their last 21 away games

2016-17 Premier League appearances

	P	G	Y	R
D Agyei	0 (3)	-	-	-
S Arfield	23 (8)	1	3	-
P Bamford	0 (6)	-	-	-
A Barnes	20 (8)	6	7	1
J Barton	12 (2)	1	4	-
G Boyd	33 (3)	2	3	-
R Brady	7 (7)	1	1	-
S Defour	16 (5)	1	1	-
J Flanagan	3 (3)	-	2	-
A Gray	26 (6)	9	2	-
J Gudmundsson	10 (10)	1	1	-
T Heaton	35		1	-
J Hendrick	31 (1)	2	6	1
D Jones	1		1	-
L Jutkiewicz	0 (2)	-	-	-
M Keane	35	2	4	-
M Kightly	1 (4)	-	-	-
K Long	3	-	-	-
M Lowton	36	-	9	-
D Marney	21	1	7	-
B Mee	34	1	5	-

	P	G	Y	R
A O'Neill	0 (3)	-	-	-
P Robinson	3		-	-
J Tarkowski	4 (15)	-	1	-
S Vokes	21 (16)	10	-	-
S Ward	37	1	5	-
A Westwood	6 (3)	-	3	-

Sam Vokes (right) led the line for Burnley

CHELSEA

Nickname: The Blues
Colours: Blue
Ground: Stamford Bridge
Tel: 0371-811-1955

Capacity: 41,623
chelseafc.com

Antonio Conte achieved three Serie A titles in three seasons at Juventus and his reputation as a serial winner can be further enhanced by a successful Premier League title defence at Chelsea.

Playing in the Champions League will make it harder for the Blues, who also kick off without Eden Hazard while he recovers from an ankle operation.

However, they do not have the problems they had at the start of last term when Conte was getting his ideas across and his preferred formation in place.

After switching to three at the back Chelsea won 27, drew two and lost three of 32 games, and it was hard to pinpoint a weakness among the regular starting XI.

If they stay focused and motivated, which is highly likely with Conte in charge, Chelsea will be the team to beat.

Longest run without a loss: 13
Longest run without a win: 3
Highest/lowest league position: 1/7
Clean sheets: 16
Yellow cards: 72 **Red cards:** 0
Avg attendance: 41,507
Players used: 24
Leading scorer: D Costa 20 (7,18)

	2016-17 H	A	Last six seasons at home P	W	D	L	OV	UN	BS	CS
Chelsea										
Tottenham	W	L	6	3	3	0	5	1	3	3
Man City	W	W	6	3	2	1	4	2	4	1
Liverpool	L	D	6	1	2	3	4	2	6	0
Arsenal	W	L	6	5	0	1	4	2	3	3
Man United	W	L	6	3	2	1	4	2	4	2
Everton	W	W	6	5	1	0	4	2	3	3
Southampton	W	W	5	2	2	1	4	1	5	0
Bournemouth	W	W	2	1	0	1	1	1	0	1
West Brom	W	W	6	4	2	0	3	3	3	3
West Ham	W	W	5	3	2	0	2	3	2	3
Leicester	W	W	3	2	1	0	1	2	1	2
Stoke	W	W	6	5	1	0	3	3	3	3
Crystal Palace	L	W	4	2	0	2	3	1	3	1
Swansea	W	D	6	5	1	0	4	2	4	2
Burnley	W	D	2	1	1	0	1	1	1	1
Watford	W	W	2	1	1	0	2	0	2	0
Newcastle			5	4	0	1	2	3	1	3
Brighton	-	-	-	-	-	-	-	-	-	-
Huddersfield	-	-	-	-	-	-	-	-	-	-

Season	Division	Pos	P	W	D	L	F	A	GD	Pts
2016-17	Premier League	1	38	30	3	5	85	33	+52	93
2015-16	Premier League	10	38	12	14	12	59	53	+6	50
2014-15	Premier League	1	38	26	9	3	73	32	+41	87

Over/Under 68%/32% 2nd   **Both score** 50%/50% 8th

Key stat: Chelsea have won 18 of their last 19 home games in all competitions

2016-17 Premier League appearances

	P	G	Y	R		P	G	Y	R
N Ake	1 (1)	-	1	-	Pedro	26 (9)	9	6	-
M Alonso	30 (1)	6	2	-	J Terry	6 (3)	1	1	-
C Azpilicueta	38	1	4	-	Willian	15 (19)	8	3	-
M Batshuayi	1 (19)	5	-	-	K Zouma	3 (6)	-	-	-
A Begovic	2		-	-					
G Cahill	36 (1)	6	5	-					
N Chalobah	1 (9)	-	2	-					
D Costa	35	20	10	-					
T Courtois	36	-	1	-					
C Fabregas	13 (16)	5	8	-					
E Hazard	36	16	3	-					
B Ivanovic	6 (7)	-	2	-					
N Kante	35	1	9	-					
Kenedy	1		-	-					
R Loftus-Cheek	0 (6)	-	-	-					
D Luiz	33	1	6	-					
N Matic	30 (5)	1	4	-					
V Moses	29 (5)	3	4	-					
Ola Aina	0 (3)	-	-	-					
Oscar	5 (4)	-	1	-					

The Blues will start off without Eden Hazard

CRYSTAL PALACE

Nickname: The Eagles
Colours: Red and blue
Ground: Selhurst Park
Tel: 020-8768-6000

Capacity: 26,309
cpfc.co.uk

Premier League survival was the only target on Crystal Palace's agenda at the start of the year, but they are eyeing up a top-half finish in 2017-18.

Palace excelled during an eight-game spell from late February to late April, winning six matches including away to Chelsea (2-1) and Liverpool (2-1) and at home to Arsenal (3-0).

Christian Benteke and Wilfried Zaha starred and the defence looked stronger after the loan signing of Mamadou Sakho from Liverpool. And while Sam Allardyce has moved on, he has been replaced by Frank De Boer and Palace are progressing nicely after four seasons in the top flight.

However, a big improvement in their home record – won six, drawn two and lost 11 – is needed for dreams of a top-half finish to become reality.

Longest run without a loss: 5
Longest run without a win: 8
Highest/lowest league position: 8/19
Clean sheets: 7
Yellow cards: 77 **Red cards:** 0
Avg attendance: 25,160
Players used: 31
Leading scorer: C Benteke 15 (3,13)

	2016-17 H	A	Last six seasons at home P	W	D	L	OV	UN	BS	CS
Chelsea	L	W	4	1	0	3	2	2	1	1
Tottenham	L	L	4	1	0	3	2	2	2	0
Man City	L	L	4	1	0	3	2	2	2	0
Liverpool	L	W	4	1	1	2	4	0	4	0
Arsenal	W	L	4	0	1	3	3	1	2	1
Man United	L	L	4	0	1	3	2	2	2	1
Everton	L	D	4	0	2	2	0	4	0	2
Southampton	W	L	5	2	0	3	2	3	1	2
Bournemouth	D	W	2	0	1	1	1	1	2	0
West Brom	L	W	4	2	0	2	1	3	1	1
West Ham	L	L	5	1	1	3	3	2	3	1
Leicester	D	L	5	1	2	2	3	2	3	1
Stoke	W	L	4	3	1	0	2	2	3	1
Crystal Palace										
Swansea	L	L	4	1	1	2	1	3	1	2
Burnley	L	L	4	2	1	1	1	3	1	2
Watford	W	D	4	2	0	2	3	1	2	2
Newcastle			3	1	1	1	2	1	2	0
Brighton			2	1	1	0	1	1	1	1
Huddersfield			1	0	1	0	0	1	1	0

Season	Division	Pos	P	W	D	L	F	A	GD	Pts
2016-17	Premier League	14	38	12	5	21	50	63	-13	41
2015-16	Premier League	15	38	11	9	18	39	51	-12	42
2014-15	Premier League	10	38	13	9	16	47	51	-4	48

Over/Under 55%/45% 9th

Both score 47%/53% 15th

Key stat: Crystal Palace lost 11 home games – the third-successive season that their tally of home defeats has reached double figures

2016-17 Premier League appearances

	P	G		Y	R
C Benteke	36	15		10	-
J Benteke	0 (1)	-		-	-
Y Bolasie	1 (1)	-		1	-
Y Cabaye	25 (7)	4		7	-
F Campbell	0 (12)	1		-	-
S Dann	19 (4)	3		2	-
D Delaney	21 (9)	-		8	-
M Flamini	3 (7)	-		-	-
E Fryers	0 (8)	-		-	-
W Hennessey	29	-		1	-
M Jedinak	1	-		-	-
S Kaikai	0 (1)	-		-	-
M Kelly	25 (4)	-		4	-
J Ledley	13 (5)	1		1	-
Lee Chung-Yong	4 (11)	-		-	-
S Mandanda	9	-		-	-
J McArthur	24 (5)	5		5	-
L Milivojevic	14	2		4	-
J Mutch	0 (4)	-		-	-
P N'Diaye Souare	3	-		-	-
J Puncheon	35 (1)	-		9	-
L Remy	1 (4)	-		-	-

	P	G		Y	R
M Sakho	8	-		-	-
B Sako	0 (7)	-		-	-
J Schlupp	11 (4)	-		-	-
J Tomkins	23 (1)	3		4	-
A Townsend	30 (6)	3		4	-
J Ward	38	-		7	-
C Wickham	4 (4)	2		1	-
W Zaha	34 (1)	7		8	-
P van Aanholt	8 (3)	2		1	-

Palace are aiming to improve their home form

EVERTON

Nickname: The Toffees
Colours: Blue and white
Ground: Goodison Park
Tel: 0151-530-5300

Capacity: 39,572
evertonfc.com

Everton enjoyed a very good season, increasing their points tally from 47 to 61, but ended up detached in seventh – eight points outside the top six and 15 ahead of eighth.

The question is do they improve and get closer to those above them or will they sink nearer to the chasing pack?

Judging by the signings of Wayne Rooney, Jordan Pickford, Michael Keane, Davy Klaassen and Sandro Ramirez, there seems to be plenty of ambition in the boardroom but it will take a massive effort to catch the teams above them.

Last season they were far too reliant on Romelu Lukaku, with the departed Belgian scoring 25 of their 62 goals. They also struggled on the road – winning just four away games – and won only twice against the top six, losing six times.

Longest run without a loss: 9
Longest run without a win: 5
Highest/lowest league position: 5/9
Clean sheets: 13
Yellow cards: 73 **Red cards:** 2
Avg attendance: 39,310
Players used: 27
Leading scorer: R Lukaku 25 (7,17)

	2016-17		Last six seasons at home							
	H	A	P	W	D	L	OV	UN	BS	CS
Chelsea	L	L	6	3	0	3	4	2	3	2
Tottenham	D	L	6	2	3	1	1	5	3	2
Man City	W	D	6	3	1	2	2	4	2	3
Liverpool	L	L	6	0	4	2	2	4	3	1
Arsenal	W	L	6	2	2	2	3	3	3	1
Man United	D	D	6	3	1	2	2	4	1	3
Everton										
Southampton	W	L	5	4	1	0	3	2	3	2
Bournemouth	W	L	2	2	0	0	2	0	2	0
West Brom	W	W	6	3	2	1	2	4	1	4
West Ham	W	D	5	4	0	1	2	3	2	3
Leicester	W	W	3	1	1	1	3	0	3	0
Stoke	W	D	6	3	0	3	2	4	1	3
Crystal Palace	D	W	4	0	2	2	2	2	4	0
Swansea	D	L	6	2	3	1	2	4	3	3
Burnley	W	L	2	2	0	0	1	1	1	1
Watford	W	L	2	1	1	0	1	1	1	1
Newcastle			5	4	1	0	5	0	3	2
Brighton			-	-	-	-	-	-	-	-
Huddersfield			-	-	-	-	-	-	-	-

Season	Division	Pos	P	W	D	L	F	A	GD	Pts
2016-17	Premier League	7	38	17	10	11	62	44	+18	61
2015-16	Premier League	11	38	11	14	13	59	55	+4	47
2014-15	Premier League	11	38	12	11	15	48	50	-2	47

Over/Under 50%/50% 12th   **Both score** 50%/50% 8th

Key stat: Everton collected 43 points from home games last season – their highest total in the Premier League and their best effort since 1989-90

2016-17 Premier League appearances

	P	G		Y	R
L Baines	32	2		4	-
R Barkley	32 (4)	5		5	-
G Barry	23 (10)	2		10	-
Y Bolasie	12 (1)	1		2	-
D Calvert-Lewin	5 (6)	1		1	-
T Cleverley	4 (6)	-		1	-
S Coleman	26	4		3	-
T Davies	18 (6)	2		4	-
G Deulofeu	4 (7)	-		1	-
R Funes Mori	16 (7)	-		-	-
I Gueye	32 (1)	1		11	-
M Holgate	16 (2)	-		2	-
P Jagielka	25 (2)	3		5	1
J Kenny	0 (1)	-		-	-
A Kone	0 (6)	-		-	-
A Lennon	6 (5)	-		-	-
A Lookman	3 (5)	1		-	-
R Lukaku	36 (1)	25		3	-
J McCarthy	7 (5)	1		2	-
K Mirallas	23 (12)	4		2	-
B Oviedo	6	-		3	-

	P	G		Y	R
M Pennington	2 (1)			-	-
J Robles	19 (1)	-		2	-
M Schneiderlin	12 (2)	1		2	-
M Stekelenburg	19	-		2	-
E Valencia	5 (16)	3		1	-
A Williams	35 (1)	1		7	1

Everton starlet Tom Davies impressed last term

HUDDERSFIELD

Nickname: The Terriers
Colours: Blue and white
Ground: John Smith's Stadium   **Capacity:** 24,500
Tel: 01484-484-112   htafc.com

Huddersfield went from Championship strugglers to playoff winners in the space of a year but must find another big improvement to stay in the top flight.

The Terriers went up despite a minus-two goal difference but regular viewers of second-tier football would testify to the quality and intensity of their football.

It was a team effort although attackers Elias Kachunga and Nahki Wells contributed goal tallies of 12 and ten.

Adding quality up front is essential and there is room for improvement at the back as their tally of 58 goals conceded was one more than relegated Wigan.

Huddersfield have often been astute in the transfer market and now have the benefit of a far bigger budget. However, they will have to spend wisely if they are to stand a good chance of survival.

Longest run without a loss: 7
Longest run without a win: 5
Highest/lowest league position: 1/8
Clean sheets: 12
Yellow cards: 87 **Red cards:** 4
Avg attendance: 20,342
Players used: 25
Leading scorer: E Kachunga 12 (7,11)

	2016-17 H	A	Last six seasons at home P	W	D	L	OV	UN	BS	CS
Chelsea	-	-	-	-	-	-	-	-	-	-
Tottenham	-	-	-	-	-	-	-	-	-	-
Man City	-	-	-	-	-	-	-	-	-	-
Liverpool	-	-	-	-	-	-	-	-	-	-
Arsenal	-	-	-	-	-	-	-	-	-	-
Man United	-	-	-	-	-	-	-	-	-	-
Everton	-	-	-	-	-	-	-	-	-	-
Southampton	-	-	-	-	-	-	-	-	-	-
Bournemouth			3	1	0	2	2	1	1	0
West Brom	-	-	-	-	-	-	-	-	-	-
West Ham	-	-	-	-	-	-	-	-	-	-
Leicester			2	0	0	2	0	2	0	0
Stoke	-	-	-	-	-	-	-	-	-	-
Crystal Palace			1	1	0	0	0	1	0	1
Swansea	-	-	-	-	-	-	-	-	-	-
Burnley			3	2	0	1	2	1	2	1
Watford			3	1	0	2	3	0	3	0
Newcastle	L	W	1	0	0	1	1	0	1	0
Brighton	W	L	5	1	3	1	2	3	5	0
Huddersfield										

Season	Division	Pos	P	W	D	L	F	A	GD	Pts
2016-17	Championship	5	46	25	6	15	56	58	-2	81
2015-16	Championship	19	46	13	12	21	59	70	-11	51
2014-15	Championship	16	46	13	16	17	58	75	-17	55

Over/Under 48%/52% 13th   **Both score** 52%/48% 14th

Key stat: Huddersfield scored 56 league goals last season. The lowest of any promoted team since Birmingham, who scored 54 goals in 2008-09

2016-17 Championship appearances

	P	G	Y	R
P Billing	13 (11)	2	4	-
I Brown	12 (3)	4	3	-
H Bunn	6 (10)	-	1	-
J Coleman	3 (2)	-	-	-
M Cranie	7 (7)	-	1	-
J Gorenc-Stankovic	4 (3)	-	2	-
M Hefele	28 (9)	3	6	-
J Hogg	33 (4)	1	6	-
T Holmes-Dennis	7 (2)	-	2	-
M Hudson	17 (5)	-	6	-
E Kachunga	41 (1)	12	6	-
J Lolley	8 (11)	1	-	-
C Lowe	39 (2)	2	8	-
A Mooy	42 (3)	4	6	-
K Palmer	16 (8)	4	4	-
I Paurevic	0 (1)	-	-	-
J Payne	10 (13)	2	1	1
C Quaner	9 (7)	2	2	-
S Scannell	8 (7)	-	1	-
C Schindler	43 (1)	2	4	-

	P	G	Y	R
T Smith	40 (2)	4	6	-
D Ward	43	-	-	1
N Wells	31 (12)	10	4	-
D Whitehead	10 (6)	-	6	1
R van La Parra	36 (4)	2	4	1

Penalty shootout success sent Huddersfield up

LEICESTER

Nickname: The Foxes
Colours: Blue
Ground: King Power Stadium **Capacity:** 32,500
Tel: 0344-815-5000 lcfc.co.uk

Craig Shakespeare has earned a three-year deal as Leicester's new manager but needs to carefully manage expectations if he is to get through his first season as a Premier League manager.

The Leicester board showed a ruthless streak in their sacking of Claudio Ranieri, although their stance was justified by a sudden improvement in results.

The Foxes racked up 23 points from 13 games under Shakespeare but may struggle to carry on in the same vein.

They have have lacked a driving force in midfield since Ngolo Kante's departure and no longer have the carrot of Champions League football to entice new signings. The squad looks equipped for mid-table but major improvements would be needed for fans to start dreaming of a return to European football.

Longest run without a loss: 5
Longest run without a win: 6
Highest/lowest league position: 9/17
Clean sheets: 9
Yellow cards: 72 **Red cards:** 1
Avg attendance: 31,893
Players used: 25
Leading scorer: J Vardy 13 (4,10)

	2016-17		Last six seasons at home							
	H	A	P	W	D	L	OV	UN	BS	CS
Chelsea	L	L	3	1	0	2	3	0	2	0
Tottenham	L	D	3	0	1	2	2	1	3	0
Man City	W	L	3	1	1	1	1	2	1	1
Liverpool	W	L	3	2	0	1	2	1	2	1
Arsenal	D	L	3	0	2	1	1	2	2	1
Man United	L	L	3	1	1	1	2	1	2	0
Everton	L	L	3	1	1	1	2	1	2	0
Southampton	D	L	4	3	1	0	1	3	1	3
Bournemouth	D	L	3	1	2	0	1	2	2	1
West Brom	L	W	3	0	1	2	2	1	2	0
West Ham	W	W	4	2	1	1	3	1	3	1
Leicester										
Stoke	W	D	3	2	0	1	1	2	0	2
Crystal Palace	W	D	5	3	0	2	3	2	2	2
Swansea	W	L	3	3	0	0	2	1	1	2
Burnley	W	L	5	2	3	0	3	2	3	2
Watford	W	L	5	3	1	1	4	1	3	2
Newcastle			2	2	0	0	1	1	0	2
Brighton			3	2	0	1	2	1	2	2
Huddersfield			2	2	0	0	2	0	2	0

Season	Division	Pos	P	W	D	L	F	A	GD	Pts
2016-17	Premier League	12	38	12	8	18	48	63	-15	44
2015-16	Premier League	1	38	23	12	3	68	36	+32	81
2014-15	Premier League	14	38	11	8	19	46	55	-9	41

Over/Under 63%/37% 4th   **Both score** 53%/47% 7th

Key stat: Leicester improved in the second half of the season but finished the lowest of any defending champion since Leeds, who were 17th in 1992-93

2016-17 Premier League appearances

	P G		Y	R
M Albrighton	29 (4)	2	5	-
D Amartey	17 (7)	1	3	-
Y Benalouane	11	-	4	-
B Chilwell	7 (5)	1	2	-
D Drinkwater	27 (2)	1	6	-
C Fuchs	35 (1)	2	10	-
D Gray	9 (21)	1	2	-
L Hernandez	3 (1)	-	1	-
R Huth	33	2	9	-
M James	0 (1)	-	-	-
A King	15 (8)	1	4	-
R Mahrez	33 (3)	6	4	-
N Mendy	4	-	1	-
W Morgan	27	1	3	-
A Musa	7 (14)	2	1	-
O Ndidi	17	2	-	-
S Okazaki	21 (9)	3	1	-
J Schlupp	1 (3)	-	-	-
K Schmeichel	30		1	-
D Simpson	34 (1)	-	12	-
I Slimani	13 (10)	7	1	-

	P G		Y	R
L Ulloa	3 (13)	1	-	-
J Vardy	33 (2)	13	2	1
M Wasilewski	1	-	-	-
R Zieler	8 (1)	-		

Leicester failed to replicate their 2015-16 form

LIVERPOOL

Nickname: The Reds
Colours: Red
Ground: Anfield
Tel: 0151-264-2500

Capacity: 54,074
liverpoolfc.tv

Jurgen Klopp was brought to Liverpool to re-establish them as Champions League regulars, but he may struggle to achieve a top-four finish this season.

Liverpool's style of play is suited to European football and they may have a good run in the Champions League.

However, the extra workload places big demands on their squad, which looked wafer-thin at times last season.

There was no quality focal point up top and they lacked pace when Sadio Mane was injured – a problem perhaps lessened by the capture of Mohamed Salah.

At their best the Reds were capable of beating the best, as can be seen by their points haul of 20 against the top six. But they often struggled to get the basics right in defence and ended up losing six matches to teams outside the top eight.

Longest run without a loss: 11
Longest run without a win: 5
Highest/lowest league position: 1/5
Clean sheets: 12
Yellow cards: 54 **Red cards:** 0
Avg attendance: 53,039 **Players used:** 23
Leading scorers: P Coutinho 13 (1,11)
S Mane 13 (6,11)

	2016-17		Last six seasons at home							
	H	A	P	W	D	L	OV	UN	BS	CS
Chelsea	D	W	6	1	3	2	3	3	5	0
Tottenham	W	D	6	4	2	0	3	3	3	3
Man City	W	D	6	4	2	0	4	2	4	2
Liverpool										
Arsenal	W	W	6	2	2	2	5	1	5	0
Man United	D	D	6	1	2	3	2	4	3	2
Everton	W	W	6	4	2	0	4	2	2	4
Southampton	D	D	5	2	2	1	4	2	2	
Bournemouth	D	L	2	1	1	0	1	1	1	1
West Brom	W	W	6	3	1	2	4	2	4	0
West Ham	D	W	5	2	2	1	3	2	2	2
Leicester	W	L	3	2	1	0	2	1	2	1
Stoke	W	W	6	4	2	0	2	4	2	4
Crystal Palace	L	W	4	1	0	3	4	0	4	0
Swansea	L	W	6	4	1	1	4	2	3	3
Burnley	W	L	2	2	0	0	1	1	1	1
Watford	W	W	2	2	0	0	1	1	1	1
Newcastle			5	3	2	0	3	2	4	1
Brighton	-	-	-	-	-	-	-	-	-	-
Huddersfield	-	-	-	-	-	-	-	-	-	-

Season	Division	Pos	P	W	D	L	F	A	GD	Pts
2016-17	Premier League	4	38	22	10	6	78	42	+36	76
2015-16	Premier League	8	38	16	12	10	63	50	+13	60
2014-15	Premier League	6	38	18	8	12	52	48	+4	62

Over/Under 61%/39% 6th   **Both score** 63%/37% 1st

Key stat: Liverpool had the best record against the big six last season, winning five and drawing five of the ten fixtures

2016-17 Premier League appearances

	P	G	Y	R
T Alex-Arnold	2 (5)	-	-	-
E Can	26 (6)	5	6	-
N Clyne	37	-	-	-
P Coutinho	28 (3)	13	2	-
M Grujic	0 (5)	-	1	-
J Henderson	24	1	8	-
L Karius	10	-	-	-
R Klavan	15 (5)	-	3	-
A Lallana	27 (4)	8	3	-
D Lovren	29	2	6	-
Lucas	12 (12)	-	4	-
S Mane	26 (1)	13	4	-
J Matip	27 (2)	1	3	-
S Mignolet	28	-	-	-
J Milner	36	7	5	-
A Moreno	2 (10)	-	1	-
D Origi	14 (20)	7	-	-
Ovie Ejaria	0 (2)	-	-	-
R Firmino	34 (1)	11	5	-
K Stewart	0 (4)	-	-	-

	P	G	Y	R
D Sturridge	7 (13)	3	1	-
G Wijnaldum	33 (3)	6	2	-
B Woodburn	1 (4)	-	-	-

Jurgen Klopp's team entertained last season

MANCHESTER CITY

Nickname: The Citizens
Colours: Sky blue and white
Ground: Etihad Stadium
Tel: 0161 444 1894

Capacity: 55,097
mcfc.co.uk

Pep Guardiola's first year at Manchester City has been a major disappointment but that has done nothing to dampen market expectations, with the Citizens topping the title betting.

They have a obvious chance given the quality they possess up front, but there are ongoing doubts over whether they have the mental strength and defensive know-how to finish top of the pile.

Guardiola's certainty in his beliefs has been a strength at previous clubs but he may have to modify his tactics to make them more suited to English football.

City often looked unsettled when they were pressed and their record in the biggest games – two wins from 12 against the top seven and none from six against the top four – was very poor and will need to improve.

Longest run without a loss: 8
Longest run without a win: 4
Highest/lowest league position: 1/5
Clean sheets: 12
Yellow cards: 71 **Red cards:** 4
Avg attendance: 54,018
Players used: 25
Leading scorer: S Aguero 20 (6,15)

	2016-17 H	A	Last six seasons at home P	W	D	L	OV	UN	BS	CS
Chelsea	L	L	6	3	1	2	3	3	3	2
Tottenham	D	L	6	4	1	1	6	0	5	1
Man City										
Liverpool	D	L	6	3	2	1	5	1	5	1
Arsenal	W	D	6	3	2	1	3	3	4	1
Man United	D	W	6	3	1	2	2	4	2	3
Everton	D	L	6	3	3	0	1	5	3	3
Southampton	D	W	5	4	1	0	3	2	4	1
Bournemouth	W	W	2	2	0	0	2	0	1	1
West Brom	W	W	6	6	0	0	5	1	3	3
West Ham	W	W	5	4	0	1	3	2	3	2
Leicester	W	L	3	2	0	1	2	1	2	1
Stoke	D	W	6	4	1	1	3	3	0	5
Crystal Palace	W	W	4	4	0	0	3	1	0	4
Swansea	W	W	6	6	0	0	5	1	3	3
Burnley	W	W	2	1	1	0	2	0	2	0
Watford	W	W	2	2	0	0	0	2	0	2
Newcastle			5	5	0	0	5	0	2	3
Brighton			-	-	-	-	-	-	-	-
Huddersfield			-	-	-	-	-	-	-	-

Season	Division	Pos	P	W	D	L	F	A	GD	Pts
2016-17	Premier League	3	38	23	9	6	80	39	+41	78
2015-16	Premier League	4	38	19	9	10	71	41	+30	66
2014-15	Premier League	2	38	24	7	7	83	38	+45	79

Over/Under 71%/29% 1st   **Both score** 61%/39% 2nd

Key stat: Manchester City have not lost a home match in 2017 and are unbeaten at the Etihad in 15 games

2016-17 Premier League appearances

	P	G		Y	R
S Aguero	25 (6)	20		4	1
C Bravo	22	-		-	-
W Caballero	16 (1)	-		-	-
G Clichy	24 (1)	1		2	-
K De Bruyne	33 (3)	6		4	-
F Delph	2 (5)	1		1	-
Fernandinho	31 (1)	2		4	2
Fernando	5 (10)	-		3	-
G Jesus	8 (2)	7		2	-
A Garcia	1 (3)	-		-	-
I Gundogan	9 (1)	3		-	-
K Iheanacho	5 (15)	4		-	-
A Kolarov	27 (2)	1		6	-
V Kompany	10 (1)	3		5	-
S Nasri	0 (1)	-		-	-
J Navas	12 (12)	-		2	-
Nolito	9 (10)	4		3	1
N Otamendi	29 (1)	1		9	-
B Sagna	14 (3)	-		2	-
L Sane	20 (6)	5		4	-
D Silva	31 (3)	4		6	-

	P	G		Y	R
R Sterling	29 (4)	7		7	-
J Stones	23 (4)	-		1	-
Y Toure	22 (3)	5		4	-
P Zabaleta	11 (8)	1		2	-

Gabriel Jesus made a strong start at the Etihad

MANCHESTER UNITED

Nickname: The Red Devils
Colours: Red and white
Ground: Old Trafford
Tel: 0161-868-8000

Capacity: 75,643
manutd.com

Manchester United finished last season with two major cups and Champions League qualification but they fell a long way short in the league and may struggle to bridge the gap to the teams above.

A better season can be expected from Paul Pogba but United need improvements in other areas if they are to get into the top four, let alone challenge for the title.

They scored just 54 goals, which was 32 fewer than Tottenham, 31 less than Chelsea and one inferior to Bournemouth.

Their lack of potency was the main reason behind so many draws, including ten from 19 games at Old Trafford.

Offering Champions League football makes it easier to attract the likes of Romelu Lukaku, but even he may struggle to fill the void left by Zlatan Ibrahimovic.

Longest run without a loss: 25
Longest run without a win: 5
Highest/lowest league position: 5/8
Clean sheets: 17
Yellow cards: 79 **Red cards:** 2
Avg attendance: 75,289
Players used: 31
Leading scorer: Z Ibrahimovic 17 (4,14)

	2016-17		Last six seasons at home							
	H	A	P	W	D	L	OV	UN	BS	CS
Chelsea	W	L	6	2	3	1	1	5	2	3
Tottenham	W	L	6	4	0	2	4	2	2	4
Man City	L	D	6	1	1	4	5	1	4	1
Liverpool	D	D	6	4	1	1	5	1	4	1
Arsenal	D	L	6	4	2	0	3	3	5	1
Man United										
Everton	D	D	6	3	2	1	2	4	3	2
Southampton	W	D	5	2	1	2	1	4	2	1
Bournemouth	D	W	2	1	1	0	1	1	2	0
West Brom	D	W	6	3	1	2	1	5	1	4
West Ham	D	W	5	3	2	0	2	3	3	2
Leicester	W	W	3	2	1	0	2	1	3	0
Stoke	D	D	6	5	1	0	4	2	4	2
Crystal Palace	W	W	4	4	0	0	0	4	0	4
Swansea	D	W	6	4	1	1	3	3	4	2
Burnley	D	W	2	1	1	0	1	1	1	1
Watford	W	L	2	2	0	0	0	2	0	2
Newcastle			5	2	2	1	2	3	3	1
Brighton	-	-	-	-	-	-	-	-	-	-
Huddersfield	-	-	-	-	-	-	-	-	-	-

Season	Division	Pos	P	W	D	L	F	A	GD	Pts
2016-17	Premier League	6	38	18	15	5	54	29	+25	69
2015-16	Premier League	5	38	19	9	10	49	35	+14	66
2014-15	Premier League	4	38	20	10	8	62	37	+25	70

Over/Under 34%/66% 20th   **Both score** 50%/50% 8th

Key stat: Manchester United drew ten home games last term – the joint-highest of any team in Premier League history

2016-17 Premier League appearances

	P	G		Y	R
E Bailly	24 (1)	-		4	-
D Blind	20 (3)	1		2	-
M Carrick	18 (5)	-		2	-
M Darmian	15 (3)	-		3	-
M Depay	0 (4)	-		1	-
M Fellaini	18 (10)	1		9	1
T Fosu-Mensah	1 (3)	-		-	-
A Gomes	0 (1)	-		-	-
J Harrop	1	1		-	-
A Herrera	27 (4)	1		6	1
Z Ibrahimovic	27 (1)	17		7	-
J Pereira	1	-		-	-
P Jones	18	-		2	-
J Lingard	18 (7)	1		3	-
A Martial	18 (7)	4		2	-
J Mata	19 (6)	6		3	-
S McTominay	1 (1)	-		1	-
D Mitchell	1	-		-	-
H Mkhitaryan	15 (9)	4		1	-
P Pogba	29 (1)	5		7	-
M Rashford	16 (16)	5		3	-
M Rojo	18 (3)	1		5	-

	P	G		Y	R
S Romero	2	-		-	-
W Rooney	15 (10)	5		8	-
M Schneiderlin	0 (3)	-		-	-
L Shaw	9 (2)	-		1	-
C Smalling	13 (5)	1		-	-
A Tuanzebe	4	-		-	-
L Valencia	27 (1)	1		5	-
A Young	8 (4)	-		2	-
D de Gea	35	-		2	-

Jose got his hands on yet more silverware

NEWCASTLE

Nickname: The Magpies
Colours: Black and white
Ground: St James' Park
Tel: 0844-372-1892

Capacity: 52,354
nufc.co.uk

Newcastle return to the Premier League with a second-tier title under their belts but cannot afford any complacency if they are to re-establish themselves in the Premier League.

Improvements must be made and Mike Ashley needs to be bold in the market, as Newcastle return to the top flight with a squad which looks little better than the one with which they were relegated.

Key men Dwight Gayle and Jamaal Lascelles still have a bit to prove in the Premier League and Aleksandr Mitrovic seemed to go backwards during his year in the Championship.

However, the positivity among the crowd has returned and Newcastle – enhanced by some summer additions – look the most likely of the promoted trio to have a comfortable season.

Longest run without a loss: 11
Longest run without a win: 3
Highest/lowest league position: 1/5
Clean sheets: 19
Yellow cards: 80 **Red cards:** 3
Avg attendance: 51,106
Players used: 30
Leading scorer: D Gayle 23 (8,14)

	2016-17 H	A	Last six seasons at home P	W	D	L	OV	UN	BS	CS
Chelsea			5	3	1	1	4	1	3	1
Tottenham			5	2	1	2	5	0	4	0
Man City			5	0	1	4	1	4	2	0
Liverpool			5	3	1	1	2	3	1	3
Arsenal			5	0	1	4	1	4	1	1
Man United			5	1	1	3	4	1	1	1
Everton			5	2	0	3	4	1	3	0
Southampton			4	1	2	1	3	1	4	0
Bournemouth			1	0	0	1	1	0	1	0
West Brom			5	3	1	1	3	2	4	1
West Ham			4	2	1	1	3	1	3	2
Leicester			2	1	0	1	1	1	0	1
Stoke			5	3	2	0	3	2	3	2
Crystal Palace			3	2	1	0	1	2	1	2
Swansea			5	1	1	3	4	1	3	2
Burnley			1	0	1	0	1	0	1	0
Watford			1	0	0	1	1	0	1	0
Newcastle										
Brighton	W	W	1	1	0	0	0	1	0	1
Huddersfield	L	W	1	0	0	1	1	0	1	0

Season	Division	Pos	P	W	D	L	F	A	GD	Pts
2016-17	Championship	1	46	29	7	10	85	40	+45	94
2015-16	Premier League	18	38	9	10	19	44	65	-21	37
2014-15	Premier League	15	38	10	9	19	40	63	-23	39

Over/Under 54%/46% 7th   **Both score** 48%/52% 19th

Key stat: Newcastle conceded 17 goals on their league travels last season – the equal lowest in the Football League alongside Plymouth and Luton

2016-17 Championship appearances

	P	G	Y	R
R Aarons	1 (3)	-	-	-
S Ameobi	0 (4)	-	-	-
V Anita	24 (3)	-	1	1
A Armstrong	0 (2)	-	-	-
C Atsu	15 (17)	5	2	-
A Perez	25 (11)	9	2	-
C Clark	34	3	3	-
J Colback	24 (5)	-	10	-
K Darlow	34		3	-
M Diame	27 (10)	3	4	-
P Dummett	44 (1)	-	8	1
R Elliot	3		-	-
J Gamez	2 (3)	-	-	-
D Gayle	26 (6)	23	3	-
Y Gouffran	33 (6)	5	3	-
M Haidara	0 (1)	-	-	-
G Hanley	5 (5)	1	1	-
I Hayden	28 (5)	2	7	-
D Janmaat	2		1	-
J Lascelles	41 (2)	3	6	-
A Lazaar	0 (4)	-	-	-
C Mbemba	12	1		-
A Mitrovic	11 (14)	4	3	-

	P	G	Y	R
D Murphy	7 (8)	5	-	-
M Ritchie	40 (2)	12	9	-
M Sels	9		-	-
J Shelvey	38 (4)	5	10	1
J Sterry	0 (2)	-	-	-
C Tiote	0 (1)	-	-	-
D Yedlin	21 (6)	1	3	-

Newcastle were promoted as champions

SOUTHAMPTON

Nickname: The Saints
Colours: Red and white
Ground: St Mary's Stadium **Capacity:** 32,689
Tel: 0845-688-9448 saintsfc.co.uk

It shows just how far Southampton have come that there was a sense of frustration after a campaign which featured European football, a Wembley cup final and an eighth-place finish – leading to the departure of manager Claude Puel and the arrival of Mauricio Pellegrino.

They didn't have much luck with injuries – Virgil van Dijk and Charlie Austin were out for long periods – and were the only team to play three games in six days over the Christmas period.

However, Southampton's points tally (46) was 17 fewer than the season before.

An improvement looks likely even if some key players depart. Southampton are usually astute in the transfer market and can anticipate a big contribution from classy forward Manolo Gabbiadini in his first full season in England.

Longest run without a loss: 5
Longest run without a win: 5
Highest/lowest league position: 7/13
Clean sheets: 14
Yellow cards: 60 **Red cards:** 2
Avg attendance: 30,936
Players used: 26
Leading scorer: N Redmond 7 (1,6)

	2016-17 H	A	Last six seasons at home P	W	D	L	OV	UN	BS	CS
Chelsea	L	L	5	1	1	3	3	2	3	0
Tottenham	L	L	5	0	1	4	4	1	4	0
Man City	L	D	5	2	1	2	4	1	3	0
Liverpool	D	D	5	2	1	2	3	2	2	1
Arsenal	L	L	5	2	2	1	2	3	2	2
Man United	D	L	5	0	2	3	3	2	4	1
Everton	W	L	5	3	1	1	2	3	0	4
Southampton										
Bournemouth	D	W	2	1	1	0	0	2	0	2
West Brom	L	W	5	2	1	2	3	2	1	3
West Ham	L	W	6	2	3	1	1	5	2	4
Leicester	W	D	4	2	1	1	2	2	1	2
Stoke	L	D	5	1	2	2	1	4	2	1
Crystal Palace	W	L	5	5	0	0	2	3	2	3
Swansea	W	L	5	3	1	1	1	4	2	2
Burnley	W	L	3	3	0	0	1	2	1	2
Watford	D	W	3	2	1	0	1	2	1	2
Newcastle			4	4	0	0	3	1	1	3
Brighton			1	1	0	0	1	0	0	1
Huddersfield			-	-	-	-	-	-	-	-

Season	Division	Pos	P	W	D	L	F	A	GD	Pts
2016-17	Premier League	8	38	12	10	16	41	48	-7	46
2015-16	Premier League	6	38	18	9	11	59	41	+18	63
2014-15	Premier League	7	38	18	6	14	54	33	+21	60

Over/Under 50%/50% 12th   **Both score** 42%/58% 18th

Key stat: Southampton won six home league games – the lowest for a top-eight side since Liverpool in 2011-12 (finished eighth and also won six at home)

2016-17 Premier League appearances

	P	G		Y	R
C Austin	11 (4)	6	▮▮▮▮	1	-
R Bertrand	28	2	▮	3	-
S Boufal	12 (12)	1	▮	5	-
M Caceres	1	-		-	-
J Clasie	12 (4)	1	▮	3	-
S Davis	29 (3)	-		3	-
J Fonte	17	-		2	-
F Forster	38	-		3	-
M Gabbiadini	10 (1)	4	▮▮▮	1	-
P Hojbjerg	14 (8)	-		2	-
S Long	10 (22)	3	▮	2	-
C Martina	6 (3)	-		-	-
S McQueen	5 (8)	-		-	-
J Pied	1 (3)	-		-	-
N Redmond	32 (5)	7	▮▮▮▮▮	2	1
H Reed	1 (2)	-		-	-
J Rodriguez	9 (15)	5	▮▮▮	-	-
O Romeu	35	1	▮	11	-
J Sims	1 (6)	-		-	-
C Soares	30	-		7	-
J Stephens	15 (2)	-		1	-

	P	G		Y	R
D Tadic	30 (3)	3	▮▮	4	-
M Targett	5	-		-	-
J Ward-Prowse	22 (8)	4	▮▮	4	-
M Yoshida	23	1	▮	2	-
V van Dijk	21	1	▮	4	1

Southampton enjoyed another solid campaign

STOKE

Nickname: The Potters
Colours: Red and white
Ground: bet365 Stadium
Tel: 01782-367-598

Capacity: 27,902
stokecityfc.com

Stoke have been a progressive club so last season's 13th place was disappointing.

Owner Peter Coates has invested heavily and warns against expecting another spending spree.

However, the squad looks in need of fresh blood, especially up front. Saido Berahino has struggled and Peter Crouch finished the campaign as the club's top league scorer with seven goals.

However, Stoke should be stronger in the goalkeeping position with Jack Butland fully recovered from injury – the England international made just five league appearances last term.

Stoke started slowly start last season, taking three points from their first seven games, and the fixture list again looks unkind as they face eight of last term's top-half teams in their first nine matches.

Longest run without a loss: 6
Longest run without a win: 7
Highest/lowest league position: 9/19
Clean sheets: 11
Yellow cards: 71 **Red cards:** 2
Avg attendance: 27,117
Players used: 26
Leading scorer: P Crouch 7 (2,7)

	2016-17 H	A	Last six seasons at home P	W	D	L	OV	UN	BS	CS
Chelsea	L	L	6	2	1	3	3	3	2	2
Tottenham	L	L	6	2	0	4	5	1	2	1
Man City	L	D	6	1	3	2	2	4	4	2
Liverpool	L	L	6	3	0	3	4	2	4	1
Arsenal	L	L	6	2	3	1	2	4	3	3
Man United	D	D	6	2	3	1	1	5	4	1
Everton	D	L	6	1	4	1	1	5	4	1
Southampton	D	W	5	1	3	1	3	2	4	1
Bournemouth	L	D	2	1	0	1	1	1	1	0
West Brom	D	L	6	1	3	2	1	5	2	3
West Ham	D	D	5	2	2	1	3	2	3	1
Leicester	D	L	3	0	2	1	2	1	2	0
Stoke										
Crystal Palace	W	L	4	2	0	2	3	1	3	1
Swansea	W	L	6	4	2	0	3	3	4	2
Burnley	W	L	2	1	0	1	1	1	1	1
Watford	W	W	2	1	0	1	0	2	0	1
Newcastle			5	4	0	1	2	3	2	3
Brighton	-	-	-	-	-	-	-	-	-	-
Huddersfield	-	-	-	-	-	-	-	-	-	-

Season	Division	Pos	P	W	D	L	F	A	GD	Pts
2016-17	Premier League	13	38	11	11	16	41	56	-15	44
2015-16	Premier League	9	38	14	9	15	41	55	-14	51
2014-15	Premier League	9	38	15	9	14	48	45	+3	54

Over/Under 39%/61% 19th

Both score 50%/50% 8th

Key stat: Stoke's 13th-place finish marked the first time they have finished lower than the previous season since 2011-12

2016-17 Premier League appearances

	P	G		Y	R
C Adam	17 (7)	1		7	-
I Afellay	3 (9)	-		-	-
J Allen	34 (2)	6		9	-
M Arnautovic	32	6		9	1
P Bardsley	14 (1)	-		5	1
S Berahino	8 (5)	-		-	-
M Biram Diouf	15 (12)	1		3	-
W Bony	9 (1)	2		1	-
J Butland	5	-		-	-
G Cameron	18 (1)	-		1	-
P Crouch	13 (14)	7		3	-
S Given	5	-		1	-
L Grant	28	-		1	-
G Imbula	9 (3)	-		1	-
G Johnson	21 (2)	-		1	-
B Krkic	5 (4)	3		1	-
B Martins Indi	35	1		4	-
M Muniesa	7 (3)	1		2	-
J Ngoy	0 (5)	-		-	-
E Pieters	35 (1)	-		5	-
X Shaqiri	21	4		2	-

	P	G		Y	R
R Shawcross	35	1		6	-
R Sobhi	8 (9)	-		2	-
J Walters	13 (10)	4		1	-
G Whelan	26 (4)	-		5	-
P Wollscheid	2	-		1	-

Jack Butland is set to be back in the Stoke goal

SWANSEA

Nickname: The Swans
Colours: White
Ground: Liberty Stadium
Tel: 01792-616-600

Capacity: 20,972
swanseacity.net

Swansea secured their Premier League survival after collecting a remarkable haul of 13 points from their final five games of 2016-17 and will be working hard over the summer to avoid getting into similar difficulty next season.

The obvious area for improvement is in defence as they conceded 70 goals last term – second only to Hull and 17 more than relegated Middlesbrough.

Offensively, there was lots to like about the Swans as Fernando Llorente helped himself to 15 goals while Gylfi Sigurdsson was third on the assist table with 13.

They also now seem to have the right manager in charge. Paul Clement inherited a disjointed, confidence-shot side when he arrived in January, but led them to nine wins, two draws and eight defeats during his 19 games in charge.

Longest run without a loss: 5
Longest run without a win: 11
Highest/lowest league position: 15/20
Clean sheets: 8
Yellow cards: 56 **Red cards:** 0
Avg attendance: 20,619
Players used: 27
Leading scorer: F Llorente 15 (5,11)

2016-17	H	A	P	W	D	L	OV	UN	BS	CS

2016-17			Last six seasons at home							
	H	A	P	W	D	L	OV	UN	BS	CS
Chelsea	D	L	6	1	3	2	2	4	3	1
Tottenham	L	L	6	0	2	4	5	1	6	0
Man City	L	L	6	1	2	3	3	3	4	2
Liverpool	L	W	6	2	2	2	3	3	3	2
Arsenal	L	L	6	2	0	4	5	1	3	0
Man United	L	D	6	2	1	3	4	2	5	0
Everton	W	D	6	1	2	3	2	4	2	2
Southampton	W	L	5	1	1	3	1	4	1	1
Bournemouth	L	L	2	0	1	1	2	0	1	0
West Brom	W	L	6	5	0	1	5	1	3	3
West Ham	L	L	5	1	3	1	2	3	2	3
Leicester	W	L	3	2	0	1	2	0	2	2
Stoke	W	L	6	4	1	1	2	4	2	3
Crystal Palace	W	W	4	1	3	0	1	3	4	0
Swansea										
Burnley	W	W	2	2	0	0	1	1	1	1
Watford	D	L	2	1	1	0	0	2	0	2
Newcastle			5	3	1	1	2	3	1	3
Brighton			-	-	-	-	-	-	-	-
Huddersfield			-	-	-	-	-	-	-	-

Season	Division	Pos	P	W	D	L	F	A	GD	Pts
2016-17	Premier League	15	38	12	5	21	45	70	-25	41
2015-16	Premier League	12	38	12	11	15	42	52	-10	47
2014-15	Premier League	8	38	16	8	14	46	49	-3	56

Over/Under 63%/37% 4th   **Both score** 55%/45% 4th

Key stat: Swansea collected 29 points after the turn of the year – more than any team who finished outside the top seven

2016-17 Premier League appearances

	P	G	Y	R
J Amat	15 (2)	-	5	-
J Ayew	9 (5)	1	1	-
M Barrow	12 (6)	-	1	-
B Baston	4 (14)	1	-	-
L Britton	16	-	3	-
T Carroll	16 (1)	1	1	-
J Cork	25 (5)	-	7	-
N Dyer	3 (5)	-	-	-
L Fabianski	37	-	1	-
L Fer	27 (7)	6	9	-
F Fernandez	27	-	7	-
J Fulton	9 (2)	-	2	-
Ki Sung-Yueng	13 (10)	-	3	-
S Kingsley	12 (1)	-	-	-
F Llorente	28 (5)	15	2	-
A Mawson	27	4	1	-
O McBurnie	0 (5)	-	-	-
J Montero	2 (11)	-	-	-
L Narsingh	3 (10)	-	-	-
K Naughton	31	1	5	-
K Nordfeldt	1	-	-	-
M Olsson	14 (1)	2	2	-

	P	G	Y	R
A Rangel	8 (10)	1	1	-
W Routledge	24 (3)	3	1	-
G Sigurdsson	37 (1)	9	2	-
N Taylor	11	-	1	-
M van der Hoorn	7 (1)	1	1	-

Swansea's attacking quality shone in adversity

TOTTENHAM

Nickname: Spurs
Colours: White and navy blue
Ground: Wembley (temporary)
Tel: 0344-499-5000

Capacity: 90,000
tottenhamhotspur.com

Tottenham have been getting better year on year under Mauricio Pochettino but may take a small backwards step in the season they are to spend at Wembley.

Replicating last season's home record (17 wins two draws and no defeats) will be nigh-on impossible but Pochettino's young team should continue to develop and Champions League qualification can be achieved for a third successive season.

Last term, Spurs had the league's top scorer, Harry Kane, and the division's highest scoring midfielder in Dele Alli.

They also had the best defensive record – conceding seven goals fewer than Chelsea – and the best goal difference (plus 60). There are bound to be some teething problems at Wembley but Spurs' home form should improve as the season goes on.

Longest run without a loss: 12
Longest run without a win: 4
Highest/lowest league position: 2/5
Clean sheets: 17
Yellow cards: 62 **Red cards:** 0
Avg attendance: 31,639
Players used: 24
Leading scorer: H Kane 29 (9,16)

	2016-17		Last six seasons at home							
	H	A	P	W	D	L	OV	UN	BS	CS
Chelsea	W	L	6	2	3	1	2	4	4	2
Tottenham										
Man City	W	D	6	3	0	3	4	2	4	1
Liverpool	D	L	6	2	2	2	4	2	2	2
Arsenal	W	D	6	4	1	1	4	2	4	1
Man United	W	L	6	2	3	1	4	2	4	2
Everton	W	D	6	4	2	0	3	3	3	3
Southampton	W	W	5	4	0	1	3	2	3	2
Bournemouth	W	D	2	2	0	0	2	0	0	2
West Brom	W	D	6	2	3	1	1	5	3	2
West Ham	W	L	5	3	1	1	5	0	4	0
Leicester	D	W	3	1	1	1	1	2	2	0
Stoke	W	W	6	2	3	1	4	2	3	3
Crystal Palace	W	W	4	3	1	0	0	4	0	4
Swansea	W	W	6	6	0	0	4	2	3	3
Burnley	W	W	2	2	0	0	2	0	2	0
Watford	W	W	2	2	0	0	1	1	0	2
Newcastle			5	2	0	3	4	1	3	1
Brighton			-	-	-	-	-	-	-	-
Huddersfield			-	-	-	-	-	-	-	-

Season	Division	Pos	P	W	D	L	F	A	GD	Pts
2016-17	Premier League	2	38	26	8	4	86	26	+60	86
2015-16	Premier League	3	38	19	13	6	69	35	+34	70
2014-15	Premier League	5	38	19	7	12	58	53	+5	64

Over/Under 53%/47% 11th   **Both score** 47%/53% 15th

Key stat: Tottenham's goal difference of plus 60 was the highest ever by a team which failed to win the Premier League

2016-17 Premier League appearances

	P	G		Y	R
T Alderweireld	30	1		1	-
D Alli	35 (2)	18		4	-
T Carroll	1 (1)	-		1	-
B Davies	18 (5)	1		1	-
M Dembele	24 (6)	1		5	-
E Dier	34 (2)	2		6	-
C Eriksen	36	8		-	-
Heung-Min Son	23 (11)	14		2	-
V Janssen	7 (20)	2		-	-
H Kane	29 (1)	29		3	-
E Lamela	6 (3)	1		1	-
F Lesniak	0 (1)	-		-	-
H Lloris	34	-		-	-
G Nkoudou	0 (8)	-		-	-
J Onomah	0 (5)	-		-	-
D Rose	18	2		8	-
M Sissoko	8 (17)	-		3	-
K Trippier	6 (6)	-		1	-
J Vertonghen	33	-		5	-
M Vorm	4 (1)	-		-	-

	P	G		Y	R
K Walker	31 (2)	-		8	-
V Wanyama	35 (1)	4		10	-
K Wimmer	4 (1)	-		3	-
H Winks	3 (18)	1		1	-

Tottenham hotshots Harry Kane and Dele Alli

WATFORD

Watford

Nickname: The Hornets
Colours: Yellow and red
Ground: Vicarage Road
Tel: 01923-49600

Capacity: 21,977
watfordfc.co.uk

Watford's hierarchy have swung the axe again, replacing Walter Mazzarri with Marco Silva, but their latest appointment looks an astute one.

The Hornets finished last season with six defeats and the players seemingly reluctant to fight for Mazzarri's future.

However, they were never in serious danger despite a raft of injuries.

Some were to key players and the loss of attacking midfielder Roberto Pereyra – not seen again since a knee injury in December – was particularly damaging.

Pereyra should play a bigger role and can link up with Abdoulaye Doucoure, impressive in the second half of last season, and new-signing Will Hughes.

Watford will continue to be innovative in the transfer market and can extend their Premier League stay to three years.

Longest run without a loss: 4
Longest run without a win: 7
Highest/lowest league position: 7/17
Clean sheets: 7
Yellow cards: 87 **Red cards:** 5
Avg attendance: 20,571
Players used: 33
Leading scorer: T Deeney 10 (3,10)

	2016-17		Last six seasons at home							
	H	A	P	W	D	L	OV	UN	BS	CS
Chelsea	L	L	2	0	1	1	1	1	1	1
Tottenham	L	L	2	0	0	2	2	0	2	0
Man City	L	L	2	0	2	2	0	1	0	
Liverpool	L	L	2	1	0	1	1	1	0	1
Arsenal	L	W	2	0	0	2	2	0	1	0
Man United	W	L	2	1	0	1	2	0	2	0
Everton	W	L	2	1	1	0	1	1	2	0
Southampton	L	D	3	0	1	2	2	1	1	1
Bournemouth	D	D	4	1	3	0	2	2	3	1
West Brom	W	L	2	1	1	0	0	2	0	2
West Ham	D	W	3	1	1	1	1	2	1	1
Leicester	W	L	5	3	0	2	4	1	3	0
Stoke	L	L	2	0	0	2	1	1	1	0
Crystal Palace	D	L	4	0	2	2	1	3	2	0
Swansea	W	D	2	2	0	0	0	2	0	2
Burnley	W	L	4	2	2	0	3	1	4	0
Watford										
Newcastle			1	1	0	0	1	0	1	0
Brighton			4	2	1	1	0	4	1	2
Huddersfield			3	2	0	1	3	0	2	1

Season	Division	Pos	P	W	D	L	F	A	GD	Pts
2016-17	Premier League	17	38	11	7	20	40	68	-28	40
2015-16	Premier League	13	38	12	9	17	40	50	-10	45
2014-15	Championship	2	46	27	8	11	91	50	+41	89

Over/Under 47%/53% 15th   **Both score** 47%/53% 15th

Key stat: Watford scored just 15 away goals last season and nine of them were against London clubs

2016-17 Premier League appearances

	P	G		Y	R
N Amrabat	25 (4)	-		4	-
V Behrami	26 (1)	-		7	-
M Britos	27	1		8	2
E Capoue	37	7		5	-
C Cathcart	13 (2)	-		3	-
T Cleverley	16 (1)	-		4	-
T Deeney	31 (6)	10		7	-
A Doucoure	14 (6)	1		4	-
H Gomes	38	-		1	-
A Guedioura	9 (3)	-		2	-
J Holebas	33	2		14	-
O Ighalo	14 (4)	1		1	-
I Success	2 (17)	1		2	-
D Janmaat	18 (9)	2		2	-
C Kabasele	7 (9)	2		1	-
Y Kaboul	22	2		2	-
A Mariappa	6 (1)	-		-	-
B Mason	1 (1)	-		-	-
M Niang	15 (1)	2		2	-
S Okaka	10 (9)	4		5	-
C Pantilimon	0 (2)	-		-	-
D Pereira	0 (2)	-		-	-

	P	G		Y	R
R Pereyra	12 (1)	2		2	1
S Prodl	32 (1)	1		11	1
J Sinclair	1 (4)	-		-	-
B Watson	0 (4)	-		-	1
M Zarate	3	-		-	-
J Zuniga	6 (15)	1		1	-

Note: players with only one substitute appearance omitted

Watford finished 17th in last season's table

WEST BROM

Nickname: The Baggies/Throstles/Albion
Colours: Navy blue and white
Ground: The Hawthorns **Capacity:** 26,500
Tel: 0871-271-1100 wba.co.uk

Tony Pulis has never been relegated in his managerial career and that is unlikely to change over the next 12 months.

However, his West Brom side were poor in the last three months of the campaign, collecting just five points from 12 games, and Pulis must find a way of lifting the mood and ensuring the poor run does not extend into 2017-18.

He may be helped by the fixture list. West Brom do not face any of last season's top eight in the opening five games and have a great opportunity to fly out of the blocks.

However, anything other than a strong start will increase the doubts among supporters, some of whom are becoming frustrated with the defensive style of play and concerned by the departure of captain Darren Fletcher to Stoke.

Longest run without a loss: 5
Longest run without a win: 9
Highest/lowest league position: 7/16
Clean sheets: 6
Yellow cards: 80 **Red cards:** 0
Avg attendance: 23,876
Players used: 23
Leading scorer: J Rondon 8 (2,6)

	2016-17		Last six seasons at home							
	H	A	P	W	D	L	OV	UN	BS	CS
Chelsea	L	L	6	3	1	2	3	3	3	2
Tottenham	D	L	6	0	3	3	3	3	4	0
Man City	L	L	6	0	1	5	5	1	3	1
Liverpool	L	L	6	1	3	2	1	5	2	2
Arsenal	W	L	6	2	1	3	4	2	5	0
Man United	L	D	6	1	2	3	4	2	3	1
Everton	L	L	6	1	1	4	2	4	3	1
Southampton	L	W	5	2	1	2	0	5	0	3
Bournemouth	W	L	2	1	0	1	2	0	2	0
West Brom										
West Ham	W	D	5	2	1	2	3	2	2	2
Leicester	L	W	3	0	0	3	2	1	2	0
Stoke	W	D	6	3	0	3	2	4	2	2
Crystal Palace	L	W	4	2	1	1	2	2	2	1
Swansea	W	L	6	3	1	2	3	3	4	1
Burnley	W	D	2	2	0	0	2	0	0	2
Watford	W	L	2	1	0	1	1	1	1	0
Newcastle			5	2	1	2	1	4	2	2
Brighton			-	-	-	-	-	-	-	-
Huddersfield			-	-	-	-	-	-	-	-

Season	Division	Pos	P	W	D	L	F	A	GD	Pts
2016-17	Premier League	10	38	12	9	17	43	51	-8	45
2015-16	Premier League	14	38	10	13	15	34	48	-14	43
2014-15	Premier League	13	38	11	11	16	38	51	-13	44

Over/Under 47%/53% 15th **Both score** 50%/50% 8th

Key stat: West Brom kept the most settled team last season, making just 49 changes from the first game to the 38th.

2016-17 Premier League appearances

	P	G	Y	R
S Berahino	3 (1)	-	1	-
C Brunt	27 (4)	3	5	-
N Chadli	27 (4)	5	2	-
C Dawson	37	4	10	-
J Evans	30 (1)	2	8	-
S Field	4 (4)	-	2	-
D Fletcher	37 (1)	2	-	-
B Foster	38		2	-
B Galloway	3		-	-
C Gardner	2 (7)	-	1	-
R Lambert	0 (1)	-	-	-
J Leko	0 (9)	-	-	-
J Livermore	15 (1)	-	2	-
G McAuley	36	6	5	-
J McClean	13 (21)	1	9	-
J Morrison	17 (14)	5	3	-
A Nyom	29 (3)	-	8	-
J Olsson	7	-	3	-
M Phillips	26 (1)	4	2	-

	P	G	Y	R
H Robson-Kanu	5 (24)	3	3	-
J Rondon	32 (6)	8	2	-
M Wilson	3 (1)	-	3	-
C Yacob	27 (6)	-	9	-

Gareth McAuley scored five goals last term

WEST HAM

Nickname: The Hammers/Irons
Colours: Claret and blue
Ground: London Stadium
Tel: 0333-030-1966
Capacity: 57,000
whufc.com

West Ham had a difficult first season at the London Stadium and will hope to do much better now they have had a chance to get used to their new home.

There were some major positives towards the end of the season with the Hammers losing just one of their last seven games and ending Tottenham's title challenge with a 1-0 victory in Stratford.

Improvement will be expected but home results could continue to disappoint with West Ham fans struggling to recreate the vibrant, sometimes intimidating atmosphere which regularly unsettled visiting teams at Upton Park.

On the pitch there are problems too. There are obvious issues up front – no West Ham player reached double figures – but the signing of right-back Pablo Zabaleta should improve the defence.

Longest run without a loss: 5
Longest run without a win: 7
Highest/lowest league position: 9/18
Clean sheets: 10
Yellow cards: 82 **Red cards:** 5
Avg attendance: 56,970
Players used: 29
Leading scorer: M Antonio 9 (4,8)

2016-17	H	A	\multicolumn{8}{Last six seasons at home}

	H	A	P	W	D	L	OV	UN	BS	CS
Chelsea	L	L	5	2	0	3	4	1	3	0
Tottenham	W	L	5	3	0	2	1	4	1	3
Man City	L	L	5	1	2	2	4	1	3	1
Liverpool	L	D	5	2	0	3	4	1	3	1
Arsenal	L	L	5	0	1	4	5	0	5	0
Man United	L	D	5	1	2	2	2	3	3	0
Everton	D	L	5	0	2	3	3	2	4	1
Southampton	L	W	6	3	1	2	5	1	5	0
Bournemouth	W	L	2	1	0	1	1	1	1	1
West Brom	D	L	5	1	4	0	3	2	5	0
West Ham										
Leicester	L	L	4	2	0	2	3	1	3	1
Stoke	D	D	5	0	4	1	0	5	3	1
Crystal Palace	W	W	5	1	2	2	3	2	2	2
Swansea	W	W	5	4	0	1	2	3	2	3
Burnley	W	W	3	2	0	1	1	2	1	2
Watford	L	D	3	1	1	1	2	1	3	0
Newcastle			4	2	1	1	1	3	1	3
Brighton			1	1	0	0	1	0	0	1
Huddersfield			-	-	-	-	-	-	-	-

Season	Division	Pos	P	W	D	L	F	A	GD	Pts
2016-17	Premier League	11	38	12	9	17	47	64	-17	45
2015-16	Premier League	7	38	16	14	8	65	51	+14	62
2014-15	Premier League	12	38	12	11	15	44	47	-3	47

Over/Under 58%/42% 8th

Both score 55%/45% 4th

Key stat: West Ham scored 19 home goals in their first season at the London Stadium. Their lowest tally in the top flight since 1988-89

2016-17 Premier League appearances

	P	G	Y	R		P	G	Y	R
Adrian	16	-	1	-	W Reid	30	2	9	1
M Antonio	29	9	5	1	D Rice	0 (1)	-	-	-
A Arbeloa	1 (2)	-	3	-	D Sakho	2 (2)	1	-	-
A Ayew	16 (9)	6	1	-	R Snodgrass	8 (7)	-	-	-
S Byram	13 (5)	-	6	1	G Tore	3 (2)	-	-	-
J Calleri	4 (12)	1	-	-	E Valencia	3	-	-	-
A Carroll	15 (3)	7	3	-	S Zaza	5 (3)	-	2	-
J Collins	19 (3)	2	3	-					
A Cresswell	24 (2)	-	3	1					
S Feghouli	11 (10)	3	1	1					
E Fernandes	8 (20)	-	4	-					
A Fletcher	2 (14)	-	2	-					
J Fonte	16	-	2	-					
C Kouyate	31	1	3	-					
M Lanzini	31 (4)	8	9	-					
A Masuaku	11 (2)	-	1	-					
M Noble	29 (1)	3	10	-					
H Nordtveit	11 (5)	-	2	-					
P Obiang	21 (1)	1	7	-					
A Ogbonna	20	-	2	-					
D Payet	17 (1)	2	2	-					
D Randolph	22	-	1	-					

West Ham's Michail Antonio played a key role

Premier League stats 2016-17

Key Points in all tables (except the league table) do not include any deductions imposed by the league.
POS H A Overall league position, rank from home games only, rank from away games only **Sup** Average match supremacy **GFA** Goals For Average **GAA** Goals Against Average **PGA** Points Gained Average

Premier League 2016-17					Home					Away						
Pos	H	A		P	W	D	L	F	A	W	D	L	F	A	GD	Pts
1	2	1	Chelsea (CL)	38	17	0	2	55	17	13	3	3	30	16	52	93
2	1	5	Tottenham (CL)	38	17	2	0	47	9	9	6	4	39	17	60	86
3	6	2	Man City (CL)	38	11	7	1	37	17	12	2	5	43	22	41	78
4	5	4	Liverpool (CL)	38	12	5	2	45	18	10	5	4	33	24	36	76
5	3	6	Arsenal (EL)	38	14	3	2	39	16	9	3	7	38	28	33	75
6	7	3	Man Utd (CL)	38	8	10	1	26	12	10	5	4	28	17	25	69
7	4	10	Everton (EL)	38	13	4	2	42	16	4	6	9	20	28	18	61
8	17	7	Southampton	38	6	6	7	17	21	6	4	9	24	27	-7	46
9	10	13	Bournemouth	38	9	4	6	35	29	3	6	10	20	38	-12	46
10	11	12	West Brom	38	9	2	8	27	22	3	7	9	16	29	-8	45
11	16	9	West Ham	38	7	4	8	19	31	5	5	9	28	33	-17	45
12	8	17	Leicester	38	10	4	5	31	25	2	4	13	17	38	-15	44
13	14	11	Stoke	38	7	6	6	24	24	4	5	10	17	32	-15	44
14	18	8	Crystal Palace	38	6	2	11	24	25	6	3	10	26	38	-13	41
15	15	14	Swansea	38	8	3	8	27	34	4	2	13	18	36	-25	41
16	9	19	Burnley	38	10	3	6	26	20	1	4	14	13	35	-16	40
17	12	15	Watford	38	8	4	7	25	29	3	3	13	15	39	-28	40
18	13	20	Hull (R)	38	8	4	7	28	35	1	3	15	9	45	-43	34
19	19	16	Middlesbrough (R)	38	4	6	9	17	23	1	7	11	10	30	-26	28
20	20	18	Sunderland (R)	38	3	5	11	16	34	3	1	15	13	35	-40	24

Best attack

		GF	GFA
1	Tottenham	86	2.26
2	Chelsea	85	2.24
3	Man City	80	2.11
4	Liverpool	78	2.05
5	Arsenal	77	2.03
6	Everton	62	1.63
7	Bournemouth	55	1.45
8	Man Utd	54	1.42
9	Crystal Palace	50	1.32
10	Leicester	48	1.26
11	West Ham	47	1.24
12	Swansea	45	1.18
13	West Brom	43	1.13
14	Southampton	41	1.08
15	Stoke	41	1.08
16	Watford	40	1.05
17	Burnley	39	1.03
18	Hull	37	0.97
19	Sunderland	29	0.76
20	Middlesbrough	27	0.71

Best defence

		GA	GAA
1	Tottenham	26	0.68
2	Man Utd	29	0.76
3	Chelsea	33	0.87
4	Man City	39	1.03
5	Liverpool	42	1.11
6	Arsenal	44	1.16
7	Everton	44	1.16
8	Southampton	48	1.26
9	West Brom	51	1.34
10	Middlesbrough	53	1.39
11	Burnley	55	1.45
12	Stoke	56	1.47
13	Leicester	63	1.66
14	Crystal Palace	63	1.66
15	West Ham	64	1.68
16	Bournemouth	67	1.76
17	Watford	68	1.79
18	Sunderland	69	1.82
19	Swansea	70	1.84
20	Hull	80	2.11

Top scorers

	Team	Goals scored	
H Kane	Tottenham	29	▮▮▮▮▮▮▮▮▮▮▮▮▮▮▮▮▮▮▮▮▮▮▮▮▮▮▮▮▮
R Lukaku	Everton	25	▮▮▮▮▮▮▮▮▮▮▮▮▮▮▮▮▮▮▮▮▮▮▮▮▮
A Sanchez	Arsenal	24	▮▮▮▮▮▮▮▮▮▮▮▮▮▮▮▮▮▮▮▮▮▮▮▮
S Aguero	Man City	20	▮▮▮▮▮▮▮▮▮▮▮▮▮▮▮▮▮▮▮▮
D Costa	Chelsea	20	▮▮▮▮▮▮▮▮▮▮▮▮▮▮▮▮▮▮▮▮
D Alli	Tottenham	18	▮▮▮▮▮▮▮▮▮▮▮▮▮▮▮▮▮▮
Z Ibrahimovic	Man Utd	17	▮▮▮▮▮▮▮▮▮▮▮▮▮▮▮▮▮
E Hazard	Chelsea	16	▮▮▮▮▮▮▮▮▮▮▮▮▮▮▮▮
J King	Bournemouth	16	▮▮▮▮▮▮▮▮▮▮▮▮▮▮▮▮
C Benteke	C Palace	15	▮▮▮▮▮▮▮▮▮▮▮▮▮▮▮
J Defoe	Sunderland	15	▮▮▮▮▮▮▮▮▮▮▮▮▮▮▮
F Llorente	Swansea	15	▮▮▮▮▮▮▮▮▮▮▮▮▮▮▮
S Heung-Min	Tottenham	14	▮▮▮▮▮▮▮▮▮▮▮▮▮▮
P Coutinho	Liverpool	13	▮▮▮▮▮▮▮▮▮▮▮▮▮
S Mane	Liverpool	13	▮▮▮▮▮▮▮▮▮▮▮▮▮
J Vardy	Leicester	13	▮▮▮▮▮▮▮▮▮▮▮▮▮
O Giroud	Arsenal	12	▮▮▮▮▮▮▮▮▮▮▮▮
R Firmino	Liverpool	11	▮▮▮▮▮▮▮▮▮▮▮
T Deeney	Watford	10	▮▮▮▮▮▮▮▮▮▮
S Vokes	Burnley	10	▮▮▮▮▮▮▮▮▮▮
T Walcott	Arsenal	10	▮▮▮▮▮▮▮▮▮▮

Over 2.5 goals

	H	A	%
Man City	12	15	71%
Chelsea	17	9	68%
Arsenal	11	14	66%
Leicester	12	12	63%
Swansea	13	11	63%

Under 2.5 goals

	H	A	%
Man United	15	10	66%
Stoke	11	12	61%
Middlesbrough	10	11	55%
Sunderland, Watford, West Brom			53%

Both to score

	H	A	%
Liverpool	13	11	63%
Arsenal	10	13	61%
Man City	14	9	61%
Bournemouth, Swansea, West Ham			55%

Both not to score

	H	A	%
Sunderland		11	13	63%
Middlesbrough	10	12	58%
Southampton	12	10	58%
Crystal Palace, Tottenham, Watford			53%

Premier League results 2016-17

	Arsenal	Bournemouth	Burnley	Chelsea	Crystal Palace	Everton	Hull	Leicester	Liverpool	Man City	Man United	Middlesbrough	Southampton	Stoke	Sunderland	Swansea	Tottenham	Watford	West Brom	West Ham
Arsenal		3-1	2-1	3-0	2-0	3-1	2-0	1-0	3-4	2-2	2-0	0-0	2-1	3-1	2-0	3-2	1-1	1-2	1-0	3-0
Bournemouth	3-3		2-1	1-3	0-2	1-0	6-1	1-0	4-3	0-2	1-3	4-0	1-3	2-2	1-2	2-0	0-0	2-2	1-0	3-2
Burnley	0-1	3-2		1-1	3-2	2-1	1-1	1-0	2-0	1-2	0-2	1-0	1-0	1-0	4-1	0-1	0-2	2-0	2-2	1-2
Chelsea	3-1	3-0	3-0		1-2	5-0	2-0	3-0	1-2	2-1	4-0	3-0	4-2	4-2	5-1	3-1	2-1	4-3	1-0	2-1
Crystal Palace	3-0	1-1	0-2	0-1		0-1	4-0	2-2	2-4	1-2	1-2	1-0	3-0	4-1	0-4	1-2	0-1	1-0	0-1	0-1
Everton	2-1	6-3	3-1	0-3	1-1		4-0	4-2	0-1	4-0	1-1	3-1	3-0	1-0	2-0	1-1	1-1	1-0	3-0	2-0
Hull	1-4	3-1	1-1	0-2	3-3	2-2		2-1	2-0	0-3	0-1	4-2	2-1	0-2	0-2	2-1	1-7	2-0	1-1	2-1
Leicester	0-0	1-1	3-0	0-3	3-1	0-2	3-1		3-1	4-2	0-3	2-2	0-0	2-0	2-0	2-1	1-6	3-0	1-2	1-0
Liverpool	3-1	2-2	2-1	1-1	1-2	3-1	5-1	4-1		1-0	0-0	3-0	0-0	4-1	2-0	2-3	2-0	6-1	2-1	2-2
Man City	2-1	4-0	2-1	1-3	5-0	1-1	3-1	2-1	1-1		0-0	1-1	1-1	0-0	2-1	2-1	2-2	2-0	3-1	3-1
Man United	1-1	1-1	0-0	2-0	2-0	1-1	0-0	4-1	1-1	1-2		2-1	2-0	1-1	3-1	1-1	1-0	2-0	0-0	1-1
Middlesbrough	1-2	2-0	0-0	0-1	1-2	0-0	1-0	0-0	0-3	2-2	1-3		1-2	1-1	1-0	3-0	1-2	0-1	1-1	1-3
Southampton	0-2	0-0	3-1	0-2	3-1	1-0	0-0	3-0	0-0	0-3	0-0	1-0		0-1	1-1	1-0	1-4	1-1	1-2	1-3
Stoke	1-4	0-1	2-0	1-2	1-0	1-1	3-1	2-2	1-2	1-4	1-1	2-0	0-0		2-0	3-1	0-4	2-0	1-1	0-0
Sunderland	1-4	0-1	0-0	0-1	2-3	0-3	3-0	2-1	2-2	0-2	0-3	1-2	0-4	1-3		0-2	0-0	1-0	1-1	2-2
Swansea	0-4	0-3	3-2	2-2	5-4	1-0	0-2	2-0	1-2	1-3	1-3	0-0	2-1	2-0	3-0		1-3	0-0	2-1	1-4
Tottenham	2-0	4-0	2-1	2-0	1-0	3-2	3-0	1-1	1-1	2-0	2-1	1-0	2-1	4-0	1-0	5-0		4-0	4-0	3-2
Watford	1-3	2-2	2-1	1-2	1-1	3-2	1-0	2-1	0-1	0-5	3-1	0-0	3-4	0-1	1-0	1-0	1-4		2-0	1-1
West Brom	3-1	2-1	4-0	0-1	0-2	1-2	3-1	0-1	0-1	0-4	0-2	0-0	0-1	1-0	2-0	3-1	1-1	3-1		4-2
West Ham	1-5	1-0	1-0	1-2	3-0	0-0	1-0	2-3	0-4	0-4	0-2	1-1	0-3	1-1	1-0	1-0	1-0	1-0	2-4	2-2	

Record when first to score

		P	W	D	L	F	A	Sup	PGA	Pts
1	Tottenham	24	22	1	1	67	12	+2.29	2.8	67
2	Leicester	12	11	1	0	30	12	+1.5	2.8	34
3	Chelsea	30	26	3	1	72	20	+1.73	2.7	81
4	Man City	25	21	3	1	64	17	+1.88	2.6	66
5	Arsenal	25	21	1	3	62	20	+1.68	2.6	64
6	Man Utd	22	17	5	0	46	12	+1.55	2.5	56
7	Everton	19	14	4	1	47	14	+1.74	2.4	46
8	Swansea	13	10	1	2	24	14	+0.77	2.4	31
9	Liverpool	24	17	5	2	58	22	+1.5	2.3	56
10	Crystal Palace	12	9	1	2	27	11	+1.33	2.3	28
11	Burnley	17	11	2	4	29	17	+0.71	2.1	35
12	Watford	14	9	3	2	22	16	+0.43	2.1	30
13	Stoke	19	11	5	3	29	18	+0.58	2	38
14	West Brom	16	9	5	2	31	16	+0.94	2	32
15	Sunderland	8	5	1	2	14	9	+0.63	2	16
16	West Ham	17	10	3	4	27	17	+0.59	1.9	33
17	Southampton	15	9	1	5	24	14	+0.67	1.9	28
18	Bournemouth	19	10	5	4	36	26	+0.53	1.8	35
19	Hull	10	5	3	2	19	18	+0.1	1.8	18
20	Middlesbrough	12	5	4	3	18	13	+0.42	1.6	19

Record when keeping a clean sheet

		P	W	D	F	Sup	PGA	Pts
1	Chelsea	16	16	0	38	+2.38	3	48
2	Crystal Palace	7	7	0	16	+2.29	3	21
3	Tottenham	17	15	2	40	+2.35	2.8	47
4	Arsenal	13	11	2	23	+1.77	2.7	35
5	Everton	13	11	2	26	+2	2.7	35
6	Man City	12	10	2	34	+2.83	2.7	32
7	West Ham	10	8	2	10	+1	2.6	26
8	Bournemouth	10	8	2	14	+1.40	2.6	26
9	Liverpool	12	9	3	18	+1.50	2.5	30
10	Stoke	11	8	3	13	+1.18	2.5	27
11	Swansea	8	6	2	11	+1.38	2.5	20
12	Burnley	10	7	3	10	+1	2.4	24
13	Watford	7	5	2	6	+0.86	2.4	17
14	Man Utd	17	11	6	22	+1.29	2.3	39
15	Leicester	9	6	3	12	+1.33	2.3	21
16	West Brom	6	4	2	8	+1.33	2.3	14
17	Sunderland	6	4	2	10	+1.67	2.3	14
18	Hull	5	3	2	6	+1.20	2.2	11
19	Southampton	14	7	7	14	+1	2	28
20	Middlesbrough	11	4	7	7	+0.64	1.7	19

Familiarity could breed success in a section lacking stand out title candidates

I t's hard to recall a Championship line-up featuring as few standout title contenders as we see in 2017-18, writes Dan Sait. That Aston Villa, a team who were utterly unconvincing en route to a 13th-place finish last term and have done little bar sign 36-year-old John Terry so far this summer, could go off favourites adds weight to that claim. As does the fact that 13 teams are within ten points of each other at the top of the winner market.

All three teams relegated into the division have clear issues and deserved to go down, but all three have made interesting changes.

Middlesbrough struggled for creativity even during their 2016 promotion campaign and while incoming manager Garry Monk is a promising appointment, it's not easy adding attacking impetus to a defensive team. Boro should be a threat but are too short at 7-1.

Simon Grayson seems an entirely sensible managerial appointment for Sunderland but the squad needs reinvigorating and it will be a tricky task getting the Black Cats to purr again after so many years of decline.

The detached leadership at Hull makes them hard to trust as it feels difficult backing a team owned by someone so obviously uninterested in his club as Assem Allam.

However, new manager Leonid Slutsky could easily prove a few doubters wrong and his friendship with Roman Abramovich should result in some decent Chelsea loanees. Even if a few players depart, Hull still have a decent squad and most are experienced at this level. At generous prices the Tigers look a reasonable outside punt for promotion.

More convincing are the claims of Fulham and Sheffield Wednesday, with preference going to the latter on account of their price.

The Owls have been in the promotion mix for the last two years, missing out in the playoffs both times, and are well placed to step up in what looks a weaker section.

The capture of George Boyd should offer the creativity that was sometimes lacking last term and Wednesday are a stable, well run and well managed club. And, unlike many of their rivals, the lack of summer upheaval means they should hit their stride early.

The same applies to a Fulham side who seem to have turned a corner after a couple of years in the doldrums. Manager Slavisa Jokanovic led Watford up in 2015 and is settled at a club with a young squad who should only improve. That they finished last season so strongly bodes well, as does the fact that the likes of Ryan Sessegnon turned down top-flight suitors to stay put. It suggests Jokanovic has something exciting going on.

At the other end, cash-strapped Bolton and Millwall look overpriced to slip straight back down. It's hard to buy the argument that Millwall's poor League One form was a result of the cup exertions when their best league form came during their cup run.

QPR look a big price to join them given their struggles last term and the potential of landing a massive Financial Fair Play fine.

Recommendations

Sheffield Wednesday to win, 11-1
Fulham to be promoted, 3-1
Hull to be promoted, 11-2
Millwall to be relegated, 12-5
Bolton to be relegated, 13-5
QPR to be relegated, 9-2

Ross Wallace and Fernando Forestieri were key men for the Owls last season

ASTON VILLA AVFC

Nickname: The Villans
Colours: Claret and blue
Ground: Villa Park (42,790)
Tel: 0121-327-2299   avfc.co.uk

Aston Villa always looked underpriced to bounce straight back up and so it proved, with new owner Tony Xia now aware of the scale of the task he has taken on.

Roberto Di Matteo won just one of his 11 games as manager, but replacement Steve Bruce fared little better after the honeymoon wore off, claiming two points in 11 games over the turn of the year.

Adding John Terry's experience should help but far more work is needed to justify Villa's position as league favourites.

Longest run without win/loss: 10/7
High/low league position: 10/20
Clean sheets: 14 **Yellow cards:** 90 **Red:** 4
Avg attendance: 32,107 **Players used:** 35
Leading scorer: J Kodjia 19 (11,16)
Key stat: Aston Villa won just two away games at teams finishing outside the bottom two last season

	2016-17 H	A	P	W	D	L	OV	UN	BS	CS
Hull			2	2	0	0	2	0	2	0
Middlesbrough			-	-	-	-	-	-	-	-
Sunderland			5	1	4	0	2	3	2	3
Reading	L	W	2	1	0	1	1	1	1	1
Sheffield Wed	W	L	1	1	0	0	0	1	0	1
Fulham	W	L	4	2	1	1	1	3	2	2
Leeds	D	L	1	0	1	0	0	1	1	0
Norwich	W	L	5	4	1	0	2	3	3	2
Derby	W	D	1	1	0	0	0	1	0	1
Brentford	D	L	1	0	1	0	0	1	1	0
Preston	D	L	1	0	1	0	1	0	1	0
Cardiff	W	L	2	2	0	0	1	1	1	1
Aston Villa										
Barnsley	L	D	1	0	0	1	1	0	1	0
Wolves	D	L	2	0	2	0	0	2	1	1
Ipswich	L	D	1	0	0	1	0	1	0	0
Bristol City	W	L	1	1	0	0	0	1	0	1
QPR	W	W	4	2	2	0	3	1	3	1
Birmingham	W	D	1	1	0	0	0	1	0	1
Burton	W	D	1	1	0	0	1	0	1	0
Nottm Forest	D	L	1	0	1	0	1	0	1	0
Sheffield United			-	-	-	-	-	-	-	-
Bolton			1	0	0	1	1	0	1	0
Millwall			-	-	-	-	-	-	-	-

Season	Division	Pos	P	W	D	L	F	A	GD	Pts
2016-17	Championship	13	46	16	14	16	47	48	-1	62
2015-16	Premier League	20	38	3	8	27	27	76	-49	17
2014-15	Premier League	17	38	10	8	20	31	57	-26	38

Over/Under 28%/72% 24th   **Both score** 46%/54% 20th

BARNSLEY

Nickname: Tykes
Colours: Red and white
Ground: Oakwell (23,009)
Tel: 01226-211-211   barnsleyfc.co.uk

Fans favourite Paul Heckingbottom is rapidly showing himself to be the real deal in the Oakwell dugout.

The Tykes went off third favourites to go straight back down to League One but never even flirted with the drop despite losing captain Conor Hourihane and top scorer Sam Winnall in January, as well as assistant Tommy Wright in September.

Barnsley's tight budget will always have vultures circling, but Heckingbottom has fended them off in some style thus far.

Longest run without win/loss: 8/4
High/low league position: 4/18
Clean sheets: 14 **Yellow cards:** 76 **Red:** 5
Avg attendance: 13,857 **Players used:** 32
Leading scorer: S Winnall 11 (3,9)
Key stat: Just two sides were worse at holding on when scoring first, with Barnsley winning just 13 of 23 games in which they did so

	2016-17 H	A	P	W	D	L	OV	UN	BS	CS
Hull			2	2	0	0	1	1	1	1
Middlesbrough			3	2	0	1	2	1	2	1
Sunderland			-	-	-	-	-	-	-	-
Reading	L	D	3	0	1	2	2	1	2	0
Sheffield Wed	D	L	3	0	2	1	0	3	2	0
Fulham	L	L	1	0	0	1	1	0	1	0
Leeds	W	L	4	3	0	1	2	2	2	1
Norwich	W	L	1	1	0	0	1	0	1	0
Derby	W	L	4	2	1	1	2	2	3	1
Brentford	D	W	1	0	1	0	0	1	1	0
Preston	D	W	2	0	2	0	0	2	1	1
Cardiff	D	W	3	0	1	2	1	2	1	1
Aston Villa	D	W	1	0	1	0	0	1	1	0
Barnsley										
Wolves	L	W	2	1	0	1	2	0	2	0
Ipswich	D	L	4	0	3	1	2	2	4	0
Bristol City	D	L	4	1	2	1	3	1	3	1
QPR	W	L	2	1	0	1	2	0	2	0
Birmingham	D	W	4	0	1	3	4	0	3	0
Burton	D	D	2	1	1	0	0	2	1	1
Nottm Forest	L	W	4	1	1	2	2	2	3	1
Sheffield United			2	0	1	1	0	2	1	0
Bolton			2	0	0	2	1	1	1	0
Millwall			4	3	0	1	2	2	2	2

Season	Division	Pos	P	W	D	L	F	A	GD	Pts
2016-17	Championship	14	46	15	13	18	64	67	-3	58
2015-16	League One	6	46	22	8	16	70	54	+16	74
2014-15	League One	11	46	17	11	18	62	61	+1	62

Over/Under 50%/50% 11th   **Both score** 54%/46% 9th

BIRMINGHAM

Nickname: Blues
Colours: Blue
Ground: St Andrews (30,015)
Tel: 0121-772-0101   bcfc.com

Sacking Gary Rowett, who led Blues to consecutive top-ten finishes and a top-six charge in 2016-17, to replace him with Gianfranco Zola was absurd.

Zola tried to play a more attractive style but the quality of his squad wasn't up to it and Birmingham duly plummeted.

Harry Redknapp replaced Zola but only succeeded in his rescue mission thanks to Blues' final two opponents downing tools – Huddersfield rested their entire first team and Bristol City were in party mode.

Longest run without win/loss: 10/7
High/low league position: 4/21
Clean sheets: 11 **Yellow cards:** 95 **Red:** 6
Avg attendance: 18,717 **Players used:** 30
Leading scorer: L Jutkiewicz 11 (5,11)
Key stat: Birmingham required 13.08 shots for every goal they scored last season – only Wigan were less effective in front of goal

	2016-17 H	A	Last six seasons at home P	W	D	L	OV	UN	BS	CS
Hull			3	1	1	1	1	2	1	2
Middlesbrough			5	2	3	0	4	1	4	1
Sunderland			-	-	-	-	-	-	-	-
Reading	L	D	5	3	0	2	3	2	3	1
Sheffield Wed	W	L	5	2	1	2	3	2	3	1
Fulham	W	W	3	1	1	1	1	2	2	1
Leeds	L	W	6	2	1	3	3	3	4	2
Norwich	W	L	2	1	1	0	1	1	0	2
Derby	L	L	6	1	3	2	5	1	5	0
Brentford	L	W	3	2	0	1	2	1	2	1
Preston	D	L	2	0	2	0	2	0	2	0
Cardiff	D	D	5	1	3	1	0	5	1	3
Aston Villa	D	L	1	0	1	0	0	1	1	0
Barnsley	L	D	4	0	2	2	2	2	2	0
Wolves	L	W	4	1	0	3	3	1	3	0
Ipswich	W	D	6	3	2	1	4	2	4	1
Bristol City	W	W	4	3	1	0	2	2	2	2
QPR	L	D	3	1	0	2	2	1	2	0
Birmingham										
Burton	L	L	1	0	0	1	0	1	0	0
Nottm Forest	D	L	6	2	2	2	3	3	3	2
Sheffield United			-	-	-	-	-	-	-	-
Bolton			4	2	0	2	2	2	2	1
Millwall			4	2	1	1	2	2	1	2

Season	Division	Pos	P	W	D	L	F	A	GD	Pts
2016-17	Championship	19	46	13	14	19	45	64	-19	53
2015-16	Championship	10	46	16	15	15	53	49	+4	63
2014-15	Championship	10	46	16	15	15	54	64	-10	63

Over/Under 46%/54% 16th   **Both score** 54%/46% 9th

BOLTON

Nickname: The Trotters
Colours: White and blue
Ground: Macron Stadium (28,723)
Tel: 01204-673-673   bwfc.co.uk

Bouncing back from relegation was an impressive achievement for a Bolton side who started the season with five teams above them in the antepost betting.

Phil Parkinson deserves huge credit given the club is under a transfer embargo and paddling hard just to stay afloat – cobbling together a patchwork team of free signings and loanees is no mean feat.

But second-tier survival likely depends on the club securing investment as the step up could push a thin squad too far.

Longest run without win/loss: 7/9
High/low league position: 1/8
Clean sheets: 18 **Yellow cards:** 75 **Red:** 2
Avg attendance: 14,934 **Players used:** 32
Lead scorers: Wheater, Clough, Madine, Vela 9
Key stat: Bolton won almost as many away games in League One last season (12) as they won at home (13)

	2016-17 H	A	Last six seasons at home P	W	D	L	OV	UN	BS	CS
Hull			2	2	0	0	1	1	1	1
Middlesbrough			4	1	1	2	4	0	4	0
Sunderland			1	0	0	1	0	1	0	0
Reading			3	0	2	1	0	3	2	0
Sheffield Wed			4	0	3	1	0	4	1	2
Fulham			3	1	1	1	3	0	2	0
Leeds			4	0	3	1	1	3	3	0
Norwich			2	0	0	2	2	0	2	0
Derby			4	1	2	1	1	3	1	2
Brentford			2	1	1	0	1	1	2	0
Preston			1	0	0	1	1	0	1	0
Cardiff			3	2	0	1	3	0	2	1
Aston Villa			1	0	0	1	0	1	1	0
Barnsley			2	1	1	0	0	2	1	1
Wolves			4	2	2	0	2	2	3	1
Ipswich			4	0	3	1	2	2	3	1
Bristol City			2	1	1	0	1	1	1	1
QPR			3	1	1	1	1	2	2	0
Birmingham			4	1	1	2	2	2	2	0
Burton			-	-	-	-	-	-	-	-
Nottm Forest			4	0	4	0	2	2	4	0
Sheffield United	W	L	1	1	0	0	0	1	0	1
Bolton										
Millwall	W	W	4	3	1	0	1	3	2	2

Season	Division	Pos	P	W	D	L	F	A	GD	Pts
2016-17	League One	2	46	25	11	10	68	36	+32	86
2015-16	Championship	24	46	5	15	26	41	81	-40	30
2014-15	Championship	18	46	13	12	21	54	67	-13	51

Over/Under 37%/63% 22nd   **Both score** 43%/57% 23rd

BRENTFORD

Nickname: The Bees
Colours: Red
Ground: Griffin Park (12,300)
Tel: 0208-847-2511   brentfordfc.co.uk

Brentford continue to provide many of the Championship's brightest moments of attacking play, but the fact that the Bees never seriously challenged for the top six will concern manager Dean Smith.

Goals remain easy to come by – although keeping hold of Jota and Lasse Vibe will be essential if that is to continue – but the team struggled defensively and was one of the most inconsistent in the division, lurching from defeat to lowly Rotherham to victory over Brighton.

Longest run without win/loss: 4/4
High/low league position: 6/18
Clean sheets: 13 **Yellow cards:** 74 **Red:** 2
Avg attendance: 10,491 **Players used:** 30
Leading scorer: L Vibe 15 (4,11)
Key stat: Brentford had the third-most shots on target in the Championship last season

	2016-17 H	A	Last six seasons at home P	W	D	L	OV	UN	BS	CS
Hull			1	0	0	1	0	1	0	0
Middlesbrough			2	0	0	2	0	2	0	0
Sunderland			-	-	-	-	-	-	-	-
Reading	W	L	3	2	0	1	3	0	3	0
Sheffield Wed	D	W	4	0	2	2	2	2	3	1
Fulham	L	D	3	2	0	1	2	1	1	1
Leeds	W	L	3	2	1	0	0	3	1	2
Norwich	D	L	2	0	1	1	1	1	0	1
Derby	W	D	3	2	0	1	3	0	2	1
Brentford										
Preston	W	L	5	4	0	1	3	2	2	3
Cardiff	D	L	3	1	1	1	3	0	3	0
Aston Villa	W	D	1	1	0	0	1	0	0	1
Barnsley	L	D	1	0	0	1	0	1	0	0
Wolves	L	L	4	2	0	2	4	0	1	2
Ipswich	W	D	3	1	1	1	2	1	2	1
Bristol City	W	W	3	2	1	0	1	2	2	1
QPR	W	W	2	2	0	0	1	1	1	1
Birmingham	L	W	3	0	1	2	1	2	2	0
Burton	W	W	1	1	0	0	1	0	1	0
Nottm Forest	W	W	3	2	1	0	2	1	2	1
Sheffield United			3	2	0	1	1	2	1	1
Bolton			2	1	1	0	2	0	2	0
Millwall			1	0	1	0	1	0	1	0

Season	Division	Pos	P	W	D	L	F	A	GD	Pts
2016-17	Championship	10	46	18	10	18	75	65	+10	64
2015-16	Championship	9	46	19	8	19	72	67	+5	65
2014-15	Championship	5	46	23	9	14	78	59	+19	78

Over/Under 57%/43% 4th   **Both score** 59%/41% 4th

BRISTOL CITY

Nickname: The Robins
Colours: Red and white
Ground: Ashton Gate (27,000)
Tel: 0117-963-0600   bcfc.co.uk

Manager Lee Johnson kept Bristol City playing attactive football even in the heat of a relegation fight and picked up some impressive results along the way, but the Robins must develop a harder edge if they are to avoid another scrap.

The loss of Tammy Abraham may look a blow, but the Chelsea loanee's impressive tally was undoubtedly boosted by City's emphasis on attack. The summer focus must surely be more on toughening up in midfield and adding defensive nous.

Longest run without win/loss: 9/5
High/low league position: 5/22
Clean sheets: 9 **Yellow cards:** 77 **Red:** 1
Avg attendance: 19,256 **Players used:** 32
Leading scorer: T Abraham 23 (5,18)
Key stat: Only Newcastle and Fulham took more shots in the second tier, but while they both scored 85 goals Bristol City netted just 60

	2016-17 H	A	Last six seasons at home P	W	D	L	OV	UN	BS	CS
Hull			3	0	2	1	1	2	3	0
Middlesbrough			3	2	0	1	0	3	0	2
Sunderland			-	-	-	-	-	-	-	-
Reading	L	L	3	0	0	3	2	1	2	0
Sheffield Wed	D	L	3	1	2	0	2	1	3	0
Fulham	L	W	2	0	0	2	1	1	1	0
Leeds	W	L	4	1	1	2	3	1	2	1
Norwich	D	L	1	0	1	0	0	1	1	0
Derby	D	D	4	0	2	2	1	3	3	0
Brentford	L	L	3	0	0	3	2	1	2	0
Preston	L	L	4	0	1	3	2	2	3	0
Cardiff	L	L	4	1	0	3	3	1	3	0
Aston Villa	W	L	1	1	0	0	1	0	1	0
Barnsley	W	D	4	3	1	0	3	1	3	1
Wolves	W	L	4	2	0	2	3	1	3	1
Ipswich	W	L	4	3	0	1	3	1	2	1
Bristol City										
QPR	W	L	2	1	1	0	1	1	2	0
Birmingham	L	L	4	0	1	3	0	4	0	1
Burton	D	W	1	0	1	0	0	1	0	1
Nottm Forest	W	L	4	3	1	0	1	3	1	3
Sheffield United			2	0	0	2	1	1	1	0
Bolton			2	1	0	1	2	0	1	1
Millwall			2	1	1	0	0	2	1	1

Season	Division	Pos	P	W	D	L	F	A	GD	Pts
2016-17	Championship	17	46	15	9	22	60	66	-6	54
2015-16	Championship	18	46	13	13	20	54	71	-17	52
2014-15	League One	1	46	29	12	5	96	38	+58	99

Over/Under 54%/46% 7th   **Both score** 54%/46% 9th

BURTON

Nickname: The Brewers
Colours: Yellow and black
Ground: Pirelli Stadium (6,912)
Tel: 01283-565938   burtonalbionfc.co.uk

Nigel Clough proved the critics wrong, defying the odds to keep tiny Burton up with a game to spare and providing some entertaining football along the way.

After underwhelming spells at Derby and Sheffield United, Clough returned to a club that just seems a natural fit, having now masterminded two promotions and an unlikely second-tier survival act at the 6,912 capacity Pirelli Stadium.

The budget and squad counts against Burton but they don't lack togetherness.

Longest run without win/loss: 5/6
High/low league position: 15/22
Clean sheets: 10 **Yellow cards:** 80 **Red:** 1
Avg attendance: 5,227 **Players used:** 30
Leading scorer: J Irvine 10 (6,10)
Key stat: Burton had an average attendance of just 5,228 last term – even second-fewest Rotherham had nearly double that at 9,783

	2016-17 H	A	Last six seasons at home P	W	D	L	OV	UN	BS	CS
Hull			-	-	-	-	-	-	-	-
Middlesbrough			-	-	-	-	-	-	-	-
Sunderland			-	-	-	-	-	-	-	-
Reading	L	L	1	0	0	1	1	0	1	0
Sheffield Wed	W	D	1	1	0	0	1	0	1	0
Fulham	L	D	1	0	0	1	0	1	0	0
Leeds	W	L	1	1	0	0	1	0	1	0
Norwich	W	L	1	1	0	0	1	0	1	0
Derby	W	D	1	1	0	0	0	1	0	1
Brentford	L	L	1	0	0	1	1	0	1	0
Preston	L	D	1	0	0	1	0	1	0	0
Cardiff	W	L	1	1	0	0	0	1	0	1
Aston Villa	D	L	1	0	1	0	0	1	1	0
Barnsley	D	D	2	0	2	0	0	2	0	2
Wolves	W	D	1	1	0	0	1	0	1	0
Ipswich	L	L	1	0	0	1	0	1	0	0
Bristol City	L	D	1	0	0	1	1	0	1	0
QPR	D	W	1	0	1	0	0	1	1	0
Birmingham	W	W	1	1	0	0	0	1	0	1
Burton										
Nottm Forest	W	L	1	1	0	0	0	1	0	1
Sheffield United			1	0	1	0	0	1	0	1
Bolton			-	-	-	-	-	-	-	-
Millwall			1	1	0	0	1	0	1	0

Season	Division	Pos	P	W	D	L	F	A	GD	Pts
2016-17	Championship	20	46	13	13	20	49	63	-14	52
2015-16	League One	2	46	25	10	11	57	37	+20	85
2014-15	League Two	1	46	28	10	8	69	39	+30	94

Over/Under 41%/59% 19th   **Both score** 57%/43% 6th

CARDIFF

Nickname: The Bluebirds
Colours: Red
Ground: Cardiff City Stadium (33,300)
Tel: 0845-365-1115   cardiffcityfc.co.uk

He may be a bit of a Marmite character but it's hard to argue Neil Warnock isn't a hugely effective Championship manager.

His latest rescue act came in the Welsh capital, digging Cardiff out of the mire after Paul Trollope's Bluebirds had slipped to second-bottom in mid-October.

By early 2017 Warnock had dragged Cardiff safely into midtable with the side not just tightening up defensively but scoring more than twice as many goals per game as under Trollope.

Longest run without win/loss: 5/4
High/low league position: 12/24
Clean sheets: 11 **Yellow cards:** 70 **Red:** 3
Avg attendance: 16,564 **Players used:** 33
Leading scorer: K Zohore 12 (2,9)
Key stat: Cardiff's points-per-game ratio last season more than doubled from 0.73 under Paul Trollope to 1.54 under Neil Warnock

	2016-17 H	A	Last six seasons at home P	W	D	L	OV	UN	BS	CS
Hull			4	1	0	3	3	1	1	0
Middlesbrough			4	2	0	2	1	3	1	2
Sunderland			1	0	1	0	1	0	1	0
Reading	L	L	4	3	0	1	2	2	2	1
Sheffield Wed	D	L	4	2	2	0	2	2	3	1
Fulham	D	D	4	2	2	0	2	2	3	1
Leeds	L	W	5	2	1	2	2	3	3	0
Norwich	L	L	3	1	0	2	2	1	2	0
Derby	L	W	5	2	1	2	1	4	2	1
Brentford	W	D	3	2	0	1	3	0	3	0
Preston	W	L	2	2	0	0	1	1	1	1
Cardiff										
Aston Villa	W	L	2	1	1	0	0	2	0	2
Barnsley	L	D	3	1	1	1	2	1	3	0
Wolves	W	L	4	3	0	1	2	2	2	1
Ipswich	W	D	5	3	2	0	3	2	3	2
Bristol City	W	W	4	3	1	0	3	1	3	1
QPR	L	L	2	0	1	1	0	2	0	1
Birmingham	D	D	5	3	2	0	1	4	3	2
Burton	W	L	1	1	0	0	0	1	0	1
Nottm Forest	W	W	5	4	1	0	2	3	2	3
Sheffield United										
Bolton			3	1	1	1	2	1	2	0
Millwall			3	1	2	0	0	3	0	3

Season	Division	Pos	P	W	D	L	F	A	GD	Pts
2016-17	Championship	12	46	17	11	18	60	61	-1	62
2015-16	Championship	8	46	17	17	12	56	51	+5	68
2014-15	Championship	11	46	16	14	16	57	61	-4	62

Over/Under 50%/50% 11th   **Both score** 52%/48% 14th

DERBY

Nickname: The Rams
Colours: White and black
Ground: Pride Park Stadium (33,597)
Tel: 0871-472-1884   dcfc.co.uk

For the first time in four seasons there was no promotion heartbreak, but that's no positive for Rams fans worried about slipping back into midtable obscurity.

More managerial upheaval didn't help but Derby got off to a dire start under Nigel Pearson and his October departure came as no shock. Steve McClaren returned but was also sacked, rather more harshly, after five months. Gary Rowett is the next man in the firing line and looks likely to focus on industry over creativity.

Longest run without win/loss: 6/10
High/low league position: 5/22
Clean sheets: 17 **Yellow cards:** 67 **Red:** 2
Avg attendance: 29,042 **Players used:** 28
Leading scorer: T Ince 14 (5,12)
Key stat: Gary Rowett became the fifth permanent manager to work for Derby in under two years

	2016-17 H	A	P	W	D	L	OV	UN	BS	CS
Hull			3	1	0	2	2	1	1	1
Middlesbrough			5	2	1	2	2	3	3	0
Sunderland			-	-	-	-	-	-	-	-
Reading	W	D	5	1	1	3	3	2	3	0
Sheffield Wed	W	L	5	3	2	0	3	2	3	2
Fulham	W	D	3	3	0	0	2	1	2	1
Leeds	W	L	6	5	0	1	3	3	3	3
Norwich	W	L	2	1	1	0	1	1	1	1
Derby										
Brentford	D	L	3	1	2	0	0	3	1	2
Preston	D	W	2	0	2	0	0	2	1	1
Cardiff	L	W	5	1	2	2	3	2	3	1
Aston Villa	D	L	1	0	1	0	0	1	0	1
Barnsley	W	L	4	3	1	0	2	2	3	1
Wolves	W	W	4	3	1	0	3	1	2	2
Ipswich	L	W	6	0	3	3	1	5	2	1
Bristol City	D	D	4	3	1	0	4	0	2	2
QPR	W	W	3	3	0	0	0	3	0	3
Birmingham	W	W	6	3	2	1	4	2	4	1
Burton	D	L	1	0	1	0	0	1	0	1
Nottm Forest	W	D	6	4	1	1	3	3	2	4
Sheffield United			-	-	-	-	-	-	-	-
Bolton			4	2	2	0	2	2	3	1
Millwall			4	2	1	1	1	3	0	3

Season	Division	Pos	P	W	D	L	F	A	GD	Pts
2016-17	Championship	9	46	18	13	15	54	50	+4	67
2015-16	Championship	5	46	21	15	10	66	43	+23	78
2014-15	Championship	8	46	21	14	11	85	56	+29	77

Over/Under 39%/61% 22nd **Both score** 37%/63% 24th

FULHAM

Nickname: The Cottagers
Colours: White and black
Ground: Craven Cottage (25,700)
Tel: 0843-208-1222   fulhamfc.com

Fulham landed hard in the Championship, finishing 17th in their first season back in the second tier and 20th in 2015-16, but they finally hit their straps last term.

Playoff heartache followed their sixth-place finish but the Cottagers were hugely impressive over the second half of the season, finishing the campaign with a run of 11 wins in their final 17 matches.

Manager Slavisa Jokanovic has earned second-tier promotion previously with Watford and will be looking for a repeat.

Longest run without win/loss: 6/8
High/low league position: 6/14
Clean sheets: 11 **Yellow cards:** 80 **Red:** 4
Avg attendance: 19,198 **Players used:** 27
Leading scorer: T Cairney 12 (4,12)
Key stat: Fulham won five of their last six road trips, winning at top-eight rivals Huddersfield, Newcastle, Norwich and Sheffield Wednesday

	2016-17 H	A	P	W	D	L	OV	UN	BS	CS
Hull			2	0	1	1	1	1	1	0
Middlesbrough			2	1	0	1	1	1	1	0
Sunderland			3	1	0	2	3	0	3	0
Reading	W	L	4	3	0	1	4	0	3	1
Sheffield Wed	D	W	3	1	1	1	1	2	1	1
Fulham										
Leeds	D	D	3	0	2	1	1	2	2	0
Norwich	D	W	5	4	1	0	3	2	2	3
Derby	D	L	3	1	2	0	1	2	2	1
Brentford	D	W	3	0	2	1	2	1	3	0
Preston	W	W	2	1	1	0	1	1	2	0
Cardiff	D	D	4	1	2	1	3	1	4	0
Aston Villa	W	L	4	3	1	0	1	3	1	3
Barnsley	W	W	1	1	0	0	0	1	0	1
Wolves	L	D	4	1	0	3	3	1	1	1
Ipswich	W	W	3	1	0	2	3	0	3	0
Bristol City	L	L	2	0	0	2	2	0	1	0
QPR	L	D	4	3	0	1	4	0	2	2
Birmingham	L	L	3	0	1	2	1	2	2	0
Burton	D	W	1	0	1	0	0	1	1	0
Nottm Forest	W	D	3	2	0	1	3	0	3	0
Sheffield United			-	-	-	-	-	-	-	-
Bolton			3	3	0	0	1	2	0	3
Millwall			1	0	0	1	0	1	0	0

Season	Division	Pos	P	W	D	L	F	A	GD	Pts
2016-17	Championship	6	46	22	14	10	85	57	+28	80
2015-16	Championship	20	46	12	15	19	66	79	-13	51
2014-15	Championship	17	46	14	10	22	62	83	-21	52

Over/Under 57%/43% 4th **Both score** 65%/35% 1st

HULL

Nickname: The Tigers
Colours: Amber and black
Ground: The KCOM Stadium (25,404)
Tel: 0870-837-0003 hullcityafc.net

A calamitous pre-season caught up with Hull, with the squad threadbare as the Premier League campaign kicked off.

The January arrivals of Marco Silva and some shrewd signings resulted in an upturn, but it couldn't save the Tigers.

Silva's departure is a blow, as is the lack of interest shown by owner Assem Allam who will offer a shoestring budget.

However, incoming manager Leonid Slutsky could prove a few wrong and his links to Roman Abramovich won't hurt.

Longest run without win/loss: 9/2
High/low league position: 15/20
Clean sheets: 5 **Yellow cards:** 67 **Red:** 5
Avg attendance: 20,761 **Players used:** 28
Leading scorer: R Snodgrass 7 (2,7)
Key stat: Maintained over a full season, Hull's points per game won under Marco Silva (from January) would have seen them finish 13th

	2016-17 H	A	Last six seasons at home P	W	D	L	OV	UN	BS	CS
Hull										
Middlesbrough	W	L	4	4	0	0	3	1	2	2
Sunderland	L	L	3	1	1	1	0	3	1	1
Reading			2	2	0	0	1	1	1	1
Sheffield Wed			2	0	1	1	1	1	1	1
Fulham			2	2	0	0	2	0	1	1
Leeds			3	1	2	0	1	2	1	2
Norwich			1	1	0	0	0	1	0	1
Derby			3	1	0	2	1	2	1	0
Brentford			1	1	0	0	0	1	0	1
Preston			1	1	0	0	0	1	0	1
Cardiff			4	2	2	0	2	2	3	1
Aston Villa			2	1	1	0	0	2	0	2
Barnsley			2	2	0	0	1	1	1	1
Wolves			2	2	0	0	2	0	2	0
Ipswich			3	2	1	0	3	0	2	1
Bristol City			3	2	1	0	2	1	0	3
QPR			2	1	1	0	1	1	2	0
Birmingham			3	3	0	0	2	1	2	1
Burton			-	-	-	-	-	-	-	-
Nottm Forest			3	1	1	1	2	1	3	0
Sheffield United			-	-	-	-	-	-	-	-
Bolton			2	2	0	0	1	1	1	1
Millwall			2	2	0	0	1	1	1	1

Season	Division	Pos	P	W	D	L	F	A	GD	Pts
2016-17	Premier League	18	38	9	7	22	37	80	-43	34
2015-16	Championship	4	46	24	11	11	69	35	+34	83
2014-15	Premier League	18	38	8	11	19	33	51	-18	35

Over/Under 55%/45% 9th   **Both score** 50%/50% 8th

IPSWICH

Nickname: Town/Tractor Boys
Colours: Blue and white
Ground: Portman Road (30,311)
Tel: 01473-400-500 itfc.co.uk

After several seasons of overachievement Ipswich finally slipped to a position more befitting of their expenditure.

Some fans bemoan the direct approach adopted by Mick McCarthy, but it was only by playing to their strengths that the Tractor Boys ever flirted with the top six.

Repeatedly selling star men is catching up with Ipswich and it's telling that only four second-tier sides scored fewer goals. Moreover, none had fewer shots. If their conversion rates drops, so might they.

Longest run without win/loss: 8/8
High/low league position: 11/17
Clean sheets: 11 **Yellow cards:** 75 **Red:** 0
Avg attendance: 16,980 **Players used:** 32
Leading scorer: T Lawrence 9 (4,7)
Key stat: Ipswich were the Championship's draw kings last season, with 16 of their 46 games (34.8 per cent) ending all-square

	2016-17 H	A	Last six seasons at home P	W	D	L	OV	UN	BS	CS
Hull			3	0	0	3	1	2	1	0
Middlesbrough			5	3	1	1	2	3	2	2
Sunderland			-	-	-	-	-	-	-	-
Reading	D	L	5	2	1	2	3	2	3	1
Sheffield Wed	L	W	5	3	0	2	4	1	3	0
Fulham	L	L	3	1	1	1	1	2	2	0
Leeds	D	L	6	4	1	1	5	1	5	1
Norwich	D	D	2	0	1	1	0	2	1	0
Derby	L	W	6	2	0	4	3	3	2	1
Brentford	D	L	3	0	2	1	2	1	3	0
Preston	W	D	2	1	1	0	0	2	1	1
Cardiff	D	L	5	2	2	1	3	2	3	2
Aston Villa	D	W	1	0	1	0	0	1	0	1
Barnsley	W	D	4	2	2	0	1	3	3	1
Wolves	D	D	4	1	2	1	2	2	2	1
Ipswich										
Bristol City	W	L	4	2	2	0	3	1	3	1
QPR	W	L	3	2	0	1	3	0	2	1
Birmingham	D	L	6	3	3	0	2	4	5	1
Burton	W	L	1	1	0	0	0	1	0	1
Nottm Forest	L	L	6	3	1	2	3	3	4	1
Sheffield United			-	-	-	-	-	-	-	-
Bolton			4	4	0	0	0	4	0	4
Millwall			4	3	0	1	3	1	0	3

Season	Division	Pos	P	W	D	L	F	A	GD	Pts
2016-17	Championship	16	46	13	16	17	48	58	-10	55
2015-16	Championship	7	46	18	15	13	53	51	+2	69
2014-15	Championship	6	46	22	12	12	72	54	+18	78

Over/Under 41%/59% 19th   **Both score** 50%/50% 18th

LEEDS

Nickname: United
Colours: White
Ground: Elland Road (37,890)
Tel: 0871-334-1919   leedsunited.com

Just as it seems Leeds might be getting somewhere they lose their key man, with manager Garry Monk departing.

He leaves big shoes to fill for incoming gaffer Thomas Christiansen, as Monk had brought a bit of stability and decent football to a club starved of both.

On the plus side, Massimo Cellino has sold up, which should result in greater focus on the pitch than in the boardroom. But holding onto the division's top scorer, Chris Wood, would seem imperative.

Longest run without win/loss: 5/7
High/low league position: 3/15
Clean sheets: 15 **Yellow cards:** 85 **Red:** 3
Avg attendance: 27,697 **Players used:** 25
Leading scorer: C Wood 27 (14,23)
Key stat: Chris Wood scored almost half of Leeds' 61 league goals last term (44 per cent)

	2016-17 H	A	Last six seasons at home P	W	D	L	OV	UN	BS	CS
Hull			3	2	0	1	3	0	3	0
Middlesbrough			5	3	1	1	2	3	2	2
Sunderland			-	-	-	-	-	-	-	-
Reading	W	L	5	2	1	2	2	3	2	2
Sheffield Wed	W	W	5	2	3	0	1	4	4	1
Fulham	D	D	3	0	2	1	0	3	2	0
Leeds										
Norwich	D	W	2	0	1	1	1	1	1	0
Derby	W	L	6	2	2	2	2	4	3	2
Brentford	W	L	3	1	1	1	0	3	1	1
Preston	W	W	2	2	0	0	1	1	0	2
Cardiff	L	W	5	1	1	3	1	4	2	1
Aston Villa	W	D	1	1	0	0	0	1	0	1
Barnsley	W	L	4	2	1	1	2	2	2	2
Wolves	L	W	4	2	0	2	2	2	2	1
Ipswich	W	D	6	4	1	1	2	4	3	2
Bristol City	W	L	4	4	0	0	2	2	2	2
QPR	D	L	3	0	2	1	0	3	1	1
Birmingham	L	W	6	1	1	4	3	3	3	1
Burton	W	L	1	1	0	0	0	1	0	1
Nottm Forest	W	L	6	2	1	3	2	4	2	2
Sheffield United			-	-	-	-	-	-	-	-
Bolton			4	3	0	1	2	2	2	2
Millwall			4	4	0	0	1	3	1	3

Season	Division	Pos	P	W	D	L	F	A	GD	Pts
2016-17	Championship	7	46	22	9	15	61	47	+14	75
2015-16	Championship	13	46	14	17	15	50	58	-8	59
2014-15	Championship	15	46	15	11	20	50	61	-11	56

Over/Under 37%/63% 23rd   **Both score** 46%/54% 20th

MIDDLESBROUGH

Nickname: Boro
Colours: Red and white
Ground: Riverside Stadium (34,742)
Tel: 0844-499-6789   mfc.co.uk

Defence solidity won Boro promotion but it soon became clear that it wouldn't be enough to keep them in the top flight.

Middlesbrough scored just 27 goals – the worst top-flight tally since 2009-10 – so it was no surprise when Aitor Karanka, who had a fractious relationship with many at the club, was sacked in March.

But owner Steve Gibson was quick to admit his mistakes and has the hunger to get the club back on track, with the appointment of Garry Monk a good start.

Longest run without win/loss: 16/3
High/low league position: 13/19
Clean sheets: 11 **Yellow cards:** 78 **Red:** 1
Avg attendance: 30,449 **Players used:** 27
Leading scorer: A Negredo 9 (5,7)
Key stat: Middlesbrough won just one of their final 21 Premier League matches last season, failing to score in 12 of those games

	2016-17 H	A	Last six seasons at home P	W	D	L	OV	UN	BS	CS
Hull	W	L	4	4	0	0	0	4	0	4
Middlesbrough										
Sunderland	W	W	1	1	0	0	0	1	0	1
Reading			4	2	0	2	2	2	1	1
Sheffield Wed			4	2	1	1	2	2	3	1
Fulham			2	1	1	0	0	2	0	2
Leeds			5	2	1	2	1	4	0	3
Norwich			1	1	0	0	1	0	0	1
Derby			5	4	1	0	1	4	1	4
Brentford			2	2	0	0	2	0	1	1
Preston			1	1	0	0	0	1	0	1
Cardiff			4	3	0	1	3	1	3	0
Aston Villa			-	-	-	-	-	-	-	-
Barnsley			3	2	0	1	2	1	2	1
Wolves			3	3	0	0	2	1	2	1
Ipswich			5	3	2	0	1	4	1	4
Bristol City			3	0	1	2	1	2	0	2
QPR			2	1	0	1	1	1	1	1
Birmingham			5	3	1	1	2	3	2	2
Burton			-	-	-	-	-	-	-	-
Nottm Forest			5	3	1	1	2	3	2	2
Sheffield United			-	-	-	-	-	-	-	-
Bolton			4	4	0	0	2	2	1	3
Millwall			4	1	1	2	3	1	3	1

Season	Division	Pos	P	W	D	L	F	A	GD	Pts
2016-17	Premier League	19	38	5	13	20	27	53	-26	28
2015-16	Championship	2	46	26	11	9	63	31	+32	89
2014-15	Championship	4	46	25	10	11	68	37	+31	85

Over/Under 45%/55% 18th   **Both score** 42%/58% 18th

MILLWALL

Nickname: The Lions
Colours: Blue and white
Ground: The Den (20,146)
Tel: 020-7232-1222   millwallfc.co.uk

Playoff glory swiftly laid to rest the ghosts of Millwall's 2016 playoff final defeat and capped a season which saw the Lions beat Leicester, Watford and Bournemouth en route to the FA Cup quarter-finals.

The concern will be that Millwall were only good enough to sneak a League One playoff place on the final day of term. And while cup exertions have been blamed for a dip in league form, all four cup clashes against top-flight sides came during their best league run of 16 games unbeaten.

Longest run without win/loss: 6/16
High/low league position: 5/19
Clean sheets: 14 **Yellow cards:** 81 **Red:** 1
Avg attendance: 9,340 **Players used:** 25
Leading scorer: L Gregory 17 (10,13)
Key stat: Millwall had only the tenth-best away record in League One last season

	2016-17 H	A	Last six seasons at home P	W	D	L	OV	UN	BS	CS
Hull			2	1	0	1	0	2	0	1
Middlesbrough			4	1	0	3	3	1	3	0
Sunderland			-	-	-	-	-	-	-	-
Reading			3	0	1	2	2	1	1	1
Sheffield Wed			3	0	1	2	2	1	3	0
Fulham			1	0	1	0	0	1	0	1
Leeds			4	3	0	1	0	4	0	3
Norwich			1	0	0	1	1	0	1	0
Derby			4	1	2	1	3	1	3	1
Brentford			1	0	0	1	1	0	1	0
Preston			-	-	-	-	-	-	-	-
Cardiff			3	1	1	1	0	3	0	2
Aston Villa			-	-	-	-	-	-	-	-
Barnsley			4	1	1	2	2	2	2	2
Wolves			2	0	1	1	1	1	1	0
Ipswich			4	2	1	1	2	2	2	2
Bristol City			2	1	0	1	2	0	2	0
QPR			1	0	1	0	1	0	1	0
Birmingham			4	0	1	3	4	0	3	0
Burton			1	1	0	0	0	1	0	1
Nottm Forest			4	1	2	1	1	3	1	2
Sheffield United	W	L	2	2	0	0	1	1	1	1
Bolton	L	L	4	1	1	2	1	3	2	0
Millwall										

Season	Division	Pos	P	W	D	L	F	A	GD	Pts
2016-17	League One	6	46	20	13	13	66	57	+9	73
2015-16	League One	4	46	24	9	13	73	49	+24	81
2014-15	Championship	22	46	9	14	23	42	76	-34	41

Over/Under 54%/46% 7th   **Both score** 52%/48% 10th

NORWICH

Nickname: The Canaries
Colours: Yellow and green
Ground: Carrow Road (27,220)
Tel: 01603-760-760   canaries.co.uk

Only their third-choice kit was more offensive than Norwich last season, with all-out attack making them the joint-most potent second-tier side but also leading to the concession of a massive 25 goals in seven road trips to the teams above them.

But thrashing Reading 7-1, Brentford 5-0 and beating Brighton 2-0 hints at a lack of organisation rather than quality.

Alex Neil duly paid the price, replaced by the latest reserve-team coach to be poached from Dortmund, Daniel Farke.

Longest run without win/loss: 6/6
High/low league position: 1/12
Clean sheets: 11 **Yellow cards:** 78 **Red:** 7
Avg attendance: 26,335 **Players used:** 28
Leading scorer: C Jerome 16 (6,15)
Key stat: Norwich were the most efficient goalscorers in the Championship, scoring with every 7.68 shots on goal

	2016-17 H	A	Last six seasons at home P	W	D	L	OV	UN	BS	CS
Hull			1	1	0	0	0	1	0	1
Middlesbrough			1	0	0	1	0	1	0	0
Sunderland			4	3	0	1	3	1	2	1
Reading	W	L	3	2	0	1	3	0	3	0
Sheffield Wed	D	L	2	1	1	0	0	2	0	2
Fulham	L	D	5	1	2	2	3	2	4	1
Leeds	L	D	2	0	1	1	1	1	2	0
Norwich										
Derby	W	L	2	1	1	0	1	1	1	1
Brentford	W	D	2	1	0	1	2	0	1	1
Preston	L	W	1	0	0	1	0	1	0	0
Cardiff	W	W	3	2	1	0	2	1	2	1
Aston Villa	W	L	5	3	0	2	1	4	1	3
Barnsley	W	L	1	1	0	0	0	1	0	1
Wolves	W	W	3	3	0	0	2	1	2	1
Ipswich	D	D	2	1	1	0	0	2	1	1
Bristol City	W	D	1	1	0	0	0	1	0	1
QPR	W	L	3	2	1	0	2	1	2	1
Birmingham	W	L	2	1	1	0	1	1	1	1
Burton	W	L	1	1	0	0	1	0	1	0
Nottm Forest	W	W	2	2	0	0	2	0	2	0
Sheffield United			-	-	-	-	-	-	-	-
Bolton			2	2	0	0	1	1	1	1
Millwall			1	1	0	0	1	0	1	0

Season	Division	Pos	P	W	D	L	F	A	GD	Pts
2016-17	Championship	8	46	20	10	16	85	69	+16	70
2015-16	Premier League	19	38	9	7	22	39	67	-28	34
2014-15	Championship	3	46	25	11	10	88	48	+40	86

Over/Under 70%/30% 1st   **Both score** 63%/37% 2nd

NOTTINGHAM FOREST

Nickname: Forest
Colours: Red and white
Ground: City Ground (30,455)
Tel: 0115-982-4444   nottinghamforest.co.uk

Forest fans won't be sorry to see the back of owner Fawaz Al Hasawi, who saw the club slip lower in each of his final four seasons. And while Evangelos Marinakis arrives with a sackful of baggage, he is no novice and has been quick to implement some much-needed structure at the club.

The appointment of Mark Warburton looks a positive, with Forest enjoying a swift upturn in results under their new manager last term, and the academy has been turning out some real quality.

Longest run without win/loss: 7/4
High/low league position: 13/21
Clean sheets: 8 **Yellow cards:** 96 **Red:** 9
Avg attendance: 20,332 **Players used:** 38
Leading scorer: B Assombalonga 14 (8,9)
Key stat: Forest had a midtable-level home record last term but only Rotherham had a worse away record in the Championship

	2016-17 H	A	P	W	D	L	OV	UN	BS	CS
Hull			3	0	0	3	1	2	1	0
Middlesbrough			5	2	2	1	3	2	3	2
Sunderland			-	-	-	-	-	-	-	-
Reading	W	L	5	4	0	1	4	1	3	2
Sheffield Wed	L	L	5	1	1	3	3	2	2	1
Fulham	D	L	3	2	1	0	2	1	2	1
Leeds	W	L	6	3	2	1	4	2	5	0
Norwich	L	L	2	1	0	1	2	0	2	0
Derby	D	L	6	2	2	2	2	4	3	2
Brentford	L	L	3	0	0	3	3	0	2	0
Preston	D	D	2	1	1	0	0	2	1	1
Cardiff	L	L	5	1	0	4	4	1	4	0
Aston Villa	W	D	1	1	0	0	1	0	1	0
Barnsley	L	W	4	1	2	1	1	3	1	2
Wolves	L	L	4	1	1	2	2	2	3	0
Ipswich	W	W	6	3	3	0	3	3	3	3
Bristol City	W	L	4	2	0	2	1	3	1	2
QPR	D	L	3	1	2	0	0	3	1	2
Birmingham	W	D	6	2	2	2	4	2	5	1
Burton	W	L	1	1	0	0	1	0	1	0
Nottm Forest										
Sheffield United			-	-	-	-	-	-	-	-
Bolton			4	3	1	0	3	1	2	2
Millwall			4	1	0	3	3	1	3	0

Season	Division	Pos	P	W	D	L	F	A	GD	Pts
2016-17	Championship	21	46	14	9	23	62	72	-10	51
2015-16	Championship	16	46	13	16	17	43	47	-4	55
2014-15	Championship	14	46	15	14	17	71	69	+2	59

Over/Under 57%/43% 4th   **Both score** 57%/43% 6th

PRESTON

Nickname: The Lilywhites/North End
Colours: White and navy blue
Ground: Deepdale (23,408)
Tel: 0344-856-1964   pnefc.co.uk

Given the limited budget at Deepdale Preston once again overachieved, with manager Simon Grayson deserving of all the praise that came his way.

However, Grayson's June departure comes as a blow to Preston's prospects as will the loss of Aiden McGeady, who lit up Deepdale while on loan.

It's hard to knock a club who have so outperformed expectations in recent seasons, but new manager Alex Neil has a lot to prove and a lot to live up to.

Longest run without win/loss: 6/6
High/low league position: 8/20
Clean sheets: 12 **Yellow cards:** 83 **Red:** 5
Avg attendance: 12,614 **Players used:** 29
Leading scorer: J Hugill 12 (3,11)
Key stat: Preston scored 19 first-half goals at Deepdale – the second-best home record in the second tier – but they also conceded a hefty 14

	2016-17 H	A	P	W	D	L	OV	UN	BS	CS
Hull			1	1	0	0	0	1	0	1
Middlesbrough			1	0	1	0	0	1	0	1
Sunderland			-	-	-	-	-	-	-	-
Reading	W	L	2	2	0	0	1	1	0	2
Sheffield Wed	D	L	3	1	1	1	0	3	1	1
Fulham	L	L	2	0	0	2	2	0	2	0
Leeds	L	L	2	0	1	1	1	1	2	0
Norwich	L	W	1	0	0	1	1	0	1	0
Derby	L	D	2	0	0	2	1	1	1	0
Brentford	W	L	5	1	1	3	4	1	4	0
Preston										
Cardiff	W	L	2	1	1	0	1	1	0	2
Aston Villa	W	D	1	1	0	0	0	1	0	1
Barnsley	L	D	2	1	0	1	1	1	1	1
Wolves	D	L	3	0	3	0	0	3	1	2
Ipswich	D	L	2	0	1	1	1	1	2	0
Bristol City	W	W	4	2	2	0	1	3	2	2
QPR	W	W	2	1	1	0	1	1	2	0
Birmingham	W	D	2	1	1	0	1	1	2	0
Burton	D	W	1	0	1	0	0	1	1	0
Nottm Forest	D	D	2	1	1	0	0	2	1	1
Sheffield United			4	0	2	2	1	3	2	1
Bolton			1	0	1	0	0	1	0	1
Millwall			-	-	-	-	-	-	-	-

Season	Division	Pos	P	W	D	L	F	A	GD	Pts
2016-17	Championship	11	46	16	14	16	64	63	+1	62
2015-16	Championship	11	46	15	17	14	45	45	0	62
2014-15	League One	3	46	25	14	7	79	40	+39	89

Over/Under 54%/46% 7th   **Both score** 59%/41% 4th

QPR

Nickname: The R's
Colours: Blue and white
Ground: Loftus Road (18,439)
Tel: 020-8743-0262   qpr.co.uk

Only victory on the penultimate weekend saved QPR from a surprise relegation, but it would be less of a shock if the R's were to struggle again in 2017-18.

Jimmy Floyd Hasselbaink failed to inspire at the helm but his replacement, returning manager Ian Holloway, inherits a squad lacking identity after such heavy player turnover in recent years.

Key for the R's, however, will be the imminent decision on whether the EFL's Financial Fair Play sanctions are upheld.

Longest run without win/loss: 6/5
High/low league position: 13/20
Clean sheets: 7 **Yellow cards:** 92 **Red:** 5
Avg attendance: 14,615 **Players used:** 37
Leading scorer: I Sylla 10 (4,10)
Key stat: QPR scored a dismal five first-half goals away from home last season – the lowest tally in the second tier

READING

Nickname: The Royals
Colours: Blue and white
Ground: Madejski Stadium (24,161)
Tel: 0118 968-1100   readingfc.co.uk

Third place rather flattered Reading, who were efficient rather than impressive.

They were unbeaten at home against top-half teams but took some hammerings on the road – 7-1 at Norwich and 5-0 at Fulham – suggesting the Royals may owe more to good fortune than the average automatic-promotion chaser.

Having the second-best goals to shots conversion rate in the division was key but will be hard to replicate, indicating Reading could well have overachieved.

Longest run without win/loss: 4/6
High/low league position: 3/8
Clean sheets: 15 **Yellow cards:** 94 **Red:** 4
Avg attendance: 17,504 **Players used:** 28
Leading scorer: Y Kermorgant 18 (7,15)
Key stat: Reading scored with every 7.97 shots on goal last term – only Norwich were more efficient in front of goal

	2016-17		Last six seasons at home							
	H	A	P	W	D	L	OV	UN	BS	CS
Hull			2	0	0	2	1	1	1	0
Middlesbrough			2	1	0	1	1	1	1	1
Sunderland			3	2	0	1	2	1	2	1
Reading	D	W	4	0	3	1	1	3	4	0
Sheffield Wed	L	L	3	1	1	1	2	1	2	1
Fulham	D	W	4	1	1	2	2	2	3	0
Leeds	W	D	3	2	1	0	1	2	1	2
Norwich	W	L	3	1	1	1	2	1	2	1
Derby	L	L	3	2	0	1	1	2	1	1
Brentford	L	L	2	1	0	1	1	1	0	1
Preston	L	L	2	0	1	1	0	2	0	1
Cardiff	W	W	2	1	1	0	2	0	2	0
Aston Villa	L	L	4	1	2	1	0	4	2	1
Barnsley	W	L	2	2	0	0	1	1	1	1
Wolves	L	W	3	0	1	2	2	1	3	0
Ipswich	W	L	3	3	0	0	1	2	1	2
Bristol City	W	L	2	2	0	0	0	2	0	2
QPR										
Birmingham	D	W	3	2	1	0	0	3	1	2
Burton	L	D	1	0	0	1	1	0	1	0
Nottm Forest	W	D	3	2	0	1	2	1	2	1
Sheffield United	-	-	-	-	-	-	-	-	-	-
Bolton			3	2	0	1	3	0	2	0
Millwall			1	0	1	0	0	1	1	0

Season	Division	Pos	P	W	D	L	F	A	GD	Pts
2016-17	Championship	18	46	15	8	23	52	66	-14	53
2015-16	Championship	12	46	14	18	14	54	54	0	60
2014-15	Premier League	20	38	8	6	24	42	73	-31	30

Over/Under 54%/46% 7th   **Both score** 57%/43% 6th

	2016-17		Last six seasons at home							
	H	A	P	W	D	L	OV	UN	BS	CS
Hull			2	0	0	2	1	1	1	0
Middlesbrough			4	2	2	0	0	4	0	4
Sunderland			1	1	0	0	1	0	1	0
Reading										
Sheffield Wed	W	W	4	2	1	1	1	3	2	1
Fulham	W	L	4	2	2	0	3	1	2	2
Leeds	W	L	5	3	1	1	0	5	0	4
Norwich	W	L	3	2	1	0	2	1	2	1
Derby	D	L	5	0	3	2	2	3	2	1
Brentford	W	L	3	1	0	2	2	1	2	0
Preston	W	L	2	1	0	1	1	1	1	1
Cardiff	W	W	4	1	2	1	2	2	4	0
Aston Villa	L	W	2	0	0	2	2	0	2	0
Barnsley	D	W	3	0	2	1	2	1	2	1
Wolves	W	L	3	1	2	0	2	1	2	1
Ipswich	W	D	5	5	0	0	3	2	3	2
Bristol City	W	W	3	3	0	0	1	2	1	2
QPR	L	D	4	0	2	2	0	4	1	1
Birmingham	D	W	5	2	1	2	0	5	0	3
Burton	W	W	1	1	0	0	1	0	0	1
Nottm Forest	W	L	5	3	1	1	2	3	2	2
Sheffield United	-	-	-	-	-	-	-	-	-	-
Bolton			3	2	1	0	2	1	2	1
Millwall			3	1	2	0	2	1	3	0

Season	Division	Pos	P	W	D	L	F	A	GD	Pts
2016-17	Championship	3	46	26	7	13	68	64	+4	85
2015-16	Championship	17	46	13	13	20	52	59	-7	52
2014-15	Championship	19	46	13	11	22	48	69	-21	50

Over/Under 59%/41% 3rd   **Both score** 52%/48% 14th

SHEFFIELD UNITED

Nickname: The Blades
Colours: Red and white
Ground: Bramall Lane (32,702)
Tel: 0114-253-720   sufc.co.uk

After years frustrating their backers, the Blades at last lived up to the hype to end their six-year spell in League One.

The man who finally unlocked the obvious potential at Bramall Lane was Chris Wilder, appointed last summer following his promotion successes at both Oxford United and Northampton.

His impact was swift and impressive with United collecting 100 league points – up 34 from 2015-16. The Blades will have loftier ambitions than mere survival.

Longest run without win/loss: 4/17
High/low league position: 1/12
Clean sheets: 17 **Yellow cards:** 73 **Red:** 1
Avg attendance: 21,892 **Players used:** 29
Leading scorer: B Sharp 30 (9,23)
Key stat: United finished League One unbeaten in 17 games (winning 13) but failed to win away at any of the rest of the top six

	2016-17 H	A	Last six seasons at home P	W	D	L	OV	UN	BS	CS
Hull	-	-	-	-	-	-	-	-	-	-
Middlesbrough	-	-	-	-	-	-	-	-	-	-
Sunderland	-	-	-	-	-	-	-	-	-	-
Reading	-	-	-	-	-	-	-	-	-	-
Sheffield Wed			1	0	1	0	1	0	1	0
Fulham	-	-	-	-	-	-	-	-	-	-
Leeds	-	-	-	-	-	-	-	-	-	-
Norwich	-	-	-	-	-	-	-	-	-	-
Derby	-	-	-	-	-	-	-	-	-	-
Brentford			3	1	2	0	1	2	1	2
Preston			4	2	1	1	2	2	2	1
Cardiff	-	-	-	-	-	-	-	-	-	-
Aston Villa	-	-	-	-	-	-	-	-	-	-
Barnsley			2	0	1	1	0	2	0	1
Wolves			1	0	0	1	0	1	0	0
Ipswich	-	-	-	-	-	-	-	-	-	-
Bristol City			2	1	0	1	2	0	1	1
QPR	-	-	-	-	-	-	-	-	-	-
Birmingham	-	-	-	-	-	-	-	-	-	-
Burton			1	0	0	1	0	1	0	0
Nottm Forest	-	-	-	-	-	-	-	-	-	-
Sheffield United										
Bolton	W	L	1	1	0	0	0	1	0	1
Millwall	W	L	2	1	0	1	1	1	1	1

Season	Division	Pos	P	W	D	L	F	A	GD	Pts
2016-17	League One	1	46	30	10	6	92	47	+45	100
2015-16	League One	11	46	18	12	16	64	59	+5	66
2014-15	League One	5	46	19	14	13	66	53	+13	71

Over/Under 61%/39% 4th   **Both score** 54%/46% 7th

SHEFFIELD WED

Nickname: The Owls
Colours: Blue and white
Ground: Hillsborough (39,732)
Tel: 03700-20-1867   swfc.co.uk

Back-to-back promotion playoff failures will have hurt Wednesday fans but they have good reason to remain optimistic.

The squad is in good shape and coach Carlos Carvalhal has proven himself at this level, so his contract extension is a boost. The way in which owner Dejphon Chansiri is building the club in a sensible, low-key fashion can only bode well, too.

More ruthlessness is needed in front of goal but Wednesday dominated most matches – even many of those they lost.

Longest run without win/loss: 4/7
High/low league position: 4/14
Clean sheets: 16 **Yellow cards:** 72 **Red:** 7
Avg attendance: 27,129 **Players used:** 30
Leading scorer: F Forestieri 12 (7,12)
Key stat: Wednesday had more shots, corners and possession in five of six home defeats, the exception when resting players against Fulham

	2016-17 H	A	Last six seasons at home P	W	D	L	OV	UN	BS	CS
Hull			2	0	1	1	0	2	1	0
Middlesbrough			4	3	0	1	1	3	1	3
Sunderland	-	-	-	-	-	-	-	-	-	-
Reading	L	L	4	2	1	1	1	3	2	1
Sheffield Wed										
Fulham	L	D	3	1	1	1	2	1	3	0
Leeds	L	L	5	2	1	2	2	3	2	2
Norwich	W	D	2	1	1	0	1	1	1	1
Derby	W	L	5	1	3	1	2	3	2	2
Brentford	L	D	4	2	1	1	2	2	1	3
Preston	W	D	3	3	0	0	2	1	2	1
Cardiff	W	D	4	2	1	1	1	3	1	2
Aston Villa	W	L	1	1	0	0	0	1	0	1
Barnsley	W	D	3	3	0	0	1	2	1	2
Wolves	D	W	4	1	2	1	1	3	1	2
Ipswich	L	W	5	0	4	1	1	4	5	0
Bristol City	W	W	3	2	0	1	2	1	2	1
QPR	W	W	3	2	1	0	1	2	1	2
Birmingham	W	L	5	4	1	0	4	1	2	3
Burton	D	L	1	0	1	0	0	1	1	0
Nottm Forest	W	W	5	2	0	3	1	4	1	1
Sheffield United			1	1	0	0	0	1	0	1
Bolton			4	1	0	3	4	0	4	0
Millwall			3	1	2	0	2	1	3	0

Season	Division	Pos	P	W	D	L	F	A	GD	Pts
2016-17	Championship	4	46	24	9	13	60	45	+15	81
2015-16	Championship	6	46	19	17	10	66	45	+21	74
2014-15	Championship	13	46	14	18	14	43	49	-6	60

Over/Under 43%/57% 18th   **Both score** 54%/46% 9th

SUNDERLAND

Nickname: The Black Cats/Mackems
Colours: Red and white
Ground: Stadium of Light (49,000)
Tel: 0371-911-1200   safc.com

David Moyes' stock continued to slide during a dismal spell as Sunderland manager but the club looked destined for the second tier long before he arrived.

The Black Cats survived by the skin of their teeth in the four seasons leading up to relegation, with a lack of continuity in the dugout and weak leadership from the boardroom producing poor focus.

Goals were scarce – departee Jermain Defoe netted 15 of just 29 goals – and the squad lacks commitment and quality.

Longest run without win/loss: 10/2
High/low league position: 18/20
Clean sheets: 6 **Yellow cards:** 81 **Red:** 4
Avg attendance: 41,286 **Players used:** 31
Leading scorer: J Defoe 15 (3,12)
Key stat: Sunderland had the worst home record in the Premier League last season, winning just three home games and losing 11

	2016-17 H	2016-17 A	P	W	D	L	OV	UN	BS	CS
Hull	W	W	3	1	0	2	2	1	1	1
Middlesbrough	L	L	1	0	0	1	1	0	1	0
Sunderland										
Reading			1	1	0	0	1	0	0	1
Sheffield Wed			-	-	-	-	-	-	-	-
Fulham			3	0	2	1	1	2	1	1
Leeds			-	-	-	-	-	-	-	-
Norwich			4	1	2	1	2	2	2	2
Derby			-	-	-	-	-	-	-	-
Brentford			-	-	-	-	-	-	-	-
Preston			-	-	-	-	-	-	-	-
Cardiff			1	1	0	0	1	0	0	1
Aston Villa			5	1	1	3	3	2	2	0
Barnsley			-	-	-	-	-	-	-	-
Wolves			1	0	1	0	0	1	0	1
Ipswich			-	-	-	-	-	-	-	-
Bristol City			-	-	-	-	-	-	-	-
QPR			3	1	1	1	1	2	1	1
Birmingham			-	-	-	-	-	-	-	-
Burton			-	-	-	-	-	-	-	-
Nottm Forest			-	-	-	-	-	-	-	-
Sheffield United			-	-	-	-	-	-	-	-
Bolton			1	0	1	0	1	0	1	0
Millwall			-	-	-	-	-	-	-	-

Season	Division	Pos	P	W	D	L	F	A	GD	Pts
2016-17	Premier League	20	38	6	6	26	29	69	-40	24
2015-16	Premier League	17	38	9	12	17	48	62	-14	39
2014-15	Premier League	16	38	7	17	14	31	53	-22	38

Over/Under 47%/53% 15th   **Both score** 37%/63% 20th

WOLVES

Nickname: Wolves
Colours: Gold and black
Ground: Molineux (31,700)
Tel: 0871-222-2220   wolves.co.uk

Solid squad, decent stadium, wealthy investors and the odd ambitious signing – it's easy to see why Wolves are usually involved in the promotion discussions.

But Wolves have looked no more than a mid-table Championship side since their 2012 relegation and, despite all the money, the current owners fail to inspire.

Managers come and go too swiftly to offer stability – there have been four in ten months – and player recruitment seems to target profit rather than progress.

Longest run without win/loss: 9/6
High/low league position: 8/21
Clean sheets: 13 **Yellow cards:** 95 **Red:** 4
Avg attendance: 21,570 **Players used:** 35
Lead scorers: Edwards 10 (2,9) Costa 10 (2,10)
Key stat: Wolves had the same points, same goals against and just one more goal scored in 2016-17 than in 2015-16

	2016-17 H	2016-17 A	P	W	D	L	OV	UN	BS	CS
Hull			2	1	1	0	0	2	1	1
Middlesbrough			3	2	0	1	2	1	2	1
Sunderland			1	1	0	0	1	0	1	0
Reading	W	L	3	2	0	1	1	2	1	2
Sheffield Wed	L	D	4	3	0	1	2	2	1	2
Fulham	D	W	4	3	1	0	3	1	2	2
Leeds	L	W	4	1	1	2	3	1	3	0
Norwich	L	L	3	1	1	1	2	1	2	1
Derby	L	L	4	2	1	1	2	2	3	1
Brentford	W	W	4	2	1	1	2	2	2	1
Preston	W	D	3	2	0	1	1	2	1	2
Cardiff	W	L	4	2	0	2	3	1	3	1
Aston Villa	W	D	2	1	0	1	1	1	1	1
Barnsley	L		2	1	0	1	2	0	1	0
Wolves										
Ipswich	D	D	4	0	3	1	0	4	1	2
Bristol City	W		4	4	0	0	4	0	4	0
QPR	L	W	3	0	0	3	3	0	2	0
Birmingham	L	W	4	1	2	1	1	3	1	3
Burton	D	L	1	0	1	0	0	1	1	0
Nottm Forest	W	W	4	1	2	2	2	2	2	1
Sheffield United			1	1	0	0	0	1	0	1
Bolton			4	1	2	1	3	1	3	1
Millwall			2	1	0	1	1	1	1	0

Season	Division	Pos	P	W	D	L	F	A	GD	Pts
2016-17	Championship	15	46	16	10	20	54	58	-4	58
2015-16	Championship	14	46	14	16	16	53	58	-5	58
2014-15	Championship	7	46	22	12	12	70	56	+14	78

Over/Under 48%/52% 13th   **Both score** 52%/48% 14th

Championship stats 2016-17

Key Points in all tables (except the league table) do not include any deductions imposed by the league.
POS H A Overall league position, rank from home games only, rank from away games only **Sup** Average match supremacy **GFA** Goals For Average **GAA** Goals Against Average **PGA** Points Gained Average

			Championship 2016-17		Home					Away						
Pos	H	A		P	W	D	L	F	A	W	D	L	F	A	GD	Pts
1	4	1	Newcastle (P)	46	15	3	5	49	23	14	4	5	36	17	45	94
2	1	3	Brighton (P)	46	17	3	3	46	14	11	6	6	28	26	34	93
3	2	6	Reading	46	16	5	2	35	16	10	2	11	33	48	4	85
4	5	4	Sheffield Wed	46	15	2	6	36	22	9	7	7	24	23	15	81
5	6	5	Huddersfield (P)	46	15	2	6	34	26	10	4	9	22	32	-2	81
6	13	2	Fulham	46	10	8	5	45	32	12	6	5	40	25	28	80
7	7	9	Leeds	46	14	4	5	32	16	8	5	10	29	31	14	75
8	3	18	Norwich	46	15	4	4	55	22	5	6	12	30	47	16	70
9	9	11	Derby	46	11	8	4	33	20	7	5	11	21	30	4	67
10	12	10	Brentford	46	11	5	7	42	25	7	5	11	33	40	10	64
11	11	14	Preston	46	11	6	6	40	26	5	8	10	24	37	1	62
12	15	12	Cardiff	46	11	4	8	31	26	6	7	10	29	35	-1	62
13	8	21	Aston Villa	46	12	8	3	33	20	4	6	13	14	28	-1	62
14	20	8	Barnsley	46	6	11	6	32	33	9	2	12	32	34	-3	58
15	22	7	Wolves	46	8	4	11	25	30	8	6	9	29	28	-4	58
16	16	17	Ipswich	46	8	10	5	30	24	5	6	12	18	34	-10	55
17	14	22	Bristol City	46	11	4	8	33	26	4	5	14	27	40	-6	54
18	18	15	QPR	46	9	4	10	30	32	6	4	13	22	34	-14	53
19	21	13	Birmingham	46	8	5	10	25	31	5	9	9	20	33	-19	53
20	19	16	Burton	46	9	4	10	28	30	4	9	10	21	33	-14	52
21	10	23	Nottm Forest	46	12	4	7	42	30	2	5	16	20	42	-10	51
22	17	20	Blackburn (R)	46	8	8	7	29	30	4	7	12	24	35	-12	51
23	23	19	Wigan (R)	46	5	8	10	19	26	5	4	14	21	31	-17	42
24	24	24	Rotherham (R)	46	5	6	12	23	34	0	2	21	17	64	-58	23

Best attack

		GF	GFA
1	Newcastle	85	1.85
2	Fulham	85	1.85
3	Norwich	85	1.85
4	Brentford	75	1.63
5	Brighton	74	1.61
6	Reading	68	1.48
7	Preston	64	1.39
8	Barnsley	64	1.39
9	Nottm Forest	62	1.35
10	Leeds	61	1.33
11	Sheff Wed	60	1.3
12	Cardiff	60	1.3
13	Bristol City	60	1.3
14	Huddersfield	56	1.22
15	Derby	54	1.17
16	Wolves	54	1.17
17	Blackburn	53	1.15
18	QPR	52	1.13
19	Burton	49	1.07
20	Ipswich	48	1.04
21	Aston Villa	47	1.02
22	Birmingham	45	0.98
23	Wigan	40	0.87
24	Rotherham	40	0.87

Best defence

		GA	GAA
1	Newcastle	40	0.87
2	Brighton	40	0.87
3	Sheff Wed	45	0.98
4	Leeds	47	1.02
5	Aston Villa	48	1.04
6	Derby	50	1.09
7	Fulham	57	1.24
8	Wigan	57	1.24
9	Huddersfield	58	1.26
10	Wolves	58	1.26
11	Ipswich	58	1.26
12	Cardiff	61	1.33
13	Preston	63	1.37
14	Burton	63	1.37
15	Reading	64	1.39
16	Birmingham	64	1.39
17	Brentford	65	1.41
18	Blackburn	65	1.41
19	Bristol City	66	1.43
20	QPR	66	1.43
21	Barnsley	67	1.46
22	Norwich	69	1.5
23	Nottm Forest	72	1.57
24	Rotherham	98	2.13

Top scorers

	Team	Goals scored	
C Wood	Leeds	27	▮▮▮▮▮▮▮▮▮▮▮▮▮▮▮▮▮▮▮▮▮▮▮▮▮▮▮
T Abraham	Bristol City	23	▮▮▮▮▮▮▮▮▮▮▮▮▮▮▮▮▮▮▮▮▮▮▮
D Gayle	Newcastle	23	▮▮▮▮▮▮▮▮▮▮▮▮▮▮▮▮▮▮▮▮▮▮▮
G Murray	Brighton	23	▮▮▮▮▮▮▮▮▮▮▮▮▮▮▮▮▮▮▮▮▮▮▮
J Kodjia	Aston Villa	19	▮▮▮▮▮▮▮▮▮▮▮▮▮▮▮▮▮▮▮
Y Kermorgant	Reading	18	▮▮▮▮▮▮▮▮▮▮▮▮▮▮▮▮▮▮

Over 2.5 goals

	H	A	%
Norwich	15	17	70%
Rotherham	10	18	61%
Reading	12	15	59%
Brentford	13	13	57%
Fulham	16	10	57%
Nottm Forest	14	12	57%

Under 2.5 goals

	H	A	%
Aston Villa	15	18	72%
Leeds	16	13	63%
Derby	14	14	61%
Burton	13	14	59%
Ipswich	14	13	59%
Wigan	15	12	59%

Both to score

	H	A	%
Fulham	17	13	65%
Blackburn	14	15	63%
Norwich	13	16	63%
Brentford	11	16	59%
Preston	15	12	59%

Both not to score

	H	A	%
Derby	14	15	63%
Brighton	14	14	61%
Wigan	15	12	59%
Aston Villa	10	15	54%
Leeds	16	9	54%

SOCCERBASE.COM

Championship results 2016-17

	Aston Villa	Barnsley	Birmingham	Blackburn	Brentford	Brighton	Bristol City	Burton	Cardiff	Derby	Fulham	Huddersfield	Ipswich	Leeds	Newcastle	Norwich	Nottm Forest	Preston	QPR	Reading	Rotherham	Sheffield Wed	Wigan	Wolves
Aston Villa		1-3	1-0	2-1	1-1	1-1	2-0	2-1	3-1	1-0	1-0	1-1	0-1	1-1	1-1	2-0	2-2	2-2	1-0	1-3	3-0	2-0	1-0	1-1
Barnsley	1-1		2-2	2-0	1-1	0-2	2-2	1-1	0-0	2-0	2-4	1-1	1-1	3-2	0-2	2-1	2-5	0-0	3-2	1-2	4-0	1-1	0-0	1-3
Birmingham	1-1	0-3		1-0	1-3	1-2	1-0	0-2	0-0	1-2	1-0	2-0	2-1	1-3	0-0	3-0	0-0	2-2	1-4	0-1	4-2	2-1	0-1	1-3
Blackburn	1-0	0-2	1-1		3-2	2-3	1-1	2-2	1-1	1-0	0-1	1-1	0-0	1-2	1-0	1-4	2-1	2-2	1-0	2-3	4-2	0-1	1-0	1-1
Brentford	3-0	0-2	1-2	1-3		3-3	2-0	2-1	2-2	4-0	0-2	0-1	2-0	2-0	1-2	0-0	1-0	5-0	3-1	4-1	4-2	1-1	0-0	1-2
Brighton	1-1	2-0	3-1	1-0	0-2		0-1	4-1	1-0	3-0	2-1	1-0	1-1	2-0	1-2	5-0	3-0	2-2	3-0	3-0	3-0	2-1	2-1	1-0
Bristol City	3-1	3-2	0-1	1-0	0-1	0-2		0-0	2-3	1-1	0-2	4-0	2-0	1-0	0-1	1-1	2-1	1-2	2-1	2-3	1-0	2-2	2-1	3-1
Burton	1-1	0-0	2-0	1-1	3-5	0-1	1-2		2-0	1-0	0-2	0-0	1-2	2-1	1-2	2-1	1-0	0-1	1-1	2-4	2-1	3-1	0-2	2-1
Cardiff	1-0	3-4	1-1	2-1	2-1	0-0	2-1	1-0		0-2	2-2	3-2	3-1	0-2	0-2	0-1	1-0	2-0	0-2	0-1	5-0	1-0	0-1	2-1
Derby	0-0	2-1	1-0	1-2	0-0	0-0	3-3	0-0	3-4		4-2	1-1	0-1	1-0	0-2	1-0	3-0	1-1	1-0	3-2	3-2	2-0	0-0	3-1
Fulham	3-1	2-0	0-1	2-2	1-1	1-2	0-4	1-1	2-2	2-2		5-0	3-1	1-1	1-0	2-2	3-2	3-1	1-2	5-0	2-1	1-1	3-2	1-3
Huddersfield	1-0	2-1	1-1	1-1	2-1	3-1	2-1	0-1	0-3	1-0	1-4		2-0	2-1	1-3	3-0	2-1	3-2	2-1	1-0	2-1	0-1	1-2	1-0
Ipswich	0-0	4-2	1-1	3-2	1-1	0-0	2-1	2-0	1-1	0-3	0-2	0-1		1-1	3-1	1-1	0-2	1-0	3-0	2-2	2-2	0-1	3-0	0-0
Leeds	2-0	2-1	1-2	2-1	1-0	2-0	2-1	2-0	0-2	1-0	1-1	0-1	1-0		0-2	3-3	2-0	3-0	0-0	2-0	3-0	1-0	1-1	0-1
Newcastle	2-0	3-0	4-0	0-1	3-1	2-0	2-1	0-1	1-1	3-2	1-1	3-0	1-1			4-3	3-1	4-1	2-2	4-1	4-0	0-1	2-1	0-2
Norwich	1-0	2-0	2-0	2-2	5-0	2-0	1-0	3-1	3-2	3-0	1-3	1-2	1-1	2-3	2-2		5-1	0-1	4-0	3-1	0-0	2-1		3-1
Nottm Forest	2-1	0-1	3-1	0-1	2-3	3-0	1-0	4-3	1-2	2-2	1-1	2-0	3-0	3-1	2-1	1-2		1-1	1-1	3-2	2-0	1-1	4-3	0-2
Preston	2-0	1-2	2-1	3-2	4-2	2-0	5-0	1-1	3-0	0-1	1-2	3-1	1-1	1-4	1-2	1-3	1-1		2-1	3-0	1-1	1-1		0-0
QPR	0-1	2-1	1-1	1-1	0-2	1-2	1-0	1-2	2-1	0-1	1-1	1-2	2-1	3-0	0-6	2-1	2-0	0-2		1-1	5-1	1-2	2-1	1-2
Reading	1-2	0-0	0-0	3-1	3-2	2-2	2-1	3-0	2-1	1-1	1-0	1-0	2-1	1-0	0-0	3-1	2-0	1-0	0-1		2-1	2-1	1-0	2-1
Rotherham	0-2	0-1	1-1	1-1	1-0	0-2	2-2	1-2	1-2	1-1	0-1	2-3	1-0	1-2	0-1	2-1	2-2	1-3	1-0	0-1		0-2	3-2	2-2
Sheffield Wed	1-0	2-0	3-0	2-1	1-2	1-2	3-2	1-1	1-0	2-1	1-2	2-0	1-2	0-2	2-1	5-1	2-1	2-1	1-0	0-2	1-0		2-1	0-0
Wigan	0-2	3-2	1-1	3-0	2-1	0-1	0-1	0-0	0-0	0-1	0-0	0-1	2-3	1-1	0-2	2-2	0-0	0-0	0-1	0-3	3-2	0-1		2-1
Wolves	1-0	0-4	1-2	0-0	3-1	0-2	3-2	1-1	3-1	2-3	4-4	0-1	0-0	0-1	0-1	1-2	1-0	1-0	1-2	2-0	1-0	0-2	0-1	

Record when first to score

		P	W	D	L	F	A	Sup	PGA	Pts
1	Brighton	27	25	1	1	58	13	+1.67	2.8	76
2	Reading	26	24	1	1	53	25	+1.08	2.8	73
3	Newcastle	33	28	4	1	76	22	+1.64	2.7	88
4	Huddersfield	27	22	4	1	41	18	+0.85	2.6	70
5	Leeds	25	21	3	1	45	12	+1.32	2.6	66
6	Burton	15	12	3	0	27	12	+1	2.6	39
7	Sheff Wed	26	20	4	2	40	15	+0.96	2.5	64
8	QPR	18	14	3	1	35	13	+1.22	2.5	45
9	Norwich	26	19	6	1	67	25	+1.62	2.4	63
10	Preston	20	14	5	1	43	17	+1.3	2.4	47
11	Wolves	18	14	2	2	33	17	+0.89	2.4	44
12	Fulham	24	17	5	2	49	21	+1.17	2.3	56
13	Brentford	23	17	2	4	57	26	+1.35	2.3	53
14	Derby	23	16	4	3	37	20	+0.74	2.3	52
15	Wigan	11	8	1	2	17	8	+0.82	2.3	25
16	Ipswich	21	13	7	1	38	21	+0.81	2.2	46
17	Blackburn	14	9	4	1	18	10	+0.57	2.2	31
18	Aston Villa	25	15	8	2	36	18	+0.72	2.1	53
19	Cardiff	18	11	5	2	35	18	+0.94	2.1	38
20	Bristol City	17	11	3	3	32	15	+1	2.1	36
21	Birmingham	20	12	5	3	31	21	+0.5	2	41
22	Barnsley	23	13	5	5	45	31	+0.61	1.9	44
23	Nottm Forest	21	11	5	5	43	31	+0.57	1.8	38
24	Rotherham	17	5	6	6	26	30	-0.24	1.2	21

Record when keeping a clean sheet

		P	W	D	F	Sup	PGA	Pts
1	Huddersfield	12	12	0	15	+1.25	3	36
2	Rotherham	3	3	0	3	+1	3	9
3	Leeds	15	14	1	25	+1.67	2.9	43
4	Newcastle	19	17	2	39	+2.05	2.8	53
5	Sheff Wed	16	14	2	20	+1.25	2.8	44
6	Fulham	11	10	1	23	+2.09	2.8	31
7	Bristol City	9	8	1	15	+1.67	2.8	25
8	Brighton	21	18	3	38	+1.81	2.7	57
9	Aston Villa	14	12	2	19	+1.36	2.7	38
10	QPR	7	6	1	10	+1.43	2.7	19
11	Reading	15	12	3	18	+1.20	2.6	39
12	Norwich	11	9	2	21	+1.91	2.6	29
13	Blackburn	9	7	2	7	+0.78	2.6	23
14	Brentford	13	10	3	24	+1.85	2.5	33
15	Preston	12	9	3	20	+1.67	2.5	30
16	Nottm Forest	8	6	2	13	+1.63	2.5	20
17	Derby	17	12	5	20	+1.18	2.4	41
18	Barnsley	14	9	5	21	+1.50	2.3	32
19	Cardiff	11	7	4	15	+1.36	2.3	25
20	Birmingham	11	7	4	10	+0.91	2.3	25
21	Wolves	13	8	5	11	+0.85	2.2	29
22	Burton	10	6	4	9	+0.90	2.2	22
23	Ipswich	11	6	5	11	+1	2.1	23
24	Wigan	13	5	8	8	+0.62	1.8	23

Bloodied Blackburn ready to dust themselves down and hit the comeback trail

Blackburn will play in the third tier of English football for the first time in 37 years after relegation, which also made them the first ever Premier League champions to drop so low, writes Mark Langdon. However, sacked manager Owen Coyle has much to answer for because he played a large part in relegating a club who should never have gone down and Rovers can make a swift return to the Championship.

Replacement Tony Mowbray lost only three of his 15 Championship games but by then the damage had already been done. But Mowbray says he is extremely happy with the budget that he has to work with and Blackburn can follow Sheffield United's lead of last season by justifying the favourites tag.

Mowbray's first signing of the summer spoke volumes as Peter Whittingham made his way to Ewood Park and that was an immediate positive in three different aspects.

First, Whittingham showed at Cardiff that he is a class midfielder. Second, he is an ideal man to get Rovers playing the passing style Mowbray will demand. Lastly, it validates the claims of a healthy budget as the former Aston Villa man reportedly turned down Championship clubs in favour of the move.

It's not a particularly strong section with Wigan unable to enjoy the same financial advantage they had over other clubs in the division last time the Latics were at this level.

Portsmouth, who lost manager Paul Cook to Wigan, have been given massive respect by the layers but there does not appear to be huge value in backing the League Two champions. Bradford had no excuses last term and have struggled with recruitment, while the likes of MK Dons and Charlton were miles off the pace last season.

Oxford must overcome the loss of manager Michael Appleton, but Peterborough, thanks to the signing of non-league goal machine Ricky Miller, should enjoy a better campaign.

However, Bury may be worth a promotion punt. James Vaughan looks set to leave but Lee Clark had shown ambition in the transfer market prior to his exit, signing Joe Murphy, Jermaine Beckford, Adam Thompson, Phil Edwards, Eoghan O'Connell, Callum Reilly, Joe Skarz, Stephen Dawson and Jay O'Shea, so the funds are likely to be reinvested.

There is a certain amount of risk in backing Bury just in case the cash doesn't last the season but at the prices there are worse bets.

Promoted Blackpool and Oldham, who improved under returning gaffer John Sheridan, head the relegation market but two other candidates stand out.

Gillingham won only four matches after Christmas and in those victories scored five penalties, which is unsustainable. The Kent side only just survived on the final day and the decision to stick with manager Adrian Pennock went down badly with supporters.

Wimbledon stayed up comfortably but second-season syndrome could strike a club who struggled as the campaign went on, particularly up front. Therefore the loss of forward Tom Elliott to Millwall is a big blow.

Recommendations
Blackburn to win (each-way), 5-1
Bury to be promoted, 9-1
Wimbledon to be relegated, 4-1
Gillingham to be relegated, 7-4

Rovers were vastly improved after Tony Mowbray took over from Owen Coyle

AFC WIMBLEDON

Nickname: The Wombles
Colours: Blue and yellow
Ground: Cherry Red Records Stadium (4,850)
Tel: 0208-547-3528   afcwimbledon.co.uk

It was a solid first season in the third tier of English football and no doubt Neal Ardley would have taken survival at the start of the campaign given AFC Wimbledon are said to have one of the lower budgets in the division.

If Ardley wants to improve on Wimbledon's 15th-place finish over the summer then goals will need to be added to a squad that scored only 52. They also finished poorly which suggests a lack of depth was a problem in the latter stages.

Longest run without win/loss: 6/8
High/low league position: 5/21
Clean sheets: 14 **Yellow cards:** 70 **Red:** 3
Avg attendance: 4,480 **Players used:** 29
Leading scorer: L Taylor 10 (3,10)
Key stat: Wimbledon have won only one of their last 15 away league matches

	2016-17		Last six seasons at home							
	H	A	P	W	D	L	OV	UN	BS	CS
Blackburn			-	-	-	-	-	-	-	-
Wigan			-	-	-	-	-	-	-	-
Rotherham			2	0	0	2	1	1	1	0
Scunthorpe	L	W	2	1	0	1	2	0	2	0
Fleetwood Town	D	D	3	2	1	0	2	1	2	1
Bradford	L	L	3	2	0	1	3	0	3	0
Southend	L	L	5	0	1	4	2	3	1	1
Oxford Utd	W	W	6	1	1	4	3	3	2	1
Rochdale	W	D	3	1	0	2	3	0	2	0
Bristol Rovers	L	L	5	1	2	2	2	3	2	2
Peterborough	D	W	1	0	1	0	0	1	0	1
MK Dons	W	L	1	1	0	0	0	1	0	1
Charlton	D	W	1	0	1	0	0	1	1	0
Walsall	W	L	1	1	0	0	0	1	0	1
AFC Wimbledon										
Northampton	L	D	6	0	3	3	2	4	3	0
Oldham	D	D	1	0	1	0	0	1	0	1
Shrewsbury	D	L	3	1	2	0	2	1	3	0
Bury	W	W	3	2	0	1	2	1	2	0
Gillingham	W	D	3	2	0	1	1	2	1	1
Portsmouth			3	2	0	1	1	2	0	2
Plymouth			5	0	3	2	1	4	3	1
Doncaster			-	-	-	-	-	-	-	-
Blackpool			-	-	-	-	-	-	-	-

Season	Division	Pos	P	W	D	L	F	A	GD	Pts
2016-17	League One	15	46	13	18	15	52	55	-3	57
2015-16	League Two	7	46	21	12	13	64	50	+14	75
2014-15	League Two	15	46	14	16	16	54	60	-6	58

Over/Under 48%/52% 12th   **Both score** 50%/50% 14th

BLACKBURN

Nickname: Rovers
Colours: Blue and white
Ground: Ewood Park (31,367)
Tel: 01254-372-001   rovers.co.uk

Many will blame Venky's for Blackburn's relegation due to a lack of investment and for destabilising Rovers as a football club but if the controversial owners were at fault for last season's demotion it was because they placed too much faith in failing manager Owen Coyle.

Things improved dramatically under Tony Mowbray when he was appointed in February but it was too late by then even though they lost just three matches, with two of those at Brighton and Reading.

Longest run without win/loss: 7/7
High/low league position: 20/23
Clean sheets: 9 **Yellow cards:** 83 **Red:** 4
Avg attendance: 12,687 **Players used:** 31
Leading scorer: D Graham 12 (2,10)
Key stat: Rovers lost only three of their 15 matches when Tony Mowbray was in charge

	2016-17		Last six seasons at home							
	H	A	P	W	D	L	OV	UN	BS	CS
Blackburn										
Wigan	W	L	4	3	0	1	2	2	2	1
Rotherham	W	D	3	3	0	0	2	1	2	1
Scunthorpe			-	-	-	-	-	-	-	-
Fleetwood Town			-	-	-	-	-	-	-	-
Bradford			-	-	-	-	-	-	-	-
Southend			-	-	-	-	-	-	-	-
Oxford Utd			-	-	-	-	-	-	-	-
Rochdale			-	-	-	-	-	-	-	-
Bristol Rovers			-	-	-	-	-	-	-	-
Peterborough			1	0	0	1	1	0	1	0
MK Dons			1	1	0	0	1	0	1	0
Charlton			4	2	0	2	2	2	1	2
Walsall			-	-	-	-	-	-	-	-
AFC Wimbledon			-	-	-	-	-	-	-	-
Northampton			-	-	-	-	-	-	-	-
Oldham			-	-	-	-	-	-	-	-
Shrewsbury			-	-	-	-	-	-	-	-
Bury			-	-	-	-	-	-	-	-
Gillingham			-	-	-	-	-	-	-	-
Portsmouth			-	-	-	-	-	-	-	-
Plymouth			-	-	-	-	-	-	-	-
Doncaster			1	1	0	0	0	1	0	1
Blackpool			3	1	2	0	0	3	2	1

Season	Division	Pos	P	W	D	L	F	A	GD	Pts
2016-17	Championship	22	46	12	15	19	53	65	-12	51
2015-16	Championship	15	46	13	16	17	46	46	0	55
2014-15	Championship	9	46	17	16	13	66	59	+7	67

Over/Under 46%/54% 16th   **Both score** 63%/37% 2nd

BLACKPOOL

Nickname: The Seasiders/Tangerines
Colours: Tangerine and white
Ground: Bloomfield Road (17,338)
Tel: 01253-685000   blackpoolfc.co.uk

Blackpool are a prime example that not all clubs need to be run perfectly to have success as the Tangerines bounced back to League One via the playoffs.

It was not easy for manager Gary Bowyer and the squad with the majority of their supporters boycotting home matches in protest at the club ownership. But eventually that was overcome thanks to a strong finish which saw Blackpool finish seventh on the final day before beating Luton and Exeter in the playoffs.

Longest run without win/loss: 6/9
High/low league position: 5/18
Clean sheets: 15 **Yellow cards:** 73 **Red:** 2
Avg attendance: 3,456 **Players used:** 27
Leading scorer: K Vassell 11 (2,9)
Key stat: Blackpool lost only five League Two matches after Christmas

	2016-17 H	A	Last six seasons at home P	W	D	L	OV	UN	BS	CS
Blackburn			3	1	1	1	2	1	2	1
Wigan			3	1	0	2	2	1	1	1
Rotherham			1	0	1	0	0	1	1	0
Scunthorpe			1	1	0	0	1	0	0	1
Fleetwood Town			1	1	0	0	0	1	0	1
Bradford			1	0	0	1	0	1	0	0
Southend			1	1	0	0	0	1	0	1
Oxford Utd			-	-	-	-	-	-	-	-
Rochdale			1	0	0	1	0	1	0	0
Bristol Rovers			-	-	-	-	-	-	-	-
Peterborough			3	2	0	1	1	2	1	1
MK Dons			-	-	-	-	-	-	-	-
Charlton			3	0	0	3	2	1	0	0
Walsall			1	0	0	1	1	0	0	0
AFC Wimbledon			-	-	-	-	-	-	-	-
Northampton			-	-	-	-	-	-	-	-
Oldham			1	0	1	0	0	1	0	1
Shrewsbury			1	0	0	1	1	0	1	0
Bury			1	0	1	0	0	1	1	0
Gillingham			1	1	0	0	0	1	0	1
Portsmouth	W	L	2	1	1	0	1	1	2	0
Plymouth	L	W	1	0	0	1	0	1	0	0
Doncaster	W	W	4	2	1	1	2	2	3	0
Blackpool										

Season	Division	Pos	P	W	D	L	F	A	GD	Pts
2016-17	League Two	7	46	18	16	12	69	46	+23	70
2015-16	League One	22	46	12	10	24	40	63	-23	46
2014-15	Championship	24	46	4	14	28	36	91	-55	26

Over/Under 50%/50% 13th   **Both score** 50%/50% 16th

BRADFORD

Nickname: The Bantams
Colours: Claret and amber
Ground: Valley Parade (25,136)
Tel: 0871-978-1911   bradfordcityfc.co.uk

It was another near miss for Bradford as they lost in the playoffs for a second successive season, this time 1-0 to Millwall in the Wembley final after matching last season's fifth-place finish.

Along with Tottenham, Bradford were the only side in English football to go unbeaten at home in the 2016-17 season, but too many draws – 12 in total at Valley Parade – held the Bantams back. They actually won only one more home game than relegated Port Vale's ten.

Longest run without win/loss: 5/12
High/low league position: 2/5
Clean sheets: 16 **Yellow cards:** 49 **Red:** 0
Avg attendance: 18,167 **Players used:** 30
Leading scorer: J Hiwula-Mayifuila 9 (3,9)
Key stat: Bradford were the only team not to have a player sent off in League One last season

	2016-17 H	A	Last six seasons at home P	W	D	L	OV	UN	BS	CS
Blackburn			-	-	-	-	-	-	-	-
Wigan			1	0	1	0	0	1	1	0
Rotherham			3	0	0	3	1	2	1	0
Scunthorpe	D	L	3	1	2	0	0	3	1	2
Fleetwood Town	W	L	4	3	1	0	3	1	3	1
Bradford										
Southend	D	L	4	2	2	0	1	3	2	2
Oxford Utd	W	L	3	2	1	2	1	2	2	1
Rochdale	W	D	4	1	1	2	4	0	3	1
Bristol Rovers	D	D	3	1	2	0	2	1	3	0
Peterborough	W	W	4	2	0	2	0	4	0	2
MK Dons	D	W	3	2	1	0	2	1	2	1
Charlton	D	D	1	0	1	0	0	1	0	1
Walsall	W	D	4	2	1	1	1	3	1	2
AFC Wimbledon	W	W	3	2	0	1	3	0	2	1
Northampton	W	W	3	3	0	0	1	2	1	2
Oldham	D	W	4	2	1	1	1	3	2	2
Shrewsbury	W	L	4	3	1	0	2	2	3	1
Bury	D	W	2	1	1	0	1	1	2	0
Gillingham	D	D	6	0	4	2	3	3	5	0
Portsmouth			-	-	-	-	-	-	-	-
Plymouth			2	1	1	0	0	2	1	1
Doncaster			2	1	0	1	2	0	2	0
Blackpool			1	1	0	0	0	1	0	1

Season	Division	Pos	P	W	D	L	F	A	GD	Pts
2016-17	League One	5	46	20	19	7	62	43	+19	79
2015-16	League One	5	46	23	11	12	55	40	+15	80
2014-15	League One	7	46	17	14	15	55	55	0	65

Over/Under 39%/61% 20th   **Both score** 54%/46% 7th

BRISTOL ROVERS

Nickname: The Pirates/The Gas
Colours: Blue and white
Ground: Memorial Stadium (12,300)
Tel: 01179-096-648   bristolrovers.co.uk

After successive promotions to League One it was always a tough ask for Bristol Rovers to land a hat-trick and Darrell Clarke's men should be satisfied with a tenth-place finish.

Rovers were much better in Bristol, where they scored 42 times compared to just 26 away, and Clarke needs to find a solution to that travel-sickness. The Gas ended the regular season with an away goal difference of minus 18 and a road record of just five victories.

Longest run without win/loss: 6/9
High/low league position: 5/21
Clean sheets: 12 **Yellow cards:** 77 **Red:** 3
Avg attendance: 9,302 **Players used:** 33
Leading scorer: M Taylor 16 (3,12)
Key stat: Only two teams – Sheffield United and MK Dons – stopped Rovers from scoring in their home league matches

	2016-17 H	A	Last six seasons at home P	W	D	L	OV	UN	BS	CS
Blackburn	-	-	-	-	-	-	-	-	-	-
Wigan	-	-	-	-	-	-	-	-	-	-
Rotherham			2	1	0	1	2	0	2	0
Scunthorpe	D	L	2	0	2	0	0	2	1	1
Fleetwood Town	W	L	3	1	1	1	2	1	2	1
Bradford	D	D	3	1	2	0	2	1	3	0
Southend	W	D	4	2	1	1	1	3	1	3
Oxford Utd	W	W	5	1	2	2	1	4	2	1
Rochdale	D	D	3	1	1	1	3	0	3	0
Bristol Rovers										
Peterborough	L	L	1	0	0	1	1	0	1	0
MK Dons	D	D	1	0	1	0	0	1	0	1
Charlton	L	L	1	0	0	1	1	0	1	0
Walsall	D	L	1	0	1	0	0	1	1	0
AFC Wimbledon	W	W	5	5	0	0	2	3	1	4
Northampton	W	W	5	4	0	1	3	2	2	2
Oldham	W	W	1	1	0	0	0	1	0	1
Shrewsbury	W	L	2	2	0	0	0	2	0	2
Bury	W	L	2	1	1	0	1	1	2	0
Gillingham	W	L	3	1	1	1	2	1	2	0
Portsmouth			2	1	0	1	1	1	1	1
Plymouth			4	2	1	1	3	1	4	0
Doncaster			-	-	-	-	-	-	-	-
Blackpool			-	-	-	-	-	-	-	-

Season	Division	Pos	P	W	D	L	F	A	GD	Pts
2016-17	League One	10	46	18	12	16	68	70	-2	66
2015-16	League Two	3	46	26	7	13	77	46	+31	85
2014-15	Conference	2	46	25	16	5	73	34	+39	91

Over/Under 54%/46% 7th   **Both score** 63%/37% 3rd

BURY

Nickname: The Shakers
Colours: White and blue
Ground: Gigg Lane (11,840)
Tel: 0161-764-4881   buryfc.co.uk

Life is rarely dull at Gigg Lane and it was the same again last season as Bury failed to make the most of a blistering start and actually finished the season fending off the threat of relegation.

Using three managers – David Flitcroft, Chris Brass and Lee Clark – is rarely a positive sign and Bury's inconsistency was shown when a five-match winning league sequence was followed by 12 straight defeats. James Vaughan starred with 24 goals and will need replacing.

Longest run without win/loss: 16/6
High/low league position: 2/22
Clean sheets: 12 **Yellow cards:** 103 **Red:** 7
Avg attendance: 3,845 **Players used:** 37
Leading scorer: J Vaughan 24 (9,16)
Key stat: No team in League One gained fewer corners than Bury's flag-kick total of 180

	2016-17 H	A	Last six seasons at home P	W	D	L	OV	UN	BS	CS
Blackburn	-	-	-	-	-	-	-	-	-	-
Wigan			1	0	1	0	1	0	1	0
Rotherham	-	-	-	-	-	-	-	-	-	-
Scunthorpe	L	L	5	1	2	2	4	1	4	1
Fleetwood Town	D	D	3	0	2	1	2	1	2	1
Bradford	L	D	2	0	1	1	0	2	0	1
Southend	L	L	4	1	1	2	2	2	3	0
Oxford Utd	L	L	3	0	1	2	1	2	2	0
Rochdale	L	L	4	0	2	2	1	3	1	2
Bristol Rovers	W	L	2	2	0	0	2	0	1	1
Peterborough	W	L	2	2	0	0	2	0	2	0
MK Dons	D	W	3	0	2	1	1	2	1	2
Charlton	W	W	2	1	0	1	1	1	1	1
Walsall	D	D	4	1	2	1	3	1	4	0
AFC Wimbledon	L	L	3	1	1	1	2	1	2	1
Northampton	W	L	3	2	1	0	2	1	2	1
Oldham	L	D	4	0	2	2	0	4	1	1
Shrewsbury	W	L	4	2	2	0	3	1	3	1
Bury										
Gillingham	L	L	2	0	0	2	1	1	1	0
Portsmouth			3	2	1	0	2	1	1	2
Plymouth			2	2	0	0	2	0	1	1
Doncaster			2	2	0	0	2	0	2	0
Blackpool			1	1	0	0	1	0	1	0

Season	Division	Pos	P	W	D	L	F	A	GD	Pts
2016-17	League One	19	46	13	11	22	61	73	-12	50
2015-16	League One	14	46	16	12	18	56	73	-17	60
2014-15	League Two	3	46	26	7	13	60	40	+20	85

Over/Under 61%/39% 4th   **Both score** 59%/41% 5th

CHARLTON

Nickname: Addicks
Colours: Red and white
Ground: The Valley (27,111)
Tel: 020-8333-4000   cafc.co.uk

There are a number of poorly run clubs in the Football League and Charlton's long-suffering supporters would suggest their owner, Roland Duchatelet, is among the worst in English football.

The constant fan protests may well be justified, but it does not make life easy for the team. Charlton were joint-second favourites in the ante-post title betting at 11-1 but never looked like challenging for promotion despite Karl Robinson replacing Russell Slade in the hotseat.

Longest run without win/loss: 8/7
High/low league position: 11/18
Clean sheets: 10 **Yellow cards:** 78 **Red:** 6
Avg attendance: 11,162 **Players used:** 33
Leading scorer: R Holmes 13 (6,10)
Key stat: Both teams scored in 16 of Charlton's 23 away league games last term

	2016-17		Last six seasons at home							
---	H	A	P	W	D	L	OV	UN	BS	CS
Blackburn			4	0	2	2	2	2	4	0
Wigan			2	1	1	0	1	1	1	1
Rotherham			2	0	2	0	0	2	2	0
Scunthorpe	W	D	2	1	1	0	2	0	2	0
Fleetwood Town	D	D	1	0	1	0	0	1	1	0
Bradford	D	D	1	0	1	0	0	1	1	0
Southend	W	D	1	1	0	0	1	0	1	0
Oxford Utd	L	D	1	0	0	1	0	1	0	0
Rochdale	L	D	2	0	1	1	0	2	1	0
Bristol Rovers	W	W	1	1	0	0	1	0	1	0
Peterborough	L	L	2	1	0	1	0	2	0	1
MK Dons	L	W	3	1	1	1	1	2	1	1
Charlton										
Walsall	D	W	2	1	1	0	0	2	1	1
AFC Wimbledon	L	D	1	0	0	1	1	0	1	0
Northampton	D	L	1	0	1	0	0	1	1	0
Oldham	D	L	2	0	2	0	0	2	2	0
Shrewsbury	W	L	1	1	0	0	1	0	0	1
Bury	L	L	2	0	1	1	0	2	1	0
Gillingham	W	D	1	1	0	0	1	0	0	1
Portsmouth			-	-	-	-	-	-	-	-
Plymouth			-	-	-	-	-	-	-	-
Doncaster			1	1	0	0	0	1	0	1
Blackpool			3	1	2	0	2	1	2	1

Season	Division	Pos	P	W	D	L	F	A	GD	Pts
2016-17	League One	13	46	14	18	14	60	53	+7	60
2015-16	Championship	22	46	9	13	24	40	80	-40	40
2014-15	Championship	12	46	14	18	14	54	60	-6	60

Over/Under 41%/59% 18th   **Both score** 59%/41% 5th

DONCASTER

Nickname: Rovers
Colours: Red and white
Ground: Keepmoat Stadium (15,231)
Tel: 01302-764-664   doncasterroversfc.co.uk

The main task of promotion was completed nice and early by Doncaster, who marched back to the third tier of English football at the first attempt, but for those who backed Darren Ferguson's men for the title it was a heartbreaker.

Rovers eventually finished third having traded at 1-50 for the title after coasting over the finishing line, claiming one point from their last five matches. It could easily be argued Donny were better than their final points tally of 85.

Longest run without win/loss: 5/10
High/low league position: 1/4
Clean sheets: 12 **Yellow cards:** 81 **Red:** 2
Avg attendance: 6,021 **Players used:** 29
Leading scorer: J Marquis 26 (5,19)
Key stat: Doncaster were the highest away scorers in League Two last season with 45 goals

	2016-17		Last six seasons at home							
---	H	A	P	W	D	L	OV	UN	BS	CS
Blackburn			1	1	0	0	0	1	0	1
Wigan			2	2	0	0	2	0	1	1
Rotherham			-	-	-	-	-	-	-	-
Scunthorpe			3	2	0	1	2	1	1	1
Fleetwood Town			2	1	1	0	0	2	0	2
Bradford			2	0	0	2	1	1	0	0
Southend			1	0	1	0	0	1	0	1
Oxford Utd			-	-	-	-	-	-	-	-
Rochdale			2	0	1	1	0	2	1	0
Bristol Rovers			-	-	-	-	-	-	-	-
Peterborough			3	0	1	2	1	2	2	0
MK Dons			2	0	2	0	0	2	0	2
Charlton			1	1	0	0	1	0	0	1
Walsall			3	0	0	3	2	1	2	0
AFC Wimbledon			-	-	-	-	-	-	-	-
Northampton			-	-	-	-	-	-	-	-
Oldham			3	1	1	1	0	3	1	1
Shrewsbury			2	1	0	1	0	2	0	1
Bury			2	1	1	0	1	1	2	0
Gillingham			2	0	1	1	2	0	1	0
Portsmouth	W	W	3	1	1	1	2	1	3	0
Plymouth	L	L	1	0	0	1	0	1	0	0
Doncaster										
Blackpool	L	L	4	0	0	4	2	2	2	0

Season	Division	Pos	P	W	D	L	F	A	GD	Pts
2016-17	League Two	3	46	25	10	11	85	55	+30	85
2015-16	League One	21	46	11	13	22	48	64	-16	46
2014-15	League One	13	46	16	13	17	58	62	-4	61

Over/Under 59%/41% 3rd   **Both score** 67%/33% 2nd

FLEETWOOD TOWN

Nickname: The Cod Army
Colours: Red and white
Ground: Highbury Stadium (5,311)
Tel: 01253-775080   fleetwoodtownfc.com

Few managers earned as much praise without gaining promotion as Uwe Rosler after he led Fleetwood to fourth spot in League One before losing a tight playoff semi-final to Bradford.

Defence was key for the Cod Army, who managed 20 league shutouts and conceded just 43 goals. Only promoted Bolton conceded fewer but maybe Town need to improve their attacking output having finished in the bottom half in the shots and shots-on-target final standings.

Longest run without win/loss: 5/18
High/low league position: 2/15
Clean sheets: 20 **Yellow cards:** 69 **Red:** 1
Avg attendance: 3,272 **Players used:** 30
Leading scorer: D Ball 14 (4,13)
Key stat: The Cod Army claimed a divisional-high 20 clean sheets in League One last term

| | 2016-17 | | Last six seasons at home | | | | | | | |
	H	A	P	W	D	L	OV	UN	BS	CS
Blackburn			-	-	-	-	-	-	-	-
Wigan			1	0	0	1	1	0	1	0
Rotherham			1	0	1	0	0	1	1	0
Scunthorpe	D	W	4	1	2	1	3	1	3	0
Fleetwood Town										
Bradford	W	L	4	1	2	1	2	2	3	0
Southend	D	W	4	0	4	0	0	4	3	1
Oxford Utd	W	W	3	2	1	0	1	2	1	2
Rochdale	D	L	5	1	3	1	1	4	1	3
Bristol Rovers	W	L	3	2	0	1	3	0	2	0
Peterborough	W	W	3	2	1	0	0	3	1	2
MK Dons	L	W	2	0	0	2	2	0	1	0
Charlton	D	D	1	0	1	0	1	0	1	0
Walsall	W	W	3	1	0	2	1	2	1	0
AFC Wimbledon	D	D	3	0	3	0	0	3	1	2
Northampton	W	D	3	3	0	0	1	2	0	3
Oldham	W	L	3	1	1	1	0	3	1	1
Shrewsbury	W	W	2	1	1	0	1	1	0	2
Bury	D	D	3	2	1	0	1	2	1	2
Gillingham	W	W	4	3	1	0	3	1	3	1
Portsmouth			1	1	0	0	1	0	1	0
Plymouth			2	1	0	1	2	0	0	1
Doncaster			2	1	1	0	1	1	1	1
Blackpool			1	0	1	0	0	1	0	1

Season	Division	Pos	P	W	D	L	F	A	GD	Pts
2016-17	League One	4	46	23	13	10	64	43	+21	82
2015-16	League One	19	46	12	15	19	52	56	-4	51
2014-15	League One	10	46	17	12	17	49	52	-3	63

Over/Under 46%/54% 15th   **Both score** 52%/48% 10th

GILLINGHAM

Nickname: Gills
Colours: Blue and white
Ground: Priestfield Stadium (11,582)
Tel: 01634-300-000   gillinghamfootballclub.com

Gillingham looked a good side when beating Southend 3-1 on the opening day of the season, but one swallow does not make a summer and the Kent outfit stayed up by only one point.

Justin Edinburgh's departure did not seem to make any notable difference and if anything things got even worse under Adrian Pennock. Gills were a defensive joke for much of the campaign, keeping only three clean sheets and conceding a whopping 49 goals in away matches.

Longest run without win/loss: 11/5
High/low league position: 8/20
Clean sheets: 3 **Yellow cards:** 110 **Red:** 7
Avg attendance: 6,129 **Players used:** 33
Leading scorer: J Wright 13 (5,9)
Key stat: Both teams to score backers collected in 34 of Gillingham's league matches last season

| | 2016-17 | | Last six seasons at home | | | | | | | |
	H	A	P	W	D	L	OV	UN	BS	CS
Blackburn			-	-	-	-	-	-	-	-
Wigan			1	1	0	0	1	0	1	0
Rotherham			3	1	1	1	1	2	1	2
Scunthorpe	W	L	3	2	0	1	3	0	2	0
Fleetwood Town	L	L	4	1	1	2	3	1	3	0
Bradford	D	D	6	3	2	1	2	4	2	3
Southend	W	W	4	2	1	1	2	2	3	1
Oxford Utd	L	L	3	1	0	2	0	3	0	1
Rochdale	W	L	4	3	0	1	2	2	1	3
Bristol Rovers	W	L	3	3	0	0	3	0	2	1
Peterborough	L	D	4	2	1	1	3	1	3	0
MK Dons	W	L	3	3	0	0	2	1	2	1
Charlton	D	L	1	0	1	0	0	1	1	0
Walsall	D	W	4	0	3	1	2	2	3	1
AFC Wimbledon	D	D	3	0	2	1	3	0	3	0
Northampton	W	D	3	3	0	0	2	1	2	1
Oldham	L	L	4	1	1	2	3	1	3	0
Shrewsbury	D	W	4	0	2	2	1	3	3	0
Bury	W	W	2	2	0	0	2	0	2	0
Gillingham										
Portsmouth			-	-	-	-	-	-	-	-
Plymouth			2	2	0	0	2	0	1	1
Doncaster			2	1	1	0	0	2	1	1
Blackpool			1	1	0	0	1	0	1	0

Season	Division	Pos	P	W	D	L	F	A	GD	Pts
2016-17	League One	20	46	12	14	20	59	79	-20	50
2015-16	League One	9	46	19	12	15	71	56	+15	69
2014-15	League One	12	46	16	14	16	65	66	-1	62

Over/Under 65%/35% 1st   **Both score** 74%/26% 1st

LEAGUE ONE

MK DONS

Nickname: The Dons
Colours: White
Ground: stadium:mk (30,500)
Tel: 01908-622-922   mkdons.co.uk

MK Dons may not get too much love from the neutrals, but the Milton Keynes crew certainly have their fair share of supporters when it comes to betting – the market makers are again sweet on them despite another poor season for the Dons.

MK Dons were continually overrated in the 1X2 markets and regularly let their backers down, particularly at home where they triumphed only seven times. That was the same home win tally as relegated pair Swindon and Chesterfield.

Longest run without win/loss: 8/6
High/low league position: 9/21
Clean sheets: 13 **Yellow cards:** 105 **Red:** 2
Avg attendance: 10,307 **Players used:** 29
Leading scorer: K Agard 12 (5,10)
Key stat: The Dons failed to score in eight of their 23 home games – only Oldham (11) had a worse record

	2016-17 H	A	Last six seasons at home P	W	D	L	OV	UN	BS	CS
Blackburn			1	1	0	0	1	0	0	1
Wigan	-	-	-	-	-	-	-	-	-	-
Rotherham			2	1	0	1	2	0	1	0
Scunthorpe	L	L	4	1	1	2	0	4	0	2
Fleetwood Town	L	W	2	1	0	1	1	1	1	0
Bradford	L	D	3	0	0	3	3	0	3	0
Southend	L	W	1	0	0	1	1	0	0	0
Oxford Utd	D	L	1	0	1	0	0	1	0	1
Rochdale	D	W	3	1	2	0	3	0	3	0
Bristol Rovers	D	D	1	0	1	0	1	0	1	0
Peterborough	L	W	3	1	0	2	1	2	0	1
MK Dons										
Charlton	L	W	3	1	1	1	0	3	1	1
Walsall	D	W	5	1	1	3	2	3	2	1
AFC Wimbledon	W	L	1	1	0	0	0	1	0	1
Northampton	W	L	1	1	0	0	1	0	1	0
Oldham	W	W	5	5	0	0	3	2	1	4
Shrewsbury	W	W	3	2	0	1	3	0	3	0
Bury	L	D	3	1	1	1	2	1	3	0
Gillingham	W	L	3	2	0	1	2	1	2	0
Portsmouth			1	0	1	0	1	0	1	0
Plymouth	-	-	-	-	-	-	-	-	-	-
Doncaster			2	2	0	0	2	0	0	2
Blackpool	-	-	-	-	-	-	-	-	-	-

Season	Division	Pos	P	W	D	L	F	A	GD	Pts
2016-17	League One	12	46	16	13	17	60	58	+2	61
2015-16	Championship	23	46	9	12	25	39	69	-30	39
2014-15	League One	2	46	27	10	9	101	44	+57	91

Over/Under 48%/52% 12th   **Both score** 50%/50% 14th

NORTHAMPTON

Nickname: The Cobblers
Colours: Claret and white
Ground: Sixfields Stadium (7,653)
Tel: 01604-683-700   ntfc.co.uk

It was always likely to be a tricky season for Northampton after gaining promotion from League Two as champions.

Manager Chris Wilder departed for Sheffield United – where he easily claimed another title – and replacement Rob Page struggled with 16 defeats before getting sacked in January as Justin Edinburgh arrived at Sixfields.

A poor finish of no wins in eight left the suggestion work needed to be done over the summer to finish in the top half.

Longest run without win/loss: 8/7
High/low league position: 5/18
Clean sheets: 9 **Yellow cards:** 74 **Red:** 5
Avg attendance: 6,650 **Players used:** 32
Lead scorers: O'Toole 10 (4,9) Richards 10 (4,8)
Key stat: Eight of Northampton's nine home league defeats last season were by one goal

	2016-17 H	A	Last six seasons at home P	W	D	L	OV	UN	BS	CS
Blackburn	-	-	-	-	-	-	-	-	-	-
Wigan	-	-	-	-	-	-	-	-	-	-
Rotherham			2	1	1	0	1	1	2	0
Scunthorpe	L	D	2	0	1	1	1	1	2	0
Fleetwood Town	D	L	3	2	1	0	1	2	2	1
Bradford	L	L	3	0	0	3	2	1	2	0
Southend	W	D	5	2	2	1	4	1	4	1
Oxford Utd	D	W	6	4	1	1	3	3	3	3
Rochdale	L	D	3	1	0	2	3	0	2	0
Bristol Rovers	L	L	5	2	2	1	3	2	3	2
Peterborough	L	L	1	0	0	1	0	1	0	0
MK Dons	W	L	1	1	0	0	1	0	1	0
Charlton	W	D	1	1	0	0	1	0	1	0
Walsall	W	L	1	1	0	0	0	1	0	1
AFC Wimbledon	D	W	6	3	3	0	1	5	2	4
Northampton										
Oldham	L	D	1	0	0	1	0	1	0	0
Shrewsbury	D	W	3	0	2	1	1	2	3	0
Bury	W	L	3	1	0	2	3	0	2	0
Gillingham	D		3	0	2	1	1	2	2	1
Portsmouth			3	1	0	2	1	2	1	1
Plymouth			5	1	1	3	1	4	1	2
Doncaster	-	-	-	-	-	-	-	-	-	-
Blackpool	-	-	-	-	-	-	-	-	-	-

Season	Division	Pos	P	W	D	L	F	A	GD	Pts
2016-17	League One	16	46	14	11	21	60	73	-13	53
2015-16	League Two	1	46	29	12	5	82	46	+36	99
2014-15	League Two	12	46	18	7	21	67	62	+5	61

Over/Under 63%/37% 2nd   **Both score** 61%/39% 4th

OLDHAM

Nickname: The Latics
Colours: Blue
Ground: Boundary Park (13,500)
Tel: 08712-262-235   oldhamathletic.co.uk

Home is where the heart is for Oldham, who adjusted better than their opponents to the awful Boundary Park surface to eventually stay up relatively comfortably once John Sheridan replaced Stephen Robinson as manager in January.

Bradford were the only side to win at Oldham in 2017 but Sheridan must get more out of his team going forward after scoring only 31 goals last term. No player reached double figures and on-loan Lee Erwin top-scored with just eight goals.

Longest run without win/loss: 10/5
High/low league position: 17/24
Clean sheets: 18 **Yellow cards:** 81 **Red:** 7
Avg attendance: 4,514 **Players used:** 32
Leading scorer: L Erwin 8 (3,7)
Key stat: Oldham failed to score in 25 league games last season – seven more than any other side in the division

	2016-17 H	A	Last six seasons at home P	W	D	L	OV	UN	BS	CS
Blackburn			-	-	-	-	-	-	-	-
Wigan			1	0	1	0	0	1	1	0
Rotherham			1	0	0	1	0	1	0	0
Scunthorpe	W	L	5	2	1	2	3	2	4	1
Fleetwood Town	W	L	3	3	0	0	0	3	0	3
Bradford	L	D	4	1	1	2	3	1	4	0
Southend	L	L	2	0	0	2	1	1	1	0
Oxford Utd	W	D	1	1	0	0	1	0	1	0
Rochdale	D	L	4	2	1	1	2	2	2	2
Bristol Rovers	L	L	1	0	0	1	0	1	0	0
Peterborough	W	D	4	2	1	1	2	2	3	1
MK Dons	L	L	5	2	0	3	4	1	4	0
Charlton	W	D	2	1	0	1	0	2	0	1
Walsall	D	L	6	3	2	1	2	4	3	2
AFC Wimbledon	D	D	1	0	1	0	0	1	0	1
Northampton	D	W	1	0	1	0	0	1	0	1
Oldham										
Shrewsbury	L	L	4	1	1	2	2	2	3	1
Bury	D	W	4	0	1	3	1	3	1	1
Gillingham	W	W	4	3	1	0	1	3	1	3
Portsmouth			1	1	0	0	0	1	0	1
Plymouth			-	-	-	-	-	-	-	-
Doncaster			3	0	1	2	3	0	3	0
Blackpool			1	1	0	0	0	1	0	1

Season	Division	Pos	P	W	D	L	F	A	GD	Pts
2016-17	League One	17	46	12	17	17	31	44	-13	53
2015-16	League One	17	46	12	18	16	44	58	-14	54
2014-15	League One	15	46	14	15	17	54	67	-13	57

Over/Under 20%/80% 24th   **Both score** 28%/72% 24th

OXFORD UNITED

Nickname: The U's
Colours: Yellow
Ground: The Kassam Stadium (12,500)
Tel: 01865-337500   oufc.co.uk

Cup kings Oxford made a splash in the knockout competitions and United will be hoping a solid first season back in League One can lay the foundations for a promotion push this term.

Michael Appleton's side went to Wembley after reaching the Football League Trophy final and also reached the FA Cup fifth round before losing 3-2 at Premier League Middlesbrough. Oxford play nice football and were better than their final position of eighth suggests.

Longest run without win/loss: 4/5
High/low league position: 8/19
Clean sheets: 16 **Yellow cards:** 78 **Red:** 1
Avg attendance: 8,297 **Players used:** 27
Leading scorer: C Maguire 13 (2,11)
Key stat: United drew the fewest matches in League One (nine)

	2016-17 H	A	Last six seasons at home P	W	D	L	OV	UN	BS	CS
Blackburn			-	-	-	-	-	-	-	-
Wigan			-	-	-	-	-	-	-	-
Rotherham			2	1	0	1	2	0	1	0
Scunthorpe	W	D	2	1	0	1	1	1	1	0
Fleetwood Town	L	L	3	0	0	3	2	1	2	0
Bradford	W	L	3	1	1	1	0	3	1	1
Southend	L	L	5	1	0	4	1	4	1	1
Oxford Utd										
Rochdale	W	W	3	2	1	0	1	2	1	2
Bristol Rovers	L	L	5	1	0	4	2	3	1	1
Peterborough	W	W	1	1	0	0	1	0	1	0
MK Dons	W	D	1	1	0	0	0	1	0	1
Charlton	D	W	1	0	1	0	0	1	1	0
Walsall	D	D	1	0	1	0	0	1	0	1
AFC Wimbledon	L	L	6	4	1	1	3	3	3	3
Northampton	L	D	6	3	1	2	1	5	2	2
Oldham	D	W	1	0	1	0	0	1	1	0
Shrewsbury	W	L	3	2	0	1	0	3	0	2
Bury	W	W	3	3	0	0	3	0	3	0
Gillingham	W	W	3	1	2	0	0	3	0	3
Portsmouth			3	0	2	1	0	3	1	1
Plymouth			5	3	1	1	3	2	3	2
Doncaster			-	-	-	-	-	-	-	-
Blackpool			-	-	-	-	-	-	-	-

Season	Division	Pos	P	W	D	L	F	A	GD	Pts
2016-17	League One	8	46	20	9	17	65	52	+13	69
2015-16	League Two	2	46	24	14	8	84	41	+43	86
2014-15	League Two	13	46	15	16	15	50	49	+1	61

Over/Under 48%/52% 12th   **Both score** 52%/48% 10th

PETERBOROUGH

Nickname: The Posh
Colours: Blue
Ground: London Road (14,084)
Tel: 01733-563 947   theposh.com

Those who use Twitter regularly probably won't need reminding of just how frustrated Peterbough's outspoken owner Darragh MacAnthony was with a disappointing 11th-place finish.

MacAnthony felt the team should have been aiming for promotion but they were the definition of average, with a goal difference of zero to go with their mid-table position. Posh were in the playoff zone at Christmas but tailed off poorly in the second half of the campaign.

Longest run without win/loss: 6/5
High/low league position: 5/13
Clean sheets: 10 **Yellow cards:** 78 **Red:** 6
Avg attendance: 5,581 **Players used:** 36
Leading scorer: T Nichols 10 (2,9)
Key stat: Only Oxford (5.6) averaged more shots on target than Peterborough's 5.4 in League One

	2016-17 H	A	Last six seasons at home P	W	D	L	OV	UN	BS	CS
Blackburn			1	0	0	1	1	0	1	0
Wigan			1	0	0	1	1	0	1	0
Rotherham			1	0	0	1	0	1	0	0
Scunthorpe	L	D	3	0	0	3	1	2	1	0
Fleetwood Town	L	L	3	2	0	1	2	1	2	1
Bradford	L	L	4	2	0	2	2	2	1	1
Southend	L	D	2	0	1	1	1	1	1	1
Oxford Utd	L	L	1	0	0	1	1	0	1	0
Rochdale	W	W	3	2	0	1	3	0	3	0
Bristol Rovers	W	W	1	1	0	0	1	0	1	0
Peterborough										
MK Dons	L	W	3	2	0	1	3	0	2	0
Charlton	W	W	2	1	1	0	1	1	1	1
Walsall	D	L	4	0	4	0	0	4	2	2
AFC Wimbledon	L	D	1	0	0	1	0	1	0	0
Northampton	W	W	1	1	0	0	1	0	0	1
Oldham	D	L	4	1	2	1	3	1	4	0
Shrewsbury	W	D	3	2	1	0	1	2	2	1
Bury	W	L	2	1	0	1	2	0	2	0
Gillingham	D	W	4	1	2	1	1	3	3	1
Portsmouth			1	0	0	1	1	0	0	0
Plymouth			-	-	-	-	-	-	-	-
Doncaster			3	1	1	1	2	1	1	2
Blackpool			3	2	0	1	3	0	3	0

Season	Division	Pos	P	W	D	L	F	A	GD	Pts
2016-17	League One	11	46	17	11	18	62	62	0	62
2015-16	League One	13	46	19	6	21	82	73	+9	63
2014-15	League One	9	46	18	9	19	53	56	-3	63

Over/Under 43%/57% 17th   **Both score** 50%/50% 14th

PLYMOUTH

Nickname: The Pilgrims
Colours: Green and white
Ground: Home Park (17,441)
Tel: 01752-562 561   pafc.co.uk

Derek Adams used the heartbreak of Plymouth's 2016 League Two playoff final defeat at the hands of AFC Wimbledon to make sure there was to be no mistake last term in the automatic promotion race.

Argyle started slowly with successive league defeats but didn't lose again until November as they concentrated on being difficult to break down. Plymouth were also a threat on the counter-attack and set-piece master Graham Carey racked up an impressive 15 assists.

Longest run without win/loss: 4/14
High/low league position: 1/3
Clean sheets: 15 **Yellow cards:** 77 **Red:** 1
Avg attendance: 9,652 **Players used:** 26
Leading scorer: G Carey 14 (7,12)
Key stat: Argyle won as many away League Two matches last season (13) as they did at Home Park

	2016-17 H	A	Last six seasons at home P	W	D	L	OV	UN	BS	CS
Blackburn			-	-	-	-	-	-	-	-
Wigan			-	-	-	-	-	-	-	-
Rotherham			2	0	0	2	1	1	1	0
Scunthorpe			1	0	0	1	0	1	0	0
Fleetwood Town			2	1	0	1	1	1	1	0
Bradford			2	1	1	0	0	2	0	2
Southend			4	1	3	0	1	3	3	1
Oxford Utd			5	0	2	3	2	3	3	0
Rochdale			2	2	0	0	1	1	1	1
Bristol Rovers			4	1	3	0	0	4	3	1
Peterborough			-	-	-	-	-	-		
MK Dons			-	-	-	-	-	-		
Charlton			-	-	-	-	-	-		
Walsall			-	-	-	-	-	-		
AFC Wimbledon			5	0	1	4	3	2	4	0
Northampton			5	4	0	1	3	2	3	2
Oldham			-	-	-	-	-	-		
Shrewsbury			2	2	0	0	0	2	0	2
Bury			2	1	0	1	1	1	1	0
Gillingham			2	0	1	1	1	1	1	0
Portsmouth	D	D	4	1	2	1	3	1	3	1
Plymouth										
Doncaster	W	W	1	1	0	0	0	1	0	1
Blackpool	L	W	1	0	0	1	1	0	0	0

Season	Division	Pos	P	W	D	L	F	A	GD	Pts
2016-17	League Two	2	46	26	9	11	71	46	+25	87
2015-16	League Two	5	46	24	9	13	72	46	+26	81
2014-15	League Two	7	46	20	11	15	55	37	+18	71

Over/Under 46%/54% 18th   **Both score** 50%/50% 16th

PORTSMOUTH

Nickname: Pompey
Colours: Blue and white
Ground: Fratton Park (21,100)
Tel: 023-9273-4129   portsmouthfc.co.uk

It was fourth time lucky for Portsmouth as they finally escaped England's basement division and did so in style, coming up as champions.

That looked an unlikely accolade for much of the season and Pompey did not even hit top spot until the final few minutes of the season, roaring home with ten wins in their last 12 games.

Portsmouth conceded just 40 goals, the fewest in League Two, and nobody claimed more than their tally of 26 wins.

Longest run without win/loss: 3/8
High/low league position: 1/7
Clean sheets: 19 **Yellow cards:** 77 **Red:** 2
Avg attendance: 16,823 **Players used:** 25
Leading scorer: K Naismith 13 (3,12)
Key stat: Portsmouth's goal difference of plus 39 was the best for a title-winning League Two side since the 2011-12 season

	2016-17 H	A	P	W	D	L	OV	UN	BS	CS
Blackburn	-	-	-	-	-	-	-	-	-	-
Wigan	-	-	-	-	-	-	-	-	-	-
Rotherham	-	-	-	-	-	-	-	-	-	-
Scunthorpe			2	1	0	1	2	0	2	0
Fleetwood Town			1	0	0	1	0	1	0	0
Bradford	-	-	-	-	-	-	-	-	-	-
Southend			2	0	0	2	2	0	2	0
Oxford Utd			3	0	1	2	1	2	1	1
Rochdale			1	1	0	0	1	0	0	1
Bristol Rovers			2	2	0	0	2	0	2	0
Peterborough			1	0	0	1	1	0	1	0
MK Dons			1	0	1	0	0	1	1	0
Charlton	-	-	-	-	-	-	-	-	-	-
Walsall			1	0	0	1	1	0	1	0
AFC Wimbledon			3	1	1	1	0	3	0	2
Northampton			3	1	1	1	3	2	1	2
Oldham			1	0	0	1	0	1	0	0
Shrewsbury			2	1	0	1	1	1	1	0
Bury			3	2	0	1	0	3	0	2
Gillingham	-	-	-	-	-	-	-	-	-	-
Portsmouth										
Plymouth	D	D	4	1	2	1	3	1	4	0
Doncaster	L	L	3	1	0	2	2	1	2	0
Blackpool	W	L	2	2	0	0	2	0	2	

Season	Division	Pos	P	W	D	L	F	A	GD	Pts
2016-17	League Two	1	46	26	9	11	79	40	+39	87
2015-16	League Two	6	46	21	15	10	75	44	+31	78
2014-15	League Two	16	46	14	15	17	52	54	-2	57

Over/Under 48%/52% 15th   **Both score** 46%/54% 23rd

ROCHDALE

Nickname: The Dale
Colours: Blue and black
Ground: Spotland (10,500)
Tel: 0844-826-1907   rochdaleafc.co.uk

It was another playoff near-miss for Rochdale, who were five points short of the top six in 2015-16 and four adrift last season, but Keith Hill can once again be proud of the efforts of his team.

Hill's side usually outperform their budget, although Dale will be kicking themselves at a missed opportunity having won only six League One matches in 2017. A knee injury to nine-goal Steve Davies in mid-January certainly did not help Rochdale in that regard.

Longest run without win/loss: 10/7
High/low league position: 4/24
Clean sheets: 14 **Yellow cards:** 84 **Red:** 8
Avg attendance: 3,556 **Players used:** 29
Leading scorer: I Henderson 15 (7,13)
Key stat: Spotland was the place for entertainment with 73 League One goals scored – the most of any venue in the division

	2016-17 H	A	P	W	D	L	OV	UN	BS	CS
Blackburn	-	-	-	-	-	-	-	-	-	-
Wigan			1	0	0	1	0	1	0	0
Rotherham			1	0	0	1	1	0	1	0
Scunthorpe	W	L	5	4	0	1	4	1	3	1
Fleetwood Town	W	D	5	2	1	2	2	3	2	2
Bradford	D	L	4	0	2	2	1	3	2	1
Southend	W	L	4	3	0	1	4	0	2	1
Oxford Utd	L	L	3	2	0	1	2	1	0	2
Rochdale										
Bristol Rovers	D	D	3	2	1	0	1	2	1	2
Peterborough	L	L	3	1	0	2	1	2	1	1
MK Dons	L	D	3	0	0	3	2	1	2	0
Charlton	D	W	2	0	1	1	2	0	2	0
Walsall	W	W	4	2	1	1	4	0	2	2
AFC Wimbledon	D	L	3	0	1	2	1	2	2	0
Northampton	D	W	3	1	2	0	1	2	2	1
Oldham	W	D	4	2	1	1	2	2	1	2
Shrewsbury	W	L	2	2	0	0	2	0	2	0
Bury	W	W	4	4	0	0	2	2	0	4
Gillingham	W	L	4	1	3	0	1	3	4	0
Portsmouth			1	1	0	0	1	0	0	1
Plymouth			2	2	0	0	1	1	0	2
Doncaster			2	0	1	1	2	0	2	0
Blackpool			1	1	0	0	1	0	0	1

Season	Division	Pos	P	W	D	L	F	A	GD	Pts
2016-17	League One	9	46	19	12	15	71	62	+9	69
2015-16	League One	10	46	19	12	15	68	61	+7	69
2014-15	League One	8	46	19	6	21	72	66	+6	63

Over/Under 57%/43% 6th   **Both score** 48%/52% 19th

ROTHERHAM

Nickname: The Millers
Colours: Red and white
Ground: New York Stadium (12,021)
Tel: 08444-140-733   themillers.co.uk

Rotherham started their campaign of woe with a 2-2 draw against ten-man Wolves having let slip a two-goal advantage, and things just got worse from there onwards.

The not-so-merry-Millers won just two matches in all competitions before Christmas and were relegated from the Championship on April 1, although their fate was virtually sealed long before that.

United conceded an eye-watering 98 goals and gained only 23 points, 28 adrift of safety in a truly shocking season.

Longest run without win/loss: 17/3
High/low league position: 21/24
Clean sheets: 3 **Yellow cards:** 80 **Red:** 3
Avg attendance: 9,348 **Players used:** 35
Leading scorer: D Ward 11 (4,9)
Key stat: Rotherham were relegated with a goal difference of minus 58. The next worst in the Championship was minus 19

	2016-17 H	A	Last six seasons at home P	W	D	L	OV	UN	BS	CS
Blackburn	D	L	3	1	1	1	0	3	1	1
Wigan	W	L	2	1	0	1	2	0	2	0
Rotherham										
Scunthorpe			-	-	-	-	-	-	-	-
Fleetwood Town			1	1	0	0	1	0	1	0
Bradford			3	2	1	0	2	1	0	3
Southend			2	0	0	2	2	0	0	0
Oxford Utd			2	2	0	0	1	1	1	1
Rochdale			1	0	0	1	1	0	1	0
Bristol Rovers			2	0	0	2	1	1	1	0
Peterborough			1	0	0	1	0	1	0	0
MK Dons			2	0	1	1	2	0	2	0
Charlton			2	0	1	1	1	1	2	0
Walsall			1	0	1	0	0	1	1	0
AFC Wimbledon			2	2	0	0	0	2	0	2
Northampton			2	1	1	0	1	1	2	0
Oldham			1	1	0	0	1	0	1	0
Shrewsbury			2	0	2	0	1	1	2	0
Bury			-	-	-	-	-	-	-	-
Gillingham			3	2	0	1	3	0	2	1
Portsmouth			-	-	-	-	-	-	-	-
Plymouth			2	2	0	0	0	2	0	2
Doncaster			-	-	-	-	-	-	-	-
Blackpool			1	0	1	0	0	1	1	0

Season	Division	Pos	P	W	D	L	F	A	GD	Pts
2016-17	Championship	24	46	5	8	33	40	98	-58	23
2015-16	Championship	21	46	13	10	23	53	71	-18	49
2014-15	Championship	21	46	11	16	19	46	67	-21	46

Over/Under 61%/39% 2nd   **Both score** 54%/46% 9th

SCUNTHORPE

Nickname: The Iron
Colours: Claret and blue
Ground: Glanford Park (9,088)
Tel: 01724-840139   scunthorpe-united.co.uk

Anyone who backed Scunthorpe at 20-1 each-way to win League One last season at least got some money back after their third-place finish, but the Iron missed out in the playoffs after losing to Millwall in the semi-finals.

Scunthorpe were leading the division at Christmas but a nine-match winless run where only three points were collected in early February through to mid-March killed the Iron even though they finished with five straight victories.

Longest run without win/loss: 9/8
High/low league position: 1/5
Clean sheets: 13 **Yellow cards:** 77 **Red:** 3
Avg attendance: 4,536 **Players used:** 28
Leading scorer: J Morris 19 (5,16)
Key stat: Top scorer Josh Morris, who notched 19 times in the league, fired blanks in each of his last 12 matches

	2016-17 H	A	Last six seasons at home P	W	D	L	OV	UN	BS	CS
Blackburn			-	-	-	-	-	-	-	-
Wigan			1	0	1	0	0	1	1	0
Rotherham			-	-	-	-	-	-	-	-
Scunthorpe										
Fleetwood Town	L	D	4	1	1	2	0	4	0	2
Bradford	W	D	3	1	1	1	1	2	2	0
Southend	W	L	3	2	1	0	2	1	1	2
Oxford Utd	D	L	2	1	1	0	0	2	1	1
Rochdale	W	L	5	4	1	0	3	2	3	2
Bristol Rovers	W	D	2	1	1	0	1	1	2	0
Peterborough	D	W	3	1	1	1	1	2	1	1
MK Dons	W	W	4	1	1	2	3	1	2	0
Charlton	D	L	2	0	2	0	0	2	1	1
Walsall	D	W	5	1	2	2	1	4	2	1
AFC Wimbledon	L	W	2	0	1	1	1	1	1	1
Northampton	D	W	2	0	2	0	0	2	2	0
Oldham	W	L	5	1	2	2	2	3	3	1
Shrewsbury	L	W	3	1	1	1	1	2	1	1
Bury	W	W	5	2	1	2	5	0	5	0
Gillingham	W	L	3	2	1	0	2	1	1	2
Portsmouth			2	2	0	0	2	0	2	0
Plymouth			1	1	0	0	0	1	0	1
Doncaster			3	1	0	2	2	1	2	1
Blackpool			1	0	0	1	0	0	1	0

Season	Division	Pos	P	W	D	L	F	A	GD	Pts
2016-17	League One	3	46	24	10	12	80	54	+26	82
2015-16	League One	7	46	21	11	14	60	47	+13	74
2014-15	League One	16	46	14	14	18	62	75	-13	56

Over/Under 63%/37% 2nd   **Both score** 65%/35% 2nd

SHREWSBURY

Nickname: The Shrews
Colours: Blue and amber
Ground: New Meadow (9,875)
Tel: 01743-289177   shrewsburytown.com

The decision of Shrewsbury's board to sack Micky Mellon and replace him with Grimsby's Paul Hurst will go down as one of the best managerial changes of the campaign.

Shrewsbury were bottom with ten points from their opening 15 matches before Hurst arrived, already five points from safety and on a run of ten matches without a win. Shrews eventually finished 18th, with nine of their last 11 games featuring under 2.5 goals.

Longest run without win/loss: 10/6
High/low league position: 17/24
Clean sheets: 11 **Yellow cards:** 90 **Red:** 9
Avg attendance: 5,507 **Players used:** 33
Leading scorer: L Dodds 8 (4,6)
Key stat: Bad boys Shrewsbury had the most red cards in League One last season with nine

	2016-17		Last six seasons at home							
	H	A	P	W	D	L	OV	UN	BS	CS
Blackburn			-	-	-	-	-	-	-	-
Wigan			1	0	0	1	1	0	1	0
Rotherham			2	1	0	1	2	0	1	0
Scunthorpe	L	W	3	0	1	2	1	2	1	0
Fleetwood Town	L	L	2	0	1	1	0	2	1	0
Bradford	W	L	4	3	1	0	1	3	2	2
Southend	W	D	4	2	1	1	2	2	3	1
Oxford Utd	W	L	3	2	1	0	1	2	1	2
Rochdale	W	L	2	2	0	0	0	2	0	2
Bristol Rovers	W	L	2	2	0	0	0	2	0	2
Peterborough	D	L	3	0	1	2	2	1	3	0
MK Dons	L	L	3	0	2	1	1	2	1	1
Charlton	W	L	1	1	0	0	1	0	1	0
Walsall	D	L	4	1	1	2	1	3	2	1
AFC Wimbledon	W	D	3	2	1	0	1	2	1	2
Northampton	L	D	3	0	1	2	2	1	3	0
Oldham	W	W	4	2	0	2	1	3	1	2
Shrewsbury										
Bury	W	L	4	3	1	0	2	2	1	3
Gillingham	L	D	4	2	1	1	2	2	2	2
Portsmouth			2	2	0	0	2	0	2	0
Plymouth			2	0	1	1	0	2	1	0
Doncaster			2	0	0	2	2	0	2	0
Blackpool			1	1	0	0	0	1	0	1

Season	Division	Pos	P	W	D	L	F	A	GD	Pts
2016-17	League One	18	46	13	12	21	46	63	-17	51
2015-16	League One	20	46	13	11	22	58	79	-21	50
2014-15	League Two	2	46	27	8	11	67	31	+36	89

Over/Under 41%/59% 18th   **Both score** 54%/46% 7th

SOUTHEND

Nickname: The Shrimpers
Colours: Blue
Ground: Roots Hall (12,392)
Tel: 01702-304-050   southendunited.co.uk

They looked like relegation fodder at the start of the season and promotion contenders in the middle part of the campaign, but a poor finish saw Southend miss out on the top six by just one point.

The signing of troubled striker Nile Ranger (who was jailed in late May) had been huge for Phil Brown's boys. Southend won 12 and drew four of their 20 matches with Ranger in the starting 11 but without him the win ratio dropped from 60 per cent to just 31.

Longest run without win/loss: 4/13
High/low league position: 6/23
Clean sheets: 14 **Yellow cards:** 85 **Red:** 5
Avg attendance: 7,432 **Players used:** 30
Leading scorer: S Cox 16 (4,14)
Key stat: Southend won only three of their opening 12 league matches last season

	2016-17		Last six seasons at home							
	H	A	P	W	D	L	OV	UN	BS	CS
Blackburn			-	-	-	-	-	-	-	-
Wigan			1	0	1	0	0	1	0	1
Rotherham			2	0	1	1	0	2	1	0
Scunthorpe	W	L	3	2	0	1	2	1	2	0
Fleetwood Town	L	D	4	1	2	1	1	3	2	1
Bradford	W	D	4	1	1	2	2	2	1	1
Southend										
Oxford Utd	W	W	5	4	1	0	3	2	3	2
Rochdale	W	L	4	2	2	0	3	1	4	0
Bristol Rovers	D	L	4	0	4	0	0	4	3	1
Peterborough	D	W	2	1	1	0	1	1	2	0
MK Dons	L	W	1	0	0	1	1	0	1	0
Charlton	D	L	1	0	1	0	0	1	1	0
Walsall	W	D	2	1	0	1	1	1	1	0
AFC Wimbledon	W	W	5	2	0	3	2	3	1	2
Northampton	D	L	5	2	2	1	3	2	3	2
Oldham	W	W	2	1	0	1	1	1	0	1
Shrewsbury	D	L	4	2	1	1	1	3	1	2
Bury	W	W	4	2	2	0	1	3	2	2
Gillingham	L	L	4	1	1	2	1	3	2	1
Portsmouth			2	2	0	0	1	1	1	1
Plymouth			4	2	1	1	0	4	0	3
Doncaster			1	0	0	1	1	0	0	0
Blackpool			1	1	0	0	0	1	0	1

Season	Division	Pos	P	W	D	L	F	A	GD	Pts
2016-17	League One	7	46	20	12	14	70	53	+17	72
2015-16	League One	15	46	16	11	19	58	64	-6	59
2014-15	League Two	5	46	24	12	10	54	38	+16	84

Over/Under 50%/50% 10th   **Both score** 50%/50% 14th

WALSALL

Nickname: The Saddlers
Colours: Red and white
Ground: Bescot Stadium (11,300)
Tel: 01922-622-791   saddlers.co.uk

The season before last was fantastic for Walsall, who finished third before missing out in the playoffs, but bookmakers rated them 25-1 shots for the League One title last term and the Bescot boys lived down to those expectations.

Jon Whitney's side never looked like recovering from the loss of influential players and, if anything, 14th was a touch generous given Walsall's shot ratio (share of match shots) was just 0.45 – only four teams had worse shot stats.

Longest run without win/loss: 6/6
High/low league position: 9/18
Clean sheets: 13 **Yellow cards:** 61 **Red:** 3
Avg attendance: 5,071 **Players used:** 27
Leading scorer: E Oztumer 15 (6,14)
Key stat: Saddlers lost six and drew three of their last ten matches in League One last term

	2016-17 H	A	Last six seasons at home P	W	D	L	OV	UN	BS	CS
Blackburn			-	-	-	-	-	-	-	-
Wigan			1	0	0	1	1	0	1	0
Rotherham			1	0	1	0	0	1	1	0
Scunthorpe	L	D	5	0	2	3	4	1	4	1
Fleetwood Town	L	L	3	2	0	1	1	2	1	1
Bradford	D	L	4	1	2	1	3	2	2	1
Southend	D	L	2	1	1	0	0	2	0	2
Oxford Utd	D	D	1	0	1	0	0	1	1	0
Rochdale	L	L	4	1	1	2	2	2	1	1
Bristol Rovers	W	D	1	1	0	0	1	0	1	0
Peterborough	W	D	4	3	1	0	0	4	0	4
MK Dons	L	D	5	1	1	3	2	3	2	1
Charlton	L	D	2	0	1	1	1	1	2	0
Walsall										
AFC Wimbledon	W	L	1	1	0	0	1	0	1	0
Northampton	W	L	1	1	0	0	1	0	1	0
Oldham	W	D	6	4	1	1	1	5	2	3
Shrewsbury	W	D	4	4	0	0	3	1	3	1
Bury	D	D	4	0	2	2	2	2	3	0
Gillingham	L	D	4	1	2	1	2	2	4	0
Portsmouth			1	1	0	0	0	1	0	1
Plymouth			-	-	-	-	-	-	-	-
Doncaster			3	2	0	1	2	1	0	2
Blackpool			1	0	1	0	0	1	1	0

Season	Division	Pos	P	W	D	L	F	A	GD	Pts
2016-17	League One	14	46	14	16	16	51	58	-7	58
2015-16	League One	3	46	24	12	10	71	49	+22	84
2014-15	League One	14	46	14	17	15	50	54	-4	59

Over/Under 35%/65% 23rd   **Both score** 52%/48% 10th

WIGAN

Nickname: The Latics
Colours: Blue and white
Ground: DW Stadium (25,133)
Tel: 01942-774-000   wiganlatics.co.uk

Wigan romped to the title the last time they were in League One and will be hoping to do the same again following their one-season stay up in the Championship.

It's never a good sign when two managers are sacked in the same campaign but that was the story for the goal-shy Latics. Gary Caldwell was given the boot in October and replacement Warren Joyce was gone in March, with Graham Barrow taking them down.

Longest run without win/loss: 7/4
High/low league position: 21/24
Clean sheets: 13 **Yellow cards:** 87 **Red:** 0
Avg attendance: 11,762 **Players used:** 41
Leading scorer: N Powell 6 (0,4)
Key stat: No team scored fewer second-tier goals than Wigan, who went down with 40 – the same as rock-bottom Rotherham

	2016-17 H	A	Last six seasons at home P	W	D	L	OV	UN	BS	CS
Blackburn	W	L	4	2	2	0	3	1	3	1
Wigan										
Rotherham	W	L	2	1	0	1	2	0	2	0
Scunthorpe			1	1	0	0	1	0	0	1
Fleetwood Town			1	1	0	0	1	0	1	0
Bradford			1	1	0	0	0	1	0	1
Southend			1	1	0	0	1	0	1	0
Oxford Utd			-	-	-	-	-	-	-	-
Rochdale			1	1	0	0	0	1	0	1
Bristol Rovers			-	-	-	-	-	-	-	-
Peterborough			1	0	1	0	0	1	1	0
MK Dons			-	-	-	-	-	-	-	-
Charlton			2	1	0	1	2	0	1	0
Walsall			1	0	1	0	0	1	0	1
AFC Wimbledon			-	-	-	-	-	-	-	-
Northampton			-	-	-	-	-	-	-	-
Oldham			1	0	1	0	0	1	0	1
Shrewsbury			1	1	0	0	0	1	0	1
Bury			1	1	0	0	1	0	0	1
Gillingham			1	1	0	0	1	0	1	0
Portsmouth			-	-	-	-	-	-	-	-
Plymouth			-	-	-	-	-	-	-	-
Doncaster			2	0	2	0	1	1	1	1
Blackpool			3	1	0	2	0	3	0	1

Season	Division	Pos	P	W	D	L	F	A	GD	Pts
2016-17	Championship	23	46	10	12	24	40	57	-17	42
2015-16	League One	1	46	24	15	7	82	45	+37	87
2014-15	Championship	23	46	9	12	25	39	64	-25	39

Over/Under 41%/59% 19th   **Both score** 41%/59% 22nd

League One stats 2016-17

Key Points in all tables (except the league table) do not include any deductions imposed by the league.
POS H A Overall league position, rank from home games only, rank from away games only **Sup** Average match supremacy **GFA** Goals For Average **GAA** Goals Against Average **PGA** Points Gained Average

Pos	H	A	League One 2016-17	P	W	D	L	F	A	W	D	L	F	A	GD	Pts
					Home					Away						
1	1	1	Sheff Utd (P)	46	17	3	3	42	16	13	7	3	50	31	45	100
2	4	2	Bolton (P)	46	13	7	3	35	16	12	4	7	33	20	32	86
3	2	5	Scunthorpe	46	14	6	3	46	22	10	4	9	34	32	26	82
4	8	3	Fleetwood	46	12	8	3	34	20	11	5	7	30	23	21	82
5	5	6	Bradford	46	11	12	0	36	17	9	7	7	26	26	19	79
6	6	10	Millwall (P)	46	13	6	4	34	17	7	7	9	32	40	9	73
7	9	8	Southend	46	11	7	5	39	27	9	5	9	31	26	17	72
8	11	7	Oxford Utd	46	11	4	8	33	27	9	5	9	32	25	13	69
9	3	13	Rochdale	46	13	7	3	48	25	6	5	12	23	37	9	69
10	7	14	Bristol Rovers	46	13	6	4	42	26	5	6	12	26	44	-2	66
11	15	9	Peterborough	46	9	6	8	39	33	8	5	10	23	29	0	62
12	23	4	MK Dons	46	7	6	10	29	37	9	7	7	31	21	2	61
13	13	11	Charlton	46	9	8	6	31	19	5	10	8	29	34	7	60
14	10	16	Walsall	46	11	5	7	34	29	3	11	9	17	29	-7	58
15	18	12	AFC Wimbledon	46	8	8	7	34	25	5	10	8	18	30	-3	57
16	19	15	Northampton	46	9	5	9	35	29	5	6	12	25	44	-13	53
17	17	17	Oldham	46	8	9	6	19	18	4	8	11	12	26	-13	53
18	14	21	Shrewsbury	46	10	5	8	26	26	3	7	13	20	37	-17	51
19	21	18	Bury	46	9	3	11	36	33	4	8	11	25	40	-12	50
20	16	20	Gillingham	46	8	9	6	32	30	4	5	14	27	49	-20	50
21	12	22	Port Vale (R)	46	10	6	7	32	31	2	7	14	13	39	-25	49
22	22	19	Swindon (R)	46	7	6	10	23	24	4	5	14	21	42	-22	44
23	20	24	Coventry (R)	46	8	7	8	22	24	1	5	17	15	44	-31	39
24	24	23	Chesterfield (R)	46	7	5	11	26	39	2	5	16	17	39	-35	37

Best attack

		GF	GFA
1	Sheff Utd	92	2
2	Scunthorpe	80	1.74
3	Rochdale	71	1.54
4	Southend	70	1.52
5	Bolton	68	1.48
6	Bristol Rovers	68	1.48
7	Millwall	66	1.43
8	Oxford Utd	65	1.41
9	Fleetwood	64	1.39
10	Bradford	62	1.35
11	Peterborough	62	1.35
12	Bury	61	1.33
13	MK Dons	60	1.3
14	Charlton	60	1.3
15	Northampton	60	1.3
16	Gillingham	59	1.28
17	Wimbledon	52	1.13
18	Walsall	51	1.11
19	Shrewsbury	46	1
20	Port Vale	45	0.98
21	Swindon	44	0.96
22	Chesterfield	43	0.93
23	Coventry	37	0.8
24	Oldham	31	0.67

Best defence

		GA	GAA
1	Bolton	36	0.78
2	Fleetwood	43	0.93
3	Bradford	43	0.93
4	Oldham	44	0.96
5	Sheff Utd	47	1.02
6	Oxford Utd	52	1.13
7	Southend	53	1.15
8	Charlton	53	1.15
9	Scunthorpe	54	1.17
10	Wimbledon	55	1.2
11	Millwall	57	1.24
12	MK Dons	58	1.26
13	Walsall	58	1.26
14	Rochdale	62	1.35
15	Peterborough	62	1.35
16	Shrewsbury	63	1.37
17	Swindon	66	1.43
18	Coventry	68	1.48
19	Bristol Rovers	70	1.52
20	Port Vale	70	1.52
21	Northampton	73	1.59
22	Bury	73	1.59
23	Chesterfield	78	1.7
24	Gillingham	79	1.72

Top scorers

	Team	Goals scored
B Sharp	Sheff Utd	30
J Vaughan	Bury	24
J Morris	Scunthorpe	19
L Gregory	Millwall	17
S Cox	Southend	16
I Henderson	Rochdale	15
E Oztumer	Walsall	15

Over 2.5 goals

	H	A	%
Gillingham	12	18	65%
Northampton	15	14	63%
Scunthorpe	14	15	63%
Bury	15	13	61%
Sheffield Utd	11	17	61%

Under 2.5 goals

	H	A	%
Oldham	19	18	80%
Walsall	12	18	65%
Bolton	13	16	63%
Bradford	14	14	61%
Coventry	15	13	61%

Both to score

	H	A	%
Gillingham	18	16	74%
Scunthorpe	14	16	65%
Bristol Rovers	15	14	63%
Northampton	15	13	61%
Bury, Charlton			59%

Both not to score

	H	A	%
Oldham	17	16	72%
Bolton	11	15	57%
Coventry, Port Vale, Rochdale, Swindon			52%

SOCCERBASE.COM

League One results 2016-17

	AFC Wimbledon	Bolton	Bradford	Bristol Rovers	Bury	Charlton	Chesterfield	Coventry	Fleetwood	Gillingham	Millwall	MK Dons	Northampton	Oldham	Oxford Utd	Peterborough	Port Vale	Rochdale	Scunthorpe	Sheffield United	Shrewsbury	Southend	Swindon	Walsall
AFC Wimbledon		1-2	2-3	0-1	5-1	1-1	2-1	1-1	2-2	2-0	2-2	2-0	0-1	0-0	2-1	0-0	4-0	3-1	1-2	2-3	1-1	0-2	0-0	1-0
Bolton	1-1		0-0	1-1	0-0	1-2	0-0	1-0	2-1	4-0	2-0	1-1	2-1	2-0	0-2	3-0	3-1	1-0	2-1	1-0	2-1	1-1	1-2	4-1
Bradford	3-0	2-2		1-1	1-1	0-0	2-0	3-1	2-1	2-2	1-1	2-2	1-0	1-1	1-0	1-0	0-0	4-0	0-0	3-3	2-0	1-1	2-1	1-0
Bristol Rovers	2-0	1-2	1-1		4-2	1-5	2-1	4-1	2-1	2-1	3-4	0-0	5-0	1-0	2-1	1-2	2-1	2-2	1-1	0-0	2-0	2-0	1-0	1-1
Bury	1-2	0-2	0-2	3-0		2-0	2-1	2-1	0-0	1-2	2-3	0-0	3-0	0-1	2-3	5-1	4-1	0-1	1-2	1-3	2-1	1-4	1-0	3-3
Charlton	1-2	1-1	1-1	4-1	0-1		1-0	3-0	1-1	3-0	0-0	0-2	1-1	1-1	0-1	0-2	2-0	0-1	2-1	1-1	3-0	2-1	3-0	1-1
Chesterfield	0-0	1-0	0-1	3-2	1-2	1-2		1-0	0-1	3-3	1-3	0-0	3-1	0-1	0-4	3-3	1-0	1-3	0-3	1-4	1-1	0-4	3-1	2-0
Coventry	2-2	2-2	0-2	1-0	0-0	1-1	2-0		0-1	2-1	0-2	1-2	1-1	0-0	2-1	1-0	2-1	2-0	0-1	1-2	0-0	0-2	1-3	1-0
Fleetwood	0-0	2-4	1-3	0-0	2-2	2-1	2-0			2-1	1-0	1-4	3-0	1-0	2-0	2-0	0-0	0-0	2-2	1-1	3-0	1-1	0-1	2-1
Gillingham	2-2	0-4	1-1	3-1	2-1	1-1	1-1	2-1	2-3		1-1	1-0	2-1	1-2	0-1	1-1	3-0	3-2	1-2	1-1	2-1	1-1	1-1	
Millwall	0-0	0-2	1-1	4-0	0-0	3-1	0-0	1-1	2-1	2-1		2-1	3-0	3-0	0-3	1-0	2-0	2-3	3-1	2-1	0-1	1-0	2-0	0-0
MK Dons	1-0	1-1	1-2	3-3	1-3	0-1	2-3	1-0	0-1	3-2	2-2		5-3	1-0	0-0	0-2	0-1	2-2	0-1	0-3	2-1	0-3	3-2	1-1
Northampton	0-0	0-1	1-2	2-3	3-2	2-1	3-1	3-0	1-1	0-0	1-3	3-2		1-2	0-0	0-1	2-1	2-3	1-2	1-2	1-1	4-0	2-1	2-0
Oldham	0-0	1-0	1-2	0-2	0-0	1-0	0-0	3-2	2-0	1-0	0-0	0-2	0-0		2-1	2-0	0-0	1-1	2-0	1-1	2-3	0-2	0-2	0-0
Oxford Utd	1-3	2-4	1-0	0-2	5-1	1-1	1-1	4-1	1-3	1-0	1-2	1-0	0-1	1-1		2-1	2-0	1-0	2-1	2-3	2-0	0-2	2-0	0-0
Peterborough	0-1	1-0	0-1	4-2	3-1	2-0	5-2	1-1	1-2	1-1	5-1	0-4	3-0	1-1	1-2		2-2	3-1	0-2	0-1	2-1	1-4	2-2	1-1
Port Vale	2-0	0-2	1-2	1-1	2-1	1-0	0-2	2-1	2-1	3-0	0-0	2-3	2-2	2-2	0-3			1-0	3-1	0-3	2-1	2-0	3-2	0-1
Rochdale	1-1	1-0	1-1	0-0	2-0	3-3	3-0	2-0	4-1	3-3	0-1	1-1	1-0	0-4	2-3	3-0			3-2	3-3	2-1	3-0	4-0	4-0
Scunthorpe	1-2	1-0	3-2	3-1	3-2	0-0	3-1	3-1	0-2	5-0	3-0	2-1	1-0	1-1	1-1	3-2	2-1			2-2	0-1	4-0	4-1	0-0
Sheffield United	4-0	2-0	3-0	1-0	1-0	2-1	3-2	2-0	0-2	2-2	2-0	2-1	1-0	2-0	2-1	1-0	4-0	1-1	1-1		2-1	0-3	4-0	0-1
Shrewsbury	2-1	0-2	1-0	2-0	2-1	4-3	2-1	0-0	0-1	2-3	1-2	0-1	2-4	1-0	2-1	1-0	0-0	1-0	0-3			1-0	1-1	1-1
Southend	3-0	0-1	3-0	1-1	1-0	1-1	1-0	3-1	0-2	1-3	3-1	1-2	2-2	3-0	2-1	1-1	1-1	2-1	3-1	2-4	1-1		1-1	3-2
Swindon	0-0	0-1	1-0	1-2	1-2	3-0	0-1	1-0	1-1	3-1	1-0	1-1	1-3	0-0	1-2	0-1	1-0	3-0	1-2	2-4	1-1	0-0		0-2
Walsall	3-1	1-0	1-1	3-1	3-3	1-2	1-0	1-1	0-1	1-2	2-1	1-4	2-1	2-0	1-1	2-0	0-1	0-2	1-4	4-1	3-2	0-0	1-0	

Record when first to score

		P	W	D	L	F	A	Sup	PGA	Pts
1	Sheff Utd	28	23	5	0	68	25	+1.54	2.6	74
2	Millwall	22	18	4	0	51	19	+1.45	2.6	58
3	MK Dons	20	16	3	1	47	22	+1.25	2.5	51
4	Peterborough	17	13	3	1	41	16	+1.47	2.5	42
5	Bolton	28	21	5	2	52	17	+1.25	2.4	68
6	Southend	25	18	6	1	52	16	+1.44	2.4	60
7	Bradford	22	16	5	1	36	12	+1.09	2.4	53
8	Fleetwood	29	21	4	4	53	26	+0.93	2.3	67
9	Scunthorpe	26	19	4	3	52	22	+1.15	2.3	61
10	Rochdale	26	18	6	2	57	23	+1.31	2.3	60
11	Oxford Utd	23	17	2	4	46	16	+1.3	2.3	53
12	Shrewsbury	15	11	2	2	23	12	+0.73	2.3	35
13	Wimbledon	13	9	3	1	30	11	+1.46	2.3	30
14	Oldham	17	11	5	1	20	12	+0.47	2.2	38
15	Charlton	20	12	6	2	37	18	+0.95	2.1	42
16	Bristol Rovers	19	12	3	4	35	19	+0.84	2.1	39
17	Walsall	23	13	8	2	39	23	+0.7	2	47
18	Port Vale	16	9	5	2	25	14	+0.69	2	32
19	Chesterfield	14	8	2	4	25	21	+0.29	1.9	26
20	Northampton	25	14	4	7	46	31	+0.6	1.8	46
21	Bury	19	11	2	6	37	26	+0.58	1.8	35
22	Coventry	19	9	7	3	29	23	+0.32	1.8	34
23	Swindon	17	9	4	4	23	17	+0.35	1.8	31
24	Gillingham	20	7	7	6	28	24	+0.2	1.4	28

Record when keeping a clean sheet

		P	W	D	F	Sup	PGA	Pts
1	Sheff Utd	17	16	1	37	+2.18	2.9	49
2	Peterborough	10	9	1	16	+1.60	2.8	28
3	Bolton	18	15	3	29	+1.61	2.7	48
4	Southend	14	12	2	29	+2.07	2.7	38
5	Rochdale	14	12	2	27	+1.93	2.7	38
6	Oxford Utd	16	13	3	25	+1.56	2.6	42
7	Fleetwood	20	15	5	25	+1.25	2.5	50
8	Bradford	16	12	4	21	+1.31	2.5	40
9	Scunthorpe	13	10	3	22	+1.69	2.5	33
10	Bristol Rovers	12	9	3	18	+1.50	2.5	30
11	Shrewsbury	11	8	3	10	+0.91	2.5	27
12	Charlton	10	7	3	16	+1.60	2.4	24
13	Swindon	12	8	4	13	+1.08	2.3	28
14	Gillingham	3	2	1	4	+1.33	2.3	7
15	Walsall	13	8	5	11	+0.85	2.2	29
16	MK Dons	13	8	5	13	+1	2.2	29
17	Coventry	10	6	4	9	+0.90	2.2	22
18	Millwall	14	8	6	18	+1.29	2.1	30
19	Port Vale	11	6	5	8	+0.73	2.1	23
20	Northampton	9	5	4	11	+1.22	2.1	19
21	Chesterfield	11	5	5	6	+0.60	2	20
22	Oldham	18	8	10	11	+0.61	1.9	34
23	Bury	12	5	7	10	+0.83	1.8	22
24	Wimbledon	14	5	9	10	+0.71	1.7	24

Playoff disappointment should spur on Hatters for automatic promotion push

L uton have endured a miserable summer trying to get over the disappointment of missing out on promotion but the Hatters can make amends this term, writes Mark Langdon. Nathan Jones saw his Luton side finish in fourth place last season, six points clear of the rest, but they lost a dramatic playoff semi-final to eventual winners Blackpool when goalkeeper Stuart Moore made a decisive blunder.

Jones has rectified that position with the signing of Czech international keeper Marek Stech, who was superb for Yeovil before moving to Sparta Prague where he understandably struggled for playing time.

Stech should be much better back at this level and Jones has also moved to solve another area he considered a weakness and that was central midfield. Brentford's Alan McCormack will make sure Luton's technical players won't be bullied this term.

Danny Hylton scored 21 times last term and Jones has been promised more funds after Cameron McGeehan, who had been sidelined from January with a broken leg in any case, was sold to Barnsley.

There's no Portsmouth or Doncaster in the fourth tier this term and Luton may not even need to improve to come out on top, although favourites Mansfield are respected. Manager Steve Evans has done most of his shopping in League One and the Stags should be right up there, but Luton offer better value.

Coventry and Swindon are big clubs at this level and may get stronger as the season unfolds, but both were in turmoil as they dropped last term and need plenty of work.

Lincoln should be flying from the start and the National League winners are interesting. However, like Mansfield, that is reflected in the betting and three at bigger prices who could go well are Notts County – a side who were unrecognisable under Kevin Nolan last

season – a young Exeter squad with the scope to improve and Accrington.

Of the trio Accy stand out as they can hit the ground running, something that was not possible last term after the loss of key men.

Stanley were sensational in the second part of the season, losing just twice in 18 games – a that run included victories away at top-seven finishers Exeter and Plymouth as well as draws at Doncaster and Blackpool.

A settled Accy team look ready for a bigger push than the prices suggest and it's worth remembering just how highly they were rated by the influential betting syndicates last term as they nearly went off favourites at Plymouth.

The relegation market is tricky but it would be something of a surprise if Crawley were comfortably away from danger.

They have taken a big risk in making Harry Kewell their manager seeing as the Australian was released by Watford Under-23s last term and knows little of the division.

Morecambe are obvious candidates and gaffer Jim Bentley understands the level he is working at and those looking for a bigger price may want to consider Chesterfield, who have had a difficult 12 months.

Recommendations

Luton to win (each-way), 8-1
Accrington to be promoted, 11-2
Crawley to be relegated, 4-1

Isaac Vassell's playoff semi-final strike wasn't enough to take Luton up

ACCRINGTON

Nickname: Stanley
Colours: Red
Ground: Crown Ground (5,057)
Tel: 01254-356950   accringtonstanley.co.uk

If there was one hard-luck story from last season's League Two then it was definitely Accrington, a side ridiculously fighting for relegation at one stage before finishing five points outside the playoffs.

That still was not good enough for a top-half finish as Accy were unable to recover from a terrible start, caused by a playoff hangover, the loss of key men in the summer and rotten misfortune. Only Luton, Portsmouth and Doncaster had more shots on target than Stanley.

Longest run without win/loss: 9/15
High/low league position: 7/22
Clean sheets: 13 **Yellow cards:** 87 **Red:** 8
Avg attendance: 1,699 **Players used:** 30
Leading scorer: B Kee 13 (7,10)
Key stat: No team had more players sent off than Accrington's eight dismissals in League Two last season

	2016-17 H	A	Last six seasons at home P	W	D	L	OV	UN	BS	CS
Port Vale			2	1	1	0	1	1	1	1
Swindon			1	0	0	1	0	1	0	0
Coventry			-	-	-	-	-	-	-	-
Chesterfield			2	2	0	0	1	1	1	1
Luton	L	L	3	0	2	1	2	1	3	0
Exeter	L	W	5	1	0	4	5	0	4	0
Carlisle	D	D	3	1	2	0	1	2	3	0
Colchester	W	W	1	1	0	0	1	0	1	0
Wycombe	D	D	5	0	4	1	1	4	4	0
Stevenage	L	W	3	0	2	1	1	2	1	1
Cambridge U	W	L	3	2	1	0	1	2	2	1
Mansfield	D	D	4	2	2	0	1	3	3	1
Accrington										
Grimsby	D	L	1	0	1	0	0	1	1	0
Barnet	W	L	4	2	1	1	3	1	2	1
Notts County	W	W	2	2	0	0	1	1	1	1
Crewe	W	W	2	1	0	1	1	1	1	0
Morecambe	L	W	6	3	2	1	4	2	5	1
Crawley	W	D	3	2	0	1	1	2	1	1
Yeovil	D	D	2	1	1	0	1	1	2	0
Cheltenham	D	L	5	0	3	2	1	4	3	0
Newport County	L	L	4	0	2	2	3	1	3	0
Lincoln			-	-	-	-	-	-	-	-
Forest Green			-	-	-	-	-	-	-	-

Season	Division	Pos	P	W	D	L	F	A	GD	Pts
2016-17	League 2	13	46	17	14	15	59	56	+3	65
2015-16	League 2	4	46	24	13	9	74	48	+26	85
2014-15	League 2	17	46	15	11	20	58	77	-19	56

Over/Under 39%/61% 24th   **Both score** 50%/50% 16th

BARNET

Nickname: The Bees
Colours: Black and amber
Ground: The Hive Stadium (6,418)
Tel: 020 8381 3800   barnetfc.com

Only goal difference separated Barnet from the playoff positions until manager Martin Allen made the unusual decision to drop down a level to Eastleigh in December and the Bees never really recovered from that body blow.

Rossi Eames and Henry Newman looked as if they could have steadied the ship before being replaced by Kevin Nugent. There was also a reliance on 26-goal John Akinde with Curtis Weston next in the goal charts with six goals.

Longest run without win/loss: 7/8
High/low league position: 7/23
Clean sheets: 11 **Yellow cards:** 67 **Red:** 3
Avg attendance: 2,260 **Players used:** 40
Leading scorer: J Akinde 26 (10,22)
Key stat: Only promoted pair Portsmouth and Blackpool as well as Accrington had more shots than Barnet in League Two last term

	2016-17 H	A	Last six seasons at home P	W	D	L	OV	UN	BS	CS
Port Vale			2	0	1	1	1	1	1	1
Swindon			1	0	0	1	0	1	0	0
Coventry			-	-	-	-	-	-	-	-
Chesterfield			1	0	0	1	0	1	0	0
Luton	L	L	3	1	0	2	2	1	2	0
Exeter	L	L	3	1	0	2	2	1	2	1
Carlisle	L	D	2	0	1	1	0	2	0	1
Colchester	D	L	1	0	1	0	0	1	1	0
Wycombe	L	W	3	1	0	2	0	3	0	1
Stevenage	L	L	2	1	0	1	2	0	2	0
Cambridge U	L	D	3	0	2	1	1	2	1	1
Mansfield	L	W	2	0	0	2	1	1	1	0
Accrington	W	L	4	1	2	1	1	3	2	2
Grimsby	W	D	3	2	0	1	3	0	3	0
Barnet										
Notts County	W	L	2	2	0	0	2	0	2	0
Crewe	D	L	2	1	1	0	2	0	2	0
Morecambe	D	W	4	1	2	1	2	2	2	1
Crawley	D	D	3	1	1	1	3	0	3	0
Yeovil	D	D	2	0	1	1	2	0	2	0
Cheltenham	W	D	3	1	2	0	2	1	2	0
Newport County	D	D	2	1	1	0	2	0	2	0
Lincoln			2	0	1	1	1	1	2	0
Forest Green			2	1	0	1	2	0	2	0

Season	Division	Pos	P	W	D	L	F	A	GD	Pts
2016-17	League 2	15	46	14	15	17	57	64	-7	57
2015-16	League 2	15	46	17	11	18	67	68	-1	62
2014-15	Conference	1	46	28	8	10	94	46	+48	92

Over/Under 46%/54% 18th   **Both score** 59%/41% 6th

CAMBRIDGE UNITED

Nickname: The U's
Colours: Yellow and black
Ground: Abbey Stadium (8,127)
Tel: 01223-566500   cambridge-united.co.uk

Cambridge went into the final match of the season still in the hunt for a playoff spot and their final League Two position of 11th was unjust according to manager Shaun Derry.

"It really hurts to finish 11th," moaned Derry, but Cambridge have only themselves to blame after making a terrible start with only three points from the first 24 available. United finished strongly, however, and much of that was down to the excellent Luke Berry.

Longest run without win/loss: 8/8
High/low league position: 7/24
Clean sheets: 13 **Yellow cards:** 73 **Red:** 4
Avg attendance: 4,737 **Players used:** 31
Leading scorer: L Berry 17 (6,14)
Key stat: United won more league games away last season (ten) than they managed at home (nine)

	2016-17 H	A	Last six seasons at home P	W	D	L	OV	UN	BS	CS
Port Vale			-	-	-	-	-	-	-	-
Swindon			-	-	-	-	-	-	-	-
Coventry			-	-	-	-	-	-	-	-
Chesterfield			-	-	-	-	-	-	-	-
Luton	L	L	6	0	3	3	3	3	4	0
Exeter	W	W	3	1	0	2	1	2	1	1
Carlisle	D	W	3	1	2	0	2	1	1	2
Colchester	D	L	1	0	1	0	0	1	1	0
Wycombe	L	L	3	1	0	2	1	2	1	1
Stevenage	D	W	3	1	2	0	0	3	1	2
Cambridge U										
Mansfield	L	D	5	2	1	2	4	1	5	0
Accrington	W	L	3	1	1	1	3	0	3	0
Grimsby	L	L	4	0	1	3	1	3	1	1
Barnet	D	W	3	1	2	0	1	2	3	0
Notts County	W	W	2	2	0	0	2	0	1	1
Crewe	W	W	1	1	0	0	1	0	1	0
Morecambe	L	L	3	1	0	2	3	0	2	1
Crawley	W	W	2	1	0	1	1	1	0	1
Yeovil	W	D	2	2	0	0	1	1	0	2
Cheltenham	W	W	2	1	0	1	2	0	2	0
Newport County	W	W	5	3	2	0	3	2	2	3
Lincoln			3	3	0	0	1	2	1	2
Forest Green			3	1	2	0	1	2	2	1

Season	Division	Pos	P	W	D	L	F	A	GD	Pts
2016-17	League 2	11	46	19	9	18	58	50	+8	66
2015-16	League 2	9	46	18	14	14	66	55	+11	68
2014-15	League 2	19	46	13	12	21	61	66	-5	51

Over/Under 48%/52% 15th   **Both score** 48%/52% 19th

CARLISLE

Nickname: Cumbrians/The Blues
Colours: Blue
Ground: Brunton Park (17,949)
Tel: 01228-526-237   carlisleunited.co.uk

Quiz buffs will probably know the answer and so too will Annual readers but who was the last remaining unbeaten team in the Football League season last term?

The answer is Carlisle, who first tasted defeat on November 12 and that shock 2-0 loss at Newport was their only league reverse until the new year.

From then onwards, things fell apart for Keith Curle's outfit and their goal difference of plus one tells a gloomy story despite their sixth-place finish.

Longest run without win/loss: 7/15
High/low league position: 1/10
Clean sheets: 7 **Yellow cards:** 83 **Red:** 7
Avg attendance: 5,114 **Players used:** 32
Leading scorer: C Wyke 14 (5,11)
Key stat: Carlisle went unbeaten in their opening 15 league matches of last term

	2016-17 H	A	Last six seasons at home P	W	D	L	OV	UN	BS	CS
Port Vale			1	0	0	1	0	1	0	0
Swindon			2	1	0	1	1	1	1	
Coventry			2	1	0	1	1	0	1	
Chesterfield			1	1	0	0	1	0	1	0
Luton	D	D	3	0	1	2	1	2	1	1
Exeter	W	W	4	3	0	1	3	1	3	1
Carlisle										
Colchester	W	L	4	2	0	2	1	3	1	2
Wycombe	W	W	4	1	2	1	2	2	3	1
Stevenage	D	W	6	4	2	0	2	4	2	4
Cambridge U	L	D	3	0	1	2	2	1	1	0
Mansfield	W	L	3	2	0	1	3	0	3	0
Accrington	D	D	3	2	1	0	0	3	1	2
Grimsby	L	D	1	0	0	1	0	1	0	0
Barnet	D	W	2	1	1	0	1	1	2	0
Notts County	L	L	5	2	0	3	5	0	2	1
Crewe	L	D	3	1	1	1	1	2	1	1
Morecambe	D	D	3	0	2	1	1	2	3	0
Crawley	W	D	4	2	1	1	2	2	3	0
Yeovil	W	W	4	3	1	0	4	0	4	0
Cheltenham	D	L	2	1	1	0	0	2	1	1
Newport County	W	L	3	1	0	2	2	1	2	0
Lincoln			-	-	-	-	-			
Forest Green			-	-	-	-	-			

Season	Division	Pos	P	W	D	L	F	A	GD	Pts
2016-17	League 2	6	46	18	17	11	69	68	+1	71
2015-16	League 2	10	46	17	16	13	67	62	+5	67
2014-15	League 2	20	46	14	8	24	56	74	-18	50

Over/Under 54%/46% 7th   **Both score** 70%/30% 1st

LEAGUE TWO

CHELTENHAM

Nickname: The Robins
Colours: Red and white
Ground: Whaddon Road (7,066)
Tel: 01242-573558   ctfc.com

The two were not linked but Cheltenham's narrow escape from relegation coincided with experienced manager Gary Johnson needing a mid-season break due to a heart operation.

Cheltenham's campaign certainly was no good for the ticker as the National League champions surprisingly struggled on their return to the Football League. The Robins finished only four points above the drop zone and won just four matches before the turn of the year.

Longest run without win/loss: 7/6
High/low league position: 16/23
Clean sheets: 11 **Yellow cards:** 92 **Red:** 5
Avg attendance: 3,323 **Players used:** 33
Leading scorer: B Waters 12 (3,11)
Key stat: Only relegated Leyton Orient scored fewer goals than Cheltenham's tally of 49

	2016-17 H	A	Last six seasons at home P	W	D	L	OV	UN	BS	CS
Port Vale			2	1	1	0	0	2	1	1
Swindon			1	1	0	0	0	1	0	1
Coventry			-	-	-	-	-	-	-	-
Chesterfield			2	1	0	1	1	1	1	1
Luton	D	W	2	0	2	0	0	2	2	0
Exeter	L	L	4	2	0	2	3	1	2	2
Carlisle	W	D	2	1	1	0	0	2	0	2
Colchester	L	L	1	0	0	1	1	0	0	0
Wycombe	L	D	4	1	1	2	2	2	2	1
Stevenage	D	L	2	0	1	1	0	2	0	1
Cambridge U	L	L	2	1	0	1	1	1	1	0
Mansfield	D	D	3	0	2	1	1	2	2	1
Accrington	W	D	5	3	0	2	5	0	3	1
Grimsby	W	W	2	2	0	0	2	0	2	0
Barnet	L	L	3	2	0	1	1	2	1	2
Notts County	L	L	1	0	0	1	1	0	1	0
Crewe	W	D	2	1	0	1	0	2	0	1
Morecambe	W	W	5	3	1	1	3	2	3	2
Crawley	W	D	2	2	0	0	2	0	2	0
Yeovil	W	L	1	1	0	0	1	0	0	1
Cheltenham										
Newport County	D	D	3	0	2	1	0	3	1	1
Lincoln			1	1	0	0	0	1	0	
Forest Green			1	0	1	0	0	1	1	0

Season	Division	Pos	P	W	D	L	F	A	GD	Pts
2016-17	League 2	21	46	12	14	20	49	69	-20	50
2015-16	National League	1	46	30	11	5	87	30	+57	101
2014-15	League 2	23	46	9	14	23	40	67	-27	41

Over/Under 48%/52% 15th   **Both score** 54%/46% 11th

CHESTERFIELD

Nickname: Spireites
Colours: Blue and white
Ground: The Proact Stadium (10,400)
Tel: 01246-269300   chesterfield-fc.co.uk

The controversial signing of Ched Evans failed to help Chesterfield as they tumbled out of League One without putting up too much of a fight.

The rock-bottom Spireites produced some pathetic numbers to go along with their wooden spoon such as finishing with the worst goal difference (minus 35) and just two away wins. Chairman Dave Allen resigned and Evans scored only five league goals, the last of which came in a 5-2 loss at Peterborough in December.

Longest run without win/loss: 10/3
High/low league position: 10/24
Clean sheets: 10 **Yellow cards:** 75 **Red:** 5
Avg attendance: 5,929 **Players used:** 39
Leading scorer: K Dennis 8 (1,8)
Key stat: Chesterfield conceded at least three goals at home in eight of their 23 matches in League One last season

	2016-17 H	A	Last six seasons at home P	W	D	L	OV	UN	BS	CS
Port Vale	W	L	4	3	1	0	3	1	2	2
Swindon	W	W	3	1	0	2	3	0	1	0
Coventry	W	L	3	1	1	1	1	2	2	1
Chesterfield										
Luton			-	-	-	-	-	-	-	-
Exeter			3	1	1	1	1	2	1	1
Carlisle			1	1	0	0	1	0	1	0
Colchester			3	1	1	1	2	1	1	1
Wycombe			3	3	0	0	2	1	1	2
Stevenage			1	0	1	0	0	1	1	0
Cambridge U			-	-	-	-	-	-	-	-
Mansfield			1	0	0	1	0	1	0	0
Accrington			2	2	0	0	1	1	1	1
Grimsby			-	-	-	-	-	-	-	-
Barnet			1	0	0	1	0	1	0	0
Notts County			2	0	1	1	1	1	2	0
Crewe			2	2	0	0	1	1	1	1
Morecambe			2	1	1	0	0	2	1	1
Crawley			1	1	0	0	1	0	0	1
Yeovil			2	0	2	0	1	1	1	1
Cheltenham			2	2	0	0	1	1	1	1
Newport County			1	0	1	0	0	1	1	0
Lincoln			-	-	-	-	-	-	-	-
Forest Green			-	-	-	-	-	-	-	-

Season	Division	Pos	P	W	D	L	F	A	GD	Pts
2016-17	League 1	24	46	9	10	27	43	78	-35	37
2015-16	League 1	18	46	15	8	23	58	70	-12	53
2014-15	League 1	6	46	19	12	15	68	55	+13	69

Over/Under 52%/48% 9th   **Both score** 50%/50% 14th

COLCHESTER

Nickname: The U's
Colours: Blue and white
Ground: Colchester Community Stadium (10,105)
Tel: 01206-755100   cu-fc.com

Home is where the heart is for Colchester, who missed out on a playoff spot by just one point because of their travel sickness.

United were awesome when playing at their Essex fortress, winning 14 times which was the same as promoted pair Portsmouth and Doncaster at home. But Colchester's away form must improve after just five triumphs.

They got worse as the season went on and their only road win in the last ten came at hapless Leyton Orient.

Longest run without win/loss: 10/9
High/low league position: 5/23
Clean sheets: 13 **Yellow cards:** 65 **Red:** 1
Avg attendance: 3,973 **Players used:** 31
Leading scorer: C Porter 16 (4,13)
Key stat: United kept nine home clean sheets in League Two last season – nobody in the division could better that figure

	2016-17 H	A	Last six seasons at home P	W	D	L	OV	UN	BS	CS
Port Vale			3	2	0	1	2	1	2	1
Swindon			4	0	1	3	2	2	3	0
Coventry			4	1	0	3	3	1	3	0
Chesterfield			3	1	1	1	2	1	3	0
Luton	W	W	1	1	0	0	1	0	1	0
Exeter	L	L	2	1	0	1	1	1	1	1
Carlisle	W	L	4	2	2	0	1	3	3	1
Colchester										
Wycombe	W	W	2	1	1	0	0	2	1	1
Stevenage	W	W	4	3	0	1	3	1	1	3
Cambridge U	W	D	1	1	0	0	0	1	0	1
Mansfield	W	D	1	1	0	0	0	1	0	1
Accrington	L	L	1	0	0	1	1	0	1	0
Grimsby	W	L	1	1	0	0	1	0	1	0
Barnet	W	D	1	1	0	0	1	0	1	0
Notts County	W	L	5	2	0	3	3	2	2	0
Crewe	W	L	5	1	0	4	5	0	4	1
Morecambe	D	D	1	0	1	0	1	0	1	0
Crawley	L	D	4	0	2	2	2	2	4	0
Yeovil	W	L	4	3	1	0	1	3	1	3
Cheltenham	W	W	1	1	0	0	0	1	0	1
Newport County	D	D	1	0	1	0	0	1	0	1
Lincoln			-	-	-	-	-	-	-	-
Forest Green			-	-	-	-	-	-	-	-

Season	Division	Pos	P	W	D	L	F	A	GD	Pts
2016-17	League 2	8	46	19	12	15	67	57	+10	69
2015-16	League 1	23	46	9	13	24	57	99	-42	40
2014-15	League 1	19	46	14	10	22	58	77	-19	52

Over/Under 50%/50% 13th   **Both score** 54%/46% 11th

COVENTRY

Nickname: The Sky Blues
Colours: Sky blue
Ground: Ricoh Arena (32,609)
Tel: 024-7699-1987   ccfc.co.uk

The famous name of Coventry City will play in the fourth tier of English football for the first time since 1959 after the cash-strapped club suffered relegation in a troubled campaign as fans protested against their unpopular owners.

Managers Tony Mowbray, Mark Venus and Russell Slade all tried to save the sinking ship before Mark Robins, appointed in March, took them down. Cov won once on the road but they did at least lift the Football League Trophy.

Longest run without win/loss: 15/4
High/low league position: 18/24
Clean sheets: 10 **Yellow cards:** 65 **Red:** 4
Avg attendance: 9,111 **Players used:** 39
Leading scorer: G Thomas 5 (3,5)
Key stat: Coventry won once on the road in League One last season

	2016-17 H	A	Last six seasons at home P	W	D	L	OV	UN	BS	CS
Port Vale	W	W	4	2	1	1	3	1	3	1
Swindon	L	L	5	0	1	4	4	1	3	1
Coventry										
Chesterfield	W	L	3	2	1	0	0	3	0	3
Luton			-	-	-	-	-	-	-	-
Exeter			-	-	-	-	-	-	-	-
Carlisle			2	0	0	2	2	0	2	0
Colchester			4	2	1	1	1	3	1	2
Wycombe			-	-	-	-	-	-	-	-
Stevenage			2	1	0	1	1	1	1	1
Cambridge U			-	-	-	-	-	-	-	-
Mansfield			-	-	-	-	-	-	-	-
Accrington			-	-	-	-	-	-	-	-
Grimsby			-	-	-	-	-	-	-	-
Barnet			-	-	-	-	-	-	-	-
Notts County			3	1	0	2	2	1	1	1
Crewe			4	1	1	2	4	0	4	0
Morecambe			-	-	-	-	-	-	-	-
Crawley			3	1	2	0	3	0	3	0
Yeovil			2	1	0	1	1	1	1	0
Cheltenham			-	-	-	-	-	-	-	-
Newport County			-	-	-	-	-	-	-	-
Lincoln			-	-	-	-	-	-	-	-
Forest Green			-	-	-	-	-	-	-	-

Season	Division	Pos	P	W	D	L	F	A	GD	Pts
2016-17	League 1	23	46	9	12	25	37	68	-31	39
2015-16	League 1	8	46	19	12	15	67	49	+18	69
2014-15	League 1	17	46	13	16	17	49	60	-11	55

Over/Under 39%/61% 20th   **Both score** 48%/52% 19th

CRAWLEY

Nickname: The Red Devils
Colours: Red and white
Ground: Broadfield Stadium (5,996)
Tel: 01293-410000 crawleytownfc.com

Only Morecambe at 7-2 were a shorter price for relegation than 4-1 pokes Crawley at the start of last season so using that as a guide perhaps the Red Devils did well to finish 19th.

However, that view was not shared by the Crawley board with manager Dermot Drummy given his marching orders in May after one win in 13 matches prior to his sacking. Striker James Collins did well with 20 league goals but nobody else got close to double figures.

Longest run without win/loss: 7/5
High/low league position: 5/21
Clean sheets: 12 **Yellow cards:** 107 **Red:** 4
Avg attendance: 2,492 **Players used:** 28
Leading scorer: J Collins 20 (11,18)
Key stat: The Red Devils lived up to their nickname with a league-high 100 yellow cards last season

	2016-17		Last six seasons at home							
	H	A	P	W	D	L	OV	UN	BS	CS
Port Vale			3	1	0	2	3	0	2	0
Swindon			4	1	2	1	1	3	1	2
Coventry			3	2	0	1	2	1	2	1
Chesterfield			1	0	1	0	0	1	1	0
Luton	W	L	2	2	0	0	1	1	1	1
Exeter	L	W	2	0	0	2	1	1	1	0
Carlisle	D	L	4	0	3	1	1	3	2	1
Colchester	D	W	4	2	2	0	1	3	1	3
Wycombe	W	W	2	1	1	0	0	2	0	2
Stevenage	L	L	4	1	2	1	2	2	4	0
Cambridge U	L	L	2	1	0	1	1	1	1	1
Mansfield	D	L	2	0	1	1	1	1	1	0
Accrington	D	L	3	0	2	1	1	2	1	1
Grimsby	W	D	1	1	0	0	1	0	1	0
Barnet	D	D	3	1	1	1	1	2	1	1
Notts County	L	L	5	2	1	2	1	4	1	3
Crewe	L	W	5	1	2	2	2	3	3	1
Morecambe	L	W	3	0	2	1	1	2	3	0
Crawley										
Yeovil	W	L	4	2	0	2	0	4	0	2
Cheltenham	D	L	2	1	1	0	1	1	1	1
Newport County	W	L	2	2	0	0	1	1	1	1
Lincoln			-	-	-	-	-	-	-	-
Forest Green			-	-	-	-	-	-	-	-

Season	Division	Pos	P	W	D	L	F	A	GD	Pts
2016-17	League 2	19	46	13	12	21	53	71	-18	51
2015-16	League 2	20	46	13	8	25	45	78	-33	47
2014-15	League 1	22	46	13	11	22	53	79	-26	50

Over/Under 54%/46% 7th   **Both score** 57%/43% 10th

CREWE

Nickname: The Railwaymen
Colours: Red and white
Ground: Gresty Road (10,180)
Tel: 01270-213014 crewealex.net

The fourth-longest serving boss in English football failed to see out the season as a turbulent campaign for Crewe saw them sack Steve Davis in January and replace him with David Artell.

Alex sat 18th when they got rid of Davis and finished 17th which suggests not much improvement but in fairness to Artell, Crewe were a more solid unit under his stewardship. Crewe won nine league games to nil and Artell achieved six of those were during Artell's tenure.

Longest run without win/loss: 11/4
High/low league position: 3/21
Clean sheets: 13 **Yellow cards:** 45 **Red:** 2
Avg attendance: 3,882 **Players used:** 25
Leading scorer: C Dagnall 14 (4,10)
Key stat: Crewe collected just 45 yellow cards which was the fewest in League Two last season

	2016-17		Last six seasons at home							
	H	A	P	W	D	L	OV	UN	BS	CS
Port Vale			4	1	2	1	2	2	3	1
Swindon			5	2	2	1	2	3	3	2
Coventry			4	2	0	2	3	1	2	1
Chesterfield			2	0	1	1	1	1	1	1
Luton	L	D	1	0	0	1	1	0	1	0
Exeter	W	L	1	1	0	0	0	1	0	1
Carlisle	D	W	3	2	1	0	1	2	2	1
Colchester	W	L	5	2	2	1	2	3	2	2
Wycombe	W	L	1	1	0	0	1	0	1	0
Stevenage	L	W	3	0	0	3	3	0	2	0
Cambridge U	L	L	1	0	0	1	1	0	1	0
Mansfield	D	L	1	0	1	0	0	1	1	0
Accrington	L	L	2	1	0	1	0	2	0	1
Grimsby	W	W	1	1	0	0	1	0	0	1
Barnet	W	D	2	2	0	0	2	0	2	0
Notts County	D	D	4	0	1	3	4	0	3	0
Crewe										
Morecambe	W	D	2	1	0	1	1	1	1	0
Crawley	L	W	5	2	2	1	0	5	1	3
Yeovil	L	L	3	1	0	2	0	3	0	1
Cheltenham	D	L	2	1	1	0	0	2	0	2
Newport County	L	D	1	0	0	1	1	0	1	0
Lincoln			-	-	-	-	-	-	-	-
Forest Green			-	-	-	-	-	-	-	-

Season	Division	Pos	P	W	D	L	F	A	GD	Pts
2016-17	League 2	17	46	14	13	19	58	67	-9	55
2015-16	League 1	24	46	7	13	26	46	83	-37	34
2014-15	League 1	20	46	14	10	22	43	75	-32	52

Over/Under 57%/43% 5th   **Both score** 52%/48% 13th

EXETER

Nickname: The Grecians
Colours: Black and white
Ground: St James Park (8,830)
Tel: 01392-411243   exetercityfc.co.uk

For most teams there is nothing but heartbreak when losing in a playoff final but manager Paul Tisdale, who has been at the club for 11 years, was in a bullish mood after defeat to Blackpool in May.

"They're a good group with a lot of young developing players that we'll look to build on," said Tisdale and he has good reason to be optimistic. Only the automatically promoted trio won more games than Exeter's 21 – not bad for a team who were bottom in November.

Longest run without win/loss: 4/12
High/low league position: 4/24
Clean sheets: 13 **Yellow cards:** 71 **Red:** 2
Avg attendance: 4,166 **Players used:** 28
Leading scorer: D Wheeler 17 (6,15)
Key stat: The free-scoring Grecians racked up 75 league goals which was the most of any side not promoted last season

	2016-17 H	A	Last six seasons at home P	W	D	L	OV	UN	BS	CS
Port Vale			1	0	0	1	0	1	0	0
Swindon			-	-	-	-	-	-	-	-
Coventry			-	-	-	-	-	-	-	-
Chesterfield			3	1	0	2	1	2	1	0
Luton	D	D	3	0	2	1	1	2	2	1
Exeter										
Carlisle	L	L	4	1	2	1	2	2	2	2
Colchester	W	W	2	1	1	0	1	1	1	1
Wycombe	W	L	6	3	0	3	4	2	4	0
Stevenage	D	W	4	0	4	0	1	3	3	1
Cambridge U	L	L	3	1	1	1	2	1	2	1
Mansfield	W	W	4	1	0	3	2	2	2	1
Accrington	L	W	5	2	0	3	2	3	2	1
Grimsby	D	W	1	0	1	0	0	1	0	1
Barnet	W	W	3	1	2	0	2	1	3	0
Notts County	L	D	3	0	2	1	0	3	2	0
Crewe	W	L	1	1	0	0	1	0	0	1
Morecambe	W	W	5	1	3	1	2	3	4	0
Crawley	L	W	2	0	1	1	1	1	1	0
Yeovil	D	D	3	1	2	0	2	1	3	0
Cheltenham	W	W	4	2	1	1	1	3	1	2
Newport County	L	W	4	1	1	2	0	4	1	1
Lincoln			-	-	-	-	-	-	-	-
Forest Green			-	-	-	-	-	-	-	-

Season	Division	Pos	P	W	D	L	F	A	GD	Pts
2016-17	League 2	5	46	21	8	17	75	56	+19	71
2015-16	League 2	14	46	17	13	16	63	65	-2	64
2014-15	League 2	10	46	17	13	16	61	65	-4	64

Over/Under 59%/41% 3rd   **Both score** 48%/52% 19th

FOREST GREEN

Nickname: Rovers
Colours: Green and black
Ground: The New Lawn (5,147)
Tel: 01453 834860   forestgreenroversfc.com

If you are somebody who loves nothing more than a fat, greasy burger to scoff down during a football match then it will probably be worth giving a trip to the New Lawn a miss this season.

Forest Green's chairman Dale Vince has turned his club vegan but what they lack in meat they make up for in money with Rovers' heavy backing finally paying dividends with a playoff final success over Tranmere despite finishing nine points behind them in the regular season.

Longest run without win/loss: 6/11
High/low league position: 1/3
Clean sheets: 16 **Yellow cards:** 62 **Red:** 1
Avg attendance: 1,756 **Players used:** 30
Leading scorer: C Doidge 25 (9,22)
Key stat: Rovers were the joint-highest away scorers in the National League last season with 42 goals alongside Dagenham

	2016-17 H	A	Last six seasons at home P	W	D	L	OV	UN	BS	CS
Port Vale			-	-	-	-	-	-	-	-
Swindon			-	-	-	-	-	-	-	-
Coventry			-	-	-	-	-	-	-	-
Chesterfield			-	-	-	-	-	-	-	-
Luton			3	1	1	1	2	1	1	2
Exeter			-	-	-	-	-	-	-	-
Carlisle			-	-	-	-	-	-	-	-
Colchester			-	-	-	-	-	-	-	-
Wycombe			-	-	-	-	-	-	-	-
Stevenage			-	-	-	-	-	-	-	-
Cambridge U			3	2	1	0	2	1	3	0
Mansfield			2	0	1	1	1	1	2	0
Accrington			-	-	-	-	-	-	-	-
Grimsby			5	2	0	3	2	3	2	0
Barnet			2	0	0	2	2	0	2	0
Notts County			-	-	-	-	-	-	-	-
Crewe			-	-	-	-	-	-	-	-
Morecambe			-	-	-	-	-	-	-	-
Crawley			-	-	-	-	-	-	-	-
Yeovil			-	-	-	-	-	-	-	-
Cheltenham			1	0	1	0	1	0	1	0
Newport County			2	0	1	1	1	1	2	0
Lincoln	L	L	6	3	1	2	5	1	4	1
Forest Green										

Season	Division	Pos	P	W	D	L	F	A	GD	Pts
2016-17	National Lge	3	46	25	11	10	88	56	+32	86
2015-16	National Lge	2	46	26	11	9	69	42	+27	89
2014-15	Conference	5	46	22	16	8	80	54	+26	79

Over/Under 57%/43% 5th   **Both score** 59%/41% 6th

GRIMSBY

Nickname: The Mariners
Colours: Black and white
Ground: Blundell Park (9,052)
Tel: 01472-605-050

Last season was a slightly disappointing return to the Football League for Grimsby, who rarely looked like challenging for promotion up to League One.

Perhaps too much was expected of the Mariners, but more likely the managerial chaos at the club held them back and more stability will be needed this term.

Paul Hurst left in October and his replacement Marcus Bignot was gone after just five months with Russell Slade seeing out a mid-table finish.

Longest run without win/loss: 4/4
High/low league position: 6/15
Clean sheets: 15 **Yellow cards:** 80 **Red:** 3
Avg attendance: 5,259 **Players used:** 31
Leading scorer: O Bogle 19 (6,12)
Key stat: Both-teams-to-score backers collected in each of the Mariners' last nine matches

	2016-17 H	A	Last six seasons at home P	W	D	L	OV	UN	BS	CS
Port Vale	-	-	-	-	-	-	-	-	-	-
Swindon	-	-	-	-	-	-	-	-	-	-
Coventry	-	-	-	-	-	-	-	-	-	-
Chesterfield	-	-	-	-	-	-	-	-	-	-
Luton	D	W	4	1	1	2	2	2	3	0
Exeter	L	D	1	0	0	1	1	0	0	0
Carlisle	D	W	1	0	1	0	1	0	1	0
Colchester	W	L	1	1	0	0	0	1	0	1
Wycombe	L	L	1	0	0	1	1	0	1	0
Stevenage	W	L	1	1	0	0	1	0	1	0
Cambridge U	W	W	4	2	0	2	2	2	2	0
Mansfield	W	W	3	2	1	0	2	1	1	2
Accrington	W	D	1	1	0	0	0	1	0	1
Grimsby										
Barnet	D	L	3	2	1	0	3	0	3	0
Notts County	W	D	1	1	0	0	0	1	0	1
Crewe	L	L	1	0	0	1	0	1	0	0
Morecambe	W	L	1	1	0	0	0	1	0	1
Crawley	D	L	1	0	1	0	0	1	1	0
Yeovil	W	D	1	1	0	0	1	0	1	0
Cheltenham	L	L	2	0	0	2	0	2	0	0
Newport County	W	D	3	2	1	0	2	1	1	2
Lincoln			5	2	2	1	2	3	4	1
Forest Green			5	4	1	0	3	2	4	1

Season	Division	Pos	P	W	D	L	F	A	GD	Pts
2016-17	League 2	14	46	17	11	18	59	63	-4	62
2015-16	National Lge	4	46	22	14	10	82	45	+37	80
2014-15	Conference	3	46	25	11	10	74	40	+34	86

Over/Under 52%/48% 10th   **Both score** 46%/54% 23rd

LINCOLN

Nickname: The Imps
Colours: Red
Ground: Sincil Bank (10,120)
Tel: 01522 880011

FA Cup kings Lincoln warmed the hearts of a national with a famous run through to the quarter-finals of the grand old competition, becoming the first non-league team to do so in 100 years.

The dream was ended by Arsenal but not before Lincoln had stunned the likes of Ipswich and Brighton at home and beaten Premier League Burnley at Turf Moor. It would have been easy to get distracted by those exploits, yet the Imps won the National League with 99 points.

Longest run without win/loss: 3/12
High/low league position: 1/5
Clean sheets: 19 **Yellow cards:** 69 **Red:** 5
Avg attendance: 2,884 **Players used:** 33
Leading scorer: M Rhead 15 (3,10)
Key stat: Barrow were the last team to win at Lincoln on September 17, 23 matches ago

	2016-17 H	A	Last six seasons at home P	W	D	L	OV	UN	BS	CS
Port Vale	-	-	-	-	-	-	-	-	-	-
Swindon	-	-	-	-	-	-	-	-	-	-
Coventry	-	-	-	-	-	-	-	-	-	-
Chesterfield	-	-	-	-	-	-	-	-	-	-
Luton			3	0	2	1	1	2	2	1
Exeter			-	-	-	-	-	-	-	-
Carlisle			-	-	-	-	-	-	-	-
Colchester			-	-	-	-	-	-	-	-
Wycombe			-	-	-	-	-	-	-	-
Stevenage			-	-	-	-	-	-	-	-
Cambridge U			3	1	1	1	0	3	0	2
Mansfield			2	0	1	1	0	2	1	0
Accrington			-	-	-	-	-	-	-	-
Grimsby			5	1	1	3	3	2	4	0
Barnet			2	1	1	0	2	0	2	0
Notts County			-	-	-	-	-	-	-	-
Crewe			-	-	-	-	-	-	-	-
Morecambe			-	-	-	-	-	-	-	-
Crawley			-	-	-	-	-	-	-	-
Yeovil			-	-	-	-	-	-	-	-
Cheltenham			1	0	1	0	0	1	1	0
Newport County			2	1	0	1	1	1	1	1
Lincoln										
Forest Green	W	W	6	2	1	3	4	2	5	0

Season	Division	Pos	P	W	D	L	F	A	GD	Pts
2016-17	National Lge	1	46	30	9	7	83	40	+43	99
2015-16	National Lge	13	46	16	13	17	69	68	+1	61
2014-15	Conference	15	46	16	10	20	62	71	-9	58

Over/Under 52%/48% 11th   **Both score** 50%/50% 18th

LUTON

Nickname: The Hatters
Colours: White and black
Ground: Kenilworth Road (10,356)
Tel: 01582-411-622   lutontown.co.uk

Not everyone loves the playoff system and Luton could be forgiven for griping after finishing six points clear of their post-season rivals in League Two but losing their semi-final to Blackpool.

The Hatters were themselves eight points off the automatic trio, so there are no real hard-luck stories but Luton were a solid side for much of the campaign.

Only Portsmouth conceded fewer goals but the Hatters need to find a way to turn some of their 17 draws into victories.

Longest run without win/loss: 5/9
High/low league position: 3/8
Clean sheets: 13 **Yellow cards:** 85 **Red:** 7
Avg attendance: 8,046 **Players used:** 27
Leading scorer: D Hylton 21 (11,17)
Key stat: Luton had a joint-high of 17 League Two draws last season

	2016-17 H	A	Last six seasons at home P	W	D	L	OV	UN	BS	CS
Port Vale	-	-	-	-	-	-	-	-	-	-
Swindon	-	-	-	-	-	-	-	-	-	-
Coventry	-	-	-	-	-	-	-	-	-	-
Chesterfield	-	-	-	-	-	-	-	-	-	-
Luton										
Exeter	D	D	3	1	1	1	2	1	3	0
Carlisle	D	D	3	1	1	1	1	2	2	1
Colchester	L	L	1	0	0	1	0	1	0	0
Wycombe	W	D	3	1	0	2	2	1	2	0
Stevenage	L	L	3	1	0	2	0	3	0	1
Cambridge U	W	W	6	3	2	1	2	4	2	3
Mansfield	D	D	5	2	2	1	2	3	2	3
Accrington	W	W	3	2	0	1	0	3	0	2
Grimsby	L	D	4	0	3	1	1	3	3	1
Barnet	W	W	3	3	0	0	2	1	2	1
Notts County	W	D	2	1	0	1	1	1	1	0
Crewe	D	W	1	0	1	0	0	1	1	0
Morecambe	W	W	3	2	0	1	2	1	2	1
Crawley	W	L	2	1	0	1	1	1	1	0
Yeovil	D	W	2	0	2	0	0	2	2	0
Cheltenham	L	D	2	1	0	1	1	1	1	1
Newport County	W	D	5	3	2	0	3	2	3	2
Lincoln			3	3	0	0	2	1	1	2
Forest Green			3	1	2	0	1	2	3	0

Season	Division	Pos	P	W	D	L	F	A	GD	Pts
2016-17	League 2	4	46	20	17	9	70	43	+27	77
2015-16	League 2	11	46	19	9	18	63	61	+2	66
2014-15	League 2	8	46	19	11	16	54	44	+10	68

Over/Under 43%/57% 20th   **Both score** 63%/37% 3rd

MANSFIELD

Nickname: The Stags
Colours: Yellow and blue
Ground: Field Mill (10,000)
Tel: 01623-482-482   mansfieldtown.net

Those who believe in the old adage that the league table never lies will have to accept Mansfield were only the 12th best team in League Two last season. However, that is simply not the case.

Boss Steve Evans can be biased but he was spot on when he bemoaned minor errors being ruthlessly punished because from a statistical point of view the Stags were excellent, conceding just 132 shots on target which was second-best in the league. Expect a bold run this season.

Longest run without win/loss: 6/9
High/low league position: 7/18
Clean sheets: 16 **Yellow cards:** 86 **Red:** 5
Avg attendance: 3,774 **Players used:** 31
Leading scorer: M Green 10 (7,9)
Key stat: The Stags had the lowest both teams to score record in League Two last season with the bet landing just 19 times

	2016-17 H	A	Last six seasons at home P	W	D	L	OV	UN	BS	CS
Port Vale	-	-	-	-	-	-	-	-	-	-
Swindon	-	-	-	-	-	-	-	-	-	-
Coventry	-	-	-	-	-	-	-	-	-	-
Chesterfield			1	0	1	0	0	1	0	1
Luton	D	D	5	1	3	1	1	4	3	1
Exeter	L	L	4	0	1	3	2	2	2	1
Carlisle	W	L	3	2	1	0	1	2	2	1
Colchester	D	L	1	0	1	0	0	1	0	1
Wycombe	D	W	4	0	3	1	1	3	2	1
Stevenage	L	W	3	2	0	1	2	1	2	1
Cambridge U	D	W	5	1	3	1	2	3	2	3
Mansfield										
Accrington	D	D	4	0	1	3	3	1	3	0
Grimsby	L	L	3	2	0	1	1	2	1	1
Barnet	L	W	2	0	1	1	0	2	1	0
Notts County	W	D	2	2	0	0	2	0	1	1
Crewe	W	D	1	1	0	0	1	0	0	1
Morecambe	L	W	4	2	0	2	2	2	2	1
Crawley	W	W	2	2	0	0	2	0	1	1
Yeovil	W	D	2	1	0	1	0	2	0	1
Cheltenham	D	D	3	0	2	1	0	3	2	0
Newport County	W	W	6	5	0	1	5	1	3	3
Lincoln			2	1	1	0	1	1	1	1
Forest Green			2	2	0	0	0	2	0	2

Season	Division	Pos	P	W	D	L	F	A	GD	Pts
2016-17	League 2	12	46	17	15	14	54	50	+4	66
2015-16	League 2	12	46	17	13	16	61	53	+8	64
2014-15	League 2	21	46	13	9	24	38	62	-24	48

Over/Under 35%/65% 26th   **Both score** 41%/59% 26th

MORECAMBE

Nickname: The Shrimps
Colours: Red and white
Ground: The Globe Arena (6,476)
Tel: 01524-411-797   morecambefc.com

Morecambe are performing minor miracles every time they stay in League Two after surviving on one of the smallest budgets in the division and last season was no different as they defied the tag of relegation favourites to finish 18th.

A fast start – Jim Bentley's boys opened up with four victories in five and that included successes over Blackpool and Portsmouth – was the bedrock of survival but Morecambe finished with one win in 14 that could hint at trouble this term.

Longest run without win/loss: 9/6
High/low league position: 4/20
Clean sheets: 8 **Yellow cards:** 86 **Red:** 7
Avg attendance: 1,703 **Players used:** 28
Lead scorers: K Ellison 8 (3,7) P Mullin 8 (1,7)
Key stat: No team conceded more shots on target than Morecambe's 253 in League Two last season

	2016-17		Last six seasons at home							
	H	A	P	W	D	L	OV	UN	BS	CS
Port Vale			2	0	1	1	1	1	1	1
Swindon			1	0	0	1	0	1	0	0
Coventry			-	-	-	-	-	-	-	-
Chesterfield			2	2	0	0	1	1	1	1
Luton	L	L	3	1	0	2	2	1	1	1
Exeter	L	L	5	1	1	3	2	3	1	1
Carlisle	L	D	3	0	0	3	2	1	1	0
Colchester	D	D	1	0	1	0	0	1	1	0
Wycombe	D	L	5	0	2	3	1	4	3	0
Stevenage	L	W	3	0	1	2	1	2	1	1
Cambridge U	W	W	3	1	0	2	1	2	1	1
Mansfield	L	W	4	1	0	3	3	1	3	0
Accrington	L	W	6	1	2	3	3	3	4	2
Grimsby	W	L	1	1	0	0	0	1	0	1
Barnet	L	D	4	2	0	2	2	2	2	0
Notts County	W	W	2	2	0	0	2	0	2	0
Crewe	D	L	2	0	1	1	1	1	1	1
Morecambe										
Crawley	L	W	3	2	0	1	3	0	2	1
Yeovil	L	W	2	1	0	1	2	0	2	0
Cheltenham	L	L	5	1	2	2	2	3	2	2
Newport County	L	D	4	2	0	2	3	1	3	0
Lincoln			-	-	-	-	-	-	-	-
Forest Green			-	-	-	-	-	-	-	-

Season	Division	Pos	P	W	D	L	F	A	GD	Pts
2016-17	League 2	18	46	14	10	22	53	73	-20	52
2015-16	League 2	21	46	12	10	24	69	91	-22	46
2014-15	League 2	11	46	17	12	17	53	52	+1	63

Over/Under 52%/48% 10th   **Both score** 63%/37% 3rd

NEWPORT COUNTY

Nickname: The Exiles
Colours: Yellow and black
Ground: Rodney Parade (7,850)
Tel: 01633-481896   newport-county.co.uk

Great escapes just don't come any greater than the Houdini act performed by Mike Flynn and his Newport County squad.

Flynn replaced Graham Westley in March with the Exiles seemingly certainties to drop out of League Two.

They were 11 points adrift of safety, rock-bottom of the table and had just suffered a 4-0 home loss to Leyton Orient. However, Newport won seven of their last 12 games and stayed up thanks to Mark O'Brien's last-gasp goal on the final day.

Longest run without win/loss: 11/6
High/low league position: 22/24
Clean sheets: 12 **Yellow cards:** 105 **Red:** 5
Avg attendance: 2,861 **Players used:** 40
Leading scorer: R Bird 6 (5,5) S Rigg 6 (1,6)
Key stat: County conceded 11 goals from penalties last season

	2016-17		Last six seasons at home							
	H	A	P	W	D	L	OV	UN	BS	CS
Port Vale			-	-	-	-	-	-	-	-
Swindon			-	-	-	-	-	-	-	-
Coventry			-	-	-	-	-	-	-	-
Chesterfield			1	1	0	0	1	0	1	0
Luton	D	L	5	3	1	1	2	3	2	2
Exeter	L	W	4	0	3	1	2	2	4	0
Carlisle	W	L	3	3	0	0	1	2	1	2
Colchester	D	D	1	0	1	0	0	1	1	0
Wycombe	L	L	4	2	0	2	0	4	0	2
Stevenage	L	L	3	1	1	1	1	2	1	1
Cambridge U	L	L	5	1	1	3	2	3	3	0
Mansfield	L	L	6	3	1	2	1	5	2	3
Accrington	W	W	4	2	1	1	1	3	2	1
Grimsby	D	L	3	0	3	0	0	3	0	3
Barnet	D	D	2	0	1	1	2	0	1	0
Notts County	W	W	2	1	0	1	1	1	1	0
Crewe	D	W	1	0	1	0	0	1	1	0
Morecambe	D	W	4	0	1	3	2	2	3	0
Crawley	W	L	2	1	0	1	1	1	0	1
Yeovil	W	L	2	1	1	0	0	2	0	2
Cheltenham	D	D	3	0	2	1	1	2	2	0
Newport County										
Lincoln			2	2	0	0	1	1	1	1
Forest Green			2	0	1	1	1	1	0	1

Season	Division	Pos	P	W	D	L	F	A	GD	Pts
2016-17	League 2	22	46	12	12	22	51	73	-22	48
2015-16	League 2	22	46	10	13	23	43	64	-21	43
2014-15	League 2	9	46	18	11	17	51	54	-3	65

Over/Under 54%/46% 7th   **Both score** 61%/39% 5th

NOTTS COUNTY

Nickname: The Magpies
Colours: Black and white
Ground: Meadow Lane (19,052)
Tel: 0115-952-9000   nottscountyfc.co.uk

Kevin Nolan must have picked up a few decent tricks from former manager and close friend Sam Allardyce after an impressive start to life in the dugout.

Notts were awful in the early part of the season but, having replaced John Sheridan in January, Nolan went about improving County with ten wins from 21 matches in charge. Nolan brought in Shola Ameobi which was a terrific signing as County won eight and drew two of the 13 matches he started.

Longest run without win/loss: 13/5
High/low league position: 6/23
Clean sheets: 8 **Yellow cards:** 81 **Red:** 6
Avg attendance: 5,970 **Players used:** 33
Leading scorer: J Stead 14 (2,11)
Key stat: Notts County conceded more goals (76) than relegated Hartlepool (75) last term

	2016-17		Last six seasons at home							
	H	A	P	W	D	L	OV	UN	BS	CS
Port Vale			2	1	0	1	1	1	1	0
Swindon			3	2	0	1	1	2	0	2
Coventry			3	1	2	0	2	1	1	2
Chesterfield			2	1	0	1	0	2	0	1
Luton	D	L	2	1	1	0	1	1	1	1
Exeter	D	W	3	1	1	1	3	0	3	0
Carlisle	L	W	5	3	0	2	3	2	2	2
Colchester	W	L	5	5	0	0	4	1	4	1
Wycombe	L	W	3	0	2	1	0	3	1	1
Stevenage	D	L	5	2	1	2	1	4	2	2
Cambridge U	L	L	2	0	0	2	1	1	1	0
Mansfield	D	L	2	0	1	1	0	2	0	1
Accrington	L	L	2	0	1	1	0	2	1	0
Grimsby	D	L	1	0	1	0	1	0	1	0
Barnet	W	L	2	2	0	0	1	1	1	1
Notts County										
Crewe	D	D	4	2	2	0	2	2	3	1
Morecambe	L	L	2	0	1	1	0	2	2	0
Crawley	W	W	5	4	1	0	3	2	4	1
Yeovil	D	L	5	2	1	2	3	2	3	2
Cheltenham	W	W	1	1	0	0	1	0	1	0
Newport County	L	L	2	1	0	1	2	0	1	0
Lincoln			-	-	-	-	-	-	-	-
Forest Green			-	-	-	-	-	-	-	-

Season	Division	Pos	P	W	D	L	F	A	GD	Pts
2016-17	League 2	16	46	16	8	22	54	76	-22	56
2015-16	League 2	17	46	14	9	23	54	83	-29	51
2014-15	League 1	21	46	12	14	20	45	63	-18	50

Over/Under 63%/37% 2nd   **Both score** 59%/41% 6th

PORT VALE

Nickname: The Valiants
Colours: White and black
Ground: Vale Park (19,052)
Tel: 01782-655-800   port-vale.co.uk

Port Vale's relegation from League One was confirmed on the final day of the season and days later chairman Norman Smurthwaite stepped down from his role, admitting defeat. "In thinking outside the box last summer I have clearly seriously damaged our club," he said.

That "thinking outside the box" saw Bruno Ribeiro appointed manager with a load of foreign signings following the Portuguese boss to Port Vale. They won just four matches in 2017.

Longest run without win/loss: 9/3
High/low league position: 4/22
Clean sheets: 11 **Yellow cards:** 96 **Red:** 3
Avg attendance: 4,813 **Players used:** 37
Leading scorer: A Jones 9 (3,7)
Key stat: No team managed fewer shots in League One than Vale's 377 last season

	2016-17		Last six seasons at home							
	H	A	P	W	D	L	OV	UN	BS	CS
Port Vale										
Swindon	W	L	5	2	0	3	2	3	2	1
Coventry	L	L	4	1	1	2	1	3	2	0
Chesterfield	W	L	4	2	0	2	2	2	2	1
Luton			-	-	-	-	-	-	-	-
Exeter			1	0	0	1	0	1	0	0
Carlisle			1	1	0	0	1	0	1	0
Colchester			3	2	0	1	1	2	1	2
Wycombe			1	1	0	0	1	0	1	0
Stevenage			1	0	1	0	1	0	1	0
Cambridge U			-	-	-	-	-	-	-	-
Mansfield			-	-	-	-	-	-	-	-
Accrington			2	2	0	0	2	0	1	1
Grimsby			-	-	-	-	-	-	-	-
Barnet			2	1	0	1	2	0	1	1
Notts County			2	1	0	1	1	1	1	0
Crewe			4	1	1	2	2	2	2	1
Morecambe			2	0	0	2	1	1	0	0
Crawley			3	1	1	1	3	0	3	0
Yeovil			1	1	0	0	1	0	1	0
Cheltenham			2	1	0	1	2	0	2	0
Newport County			-	-	-	-	-	-	-	-
Lincoln			-	-	-	-	-	-	-	-
Forest Green			-	-	-	-	-	-	-	-

Season	Division	Pos	P	W	D	L	F	A	GD	Pts
2016-17	League 1	21	46	12	13	21	45	70	-25	49
2015-16	League 1	12	46	18	11	17	56	58	-2	65
2014-15	League 1	18	46	15	9	22	55	65	-10	54

Over/Under 50%/50% 10th   **Both score** 48%/52% 19th

STEVENAGE

Nickname: The Boro
Colours: White and red
Ground: Broadhall Way (6,722)
Tel: 01438-223223   stevenagefc.com

Easter saw the end of the Stevenage's unlikely hunt for promotion with the 12-1 ante-post pokes eventually falling apart with the finishing line in sight.

A 1-0 loss to Morecambe on Good Friday was bad enough but 20-goal top scorer Matt Godden got injured and they did not win again for the rest of the term.

It was still a good campaign for Boro with Godden, signed from non-league, a revelation for a side who drew just one home match all season long.

Longest run without win/loss: 6/9
High/low league position: 4/22
Clean sheets: 11 **Yellow cards:** 102 **Red:** 2
Avg attendance: 2,899 **Players used:** 31
Leading scorer: M Godden 20 (7,16)
Key stat: Stevenage drew just once at home in League Two last term

| | 2016-17 | | Last six seasons at home | | | | | | | |
	H	A	P	W	D	L	OV	UN	BS	CS
Port Vale			1	0	1	0	0	1	1	0
Swindon			2	1	0	1	1	1	0	1
Coventry			2	0	0	2	1	1	1	0
Chesterfield			1	0	1	0	1	0	1	0
Luton	W	W	3	1	1	1	2	1	2	1
Exeter	L	D	4	1	1	2	0	4	0	2
Carlisle	L	D	6	2	1	3	2	4	3	2
Colchester	L	L	4	0	1	3	2	2	2	1
Wycombe	W	L	4	2	1	1	3	1	3	1
Stevenage										
Cambridge U	L	D	3	2	0	1	2	1	2	1
Mansfield	L	W	3	1	0	2	1	2	0	1
Accrington	L	W	3	1	1	2	1	2	2	0
Grimsby	W	L	1	1	0	0	0	1	0	1
Barnet	W	W	2	1	1	0	0	2	0	2
Notts County	W	D	5	2	0	3	1	4	0	2
Crewe	L	W	3	1	1	2	1	2	1	1
Morecambe	L	W	3	1	1	1	1	2	2	0
Crawley	W	W	4	2	0	2	2	2	2	1
Yeovil	D	D	4	0	3	1	1	3	1	2
Cheltenham	W	D	2	2	0	0	2	0	2	0
Newport County	W	W	3	3	0	0	3	0	3	0
Lincoln			-	-	-	-	-	-	-	-
Forest Green			-	-	-	-	-	-	-	-

Season	Division	Pos	P	W	D	L	F	A	GD	Pts
2016-17	League 2	10	46	20	7	19	67	63	+4	67
2015-16	League 2	18	46	11	15	20	52	67	-15	48
2014-15	League 2	6	46	20	12	14	62	54	+8	72

Over/Under 57%/43% 5th   **Both score** 52%/48% 13th

SWINDON

Nickname: The Robins
Colours: Red and white
Ground: County Ground (15,728)
Tel: 0871-876-1879   swindontownfc.co.uk

One of the most bizarre appointments of last season was Tim Sherwood's arrival as director of football at Swindon when chairman Lee Power said: "He will head up all aspects – that will be transfers, that will be the way that we play, the formations and the picking of the team."

To most people that sounded like the role of a manager and the confused state surely did not help actual boss Luke Williams in their dismal relegation campaign from League One.

Longest run without win/loss: 6/4
High/low league position: 17/22
Clean sheets: 12 **Yellow cards:** 100 **Red:** 7
Avg attendance: 7,026 **Players used:** 34
Leading scorer: J Obika 6 (1,6)
Key stat: Swindon have kept one clean sheet in their last 18 away matches in all competitions

| | 2016-17 | | Last six seasons at home | | | | | | | |
	H	A	P	W	D	L	OV	UN	BS	CS
Port Vale	W	L	5	4	1	0	3	2	2	3
Swindon										
Coventry	W	W	5	2	3	0	3	2	4	1
Chesterfield	L	L	3	2	0	1	1	2	1	1
Luton			-	-	-	-	-	-	-	-
Exeter			-	-	-	-	-	-	-	-
Carlisle			2	2	0	0	2	0	1	1
Colchester			4	0	2	2	2	2	2	1
Wycombe			-	-	-	-	-	-	-	-
Stevenage			2	2	0	0	1	1	0	2
Cambridge U			-	-	-	-	-	-	-	-
Mansfield			-	-	-	-	-	-	-	-
Accrington			1	1	0	0	0	1	0	1
Grimsby			-	-	-	-	-	-	-	-
Barnet			1	1	0	0	1	0	0	1
Notts County			3	2	1	0	1	2	0	3
Crewe			5	5	0	0	4	1	2	3
Morecambe			1	1	0	0	1	0	0	1
Crawley			4	2	1	1	3	1	2	2
Yeovil			2	1	0	1	1	1	1	0
Cheltenham			1	1	0	0	0	1	0	1
Newport County			-	-	-	-	-	-	-	-
Lincoln			-	-	-	-	-	-	-	-
Forest Green			-	-	-	-	-	-	-	-

Season	Division	Pos	P	W	D	L	F	A	GD	Pts
2016-17	League 1	22	46	11	11	24	44	66	-22	44
2015-16	League 1	16	46	16	11	19	64	71	-7	59
2014-15	League 1	4	46	23	10	13	76	57	+19	79

Over/Under 46%/54% 15th   **Both score** 48%/52% 19th

WYCOMBE

Nickname: The Chairboys
Colours: Sky and navy blue
Ground: Adams Park (10,300)
Tel: 01494-472100   wwfc.com

Getting a big FA Cup away game is what all small teams dream of but for Wycombe they were never able to lift themselves following a heartbreaking last-16 exit at the hands of Tottenham.

Wanderers went to White Hart Lane fifth in League Two and oozing confidence. Twice they led at Spurs before losing a dramatic tie 4-3 and following that match Gareth Ainsworth's side suffered seven defeats in eighth which contributed to a ninth-placed finish.

Longest run without win/loss: 6/12
High/low league position: 5/22
Clean sheets: 15 **Yellow cards:** 102 **Red:** 4
Avg attendance: 3,917 **Players used:** 27
Leading scorer: A Akinfenwa 12 (6,11)
Key stat: Only Portsmouth conceded fewer home goals than Wycombe's tally of 21 in League Two last season

	2016-17 H	A	P	W	D	L	OV	UN	BS	CS
Port Vale			1	0	1	0	0	1	1	0
Swindon	-	-	-	-	-	-	-	-	-	-
Coventry	-	-	-	-	-	-	-	-	-	-
Chesterfield			3	3	0	0	2	1	2	1
Luton	D	L	3	0	2	1	0	3	2	0
Exeter	W	L	6	4	1	1	2	4	3	2
Carlisle	L	L	4	1	2	1	2	2	4	0
Colchester	L	L	2	0	1	1	0	2	0	1
Wycombe										
Stevenage	W	L	4	2	1	1	1	3	1	2
Cambridge U	W	W	3	3	0	0	0	3	0	3
Mansfield	L	D	4	2	0	2	1	3	1	1
Accrington	D	D	5	0	3	2	1	4	2	1
Grimsby	W	W	1	1	0	0	1	0	1	0
Barnet	L	W	3	0	2	1	0	3	1	1
Notts County	L	W	3	0	1	2	2	1	2	0
Crewe	W	L	1	1	0	0	1	0	1	0
Morecambe	W	D	5	2	1	2	1	4	1	2
Crawley	L	L	2	1	0	1	1	1	1	1
Yeovil	D	L	3	0	2	1	1	2	2	1
Cheltenham	D	W	4	1	2	1	3	1	4	0
Newport County	W	W	4	1	0	3	2	2	2	0
Lincoln	-	-	-	-	-	-	-	-	-	-
Forest Green	-	-	-	-	-	-	-	-	-	-

Season	Division	Pos	P	W	D	L	F	A	GD	Pts
2016-17	League 2	9	46	19	12	15	58	53	+5	69
2015-16	League 2	13	46	17	13	16	45	44	+1	64
2014-15	League 2	4	46	23	15	8	67	45	+22	84

Over/Under 37%/63% 25th   **Both score** 48%/52% 19th

YEOVIL

Nickname: The Glovers
Colours: Green and white
Ground: Huish Park (9,566)
Tel: 01935-423-662   ytfc.net

There were periods of last season when it seemed as if the Glovers had changed their name to "Yeovil Town nil" after a miserable time in front of goal.

Yeovil failed to score in 17 matches last season and scored a paltry 49 goals as they stayed up by just four points.

Darren Way's team struggled for wins – they matched relegated Hartlepool's 11 – and things could have been much worse for shot-shy Yeovil had they not scrapped their way to 17 draws.

Longest run without win/loss: 8/8
High/low league position: 7/23
Clean sheets: 12 **Yellow cards:** 70 **Red:** 2
Avg attendance: 3,535 **Players used:** 26
Leading scorer: F Zoko 8 (4,8)
Key stat: The Glovers won only 11 games last season, no team stayed up with fewer victories

	2016-17 H	A	P	W	D	L	OV	UN	BS	CS
Port Vale			1	0	1	0	0	1	1	0
Swindon			2	0	1	1	0	2	1	0
Coventry			2	0	2	0	0	2	1	1
Chesterfield			2	1	0	1	2	0	2	0
Luton	L	D	2	1	0	1	2	0	1	0
Exeter	D	D	3	0	2	1	1	2	1	1
Carlisle	L	L	4	0	1	3	2	2	1	1
Colchester	W	L	4	3	0	1	3	1	3	0
Wycombe	W	W	3	2	0	1	0	3	0	2
Stevenage	D	D	4	0	2	2	3	1	3	0
Cambridge U	D	L	2	0	1	1	1	1	2	0
Mansfield	D	L	2	0	1	1	0	2	0	1
Accrington	D	D	2	1	1	0	0	2	1	1
Grimsby	D	L	1	0	1	0	1	0	0	1
Barnet	L	D	2	0	1	1	1	1	1	0
Notts County	W	D	5	3	2	0	0	5	1	4
Crewe	W	W	3	2	1	0	1	2	1	2
Morecambe	L	W	2	0	0	2	1	1	1	0
Crawley	W	L	4	3	1	0	4	0	3	1
Yeovil										
Cheltenham	W	L	1	1	0	0	1	0	1	0
Newport County	W	L	2	2	0	0	0	2	0	2
Lincoln	-	-	-	-	-	-	-	-	-	-
Forest Green	-	-	-	-	-	-	-	-	-	-

Season	Division	Pos	P	W	D	L	F	A	GD	Pts
2016-17	League 2	20	46	11	17	18	49	64	-15	50
2015-16	League 2	19	46	11	15	20	43	59	-16	48
2014-15	League 1	24	46	10	10	26	36	75	-39	40

Over/Under 41%/59% 23rd   **Both score** 48%/52% 19th

League Two stats 2016-17

Key Points in all tables (except the league table) do not include any deductions imposed by the league. **POS H A** Overall league position, rank from home games only, rank from away games only **Sup** Average match supremacy **GFA** Goals For Average **GAA** Goals Against Average **PGA** Points Gained Average

				Home						Away						
Pos	H	A		P	W	D	L	F	A	W	D	L	F	A	GD	Pts
1	2	3	Portsmouth (P)	46	14	4	5	48	19	12	5	6	31	21	39	87
2	4	1	Plymouth (P)	46	13	3	7	41	29	13	6	4	30	17	25	87
3	1	5	Doncaster (P)	46	14	6	3	40	22	11	4	8	45	33	30	85
4	5	4	Luton	46	11	7	5	38	26	9	10	4	32	17	27	77
5	18	2	Exeter	46	8	5	10	36	29	13	3	7	39	27	19	71
6	9	7	Carlisle	46	10	7	6	34	34	8	10	5	35	34	1	71
7	6	10	Blackpool (P)	46	10	9	4	40	24	8	7	8	29	22	23	70
8	3	18	Colchester	46	14	4	5	43	27	5	8	10	24	30	10	69
9	7	12	Wycombe	46	11	6	6	29	21	8	6	9	29	32	5	69
10	11	8	Stevenage	46	11	1	11	42	33	9	6	8	25	30	4	67
11	13	6	Cambridge Utd	46	9	5	9	30	26	10	4	9	28	24	8	66
12	10	9	Mansfield	46	9	7	7	31	21	8	8	7	23	29	4	66
13	8	15	Accrington	46	10	7	6	36	29	7	7	9	23	27	3	65
14	12	14	Grimsby	46	9	6	8	32	31	8	5	10	27	32	-4	62
15	21	11	Barnet	46	6	9	8	27	31	8	6	9	30	33	-7	57
16	20	16	Notts County	46	7	7	9	25	30	9	1	13	29	46	-22	56
17	15	17	Crewe	46	8	7	8	35	26	6	6	11	23	41	-9	55
18	23	13	Morecambe	46	6	4	13	24	38	8	6	9	29	35	-20	52
19	17	21	Crawley	46	8	7	8	29	30	5	5	13	24	41	-18	51
20	14	23	Yeovil	46	8	8	7	25	24	3	9	11	24	40	-15	50
21	16	22	Cheltenham	46	8	7	8	27	25	4	7	12	22	44	-20	50
22	22	20	Newport County	46	6	8	9	26	35	6	4	13	25	38	-22	48
23	19	24	Hartlepool (R)	46	7	8	8	28	30	4	5	14	26	45	-21	46
24	24	19	Leyton Orient (R)	46	4	1	18	19	40	6	5	12	28	47	-40	36

Best attack

		GF	GFA
1	Doncaster	85	1.85
2	Portsmouth	79	1.72
3	Exeter	75	1.63
4	Plymouth	71	1.54
5	Luton	70	1.52
6	Carlisle	69	1.5
7	Blackpool	69	1.5
8	Colchester	67	1.46
9	Stevenage	67	1.46
10	Accrington	59	1.28
11	Grimsby	59	1.28
12	Wycombe	58	1.26
13	Cambridge U	58	1.26
14	Crewe	58	1.26
15	Barnet	57	1.24
16	Mansfield	54	1.17
17	Notts County	54	1.17
18	Hartlepool	54	1.17
19	Morecambe	53	1.15
20	Crawley	53	1.15
21	Newport Co	51	1.11
22	Yeovil	49	1.07
23	Cheltenham	49	1.07
24	Leyton Orient	47	1.02

Best defence

		GA	GAA
1	Portsmouth	40	0.87
2	Luton	43	0.93
3	Plymouth	46	1
4	Blackpool	46	1
5	Mansfield	50	1.09
6	Cambridge U	50	1.09
7	Wycombe	53	1.15
8	Doncaster	55	1.2
9	Exeter	56	1.22
10	Accrington	56	1.22
11	Colchester	57	1.24
12	Stevenage	63	1.37
13	Grimsby	63	1.37
14	Barnet	64	1.39
15	Yeovil	64	1.39
16	Crewe	67	1.46
17	Carlisle	68	1.48
18	Cheltenham	69	1.5
19	Crawley	71	1.54
20	Morecambe	73	1.59
21	Newport Co	73	1.59
22	Hartlepool	75	1.63
23	Notts County	76	1.65
24	Leyton Orient	87	1.89

Top scorers

		Team	Goals scored	
J Akinde		Barnet	26	▊▊▊▊▊▊▊▊▊▊▊▊▊▊▊▊▊▊▊▊▊▊▊▊▊▊
J Marquis		Doncaster	26	▊▊▊▊▊▊▊▊▊▊▊▊▊▊▊▊▊▊▊▊▊▊▊▊▊▊
D Hylton		Luton	21	▊▊▊▊▊▊▊▊▊▊▊▊▊▊▊▊▊▊▊▊▊
J Collins		Crawley	20	▊▊▊▊▊▊▊▊▊▊▊▊▊▊▊▊▊▊▊▊
M Godden		Stevenage	20	▊▊▊▊▊▊▊▊▊▊▊▊▊▊▊▊▊▊▊▊
O Bogle		Grimsby	19	▊▊▊▊▊▊▊▊▊▊▊▊▊▊▊▊▊▊▊
L Berry		Cambridge U	17	▊▊▊▊▊▊▊▊▊▊▊▊▊▊▊▊▊
D Wheeler		Exeter	17	▊▊▊▊▊▊▊▊▊▊▊▊▊▊▊▊▊

Over 2.5 goals

	H	A	%
Leyton Orient	12	18	65%
Notts County	12	17	63%
Doncaster	11	16	59%
Exeter	13	14	59%
Crewe, Stevenage			57%

Under 2.5 goals

	H	A	%
Mansfield	15	15	65%
Wycombe	16	13	63%
Accrington	12	16	61%
Yeovil	14	13	59%
Luton	11	15	57%

Both to score

	H	A	%
Carlisle	16	16	70%
Doncaster	14	17	67%
Luton	17	12	63%
Morecambe	13	16	63%
Newport Co	14	14	61%

Both not to score

	H	A	%
Mansfield	13	14	59%
Grimsby	12	13	54%
Portsmouth	10	15	54%
Cambridge U, Exeter,			
Wycombe, Yeovil			52%

League Two results 2016-17

	Accrington	Barnet	Blackpool	Cambridge Utd	Carlisle	Cheltenham	Colchester	Crawley Town	Crewe	Doncaster	Exeter	Grimsby	Hartlepool	Leyton Orient	Luton	Mansfield	Morecambe	Newport County	Notts County	Plymouth	Portsmouth	Stevenage	Wycombe	Yeovil
Accrington		1-0	2-1	2-0	1-1	1-1	2-1	1-0	3-2	3-2	1-2	1-1	2-2	5-0	1-4	1-1	2-3	1-3	2-0	0-1	1-0	0-1	2-2	1-1
Barnet	2-0		1-1	0-1	0-1	3-1	1-1	2-2	0-0	1-3	1-4	3-1	3-2	0-0	0-1	0-2	2-2	0-0	3-2	1-0	1-1	1-2	0-2	2-2
Blackpool	0-0	2-2		1-1	2-2	3-0	1-1	0-0	2-2	4-2	2-0	1-3	2-1	3-1	0-2	0-1	3-1	4-1	4-0	0-1	3-1	1-0	0-0	2-2
Cambridge U	2-1	1-1	0-0		2-2	3-1	1-1	2-0	2-1	2-3	1-0	0-1	0-1	3-0	0-3	1-3	1-2	3-2	4-0	0-1	0-1	0-0	1-2	1-0
Carlisle	1-1	1-1	1-4	0-3		1-1	2-0	3-1	0-2	2-1	3-2	1-3	3-2	2-2	0-0	5-2	1-1	2-1	1-2	1-0	0-3	1-1	1-0	2-1
Cheltenham	3-0	1-2	2-2	0-1	1-0		0-3	2-1	2-0	0-1	1-3	2-1	1-0	1-1	1-1	0-0	3-1	1-1	2-3	1-2	1-1	0-0	0-1	2-0
Colchester	1-2	2-1	3-2	2-0	4-1	2-0		2-3	4-0	1-1	2-3	3-2	2-1	0-3	2-1	2-0	2-2	0-0	2-1	0-0	0-4	4-0	1-0	2-0
Crawley Town	0-0	1-1	1-0	1-3	3-3	0-0	1-1		0-3	0-0	1-2	3-0	0-2	2-2	1-3	1-3	1-2	0-2	1-2	1-2	1-0	2-0	1-0	2-0
Crewe	0-1	4-1	1-1	1-2	1-1	0-0	2-0	0-2		2-1	2-0	5-0	3-3	3-0	1-2	1-1	1-2	2-2	1-0	2-2	1-2	2-1	0-1	0-1
Doncaster	2-2	3-2	0-1	1-0	2-2	2-0	1-0	1-1	3-1		1-3	1-0	2-1	3-1	1-1	1-0	1-1	2-0	3-1	0-1	3-1	1-0	2-2	4-1
Exeter	0-2	2-1	2-2	1-2	2-3	3-0	3-0	0-1	4-0	1-3		0-0	1-2	4-0	0-0	2-0	3-1	0-1	0-2	0-2	0-1	1-1	4-2	3-3
Grimsby	2-0	2-2	0-0	2-1	2-2	0-1	1-0	1-1	0-2	1-5	0-3		0-3	1-2	1-1	3-0	2-0	1-0	2-0	1-1	0-1	5-2	1-2	4-2
Hartlepool	2-0	0-2	0-1	0-5	1-1	2-0	1-1	1-1	4-0	2-1	3-1	0-1		1-3	1-1	0-0	3-2	2-2	1-2	1-1	0-2	2-0	0-2	1-1
Leyton Orient	1-0	1-3	1-2	1-1	1-2	0-1	1-3	3-2	0-2	1-4	0-1	0-3	2-1		1-2	1-2	0-1	0-1	2-3	0-2	0-1	3-0	0-2	0-1
Luton	1-0	3-1	1-0	2-0	1-1	2-3	0-1	2-1	1-1	3-1	1-1	1-2	3-0	2-2		1-1	3-1	2-1	2-1	1-1	1-3	0-2	4-1	1-1
Mansfield	4-4	0-1	1-0	0-0	2-0	1-1	0-0	3-1	3-0	1-1	0-1	4-0	2-0	1-1	2-0		0-1	2-1	3-1	0-2	0-1	1-2	1-1	1-0
Morecambe	1-2	0-1	2-1	2-0	0-3	1-2	1-1	2-3	0-0	1-5	0-3	1-0	1-1	1-2	0-2	1-3		0-1	4-1	2-1	2-0	0-2	1-1	1-3
Newport County	1-0	2-2	1-3	1-2	2-0	2-2	1-1	1-0	1-1	0-0	1-4	0-0	3-1	0-4	1-1	2-3	1-1		2-1	1-3	2-3	0-2	0-1	1-0
Notts County	0-2	1-0	1-0	0-1	2-3	2-1	3-1	2-1	1-0	0-1	2-2	2-2	2-1	3-1	0-0	0-0	1-2	0-3		1-2	1-3	1-1	0-2	0-0
Plymouth	0-1	0-2	0-3	2-1	2-0	1-0	2-1	2-0	2-1	2-0	3-0	0-3	1-1	2-3	0-3	2-0	1-0	6-1	0-1		2-2	4-2	3-3	4-1
Portsmouth	2-0	5-1	2-0	2-1	1-1	6-1	2-0	3-0	0-1	1-2	0-1	4-0	0-0	2-1	1-0	4-0	1-1	2-1	1-2	1-1		1-2	4-2	3-1
Stevenage	0-3	1-0	0-2	1-2	1-2	2-1	2-4	2-1	1-2	3-4	0-2	2-0	6-1	4-1	2-1	0-1	0-1	3-1	3-0	1-2	3-0		3-0	2-2
Wycombe	1-1	0-2	0-0	1-0	1-2	3-3	0-2	1-2	5-1	2-1	1-0	2-1	2-0	1-0	1-1	0-1	2-0	2-1	0-1	1-1	1-0	1-0		1-1
Yeovil	1-1	0-1	0-3	1-1	0-2	4-2	2-1	5-0	3-0	0-3	0-0	0-0	1-2	1-1	0-4	0-0	0-1	1-0	2-0	2-1	0-0	1-1	1-0	

Record when first to score

		P	W	D	L	F	A	Sup	PGA	Pts
1	Portsmouth	23	22	1	0	47	6	+1.78	2.9	67
2	Plymouth	25	22	2	1	51	14	+1.48	2.7	68
3	Doncaster	23	20	0	3	48	19	+1.26	2.6	60
4	Stevenage	21	17	3	1	41	16	+1.19	2.6	54
5	Exeter	26	19	2	5	62	28	+1.31	2.3	59
6	Grimsby	24	16	6	2	46	22	+1	2.3	54
7	Cambridge U	23	16	5	2	43	20	+1	2.3	53
8	Morecambe	16	11	3	2	25	11	+0.88	2.3	36
9	Wycombe	25	17	5	3	42	20	+0.88	2.2	56
10	Colchester	25	17	5	3	53	22	+1.24	2.2	56
11	Luton	26	16	8	2	48	20	+1.08	2.2	56
12	Blackpool	24	16	5	3	56	22	+1.42	2.2	53
13	Mansfield	24	15	7	2	43	21	+0.92	2.2	52
14	Accrington	22	14	7	1	44	21	+1.05	2.2	49
15	Notts Co	19	13	2	4	34	23	+0.58	2.2	41
16	Cheltenham	18	11	6	1	33	24	+0.5	2.2	39
17	Barnet	18	11	4	3	29	21	+0.44	2.1	37
18	Leyton Orient	11	7	2	2	23	12	+1	2.1	23
19	Carlisle	23	12	9	2	38	24	+0.61	2	45
20	Crewe	20	13	2	5	43	20	+1.15	2	41
21	Yeovil	20	10	9	1	37	20	+0.85	2	39
22	Crawley	20	11	4	5	34	24	+0.5	1.9	37
23	Newport Co	20	11	3	6	31	24	+0.35	1.8	36
24	Hartlepool	20	7	7	6	32	28	+0.2	1.4	28

Record when keeping a clean sheet

		P	W	D	F	Sup	PGA	Pts
1	Plymouth	15	14	1	23	+1.53	2.9	43
2	Morecambe	8	7	1	9	+1.13	2.8	22
3	Portsmouth	19	16	3	34	+1.79	2.7	51
4	Wycombe	15	13	2	19	+1.27	2.7	41
5	Accrington	13	11	2	21	+1.62	2.7	35
6	Doncaster	12	10	2	14	+1.17	2.7	32
7	Carlisle	7	6	1	10	+1.43	2.7	19
8	Stevenage	11	9	2	19	+1.73	2.6	29
9	Leyton Orient	5	4	1	11	+2.20	2.6	13
10	Grimsby	15	11	4	20	+1.33	2.5	37
11	Luton	13	10	3	22	+1.69	2.5	33
12	Exeter	13	10	3	26	+2	2.5	33
13	Colchester	13	10	3	23	+1.77	2.5	33
14	Cambridge U	13	10	3	22	+1.69	2.5	33
15	Barnet	11	8	3	12	+1.09	2.5	27
16	Hartlepool	8	6	2	14	+1.75	2.5	20
17	Crewe	13	9	4	22	+1.69	2.4	31
18	Mansfield	16	10	6	18	+1.13	2.3	36
19	Crawley	12	8	4	13	+1.08	2.3	28
20	Newport Co	12	8	4	11	+0.92	2.3	28
21	Cheltenham	11	7	4	11	+1	2.3	25
22	Notts Co	8	5	3	6	+0.75	2.3	18
23	Blackpool	15	9	6	20	+1.33	2.2	33
24	Yeovil	12	7	5	14	+1.17	2.2	26

Tranmere look the team to beat but Fylde are value to coast to the Football League

T he National League market is dominated by Tranmere and, with them having gone so close to promotion last season, it's difficult to argue against them being rightful favourites, writes Danny Hayes. Micky Mellon's side recorded an impressive 95 points in 2016-17 but were edged out by an excellent Lincoln side in the title race before underperforming against Forest Green in the playoff final.

The main bulk of that squad remains in place and Rovers look set to make a bold bid. However, they are a little short at 3-1 and if there is one team who could offer a bit of value against them it is AFC Fylde, led by former Tranmere player Dave Challinor.

The Coasters romped to the National League North last year, scoring 109 goals in the process. They have kept hold of Danny Rowe, who scored over 50 goals, along with key players Dan Bradley and Jamie Hardy, and have further strengthened their squad.

Henry Jones is an exciting addition from Bangor, where he could have played European football. Zaine Francis-Angol, Jordan Tunnicliffe and Lewis Montrose all performed well in the National League North and should add depth and more steel.

The Coasters are an upwardly mobile side who look sure to make an impact at this level at some point in the near future.

Also worth an interest are Dagenham & Redbridge, who were defeated by Forest Green in the playoffs. Led by the experienced John Still, they finished 11 points behind Tranmere in the league last season as inconsistency let them down in their first season back in the National League.

Still has been quick to bolster his squad, signing Boreham Wood's Morgan Ferrier and Michael Cheek from Braintree. Those two are sure to add further cutting edge to an already potent front line and further recruits are likely before the transfer window closes.

At over three times the price of Tranmere the Daggers represent value to at least close the gap between the pair and are not going to need a great deal of improvement to mount a serious title challenge.

Eastleigh are prominent in the betting but the Hampshire side went through three managers last year and their owner has vowed to reign in their spending.

They have re-appointed Richard Hill, but it could be a season of consolidation rather than promotion pushing for the Spitfires.

The two clubs relegated into the division will attract plenty of support due to their stature, but both have a bit to prove.

Leyton Orient, who contested the League One playoff final in 2015, have tumbled rapidly under the ownership of Francesco Becchetti. They avoided a winding-up order over the summer and have a new consortium in charge but need to strengthen significantly before the season commences.

Hartlepool, also blighted by financial troubles, dropped out of the Football League for the first time in 96 years. Perhaps their most noteworthy business has been the appointment of Craig Harrison, who led The New Saints to six straight Welsh titles, but both he and the club will need time to acclimatise to this level.

Tranmere lost out to Forest Green in the National League playoff final

Wrexham and Aldershot should again be in the playoff mix while it would be no surprise to see Ebbsfleet make an instant impact.

At the other end of the table, the promoted sides look strong, which should spell trouble for Guiseley. They only survived by a single point last season and their squad looks weaker this time round.

Boreham Wood could also struggle. They have a small squad and have lost some key players, so their survival chances depend on good recruitment.

In the National League North, it is difficult to look beyond Salford. They finished fourth last year and have strengthened significantly during the summer. Their squad looks vastly superior to anything else in the division and even at short odds they look the best bet. Darlington and Harrogate can also go well.

The National League South looks far more open at 6-1 the field, but it could be worth chancing Braintree to make an instant return following April's fifth-tier relegation.

The loss of manager Danny Cowley hit them hard last term, but Braintree have appointed former player Brad Quinton, who has rebuilt squad over the summer. In an open year, they appeal at 14-1.

Recommendations

Dagenham & R to win National League, 10-1
Fylde to win National League, 16-1
Salford to win National League North, 7-2
Braintree to win National League South, 14-1

National League 2016-17

Pos	H	A		P	Home W	D	L	F	A	Away W	D	L	F	A	GD	Pts
1	1	2	Lincoln (P)	46	17	4	2	48	17	13	5	5	35	23	43	99
2	2	1	Tranmere	46	16	3	4	43	19	13	5	5	36	20	40	95
3	4	4	Forest Green (P)	46	12	9	2	46	25	13	2	8	42	31	32	86
4	8	3	Dagenham & Red	46	12	5	6	37	28	14	1	8	42	25	26	84
5	3	8	Aldershot	46	15	5	3	38	13	8	8	7	28	24	29	82
6	6	6	Dover	46	13	5	5	48	28	11	2	10	37	35	22	79
7	7	9	Barrow	46	12	8	3	40	20	8	7	8	32	33	19	75
8	9	7	Gateshead	46	9	9	5	38	23	10	4	9	34	28	21	70
9	17	5	Macclesfield	46	9	3	11	30	29	11	5	7	34	28	7	68
10	10	13	Bromley	46	11	3	9	33	37	7	5	11	26	29	-7	62
11	16	12	Boreham Wood	46	8	7	8	23	21	7	6	10	26	27	1	58
12	5	23	Sutton Utd	46	13	6	4	41	25	2	7	14	20	38	-2	58
13	11	17	Wrexham	46	10	5	8	23	24	5	8	10	24	37	-14	58
14	19	10	Maidstone	46	8	5	10	29	39	8	5	10	30	36	-16	58
15	15	14	Eastleigh	46	8	7	8	28	26	6	8	9	28	37	-7	57
16	21	11	Solihull Moors	46	8	3	12	35	38	7	7	9	27	37	-13	55
17	14	18	Torquay	46	9	5	9	34	28	5	6	12	20	33	-7	53
18	12	20	Woking	46	9	7	7	32	30	5	4	14	34	50	-14	53
19	20	16	Chester	46	8	3	12	37	35	6	7	10	26	36	-8	52
20	13	22	Guiseley	46	9	6	8	32	31	4	6	13	18	36	-17	51
21	18	19	York (R)	46	7	8	8	33	31	4	9	10	22	39	-15	50
22	23	15	Braintree (R)	46	6	4	13	23	36	7	5	11	28	40	-25	48
23	22	24	Southport (R)	46	7	5	11	32	41	3	4	16	20	56	-45	39
24	24	21	North Ferriby (R)	46	6	2	15	17	40	6	1	16	15	42	-50	39

National League results

	Aldershot	Barrow	Boreham W	Braintree	Bromley	Chester	Dag & Red	Dover	Eastleigh	Forest Green	Gateshead	Guiseley	Lincoln	Macclesfield	Maidstone	North Ferriby	Solihull Moors	Southport	Sutton Utd	Torquay	Tranmere	Woking	Wrexham	York
Aldershot		2-2	2-0	2-0	4-0	0-0	3-1	1-0	0-1	0-4	3-0	1-0	0-0	1-2	1-0	2-0	2-0	2-1	2-0	1-1	3-1	4-0	2-0	0-0
Barrow	1-0		1-1	2-1	1-1	3-2	2-1	2-3	4-0	2-3	0-0	3-0	3-0	1-1	3-0	3-1	2-1	0-1	0-0	0-0	2-1	2-2	1-1	2-0
Boreham Wood	1-1	1-1		0-1	0-0	1-1	1-3	5-0	0-1	1-0	0-4	0-0	2-0	2-4	0-1	1-0	0-0	2-0	1-0	2-0	0-1	2-1	0-1	1-1
Braintree	2-0	0-2	1-2		2-2	1-2	3-2	1-2	1-1	0-1	1-4	2-0	0-4	1-3	0-0	1-0	0-1	2-0	1-0	1-3	0-1	1-3	1-2	1-1
Bromley	2-2	4-1	1-0	0-5		0-1	1-3	0-2	0-5	1-5	3-2	1-2	1-0	1-1	1-0	1-0	1-0	2-2	2-1	4-3	3-0			
Chester	2-0	1-2	0-2	1-0	1-1		3-0	5-0	0-1	1-2	1-2	2-0	2-5	2-3	1-3	3-0	0-3	2-2	4-0	1-0	2-3	2-3	1-1	0-2
Dag & Red	1-0	1-4	0-2	3-0	2-1	3-2		2-0	4-0	2-1	0-5	1-2	1-0	1-1	0-2	2-0	4-4	3-0	2-2	0-1	0-0	1-1	3-0	1-0
Dover	1-2	3-1	1-4	6-1	1-0	3-1	1-2		3-0	4-3	2-0	2-0	2-0	2-2	1-1	2-0	0-0	3-0	3-1	1-2	1-4	3-1	1-1	2-2
Eastleigh	1-1	2-0	2-2	0-2	2-1	0-3	0-1	2-4		1-1	1-1	2-1	0-1	0-1	3-0	2-0	2-0	1-1	2-1	3-0	0-2	0-1	1-1	1-1
Forest Green	2-1	0-0	2-0	1-1	1-0	2-0	1-1	1-1	1-1		1-0	3-0	2-3	3-0	2-2	0-1	2-1	5-1	1-1	5-5	2-2	4-3	3-0	2-1
Gateshead	1-1	4-1	1-1	1-1	0-2	3-0	1-0	4-2	2-2	3-1		1-1	1-2	1-1	1-2	0-1	0-0	3-0	1-0	0-0	0-1	2-1	2-2	6-1
Guiseley	1-0	1-0	3-1	0-0	1-4	1-1	0-2	0-4	1-1	0-1	1-1		2-1	1-2	2-1	1-2	1-1	2-1	2-1	2-0	1-2	1-1	2-3	6-1
Lincoln	3-3	1-2	2-0	3-0	1-0	1-0	2-0	2-0	0-0	3-1	3-0	3-1		2-1	2-0	6-1	0-0	4-0	1-3	2-1	2-1	3-2	1-0	1-1
Macclesfield	0-2	0-1	0-2	2-0	1-2	0-0	1-4	2-1	0-1	0-1	1-1	1-2	1-2		3-0	1-0	1-3	3-1	0-0	2-0	4-2	3-1	3-0	1-3
Maidstone	0-2	2-1	1-0	2-1	0-2	4-2	0-1	1-4	2-1	1-4	0-2	1-1	0-0	2-1		1-2	2-4	4-2	1-1	2-1	0-1	0-3	2-2	1-1
North Ferriby	0-3	0-1	2-4	0-0	1-2	0-1	0-4	1-2	2-1	0-3	1-0	3-2	0-1	0-2	0-2		1-4	0-1	2-1	1-0	1-4	2-1	0-0	0-1
Solihull Moors	0-2	2-4	1-1	3-3	1-0	3-2	2-5	2-3	2-0	0-1	0-2	3-2	0-1	2-3	2-0	2-0		4-0	3-0	0-1	0-3	2-2	0-1	1-2
Southport	1-1	1-4	1-0	4-5	1-2	0-1	1-4	0-1	4-3	2-0	0-3	0-1	1-1	1-2	3-2	2-4	0-0		1-1	1-2	1-1	2-1	3-2	2-0
Sutton Utd	2-0	0-0	1-0	1-2	2-0	5-2	1-0	0-6	1-1	1-2	3-0	1-0	1-1	2-0	2-2	5-1	1-3	2-2		2-0	1-0	4-1	1-0	2-2
Torquay	0-0	1-1	0-1	3-1	1-0	0-1	1-0	2-1	2-3	4-3	3-1	1-2	1-2	1-1	2-3	2-0	3-0	1-2	2-3		0-0	1-2	1-1	2-0
Tranmere	2-2	2-0	2-1	1-0	2-2	2-2	0-2	1-0	2-1	0-1	1-1	1-0	2-1	1-1	9-0	4-1	3-2	2-1		3-1		2-0		
Woking	1-2	1-1	0-0	2-3	2-1	3-1	1-3	1-3	3-3	0-1	3-0	0-0	1-3	1-0	2-4	1-1	2-1	0-0	2-1	3-1	0-3		2-0	1-1
Wrexham	0-2	2-2	2-1	0-1	2-1	0-0	0-1	0-0	0-0	3-1	0-2	3-1	1-2	0-3	1-3	1-0	1-0	1-0	1-0	1-1	0-1	2-1		2-1
York	0-1	2-1	1-1	3-0	0-2	1-1	0-2	0-1	3-1	2-2	1-3	1-1	1-4	1-0	1-1	0-1	4-0	5-3	2-2	0-0	0-0	4-1	1-3	

Promoted FA Cup quarter-finalists Lincoln had plenty of reason to celebrate last term

National League North 2016-17

	H	A		P	Home					Away					GD	Pts
					W	D	L	F	A	W	D	L	F	A		
1	3	1	AFC Fylde (P)	42	13	7	1	58	26	13	3	5	51	34	49	88
2	1	5	Kidderminster	42	16	2	3	43	15	9	5	7	33	26	35	82
3	7	3	Halifax (P)	42	12	5	4	37	16	12	3	6	44	27	38	80
4	4	7	Salford City	42	13	7	1	45	17	9	4	8	34	27	35	77
5	5	6	Darlington*	42	14	2	5	50	29	8	8	5	39	38	22	76
6	6	8	Chorley	42	13	4	4	34	20	7	10	4	26	21	19	74
7	11	2	Brackley	42	9	6	6	27	21	11	7	3	39	22	23	73
8	8	4	Stockport	42	9	8	4	34	26	10	8	3	25	15	18	73
9	2	15	Tamworth	42	15	2	4	43	28	6	4	11	30	39	6	69
10	10	9	Gloucester**	42	10	3	8	41	30	8	7	6	28	31	8	64
11	9	14	Harrogate Town	42	10	4	7	44	38	6	7	8	27	25	8	59
12	12	12	Nuneaton	42	7	8	6	33	29	7	5	9	34	40	-2	55
13	15	10	FC United	42	6	8	7	35	35	8	4	9	34	33	1	54
14	17	11	Curzon Ashton	42	6	6	9	31	36	8	4	9	32	36	-9	52
15	16	16	Boston Utd	42	7	4	10	29	33	5	7	9	25	39	-18	47
16	20	13	Bradford Park Av	42	4	5	12	22	38	8	2	11	24	36	-28	43
17	13	19	Telford	42	8	5	8	19	25	2	7	12	19	32	-19	42
18	14	18	Alfreton	42	7	7	7	30	34	4	2	15	32	61	-33	42
19	18	22	Gainsborough	42	5	8	8	27	31	3	4	14	24	53	-33	36
20	19	17	Worcester (R)	42	4	8	9	30	30	3	6	12	14	33	-19	35
21	21	20	Stalybridge (R)	42	5	1	15	23	48	3	4	14	17	41	-49	29
22	22	21	Altrincham (R)	42	1	5	15	19	47	3	4	14	21	45	-52	21

*Darlington ineligible for playoffs due to ground size restrictions; **Gloucester transferred to National League South

National League North results

	AFC Fylde	Alfreton	Altrincham	Boston Utd	Brackley	Bradford PA	Chorley	Curzon Ashton	Darlington	FC United	Gainsborough	Gloucester	Halifax	Harrogate	Kidderminster	Nuneaton	Salford City	Stalybridge	Stockport	Tamworth	Telford	Worcester
AFC Fylde		2-0	4-1	9-2	1-1	1-1	0-2	4-1	4-1	3-1	3-1	2-2	3-2	2-1	2-2	2-1	3-3	5-0	0-0	3-1	1-4	4-2
Alfreton Town	3-5		3-2	1-0	0-0	0-1	2-2	0-1	2-1	4-0	0-2	1-0	1-0	3-3	3-3	1-1	0-2	1-1	2-5	3-2	0-0	
Altrincham	0-6	1-1		0-1	1-3	2-3	2-2	2-4	2-2	0-3	2-3	0-1	0-1	0-0	1-4	1-3	0-2	0-0	2-3	1-2	0-2	
Boston Utd	0-3	3-2	0-1		2-3	1-0	3-1	3-1	1-2	2-3	1-1	2-2	1-4	0-3	1-1	1-3	2-0	0-1	0-2	3-0	3-0	0-0
Brackley Town	1-3	2-3	1-1	0-0		2-0	0-1	2-0	2-2	1-0	0-0	3-0	0-0	2-1	2-0	2-1	0-1	5-2	0-3	0-0	2-1	0-2
Bradford PA	1-4	1-0	2-1	0-2	2-1		0-3	4-4	1-2	0-0	5-1	0-1	1-3	2-3	1-3	1-1	0-2	0-1	0-2	0-0	1-1	0-3
Chorley	1-3	2-1	2-0	2-0	1-1	3-0		0-3	1-1	3-3	4-0	4-1	0-2	1-0	2-1	1-0	2-1	1-0	0-1	1-1	2-1	1-0
Curzon	3-2	5-0	2-3	4-2	0-0	1-2	1-1		1-2	1-2	1-2	0-0	4-2	1-0	1-6	2-1	0-2	0-0	1-2	1-5	1-1	1-1
Darlington	1-1	3-4	3-1	4-1	1-0	1-0	2-0	1-3		4-2	5-2	2-0	3-2	2-3	0-1	1-2	2-2	4-1	2-1	3-2	1-0	5-1
FC United	2-3	4-3	1-1	1-1	1-2	2-3	3-3	0-0	2-3		5-1	2-4	0-3	2-2	1-0	3-0	0-3	2-2	2-0	1-0	0-0	1-1
Gainsborough	1-2	0-2	2-0	1-2	1-1	1-1	0-2	0-1	3-3	1-2		1-1	3-2	0-2	1-1	2-2	1-0	2-2	0-1	3-2	3-1	1-1
Gloucester City	1-5	4-0	5-0	3-1	1-3	1-0	2-2	0-2	1-2	2-3	4-1		0-2	1-1	1-2	2-2	3-2	2-1	0-1	2-0	3-0	3-0
Halifax Town	0-1	1-0	2-2	0-0	1-3	4-0	2-1	3-0	2-2	3-1	2-1	0-1		0-1	2-0	2-0	4-2	1-0	0-4	4-0	1-1	3-0
Harrogate Town	3-3	6-3	2-2	2-0	1-2	1-0	2-1	2-2	1-4	3-1	1-3	3-1	0-3		0-2	3-1	3-3	3-1	0-1	3-4	2-1	3-0
Kidderminster	3-3	3-0	1-0	1-0	1-2	3-1	0-0	3-2	2-1	0-2	3-0	3-0	1-2	1-0		4-0	1-0	2-1	2-0	6-0	1-0	2-1
Nuneaton	4-1	4-1	4-1	2-2	2-2	1-2	1-1	0-1	1-1	1-4	2-1	1-1	2-3	2-1	0-2		0-1	2-1	1-1	1-0	1-1	1-1
Salford City	5-0	4-1	2-1	3-3	1-1	1-0	1-1	1-0	5-1	1-0	3-2	1-1	2-2	0-0	3-0	4-0		1-0	1-1	1-2	2-1	3-0
Stalybridge	2-1	2-3	0-2	3-3	0-1	4-3	0-1	1-2	0-1	2-4	3-2	1-3	1-0	2-4	0-4				1-3	0-4	0-2	0-1
Stockport	1-2	4-3	3-0	1-2	1-2	4-1	2-0	0-0	3-1	3-3	2-1	1-1	1-1	0-1	1-1	2-1	3-1			2-1	1-1	1-0
Tamworth	1-0	4-1	2-1	1-0	2-1	5-1	1-0	3-2	2-1	1-1	1-0	3-1	2-6	3-2	3-4	1-2	2-0	2-1	2-2		2-1	1-0
Telford Utd	0-1	1-1	1-0	1-2	0-6	1-3	0-0	3-1	2-0	1-0	1-1	0-2	1-2	0-0	1-0	2-4	0-2	2-0	0-0	1-0		1-0
Worcester City	1-2	5-3	3-0	0-2	1-2	0-1	0-1	1-1	2-2	0-0	2-2	2-3	1-2	2-2	0-0	2-3	1-2	4-0	0-0	1-1	2-1	

National League South 2016-17

Pos	H	A		P	W	D	L	F	A	W	D	L	F	A	GD	Pts
					Home					Away						
1	2	1	Maidenhead (P)	42	16	4	1	53	11	14	4	3	40	18	64	98
2	1	2	Ebbsfleet (P)	42	17	3	1	62	15	12	6	3	34	15	66	96
3	3	6	Dartford	42	16	3	2	49	20	9	6	6	34	25	38	84
4	4	5	Chelmsford	42	14	6	1	54	23	9	7	5	35	24	42	82
5	6	7	Poole Town*	42	12	6	3	38	19	8	5	8	25	30	14	71
6	5	8	Hungerford Town*	42	12	6	3	37	17	7	7	7	30	32	18	70
7	11	4	Hampton & R	42	9	5	7	36	28	10	7	4	45	28	25	69
8	15	3	Wealdstone	42	7	7	7	30	31	11	5	5	32	27	4	66
9	9	9	Bath City	42	10	5	6	41	24	8	3	10	30	28	19	62
10	8	14	St Albans	42	11	4	6	43	31	5	7	9	29	35	6	59
11	7	16	Eastbourne	42	12	4	5	51	30	4	6	11	31	40	12	58
12	10	12	Hemel	42	9	6	6	34	36	6	6	9	40	47	-9	57
13	12	10	East Thurrock	42	7	9	5	37	25	7	5	9	36	40	8	56
14	14	13	Oxford City	42	8	5	8	21	32	7	2	12	27	41	-25	52
15	19	11	Weston-s-Mare	42	6	4	11	33	35	8	2	11	30	34	-6	48
16	13	20	Welling	42	9	2	10	36	26	3	5	13	28	43	-5	43
17	18	15	Whitehawk	42	6	5	10	24	32	6	2	13	27	40	-21	43
18	17	17	Concord Rangers	42	6	7	8	28	37	4	5	12	29	38	-18	42
19	16	21	Truro City	42	7	5	9	29	41	4	2	15	24	58	-46	40
20	20	19	Gosport Boro (R)	42	6	3	12	23	47	3	6	12	22	54	-56	36
21	22	18	Bishop's Stort (R)	42	3	1	17	14	51	5	2	14	15	53	-75	27
22	21	22	Margate (R)	42	6	2	13	17	41	1	2	18	9	40	-55	25

*Hungerford Town & Poole Town ineligible for playoffs due to ground size restrictions

National League South results

	Bath City	Bishop's St.	Chelmsford	Concord R	Dartford	East Thurrock	Eastbourne	Ebbsfleet	Gosport Boro	Hampton & R	Hemel	Hungerford	Maidenhead	Margate	Oxford City	Poole Town	St Albans	Truro City	Wealdstone	Welling	Weston-s-M	Whitehawk
Bath City		2-0	2-2	2-2	0-1	2-1	1-1	0-1	4-0	1-1	6-0	1-1	1-5	2-0	1-3	3-0	3-0	4-0	1-2	2-1	1-2	2-1
Bishop's Stort.	0-1		1-3	1-0	0-3	0-4	1-4	0-3	0-2	0-1	0-4	1-2	0-2	0-2	0-2	1-4	1-5	0-4	0-3	2-2	2-1	0-3
Chelmsford	3-1	4-0		4-3	1-1	2-2	5-1	2-1	5-1	2-2	4-4	3-3	0-1	2-0	2-0	3-0	1-1	2-0	4-1	3-1	1-0	1-0
Concord R	0-5	0-0	2-2		1-1	1-1	3-1	0-1	2-2	2-1	2-0	2-4	0-1	0-0	3-3	3-2	3-2	0-2	0-1	0-5	1-3	3-0
Dartford	2-0	4-0	0-1	2-1		6-1	4-3	2-1	0-0	3-1	2-0	2-0	0-0	4-0	1-0	2-1	0-2	5-3	2-2	2-1	3-2	3-1
East Thurrock	2-0	2-2	1-2	1-1	1-1		1-1	1-1	5-1	2-1	2-3	0-1	0-0	1-0	2-1	1-2	1-1	5-1	1-1	1-1	5-1	2-3
Eastbourne	1-2	1-0	1-5	2-1	2-3	4-0		0-0	2-0	2-2	3-0	2-2	1-2	2-1	4-0	0-0	3-2	2-0	5-1	7-3	3-4	4-2
Ebbsfleet	1-0	8-0	2-0	4-0	1-0	6-1	4-1		2-0	1-1	2-2	1-0	2-3	4-0	1-0	4-0	3-1	4-2	4-1	5-1	2-1	1-1
Gosport Bor	1-0	0-1	0-6	2-5	0-4	1-5	3-1	1-0		1-1	0-6	1-4	0-2	1-0	0-0	0-2	4-0	3-1	1-3	1-1	1-1	2-3
Hampton & R	2-1	4-1	0-2	1-0	4-1	1-2	1-1	2-2			3-3	2-0	2-3	1-0	0-2	4-2	2-2	1-1	3-1	0-2	0-2	0-2
Hemel	3-3	3-2	2-2	2-1	2-2	1-1	0-4	1-1	1-2	1-0		2-0	2-1	3-2	2-0	2-4	2-2	0-1	1-3	2-0	0-5	2-0
Hungerford T	2-2	2-0	1-1	2-1	2-0	3-0	0-2	1-1	3-3	1-3	3-0		1-1	1-0	2-0	0-1	0-0	5-0	2-0	1-0	2-1	3-1
Maidenhead	2-1	6-0	1-0	2-0	5-0	2-1	2-1	1-2	3-0	0-0	5-0	2-2		2-0	6-1	1-1	1-1	2-0	2-0	3-0	3-0	2-1
Margate	1-0	0-3	0-2	1-5	0-2	2-1	1-1	0-1	2-0	2-4	2-1	1-1	0-3		0-5	0-2	0-2	2-1	0-1	0-3	3-1	0-2
Oxford City	1-1	3-1	2-0	2-2	1-1	0-1	1-0	1-3	1-2	0-5	1-0	0-6	1-3	1-0		0-1	2-1	1-1	0-3	2-1	0-0	1-0
Poole Town	1-0	1-0	4-0	2-1	2-3	1-1	1-1	0-2	7-0	3-3	1-1	1-1	1-0	1-0	1-3		1-0	2-0	1-1	2-1	2-0	3-1
St Albans	1-4	0-1	2-1	2-0	1-0	2-2	1-0	0-3	2-1	2-4	2-2	5-0	2-2	1-1	2-4	4-0		5-0	0-3	3-2	3-0	3-1
Truro City	1-3	1-2	2-2	1-2	0-5	0-6	2-2	1-1	0-0	2-0	0-3	2-0	3-2	0-0	3-2				1-2	1-1	1-2	4-2
Wealdstone	0-1	5-0	1-1	1-1	0-4	1-0	1-4	2-4	2-1	2-4	1-1	3-0	2-1	2-1	1-1	2-2	2-2	1-2		0-1	1-0	0-1
Welling	3-1	1-2	0-2	3-1	0-0	2-0	3-1	1-2	4-0	1-2	2-3	0-0	1-2	5-1	4-0	2-1	0-1	3-2	0-1		0-2	1-2
Weston-s-Mare	1-2	5-0	0-0	1-2	1-2	1-3	2-0	0-2	1-1	1-3	3-5	0-1	1-3	3-1	3-0	0-0	0-3	4-2	1-2	2-2		3-1
Whitehawk	0-2	1-0	0-1	0-0	1-0	2-3	1-1	0-3	4-4	1-3	1-4	1-2	1-2	2-0	3-0	2-0	1-1	2-4	0-0	1-0	0-2	

Impossible to look past the Bhoys as they bid to retain their Premiership crown

T he annual coronation of Celtic is ten months away – possibly sooner based on the speed with which they clinched the crown last season – but the battle for second spot looks an absorbing one, writes Steve Davies. This is the 11th straight season in which Celtic will go off odds-on shots and, after romping in by 30 points last term, few doubt that Brendan Rodgers' powerhouses will dot up once again.

The return of Rangers to the top flight last term added a degree of spice, and maybe even a few doubts at Parkhead. But the Gers were put in their place early on, never looked a threat and couldn't even get second.

A tame end to the campaign under Pedro Caixinha followed by a dire start to 2017-18 – they lost to Luxembourg's Progres in the Europa League – suggests Rangers still have plenty to do to be primary challengers.

For all that, they remain favourites in the 'without Celtic' market. But Aberdeen, who have been runners-up in each of the past four seasons, seem a far better alternative.

Derek McInnes remains at the helm, the exodus of players hasn't happened, one or two newcomers have arrived and there are several more big signings being lined up. The Dons have consistency on their side and that certainly puts them head and shoulders above Hearts, say, who could be anything.

The Ian Cathro revolution has backfired spectacularly and it's blind faith taking a punt on a replacement like Kyle Lafferty.

Hibs are all talk but, as Rangers found out, a returning big gun shouldn't necessarily be able to shoot for second spot as a divine right.

Hibernian may actually be a better value punt to finish in the bottom six while it does seem that the time is up for arch-survivors Hamilton, who look set for bottom spot.

Dundee United head the Championship betting but finances are tight and they only managed third place last season.

Falkirk, second for a second successive season, look a better alternative while Morton stand out as an each-way proposition. Jim Duffy was so impressive in guiding the Ton to fourth that he was named manager of the year and there is much to build on.

In League One, the consensus is that Raith, a team good enough to draw three times with Hibs last season, should bounce straight back, but they look on the short side in a pretty competitive section. I'm more persuaded by the 25-1 for Arbroath. Under promotion addict Dick Campbell, the Lichties won League Two in style and should be confident.

Peterhead are the jollies in League Two but their price could still be worth tucking into. Boss Jim McInally has overseen a summer overhaul after relegation and has been looking abroad to bolster his squad further.

In a division of mediocrity, Stirling could represent an each-way nibble given the improvements made under Dave Mackay.

Recommended bets

Aberdeen w/o Celtic, 13-10
Hibernian to finish in the bottom six
Hamilton to finish bottom, 10-3
Falkirk to win the Championship, 5-1
Morton e-w to win the Championship, 16-1
Arbroath e-w to win League One, 20-1
Peterhead to win League Two, 9-4
Stirling e-w to win League Two, 14-1

Celtic midfield man Callum McGregor celebrates during the Old Firm derby

ABERDEEN

Nickname: The Dons
Colours: Red
Ground: Pittodrie (20,866)
Tel: 01224 650-400   afc.co.uk

	2016-17		Last six seasons at home							
	H	A	P	W	D	L	OV	UN	BS	CS
Celtic	L L	L L	11	3	1	7	5	6	6	0
Aberdeen										
Rangers	W L	L W	3	1	0	2	3	0	2	0
St Johnstone	D L	D W	12	3	6	3	1	11	3	7
Hearts	D W	W W	9	3	4	2	1	8	2	6
Partick	W W	W W	6	4	2	0	2	4	1	5
Ross County	W W	L	9	6	1	2	5	4	1	6
Kilmarnock	W	W W	10	7	2	1	5	5	5	4
Motherwell	W W	W	11	5	3	3	5	6	6	3
Dundee	W	W W	6	5	1	0	2	4	1	5
Hamilton	W	L L	4	4	0	0	3	1	1	3
Hibernian			5	3	1	1	2	3	2	3

Season	Division	Pos	P	W	D	L	F	A	GD	Pts
2016-17	Premiership	2	38	24	4	10	74	35	+39	76
2015-16	Premiership	2	38	22	5	11	62	48	+14	71
2014-15	Premiership	2	38	23	6	9	57	33	+24	75

Over/Under 61%/39% 2nd   **Both score** 47%/53% 9th

Consistently second-best in Scotland after three straight runners-up spots, the market suggested third was their limit, yet Derek McInnes' men, 4-5 without the Old Firm, duly split the big two.

Still couldn't quite make a European breakthrough – undone by Maribor in the Europa League third qualifying round – they did reach both domestic cup finals.

McInnes' stock continues to rise and he surprised (and delighted) fans when turning down the Sunderland job in June.

Longest run without win/loss: 2/5
High/low league position: 2/4
Clean sheets: 14 **Yellow cards:** 61 **Red:** 4
Avg attendance: 12,562 **Players used:** 21
Leading scorer: A Rooney 12 (3,9)
Key stat: Aberdeen signed off without a draw in 22 league games and have drawn just one league away game since November 2015

Top league scorers	P	G		Y	R
A Rooney	32 (6)	12		-	-
N McGinn	30 (6)	10		1	-
J Hayes	32	9		6	-
R Christie	7 (6)	6		-	-
A Considine	36	6		7	-
J Stockley	8 (19)	5		3	2
K McLean	37 (1)	4		3	-
A O'Connor	25 (7)	3		2	-
P Pawlett	6 (12)	3		3	-
A Taylor	28 (3)	3		4	-
S Wright	1 (4)	3		-	-

CELTIC

Nickname: The Bhoys
Colours: Green and white
Ground: Celtic Park (60,411)
Tel: 0871-226-1888   celticfc.net

	2016-17		Last six seasons at home							
	H	A	P	W	D	L	OV	UN	BS	CS
Celtic										
Aberdeen	W W	W W	11	11	0	0	9	2	8	3
Rangers	W D	W W	4	3	1	0	2	2	2	2
St Johnstone	W W	W W	12	9	1	2	6	6	5	5
Hearts	W W	W W	9	8	1	0	4	5	2	7
Partick	W D	W W	6	5	1	0	0	6	1	5
Ross County	W	W D	8	5	3	0	2	6	3	5
Kilmarnock	W W	W	9	7	1	1	6	3	5	3
Motherwell	W W	W	11	9	1	1	5	6	2	9
Dundee	W	W W	7	6	1	0	5	2	2	5
Hamilton	W W	W	5	4	0	1	2	3	1	3
Hibernian			4	2	2	0	2	2	1	3

Season	Division	Pos	P	W	D	L	F	A	GD	Pts
2016-17	Premiership	1	38	34	4	0	106	25	+81	106
2015-16	Premiership	1	38	26	8	4	93	31	+62	86
2014-15	Premiership	1	38	29	5	4	84	17	+67	92

Over/Under 63%/37% 1st   **Both score** 50%/50% 6th

The low was obvious – losing 1-0 at Lincoln Red Imps in a Champions League qualifier. They would go on to fail to win any of six Champions League group ties.

But the rest was all highs in Brendan Rodgers' debut season. Favourites for an 11th-straight season, league glory was never in doubt – they won it with eight games in hand, collecting 106 points.

The Bhoys twice thrashed Rangers 5-1, won the domestic treble and claimed an unbeaten Premiership campaign.

Longest run without win/loss: 1/38
High/low league position: 1/1
Clean sheets: 19 **Yellow cards:** 56 **Red:** 2
Avg attendance: 54,477 **Players used:** 32
Leading scorer: S Sinclair 21 (7,18)
Key stat: The top scorers in Scotland with 106 goals, Celtic haven't failed to score in a league game since April 2016

Top league scorers	P	G		Y	R
S Sinclair	30 (5)	21		2	-
M Dembele	20 (9)	17		3	-
S Armstrong	25 (6)	15		1	-
L Griffiths	15 (8)	12		4	-
P Roberts	20 (12)	9		1	-
T Rogic	15 (7)	7		1	-
J Forrest	23 (5)	6		2	-
C McGregor	20 (11)	6		2	1
D Boyata	17	5		3	-

Eight players scored one goal

DUNDEE

Nickname: The Dark Blues
Colours: Blue and white
Ground: Dens Park (11,506)
Tel: 01382-889966　　　dundeefc.co.uk

Last season was a topsy-turvy one at Dens Park. Dundee were bottom at the end of October after winning just one of their first 11 games, yet were sixth by February.

The roller-coaster continued with seven straight defeats, which cost Paul Hartley his job and left caretaker Neil McCann five games to save a club he twice played for. McCann duly pulled it off and was rewarded with the job on a full-time basis, although a last-day 4-0 hammering at Hamilton hints at problems ahead.

Longest run without win/loss: 10/4
High/low league position: 6/12
Clean sheets: 6 **Yellow cards:** 67 **Red:** 3
Avg attendance: 6,460 **Players used:** 25
Leading scorer: M Haber 8 (2,7)
Key stat: Dundee failed to score in a Premiership-high 16 games last term and did not find the net in four of their last six at home

| | 2016-17 | | Last six seasons at home | | | | | | | |
	H	A	P	W	D	L	OV	UN	BS	CS
Celtic	L L	L	6	0	2	4	2	4	3	1
Aberdeen	L L	L	8	0	3	5	4	4	6	0
Rangers	L W	L	2	1	0	1	2	0	2	0
St Johnstone	W	L L	7	3	2	2	4	3	4	2
Hearts	W	L L	5	3	0	2	2	3	2	2
Partick	L L	L	7	1	2	4	1	6	2	1
Ross County	D D	W L	9	1	5	3	3	6	6	1
Kilmarnock	D D	L W	8	1	5	2	2	6	6	2
Motherwell	W D W W		6	3	1	2	5	1	4	1
Dundee										
Hamilton	D L	W L	10	3	4	3	2	8	3	4
Hibernian			1	1	0	0	1	0	1	0

Season	Division	Pos	P	W	D	L	F	A	GD	Pts
2016-17	Premiership	10	38	10	7	21	38	62	-24	37
2015-16	Premiership	8	38	11	15	12	53	57	-4	48
2014-15	Premiership	6	38	11	12	15	46	57	-11	45

Over/Under 47%/53% 8th　　**Both score** 47%/53% 9th

All league scorers	P	G		Y	R
M Haber	27	8		2	-
M O'Hara	26 (2)	6		5	1
D O'Dea	35	4		1-	-
F El-Bakhtaoui	15 (15)	3		3	-
K Holt	37	3		5	-
R Loy	4 (9)	3		-	-
P McGowan	35 (1)	3		11	-
K Gadzhalov	15 (3)	2		2	-
C Wighton	19 (12)	2		-	-
C Kerr	35 (1)	1		6	-
N Low	2	1		1	-

HAMILTON

Nickname: The Accies
Colours: Red and white
Ground: New Douglas Park (5,510)
Tel: 01698-368-650　　　acciesfc.co.uk

Third-bottom in Martin Canning's first full season, the Accies dropped another place last term, surviving on the final day courtesy of a 4-0 thumping of Dundee.

Hamilton, who had been the 11-4 favourites to finish bottom, then pipped Dundee United 1-0 over two legs in a dire playoff to retain their top-flight status.

Hamilton didn't score enough goals – just 37 all season – nor win enough games, seven in total. They managed just a solitary away win all season.

Longest run without win/loss: 12/5
High/low league position: 8/12
Clean sheets: 9 **Yellow cards:** 98 **Red:** 4
Avg attendance: 2,426 **Players used:** 33
Leading scorer: A Crawford 8 (3,7)
Key stat: Hamilton struggled to win games but were also hard to beat, especially early on with ten draws in their first 16 matches

| | 2016-17 | | Last six seasons at home | | | | | | | |
	H	A	P	W	D	L	OV	UN	BS	CS
Celtic	L	L L	4	0	1	3	2	2	2	0
Aberdeen	W W	L	5	3	1	1	2	3	1	3
Rangers	L	D L	1	0	0	1	1	0	1	0
St Johnstone	D W	L	5	2	2	1	1	4	3	2
Hearts	D	L L	3	1	2	0	2	1	2	1
Partick	D	D L	9	2	5	2	3	6	5	3
Ross County	W D	D L	7	3	2	2	4	3	4	2
Kilmarnock	L D	L D	7	0	3	4	2	5	2	2
Motherwell	D L	L D	6	3	1	2	1	5	1	3
Dundee	L W	D W	9	4	2	3	6	3	6	1
Hamilton										
Hibernian			-	-	-	-	-	-	-	-

Season	Division	Pos	P	W	D	L	F	A	GD	Pts
2016-17	Premiership	11	38	7	14	17	37	56	-19	35
2015-16	Premiership	10	38	11	10	17	42	63	-21	43
2014-15	Premiership	7	38	15	8	15	50	53	-3	53

Over/Under 39%/61% 11th　　**Both score** 50%/50% 6th

Top league scorers	P	G		Y	R
A Crawford	31 (2)	8		7	-
A D'Acol	24 (5)	7		-	-
R Bingham	23 (7)	5		3	-
D Imrie	36 (1)	4		1-	-
E Brophy	7 (21)	2		-	-
M Devlin	28	2		12	-
M Donati	26 (5)	2		8	-

Seven players scored one goal

HEARTS

Nickname: Jambos
Colours: Claret and white
Ground: Tynecastle (17,480)
Tel: 0333-043-1874   heartsfc.co.uk

A dire season at Tynecastle. Second in late November, head coach Robbie Neilsen left for MK Dons and the rot set in.

New rookie boss Ian Cathro, a former assistant at Valencia and Newcastle, took the reins in December and things went from bad to worse.

Nine players arrived in January and six of those subsequently left as Hearts' campaign petered out spectacularly – they won just two of their last 14 games to finish fifth and split opinions on Cathro.

Longest run without win/loss: 6/6
High/low league position: 3/5
Clean sheets: 10 **Yellow cards:** 70 **Red:** 4
Avg attendance: 16,338 **Players used:** 33
Leading scorer: J Walker 12 (2,8)
Key stat: The campaign ended terribly with two wins in Hearts' last 16 games, including an ignominious cup exit at hands of rivals Hibs

HIBERNIAN

Nickname: The Hibees
Colours: Green and white
Ground: Easter Road (20,421)
Tel: 0131-661-2159   hibernianfc.co.uk

Neil Lennon's first season in charge was a triumphant one as Hibs won the Championship by nine points to end a three-year exile from the top flight.

Another highlight was beating Hearts on the way to a Scottish Cup semi-final, where they were pipped by Aberdeen – though Lennon promptly proclaimed his team was the second best in Scotland.

There was European disappointment, however, when they lost to Brondby on penalties in their one Europa League tie.

Longest run without win/loss: 4/10
High/low league position: 1/2
Clean sheets: 16 **Yellow cards:** 64 **Red:** 5
Avg attendance: 9,427 **Players used:** 28
Leading scorer: J Cummings 19 (8,15)
Key stat: Hibs have only failed to score in one of their last 24 home matches, a 0-0 draw with Morton in March

HEARTS

	2016-17 H	2016-17 A	Last six seasons at home P	W	D	L	OV	UN	BS	CS
Celtic	L L	L L	9	1	1	7	7	2	4	1
Aberdeen	L L	D L	9	5	1	3	6	3	5	3
Rangers	W W	L L	6	3	1	2	3	3	2	2
St Johnstone	D	L L L	9	4	2	3	5	4	4	3
Hearts										
Partick	D D	W L	6	2	2	2	3	3	3	2
Ross County	D L		8	3	4	1	3	5	4	3
Kilmarnock	W	L D	8	3	1	4	5	3	2	3
Motherwell	W	W W	8	5	0	3	5	5	1	5
Dundee	W W	L	5	3	1	1	0	5	1	3
Hamilton	W W	D	3	3	0	0	2	1	1	2
Hibernian			8	5	2	1	2	6	3	5

Season	Division	Pos	P	W	D	L	F	A	GD	Pts
2016-17	Premiership	5	38	12	10	16	55	52	+3	46
2015-16	Premiership	3	38	18	11	9	59	40	+19	65
2014-15	Championship	1	36	29	4	3	96	26	+70	91

Over/Under 53%/47% 5th   **Both score** 42%/58% 12th

Top league scorers	P	G		Y	R
J Walker	28 (6)	12		7	1
C Paterson	20	8		5	-
Esmael	15	7		3	1
B Johnsen	22 (12)	6		3	-
Arnaud Djoum	30 (3)	5		4	-
S Nicholson	13 (6)	4		1	1
D Cowie	34	3		1	-
R Muirhead	6 (12)	2		2	-

Eight players scored one goal

HIBERNIAN

	2016-17 H	2016-17 A	Last six seasons at home P	W	D	L	OV	UN	BS	CS
Celtic			5	1	1	3	2	3	1	1
Aberdeen			6	0	3	3	0	6	0	3
Rangers			5	3	0	2	3	2	2	1
St Johnstone			5	2	1	2	3	2	3	2
Hearts			7	2	3	2	3	4	5	2
Partick			2	0	2	0	0	2	2	0
Ross County			3	1	1	1	1	2	1	1
Kilmarnock			6	2	2	2	3	3	3	1
Motherwell			5	0	2	3	2	3	3	0
Dundee			3	2	1	0	1	2	1	2
Hamilton			-	-	-	-	-	-	-	-
Hibernian										

Season	Division	Pos	P	W	D	L	F	A	GD	Pts
2016-17	Championship	1	36	19	14	3	59	25	+34	71
2015-16	Championship	3	36	21	7	8	59	34	+25	70
2014-15	Championship	2	36	21	7	8	70	32	+38	70

Over/Under 42%/58% 7th   **Both score** 50%/50% 8th

Top league scorers	P	G		Y	R
J Cummings	26 (6)	19		2	1
M Boyle	22 (12)	8		2	-
G Holt	22 (8)	5		6	-
J Keatings	12 (12)	5		3	-
B Graham	8 (20)	4		4	-
J McGinn	27 (2)	4		4	-
K Commons	5	2		-	-
D Gray	32 (1)	2		6	-
P Hanlon	21 (1)	2		2	-
D McGregor	35	2		5	1

Two players scored one goal

KILMARNOCK

Nickname: Killie
Colours: Blue and white
Ground: Rugby Park (17,889)
Tel: 01563 545-300   kilmarnockfc.co.uk

Killie spent much of the first half of the season in the bottom three, though when Lee Clark quit in February to move to Bury after exactly a year at Rugby Park, Kilmarnock were in sixth place.

Lee McCulloch took temporary charge and, with just three defeats in his first ten matches, relegation was never a worry even if they missed out on the top six.

McCulloch was given the job full-time in June with a vow to gain consistency – Killie used 37 players last term.

Longest run without win/loss: 6/4
High/low league position: 6/11
Clean sheets: 10 **Yellow cards:** 72 **Red:** 2
Avg attendance: 5,199 **Players used:** 35
Lead scorers: K Boyd 8 (6,8) S Coulibaly 8 (4,8)
Key stat: Had a season-high five 0-0 draws last season and their 36-goal tally was the lowest in the division

MOTHERWELL

Nickname: The Steelmen
Colours: Amber and claret
Ground: Fir Park (13,677)
Tel: 01698-333-333   motherwellfc.co.uk

Second from bottom and staring at a relegation playoff, Motherwell won two of their last three matches to survive.

But it was yet another disappointing campaign for a club who were runners-up behind Celtic as recently as 2013-14.

Mark McGhee was sacked in February after a four-game losing streak which saw them ship 17 goals and he was replaced by Stephen Robinson, recently fired by Oldham. After a two-week trial he was made manager on a permanent basis.

Longest run without win/loss: 5/4
High/low league position: 5/11
Clean sheets: 5 **Yellow cards:** 68 **Red:** 3
Avg attendance: 4,450 **Players used:** 30
Leading scorer: L Moult 15 (5,11)
Key stat: Motherwell conceded two goals or more in 19 (exactly half) of their 38 matches in 2016-17

Kilmarnock

	2016-17 H	A	Last six seasons at home P	W	D	L	OV	UN	BS	CS
Celtic	L	L L	9	0	2	7	6	3	4	0
Aberdeen	L L	L	10	1	2	7	5	5	5	1
Rangers	D D	L	3	1	2	0	0	3	1	2
St Johnstone	L	W W	9	2	2	5	5	4	4	3
Hearts	W D	L	9	4	4	1	2	7	3	5
Partick	D D	D	8	2	3	3	6	2	6	1
Ross County	W L	L W	9	3	1	5	7	2	4	2
Kilmarnock										
Motherwell	L L	D L	10	3	1	6	4	6	4	4
Dundee	W L	D D	7	1	2	4	3	4	2	3
Hamilton	D	W D W	5	1	1	3	2	3	2	2
Hibernian			6	1	2	3	4	2	6	0

Season	Division	Pos	P	W	D	L	F	A	GD	Pts
2016-17	Premiership	8	38	9	14	15	36	56	-20	41
2015-16	Premiership	11	38	9	9	20	41	64	-23	36
2014-15	Premiership	10	38	11	8	19	44	59	-15	41

Over/Under 42%/58% 10th   **Both score** 55%/45% 5th

Top league scorers	P	G		Y	R
K Boyd	22 (5)	8		2	-
S Coulibaly	18 (3)	8		1	-
C Sammon	14 (1)	5		1	-
R McKenzie	25 (3)	4		5	-
J Jones	29 (8)	3		2	-
S Longstaff	16	3		1	-
S Boyd	18 (1)	1		4	-
G Dicker	36	1		1-	-
A Frizzell	8 (7)	1		-	-
M Smith	7 (3)	1		-	-
S Smith	25 (1)	1		5	-

Motherwell

	2016-17 H	A	Last six seasons at home P	W	D	L	OV	UN	BS	CS
Celtic	L	L L	11	2	1	8	8	3	6	0
Aberdeen	L	L L	9	4	1	4	6	3	6	2
Rangers	L	L D	3	0	0	3	2	1	1	0
St Johnstone	L L	D	13	6	2	5	9	4	9	2
Hearts	L L	L	9	5	2	2	6	3	4	4
Partick	W	D L	7	6	1	0	3	4	3	4
Ross County	W L	D W	10	5	3	2	6	4	8	1
Kilmarnock	D W	W W	10	4	4	2	5	5	6	3
Motherwell										
Dundee	D	L L L	7	1	2	4	4	3	5	1
Hamilton	W D	D W	5	2	2	1	4	1	2	2
Hibernian			4	3	0	1	3	1	2	1

Season	Division	Pos	P	W	D	L	F	A	GD	Pts
2016-17	Premiership	9	38	10	8	20	46	69	-23	38
2015-16	Premiership	5	38	15	5	18	47	63	-16	50
2014-15	Premiership	11	38	10	6	22	38	63	-25	36

Over/Under 55%/45% 4th   **Both score** 61%/39% 4th

Top league scorers	P	G		Y	R
L Moult	30 (1)	15		7	-
S McDonald	34 (1)	9		6	1
L Ainsworth	10 (20)	4		1	-
C Cadden	36	3		4	-
R Bowman	11 (13)	2		2	-
J McFadden	0 (6)	2		-	-
C McHugh	19	2		5	1

Seven players scored one goal

PARTICK

Nickname: The Jags
Colours: Yellow and red
Ground: Firhill Stadium (10,102)
Tel: 0141-579-1971   ptfc.co.uk

Thistle produced one of the great turnarounds of 2016-17. Alan Archibald's men were rock bottom the week before Christmas, having won just three of their first 18 matches, but rose to claim sixth spot, their best finish for 27 years.

They were 4-1 last summer to finish in the top six, and managed it despite netting just 38 goals in 38 games.

Inevitably, the impressive Jags' boss has been linked this summer with moves to jobs in England.

Longest run without win/loss: 8/8
High/low league position: 6/12
Clean sheets: 9 **Yellow cards:** 66 **Red:** 4
Avg attendance: 3,946 **Players used:** 27
Leading scorer: K Doohlan 14 (8,12)
Key stat: There were two or three goals scored in 24 (63 percent) of Partick's 38 top-flight games last season

RANGERS

Nickname: The Gers
Colours: Blue
Ground: Ibrox Stadium (50,817)
Tel: 0871-702-1972   rangers.co.uk

Pedro Caixinha was under pressure when he took over in March and four months on that pressure is through the roof after an embarrassing Europa League exit.

The Gers' first year back in the top flight never really caught fire. Six meetings with Celtic yielded five defeats – two by 5-1 scorelines – and a solitary draw.

Any chance of challenging Celtic vanished with a run of one win in seven during which time boss Mark Warburton was shown the door.

Longest run without win/loss: 4/7
High/low league position: 2/7
Clean sheets: 12 **Yellow cards:** 72 **Red:** 4
Avg attendance: 48,941 **Players used:** 30
Leading scorer: K Miller 11 (7,10)
Key stat: Both teams scored in 25 of Rangers' 38 league games – their last four were all 2-1 scorelines

Partick tables

	2016-17 H	A	P	W	D	L	OV	UN	BS	CS
Celtic	L L	L D	7	0	0	7	6	1	4	0
Aberdeen	L L	L L	7	1	0	6	5	2	3	0
Rangers	L L	L L	2	0	0	2	2	0	2	0
St Johnstone	L L	W L	6	2	1	3	1	5	0	3
Hearts	L W	D D	5	1	1	3	3	2	3	1
Partick										
Ross County	D W	W	9	3	2	4	5	4	5	2
Kilmarnock	D	D D	7	0	6	1	2	5	5	2
Motherwell	D W	L	6	4	1	1	2	4	3	3
Dundee	W	W W	7	1	2	4	2	5	3	2
Hamilton	D W	D	10	5	4	1	5	5	5	5
Hibernian			2	1	0	1	1	1	1	0

Season	Division	Pos	P	W	D	L	F	A	GD	Pts
2016-17	Premiership	6	38	10	12	16	38	54	-16	42
2015-16	Premiership	9	38	12	10	16	41	50	-9	46
2014-15	Premiership	8	38	12	10	16	48	44	+4	46

Over/Under 37%/63% 12th   **Both score** 50%/50% 6th

All league scorers	P	G	Y	R
K Doohlan	29 (8)	14	1	-
L Lindsay	36	6	3	-
C Erskine	25 (11)	5	3	-
S Welsh	18 (3)	3	5	1
A Azeez	19 (19)	2	5	-
S Lawless	24 (6)	2	3	-
D Amoo	14 (11)	1	2	-
A Barton	30 (1)	1	2	-
C Booth	31	1	6	-
R Edwards	33 (5)	1	6	-
A Osman	30 (1)	1	7	1

Rangers tables

	2016-17 H	A	P	W	D	L	OV	UN	BS	CS
Celtic	L L	L D	4	2	0	2	4	0	4	0
Aberdeen	W L	L W	4	2	1	1	2	2	3	1
Rangers										
St Johnstone	D W	D W	3	1	2	0	1	2	2	1
Hearts	W W	L L	6	3	1	2	4	2	5	1
Partick	W W	W W	2	2	0	0	2	0	2	0
Ross County	D D	D	2	0	2	0	0	2	1	1
Kilmarnock	W	D D	3	2	0	1	1	2	0	2
Motherwell	W D	W	4	2	2	0	2	2	2	2
Dundee	W	W L	1	1	0	0	0	1	0	1
Hamilton	D W	W	2	1	1	0	1	1	1	1
Hibernian			6	4	0	2	3	3	2	3

Season	Division	Pos	P	W	D	L	F	A	GD	Pts
2016-17	Premiership	3	38	19	10	9	56	44	+12	67
2015-16	Championship	1	36	25	6	5	88	34	+54	81
2014-15	Championship	3	36	19	10	7	69	39	+30	67

Over/Under 53%/47% 5th   **Both score** 66%/34% 1st

Top league scorers	P	G	Y	R
K Miller	32 (5)	11	1	-
M Waghorn	20 (12)	8	6	-
J Garner	21 (10)	7	9	-
B McKay	28 (7)	5	-	-
E Hyndman	13	4	1	-
J Dodoo	5 (15)	3	1	-
H Forrester	7 (14)	3	2	-
A Halliday	24 (8)	3	4	-
C Hill	23 (1)	3	6	1
L Wallace	27	3	4	-
J Toral	12	2	5	-
Four players scored one goal				

ROSS COUNTY

Nickname: County
Colours: Blue, red and white
Ground: Victoria Park (6,541)
Tel: 01349-860860 rosscountyfootballclub.co.uk

	2016-17		Last six seasons at home							
	H	A	P	W	D	L	OV	UN	BS	CS
Celtic	L D	L	9	1	3	5	6	3	6	0
Aberdeen	W	L L	7	4	1	2	3	4	4	2
Rangers	D	D D	1	0	1	0	0	1	1	0
St Johnstone	L L	W	9	3	0	6	4	5	4	3
Hearts	D	D W	6	1	2	3	6	0	5	0
Partick	L	D L	9	4	2	3	5	4	5	4
Ross County										
Kilmarnock	W L	L W	9	4	1	4	6	3	6	2
Motherwell	D L	L W	9	3	2	4	7	2	6	3
Dundee	L W	D D	8	5	2	1	5	3	6	2
Hamilton	D W	L D	8	6	1	1	4	4	5	2
Hibernian			4	3	0	1	1	3	1	2

Season	Division	Pos	P	W	D	L	F	A	GD	Pts
2016-17	Premiership	7	38	11	13	14	48	58	-10	46
2015-16	Premiership	6	38	14	6	18	55	61	-6	48
2014-15	Premiership	9	38	12	8	18	46	63	-17	44

Over/Under 53%/47% 5th   **Both score** 66%/34% 1st

All league scorers	P	G		Y	R
L Boyce	34	23		7	-
C Curran	26 (8)	5		6	-
A Schalk	15 (17)	5		1	-
J McEveley	19 (3)	3		1-	1
C Routis	23 (7)	3		6	-
M Gardyne	28 (5)	2		4	-
C Burke	4 (2)	1		1	-
T Chow	26 (4)	1		8	1
A Davies	31	1		7	-
R Dow	13 (10)	1		4	-
J Franks	9 (9)	1		-	-
M Woods	27 (2)	1		6	-

Failed to repeat the previous season's top-half heroics – indeed, Jim McIntyre's third year in charge was a dicier affair.

The Staggies were bottom after 13 games after a run of ten games without a win. Even by the end of February they were only three points off the foot.

They finished the season spectacularly, however, with Liam Boyce scoring nine goals in eight games to become the league's top scorer – a feat which earned him a £500,000 switch to Burton.

Longest run without win/loss: 10/8
High/low league position: 6/12
Clean sheets: 7 **Yellow cards:** 86 **Red:** 5
Avg attendance: 4,004 **Players used:** 31
Leading scorer: L Boyce 23 (8,15)
Key stat: County rounded off 2016-17 in style by taking 18 points out of a possible 24 during an unbeaten eight-game run

ST JOHNSTONE

Nickname: The Saints
Colours: Blue and white
Ground: McDiarmid Park (10,696)
Tel: 01738-459090   perthstjohnstonefc.co.uk

	2016-17		Last six seasons at home							
	H	A	P	W	D	L	OV	UN	BS	CS
Celtic	L L	L L	12	2	3	7	8	4	7	1
Aberdeen	D L	D W	10	3	2	5	6	4	6	3
Rangers	D L	D L	5	0	1	4	3	2	3	0
St Johnstone										
Hearts	W W W D		9	6	3	0	3	6	3	6
Partick	L W	W W	7	2	2	3	3	4	5	2
Ross County	L	W W	8	2	4	2	4	4	6	1
Kilmarnock	L L	W	9	6	1	3	4	5	4	3
Motherwell	D	W W	9	6	1	2	6	3	5	3
Dundee	W W	L	6	4	1	1	1	5	2	3
Hamilton	W	D L	4	2	1	1	2	2	1	2
Hibernian			4	2	0	2	2	2	2	1

Season	Division	Pos	P	W	D	L	F	A	GD	Pts
2016-17	Premiership	4	38	17	7	14	50	46	+4	58
2015-16	Premiership	4	38	16	8	14	55	43	+12	56
2014-15	Premiership	4	38	16	9	13	34	34	0	57

Over/Under 47%/53% 8th   **Both score** 47%/53% 9th

Top league scorers	P	G		Y	R
S MacLean	30 (2)	10		8	-
D Swanson	28 (2)	10		7	1
L Craig	27 (9)	5		1-	-
G Cummins	17 (13)	5		4	-
C Kane	14 (11)	5		4	-
S Anderson	26	3		5	-
M Davidson	19 (4)	3		8	-
B Alston	25 (10)	2		2	-

Six players scored one goal

Saints enter the new campaign on the back of a third straight top-six finish under inspirational boss Tommy Wright.

Finishing 12 points clear of Hearts in fourth was a magnificent achievement which earned St Johnstone a place in the Europa League.

That they pulled that off despite losing eight home games – more than Inverness who finished bottom – was even more remarkable. Signed off without a draw in their last 19 league matches.

Longest run without win/loss: 4/5
High/low league position: 4/5
Clean sheets: 15 **Yellow cards:** 76 **Red:** 2
Avg attendance: 4,368 **Players used:** 25
Lead scorers: MacLean 10 (2,9) Swanson 10 (3,10)
Key stat: The Saints were level at half-time on a league-high 18 occasions, yet only ended up with seven draws in total

Scottish Premiership stats 2016-17

Key Points in all tables (except the league table) do not include any deductions imposed by the league.
POS H A Overall league position, rank from home games only, rank from away games only **Sup** Average match supremacy **GFA** Goals For Average **GAA** Goals Against Average **PGA** Points Gained Average

Scottish Premiership 2016-17				Home				Away							
Pos	H	A		P	W	D	L	F	A	W	D	L	F	A	GD	Pts
1	1	1	Celtic (CL)	38	17	2	0	47	8	17	2	0	59	17	81	106
2	2	2	Aberdeen (EL)	38	12	3	4	34	16	12	1	6	40	19	39	76
3	3	4	Rangers (EL)	38	11	5	3	31	18	8	5	6	25	26	12	67
4	5	3	St Johnstone (EL)	38	8	3	8	25	25	9	4	6	25	21	4	58
5	4	10	Hearts	38	9	5	5	36	20	3	5	11	19	32	3	46
6	9	8	Partick	38	6	5	9	21	32	4	7	7	17	22	-16	42
7	7	5	Ross County	38	6	5	7	28	31	5	8	7	20	27	-10	46
8	11	6	Kilmarnock	38	4	7	8	18	23	5	7	7	18	33	-20	41
9	12	7	Motherwell	38	5	3	11	27	37	5	5	9	19	32	-23	38
10	10	9	Dundee	38	5	5	9	19	30	5	2	12	19	32	-24	37
11	6	12	Hamilton*	38	6	7	6	22	20	1	7	11	15	36	-19	35
12	8	11	Inverness CT (R)	38	5	8	6	27	33	2	5	12	17	38	-27	34

*Hamilton avoided relegation by winning playoff

Best attack

		GF	GFA
1	Celtic	106	2.79
2	Aberdeen	74	1.95
3	Rangers	56	1.47
4	Hearts	55	1.45
5	St Johnstone	50	1.32
6	Ross County	48	1.26
7	Motherwell	46	1.21
8	Inverness CT	44	1.16
9	Partick	38	1
10	Dundee	38	1
11	Hamilton	37	0.97
12	Kilmarnock	36	0.95

Best defence

		GA	GAA
1	Celtic	25	0.66
2	Aberdeen	35	0.92
3	Rangers	44	1.16
4	St Johnstone	46	1.21
5	Hearts	52	1.37
6	Partick	54	1.42
7	Kilmarnock	56	1.47
8	Hamilton	56	1.47
9	Ross County	58	1.53
10	Dundee	62	1.63
11	Motherwell	69	1.82
12	Inverness CT	71	1.87

Top scorers

	Team	Goals scored	
L Boyce	Ross County	23	|||||||||||||||||||||||
S Sinclair	Celtic	21	|||||||||||||||||||||
M Dembele	Celtic	17	|||||||||||||||||
S Armstrong	Celtic	15	|||||||||||||||
L Moult	Motherwell	15	|||||||||||||||
K Doohan	Partick	14	||||||||||||||
J Griffiths	Celtic	12	||||||||||||
A Rooney	Aberdeen	12	||||||||||||
J Walker	Hearts	12	||||||||||||
K Miller	Rangers	11	|||||||||||
N McGinn	Aberdeen	10	||||||||||
D Swanson	St Johnstone	10	||||||||||

Record when first to score

		P	W	D	L	F	A	Sup	PGA	Pts
1	Aberdeen	22	21	1	0	61	12	+2.23	2.9	64
2	St Johnstone	17	16	1	0	29	4	+1.47	2.9	49
3	Celtic	35	31	4	0	94	20	+2.11	2.8	97
4	Rangers	19	16	2	1	36	11	+1.32	2.6	50
5	Hearts	15	11	3	1	38	12	+1.73	2.4	36
6	Dundee	12	9	2	1	21	12	+0.75	2.4	29
7	Ross County	16	10	5	1	33	20	+0.81	2.2	35
8	Inverness CT	11	7	3	1	23	16	+0.64	2.2	24
9	Motherwell	14	9	2	3	32	26	+0.43	2.1	29
10	Partick	16	9	5	2	24	12	+0.75	2	32
11	Hamilton	18	7	9	2	25	15	+0.56	1.7	30
12	Kilmarnock	19	8	7	4	28	24	+0.21	1.6	31

Record when keeping a clean sheet

		P	W	D	F	Sup	PGA	Pts
1	Celtic	19	19	0	45	+2.37	3	57
2	St Johnstone	15	13	2	23	+1.53	2.7	41
3	Rangers	12	10	2	21	+1.75	2.7	32
4	Aberdeen	14	11	3	32	+2.29	2.6	36
5	Partick	9	7	2	12	+1.33	2.6	23
6	Hamilton	9	7	2	13	+1.44	2.6	23
7	Hearts	10	7	3	19	+1.90	2.4	24
8	Dundee	6	4	2	7	+1.17	2.3	14
9	Inverness CT	3	2	1	5	+1.67	2.3	7
10	Ross County	7	4	3	8	+1.14	2.1	15
11	Kilmarnock	10	5	5	9	+0.90	2	20
12	Motherwell	5	2	3	3	+0.60	1.8	9

Over 2.5 goals

	H	A	%
Celtic	8	16	63%
Aberdeen	9	14	61%
Inverness CT	13	10	61%
Motherwell	13	8	55%
Hearts, Rangers, Ross Co			53%

Under 2.5 goals

	H	A	%
Partick	10	14	63%
Hamilton	13	10	61%
Kilmarnock	11	11	58%
Dundee	11	9	53%
St Johnstone	10	10	53%

Both to score

	H	A	%
Inverness CT	15	10	66%
Rangers	11	14	66%
Ross County	14	11	66%
Motherwell	11	12	61%
Kilmarnock	10	11	55%

Both not to score

	H	A	%
Hearts	10	12	58%
Aberdeen	12	8	53%
Dundee	9	11	53%
St Johnstone	10	10	53%
Celtic, Hamilton, Partick			50%

SCOTTISH PREMIERSHIP

Scottish Premiership results 2016-17

	Aberdeen	Celtic	Dundee	Hamilton	Hearts	Inverness CT	Kilmarnock	Motherwell	Partick	Rangers	Ross County	St Johnstone
Aberdeen		0-1/1-3	3-0	2-1	0-0/2-0	1-1/1-0	5-1	7-2/1-0	2-1/2-0	2-1/0-3	4-0/1-0	0-0/0-2
Celtic	4-1/1-0		2-1	1-0/2-0	4-0/2-0	3-0	6-1/3-1	2-0/2-0	1-0/1-1	5-1/1-1	2-0	1-0/4-1
Dundee	1-3/0-7	0-1/1-2		1-1/0-2	3-2	2-1/0-2	1-1/1-1	2-0	0-2/0-1	1-2/2-1	0-0/1-1	3-0
Hamilton	1-0/1-0	0-3	0-1/4-0		3-3	1-1/3-0	1-2/1-1/0-2	1-1/0-1	1-1	1-2	1-0/1-1	1-1/1-0
Hearts	0-1/1-2	1-2/0-5	2-0/1-0	3-1/4-0		5-1/1-1	4-0	3-0	1-1/2-2	2-0/4-1	0-0/0-1	2-2
Inverness CT	1-3	2-2/0-4	3-1/2-2	1-1/2-1	3-3		1-1/1-1	1-2/3-2	0-0	0-1/2-1	2-3/1-1	2-1/0-3
Kilmarnock	0-4/1-2	0-1	2-0/0-1	0-0	2-0/0-0	1-1/2-1		1-2/1-2	2-2/1-1	1-1/0-0	3-2/1-2	0-1
Motherwell	1-3	3-4	0-0/1-5/2-3	4-2/0-0	1-3/0-3	0-3/4-2	0-0/3-1		2-0	0-2	4-1/0-1	1-2/1-2
Partick	1-2/0-6	1-4/0-5	2-0	2-2/2-0	1-2/2-0	2-0/1-1	0-0	1-1/1-0		1-2/1-2	1-1/2-1	0-2/0-1
Rangers	2-1/1-2	1-2/1-5	1-0	1-1/4-0	2-0/2-1	1-0	3-0	2-1/1-1	2-0/2-0		0-0/1-1	1-1/3-2
Ross County	2-1	0-4/2-2	1-3/2-1	1-1/3-2	2-2	3-2/4-0	2-0/1-2	1-1/1-2	1-3	1-1		0-2/1-2
St Johnstone	0-0/1-2	2-4/2-5	2-1/2-0	3-0	1-0/1-0/1-0	3-0	0-1/0-2	1-1	1-2/1-0	1-1/1-2	2-4	

Rangers hitman Martyn Waghorn

BRECHIN

Nickname: The City — Glebe Park
brechincity.com

Back in the Championship after 11 year, a strong finish to 2015-16 gave promise and Darren Dods' men delivered, finishing fourth in League One albeit with -6 goal difference.

Beat Raith and Alloa in the playoffs, despite winning only one of the four ties.

	2016-17 H	A	Last six seasons at home P	W	D	L	OV	UN	BS	CS
Inverness CT			-	-	-	-	-	-	-	-
Falkirk			-	-	-	-	-	-	-	-
Dundee United			-	-	-	-	-	-	-	-
Morton			2	1	1	0	1	1	2	0
Dunfermline			6	2	2	2	4	2	5	1
Queen of Sth			2	0	0	2	2	0	0	0
St Mirren			-	-	-	-	-	-	-	-
Dumbarton			2	0	2	0	2	0	2	0
Livingston	L L	L L	2	0	0	2	1	1	0	0
Brechin										

Season	Division	Pos	P	W	D	L	F	A	GD	Pts
2016-17	League One	4	36	15	5	16	43	49	-6	50
2015-16	League One	7	36	12	6	18	47	59	-12	42
2014-15	League One	4	36	15	14	7	58	46	+12	59

Over/Under 53%/47% 6th **Both score** 50%/50% 6th

DUMBARTON

Nickname: The Sons — Dumbarton Football Stadium
dumbartonfootballclub.com

Eighth in Stevie Aitken's first season, the Sons were eighth again, staying up on goal difference – a feat which earned Aitken a new two-year deal. The low point was losing to Bonnyrigg Rose in the cup, the first second-tier side to succumb to a junior team.

	2016-17 H	A	Last six seasons at home P	W	D	L	OV	UN	BS	CS
Inverness CT										
Falkirk	W L	L D	10	3	2	5	4	6	4	1
Dundee United	W W	L L	2	2	0	0	0	2	0	2
Morton	L W	D L	8	3	1	4	4	4	3	3
Dunfermline	D L	L L	4	0	1	3	1	3	1	0
Queen of Sth	D L	W W	8	1	2	5	4	4	2	2
St Mirren	D D	W D	4	2	2	0	2	2	3	1
Dumbarton										
Livingston			8	3	1	4	6	2	5	2
Brechin			2	2	0	0	1	1	1	1

Season	Division	Pos	P	W	D	L	F	A	GD	Pts
2016-17	Championship	8	36	9	12	15	46	56	-10	39
2015-16	Championship	8	36	10	7	19	35	66	-31	37
2014-15	Championship	7	36	9	7	20	36	79	-43	34

Over/Under 56%/44% 1st **Both score** 58%/42% 3rd

DUNDEE UNITED

Nickname: The Terrors — Tannadice Park
dundeeunitedfc.co.uk

United's first term out of the top flight since 1996 didn't go well – top at Christmas after a 12-game unbeaten run, they boasted the best home record but had to settle for third.

Saw off Morton and Falkirk in the playoffs before faltering against Hamilton.

	2016-17 H	A	Last six seasons at home P	W	D	L	OV	UN	BS	CS
Inverness CT			8	3	3	2	4	4	5	1
Falkirk	W D	L L	2	1	1	0	0	2	1	1
Dundee United										
Morton	W D	D D	2	1	1	0	1	1	2	0
Dunfermline	W W	W D	4	3	0	1	1	3	0	3
Queen of Sth	D D	W L	2	0	2	0	1	1	2	0
St Mirren	W W	W W	8	5	2	1	6	2	5	3
Dumbarton	W D	L L	2	1	1	0	2	0	2	0
Livingston			-	-	-	-	-	-	-	-
Brechin			-	-	-	-	-	-	-	-

Season	Division	Pos	P	W	D	L	F	A	GD	Pts
2016-17	Championship	3	36	15	12	9	50	42	+8	57
2015-16	Premiership	12	38	8	7	23	45	70	-25	28
2014-15	Premiership	5	38	17	5	16	58	56	+2	56

Over/Under 50%/50% 3rd **Both score** 56%/44% 5th

DUNFERMLINE

Nickname: The Pars — East End Park
dafc.co.uk

The runaway League One champions looked to be heading back there when in ninth spot after winning just two of their first 13 games.

An immediate nine-game unbeaten streak vaulted them to sixth and they finished four points off the playoffs at the end of term.

	2016-17 H	A	Last six seasons at home P	W	D	L	OV	UN	BS	CS
Inverness CT			2	0	2	0	1	1	2	0
Falkirk	D L	L L	4	0	1	3	1	3	2	0
Dundee United	D L	L L	3	0	1	2	2	1	3	0
Morton	W W	L W	6	2	1	3	6	0	5	0
Dunfermline										
Queen of Sth	L D	D W	2	0	1	1	0	2	1	0
St Mirren	W D	W D	4	1	3	0	1	3	3	1
Dumbarton	W W	D W	4	3	0	1	4	0	3	1
Livingston			2	1	0	1	1	1	0	1
Brechin			6	4	1	1	4	2	4	1

Season	Division	Pos	P	W	D	L	F	A	GD	Pts
2016-17	Championship	5	36	12	12	12	46	43	+3	48
2015-16	League One	1	36	24	7	5	83	30	+53	79
2014-15	League One	7	36	13	9	14	46	48	-2	48

Over/Under 39%/61% 8th **Both score** 56%/44% 5th

FALKIRK

Nickname: The Bairns Falkirk Stadium
falkirkfc.co.uk

Back-to-back second-placed finishes have yielded successive playoff defeats, with Dundee United their conquerors in May.

Peter Houston's consistent Bairns failed to score in only one game from late October and lost just twice in the league during 2017.

	2016-17 H A		Last six seasons at home P W D L OV UN BS CS							
Inverness CT			-	-	-	-	-	-	-	-
Falkirk										
Dundee United	W W	L D	2	2	0	0	2	0	1	1
Morton	D L	D D	10	5	2	3	2	8	4	3
Dunfermline	W W	D W	4	3	1	0	2	2	2	2
Queen of Sth	D D	L W	10	5	5	0	5	5	6	4
St Mirren	W D	D W	4	3	1	0	4	0	3	1
Dumbarton	W D	L W	10	4	3	3	6	4	7	3
Livingston			10	5	2	3	5	5	6	4
Brechin			-	-	-	-	-	-	-	-

Season	Division	Pos	P	W	D	L	F	A	GD	Pts
2016-17	Championship	2	36	16	12	8	58	40	+18	60
2015-16	Championship	2	36	19	13	4	61	34	+27	70
2014-15	Championship	5	36	14	11	11	48	48	0	53

Over/Under 50%/50% 3rd **Both score** 67%/33% 1st

INVERNESS CT

Nickname: Caley Caledonian Stadium
ictfc.com

Chairman Kenny Cameron's memorable six-year reign ended in relegation as they paid the price for three clean sheets all season.

Three wins in the last four couldn't save Thistle or Richie Foran and, after 13 year away, John Robertson returns as manager.

	2016-17 H A		Last six seasons at home P W D L OV UN BS CS							
Inverness CT										
Falkirk			-	-	-	-	-	-	-	-
Dundee United			11	4	4	3	7	4	7	4
Morton			-	-	-	-	-	-	-	-
Dunfermline			2	0	2	0	0	2	1	1
Queen of Sth			-	-	-	-	-	-	-	-
St Mirren			6	3	3	0	4	2	3	3
Dumbarton			-	-	-	-	-	-	-	-
Livingston			-	-	-	-	-	-	-	-
Brechin			-	-	-	-	-	-	-	-

Season	Division	Pos	P	W	D	L	F	A	GD	Pts
2016-17	Premiership	12	38	7	13	18	44	71	-27	34
2015-16	Premiership	7	38	14	10	14	54	48	+6	52
2014-15	Premiership	3	38	19	8	11	52	42	+10	65

Over/Under 61%/39% 2nd **Both score** 66%/34% 1st

LIVINGSTON

Nickname: Livi Lions Almondvale Stadium
livingstonfc.co.uk

Livingston's sole term in League One ended with them winning the title by 19 points. David Hopkins' men won their last nine, securing promotion with four games to go.

Only Celtic scored more goals than the Livi Lions in the four divisions.

	2016-17 H A		Last six seasons at home P W D L OV UN BS CS							
Inverness CT			-	-	-	-	-	-	-	-
Falkirk			10	2	2	6	6	4	7	0
Dundee United			-	-	-	-	-	-	-	-
Morton			8	0	5	3	3	5	4	2
Dunfermline			2	1	1	0	2	0	2	0
Queen of Sth			8	1	4	3	5	3	5	1
St Mirren			2	0	0	2	1	1	1	0
Dumbarton			8	2	1	5	6	2	6	2
Livingston										
Brechin	W W	W W	2	2	0	0	2	0	1	1

Season	Division	Pos	P	W	D	L	F	A	GD	Pts
2016-17	League One	1	36	26	3	7	80	32	+48	81
2015-16	Championship	9	36	8	7	21	37	51	-14	31
2014-15	Championship	8	36	8	8	20	41	53	-12	27

Over/Under 69%/31% 2nd **Both score** 56%/44% 4th

MORTON

Nickname: The Ton Cappielow Park
gmfc.net

Manager of the season Jim Duffy guided the Ton to the playoffs, which looked unlikely after they failed to win any of their first five.

Had pushed for second spot until tamely signing off with nine without a win, then defeat by Dundee United in the playoffs.

	2016-17 H A		Last six seasons at home P W D L OV UN BS CS							
Inverness CT			-	-	-	-	-	-	-	-
Falkirk	D D	D W	10	2	5	3	3	7	6	2
Dundee United	D D	L D	2	0	2	0	0	2	1	1
Morton										
Dunfermline	W L	L L	6	4	0	2	3	3	3	1
Queen of Sth	W W	W L	8	4	3	1	3	5	4	3
St Mirren	W L	D D	4	1	1	2	2	2	2	1
Dumbarton	D W	W L	8	5	2	1	4	4	2	5
Livingston			8	5	1	2	6	2	6	2
Brechin			2	0	1	1	1	1	1	0

Season	Division	Pos	P	W	D	L	F	A	GD	Pts
2016-17	Championship	4	36	13	13	10	44	41	+3	52
2015-16	Championship	5	36	11	10	15	39	42	-3	43
2014-15	League One	1	36	22	3	11	65	40	+25	69

Over/Under 39%/61% 8th **Both score** 58%/42% 3rd

QUEEN OF THE SOUTH

Nickname: The Doonhamers Palmerston Park
qosfc.com

Returning Stephen Dobbie got Queens off to a flyer and they were top after eight games.

The joy didn't last – Gavin Skelton quit after four losses and Gary Naysmith oversaw a second half of term when they were never higher than fifth or lower than seventh.

	2016-17 H	A	Last six seasons at home P	W	D	L	OV	UN	BS	CS
Inverness CT			-	-	-	-	-	-	-	-
Falkirk	W L	D D	10	4	3	3	5	5	4	5
Dundee United	L W	D D	2	1	0	1	2	0	2	0
Morton	L W	L L	8	6	1	1	6	2	3	4
Dunfermline	D L	W D	2	0	1	1	1	1	1	0
Queen of Sth										
St Mirren	L L	W W	4	1	0	3	1	3	1	1
Dumbarton	L L	D W	8	5	0	3	7	1	5	3
Livingston			8	3	2	3	5	3	5	1
Brechin			2	2	0	0	1	1	1	1

Season	Division	Pos	P	W	D	L	F	A	GD	Pts
2016-17	Championship	6	36	11	10	15	46	52	-6	43
2015-16	Championship	7	36	12	6	18	46	56	-10	42
2014-15	Championship	4	36	17	9	10	58	41+	1760	

Over/Under 53%/47% 2nd **Both score** 47%/53% 9th

ST MIRREN

Nickname: The Saints St Mirren Park
saintmirren.net

Looked doomed in February when eight points adrift with two wins to their name.

Alex Rae had long since gone as manager leaving Jack Ross to produce the great escape. From nowhere they signed off with two losses in 14 to stay up on goal difference.

	2016-17 H	A	Last six seasons at home P	W	D	L	OV	UN	BS	CS
Inverness CT			7	1	2	4	4	3	4	1
Falkirk	D L	L D	4	0	2	2	2	2	3	1
Dundee United	L W	L L	8	2	3	3	4	4	4	1
Morton	D D	L W	4	1	3	0	1	3	4	0
Dunfermline	L D	L D	4	1	2	1	2	2	2	1
Queen of Sth	L L	W W	4	2	0	2	3	1	2	1
St Mirren										
Dumbarton	L D	D D	4	1	1	2	1	3	2	1
Livingston			2	0	1	1	1	1	2	0
Brechin			-	-	-	-	-	-	-	-

Season	Division	Pos	P	W	D	L	F	A	GD	Pts
2016-17	Championship	7	36	9	12	15	52	56	-4	39
2015-16	Championship	6	36	11	9	16	44	53	-9	42
2014-15	Premiership	12	38	9	3	26	30	66	-36	30

Over/Under 44%/56% 5th **Both score** 64%/36% 2nd

The familiar black and white colours adorn St Mirren Park

Scottish Championship results 2016-17

	Ayr	Dumbarton	Dundee Utd	Dunfermline	Falkirk	Hibernian	Morton	Queen of Sth	Raith	St Mirren
Ayr		4-4/2-1	0-1/0-0	0-0/0-2	0-1/1-4	0-3/0-4	2-1/1-4	1-0/0-2	0-2/1-0	1-1/0-2
Dumbarton	0-3/2-2		1-0/1-0	2-2/0-2	2-1/0-1	0-1/0-1	0-2/1-0	0-0/1-2	0-0/4-0	1-1/2-2
Dundee Utd	3-0/2-1	2-1/2-2		1-0/1-0	1-0/1-1	1-0/0-1	2-1/1-1	1-1/3-3	2-2/3-0	2-1/3-2
Dunfermline	1-1/0-1	4-3/5-1	1-3/1-1		1-1/1-2	1-3/1-1	2-1/3-1	0-1/1-1	0-0/1-0	4-3/1-1
Falkirk	2-0/1-1	1-0/2-2	3-1/3-0	2-1/2-0		1-2/1-2	1-1/0-1	2-2/2-2	2-4/1-0	3-1/2-2
Hibernian	1-2/1-1	2-0/2-2	1-1/3-0	2-1/2-2	1-1/2-1		4-0/0-0	4-0/3-0	1-1/3-2	2-0/1-1
Morton	2-1/1-1	1-1/2-1	0-0/1-1	2-1/0-1	1-1/2-2	1-1/1-1		1-0/1-0	1-0/2-0	3-1/1-4
Queen of Sth	4-1/0-0	1-2/1-2	1-4/4-2	2-2/0-1	2-0/0-2	2-0/0-1	0-5/3-0		3-1/2-1	2-3/0-2
Raith	1-1/2-1	3-2/1-3	0-0/2-1	2-0/0-2	0-2/1-4	0-0/1-1	0-1/2-0	1-0/1-1		3-1/2-0
St Mirren	1-1/6-2	0-1/1-1	0-2/3-2	0-1/0-0	1-1/1-2	0-2/2-0	1-1/1-1	1-3/0-3	1-0/5-0	

Scottish Championship 2016-17

Pos	H	A		P	Home W	D	L	F	A	Away W	D	L	F	A	GD	Pts
1	2	1	Hibernian (P)	36	9	8	1	35	15	10	6	2	24	10	34	71
2	4	2	Falkirk	36	8	6	4	31	22	8	6	4	27	18	18	60
3	1	7	Dundee Utd	36	11	6	1	31	17	4	6	8	19	25	8	57
4	3	5	Morton	36	8	8	2	23	17	5	5	8	21	24	3	52
5	6	3	Dunfermline	36	6	7	5	28	25	6	5	7	18	18	3	48
6	9	4	Queen of Sth	36	6	3	9	25	29	5	7	6	21	23	-6	43
7	7	6	St Mirren	36	5	6	7	24	23	4	6	8	28	33	-4	39
8	8	8	Dumbarton	36	5	6	7	17	20	4	6	8	29	36	-10	39
9	5	10	Raith (R)	36	8	5	5	22	20	2	4	12	13	32	-17	39
10	10	9	Ayr (R)	36	4	4	10	13	32	3	8	7	20	30	-29	33

Best attack

		GF	GFA
1	Hibernian	59	1.64
2	Falkirk	58	1.61
3	St Mirren	52	1.44
4	Dundee Utd	50	1.39
5	Dunfermline	46	1.28
6	Queen of Sth	46	1.28
7	Dumbarton	46	1.28
8	Morton	44	1.22
9	Raith	35	0.97
10	Ayr	33	0.92

Best defence

		GA	GAA
1	Hibernian	25	0.69
2	Falkirk	40	1.11
3	Morton	41	1.14
4	Dundee Utd	42	1.17
5	Dunfermline	43	1.19
6	Queen of Sth	52	1.44
7	Raith	52	1.44
8	Dumbarton	56	1.56
9	St Mirren	56	1.56
10	Ayr	62	1.72

Top scorers

	Team	Goals scored
J Cummings	Hibernian	19
S Dobbie	Queen of Sth	19
N Clark	Dunfermline	15
T Andreu	Dundee Utd	13
R Thomson	Dumbarton	11

Lyle (Queen of Sth), Murray (Dundee) Sibbald (Falkirk) – all 10

Key Points in all tables (except the league table) do not include any deductions imposed by the league.
POS H A Position, home/away rank **Sup** Average supremacy
GFA/GAA Goals For/Against Average **PGA** Pts Gained Average

Record when first to score

		P	W	D	L	F	A	Sup	PGA	Pts
1	Dundee Utd	19	14	5	0	36	15	+1.11	2.5	47
2	Hibernian	23	17	5	1	45	12	+1.43	2.4	56
3	Falkirk	18	13	4	1	31	13	+1	2.4	43
4	Morton	20	12	8	0	33	13	+1	2.2	44
5	Queen of Sth	17	11	4	2	37	17	+1.18	2.2	37
6	Dunfermline	15	10	3	2	28	15	+0.87	2.2	33
7	Raith	16	10	4	2	29	18	+0.69	2.1	34
8	St Mirren	15	8	4	3	36	20	+1.07	1.9	28
9	Dumbarton	14	7	5	2	23	18	+0.36	1.9	26
10	Ayr	11	5	5	1	17	13	+0.36	1.8	20

Record when keeping a clean sheet

		P	W	D	F	Sup	PGA	Pts
1	Falkirk	9	9	0	15	+1.67	3	27
2	St Mirren	6	5	1	12	+2	2.7	16
3	Hibernian	16	13	3	31	+1.94	2.6	42
4	Morton	10	8	2	14	+1.40	2.6	26
5	Dundee Utd	11	8	3	13	+1.18	2.5	27
6	Dunfermline	10	7	3	10	+1	2.4	24
7	Dumbarton	7	5	2	8	+1.14	2.4	17
8	Queen of Sth	8	5	3	11	+1.38	2.3	18
9	Raith	9	5	4	9	+1	2.1	19
10	Ayr	7	4	3	6	+0.86	2.1	15

Over 2.5 goals

	H	A	%
Dumbarton	7	13	56%
Queen of Sth	11	8	53%
Dundee Utd, Falkirk			50%

Under 2.5 goals

	H	A	%
Dunfermline	10	12	61%
Morton	12	10	61%
Raith	12	10	61%

Both to score

	H	A	%
Falkirk	12	12	67%
St Mirren	9	14	64%
Dumbarton, Morton			58%

Both not to score

	H	A	%
Raith	9	12	58%
Queen of Sth	9	10	53%
Hibernian	7	11	50%

AIRDRIEONIANS

Nickname: The Diamonds Excelsior Stadium
airdriefc.com

The division's great entertainers with 27 of 36 matches producing three goals or more.

Yet it was a couple of missed penalties against Alloa in the playoffs which cost them a shot at promotion after finishing third but with the section's worst defensive record.

	2016-17 H	A	Last six seasons at home P	W	D	L	OV	UN	BS	CS
Raith			2	0	1	1	1	1	1	1
Ayr			6	3	0	3	3	3	1	3
Alloa	W L	W L	2	1	0	1	1	1	1	0
Airdrieonians										
East Fife	D D	W W	6	2	2	2	4	2	5	1
Queens Park	W W	W L	2	2	0	0	2	0	2	0
Stranraer	W L	W L	8	2	4	2	3	5	6	1
Albion	L L	W W	6	2	2	2	2	4	3	2
Arbroath			4	3	1	0	2	2	2	2
Forfar			8	3	2	3	5	3	5	1

Season	Division	Pos	P	W	D	L	F	A	GD	Pts
2016-17	League One	3	36	16	4	16	61	66	-5	52
2015-16	League One	5	36	14	7	15	48	50	-2	49
2014-15	League One	5	36	16	10	10	53	39	+14	58

Over/Under 75%/25% 1st **Both score** 69%/31% 2nd

ALBION

Nickname: The Wee Rovers Cliftonhill
albionroversfc.com

Albion lost their last four matches to finish just two points clear of Peterhead in eighth.

It was a poor finale which saw Darren Young, their most successful ever manager, surprisingly fired. Brian Kerr was promoted from the youth set-up to replace Young.

	2016-17 H	A	Last six seasons at home P	W	D	L	OV	UN	BS	CS
Raith	-	-	-	-	-	-	-	-	-	-
Ayr			4	2	0	2	3	1	2	2
Alloa	L D	D D	4	0	1	3	3	1	2	0
Airdrieonians	L L	W W	6	1	0	5	5	1	5	0
East Fife	W L	D L	8	2	2	4	3	5	3	2
Queens Park	W D	L L	6	5	1	0	2	4	3	3
Stranraer	W W	L L	6	3	0	3	4	2	3	1
Albion										
Arbroath			6	3	2	1	2	4	3	2
Forfar			6	2	2	2	4	2	5	1

Season	Division	Pos	P	W	D	L	F	A	GD	Pts
2016-17	League One	8	36	11	9	16	41	48	-7	42
2015-16	League One	6	36	13	10	13	40	44	-4	49
2014-15	League Two	1	36	22	5	9	61	33	+28	71

Over/Under 44%/56% 10th **Both score** 42%/58% 11th

Ross Callachan (right) and Greig Spence will be teammates at Raith again this season

ALLOA

Nickname: The Wasps   Recreation Park
alloaathletic.co.uk

The 11-4 favourites to bounce back after relegation from the Championship, Alloa won their first four as a signal of intent.

Manager Jack Ross then joined St Mirren, leaving Jim Goodwin to lead them to second. But they lost to Brechin in the playoff final.

	2016-17 H / A	P	W	D	L	OV	UN	BS	CS
Raith	6 1	2	3	0	6		1	2	
Ayr	2 1	1	0	1	1	1	1		
Alloa									
Airdrieonians	L W / L W	2	1	0	1	2	0	2	0
East Fife	W W / D D	4	2	2	0	2	2	3	1
Queens Park	D D / W W	4	2	2	0	2	2	2	2
Stranraer	D W / W W	6	5	1	0	4	2	3	3
Albion	D D / W D	4	2	2	0	2	2	3	1
Arbroath		2	0	0	2	1	1	1	0
Forfar		2	2	0	0	1	1	1	1

Season	Division	Pos	P	W	D	L	F	A	GD	Pts
2016-17	League One	2	36	17	11	8	69	44	+25	62
2015-16	Championship	10	36	4	9	23	22	67	-45	21
2014-15	Championship	9	36	6	9	21	34	56	-22	27

Over/Under 69%/31% 2nd   **Both score** 72%/28% 1st

ARBROATH

Nickname: The Red Lichties   Gayfield Park
arbroathfc.co.uk

Dick Campbell's first full season in charge ended with the League Two title, fittingly clinched on the road since the Lichties had gone unbeaten away since September.

It was veteran Campbell's eighth promotion as either a coach or manager.

	2016-17 H / A	P	W	D	L	OV	UN	BS	CS
Raith	-	-	-	-	-	-	-	-	-
Ayr		4	1	0	3	4	0	3	0
Alloa		2	0	0	2	1	1	1	0
Airdrieonians		4	2	1	1	3	1	3	0
East Fife		10	4	4	2	4	6	5	3
Queens Park		4	0	1	3	2	2	3	0
Stranraer		4	3	0	1	3	1	3	1
Albion		6	5	0	1	4	2	4	1
Arbroath									
Forfar	W L / W D	8	4	1	3	4	4	4	2

Season	Division	Pos	P	W	D	L	F	A	GD	Pts
2016-17	League Two	1	36	18	12	6	63	36	+27	66
2015-16	League Two	9	36	11	6	19	42	51	-9	39
2014-15	League Two	3	36	16	8	12	65	46	+19	56

Over/Under 42%/58% 9th   **Both score** 58%/42% 6th

AYR

Nickname: The Honest Men   Somerset Park
ayrunitedfc.co.uk

Back in League One after a dismal season which saw them finish bottom with the least goals scored (33) and most conceded (62).

Ten home defeats was their undoing with no wins in their last seven leaving Ian McCall's men bottom of the Championship.

	2016-17 H / A	P	W	D	L	OV	UN	BS	CS
Raith	L W / D L	4	2	1	1	1	3	2	1
Ayr									
Alloa		2	0	1	1	0	2	0	1
Airdrieonians		6	2	1	3	5	1	2	2
East Fife		4	3	0	1	3	1	3	1
Queens Park	-	-	-	-	-	-	-	-	-
Stranraer		8	5	0	3	6	2	5	1
Albion		4	3	0	1	2	2	2	1
Arbroath		4	3	0	1	1	3	1	2
Forfar		8	5	1	2	5	3	5	3

Season	Division	Pos	P	W	D	L	F	A	GD	Pts
2016-17	Championship	10	36	7	12	17	33	62	-29	33
2015-16	League One	2	36	19	4	13	65	47	+18	61
2014-15	League One	8	36	9	7	20	45	60	-15	34

Over/Under 44%/56% 5th   **Both score** 53%/47% 7th

EAST FIFE

Nickname: The Fifers   Bayview Stadium
eastfifefc.info

Third after March's 1-0 win at Livingston – they beat the champions three times – East Fife won one of their last nine to finish fifth.

Barry Smith quit to join Raith enabling Darren Young a swift return to management after being fired by Albion.

	2016-17 H / A	P	W	D	L	OV	UN	BS	CS
Raith	-	-	-	-	-	-	-	-	-
Ayr		4	0	1	3	4	0	3	0
Alloa	D D / L L	4	1	2	1	2	2	2	1
Airdrieonians	L L / D D	6	3	1	2	1	5	0	4
East Fife									
Queens Park	L D / L D	6	0	4	2	2	4	3	2
Stranraer	W D / D L	6	1	3	2	1	5	3	2
Albion	D W / L W	8	4	2	2	3	5	3	5
Arbroath		10	5	1	4	6	4	6	2
Forfar		6	4	0	2	6	0	4	2

Season	Division	Pos	P	W	D	L	F	A	GD	Pts
2016-17	League One	5	36	12	10	14	41	44	-3	46
2015-16	League Two	1	36	18	8	10	62	41	+21	62
2014-15	League Two	4	36	15	8	13	56	48	+8	53

Over/Under 50%/50% 8th   **Both score** 50%/50% 6th

FORFAR

Nickname: The Loons   Station Park
forfarathletic.co.uk

Gary Bollan's men won their first seven games and were 11 points clear after 23 matches, but then the wheels came off.

Won just two of the last 13 to blow the title but recovered to beat Annan then Peterhead in the playoffs to go straight back up.

	2016-17 H	A	P	W	D	L	OV	UN	BS	CS
Raith	-	-	-	-	-	-	-	-	-	-
Ayr			8	5	1	2	6	2	6	1
Alloa			2	0	0	2	1	1	1	0
Airdrieonians			8	2	3	3	4	4	6	1
East Fife			6	4	0	2	5	1	5	1
Queens Park	-	-	-	-	-	-	-	-	-	-
Stranraer			8	4	2	2	4	4	5	3
Albion			6	5	0	1	4	2	2	3
Arbroath	L D	L W	8	0	4	4	2	6	6	0
Forfar										

Season	Division	Pos	P	W	D	L	F	A	GD	Pts
2016-17	League Two	2	36	18	10	8	69	49	+20	64
2015-16	League One	8	36	8	10	18	48	60	-12	34
2014-15	League One	3	36	20	6	10	59	41	+18	66

Over/Under 58%/42% 4th   **Both score** 69%/31% 1st

QUEEN'S PARK

Nickname: The Spiders   Hampden Park
queensparkfc.co.uk

In the playoff places with three games left only to lose all three and finish sixth. It was a tame end to a good campaign for a Spiders side who were the division's lowest scorers.

Manager Gus McPherson is preparing for his fourth full season in charge.

	2016-17 H	A	P	W	D	L	OV	UN	BS	CS
Raith	-	-	-	-	-	-	-	-	-	-
Ayr	-	-	-	-	-	-	-	-	-	-
Alloa	L L	D D	4	0	0	4	3	1	3	0
Airdrieonians	L W	L L	2	1	0	1	2	0	2	0
East Fife	W D	W D	6	4	1	1	3	3	1	4
Queens Park										
Stranraer	L L	W D	4	2	0	2	1	3	1	1
Albion	W W	L D	6	3	1	2	2	4	2	2
Arbroath			4	3	0	1	2	2	2	1
Forfar	-	-	-	-	-	-	-	-	-	-

Season	Division	Pos	P	W	D	L	F	A	GD	Pts
2016-17	League One	6	36	12	10	14	37	51	-14	46
2015-16	League One	4	36	15	11	10	46	32	+14	56
2014-15	League Two	2	36	17	10	9	51	34	+17	61

Over/Under 42%/58% 11th   **Both score** 47%/53% 8th

RAITH

Nickname: The Rovers   Stark's Park
raithrovers.net

Back in the third tier for the first time since 2009 with a fourth manager in a year.

Gary Locke lasted eight months – fired during a five-month winless streak – and John Hughes couldn't save them. After their playoff defeat, Barry Smith was appointed.

	2016-17 H	A	P	W	D	L	OV	UN	BS	CS
Raith										
Ayr	D W	W L	4	1	2	1	2	2	3	0
Alloa			6	3	1	2	1	3	3	4
Airdrieonians			2	2	0	0	0	2	0	2
East Fife	-	-	-	-	-	-	-	-	-	-
Queens Park	-	-	-	-	-	-	-	-	-	-
Stranraer	-	-	-	-	-	-	-	-	-	-
Albion	-	-	-	-	-	-	-	-	-	-
Arbroath	-	-	-	-	-	-	-	-	-	-
Forfar	-	-	-	-	-	-	-	-	-	-

Season	Division	Pos	P	W	D	L	F	A	GD	Pts
2016-17	Championship	9	36	10	9	17	35	52	-17	39
2015-16	Championship	4	36	18	8	10	52	46	+6	62
2014-15	Championship	6	36	12	7	17	42	65	-23	43

Over/Under 39%/61% 8th   **Both score** 42%/58% 10th

STRANRAER

Nickname: The Blues   Stair Park
stranraerfc.org

Bottom of the table in mid-January after a 1-0 defeat at Stenhousemuir which saw manager Brian Reid depart Stair Park.

Stevie Farrell took the reins and transformed the Blues' fortunes with just three defeats in their last 15 games.

	2016-17 H	A	P	W	D	L	OV	UN	BS	CS
Raith	-	-	-	-	-	-	-	-	-	-
Ayr			8	5	1	2	3	5	3	4
Alloa	L L	D L	6	1	0	5	6	0	5	0
Airdrieonians	L W	L W	8	5	1	2	5	3	5	3
East Fife	D W	L D	6	4	1	1	3	3	4	2
Queens Park	L D	W W	4	0	1	3	2	2	3	0
Stranraer										
Albion	W W	L L	6	3	2	1	3	3	3	2
Arbroath			4	2	2	0	1	3	3	1
Forfar			8	4	2	2	5	3	4	2

Season	Division	Pos	P	W	D	L	F	A	GD	Pts
2016-17	League One	7	36	12	8	16	46	50	-4	44
2015-16	League One	4	36	15	6	15	43	49	-6	51
2014-15	League One	2	36	20	7	9	59	38	+21	67

Over/Under 50%/50% 8th   **Both score** 44%/56% 10th

Scottish League One results 2016-17

	Airdrieonians	Albion	Alloa	Brechin	East Fife	Livingston	Peterhead	Queens Park	Stenhousemuir	Stranraer
Airdrieonians		0-2/1-2	2-1/0-1	1-0/3-1	1-1/2-2	2-4/0-4	1-3/4-1	4-1/3-2	0-5/1-0	1-0/1-2
Albion	1-2/3-4		0-4/1-1	0-2/1-0	1-0/0-1	0-1/0-2	0-1/0-0	2-0/1-1	4-0/1-1	3-2/3-0
Alloa	1-2/2-1	0-0/1-1		1-2/6-1	2-1/3-0	1-3/2-2	4-0/0-1	1-1/2-2	4-1/2-1	2-2/1-0
Brechin	3-2/3-0	1-2/1-0	0-1/1-2		0-1/2-1	0-3/0-2	2-1/0-1	0-0/3-1	2-1/2-2	2-0/0-0
East Fife	0-1/0-4	2-2/2-0	2-2/0-0	1-2/3-2		3-1/2-1	2-0/1-2	1-2/0-0	0-1/1-0	2-0/0-0
Livingston	2-0/4-2	1-2/3-0	3-1/2-1	2-1/3-0	3-1/0-1		1-2/4-1	1-2/4-0	4-1/1-0	5-1/0-0
Peterhead	2-4/1-1	2-2/1-1	1-1/3-2	1-3/0-1	0-3/1-1	1-2/2-3		2-0/4-0	0-2/0-1	2-0/2-2
Queens Park	1-3/2-1	2-1/2-0	1-2/0-2	2-0/1-1	1-0/2-2	1-0/1-1	0-0/2-0		0-3/0-2	0-2/0-1
Stenhousemuir	2-2/4-2	1-0/0-3	2-2/2-4	1-3/1-1	0-1/3-1	0-4/0-1	2-2/3-1	1-2/0-2		0-5/1-0
Stranraer	1-2/2-1	3-2/3-0	2-5/1-2	0-1/2-0	1-1/2-1	1-2/0-1	1-0/3-3	0-2/1-1	3-1/3-0	

Scottish League One 2016-17

Pos	H	A		P	Home W	D	L	F	A	Away W	D	L	F	A	GD	Pts
1	1	1	Livingston (P)	36	13	1	4	43	16	13	2	3	37	16	48	81
2	2	2	Alloa	36	8	6	4	35	21	9	5	4	34	23	25	62
3	6	3	Airdrieonians	36	8	2	8	27	32	8	2	8	34	34	-5	52
4	4	4	Brechin (P)	36	8	3	7	22	20	7	2	9	21	29	-6	50
5	5	7	East Fife	36	7	5	6	22	20	5	5	8	19	24	-3	46
6	7	6	Queen's Park	36	7	4	7	18	21	5	6	7	19	30	-14	46
7	3	10	Stranraer	36	8	3	7	29	25	4	5	9	17	25	-4	44
8	8	9	Albion	36	6	4	8	21	22	5	5	8	20	26	-7	42
9	10	5	Peterhead (R)	36	4	6	8	25	29	6	4	8	19	30	-15	40
10	9	8	Stenhousemuir (R)	36	5	4	9	23	36	6	2	10	22	28	-19	39

Best attack

		GF	GFA
1	Livingston	80	2.22
2	Alloa	69	1.92
3	Airdrieonians	61	1.69
4	Stranraer	46	1.28
5	Stenhousemuir	45	1.25
6	Peterhead	44	1.22
7	Brechin	43	1.19
8	East Fife	41	1.14
9	Albion	41	1.14
10	Queen's Park	37	1.03

Best defence

		GA	GAA
1	Livingston	32	0.89
2	Alloa	44	1.22
3	East Fife	44	1.22
4	Albion	48	1.33
5	Brechin	49	1.36
6	Stranraer	50	1.39
7	Queen's Park	51	1.42
8	Peterhead	59	1.64
9	Stenhousemuir	64	1.78
10	Airdrieonians	66	1.83

Top scorers

	Team	Goals scored
Ryan	Airdrieonians	23
Buchanan	Livingston	22
Russell	Airdrieonians	18
McAllister	Peterhead	16
Spence	Alloa	16

Kirkpatrick (Alloa), Mullen (Livingston) – both 14

Key POS H A Overall league position, rank from home games, rank from away games **Sup** Avg match supremacy **GFA** Goals For Avg **GAA** Goals Against Avg **PGA** Points Gained Avg

Record when first to score

		P	W	D	L	F	A	Sup	PGA	Pts
1	Livingston	27	24	1	2	67	19	+1.78	2.7	73
2	Airdrieonians	16	14	1	1	35	16	+1.19	2.7	43
3	Albion	13	10	2	1	28	9	+1.46	2.5	32
4	East Fife	16	11	5	0	27	10	+1.06	2.4	38
5	Alloa	18	12	5	1	37	16	+1.17	2.3	41
6	Brechin	17	12	3	2	29	17	+0.71	2.3	39
7	Stranraer	16	12	1	3	35	17	+1.13	2.3	37
8	Stenhousemuir	15	11	1	3	32	21	+0.73	2.3	34
9	Queen's Park	15	9	3	3	24	14	+0.67	2	30
10	Peterhead	18	8	7	3	30	24	+0.33	1.7	31

Record when keeping a clean sheet

		P	W	D	F	Sup	PGA	Pts
1	Stenhousemuir	8	8	0	16	+2	3	24
2	Airdrieonians	5	5	0	8	+1.60	3	15
3	Livingston	14	13	1	31	+2.21	2.9	40
4	Alloa	9	7	2	16	+1.78	2.6	23
5	Albion	9	7	2	16	+1.78	2.6	23
6	East Fife	12	9	3	14	+1.17	2.5	30
7	Brechin	8	6	2	10	+1.25	2.5	20
8	Peterhead	8	6	2	11	+1.38	2.5	20
9	Stranraer	10	7	3	17	+1.70	2.4	24
10	Queen's Park	10	7	3	12	+1.20	2.4	24

Over 2.5 goals

	H	A	%
Airdrieonians	12	15	75%
Alloa	13	12	69%
Livingston	14	11	69%

Under 2.5 goals

	H	A	%
Queens Park	12	9	58%
Albion	12	8	56%
East Fife, Stranraer			50%

Both to score

	H	A	%
Alloa	13	13	72%
Airdrieonians	11	14	69%
Livingston, Peterhead			56%

Both not to score

	H	A	%
Albion	12	9	58%
Stranraer	7	13	56%
Queens Pk, Stenh'smuir			53%

ANNAN

Nickname: Galabankies Galabank
annanathleticfc.com

Ex-Carlisle hero Peter Murphy is the new player-manager at Galabank replacing Jim Chapman, who led Annan to the playoffs.

They weren't involved in a single 0-0 draw – nor the season before – and their matches averaged a league-high 3.3 goals per game.

	2016-17 H	2016-17 A	P	W	D	L	OV	UN	BS	CS
Peterhead			6	4	1	1	3	3	2	3
Stenhousemuir	-	-	-	-	-	-	-	-	-	-
Annan										
Montrose	L W	D W	12	7	3	2	10	2	11	1
Elgin	W W	W L	12	6	5	1	5	7	8	4
Stirling	W W	L L	8	3	3	2	6	2	7	0
Edinburgh City	D W	L L	2	1	1	0	0	2	1	1
Berwick	W W	L L	12	9	3	0	8	4	8	4
Clyde	W W	W L	12	5	1	6	6	6	6	3
Cowdenbeath	W W	D W	2	2	0	0	0	2	0	2

Season	Division	Pos	P	W	D	L	F	A	GD	Pts
2016-17	League Two	3	36	18	4	14	61	58	+3	58
2015-16	League Two	5	36	16	8	12	69	57	+12	56
2014-15	League Two	5	36	14	8	14	56	56	0	50

Over/Under 61%/39% 2nd **Both score** 67%/33% 3rd

BERWICK

Nickname: The Borderers Shielfield Park
berwickrangersfc.co.uk

Signed off without a clean sheet in their last 17 matches, hence finishing with the worst defensive record in the section and in the bottom half for a third-straight season.

John Coughlin's men left it to the final day to guarantee their league survival.

	2016-17 H	2016-17 A	P	W	D	L	OV	UN	BS	CS
Peterhead			6	1	1	4	3	3	4	0
Stenhousemuir	-	-	-	-	-	-	-	-	-	-
Annan	W W	L L	12	6	1	5	7	5	7	2
Montrose	L L	D L	12	4	4	4	9	3	8	3
Elgin	L L	L D	12	2	4	6	6	6	8	2
Stirling	W L	D D	8	5	1	2	4	4	4	3
Edinburgh City	L W	W D	2	1	0	1	2	0	2	0
Berwick										
Clyde	D W	L D	12	6	3	3	8	4	4	5
Cowdenbeath	D L	W W	2	0	1	1	1	1	2	0

Season	Division	Pos	P	W	D	L	F	A	GD	Pts
2016-17	League Two	8	36	10	10	16	50	65	-15	40
2015-16	League Two	6	36	14	7	15	45	50	-5	49
2014-15	League Two	8	36	11	10	15	60	57	+3	43

Over/Under 58%/42% 4th **Both score** 69%/31% 1st

CLYDE

Nickname: The Bully Wee Broadwood Stadium
clydefc.co.uk

Went off favourites for the second year in a row but again flopped.

Second after 13 games yet only stayed up on the final day following a four-month winless streak which cost Barry Ferguson his job. Jim Chapman is the new manager.

	2016-17 H	2016-17 A	P	W	D	L	OV	UN	BS	CS
Peterhead			6	2	0	4	1	5	1	2
Stenhousemuir	-	-	-	-	-	-	-	-	-	-
Annan	L W	L L	12	6	3	3	8	4	9	2
Montrose	W L	L D	12	5	2	5	8	4	8	3
Elgin	W W	W L	12	7	2	3	8	4	8	2
Stirling	D L	D L	8	4	1	3	5	3	6	1
Edinburgh City	D W	W D	2	1	1	0	1	1	1	1
Berwick	W D	D L	12	5	5	2	9	3	10	1
Clyde										
Cowdenbeath	W L	L L	2	1	0	1	1	1	1	0

Season	Division	Pos	P	W	D	L	F	A	GD	Pts
2016-17	League Two	9	36	10	8	18	49	64	-15	38
2015-16	League Two	7	36	17	6	13	56	45	+11	57
2014-15	League Two	6	36	13	8	15	40	50	-10	47

Over/Under 58%/42% 4th **Both score** 64%/36% 4th

COWDENBEATH

Nickname: The Blue Brazil Central Park
cowdenbeathfc.com

Gary Locke replaced Liam Fox with the Blue Brazil in trouble having lost seven in a row.

Lost just three of last 13 under Locke but still came last, with only shootout success over East Kilbride avoiding a third straight relegation. Assistant Billy Brown takes over.

	2016-17 H	2016-17 A	P	W	D	L	OV	UN	BS	CS
Peterhead			2	0	1	1	2	0	2	0
Stenhousemuir			4	1	2	1	2	2	2	2
Annan	D L	L L	2	0	1	1	1	1	1	0
Montrose	W L	W L	2	1	0	1	0	2	0	1
Elgin	L D	L D	2	0	1	1	0	2	1	0
Stirling	L L	W W	4	2	0	2	1	3	1	1
Edinburgh City	W L	D D	2	1	0	1	1	1	1	1
Berwick	L L	D W	2	0	0	2	0	2	0	0
Clyde	W W	L W	2	2	0	0	0	2	0	2
Cowdenbeath										

Season	Division	Pos	P	W	D	L	F	A	GD	Pts
2016-17	League Two	10	36	9	8	19	40	55	-15	35
2015-16	League One	9	36	11	6	19	46	72	-26	39
2014-15	Championship	10	36	7	4	25	31	86	-55	25

Over/Under 39%/61% 10th **Both score** 50%/50% 9th

EDINBURGH CITY

Nickname: City   Ainslie Park
edinburghcityfc.com

Five points adrift after ten matches, City's debut league season got off to a dismal start.

Still second-bottom at the end of February they won six of their last 11 to stay up. The lowest scorers with 38, City were the only side whose games averaged under 2.5 goals.

	2016-17 H A	Last six seasons at home P	W	D	L	OV	UN	BS	CS
Peterhead		-	-	-	-	-	-	-	-
Stenhousemuir		-	-	-	-	-	-	-	-
Annan	WW DL	2	2	0	0	0	2	0	2
Montrose	LD WL	2	0	1	1	0	2	1	0
Elgin	LW LL	2	1	0	1	2	0	1	1
Stirling	WW DL	2	2	0	0	0	2	0	2
Edinburgh City									
Berwick	LD WL	2	0	1	1	2	0	2	0
Clyde	LD DL	2	0	1	1	0	2	0	1
Cowdenbeath	DD LW	2	0	2	0	0	2	2	0

Season	Division	Pos	P	W	D	L	F	A	GD	Pts
2016-17	League Two	7	36	11	10	15	38	45	-7	43

Over/Under 39%/61% 10th   **Both score** 47%/53% 11th

ELGIN

Nickname: The Black And Whites   Borough Briggs
elgincity.com

League Two top scorer and player of the year, Shane Sutherland, missed the last two months of the season – and Elgin collapsed.

Won none of their last 12 and dropped from second at the end of February to miss out on a playoff spot on the final weekend.

	2016-17 H A	Last six seasons at home P	W	D	L	OV	UN	BS	CS
Peterhead		6	2	0	4	5	1	4	1
Stenhousemuir		-	-	-	-	-	-	-	-
Annan	LW LL	12	4	3	5	10	2	9	2
Montrose	WD WW	12	7	3	2	8	4	9	2
Elgin									
Stirling	LD WL	8	4	1	3	7	1	6	2
Edinburgh City	WW WL	2	2	0	0	2	0	1	1
Berwick	WD WW	12	8	2	2	10	2	8	4
Clyde	LW LL	12	8	2	2	5	7	6	4
Cowdenbeath	WD WD	2	1	1	0	1	1	1	1

Season	Division	Pos	P	W	D	L	F	A	GD	Pts
2016-17	League Two	5	36	14	9	13	67	47	+20	51
2015-16	League Two	2	36	17	8	11	59	46	+13	59
2014-15	League Two	7	36	12	9	15	55	58	-3	45

Over/Under 61%/39% 2nd   **Both score** 56%/44% 8th

MONTROSE

Nickname: The Gable Endies   Links Park
montrosefc.co.uk

Stewart Petrie was an unsung hero last term, transforming Montrose into a playoff outfit after eight successive bottom-half finishes.

One defeat in their last eight matches earned them that promotion shot but Peterhead proved too strong.

	2016-17 H A	Last six seasons at home P	W	D	L	OV	UN	BS	CS
Peterhead		6	3	0	3	5	1	4	1
Stenhousemuir		-	-	-	-	-	-	-	-
Annan	DL WL	12	4	4	4	7	5	8	2
Montrose									
Elgin	LL LD	12	5	2	5	11	1	7	2
Stirling	DL LW	8	1	4	3	6	2	7	1
Edinburgh City	LW WD	2	1	0	1	1	1	0	1
Berwick	DW WW	12	5	4	3	6	6	8	3
Clyde	WD LW	12	5	2	5	6	6	5	3
Cowdenbeath	LW LW	2	1	0	1	2	0	2	0

Season	Division	Pos	P	W	D	L	F	A	GD	Pts
2016-17	League Two	4	36	14	10	12	44	53	-9	52
2015-16	League Two	8	36	11	10	15	50	70	-20	43
2014-15	League Two	10	36	9	6	21	42	78	-36	33

Over/Under 56%/44% 7th   **Both score** 61%/39% 5th

PETERHEAD

Nickname: The Blue Toon   Balmoor Stadium
peterheadfc.com

Second favourites for League One, they finished second bottom, with one win in 13 after Christmas seeing them plunge.

Escaped automatic relegation on the final day only to be crushed 7-2 by Forfar in the playoff to crash into the basement.

	2016-17 H A	Last six seasons at home P	W	D	L	OV	UN	BS	CS
Peterhead									
Stenhousemuir	LL DL	6	3	1	2	2	4	2	2
Annan		6	4	1	1	4	2	4	2
Montrose		6	4	0	2	4	2	2	3
Elgin		6	2	2	2	4	2	4	1
Stirling		6	2	3	1	4	2	4	1
Edinburgh City		-	-	-	-	-	-	-	-
Berwick		6	3	2	1	2	4	3	3
Clyde		6	3	3	0	1	5	2	4
Cowdenbeath		2	1	0	1	1	1	0	1

Season	Division	Pos	P	W	D	L	F	A	GD	Pts
2016-17	League One	9	36	10	10	16	44	59	-15	40
2015-16	League One	3	36	16	11	9	72	47	+25	59
2014-15	League One	6	36	14	9	13	51	54	-3	51

Over/Under 53%/47% 6th   **Both score** 56%/44% 4th

STENHOUSEMUIR

Nickname: Warriors · Ochilview Park
stenhousemuirfc.com

Last term's relegation jollies didn't let anyone down, finishing bottom of the table.

Brown Ferguson remains at the helm and might be encouraged by a gallant end to a wretched campaign in which the Warriors took ten points from their last five games.

	2016-17		Last six seasons at home							
	H	A	P	W	D	L	OV	UN	BS	CS
Peterhead	D W	W W	6	3	1	2	6	0	6	0
Stenhousemuir										
Annan	-	-	-	-	-	-	-	-	-	-
Montrose	-	-	-	-	-	-	-	-	-	-
Elgin	-	-	-	-	-	-	-	-	-	-
Stirling			4	2	0	2	4	0	2	2
Edinburgh City	-	-	-	-	-	-	-	-	-	-
Berwick	-	-	-	-	-	-	-	-	-	-
Clyde	-	-	-	-	-	-	-	-	-	-
Cowdenbeath			4	2	0	2	3	1	3	0

Season	Division	Pos	P	W	D	L	F	A	GD	Pts
2016-17	League One	10	36	11	6	19	45	64	-19	39
2015-16	League One	8	36	11	7	18	46	80	-34	40
2014-15	League One	9	36	8	5	23	42	63	-21	29

Over/Under 61%/39% 4th **Both score** 47%/53% 8th

STIRLING

Nickname: The Binos · Forthbank Stadium
stirlingalbionfc.co.uk

Stuart McLaren was sacked after a dire start and the Binos were still bottom in December.

Dave Mackay was appointed to right the ship and seven wins in eight saw him earn manager-of-the-month recognition and helped Stirling to a sixth-place finish.

	2016-17		Last six seasons at home							
	H	A	P	W	D	L	OV	UN	BS	CS
Peterhead			6	3	0	3	3	3	3	2
Stenhousemuir			4	2	1	1	4	0	3	0
Annan	W W	L L	8	6	1	1	4	4	5	2
Montrose	W L	D W	8	5	1	2	6	2	5	3
Elgin	L W	D W	8	2	4	2	4	4	5	2
Stirling										
Edinburgh City	D W	L L	2	1	1	0	0	2	1	1
Berwick	D D	L W	8	5	2	1	6	2	6	2
Clyde	D W	D W	8	3	2	3	3	5	4	2
Cowdenbeath	L L	W W	4	0	1	3	2	2	2	0

Season	Division	Pos	P	W	D	L	F	A	GD	Pts
2016-17	League Two	6	36	12	11	13	50	59	-9	47
2015-16	League Two	7	36	13	9	14	47	46	+1	48
2014-15	League One	10	36	4	8	24	35	84	-49	20

Over/Under 56%/44% 7th **Both score** 58%/42% 6th

Balmoor Stadium will host League Two football following Peterhead's relegation

Scottish League Two results 2016-17

	Annan	Arbroath	Berwick	Clyde	Cowdenbeath	Edinburgh C	Elgin	Forfar	Montrose	Stirling
Annan		1-2/2-5	3-1/2-1	3-2/1-0	2-0/1-0	1-1/1-0	1-0/1-0	1-2/1-2	2-3/5-1	3-2/4-1
Arbroath	1-1/1-2		1-1/4-1	4-0/1-0	0-0/4-1	0-1/0-1	3-2/3-2	2-0/0-1	0-0/0-1	5-3/1-1
Berwick	2-0/4-1	1-1/0-2		1-1/4-3	1-1/1-3	1-3/3-2	2-4/0-1	1-2/3-2	1-2/0-1	3-2/0-1
Clyde	2-3/2-1	3-2/1-2	3-2/1-1		5-3/0-2	0-0/3-1	2-1/3-2	0-1/2-2	2-1/1-2	1-1/2-3
Cowdenbeath	2-2/0-1	0-2/1-2	0-2/0-1	1-0/1-0		2-0/1-2	0-1/1-1	3-4/1-1	2-0/0-2	0-2/0-2
Edinburgh City	1-0/2-0	3-3/0-2	1-2/2-2	0-1/0-0	1-1/1-1		1-2/3-0	2-3/0-1	0-1/1-1	2-0/1-0
Elgin	0-2/3-2	0-1/0-0	6-0/2-2	0-2/4-1	3-1/0-0	3-0/3-1		2-2/1-1	4-1/1-1	2-3/2-2
Forfar	5-1/2-4	0-1/1-1	2-0/2-3	4-3/3-0	4-3/3-1	1-1/1-2	3-2/1-1		1-3/0-0	4-1/1-1
Montrose	2-2/2-3	1-1/1-3	0-0/2-1	2-1/1-1	1-2/2-1	0-1/3-0	0-5/0-3	1-1/1-0		2-2/1-3
Stirling	3-1/1-0	2-2/1-1	0-0/2-2	1-1/3-0	1-2/0-3	1-1/1-0	0-4/1-0	0-3/0-3	2-0/1-2	

Scottish League Two 2016-17

Pos	H	A		P	Home W	D	L	F	A	Away W	D	L	F	A	GD	Pts
1	2	1	Arbroath (P)	36	8	5	5	30	18	10	7	1	33	18	27	66
2	3	2	Forfar (P)	36	8	5	5	38	28	10	5	3	31	21	20	64
3	1	7	Annan	36	12	1	5	35	23	6	3	9	26	35	3	58
4	9	3	Montrose	36	5	6	7	22	30	9	4	5	22	23	-9	52
5	4	4	Elgin City	36	7	7	4	36	22	7	2	9	31	25	20	51
6	6	5	Stirling	36	6	6	6	20	25	6	5	7	30	34	-9	47
7	7	6	Edinburgh City	36	5	6	7	21	20	6	4	8	17	25	-7	43
8	8	9	Berwick	36	6	3	9	28	32	4	7	7	22	33	-15	40
9	5	10	Clyde	36	8	4	6	33	30	2	4	12	16	34	-15	38
10	10	8	Cowdenbeath*	36	4	3	11	15	25	5	5	8	25	30	-15	35

*Cowdenbeath avoided relegation by winning playoff

Best attack

		GF	GFA
1	Forfar	69	1.92
2	Elgin City	67	1.86
3	Arbroath	63	1.75
4	Annan	61	1.69
5	Stirling	50	1.39
6	Berwick	50	1.39
7	Clyde	49	1.36
8	Montrose	44	1.22
9	Cowdenbeath	40	1.11
10	Edinburgh City	38	1.06

Best defence

		GA	GAA
1	Arbroath	36	1
2	Edinburgh City	45	1.25
3	Elgin City	47	1.31
4	Forfar	49	1.36
5	Montrose	53	1.47
6	Cowdenbeath	55	1.53
7	Annan	58	1.61
8	Stirling	59	1.64
9	Clyde	64	1.78
10	Berwick	65	1.81

Top scorers

	Team	Goals scored	
Sutherland	Elgin City	18	IIIIIIIIIIIIIIIIII
MacDonald	Clyde	17	IIIIIIIIIIIIIIIII
Cameron	Elgin City	13	IIIIIIIIIIIII
McCord	Arbroath	13	IIIIIIIIIIIII
Thomson	Berwick	13	IIIIIIIIIIIII

Denholm (Forfar), Doris (Arbroath) – both 12

Key POS H A Overall league position, rank from home games, rank from away games **Sup** Avg match supremacy **GFA** Goals For Avg **GAA** Goals Against Avg **PGA** Points Gained Avg

Record when first to score

		P	W	D	L	F	A	Sup	PGA	Pts
1	Montrose	15	12	1	2	26	14	+0.8	2.5	37
2	Forfar	17	12	4	1	39	18	+1.24	2.4	40
3	Arbroath	21	14	6	1	44	21	+1.1	2.3	48
4	Annan	22	14	4	4	40	24	+0.73	2.1	46
5	Elgin City	21	14	3	4	57	24	+1.57	2.1	45
6	Edinburgh City	14	9	3	2	20	9	+0.79	2.1	30
7	Clyde	14	8	4	2	28	20	+0.57	2	28
8	Berwick	14	8	4	2	31	23	+0.57	2	28
9	Cowdenbeath	14	8	2	4	27	19	+0.57	1.9	26
10	Stirling	19	9	6	4	28	19	+0.47	1.7	33

Record when keeping a clean sheet

		P	W	D	F	Sup	PGA	Pts
1	Annan	8	8	0	10	+1.25	3	24
2	Stirling	9	8	1	13	+1.44	2.8	25
3	Forfar	8	7	1	14	+1.75	2.8	22
4	Edinburgh City	10	8	2	12	+1.20	2.6	26
5	Elgin City	9	7	2	23	+2.56	2.6	23
6	Arbroath	11	8	3	15	+1.36	2.5	27
7	Cowdenbeath	8	6	2	11	+1.38	2.5	20
8	Montrose	9	6	3	9	+1	2.3	21
9	Berwick	5	3	2	5	+1	2.2	11
10	Clyde	4	2	2	3	+0.75	2	8

Over 2.5 goals

	H	A	%
Annan	11	11	61%
Elgin	11	11	61%
Berwick, Clyde, Forfar			58%

Under 2.5 goals

	H	A	%
Cowdenbeath	14	8	61%
Edinburgh City	12	10	61%
Arbroath	11	10	58%

Both to score

	H	A	%
Berwick	13	12	69%
Forfar	14	11	69%
Annan	12	12	67%

Both not to score

	H	A	%
Edinburgh City	10	9	53%
Cowdenbeath	12	6	50%
Elgin		7	9	44%

Tight title race should offer more betting opportunities for well-informed punters

I've written before that one of the joys of outright betting is the different pace involved in betting on the gradual unfurling of the season's outcomes, writes Alex Deacon. In contrast to the fruit-machine velocity of match betting, I would also contend that it's a place where one's chances of coming out ahead at the end of the season are significantly greater than when plying your trade match by match.

When compared to the often fruitless slog of trying to find a significant degree of edge in match betting, the outright markets do at least offer a bastion of hope.

I say this because it is also quite surprising, when viewed over the course of a season, how amazingly predictable things can seem when viewed from a distance greater than one game from the next.

When betting in outright markets, those making a considered analysis over a much longer period of time have a much better chance of making a profit.

Also the more the time considered, the greater the advantage.

Therefore, the further we look ahead to make informed calculations of games to be played months in advance, the clearer the emerging picture.

This helps form an opinion that is more reasoned and balanced than the vast majority of reactionary opinion which helps create such liquidity in the outright markets.

And when I say outright markets I mean the half a dozen or so markets that trade for good money on the Betfair betting exchange.

For this reason, Racing & Football Outlook readers are more informed than most bettors as we print forecasted league tables throughout the season.

After the past two seasons in which the forecasts have been able to call the Premier League winners – Chelsea and Leicester – as early as Christmas, I'm all for the kind of predicable fare that we see in Europe's major leagues, with the English top-flight less dull than most but still providing value.

Predictable, that is, in terms of defining the eventual outcome of the title.

However, that is not the case when looking at the swirling pot of chaos that is the relegation zone, situated not that far below the small group of sides who aren't going to be relegated any more than once in a generation.

For the coming season, I think it is likely we will witness a battle for the title far more exciting than we have seen in the last 12 months.

You couldn't rule out that it may be all over before Christmas, but the starting Index ratings of the small group of challengers are all of a broadly similar level.

You should add to that the most significant factor of the entire pre-season – for the first time in a while we have an established manager at each of the title hopefuls.

Consequently, we should see more sustained challenges than in recent seasons and more interesting opportunities to try to stay ahead of them as the campaign unfolds.

You can follow my slow-burning, season-long advice on Twitter at @rfoindex

About the Outlook Index

Our unique ratings provide an objective view of every club. Each team has a rating, roughly on a scale of 0 to 1,000, which goes up or down with league results and takes into account the relative strength of the opposition. The tables show each team's overall rating, plus ratings for home and away form (a separate ratings system) and a Trend rating (-20 to +20). The red and blue bars show the Trend value, based on the last 60 matches but weighted towards more recent games, to help identify the teams in form. Red is hot, blue is not. The tables show final ratings for 2016-17.

Premier League

	Current	H	A		Trend
Chelsea	974	978	954		4
Tottenham	970	972	941		8
Man City	957	972	938		6
Liverpool	953	952	933		4
Arsenal	949	965	926		6
Man Utd	944	966	927		-4
Everton	911	931	874		-2
Leicester	899	930	873		-2
Southampton	899	906	900		-3
Bournemouth	898	888	866		9
West Ham	896	897	882		2
Swansea	890	903	860		6
Stoke	889	896	874		-7
Crystal Palace	887	864	889		6
Newcastle	876	891	858		-2
Burnley	874	900	845		-6
West Brom	874	884	868		-12
Watford	873	882	851		-7
Brighton	868	878	854		-9
Huddersfield	836	838	823		-10

Championship

	Current	H	A		Trend
Fulham	867	840	854		10
Hull	865	893	805		-1
Middlesbrough	860	877	824		-4
Reading	858	867	816		4
Sheff Wed	857	863	837		4
Sunderland	854	861	852		-7
Norwich	844	880	811		7
Derby	838	861	814		-2
Brentford	837	829	825		3
Leeds	836	848	818		-11
Aston Villa	832	853	798		1
Cardiff	830	844	816		0
Sheff Utd	825	807	803		10
Wolves	821	811	829		2
Barnsley	819	814	802		-5
Bristol City	819	826	785		11
Preston	815	840	810		-12
Ipswich	814	831	806		-6
Burton	813	803	782		4
Nottm Forest	811	828	783		0
QPR	806	828	792		-7
Birmingham	803	802	812		0
Bolton	799	814	776		1
Millwall	782	808	769		-3

Manchester City should put up a stronger title challenge in 2017-18

League One

	Current	H	A	Trend	
Blackburn	831	822	812		9
Wigan	799	802	787		2
Fleetwood	797	781	773		4
Bradford	790	807	774		2
Scunthorpe	788	800	768		4
Oxford Utd	776	752	771		6
Rochdale	776	788	740		0
Southend	774	772	753		-4
MK Dons	770	759	775		2
Charlton	766	778	758		2
Rotherham	766	791	739		2
Bristol Rovers	764	788	718		-3
Oldham	764	766	746		5
Portsmouth	756	749	746		11
Shrewsbury	752	759	726		1
Wimbledon	751	748	738		-2
Peterborough	751	753	745		-5
Bury	751	754	725		1
Walsall	746	765	748		-14
Gillingham	742	769	722		-2
Northampton	742	752	736		-5
Plymouth	739	733	746		1
Blackpool	734	746	726		3
Doncaster	727	757	726		-15

League Two

	Current	H	A	Trend	
Luton	737	731	729		6
Swindon	733	745	723		-2
Port Vale	732	762	713		-1
Coventry	732	760	705		5
Accrington	725	733	723		5
Colchester	725	749	694		5
Exeter	724	709	735		-2
Wycombe	722	723	716		4
Chesterfield	720	731	710		-5
Cambridge	716	717	717		-1
Mansfield	713	718	713		-1
Carlisle	712	722	722		-1
Grimsby	708	717	692		1
Lincoln	708	719	677		4
Stevenage	707	714	712		-9
Notts County	704	714	694		6
Newport County	704	713	686		11
Crewe	699	716	694		3
Yeovil	695	712	692		-5
Cheltenham	694	717	679		0
Barnet	694	705	696		-8
Crawley	686	714	670		-2
Forest Green	686	704	687		-4
Morecambe	682	675	698		-3

Scottish Premiership

	Current	H	A	Trend	
Celtic	942	963	917		3
Aberdeen	873	861	864		5
Rangers	852	904	816		7
St Johnstone	848	826	842		2
Ross County	824	807	807		8
Partick	811	800	802		-3
Kilmarnock	808	788	805		-2
Hearts	808	842	792		-11
Motherwell	796	792	792		-2
Hamilton	796	803	778		-4
Hibernian	795	812	785		0
Dundee	794	798	781		-6

National League

	Current	H	A	Trend	
Tranmere	713	704	705		5
Aldershot	702	688	672		13
Dag & Red	687	680	696		2
Dover	680	692	672		-1
Hartlepool	676	711	660		-5
Barrow	666	689	656		-4
Maidstone Utd	664	649	656		12
Gateshead	661	663	666		-8
Bromley	660	667	648		4
Woking	658	666	636		11
Leyton Orient	656	666	694		-9
Macclesfield	655	653	678		-8
Sutton United	654	676	613		7
Torquay	651	649	646		8
Fylde	650	642	647		8
Wrexham	649	663	645		-7
Guiseley	648	657	629		-6
Maidenhead	647	644	644		4
Solihull M	646	633	656		1
Eastleigh	646	668	650		-2
Halifax	640	639	640		3
Boreham Wood	638	642	646		-4
Ebbsfleet	625	645	610		-10
Chester	617	628	640		-14

Scottish Championship

	Current	H	A	Trend	
Inverness CT	802	816	785		2
Falkirk	778	789	778		2
Dundee Utd	765	807	747		-8
Dunfermline	757	739	741		8
Morton	755	762	721		-7
St Mirren	752	744	748		12
Livingston	742	729	733		9
Dumbarton	735	732	709		2
Queen Of Sth	732	741	725		-2
Brechin	668	689	656		-3

Scottish League One

	Current	H	A	Trend	
Raith	733	768	710		-6
Ayr	709	698	691		-2
Alloa	701	705	689		2
Stranraer	673	690	664		2
Airdrieonians	671	676	680		-1
Queen's Park	670	659	658		1
Albion	659	665	661		-8
East Fife	654	671	647		-9
Arbroath	643	624	661		2
Forfar	638	655	657		-12

Scottish League Two

	Current	H	A	Trend	
Peterhead	668	672	668		-1
Stenhousemuir	661	653	656		6
Annan	635	668	613		6
Montrose	630	618	628		4
Stirling	622	632	629		2
Elgin	618	650	607		-9
Edinburgh City	612	622	610		4
Cowdenbeath	610	623	641		5
Berwick	604	623	607		-1
Clyde	598	632	594		0

Spanish La Liga

	Current	H	A	Trend	
Real Madrid	1034	1050	1031		2
Barcelona	1028	1054	1015		5
Atl Madrid	1004	1022	992		4
Villarreal	969	981	956		6
Seville	965	1016	928		-4
Ath Bilbao	964	990	931		0
Real Sociedad	957	956	949		-1
Alaves	950	943	930		6
Espanyol	943	945	929		-1
Valencia	935	954	921		3
Malaga	934	950	907		12
Eibar	932	932	922		-5
Girona	927	926	920		3
Celta Vigo	922	942	916		-9
Leganes	911	917	903		2
Deportivo	911	918	901		-2
Levante	908	937	869		2
Real Betis	906	932	905		-5
Getafe	902	912	878		-4
Las Palmas	897	953	864		-11

German Bundesliga

	Current	H	A	Trend	
B Munich	1008	1022	994		1
Dortmund	964	1004	930		3
Hoffenheim	942	954	902		3
RB Leipzig	932	920	924		-2
Werder Bremen	919	908	900		4
Cologne	916	924	890		2
Augsburg	914	899	898		3
B M'gladbach	914	953	900		-3
Schalke	912	943	887		-3
Freiburg	910	916	887		1
Leverkusen	908	926	916		-5
Hamburg	903	908	870		2
Wolfsburg	901	920	899		0
H Berlin	901	933	869		-7
Frankfurt	900	925	863		-8
Mainz	889	912	879		-5
Stuttgart	880	886	882		-3
Hannover	864	874	872		1

Italian Serie A

	Current	H	A	Trend	
Juventus	981	1048	969		-4
Napoli	976	997	969		9
Roma	970	994	966		4
Atalanta	929	936	912		5
Lazio	912	937	922		-8
Fiorentina	911	964	907		-5
Inter	908	942	916		-8
Milan	903	943	916		-7
Sassuolo	897	908	906		6
Torino	894	922	894		1
Sampdoria	882	899	881		-3
Cagliari	878	910	857		5
Udinese	877	910	876		-6
Chievo	868	889	890		-8
Genoa	860	914	851		-2
Verona	860	890	866		-4
Bologna	860	882	880		-4
Empoli	857	886	869		-6
Palermo	848	876	856		5
Crotone	845	845	798		22
Benevento	808	813	794		6
Pescara	800	819	789		1
SPAL	799	802	794		6

French Ligue 1

	Current	H	A	Trend	
Paris St-G	971	997	961		2
Monaco	970	957	950		10
Nice	927	943	897		-6
Lyon	917	924	908		3
Marseille	904	922	883		6
Bordeaux	898	914	888		3
Nantes	888	888	870		1
Lille	884	890	893		1
Rennes	880	900	867		1
Angers	878	878	840		5
St Etienne	878	912	876		-6
Guingamp	875	896	837		0
Dijon	866	870	817		2
Toulouse	864	875	855		-5
Metz	864	867	822		4
Caen	849	858	862		-9
Montpellier	849	880	849		-9
Strasbourg	833	842	849		-4
Amiens	828	832	811		10
Troyes	824	844	809		-5

Portuguese Primeira Liga

	Current	H	A	Trend	
Benfica	961	986	944		-2
Porto	938	971	908		-4
Sporting Lisbon	934	941	923		-5
V Guimaraes	891	878	880		3
Feirense	871	848	855		18
Maritimo	871	899	826		1
Braga	870	915	849		-9
Rio Ave	868	869	860		1
Estoril	858	856	847		10
Boavista	855	848	851		4
Pacos Ferreira	854	874	834		3
Moreirense	854	850	840		12
Aves	850	859	843		4
Tondela	849	849	823		11
Chaves	847	857	834		-8
Belenenses	843	839	857		-8
Vitoria Setubal	834	846	809		-6
Portimonense	830	843	823		2

Dutch Eredivisie

	Current	H	A	Trend	
PSV Eindhoven	934	952	916		-1
Ajax	934	946	914		1
Feyenoord	915	930	886		-1
FC Utrecht	890	884	870		10
AZ Alkmaar	862	874	864		-8
Groningen	856	867	837		6
Vitesse	854	863	855		0
Heracles	841	852	828		2
Den Haag	839	852	819		11
Excelsior	834	831	805		12
FC Twente	833	871	822		-9
PEC Zwolle	828	854	813		-2
Heerenveen	826	852	820		-13
Roda JC	825	836	802		3
Willem II	823	826	810		-5
VVV Venlo	813	817	780		5
Sparta Rotterdam	811	827	795		1
NAC Breda	808	816	806		-3

OPT IN FOR
2% COMMISSION ON ENGLISH PREMIER LEAGUE MATCH ODDS IN AUGUST

WHEN THE **FUN** STOPS **STOP**™

Pools draws chart 2016-17   **X score-draw, 0 goalless draw**

Pools No.	Aug / Sep / Oct / Nov / Dec / Jan / Feb / Mar / Apr / May — draw pattern	X	0
	6 13 20 27 3 10 17 24 1 8 15 22 29 5 12 19 26 3 10 17 24 31 7 14 21 28 4 11 18 25 4 11 18 25 1 8 15 22 29 6		
1	- - - - - - - - - - - - 0 - X - - - - - - - - - - - - - - - - - - - X - - X - - -	3	1
2	0 - 0 X X - - - - - - - - - - - - - X - - - - - - - - - - - - - X - - - - - - - - X	5	2
3	- - - - - X - - - 0 - - 0 - - - X X - - - - X - - - - - - 0 0 - - - - - - - - - X X	6	4
4	- - - - - - - - 0 - - - - - 0 X - X - - - 0 - - - - - - - X - - X - - 0 - - X - - -	5	4
5	0 - - - - - X X - X - - - - - - - - - - - 0 X - - - - - - - - - - X - - - - 0 - X -	5	3
6	- X - - - - - - X - - - X - - X - X X - - - X - - X - - X - - - - 0 - X - 0 - 0 -	9	2
7	- - - X X - - - - X - - X - - X - - - - - - - - - - - - X - 0 - 0 - - - 0 - 5	5	3
8	- - - X - X - - - - X - 0 - X 0 - - - - - - 0 0 - - - - - - - - - - 0 - - - 4	4	5
9	- X - - - - X X - X - X - 0 - - - - - - X - X - - X - - - - - - 0 - - 8	8	2
10	- X - 0 - X - - X X X - X X - - - - - X - 0 - - - - X 0 - 0 0 - - - - X - 10	10	5
11	X - X - X - - X - - X - - X - - - 0 - X - 0 - X X - - X - - X - - X - - X 13	13	2
12	- - - - - - 0 0 0 - - - - - - - - 0 - - - - - - - - - - - - 0 - - X - - 1	1	5
13	- - 0 - X - - - X - - 0 - - - - - X - X - - - 0 0 - - - - - 4	4	4
14	0 - X X - X - 0 - - - X - X - 0 - - X X - - - X - X - X X - 0 - 11	11	4
15	- - - - - - X - X - - - - - - 0 - - - 0 - X - - 0 X - - - X - 5	5	3
16	- - X - - - - - X - - - X - X X - - - - - X - - - - - - 6	6	0
17	X - - 0 X 0 - - - X X 0 - - - X - - - - - - - - X - X - 9	9	3
18	X - - - - - X - X - - - - - - X X - - - - 0 0 - 6	6	2
19	- 0 X - - X - - - 0 - - - - X X - X - - 0 - - 0 0 - X 6	6	5
20	- - - - X - 0 X - - 0 - - - X - - 0 - X X - X X - X X - X - - X - 0 - 11	11	4
21	- - - - X X 0 - - X - - X - - X - X - - X 0 - 0 - 0 - - X 8	8	4
22	- - - - - - 0 X - 0 - 0 - - 0 X - X 0 X 0 - - 0 - - X - 5	5	7
23	- - X - X - - X - - - - X 0 - - X X 0 - - 7	7	2
24	- - X - X 0 - - - 0 - 0 - 0 - - - - X - - - 0 - 5	5	6
25	- X - - - 0 - - X X - - - - 0 - - - - X X - X X - 0 X 9	9	3
26	- - 0 X X X - - - X - - - X - - 0 X - X 0 - - X - 9	9	3
27	X 0 - - - X - X - - X - - X X - - 0 - - X - 0 - X X 9	9	3
28	X X - X - - - - X - X - - X X - X - 0 - - 0 - X 10	10	2
29	- - - X - - X - X X - - 0 - - - - - X X - X 7	7	1
30	- - - X - 0 - X - X X - - - - - X - - X 6	6	1
31	X 0 X - 0 - - X X - - - 0 0 - 0 X - X - - X X - - - X 9	9	5
32	- - - - X - - X 0 - - X - X 0 - X - 0 - - X - X X 8	8	3
33	- - - 0 X - - - X - X - - X 0 - - X - X X X - - X 0 - 9	9	3
34	X X - X - X X X 0 X - 0 - - 0 - - 0 0 - - X - X - 10	10	5
35	- - 0 - - X - - - X - - 0 - - - X - 0 - X 4	4	3
36	- - X - - - - X X - X - - - X - 0 0 - - X 7	7	2
37	- - - - X - - - X - - 0 - - X 3	3	1
38	- 0 X - - - - X X - X 0 - X - X - - 7	7	2
39	- X - - X X X X X - X - 0 - 0 - - 7	7	2
40	X - - - X - - - - 0 - 0 - X - X X - 0 - X - X 7	7	3
41	- - X - X - 0 - 0 - X - - X - X - - X - X 8	8	2
42	0 X - X - 0 X X 0 - - X - 0 - X 0 7	7	5
43	- X - - - 0 - - 0 - X X - X X - X X 7	7	2
44	X - - X - - 0 - X X - X 0 X 6	6	2
45	- X - - - X - X 0 - X 0 0 X 0 - X X - X 9	9	4
46	- - X - 0 - 0 X - X X - X 0 X - X X - 0 10	10	4
47	X 0 - X X - X - 0 X X 0 - X - X - X 11	11	3
48	- - - 0 - X 0 X 0 X X - 0 - X - X 10	10	4
49	- X X - X - X X - X X - X - X 10	10	0
X	10 11 9 10 10 15 4 9 11 11 9 7 11 14 8 4 8 9 7 7 5 10 5 8 14 4 12 11 13 10 5 9 7 7 8 7 10 5 10 12	356	
0	4 5 4 2 2 2 6 1 5 4 3 4 3 2 3 5 3 7 5 1 3 5 6 6 4 3 2 3 4 3 8 3 5 5 4 1 3 4 5 2		150

British weekend results only. European and international games used in some mid-season coupons. May 13 and May 20 coupons omitted due to British fixtures covering matches 1-10 only.

FA CUP

First round
Friday November 4, 2016
Eastleigh.......(0) 1-1 (0).......Swindon
Millwall ....(0) 1-0 (0)......Southend
Saturday November 5, 2016
Bolton...........(1) 1-0 (0)........Grimsby
Bradford ....(0) 1-2 (1)....Accrington
Braintree.......(3) 7-0 (0)....Eastbourne
Bury..............(2) 2-2 (0)..Wimbledon
Cambridge U (1) 1-1 (0)..........Dover
Charlton ....(2) 3-1 (0)....Scunthorpe
Cheltenham ..(0) 1-1 (0)..........Crewe
Colchester.....(0) 1-2 (1)..Chesterfield
Crawley ....(1) 1-1 (1).......Bristol R
Dag & Red ....(0) 0-0 (0)..........Halifax
Dartford........(2) 3-6 (3)....Sutton Utd
Exeter ....(1) 1-3 (1)........Luton
Gillingham ....(2) 2-2 (2)....... Brackley
Lincoln..........(1) 2-1 (0)....Altrincham
MK Dons.......(3) 3-2 (1).Spennymoor
Mansfield .....(0) 1-2 (1)......Plymouth
Merstham .....(0) 0-5 (2)........Oxford
Northampton (2) 6-0 (0).Harrow Boro
Oldham ....(1) 2-1 (0).....Doncaster
Peterborough (1) 2-1 (0)......Chesham
Port Vale ......(1) 1-0 (0).....Stevenage
Portsmouth ...(0) 1-2 (1)....Wycombe
Shrewsbury ..(2) 3-0 (0).........Barnet
Stockport ......(2) 2-4 (2)........ Woking
Walsall ....(0) 0-1 (1)..Macclesfield
Westfields.....(1) 1-1 (0)Curzon Ashton
Whitehawk...(1) 1-1 (0)..Stourbridge
Yeovil............(1) 2-2 (0).....Solihull M
Sunday November 6, 2016
Alfreton ....(0) 1-1 (0)..Newport Co
Blackpool......(2) 2-0 (0)Kidderminster
Boreham W ..(1) 2-2 (0).......Notts Co
Hartlepool....(0) 3-0 (0)...... Stamford
Maidstone ....(1) 1-1 (0)......Rochdale
Morecambe ..(0) 1-1 (0)......Coventry
Sheff Utd ......(3) 6-0 (0)Leyton Orient
St Albans ......(1) 3-5 (1).........Carlisle
Taunton Town(2) 2-2 (2).........Barrow
Monday November 7, 2016
Southport .....(0) 0-0 (0)....Fleetwood
First-round replays
Monday November 14, 2016
Curzon Ashton(2) 3-1 (0)....Westfields
Stourbridge...(0) 3-0 (0)...Whitehawk
Tuesday November 15, 2016
Wimbledon...(3) 5-0 (0)............ Bury
Barrow..........(0) 2-1 (0)........Taunton
Bristol R........(1) 4-2 (1)........Crawley
AET – 2-2 after 90 mins
Coventry.......(1) 2-1 (1)..Morecambe
Crewe...........(0) 1-4 (2)..Cheltenham
Fleetwood ....(1) 4-1 (0).....Southport
AET – 1-1 after 90 mins

Halifax..........(1) 2-1 (0)....Dag & Red
Newport Co ..(0) 4-1 (0)........Alfreton
AET – 1-1 after 90 mins
Notts Co ....(1) 2-0 (0).. Boreham W
Rochdale ......(2) 2-0 (0)....Maidstone
Solihull M .....(0) 1-1 (0)........... Yeovil
AET – 0-0 after 90, Solihull 4-2 on pens
Swindon ....(0) 1-3 (2)...... Eastleigh
Wednesday November 16, 2016
Brackley........(2) 4-3 (1)... Gillingham
AET – 2-2 after 90 mins
Thursday November 17, 2016
Dover ....(0) 2-4 (0) Cambridge U
AET – 1-1 after 90 mins

Second round
Friday December 2, 2016
Macclesfield..(0) 0-0 (0)..........Oxford
Saturday December 3, 2016
Blackpool......(1) 1-0 (0)....... Brackley
Carlisle ....(0) 0-2 (0)...... Rochdale
Charlton ....(0) 0-0 (0)...... MK Dons
Chesterfield ..(0) 0-5 (2).....Wycombe
Luton.............(0) 6-2 (2)....Solihull M
Plymouth ......(0) 0-0 (0)...Newport Co
Shrewsbury ..(0) 0-0 (0)......Fleetwood
Sutton Utd ....(0) 2-1 (1)..Cheltenham
Sunday December 4, 2016
Bolton...........(1) 3-2 (0)...... Sheff Utd
Bristol R.........(1) 1-2 (1).........Barrow
Cambridge U (3) 4-0 (0)...... Coventry
Curzon Ashton(2)3-4 (0).. Wimbledon
Eastleigh.......(1) 3-3 (0)..........Halifax
Millwall ....(3) 5-2 (2)...... Braintree

Notts Co ....(1) 2-2 (2)Peterborough
Port Vale ....(3) 4-0 (0).... Hartlepool
Woking.........(0) 0-3 (0)....Accrington
Monday December 5, 2016
Lincoln..........(2) 3-2 (0)........Oldham
Second-round replays
Tuesday December 13, 2016
Fleetwood ....(0) 3-2 (1).. Shrewsbury
Halifax..........(0) 0-2 (2)...... Eastleigh
MK Dons.......(1) 3-1 (1)...... Charlton
AET – 1-1 after 90 mins
Oxford ....(1) 3-0 (0). Macclesfield
Stourbridge...(0) 1-0 (0)Northampton
Tuesday December 20, 2016
Peterborough(2) 2-0 (0).......Notts Co
Wednesday December 21, 2016
Newport Co ..(0) 0-1 (0)......Plymouth
AET – 0-0 after 90 mins

Third round
Friday January 6, 2017
West Ham.....(0) 0-5 (3)... Man City
Saturday January 7, 2017
Accrington ....(1) 2-1 (0)........... Luton
Barrow..........(0) 0-2 (1)...... Rochdale
Birmingham..(1) 1-1 (1).... Newcastle
Blackpool......(0) 0-0 (0)....... Barnsley
Bolton...........(0) 0-0 (0)...... C Palace
Brentford......(5) 5-1 (1)...... Eastleigh
Brighton ....(1) 2-0 (0)...... MK Dons
Bristol City ....(0) 0-0 (0)....Fleetwood
Everton.........(0) 1-2 (0)...... Leicester
Huddersfield .(1) 4-0 (0)......Port Vale

Wycombe gave Spurs a fright in a cracking fourth-round clash

Arsenal put in an excellent FA Cup final performance

Hull ....(0) 2-0 (0)...... Swansea
Ipswich..........(1) 2-2 (1)......... Lincoln
Man Utd ....(2) 4-0 (0)........Reading
Millwall ....(1) 3-0 (0)Bournemouth
Norwich........(0) 2-2 (1)Southampton
Preston ....(1) 1-2 (0).........Arsenal
QPR ....(0) 1-2 (1)..... Blackburn
Rotherham....(0) 2-3 (1)........Oxford
Stoke ....(0) 0-2 (1)........ Wolves
Sunderland ...(0) 0-0 (0).........Burnley
Sutton Utd ....(0) 0-0 (0).. Wimbledon
Watford ....(1) 2-0 (0).........Burton
West Brom....(1) 1-2 (0).......... Derby
Wigan...........(1) 2-0 (0) Nottm Forest
Wycombe .....(0) 2-1 (0).. Stourbridge

Sunday January 8, 2017
Cardiff ....(1) 1-2 (2).........Fulham
Chelsea.........(2) 4-1 (0)Peterborough
Liverpool ......(0) 0-0 (0)......Plymouth
Middlesbro ...(0) 3-0 (0).... Sheff Wed
Tottenham ....(0) 2-0 (0)....Aston Villa

Monday January 9, 2017
Cambridge U (1) 1-2 (0)........... Leeds

Third-round replays
Tuesday January 17, 2017
Barnsley........(0) 1-2 (1)..... Blackpool
　　　　　　AET – 1-1 after 90 mins
Burnley ....(1) 2-0 (0)...Sunderland
C Palace........(0) 2-1 (0).......... Bolton
Fleetwood ....(0) 0-1 (1)....Bristol City
Lincoln..........(1) 1-0 (0)........ Ipswich
Wimbledon...(1) 1-3 (0)....Sutton Utd

Wednesday January 18, 2017
Newcastle.....(2) 3-1 (0). Birmingham
Plymouth ......(0) 0-1 (1)..... Liverpool
Southampton(0) 1-0 (0)....... Norwich

Fourth round
Friday January 27, 2017
Derby ....(2) 2-2 (1).......Leicester

Saturday January 28, 2017
Blackburn ......(2) 2-0 (0)..... Blackpool
Burnley ....(1) 2-0 (0)....Bristol City
C Palace ....(0) 0-3 (1) .... Man City
Chelsea.........(2) 4-0 (0)......Brentford
Lincoln..........(0) 3-1 (1)...... Brighton
Liverpool ......(0) 1-2 (2)........ Wolves
Middlesbro ...(0) 1-0 (0)....Accrington
Oxford ....(0) 3-0 (0)....Newcastle
Rochdale ....(0) 0-4 (1).Huddersfield
Southampton(0) 0-5 (3).........Arsenal
Tottenham ....(0) 4-3 (2).....Wycombe

Sunday January 29, 2017
Fulham ....(1) 4-1 (0)............... Hull
Man Utd ....(1) 4-0 (0)......... Wigan
Millwall ....(0) 1-0 (0).......Watford
Sutton Utd ....(0) 1-0 (0)........... Leeds

Fourth-round replays
Wednesday February 8, 2017
Leicester ....(0) 3-1 (0).......... Derby
　　　　　　AET – 1-1 after 90 mins

Fifth round
Saturday February 18, 2017
Burnley ....(0) 0-1 (0)......... Lincoln

Huddersfield .(0) 0-0 (0)...... Man City
Middlesbro ...(2) 3-2 (0).........Oxford
Millwall ....(0) 1-0 (0)......Leicester
Wolves ....(0) 0-2 (0)........ Chelsea

Sunday February 19, 2017
Blackburn .....(1) 1-2 (1).......Man Utd
Fulham ....(0) 0-3 (1)....Tottenham

Monday February 20, 2017
Sutton Utd ....(0) 0-2 (1).........Arsenal

Fifth-round replay
Wednesday March 1, 2017
Man City.......(3) 5-1 (1).Huddersfield

Quarter-finals
Saturday March 11, 2017
Arsenal ....(1) 5-0 (0)......... Lincoln
Middlesbro ...(0) 0-2 (1)..... Man City

Sunday March 12, 2017
Tottenham ....(2) 6-0 (0)........Millwall

Monday March 13, 2017
Chelsea.........(0) 1-0 (0).......Man Utd

Semi-finals
Saturday April 22, 2017
Chelsea.........(2) 4-2 (1)....Tottenham

Sunday April 23, 2017
Arsenal ....(0) 2-1 (0)..... Man City
　　　　　　AET – 1-1 after 90 mins

Final
Saturday May 27, 2017
Arsenal ....(1) 2-1 (0)........ Chelsea

First round

Tuesday August 30, 2016
Accrington....(0) 0-3 (0).........Crewe
Blackpool......(0) 2-1 (1)..Cheltenham
Bolton...........(0) 0-2 (1). Everton U23
Bradford.......(1) 1-0 (0)....Stoke U23
Bristol R........(0) 2-3 (1) Reading U23
Bury..............(1) 4-1 (1)..Morecambe
Charlton........(0) 0-0 (0)...So'ton U23
AET – 0-0 after 90, Charlton 5-4 on pens
Chesterfield..(1) 2-1 (0)..Wolves U23
Coventry.......(1) 4-2 (1). W Ham U23
Crawley.........(1) 1-0 (0)....Colchester
Fleetwood....(1) 1-0 (0)Blackpool U23
Gillingham.....(0) 1-2 (2)........Luton
Leyton Orient(1) 3-1 (0)....Stevenage
MK Dons.......(1) 2-2 (0).........Barnet
AET – 2-2 after 90, MK Dons 5-3 on pens
Mansfield.....(0) 0-2 (0).....Doncaster
Millwall........(0) 2-0 (0).....WBA U23
Northampton(0) 0-3 (1)....Wycombe
Oldham........(1) 4-5 (3)........Carlisle
Oxford.........(2) 4-2 (1)..........Exeter
Peterborough(0) 1-6 (4) Norwich U23
Plymouth......(0) 4-1 (1)..Newport Co
Port Vale.......(0) 1-0 (0)....Derby U23
Scunthorpe...(0) 2-1 (0)..M'boro U23
Sheff Utd......(0) 0-0 (0)Leicester U23
AET – 0-0 after 90, Leicester 5-4 on pens
Shrewsbury ..(0) 0-1 (1) Cambridge U
Southend......(1) 2-0 (0) Brighton U23
Walsall.........(3) 5-2 (1)......Grimsby
Wimbledon...(1) 3-0 (0)Swansea U23
Yeovil...........(4) 4-3 (2)....Portsmouth

Wednesday August 31, 2016
Notts Co.......(2) 2-1 (1)....Hartlepool

Tuesday September 6, 2016
Rochdale......(0) 1-1 (0)Sun'land U23
AET – 1-1 after 90, Rochdale 4-2 on pens

Tuesday September 13, 2016
Swindon.......(1) 2-1 (0).Chelsea U23

Tuesday October 4, 2016
Barnet..........(0) 0-5 (1) Norwich U23
Bolton..........(1) 1-0 (0).....Blackpool
Bradford.......(2) 2-1 (0)............Bury
Bristol Rovers(0) 0-0 (0)..........Yeovil
AET – 0-0 after 90, Bristol R 5-3 on pens
Cambridge U (1) 2-1 (1)..M'boro U23
Carlisle.........(1) 2-0 (0)Blackburn U23
Charlton.......(0) 0-2 (1)......Crawley
Cheltenham..(0) 2-1 (1). Everton U23
Chesterfield..(0) 1-4 (3)....Accrington
Colchester.....(1) 1-2 (1)...So'ton U23
Coventry......(2) 3-1 (1)Northampton
Crewe...........(0) 2-3 (2)..Wolves U23
Doncaster.....(0) 2-2 (1)....Derby U23
AET – 2-2 after 90, Doncaster 4-2 on pens
Fleetwood....(0) 0-2 (2)......Oldham
Grimsby.......(0) 0-1 (0)Leicester U23
Hartlepool....(0) 0-1 (0)Sun'land U23
Luton............(0) 2-0 (0).....WBA U23
Millwall........(1) 2-1 (1)... Gillingham
Morecambe..(3) 3-1 (0).... Stoke U23
Newport Co..(0) 1-2 (1)Swansea U23
Peterborough(0) 0-1 (1)......MK Dons
Port Vale.......(0) 0-1 (0).....Mansfield
Portsmouth...(0) 2-2 (1) Reading U23
AET – 2-2 after 90, Reading 4-3 on pens
Rochdale......(0) 2-1 (1).......Notts Co
Scunthorpe...(1) 2-0 (0)..Shrewsbury
Sheff Utd......(0) 1-2 (1).........Walsall
Southend......(0) 1-0 (0)Leyton Orient
Stevenage.....(0) 2-2 (1) Brighton U23
AET – 2-2 after 90, Brighton 4-3 on pens
Swindon.......(0) 0-0 (0)..........Oxford
AET – 0-0 after 90, Swindon 3-1 on pens
Wimbledon...(0) 2-1 (1).....Plymouth
Wycombe.....(1) 3-0 (0). W Ham U23

Tuesday October 18, 2016
Exeter...........(2) 3-2 (0).Chelsea U23

Tuesday November 8, 2016
Barnet..........(0) 1-2 (1)Peterborough
Blackburn U23(1)2-2 (0).......Oldham
AET – 2-2 after 90, Oldham 5-4 on pens
Brighton U23(1) 1-0 (0)Leyton Orient
Cambridge U (0) 0-2 (1)...Scunthorpe
Chelsea U23.(1) 1-1 (0)..........Oxford
AET – 1-1 after 90, Chelsea 13-12 on pens
Cheltenham..(0) 1-0 (0).........Bolton
Colchester.....(1) 1-1 (1).......Charlton
AET – 1-1 after 90, Colchester 4-3 on pens
Crewe...........(0) 0-2 (1)..Chesterfield
Derby U23....(1) 2-3 (2).....Mansfield
Doncaster.....(0) 0-0 (0).......Port Vale
AET – 0-0 after 90, Port Vale 4-3 on pens
Everton U23.(0) 1-1 (0).....Blackpool
AET – 1-1 after 90, Blackpool 5-4 on pens
Exeter...........(1) 1-1 (0).......Swindon
AET – 1-1 after 90, Swindon 4-2 on pens
Leicester U23(0) 0-1 (1).........Walsall
Luton............(0) 1-3 (0)......Millwall
M'boro U23..(0) 0-3 (0)..Shrewsbury
Newport Co..(1) 2-0 (0).. Wimbledon
Northampton(1) 1-1 (1). W Ham U23
AET – 1-1 after 90, West Ham 3-2 pens
Norwich U23 (2) 4-1 (0)......MK Dons
Portsmouth...(0) 1-0 (0).......Bristol R
Stevenage.....(2) 4-0 (0).......Southend
Stoke U23.....(0) 1-1 (0)...........Bury
AET – 1-1 after 90, Stoke 4-3 on pens
Swansea U23(2) 2-0 (0).....Plymouth
WBA U23......(0) 0-2 (1)... Gillingham
Wolves U23 ..(3) 4-0 (0)....Accrington

Wednesday November 9, 2016
Carlisle.........(3) 4-2 (0)....Fleetwood
Grimsby........(1) 2-4 (0).....Sheff Utd
Hartlepool.....(0) 1-2 (1)......Rochdale
Morecambe ..(0) 3-2 (0).....Bradford
Reading U23.(0) 0-2 (0)..........Yeovil
So'ton U23 ...(3) 4-0 (0)....Crawley
Sun'land U23(0) 2-1 (0).......Notts Co
Wycombe.....(1) 2-4 (0)......Coventry

Northern Group A – first round

	P	W	D	L	F	A	GD	Pts
Cheltenham	3	2	0	1	4	3	1	6
Blackpool	3	1	1	1	3	3	0	5
Everton U23	3	1	1	1	4	3	1	4
Bolton	3	1	0	2	1	3	-2	3

Northern Group B – first round

	P	W	D	L	F	A	GD	Pts
Wolves U23	3	2	0	1	8	4	4	6
Chesterfield	3	2	0	1	5	5	0	6
Crewe	3	1	0	2	5	5	0	3
Accrington	3	1	0	2	4	8	-4	3

Northern Group C – first round

	P	W	D	L	F	A	GD	Pts
Bradford	3	2	0	1	5	4	1	6
Morecambe	3	2	0	1	7	7	0	6
Bury	3	1	1	1	6	4	2	4
Stoke U23	3	0	1	2	2	5	-3	2

Northern Group D – first round

	P	W	D	L	F	A	GD	Pts
Carlisle	3	3	0	0	11	6	5	9
Oldham	3	1	1	1	8	7	1	5
Fleetwood	3	1	0	2	3	6	-3	3
Blackburn	3	0	1	2	2	5	-3	1

Northern Group E – first round

	P	W	D	L	F	A	GD	Pts
Doncaster	3	2	0	1	4	2	2	6
Mansfield	3	2	0	1	4	4	0	6
Port Vale	3	1	1	1	1	1	0	5
Derby U23	3	0	1	2	4	6	-2	1

Northern Group F – first round

	P	W	D	L	F	A	GD	Pts
Rochdale	3	2	1	0	5	3	2	8
S'derland U23	3	2	1	0	4	2	2	7
Notts County	3	1	0	2	4	5	-1	3
Hartlepool	3	0	0	3	2	5	-3	0

Northern Group G – first round

	P	W	D	L	F	A	GD	Pts
Scunthorpe	3	3	0	0	6	1	5	9
Cambridge	3	2	0	1	3	3	0	6
Shrewsbury	3	1	0	2	3	3	0	3
Middlesbro U23	3	0	0	3	2	7	-5	0

Northern Group H – first round

	P	W	D	L	F	A	GD	Pts
Walsall	3	3	0	0	8	3	5	9
Leicester U23	3	1	1	1	1	1	0	5
Sheff Utd	3	1	1	1	5	4	1	4
Grimsby	3	0	0	3	4	10	-6	0

Southern Group A – first round

	P	W	D	L	F	A	GD	Pts
Yeovil Town	3	2	1	0	6	3	3	7
Reading U23	3	1	1	1	5	6	-1	5
Portsmouth	3	1	1	1	6	6	0	4
Bristol Rovers	3	0	1	2	2	4	-2	2

Southern Group B – first round

	P	W	D	L	F	A	GD	Pts
Wimbledon	3	2	0	1	5	3	2	6
Swansea U23	3	2	0	1	4	4	0	6
Plymouth	3	1	0	2	5	5	0	3
Newport Co	3	1	0	2	4	6	-2	3

Southern Group C – first round

	P	W	D	L	F	A	GD	Pts
Swindon	3	1	2	0	3	2	1	7
Oxford Utd	3	1	2	0	5	3	2	5
Exeter	3	1	1	1	6	7	-1	4
Chelsea U23	3	0	1	2	4	6	-2	2

Southern Group D – first round

	P	W	D	L	F	A	GD	Pts
Coventry	3	3	0	0	11	5	6	9
Wycombe	3	2	0	1	8	4	4	6
West Ham U23	3	0	1	2	3	8	-5	2
Northampton	3	0	1	2	2	7	-5	1

Southern Group E – first round

	P	W	D	L	F	A	GD	Pts
So'ton U23	3	2	1	0	6	1	5	7
Crawley	3	2	0	1	3	4	-1	6
Charlton	3	0	2	1	1	3	-2	3
Colchester	3	0	1	2	2	4	-2	2

Southern Group F – first round

	P	W	D	L	F	A	GD	Pts
Norwich U23	3	3	0	0	15	2	13	9
MK Dons	3	1	1	1	4	6	-2	5
Peterborough	3	1	0	2	3	8	-5	3
Barnet	3	0	1	2	3	9	-6	1

Southern Group G – first round

	P	W	D	L	F	A	GD	Pts
Southend	3	2	0	1	3	4	-1	6
Brighton U23	3	1	1	1	3	4	-1	5
Stevenage	3	1	1	1	7	5	2	4
Leyton Orient	3	1	0	2	3	3	0	3

Southern Group H – first round

	P	W	D	L	F	A	GD	Pts
Millwall	3	3	0	0	7	2	5	9
Luton	3	2	0	1	5	4	1	6
Gillingham	3	1	0	2	4	4	0	3
WBA U23	3	0	0	3	0	6	-6	0

Second round
Northern section
Monday December 5, 2016
Wolves U23 ..(1) 1-1 (1)Sun'land U23
AET – 1-1 90 mins, Wolves 4-3 on pens

Tuesday December 6, 2016
Carlisle ....(0) 2-3 (2).... Mansfield
Doncaster .....(0) 1-1 (1)..... Blackpool
AET – 1-1 after 90, Blackpool 8-7 on pens
Rochdale ......(0) 0-2 (1)..Chesterfield
Scunthorpe ...(1) 1-1 (0)..Morecambe
AET – 1-1 after 90, Scunthorpe 5-3 pens

Wednesday December 7, 2016
Bradford ....(0) 1-0 (0) Cambridge U

Tuesday December 13, 2016
Walsall ....(1) 1-3 (0)........ Oldham

Tuesday January 10, 2017
Cheltenham ..(3) 6-1 (1)Leicester U23

Second round
Southern section
Tuesday December 6, 2016
Norwich U23 (0) 0-1 (0)Swansea U23
Southend ......(0) 1-1 (0).........Oxford
AET – 1-1 after 90, Oxford 4-3 on pens
Swindon ....(1) 2-3 (2)........... Luton
Wimbledon...(0) 1-2 (2) Brighton U23
Yeovil............(0) 4-1 (1)...... MK Dons

Wednesday December 7, 2016
Coventry.......(1) 1-0 (0)........Crawley
Millwall ....(0) 1-3 (0)..... Wycombe

Wednesday December 21, 2016
So'ton U23 ...(1) 1-1 (0) Reading U23
AET – 1-1 after 90, Reading 4-3 on pens

Third round
Tuesday January 10, 2017
Blackpool......(1) 1-1 (0).....Wycombe
AET – 1-1 after 90, Wycombe 5-4 on pens
Coventry.......(1) 3-0 (0) Brighton U23
Luton ....(2) 4-0 (0)...Chesterfield
Mansfield .....(0) 2-0 (0)........ Oldham
Oxford ....(2) 4-1 (1)...Scunthorpe
Swansea U23(0) 2-1 (1)...Wolves U23
Yeovil............(2) 4-2 (1) Reading U23

Tuesday January 17, 2017
Cheltenham ..(0) 0-1 (0).......Bradford

Quarter-finals
Tuesday January 24, 2017
Mansfield .....(1) 1-2 (0).....Wycombe
Swansea U23(0) 1-1 (0)...... Coventry
AET – 1-1 after 90, Coventry 4-2 on pens

Tuesday January 31, 2017
Oxford ....(0) 2-1 (0).......Bradford

Tuesday February 7, 2017
Luton ....(1) 5-2 (0)........... Yeovil

Semi-finals
Tuesday February 7, 2017
Coventry.......(2) 2-1 (0).....Wycombe

Wednesday March 1, 2017
Luton ....(0) 2-3 (1).........Oxford

Final
Sunday April 2, 2017
Coventry.......(1) 2-1 (0)..........Oxford

Coventry gave their supporters some much-needed cheer in the EFL Trophy

LEAGUE CUP

First round
Tuesday August 9, 2016

Accrington ....(0) 0-0 (0) .... Bradford
AET 0-0 after 90, Accrington 11-10 on pens
Barnet...........(0) 0-4 (2) .... Millwall
Barnsley........(1) 1-2 (0) Northampton
AET – 1-1 after 90 mins
Birmingham ..(0) 0-1 (0) .... Oxford
AET – 0-0 after 90 mins
Blackpool......(0) 4-2 (1) .... Bolton
AET – 2-2 after 90 mins
Brighton ....(0) 4-0 (0) .... Colchester
Cambridge U (0) 2-1 (0) .... Sheff Wed
AET – 1-1 after 90 mins
Carlisle ....(2) 2-1 (0) ....Port Vale
Cheltenham ..(1) 1-0 (0) .... Charlton
Coventry........(0) 3-2 (1) ...Portsmouth
AET – 2-2 after 90 mins
Derby ....(0) 1-0 (0) ....Grimsby
Doncaster .....(0) 1-2 (1) Nottm Forest
Exeter...........(0) 1-0 (0) ......Brentford
AET – 0-0 after 90 mins
Ipswich.........(0) 0-1 (0) .... Stevenage
Leyton Orient (0) 2-3 (1) .... Fulham
Mansfield .....(0) 1-3 (1) ..... Blackburn
Newport Co ..(1) 2-3 (0) .... MK Dons
Oldham ....(1) 2-1 (1) .... Wigan
Peterborough (0) 3-2 (1) .. Wimbledon
Preston ....(0) 1-0 (0) .... Hartlepool
Reading ....(2) 2-0 (0) ......Plymouth
Rochdale ....(0) 3-1 (1) ..Chesterfield
Rotherham....(0) 4-5 (1) ..Morecambe
AET – 3-3 after 90 mins
Scunthorpe ...(0) 2-0 (0) ....Notts Co
AET – 0-0 after 90 mins
Sheff Utd ......(1) 1-2 (0) .... Crewe
AET – 1-1 after 90 mins
Shrewsbury ..(1) 2-1 (1) .Huddersfield
Southend......(1) 1-3 (0) ... Gillingham
Walsall ....(0) 0-2 (0) .... Yeovil
AET – 0-0 after 90 mins
Wolves ....(1) 2-1 (1) ....Crawley
Wycombe ......(0) 0-1 (1) ....Bristol City

Wednesday August 10, 2016

Burton ....(1) 3-2 (0) .... Bury
AET – 1-1 after 90 mins
Fleetwood ....(1) 2-2 (0) .... Leeds
AET – 1-1 after 90, Leeds won 5-4 on pens
Luton............(1) 3-1 (1) ....Aston Villa
QPR ....(0) 2-2 (0) ....Swindon
AET – 1-1 after 90, QPR won 4-2 on pens

Thursday August 11, 2016

Bristol Rovers (0) 1-0 (0) .... Cardiff
AET – 0-0 after 90 mins

Second round
Tuesday August 23, 2016

Blackburn .....(1) 4-3 (2) .... Crewe
AET – 3-3 after 90 mins
Burton ....(0) 0-5 (2) ...... Liverpool
C Palace........(1) 2-0 (0) ..... Blackpool
Chelsea.........(3) 3-2 (1) Bristol Rovers
Derby ....(0) 1-1 (0) .... Carlisle
AET – 1-1 after 90, Derby won 14-13 pens
Everton ....(1) 4-0 (0) .... Yeovil

Wayne Rooney and Zlatan enjoy a League Cup bromance moment

Exeter ....(1) 1-3 (1) .... Hull
Luton.............(0) 0-1 (1) .... Leeds
Millwall ....(0) 1-2 (1) Nottm Forest
Newcastle.....(1) 2-0 (0) ..Cheltenham
Northampton (1) 2-2 (1) ... West Brom
AET – 2-2 after 90, Northampton 4-3 pens
Norwich........(2) 6-1 (0) ...... Coventry
Oxford ....(1) 2-4 (1) ...... Brighton
Peterborough (0) 1-3 (3) ...... Swansea
Preston ....(0) 2-0 (0) .... Oldham
QPR ....(1) 2-1 (1) .... Rochdale
Reading ....(0) 2-2 (1) ...... MK Dons
AET – 1-1 after 90, Reading 4-2 on pens
Scunthorpe ...(0) 1-2 (1) ....Bristol City
AET – 1-1 after 90 mins
Stevenage.....(0) 0-4 (2) ....Stoke
Watford ....(0) 1-2 (0) ... Gillingham
AET 1-1 after 90 mins
Wolves ....(2) 2-1 (1) Cambridge U

Wednesday August 24, 2016

Accrington ....(0) 1-0 (0) ....Burnley
AET – 0-0 after 90 mins
Fulham ....(0) 2-1 (1) ...Middlesbro
AET – 1-1 after 90 mins
Morecambe ..(1) 1-2 (1) Bournemouth
Sunderland ...(0) 1-0 (0) .. Shrewsbury

Third round
Tuesday September 20, 2016

Bournemouth (0) 2-3 (1) ....Preston
AET – 2-2 after 90 mins
Brighton ....(0) 1-2 (1) ....Reading
Derby ....(0) 0-3 (1) ...... Liverpool
Everton ....(0) 0-2 (1) .... Norwich
Leeds............(0) 1-0 (0) ..... Blackburn
Leicester.......(2) 2-4 (1) .... Chelsea
AET – 2-2 after 90 mins
Newcastle.....(2) 2-0 (0) .... Wolves
Nottm Forest (0) 0-4 (1) ....Arsenal

Wednesday September 21, 2016

Fulham ....(1) 1-2 (1) ....Bristol City
Northampton (1) 1-3 (1) ......Man Utd
QPR ....(0) 1-2 (0) ...Sunderland
Southampton (1) 2-0 (0) ...... C Palace

Stoke ....(1) 1-2 (1) .... Hull
Swansea........(0) 1-2 (1) ...... Man City
Tottenham ....(1) 5-0 (0) ... Gillingham
West Ham.....(0) 1-0 (0) ....Accrington

Fourth round
Tuesday October 25, 2016

Arsenal ....(1) 2-0 (0) ....Reading
Bristol City ....(0) 1-2 (1) .... Hull
Leeds.............(1) 2-2 (1) .... Norwich
AET – 1-1 after 90 mins, Leeds 3-2 on pens
Liverpool ......(1) 2-1 (0) ....Tottenham
Newcastle.....(2) 6-0 (0) ....Preston

Wednesday October 26, 2016

Man Utd ....(0) 1-0 (0) ...... Man City
Southampton (0) 1-0 (0) ...Sunderland
West Ham......(2) 2-1 (0) .... Chelsea

Quarter-finals
Tuesday November 29, 2016

Hull ....(0) 1-1 (0) .... Newcastle
AET – 0-0 after 90, Hull won 3-1 on pens
Liverpool ......(0) 2-0 (0) .... Leeds

Wednesday November 30, 2016

Arsenal ....(0) 0-2 (2) Southampton
Man Utd ....(1) 4-1 (1) .... West Ham

Semi-final, first legs
Tuesday January 10, 2017

Man Utd ....(0) 2-0 (0) .... Hull

Wednesday January 11, 2017

Southampton (1) 1-0 (0) ...... Liverpool

Semi-final, second legs
Wednesday January 25, 2017

Liverpool ......(0) 0-1 (0) Southampton
Southampton won 2-0 on aggregate

Thursday January 26, 2017

Hull ....(1) 2-1 (0) ......Man Utd
Man Utd won 3-2 on aggregate

Final
Sunday February 26, 2017

Man Utd ....(2) 3-2 (1) Southampton

SCOTTISH CUP

First round

Saturday September 24, 2016
BSC Glasgow (0) 3-1 (0).........Rothes
Beith Juniors .(0) 6-0 (0). Strathspey T
Civil Serv Strol(0)2-4 (0)Hawick Royal
Clachnacuddin (0) 1-2 (0). Stirling Univ
Dalbeattie Star(0)1-3 (0) Wick Academy
Deveronvale .(0) 0-3 (0).Gretna 2008
East Kilbride..(0) 9-1 (0)Vale of Leithen
Edinburgh Uni(0)0-1 (0)..Whitehill W
Forres Mech ..(0) 2-2 (0).Lossiemouth
Fort William ..(0) 1-4 (0).Brora Rangers
Gala Fairydean(0) 3-1 (0)..Fraserburgh
Girvan ....(0) 1-2 (0)...........Huntly
Inverurie Locos(0) 0-6 (0)Buckie Thistle
Keith.............(0) 0-1 (0). Banks o'Dee
Nairn County (0) 2-3 (0). Preston Ath.
Selkirk...........(0) 0-3 (0)....Linlithgow
Turriff U ....(0) 1-1 (0).... Bonnyrigg

Sunday September 25, 2016
Leith Athletic (0) 0-0 (0)Cumbernauld

First-round replays

Saturday October 1, 2016
Bonnyrigg .....(0) 4-1 (0)........ Turriff U
Hawick Royal (0) 6-2 (0)..Civil Service
Lossiemouth .(0) 0-4 (0). Forres Mech

Wednesday October 5, 2016
Cumbernauld(0) 1-0 (0) Leith Athletic

Second round

Saturday October 22, 2016
Annan...........(0) 0-0 (0).. East Stirling
Arbroath ....(3) 3-1 (1). Stirling Univ
BSC Glasgow (0) 0-1 (0).Beith Juniors
Banks o'Dee..(0) 2-2 (1)Formartine Utd
Berwick ....(1) 2-3 (3)Hawick Royal
Bonnyrigg .....(0) 2-1 (0)Cove Rangers
Brora Rangers .(0) 0-2 (0)...........Clyde
Buckie Thistle(0) 1-1 (1).Gretna 2008
Cowdenbeath(0)0-1 (1). East Kilbride
Cumbernauld(1) 2-2 (1). Forres Mech
Edinburgh C..(0) 0-0 (0)........... Forfar
Gala Fairydean(0) 0-4 (3)......Elgin City
Huntly...........(0) 0-2 (2).......Spartans
Linlithgow Rose(0)0-3 (1)......... Stirling
Preston Ath...(0) 0-3 (0)..... Montrose
Wick Academy (0) 4-1 (1)..Whitehill W

Second-round replays

Saturday October 29, 2016
East Stirling ..(1) 1-2 (1).......... Annan
Formartine ....(4) 7-2 (2). Banks o'Dee
Forres Mech..(1) 4-0 (0)Cumbernauld
Gretna 2008 .(0) 2-6 (2)Buckie Thistle

Tuesday November 1, 2016
Forfar ....(0) 0-1 (0). Edinburgh C

Third round

Saturday November 26, 2016
Airdrieonians (1) 1-2 (1).... Livingston

Bonnyrigg .....(0) 0-0 (0)...Dumbarton
Buckie Thistle(2) 3-5 (2). Dunfermline
Elgin City ......(3) 8-1 (1)Hawick Royal
Forres Mech..(1) 2-2 (1) Stenh'semuir
Peterhead .....(0) 0-1 (0)............ Alloa

Tuesday November 29, 2016
Albion...........(1) 2-1 (0) Queen of Sth
Brechin ....(0) 0-1 (0).............. Ayr
East Fife........(0) 1-1 (1). Edinburgh C
Queen's Park.(1) 2-0 (0)..... Montrose
St Mirren ......(3) 5-1 (0).......Spartans

Saturday December 3, 2016
Beith Juniors .(0) 0-6 (3).........Morton
Formartine ....(0) 4-0 (0).......... Annan
Stirling...........(1) 2-0 (0) Wick Academy
Stranraer.......(1) 2-1 (1). East Kilbride

Tuesday December 6, 2016
Clyde ....(3) 5-0 (0).......Arbroath

Third-round replays

Saturday December 3, 2016
Stenh'semuir..(2) 3-1 (0). Forres Mech

Tuesday December 6, 2016
Dumbarton ...(0) 0-1 (0).... Bonnyrigg

Wednesday December 7, 2016
Edinburgh C..(0) 0-1 (0)....... East Fife

Fourth round

Saturday January 21, 2017
Aberdeen......(2) 4-0 (0)..... Stranraer
Alloa.............(0) 2-3 (2). Dunfermline
Ayr ....(0) 0-0 (0) Queen's Park
Bonnyrigg .....(1) 1-8 (3).... Hibernian
Dundee.........(0) 0-2 (1)..... St Mirren
Elgin City ......(1) 1-2 (1).Inverness CT
Kilmarnock....(0) 0-1 (0)...... Hamilton
Livingston.....(0) 0-1 (1)..... East Fife
Morton ....(1) 2-0 (0)......... Falkirk
Partick ....(3) 4-0 (0)Formartine Utd
Rangers ....(0) 2-1 (0).. Motherwell
Ross County..(4) 6-2 (2)..Dundee Utd
St Johnstone .(2) 2-0 (0) Stenh'semuir
Stirling..........(1) 2-2 (1)...........Clyde

Sunday January 22, 2017
Albion...........(0) 0-3 (1)...........Celtic
Raith..............(0) 1-1 (1)........... Hearts

Fourth-round replays

Tuesday January 24, 2017
Queen's Park.(2) 2-2 (1)............... Ayr
AET – 2-2 after 90, Ayr won 5-4 on pens

Wednesday January 25, 2017
Hearts...........(1) 4-2 (1)............ Raith
AET – 1-1 after 90 mins

Tuesday January 31, 2017
Clyde ....(3) 3-2 (1)........ Stirling
AET – 1-1 after 90 mins

Fifth round

Saturday February 11, 2017
Ayr ....(0) 1-1 (0)............Clyde

Celtic ....(2) 6-0 (0).Inverness CT
Dunfermline..(1) 1-1 (0)...... Hamilton
East Fife........(0) 2-3 (1)..... St Mirren
Ross County..(0) 0-1 (0)..... Aberdeen
St Johnstone .(0) 0-1 (1)....... Partick

Sunday February 12, 2017
Hearts...........(0) 0-0 (0)..... Hibernian
Rangers ....(1) 2-1 (1).........Morton

Fifth-round replays

Tuesday February 14, 2017
Clyde ....(0) 1-2 (1)............... Ayr
AET – 1-1 after 90 mins
Hamilton.......(0) 1-1 (1). Dunfermline
AET – 1-1 after 90, Hamilton 3-0 on pens

Wednesday February 22, 2017
Hibernian......(2) 3-1 (1).......... Hearts

Quarter-finals

Saturday March 4, 2017
Hibernian......(2) 3-1 (1)............... Ayr
Rangers ....(1) 6-0 (0)..... Hamilton

Sunday March 5, 2017
Aberdeen......(1) 1-0 (0).......... Partick
Celtic ....(0) 4-1 (1)...... St Mirren

Semi-finals

Saturday April 22, 2017
Hibernian......(1) 2-3 (2)..... Aberdeen

Sunday April 23, 2017
Celtic ....(1) 2-0 (0)........Rangers

Final

Saturday May 27, 2017
Celtic ....(1) 2-1 (1)..... Aberdeen

SCOTTISH LEAGUE CUP

Group stage

Friday July 15, 2016
Airdrieonians (0) 0-1 (0)..........Partick
Arbroath ....(0) 1-1 (0)..Dundee Utd
  AET – Dundee Utd won 5-3 on pens
Cove Rangers(1) 1-2(1)–........... Raith

Saturday July 16, 2016
Albion...........(0) 0-0 (0).........Morton
  AET – Morton won 4-3 on pens
Annan...........(0) 1-2 (0)...... Stranraer
Ayr ....(1) 2-1 (0)...... Hamilton
Clyde ....(0) 1-2 (0)... Kilmarnock
Cowdenbeath(1) 1-2 (1).Inverness CT
East Fife........(0) 1-1 (1)........ Dundee
  AET – East Fife won 4-2 on pens
Elgin City ......(0) 1-3 (1).St Johnstone
Forfar ....(1) 2-2 (0)...Dumbarton
  AET – Forfar won 5-3 on pens
Livingston......(0) 2-3 (1)...... St Mirren
Montrose......(0) 0-1 (0). Ross County
Motherwell...(0) 0-2 (0)........Rangers
Queen's Park.(0) 0-2 (2) Queen of Sth
Stirling..........(1) 1-0 (0).......... Falkirk

Tuesday July 19, 2016
Alloa..............(1) 4-0 (0)Cove Rangers
Berwick ....(0) 0-0 (0).......... Albion
  AET – Albion won 5-4 on pens
Brechin ....(1) 2-1 (1).......... Stirling
Dumbarton ...(0) 0-2 (2)....... East Fife
Dundee Utd ..(4) 6-1 (1)Cowdenbeath
Dunfermline..(1) 3-0 (0).......Arbroath
Falkirk...........(2) 3-0 (0).....Elgin City
Morton ....(1) 1-0 (0)..........Clyde
Peterhead .....(2) 2-0 (0).......... Forfar
Queen of Sth.(2) 2-0 (0) Airdrieonians

Raith..............(1) 2-1 (0)..... Montrose
Rangers ....(1) 2-0 (0).......... Annan
St Mirren ......(0) 1-0 (0)................Ayr
Stenh'semuir.(0) 0-2 (1) Queen's Park
Stranraer.......(0) 3-1 (0).. East Stirling

Wednesday July 20, 2016
Edinburgh C..(0) 0-3 (2).... Livingston

Friday July 22, 2016
East Stirling ..(0) 0-3 (2)........Rangers

Saturday July 23, 2016
Airdrieonians (1) 2-1 (0) Stenh'semuir
Annan...........(1) 1-3 (1).. Motherwell
Ayr ....(1) 1-0 (0). Edinburgh C
Clyde ....(0) 1-1 (0)........ Berwick
  AET – 1-1 after 90, Clyde won 6-5 pens
Cowdenbeath(0) 0-3 (0).. Dunfermline
Dundee.........(1) 6-2 (2)...Dumbarton
East Fife........(1) 2-1 (1)...... Peterhead
Elgin City ......(2) 4-2 (1)........ Brechin
Hamilton.......(1) 3-0 (0)...... St Mirren
Inverness CT .(1) 1-1 (0)..Dundee Utd
  AET – 1-1 after 90, Dundee Utd 4-1 pens
Kilmarnock....(0) 0-2 (1)........ Morton
Montrose......(0) 0-2 (1)............ Alloa
Partick ....(0) 2-1 (0) Queen of Sth
Ross County..(0) 1-1 (1)............ Raith
  AET 1-1 after 90 mins, Raith won 4-3
  on pens
St Johnstone .(2) 3-0 (0).......... Falkirk

Monday July 25, 2016
Rangers ....(2) 3-0 (0)...... Stranraer

Tuesday July 26, 2016
Albion...........(0) 1-2 (0)............Clyde
Alloa..............(2) 3-2 (2). Ross County
Berwick ....(1) 2-3 (0)... Kilmarnock
Brechin ....(1) 1-1 (0).St Johnstone
  AET – 1-1 after 90, Brechin 4-2 on pens

Dunfermline..(1) 1-5 (2).Inverness CT
Forfar ....(1) 2-0 (0)....... East Fife
Livingston......(0) 0-2 (1)................Ayr
Motherwell...(0) 3-0 (0).. East Stirling
Peterhead .....(0) 2-1 (0)........ Dundee
Queen's Park.(1) 3-3 (3) Airdrieonians
  AET – 3-3 after 90, Airdrieonians 8-7 pens
Stenh'semuir.(0) 1-4 (0).......... Partick
Stirling..........(1) 4-1 (1)......Elgin City

Wednesday July 27, 2016
Arbroath ....(0) 0-2 (2)Cowdenbeath
Cove Rangers(1) 3-0 (0)..... Montrose
Edinburgh C..(2) 2-4 (2)...... Hamilton

Saturday July 30, 2016
Dumbarton ...(2) 3-3 (1).....Peterhead
  AET – 3-3 after 90, Peterhead 6-5 on pens
Dundee.........(3) 7-0 (0)........... Forfar
East Stirling ..(0) 0-2 (0).......... Annan
Falkirk...........(0) 2-0 (0)........Brechin
Hamilton.......(1) 2-1 (1)..... Livingston
Inverness CT .(4) 7-0 (0)....Arbroath
Kilmarnock....(0) 0-0 (0).......... Albion
  AET – 0-0 after 90, Albion 5-3 on pens
Morton ....(2) 2-0 (0)........ Berwick
Partick ....(1) 2-0 (0) Queen's Park
Queen of Sth.(0) 1-0 (0) Stenh'semuir
Raith..............(0) 0-1 (1)............ Alloa
Ross County..(1) 7-0 (0)Cove Rangers
St Johnstone .(3) 4-0 (0)......... Stirling
St Mirren ......(3) 3-0 (0). Edinburgh C
Stranraer.......(0) 0-3 (0).. Motherwell

Sunday July 31, 2016
Dundee Utd ..(0) 2-0 (0). Dunfermline

Second round

Tuesday August 9, 2016
Alloa..............(1) 1-0 (0).Inverness CT
Dundee Utd ..(3) 3-1 (0).......... Partick
Hamilton.......(1) 1-2 (0)........Morton
Hibernian......(1) 1-3 (0) Queen of Sth
Rangers ....(2) 5-0 (0).....Peterhead

Wednesday August 10, 2016
Ayr ....(1) 1-2 (2)..... Aberdeen
Celtic ....(2) 5-0 (0).. Motherwell
St Johnstone .(1) 3-2 (2).......... Hearts

Quarter-finals

Tuesday September 20, 2016
Morton ....(2) 2-1 (0)..Dundee Utd
Rangers ....(1) 5-0 (0) Queen of Sth

Wednesday September 21, 2016
Celtic ....(0) 2-0 (0)............ Alloa

Thursday September 22, 2016
Aberdeen......(0) 1-0 (0).St Johnstone

Semi-finals

Saturday October 22, 2016
Morton ....(0) 0-2 (0)..... Aberdeen

Sunday October 23, 2016
Rangers ....(0) 0-1 (1)............Celtic

Final

Sunday November 27, 2016
Aberdeen......(0) 0-3 (2)............Celtic

Spanish champions should be shorter in their bid to keep hold of La Liga title

The 2016-17 European campaign proved a mixed bag for the ante-post title favourites, writes Joe Champion. Bayern Munich and Juventus retained the domestic league titles that few expected them to lose, but Barcelona surrendered La Liga to bitter rivals Real Madrid and Paris Saint-Germain's dominance in France was finally ended by a magnificent Monaco side.

For Real, the season acted as a turning point. Having failed to win La Liga for five years, they confirmed themselves as top dogs in some style by both topping the pile in Spain and retaining the Champions League trophy. Zinedine Zidane had delivered.

Real's renaissance was marked by their consistency throughout the season. The iconic image of Barcelona's Leo Messi, shirt held aloft at the Bernabeu, briefly threatened to define the season but Real held on to a lead they rarely looked likely to relinquish.

Zidane built on the foundations of his debut season, while Barca's dismal attempt to add depth to their squad resulted in a number of poor purchases. With Andres Iniesta's influence seemingly on the wane, they appeared far too reliant on Messi.

Cristiano Ronaldo will continue to earn the majority of the plaudits but the importance of Luka Modric, Isco and Toni Kroos should not be underestimated.

The bulk of their title-winning squad will be there next season. Ronaldo and Gareth Bale should stay in the Spanish capital and while Alvaro Morata is likely to move on, Los Blancos are chasing Kylian Mbappe.

Both Antoine Griezmann and Diego Simeone look set to stay at Atletico Madrid as the club enters a new era at Wanda Metropolitano. But they will have to improve dramatically to prevent the 2017-18 La Liga campaign becoming another two-horse race.

Barca must strengthen again and this time they can't afford to get it wrong. With the bookies struggling to split them, Real look a shade overpriced to confirm the form.

Juventus are odds-on favourites to retain the Serie A title, but the gap appears to be narrowing in Italy and the Old Lady may face their biggest test for some time. They have won six consecutive Scudettos but last season's four-point winning margin was the slimmest since Antonio Conte led them back to the Serie A summit in 2011-12.

Juve's defence was rightly lauded last season during their phenomenal run to the Champions League final, but age will catch up with them at some point and the departure of Dani Alves is a negative. The Brazilian's contributions in both defence and attack will be sorely missed.

Runners-up Roma will have to replace both Mohamed Salah and Giallorossi icon Francesco Totti. While only a bit-part player last season, Totti's departure leaves a significant hole in the dressing room.

Manager Luciano Spalletti has left the Stadio Olimpico to take charge at Inter and new man Eusebio di Francesco has a big task on his hands in the eternal city.

Napoli will be in the mix again. Dries Mertens picked up the goalscoring baton in terrific style following the departure of Gonzalo Higuain last season and they remain an exciting team to watch, but Milan are emerging as the interesting outsiders.

The Rossoneri have a squad packed with young talent and, with the help of Chinese financial clout, Vincenzo Montella is able to strengthen an already improving squad.

Gianluigi Donnarumma has ended speculation about his future by signing a new San Siro deal, while a number of big signings have already arrived – most notably creative midfielder Hakan Calhanoglu and 21-year-old Portugal striker Andre Silva.

With more signings likely, Milan could prove an excellent each-way alternative to the Old Lady.

Bayern Munich retained the Bundesliga title by a comprehensive 15 points but it was second-placed RB Leipzig who provided the major talking point in Germany last season.

The Red Bull-backed club are despised by German supporters for their corporate origins but Ralph Hasenhuttl's team are anything but boring and they lit up the division in the first half of the season.

Leading lights Timo Werner, Emil Forsberg and Naby Keita have been subject to transfer speculation but the club are not in a position where they have to sell.

Peter Bosz takes charge of Dortmund and they are second favourites behind the champions. Bosz did a fine job nurturing a young Ajax side but has to reignite a Dortmund squad who were a virtual nonentity in the title race last season.

Pierre-Emerick Aubameyang could be on his way out of the club and they're not certain to finish above Leipzig. Back the Bulls in the 'without Bayern' market.

Monaco produced a seismic shock in France as they beat 1-10 shots Paris Saint-Germain to the Ligue 1 title, but Leonardo Jardim has already lost the services of Bernardo Silva to Manchester City, and Benjamin Mendy and Mbappe are among a host of players linked with a move elsewhere.

Jardim has spent some of the Silva cash, bringing in midfielder Youri Tielemans from Anderlecht and Feyenoord centre-half Terence Kongolo, but Monaco's golden generation look subject to the highest bidder.

Odds-on PSG are still the real powerhouse of French football and they are another name supposedly in the hunt for Mbappe – that purchase would be a real statement of their intent to regain the Ligue 1 title.

Neither Lyon or Marseille look up to challenging the top two. OL have lost three influential players in the shape of Alexandre Lacazette, Maxime Gonalons and Corentin Tolisso, while Marseille finished well last season but the squad looks light on firepower.

Monaco should retain enough of last season's stars to allow them to at least finish second but Nice offer a bit of value in the top-three finish market at around 3-1.

The Eaglets failed to stay in touch with the searing pace set by the top two, but they finished a long way clear of fourth-placed Lyon and should not be written off.

Nice will have to contend with Champions League football this season but Lucien Favre has done a fine job in the south of France and Nice shouldn't be such a big price in relation to some of the teams who rival them for European places.

Gianluigi Donnarumma has signed a new deal to stay on at the San Siro

ATALANTA

Atleti Azzurri d'Italia — atalanta.it

	2016-17 H	A	Last six seasons at home P	W	D	L	OV	UN	BS	CS
Juventus	D	L	6	0	1	5	3	3	2	0
Roma	W	D	6	2	2	2	5	1	6	0
Napoli	W	W	6	3	2	1	2	4	3	3
Atalanta										
Lazio	L	L	6	2	1	3	3	3	4	0
Milan	D	D	6	2	1	3	3	3	4	0
Inter	W	L	6	2	3	1	3	3	6	0
Fiorentina	D	D	6	1	1	4	1	5	1	2
Torino	W	D	5	2	0	3	3	2	3	1
Sampdoria	W	L	5	3	1	1	3	2	2	3
Cagliari	W	L	5	4	1	0	1	4	2	3
Sassuolo	D	W	4	1	2	1	1	3	3	0
Udinese	L	D	6	1	4	1	1	5	3	3
Chievo	W	W	6	4	2	0	2	4	3	3
Bologna	W	W	5	4	1	0	2	3	3	2
Genoa	W	W	6	2	1	3	2	4	2	2
Crotone	W	W	1	1	0	0	0	1	0	1
SPAL			-	-	-	-	-	-	-	-
Hellas Verona			3	0	2	1	1	2	2	1
Benevento										

Season	Division	Pos	P	W	D	L	F	A	GD	Pts
2016-17	Serie A	4	38	21	9	8	62	41	+21	72
2015-16	Serie A	13	38	11	12	15	41	47	-6	45
2014-15	Serie A	17	38	7	16	15	38	57	-19	37

Over/Under 53%/47% 13th   **Both score** 53%/47% 15th

BENEVENTO

Stadio Ciro Vigorito — beneventocalcio.club

	2016-17 H	A	Last six seasons at home P	W	D	L	OV	UN	BS	CS
Juventus			-	-	-	-	-	-	-	-
Roma			-	-	-	-	-	-	-	-
Napoli			-	-	-	-	-	-	-	-
Atalanta			-	-	-	-	-	-	-	-
Lazio			-	-	-	-	-	-	-	-
Milan			-	-	-	-	-	-	-	-
Inter			-	-	-	-	-	-	-	-
Fiorentina			-	-	-	-	-	-	-	-
Torino			-	-	-	-	-	-	-	-
Sampdoria			-	-	-	-	-	-	-	-
Cagliari			-	-	-	-	-	-	-	-
Sassuolo			-	-	-	-	-	-	-	-
Udinese			-	-	-	-	-	-	-	-
Chievo			-	-	-	-	-	-	-	-
Bologna			-	-	-	-	-	-	-	-
Genoa			-	-	-	-	-	-	-	-
Crotone			-	-	-	-	-	-	-	-
SPAL	W	L	1	1	0	0	0	1	0	1
Hellas Verona	W	D	1	1	0	0	0	1	0	1
Benevento										

Season	Division	Pos	P	W	D	L	F	A	GD	Pts
2016-17	Serie B	5	42	18	12	12	56	42	+14	65
2015-16	Lega Pro C	2	34	19	8	7	61	31	+30	65
2014-15	Lega Pro C	2	38	21	13	4	55	29	+26	76

Over/Under 43%/57% 12th   **Both score** 48%/52% 22nd

BOLOGNA

Renato Dall'Ara — bolognafc.it

	2016-17 H	A	Last six seasons at home P	W	D	L	OV	UN	BS	CS
Juventus	L	L	5	0	2	3	1	4	2	1
Roma	L	L	5	0	2	3	3	2	2	0
Napoli	L	L	5	2	1	2	4	1	3	1
Atalanta	L	L	5	3	0	2	3	2	2	1
Lazio	L	D	5	0	3	2	1	4	1	2
Milan	L	L	5	0	2	3	3	2	3	0
Inter	L	D	5	0	1	4	2	3	3	0
Fiorentina	L	L	5	2	1	2	2	3	2	1
Torino	W	L	4	1	1	2	2	2	2	1
Sampdoria	W	L	4	2	2	0	2	2	3	1
Cagliari	W	D	4	4	0	0	2	2	1	3
Sassuolo	D	W	3	0	2	1	0	3	1	1
Udinese	W	L	5	1	1	3	3	2	3	1
Chievo	W	D	5	2	2	1	3	2	2	2
Bologna										
Genoa	L	D	5	3	1	1	1	4	1	3
Crotone	W	W	2	1	0	1	0	2	0	1
SPAL			-	-	-	-	-	-	-	-
Hellas Verona			2	0	0	2	1	1	1	0
Benevento			-	-	-	-	-	-	-	-

Season	Division	Pos	P	W	D	L	F	A	GD	Pts
2016-17	Serie A	15	38	11	8	19	40	58	-18	41
2015-16	Serie A	14	38	11	9	18	33	45	-12	42
2014-15	Serie B	4	42	17	17	8	49	35	+14	68

Over/Under 45%/55% 20th   **Both score** 45%/55% 18th

CAGLIARI

Sardegna Arena — cagliaricalcio.net

	2016-17 H	A	Last six seasons at home P	W	D	L	OV	UN	BS	CS
Juventus	L	L	5	0	0	5	3	2	3	0
Roma	D	L	5	1	1	3	5	0	4	0
Napoli	L	L	5	0	2	3	2	3	1	1
Atalanta	W	L	5	3	1	1	3	2	3	2
Lazio	D	L	5	1	1	3	2	3	1	2
Milan	W	L	5	1	2	2	3	2	4	0
Inter	L	W	5	1	2	2	3	2	4	1
Fiorentina	L	L	5	2	1	2	3	2	2	2
Torino	L	L	4	2	0	2	4	0	4	0
Sampdoria	W	D	4	2	2	0	4	0	4	0
Cagliari										
Sassuolo	W	L	3	2	1	0	3	0	3	0
Udinese	W	L	5	1	1	3	2	2	2	2
Chievo	W	L	5	1	1	3	1	4	0	2
Bologna	D	L	4	1	2	1	1	3	2	1
Genoa	W	L	5	4	1	0	4	1	4	1
Crotone	W	W	2	2	0	0	0	2	0	1
SPAL			-	-	-	-	-	-	-	-
Hellas Verona			2	1	0	1	1	1	1	1
Benevento			-	-	-	-	-	-	-	-

Season	Division	Pos	P	W	D	L	F	A	GD	Pts
2016-17	Serie A	11	38	14	5	19	55	76	-21	47
2015-16	Serie B	1	42	25	8	9	78	41	+37	83
2014-15	Serie A	18	38	8	10	20	48	68	-20	34

Over/Under 68%/32% 3rd   **Both score** 66%/34% 3rd

ITALIAN SERIE A

CHIEVO

Stadio Marc'Antonio Bentegodi   chievoverona.tv

	2016-17 H	A	Last six seasons at home P	W	D	L	OV	UN	BS	CS
Juventus	L	L	6	0	1	5	4	2	3	1
Roma	L	L	6	1	3	2	2	4	2	3
Napoli	L	L	6	2	0	4	3	3	3	2
Atalanta	L	L	6	2	2	2	1	5	2	3
Lazio	D	W	6	1	2	3	3	3	2	2
Milan	L	L	6	0	3	3	1	5	1	3
Inter	W	L	6	2	0	4	1	5	1	1
Fiorentina	L	L	6	1	2	3	3	3	3	2
Torino	L	L	5	1	2	2	1	4	2	2
Sampdoria	W	D	5	3	1	1	3	2	4	0
Cagliari	W	L	5	3	2	0	0	5	0	5
Sassuolo	W	W	4	1	2	1	1	3	2	1
Udinese	D	W	6	1	4	1	3	3	4	2
Chievo										
Bologna	D	L	5	2	2	1	1	4	1	3
Genoa	D	W	6	3	1	2	3	3	3	2
Crotone	L	L	1	0	0	1	1	0	1	0
SPAL			-	-	-	-	-	-	-	-
Hellas Verona			3	0	2	1	1	2	2	0
Benevento			-	-	-	-	-	-	-	-

Season	Division	Pos	P	W	D	L	F	A	GD	Pts
2016-17	Serie A	14	38	12	7	19	43	61	-18	43
2015-16	Serie A	9	38	13	11	14	43	45	-2	50
2014-15	Serie A	13	38	10	13	15	28	41	-13	43

Over/Under 53%/47% 13th   **Both score** 55%/45% 12th

CROTONE

Stadio Ezio Scida   fccrotone.it

	2016-17 H	A	Last six seasons at home P	W	D	L	OV	UN	BS	CS
Juventus	L	L	1	0	0	1	0	1	0	0
Roma	L	L	1	0	0	1	0	1	0	0
Napoli	L	L	1	0	0	1	1	0	1	0
Atalanta	L	L	1	0	0	1	1	0	1	0
Lazio	W	L	1	1	0	0	1	0	1	0
Milan	D	L	1	0	1	0	0	1	1	0
Inter	W	L	1	1	0	0	1	0	1	0
Fiorentina	L	D	1	0	0	1	0	1	0	0
Torino	L	D	2	0	1	1	0	2	0	1
Sampdoria	D	W	2	1	1	0	0	2	1	1
Cagliari	L	L	2	1	0	1	2	0	2	0
Sassuolo	D	L	3	1	2	0	1	2	2	1
Udinese	W	L	1	1	0	0	0	1	0	1
Chievo	W	W	1	1	0	0	0	1	0	1
Crotone										
Bologna	L	L	2	0	0	2	0	2	0	0
Genoa	L	D	1	0	0	1	1	0	1	0
Crotone										
SPAL			-	-	-	-	-	-	-	-
Hellas Verona			2	1	1	0	2	0	2	0
Benevento			-	-	-	-	-	-	-	-

Season	Division	Pos	P	W	D	L	F	A	GD	Pts
2016-17	Serie A	17	38	9	7	22	34	58	-24	34
2015-16	Serie B	2	42	23	13	6	61	36	+25	82
2014-15	Serie B	17	42	12	12	18	42	52	-10	48

Over/Under 50%/50% 16th   **Both score** 53%/47% 15th

FIORENTINA

Artemio Franchi   violachannel.tv

	2016-17 H	A	Last six seasons at home P	W	D	L	OV	UN	BS	CS
Juventus	W	L	6	2	2	2	4	2	3	2
Roma	W	L	6	2	1	3	2	4	2	2
Napoli	D	L	6	0	3	3	3	3	4	0
Atalanta	D	D	6	4	2	0	4	2	3	3
Lazio	W	L	6	2	0	4	3	3	3	1
Milan	D	L	6	2	3	1	2	4	2	3
Inter	W	L	6	4	1	1	5	1	4	2
Fiorentina										
Torino	D	L	5	2	3	0	3	2	4	1
Sampdoria	D	D	5	2	3	0	2	3	4	1
Cagliari	W	W	5	2	2	1	2	3	3	2
Sassuolo	W	D	4	2	1	1	3	1	3	1
Udinese	W	W	6	6	0	0	6	0	3	3
Chievo	W	W	6	5	0	1	4	2	3	3
Bologna	W	W	5	5	0	0	1	4	0	5
Genoa	D	L	6	3	3	0	3	3	3	3
Crotone	D	W	1	0	1	0	0	1	1	0
SPAL			-	-	-	-	-	-	-	-
Hellas Verona			3	1	1	1	1	2	2	0
Benevento			-	-	-	-	-	-	-	-

Season	Division	Pos	P	W	D	L	F	A	GD	Pts
2016-17	Serie A	8	38	16	12	10	63	57	+6	60
2015-16	Serie A	5	38	18	10	10	60	42	+18	64
2014-15	Serie A	4	38	18	10	10	61	46	+15	64

Over/Under 66%/34% 5th   **Both score** 61%/39% 6th

GENOA

Luigi Ferraris   genoafc.it

	2016-17 H	A	Last six seasons at home P	W	D	L	OV	UN	BS	CS
Juventus	W	L	6	2	1	3	2	4	2	2
Roma	L	L	6	2	0	4	3	3	3	1
Napoli	D	L	6	1	2	3	3	3	3	2
Atalanta	L	L	6	0	4	2	4	2	5	0
Lazio	D	L	6	4	2	0	3	3	3	3
Milan	W	L	6	3	0	3	2	4	1	3
Inter	W	L	6	4	1	1	1	5	1	4
Fiorentina	W	D	6	1	3	2	2	4	3	2
Torino	W	L	5	3	0	2	3	2	5	0
Sampdoria	L	L	5	0	1	4	1	4	2	0
Cagliari	W	L	5	4	0	1	3	2	3	2
Sassuolo	L	L	4	2	1	1	2	2	2	1
Udinese	D	L	6	3	3	0	3	3	5	1
Chievo	L	D	6	2	0	4	4	2	4	0
Bologna	D	W	5	2	2	1	1	4	2	2
Genoa										
Crotone	D	W	1	0	1	0	1	0	1	0
SPAL			-	-	-	-	-	-	-	-
Hellas Verona			3	3	0	0	1	2	1	2
Benevento			-	-	-	-	-	-	-	-

Season	Division	Pos	P	W	D	L	F	A	GD	Pts
2016-17	Serie A	16	38	9	9	20	38	64	-26	36
2015-16	Serie A	11	38	13	7	18	45	48	-3	46
2014-15	Serie A	6	38	16	11	11	62	47	+15	59

Over/Under 50%/50% 16th   **Both score** 42%/58% 20th

HELLAS VERONA

Stadio Marc'Antonio Bentegodi — hellasverona.it

	2016-17		Last six seasons at home							
	H	A	P	W	D	L	OV	UN	BS	CS
Juventus			3	1	2	0	3	0	3	0
Roma			3	0	2	1	1	2	3	0
Napoli			3	1	0	2	1	2	0	1
Atalanta			3	3	0	0	2	1	2	1
Lazio			3	1	1	1	2	1	3	0
Milan			3	2	0	1	3	0	3	0
Inter			3	0	1	2	2	1	1	0
Fiorentina			3	0	0	3	2	1	2	0
Torino			4	0	1	3	4	0	4	0
Sampdoria			4	1	1	2	2	2	2	1
Cagliari			2	2	0	0	1	1	1	1
Sassuolo			5	4	1	0	1	4	2	3
Udinese			3	0	2	1	1	2	2	0
Chievo			3	1	0	2	1	2	1	0
Bologna			2	0	1	1	0	2	1	0
Genoa			3	1	2	0	2	1	2	1
Crotone			2	2	0	0	2	0	2	0
SPAL	D	W	1	0	1	0	0	1	0	1
Hellas Verona										
Benevento	D	L	1	0	1	0	1	0	1	0

Season	Division	Pos	P	W	D	L	F	A	GD	Pts
2016-17	Serie B	2	42	20	14	8	64	40	+24	74
2015-16	Serie A	20	38	5	13	20	34	63	-29	28
2014-15	Serie A	13	38	11	13	14	49	65	-16	46

Over/Under 38%/62% 18th   **Both score** 43%/57% 28th

INTER

San Siro — inter.it

	2016-17		Last six seasons at home							
	H	A	P	W	D	L	OV	UN	BS	CS
Juventus	W	L	6	1	2	3	4	2	5	1
Roma	L	L	6	2	1	3	4	2	3	2
Napoli	L	L	6	2	2	2	3	3	2	2
Atalanta	W	L	6	3	1	2	3	3	3	3
Lazio	W	W	6	3	1	2	6	0	5	1
Milan	D	D	6	3	3	0	2	4	3	3
Inter										
Fiorentina	W	L	6	4	0	2	4	2	4	1
Torino	W	D	5	2	1	2	3	2	3	1
Sampdoria	L	L	5	3	1	1	3	2	4	1
Cagliari	L	W	5	1	2	2	4	1	5	0
Sassuolo	L	W	4	2	0	2	2	1	2	0
Udinese	W	W	6	2	1	3	4	2	4	1
Chievo	W	L	6	4	2	0	2	4	3	3
Bologna	D	W	5	1	2	2	3	2	3	0
Genoa	W	L	6	5	1	0	2	4	3	3
Crotone	W	L	1	1	0	0	1	0	0	1
SPAL	-	-	-	-	-	-	-	-	-	-
Hellas Verona			3	2	1	0	2	1	2	1
Benevento	-	-	-	-	-	-	-	-	-	-

Season	Division	Pos	P	W	D	L	F	A	GD	Pts
2016-17	Serie A	7	38	19	5	14	72	49	+23	62
2015-16	Serie A	4	38	20	7	11	50	38	+12	67
2014-15	Serie A	8	38	14	13	11	59	48	+11	55

Over/Under 66%/34% 5th   **Both score** 61%/39% 6th

JUVENTUS

Juventus Stadium — juventus.com

	2016-17		Last six seasons at home							
	H	A	P	W	D	L	OV	UN	BS	CS
Juventus										
Roma	W	L	6	6	0	0	4	2	2	4
Napoli	W	D	6	6	0	0	4	2	2	4
Atalanta	W	D	6	6	0	0	4	2	3	3
Lazio	W	W	6	5	1	0	3	3	2	4
Milan	W	L	6	6	0	0	3	3	3	3
Inter	W	L	6	4	1	1	2	4	3	3
Fiorentina	W	L	6	6	0	0	4	2	4	2
Torino	D	W	5	4	1	0	3	2	3	2
Sampdoria	W	W	5	3	1	1	4	1	4	1
Cagliari	W	W	5	2	3	0	2	3	3	2
Sassuolo	W	W	4	4	0	0	2	2	1	3
Udinese	W	D	6	5	0	1	3	3	2	3
Chievo	W	W	6	4	2	0	1	5	3	3
Bologna	W	W	5	4	1	0	3	2	3	2
Genoa	W	W	6	4	2	0	2	4	2	4
Crotone	W	W	1	1	0	0	1	0	0	1
SPAL	-	-	-	-	-	-	-	-	-	-
Hellas Verona			3	3	0	0	3	0	1	2
Benevento	-	-	-	-	-	-	-	-	-	-

Season	Division	Pos	P	W	D	L	F	A	GD	Pts
2016-17	Serie A	1	38	29	4	5	77	27	+50	91
2015-16	Serie A	1	38	29	4	5	75	20	+55	91
2014-15	Serie A	1	38	26	9	3	72	24	+48	87

Over/Under 58%/42% 11th   **Both score** 50%/50% 17th

LAZIO

Stadio Olimpico — sslazio.it

	2016-17		Last six seasons at home							
	H	A	P	W	D	L	OV	UN	BS	CS
Juventus	L	L	6	0	1	5	1	5	1	0
Roma	L	W	6	2	1	3	4	2	4	1
Napoli	L	D	6	1	1	4	3	3	3	0
Atalanta	W	W	6	5	0	1	2	4	1	4
Lazio										
Milan	D	L	6	3	2	1	3	3	5	1
Inter	L	L	6	4	0	2	3	3	3	3
Fiorentina	W	L	6	3	1	2	3	3	2	3
Torino	W	D	5	3	2	0	4	1	4	1
Sampdoria	W	W	5	4	1	0	2	3	2	3
Cagliari	W	D	5	5	0	0	3	2	3	2
Sassuolo	W	W	4	3	0	1	3	1	3	0
Udinese	W	W	6	4	1	1	3	3	2	3
Chievo	L	D	6	2	2	2	4	2	2	2
Bologna	D	W	5	3	1	1	3	2	3	2
Genoa	W	D	6	2	0	4	2	4	2	1
Crotone	W	L	1	1	0	0	1	0	1	0
SPAL	-	-	-	-	-	-	-	-	-	-
Hellas Verona			3	2	1	0	2	1	2	1
Benevento	-	-	-	-	-	-	-	-	-	-

Season	Division	Pos	P	W	D	L	F	A	GD	Pts
2016-17	Serie A	5	38	21	7	10	74	51	+23	70
2015-16	Serie A	8	38	15	9	14	52	52	0	54
2014-15	Serie A	3	38	21	6	11	71	38	+33	69

Over/Under 61%/39% 8th   **Both score** 61%/39% 6th

ITALIAN SERIE A

MILAN

San Siro — acmilan.com

	2016-17 H	A	P	W	D	L	OV	UN	BS	CS
			Last six seasons at home							
Juventus	W	L	6	2	1	3	1	5	2	2
Roma	L	L	6	2	2	2	5	1	5	1
Napoli	L	L	6	1	2	3	3	3	3	2
Atalanta	D	D	6	2	2	1	5	0	4	
Lazio	W	D	6	3	3	0	3	3	4	2
Milan										
Inter	D	D	6	2	2	2	4	2	2	
Fiorentina	W	D	6	2	1	3	3	3	4	1
Torino	W	D	5	4	1	0	2	3	2	3
Sampdoria	L	W	5	2	1	2	1	4	2	1
Cagliari	W	L	5	5	0	0	3	2	2	3
Sassuolo	W	W	4	3	0	1	4	0	4	0
Udinese	L	L	6	3	2	1	1	5	3	2
Chievo	W	W	6	6	0	0	4	2	2	4
Bologna	W	W	5	3	1	1	2	3	2	2
Genoa	W	L	6	4	1	1	2	4	3	3
Crotone	W	D	1	1	0	0	1	0	1	0
SPAL			-	-	-	-	-	-	-	-
Hellas Verona			3	1	2	0	1	2	2	1
Benevento			-	-	-	-	-	-	-	-

Season	Division	Pos	P	W	D	L	F	A	GD	Pts
2016-17	Serie A	6	38	18	9	11	57	45	+12	63
2015-16	Serie A	7	38	15	12	11	49	43	+6	57
2014-15	Serie A	10	38	13	13	12	56	50	+6	52

Over/Under 55%/45% 12th **Both score** 58%/42% 10th

NAPOLI

Stadio San Paolo — sscnapoli.it

	2016-17 H	A	P	W	D	L	OV	UN	BS	CS
			Last six seasons at home							
Juventus	D	L	6	2	3	1	3	3	5	1
Roma	L	W	6	3	1	2	3	3	3	3
Napoli										
Atalanta	L	L	6	3	1	2	3	3	4	1
Lazio	D	W	6	3	2	1	4	2	3	3
Milan	W	W	6	4	2	0	5	1	5	1
Inter	W	W	6	5	1	0	5	1	4	2
Fiorentina	W	D	6	4	1	1	4	2	3	2
Torino	W	W	5	4	1	0	3	2	4	1
Sampdoria	W	W	5	3	2	0	3	2	3	2
Cagliari	W	W	5	4	1	0	5	0	4	1
Sassuolo	D	D	4	2	2	0	1	3	3	1
Udinese	W	W	6	5	1	0	4	2	3	3
Chievo	W	W	6	4	1	1	1	5	2	3
Bologna	W	W	5	3	1	1	4	1	3	2
Genoa	W	D	6	5	1	0	3	3	4	2
Crotone	W	W	1	1	0	0	1	0	0	1
SPAL			-	-	-	-	-	-	-	-
Hellas Verona			3	3	0	0	3	0	2	1
Benevento			-	-	-	-	-	-	-	-

Season	Division	Pos	P	W	D	L	F	A	GD	Pts
2016-17	Serie A	3	38	26	8	4	94	39	+55	86
2015-16	Serie A	2	38	25	7	6	80	32	+48	82
2014-15	Serie A	5	38	18	9	11	70	54	+16	63

Over/Under 71%/29% 1st **Both score** 63%/37% 5th

ROMA

Stadio Olimpico — asroma.it

	2016-17 H	A	P	W	D	L	OV	UN	BS	CS
			Last six seasons at home							
Juventus	W	L	6	3	2	1	2	4	4	1
Roma										
Napoli	L	W	6	4	1	1	3	3	3	3
Atalanta	D	W	6	3	2	1	2	4	4	1
Lazio	L	W	6	2	2	2	3	3	4	2
Milan	W	W	6	3	2	1	2	4	3	3
Inter	W	W	6	3	3	0	3	3	4	2
Fiorentina	W	W	6	5	0	1	5	1	4	2
Torino	W	L	5	5	0	0	4	1	3	2
Sampdoria	W	L	5	3	1	1	3	2	3	1
Cagliari	W	D	5	2	1	2	2	3	2	3
Sassuolo	W	W	4	1	3	0	3	1	4	0
Udinese	W	W	6	5	0	1	6	0	5	1
Chievo	W	W	6	5	0	1	3	3	1	4
Bologna	W	W	5	2	2	1	3	2	3	2
Genoa	W	W	6	6	0	0	3	3	2	4
Crotone	W	W	1	1	0	0	1	0	0	1
SPAL			-	-	-	-	-	-	-	-
Hellas Verona			3	2	1	0	1	2	1	2
Benevento			-	-	-	-	-	-	-	-

Season	Division	Pos	P	W	D	L	F	A	GD	Pts
2016-17	Serie A	2	38	28	3	7	90	38	+52	87
2015-16	Serie A	3	38	23	11	4	83	41	+42	80
2014-15	Serie A	2	38	19	13	6	54	31	+23	70

Over/Under 71%/29% 1st **Both score** 58%/42% 10th

SAMPDORIA

Luigi Ferraris — sampdoria.it

	2016-17 H	A	P	W	D	L	OV	UN	BS	CS
			Last six seasons at home							
Juventus	L	L	5	1	0	4	2	3	2	0
Roma	W	L	5	3	1	1	3	2	3	1
Napoli	L	L	5	0	1	4	3	2	4	0
Atalanta	W	L	5	3	1	1	2	3	2	3
Lazio	L	L	5	1	1	3	2	3	3	0
Milan	L	W	5	0	2	3	1	4	1	1
Inter	W	W	5	2	1	2	1	4	1	2
Fiorentina	D	D	5	1	2	2	3	2	2	1
Torino	W	D	6	2	3	1	3	3	4	2
Sampdoria										
Cagliari	D	L	4	2	1	1	0	4	1	2
Sassuolo	W	L	5	1	2	2	3	2	5	0
Udinese	D	D	5	2	2	1	2	3	1	3
Chievo	D	L	5	3	1	1	2	3	3	1
Bologna	W	L	4	3	1	0	1	3	2	2
Genoa	W	W	5	2	1	2	4	1	3	0
Crotone	L	D	2	1	0	1	1	1	1	1
SPAL			-	-	-	-	-	-	-	-
Hellas Verona			4	3	1	0	2	2	2	2
Benevento			-	-	-	-	-	-	-	-

Season	Division	Pos	P	W	D	L	F	A	GD	Pts
2016-17	Serie A	10	38	12	12	14	49	55	-6	48
2015-16	Serie A	15	38	10	10	18	48	61	-13	40
2014-15	Serie A	7	38	13	17	8	48	42	+6	56

Over/Under 47%/53% 19th **Both score** 71%/29% 2nd

SASSUOLO

Mapei Stadium — sassuolocalcio.it

	2016-17 H	A	Last six seasons at home P	W	D	L	OV	UN	BS	CS
Juventus	L	L	4	1	1	2	1	3	2	1
Roma	L	L	4	0	0	4	2	2	1	0
Napoli	D	D	4	1	1	2	2	2	2	0
Atalanta	L	D	4	1	2	1	2	2	1	2
Lazio	L	L	4	1	1	2	4	0	3	0
Milan	L	L	4	3	0	1	2	2	2	1
Inter	L	W	4	2	0	2	3	1	2	0
Fiorentina	D	L	4	0	2	2	2	2	3	0
Torino	D	L	5	0	4	1	0	5	2	2
Sampdoria	W	L	5	1	3	1	2	3	2	3
Cagliari	W	L	3	1	2	0	1	2	3	0
Sassuolo										
Udinese	W	W	4	1	2	1	1	3	3	1
Chievo	L	L	4	1	1	2	1	3	2	1
Bologna	L	D	3	1	0	2	1	2	1	0
Genoa	W	W	4	3	0	1	2	2	2	1
Crotone	W	D	3	3	0	0	2	1	2	1
SPAL			-	-	-	-	-	-	-	-
Hellas Verona			5	3	1	1	2	3	3	2
Benevento										

Season	Division	Pos	P	W	D	L	F	A	GD	Pts
2016-17	Serie A	12	38	13	7	18	58	63	-5	46
2015-16	Serie A	6	38	16	13	9	49	40	+9	61
2014-15	Serie A	12	38	12	13	13	49	57	-8	49

Over/Under 66%/34% 5th   **Both score** 66%/34% 3rd

SPAL

Stadio Paolo Mazza — spalferrara.it

	2016-17 H	A	Last six seasons at home P	W	D	L	OV	UN	BS	CS
Juventus			-	-	-	-	-	-	-	-
Roma			-	-	-	-	-	-	-	-
Napoli			-	-	-	-	-	-	-	-
Atalanta			-	-	-	-	-	-	-	-
Lazio			-	-	-	-	-	-	-	-
Milan			-	-	-	-	-	-	-	-
Inter			-	-	-	-	-	-	-	-
Fiorentina			-	-	-	-	-	-	-	-
Torino			-	-	-	-	-	-	-	-
Sampdoria			-	-	-	-	-	-	-	-
Cagliari			-	-	-	-	-	-	-	-
Sassuolo			-	-	-	-	-	-	-	-
Udinese			-	-	-	-	-	-	-	-
Chievo			-	-	-	-	-	-	-	-
Bologna			-	-	-	-	-	-	-	-
Genoa			-	-	-	-	-	-	-	-
Crotone			-	-	-	-	-	-	-	-
SPAL			-	-	-	-	-	-	-	-
Hellas Verona	L	D	1	0	0	1	1	0	1	0
Benevento	W	L	1	1	0	0	0	1	0	1

Season	Division	Pos	P	W	D	L	F	A	GD	Pts
2016-17	Serie B	1	42	22	12	8	66	39	+27	78
2015-16	Lega Pro B	1	34	21	8	5	59	25	+34	71
2014-15	Lega Pro B	4	38	18	8	12	46	31	+15	62

Over/Under 50%/50% 5th   **Both score** 57%/43% 7th

TORINO

Stadio Olimpico Grande Torino — torino.it

	2016-17 H	A	Last six seasons at home P	W	D	L	OV	UN	BS	CS
Juventus	L	D	5	1	0	4	3	2	3	0
Roma	W	L	5	1	3	1	2	3	5	0
Napoli	L	L	5	1	0	4	3	2	2	1
Atalanta	D	L	5	3	2	0	2	3	3	2
Lazio	D	L	5	2	2	1	1	4	2	2
Milan	D	L	5	0	4	1	3	2	5	0
Inter	D	L	5	0	3	2	2	3	2	1
Fiorentina	W	D	5	2	3	0	3	2	4	1
Torino										
Sampdoria	D	L	6	3	2	1	2	4	3	2
Cagliari	W	W	4	2	1	1	2	2	3	0
Sassuolo	W	D	5	3	0	2	3	2	2	2
Udinese	D	D	5	2	2	1	1	4	1	3
Chievo	W	W	5	4	0	1	3	2	3	2
Bologna	W	L	4	3	0	1	2	2	2	2
Genoa	W	L	5	3	2	0	3	2	3	2
Crotone	D	W	2	1	1	0	1	1	2	0
SPAL			-	-	-	-	-	-	-	-
Hellas Verona			4	0	2	2	2	2	2	1
Benevento			-	-	-	-	-	-	-	-

Season	Division	Pos	P	W	D	L	F	A	GD	Pts
2016-17	Serie A	9	38	13	14	11	71	66	+5	53
2015-16	Serie A	12	38	12	9	17	52	55	-3	45
2014-15	Serie A	9	38	14	12	12	48	45	+3	54

Over/Under 68%/32% 3rd   **Both score** 79%/21% 1st

UDINESE

Stadio Friuli — udinese.it

	2016-17 H	A	Last six seasons at home P	W	D	L	OV	UN	BS	CS
Juventus	D	L	6	0	3	3	2	4	2	2
Roma	L	L	6	1	1	4	5	2	1	
Napoli	L	L	6	2	3	1	3	3	4	2
Atalanta	D	W	6	3	3	0	2	4	4	3
Lazio	L	L	6	2	1	3	2	4	1	3
Milan	W	W	6	4	0	2	5	1	5	1
Inter	L	L	6	1	0	5	6	0	3	1
Fiorentina	D	L	6	4	2	0	4	2	4	2
Torino	D	D	5	2	1	2	3	2	3	1
Sampdoria	D	D	5	2	2	1	3	2	4	1
Cagliari	W	L	5	3	2	0	3	2	3	2
Sassuolo	L	L	4	1	1	2	1	3	1	2
Udinese										
Chievo	L	D	6	3	2	1	4	2	4	2
Bologna	W	L	5	2	2	1	0	5	1	3
Genoa	W	L	6	3	2	1	2	4	2	4
Crotone	W	L	1	1	0	0	0	1	0	1
SPAL			-	-	-	-	-	-	-	-
Hellas Verona			3	1	0	2	2	1	2	1
Benevento			-	-	-	-	-	-	-	-

Season	Division	Pos	P	W	D	L	F	A	GD	Pts
2016-17	Serie A	13	38	12	9	17	47	56	-9	45
2015-16	Serie A	17	38	10	9	19	35	60	-25	39
2014-15	Serie A	16	38	10	11	17	43	56	-13	41

Over/Under 61%/39% 8th   **Both score** 55%/45% 12th

Serie A 2016-17

Pos	H	A		P	W	D	L	F	A	W	D	L	F	A	GD	Pts
						Home					**Away**					
1	1	3	Juventus (CL)	38	18	1	0	48	9	11	3	5	29	18	50	91
2	2	2	Roma (CL)	38	16	1	2	50	18	12	2	5	40	20	52	87
3	3	1	Napoli (CL)	38	13	4	2	44	19	13	4	2	50	20	55	86
4	4	4	Atalanta (EL)	38	12	4	3	31	18	9	5	5	31	23	21	72
5	5	5	Lazio (EL)	38	12	2	5	40	23	9	5	5	34	28	23	70
6	6	7	Milan (EL)	38	12	2	5	32	20	6	7	6	25	25	12	63
7	8	6	Inter	38	11	3	5	44	22	8	2	9	28	27	23	62
8	7	9	Fiorentina	38	10	8	1	34	23	6	4	9	29	34	6	60
9	10	11	Torino	38	9	8	2	43	31	4	6	9	28	35	5	53
10	11	12	Sampdoria	38	8	6	5	28	23	4	6	9	21	32	-6	48
11	9	17	Cagliari	38	11	3	5	38	34	3	2	14	17	42	-21	47
12	15	8	Sassuolo	38	7	3	9	27	28	6	4	9	31	35	-5	46
13	12	13	Udinese	38	8	5	6	30	23	4	4	11	17	33	-9	45
14	16	10	Chievo	38	6	5	8	25	30	6	2	11	18	31	-18	43
15	13	14	Bologna	38	8	2	9	24	25	3	6	10	16	33	-18	41
16	14	18	Genoa	38	6	7	6	24	24	3	2	14	14	40	-26	36
17	17	16	Crotone	38	6	4	9	21	25	3	3	13	13	33	-24	34
18	18	15	Empoli (R)	38	5	4	10	16	29	3	4	12	13	32	-32	32
19	19	19	Palermo (R)	38	4	3	12	13	30	2	5	12	20	47	-44	26
20	20	20	Pescara (R)	38	2	5	12	19	38	1	4	14	18	43	-44	18

Serie A results 2016-17

	Atalanta	Bologna	Cagliari	Chievo	Crotone	Empoli	Fiorentina	Genoa	Inter	Juventus	Lazio	Milan	Napoli	Palermo	Pescara	Roma	Sampdoria	Sassuolo	Torino	Udinese
Atalanta		3-2	2-0	1-0	1-0	2-1	0-0	3-0	2-1	2-2	3-4	1-1	1-0	0-1	3-0	2-1	1-0	1-1	2-1	1-3
Bologna	0-2		2-1	4-1	1-0	0-0	0-1	0-1	0-1	1-2	0-2	0-1	1-7	3-1	3-1	0-3	2-0	1-1	2-0	4-0
Cagliari	3-0	1-1		4-0	2-1	3-2	3-5	4-1	1-5	0-2	0-0	2-1	0-5	2-1	1-0	2-2	2-1	4-3	2-3	2-1
Chievo	1-4	1-1	1-0		1-2	4-0	0-3	0-0	2-0	1-2	1-1	1-3	1-3	1-1	2-0	3-5	2-1	2-1	1-3	0-0
Crotone	1-3	0-1	1-2	2-0		4-1	0-1	1-3	2-1	0-2	3-1	1-1	1-2	1-1	2-1	0-2	1-1	0-0	0-2	1-0
Empoli	0-1	3-1	2-0	0-0	2-1		0-4	0-2	0-2	0-3	1-2	1-4	2-3	1-0	1-1	0-0	0-1	1-3	1-1	1-0
Fiorentina	0-0	1-0	1-0	1-0	1-1	1-2		3-3	5-4	2-1	3-2	0-0	3-3	2-1	2-2	1-0	1-1	2-1	2-2	3-0
Genoa	0-5	1-1	3-1	1-2	2-2	0-0	1-0		1-0	3-1	2-2	3-0	0-0	3-4	1-1	0-1	0-1	0-1	2-1	1-1
Inter	7-1	1-1	1-2	3-1	3-0	2-0	4-2	2-0		2-1	3-0	2-2	0-1	1-1	3-0	1-3	1-2	1-2	2-1	5-2
Juventus	3-1	3-0	4-0	2-0	3-0	2-0	2-1	4-0	1-0		2-0	2-1	2-1	4-1	3-0	1-0	4-1	3-1	1-1	2-1
Lazio	2-1	1-1	4-1	0-1	1-0	2-0	3-1	3-1	1-3	0-1		1-1	0-3	6-2	3-0	0-2	7-3	2-1	3-1	1-0
Milan	0-0	3-0	1-0	3-1	2-1	1-2	2-1	1-0	2-2	1-0	2-0		1-2	4-0	1-0	1-4	0-1	4-3	3-2	0-1
Napoli	0-2	3-1	3-1	2-0	3-0	2-0	4-1	2-0	3-0	1-1	1-1	4-2		1-1	3-1	1-3	2-1	1-1	5-3	3-0
Palermo	1-3	0-0	1-3	0-2	1-0	2-1	2-0	1-0	0-1	0-1	0-1	1-2	0-3		1-1	0-3	1-1	0-1	1-4	1-3
Pescara	0-1	0-3	1-1	0-2	0-1	0-4	1-2	5-0	1-2	0-2	2-6	1-1	2-2	2-0		1-4	1-1	1-3	0-0	1-3
Roma	1-1	3-0	1-0	3-1	4-0	2-0	4-0	3-2	2-1	3-1	1-3	1-0	1-2	4-1	3-2		3-2	3-1	4-1	4-0
Sampdoria	2-1	3-1	1-1	1-1	1-2	0-0	2-2	2-1	1-0	0-1	1-2	0-1	2-4	1-1	3-1	3-2		3-2	2-0	0-0
Sassuolo	0-3	0-1	6-2	1-3	2-1	3-0	2-2	2-0	0-1	0-2	1-2	0-1	2-2	4-1	0-3	1-3	2-1		0-0	1-0
Torino	1-1	5-1	5-1	2-1	1-1	0-0	2-1	1-0	2-2	1-3	2-2	2-2	0-5	3-1	5-3	3-1	1-1	5-3		2-2
Udinese	1-1	1-0	2-1	1-2	2-0	2-0	2-2	3-0	1-2	1-1	0-3	2-1	1-2	4-1	3-1	0-1	1-1	1-2	2-2	

Top scorers

	Team	Goals scored	
E Dzeko	Roma	29	||||||||||||||||||||||||||||
D Mertens	Napoli	28	|||||||||||||||||||||||||||
A Belotti	Torino	26	||||||||||||||||||||||||
G Higuain	Juventus	24	||||||||||||||||||||||
M Icardi	Inter	24	||||||||||||||||||||||
C Immobile	Lazio	23	|||||||||||||||||||||

Over 2.5 goals top ten

	H	A	%
Napoli	11	16	71%
Roma	15	12	71%
Cagliari	15	11	68%
Torino	14	12	68%
Fiorentina, Inter, Sassuolo			66%

Both to score top five

	H	A	%
Torino	16	14	79%
Sampdoria	13	14	71%
Cagliari	13	12	66%
Sassuolo	9	16	66%
Napoli	12	12	63%

AUGSBURG

WWK Arena   fcaugsburg.de

	2016-17 H	A	Last six seasons at home P	W	D	L	OV	UN	BS	CS
Bayern Munich	L	L	6	1	0	5	4	2	3	1
RB Leipzig	D	L	1	0	1	0	1	0	1	0
Dortmund	D	D	6	0	2	4	4	2	4	1
Hoffenheim	L	D	6	3	0	3	3	3	3	1
Cologne	W	D	4	2	2	0	2	2	2	2
Hertha	D	L	5	2	2	1	1	4	0	4
Freiburg	D	L	5	2	3	0	2	3	4	1
Werder Bremen	W	W	6	4	1	1	5	1	6	0
B M'gladbach	W	D	6	3	3	0	3	3	4	4
Schalke	D	L	6	1	4	1	2	4	4	2
E Frankfurt	D	L	5	2	3	0	2	3	3	2
Leverkusen	L	D	6	0	2	4	6	0	6	0
Augsburg										
Hamburg	W	L	6	4	0	2	4	2	3	2
Mainz	L	L	6	2	2	4	2	5	0	
Wolfsburg	L	W	6	2	2	1	5	1	4	
Stuttgart			5	4	0	1	4	1	3	2
Hannover			5	1	2	2	1	4	2	2

Season	Division	Pos	P	W	D	L	F	A	GD	Pts
2016-17	Bundesliga	13	34	9	11	14	35	51	-16	38
2015-16	Bundesliga	12	34	9	11	14	42	52	-10	38
2014-15	Bundesliga	5	34	15	4	15	43	43	0	49

Over/Under 47%/53% 13th   **Both score** 56%/44% 7th

BAYERN MUNICH

Allianz Arena   fcbayern.de

	2016-17 H	A	Last six seasons at home P	W	D	L	OV	UN	BS	CS
Bayern Munich										
RB Leipzig	W	W	1	1	0	0	1	0	0	1
Dortmund	W	L	6	3	1	2	4	2	4	0
Hoffenheim	D	L	6	4	2	0	3	3	3	3
Cologne	D	W	4	3	1	0	3	1	2	2
Hertha	W	D	5	5	0	0	3	2	1	4
Freiburg	W	W	5	5	0	0	3	2	1	4
Werder Bremen	W	W	6	6	0	0	6	0	3	3
B M'gladbach	W	W	6	2	2	2	1	5	3	1
Schalke	D	W	6	4	2	0	3	3	3	3
E Frankfurt	W	D	5	5	0	0	3	2	0	5
Leverkusen	W	D	6	5	0	1	5	1	3	3
Augsburg	W	W	6	5	0	1	5	1	2	3
Hamburg	W	W	6	6	0	0	6	0	2	4
Mainz	D	W	6	3	2	1	4	2	4	2
Wolfsburg	W	W	6	6	0	0	4	2	2	4
Stuttgart			5	5	0	0	2	3	1	4
Hannover			5	5	0	0	4	1	2	3

Season	Division	Pos	P	W	D	L	F	A	GD	Pts
2016-17	Bundesliga	1	34	25	7	2	89	22	+67	82
2015-16	Bundesliga	1	34	28	4	2	80	17	+63	88
2014-15	Bundesliga	1	34	25	4	5	80	18	+62	79

Over/Under 59%/41% 7th   **Both score** 44%/56% 14th

COLOGNE

RheinEnergieStadion   fc-koeln.de

	2016-17 H	A	Last six seasons at home P	W	D	L	OV	UN	BS	CS
Bayern Munich	L	D	4	0	0	4	2	2	1	0
RB Leipzig	D	L	1	0	1	0	0	1	0	0
Dortmund	D	D	4	2	1	1	3	1	4	0
Hoffenheim	D	L	4	2	2	0	1	3	2	2
Cologne										
Hertha	W	L	5	2	0	3	3	2	3	1
Freiburg	W	L	3	2	0	1	2	1	0	2
Werder Bremen	W	D	4	1	3	0	1	3	3	1
B M'gladbach	L	W	4	1	1	2	2	2	1	2
Schalke	D	W	4	1	1	2	2	2	3	1
E Frankfurt	W	D	3	3	0	0	2	1	2	1
Leverkusen	D	D	4	0	2	2	0	4	2	0
Augsburg	D	L	4	1	1	2	2	2	1	2
Hamburg	W	L	4	2	1	1	2	2	1	2
Mainz	W	D	4	1	3	0	0	4	1	3
Wolfsburg	W	D	4	1	2	1	2	2	2	1
Stuttgart			3	0	2	1	1	2	2	1
Hannover			3	1	1	1	0	3	1	1

Season	Division	Pos	P	W	D	L	F	A	GD	Pts
2016-17	Bundesliga	5	34	12	13	9	51	42	+9	49
2015-16	Bundesliga	9	34	10	13	11	38	42	-4	43
2014-15	Bundesliga	12	34	9	13	12	34	41	-7	40

Over/Under 53%/47% 9th   **Both score** 62%/38% 6th

DORTMUND

Westfalenstadion · bvb.de

	2016-17 H	A	P	W	D	L	OV	UN	BS	CS
Bayern Munich	W	L	6	2	2	2	1	5	1	3
RB Leipzig	W	L	1	1	0	0	0	1	0	1
Dortmund										
Hoffenheim	W	D	6	5	0	1	5	1	5	1
Cologne	D	D	4	1	3	0	2	2	1	3
Hertha	D	L	5	2	1	2	3	2	4	1
Freiburg	W	W	5	5	0	0	5	0	3	2
Werder Bremen	W	W	6	6	0	0	4	2	4	2
B M'gladbach	W	W	6	5	0	1	4	2	2	4
Schalke	D	D	6	3	2	1	3	3	2	4
E Frankfurt	W	L	5	5	0	0	4	1	2	3
Leverkusen	W	L	6	4	0	2	3	3	1	3
Augsburg	D	D	6	3	2	1	4	2	4	1
Hamburg	W	W	6	4	0	2	5	1	3	2
Mainz	W	D	6	6	0	0	4	2	4	2
Wolfsburg	W	W	6	4	1	1	6	0	5	1
Stuttgart			5	2	3	0	4	1	4	1
Hannover			5	4	0	1	2	3	2	2

Season	Division	Pos	P	W	D	L	F	A	GD	Pts
2016-17	Bundesliga	3	34	18	10	6	72	40	+32	64
2015-16	Bundesliga	2	34	24	6	4	82	34	+48	78
2014-15	Bundesliga	7	34	13	7	14	47	42	+5	46

Over/Under 62%/38% 4th **Both score** 68%/32% 2nd

EINTRACHT FRANKFURT

Commerzbank-Arena · eintracht.de

	2016-17 H	A	P	W	D	L	OV	UN	BS	CS
Bayern Munich	D	L	5	0	2	3	2	3	1	1
RB Leipzig	D	L	1	0	1	0	1	0	1	0
Dortmund	W	L	5	3	1	1	3	2	3	2
Hoffenheim	D	L	5	2	1	2	3	2	3	1
Cologne	W	L	3	3	0	0	2	1	2	1
Hertha	D	L	4	1	3	0	2	2	3	1
Freiburg	L	L	4	2	0	2	3	1	3	1
Werder Bremen	D	W	5	3	2	0	4	1	4	1
B M'gladbach	D	D	5	1	2	2	1	4	1	3
Schalke	W	W	5	3	2	0	1	4	1	4
E Frankfurt										
Leverkusen	W	L	5	3	0	2	4	1	4	0
Augsburg	W	D	5	2	2	1	2	3	4	0
Hamburg	D	W	5	2	3	0	3	2	3	2
Mainz	W	L	5	3	1	1	4	1	3	2
Wolfsburg	L	L	5	1	2	2	3	2	4	0
Stuttgart			4	1	0	3	4	0	4	0
Hannover			4	2	1	1	3	1	3	1

Season	Division	Pos	P	W	D	L	F	A	GD	Pts
2016-17	Bundesliga	11	34	11	9	14	36	43	-7	42
2015-16	Bundesliga	16	34	9	9	16	34	52	-18	36
2014-15	Bundesliga	9	34	11	10	13	56	62	-6	43

Over/Under 47%/53% 13th **Both score** 35%/65% 18th

Bayern Munich celebrate a fifth consecutive Bundesliga crown

FREIBURG

Schwarzwald-Stadion · scfreiburg.com

	2016-17 H	A	P	W	D	L	OV	UN	BS	CS
Bayern Munich	L	L	5	1	2	2	2	3	3	1
RB Leipzig	L	L	2	1	0	1	2	0	2	0
Dortmund	L	L	5	0	0	5	3	2	1	0
Hoffenheim	D	L	5	1	4	0	1	4	4	1
Cologne	W	L	3	3	0	0	2	1	2	1
Hertha	W	L	4	1	3	0	3	1	4	0
Freiburg										
Werder Bremen	L	W	5	1	1	3	4	1	4	0
B M'gladbach	W	L	5	4	1	0	2	3	2	3
Schalke	W	D	5	3	0	2	2	3	2	2
E Frankfurt	W	W	4	2	2	0	1	3	2	2
Leverkusen	W	D	5	2	2	1	2	3	2	2
Augsburg	W	D	5	4	0	1	2	3	2	3
Hamburg	W	D	5	1	2	2	2	3	1	3
Mainz	W	L	5	1	1	3	3	2	4	1
Wolfsburg	L	W	5	1	0	4	5	0	3	1
Stuttgart			4	1	0	3	4	0	3	1
Hannover			4	2	2	0	3	1	4	0

Season	Division	Pos	P	W	D	L	F	A	GD	Pts
2016-17	Bundesliga	7	34	14	6	14	42	60	-18	48
2015-16	2.Bundesliga	1	34	22	6	6	75	39	+36	72
2014-15	Bundesliga	17	34	7	13	14	36	47	-11	34

Over/Under 68%/32% 2nd **Both score** 65%/35% 4th

HAMBURG ◆ hsv.de

Volksparkstadion

	2016-17 H	2016-17 A	Last six seasons at home P	W	D	L	OV	UN	BS	CS
Bayern Munich	L	L	6	0	2	4	3	3	3	1
RB Leipzig	L	W	1	0	0	1	1	0	0	0
Dortmund	L	L	6	3	1	2	5	1	4	2
Hoffenheim	W	D	6	3	1	2	3	3	4	2
Cologne	W		4	1	1	2	2	2	3	0
Hertha	W	L	5	2	1	2	2	3	1	2
Freiburg	D	L	5	0	3	2	2	3	4	0
Werder Bremen	D	L	6	3	1	2	4	2	4	1
B M'gladbach	W	D	6	3	1	2	2	4	3	1
Schalke	W	D	6	3	0	3	4	2	3	1
E Frankfurt	L	D	5	0	2	3	2	3	2	1
Leverkusen	W	L	6	3	2	1	1	5	2	3
Augsburg	W	L	6	2	1	3	1	5	2	1
Hamburg										
Mainz	D	L	6	2	2	2	3	3	3	3
Wolfsburg	W	L	6	1	2	3	2	4	4	0
Stuttgart			5	1	1	3	3	2	2	0
Hannover			5	4	0	1	3	2	3	2

Season	Division	Pos	P	W	D	L	F	A	GD	Pts
2016-17	Bundesliga	14	34	10	8	16	33	61	-28	38
2015-16	Bundesliga	10	34	11	8	15	40	46	-6	41
2014-15	Bundesliga	16	34	9	8	17	25	50	-25	35

Over/Under 62%/38% 4th   **Both score** 47%/53% 13th

HANNOVER 96 hannover96.de

HDI-Arena

	2016-17 H	2016-17 A	Last six seasons at home P	W	D	L	OV	UN	BS	CS
Bayern Munich			5	1	0	4	4	1	3	0
RB Leipzig			-	-	-	-	-	-	-	-
Dortmund			5	1	1	3	4	1	4	0
Hoffenheim			5	3	0	2	3	2	3	2
Cologne			3	2	0	1	2	1	1	1
Hertha			4	0	3	1	1	3	4	0
Freiburg			4	2	1	1	3	1	3	1
Werder Bremen			5	3	1	1	3	2	4	1
B M'gladbach			5	3	0	2	4	1	3	1
Schalke			5	2	2	1	5	0	5	0
E Frankfurt			4	2	1	1	1	3	1	3
Leverkusen			5	1	2	2	2	3	3	1
Augsburg			5	3	1	1	2	3	2	2
Hamburg			5	3	1	1	3	2	3	1
Mainz			5	1	3	1	2	3	4	0
Wolfsburg			5	3	0	2	3	2	2	2
Stuttgart	W	W	6	2	3	1	2	4	3	3
Hannover										

Season	Division	Pos	P	W	D	L	F	A	GD	Pts
2016-17	2.Bundesliga	2	34	19	10	5	51	32	+19	67
2015-16	Bundesliga	18	34	7	4	23	31	62	-31	25
2014-15	Bundesliga	13	34	9	10	15	40	56	-16	37

Over/Under 41%/59% 17th   **Both score** 44%/56% 19th

HERTHA BERLIN herthabsc.de

Olympiastadion

	2016-17 H	2016-17 A	Last six seasons at home P	W	D	L	OV	UN	BS	CS
Bayern Munich	D		5	0	1	4	2	3	2	0
RB Leipzig	L	L	1	0	0	1	1	0	1	0
Dortmund	W	D	5	2	1	2	2	3	1	2
Hoffenheim	L	L	5	2	1	2	3	2	3	1
Cologne	W	L	5	3	2	0	2	3	2	3
Hertha										
Freiburg	W	L	4	1	1	2	2	2	2	1
Werder Bremen	L	L	5	2	2	1	2	3	3	1
B M'gladbach	W	L	5	2	0	3	4	1	3	2
Schalke	W	L	5	2	1	2	2	3	2	2
E Frankfurt	W	D	4	3	1	0	1	3	1	3
Leverkusen	L	L	5	1	1	3	3	2	3	0
Augsburg	W	D	5	2	3	0	1	4	1	4
Hamburg	W	L	5	4	0	1	3	2	1	4
Mainz	W	L	5	3	1	1	3	2	3	2
Wolfsburg	W	W	5	2	1	2	2	3	3	2
Stuttgart			4	3	0	1	2	2	2	1
Hannover			4	0	1	3	2	2	1	0

Season	Division	Pos	P	W	D	L	F	A	GD	Pts
2016-17	Bundesliga	6	34	15	4	15	43	47	-4	49
2015-16	Bundesliga	7	34	14	8	12	42	42	0	50
2014-15	Bundesliga	15	34	9	8	17	36	52	-16	35

Over/Under 41%/59% 17th   **Both score** 41%/59% 16th

HOFFENHEIM achtzehn99.de

Rhein-Neckar Arena

	2016-17 H	2016-17 A	Last six seasons at home P	W	D	L	OV	UN	BS	CS
Bayern Munich	W	D	6	1	1	4	2	4	2	2
RB Leipzig	D	L	1	0	1	0	1	0	1	0
Dortmund	D	L	6	1	4	1	3	3	5	1
Hoffenheim										
Cologne	W	D	4	1	2	1	2	2	3	1
Hertha	W	W	5	3	1	1	3	2	4	1
Freiburg	W	D	5	2	3	0	4	1	5	0
Werder Bremen	D	W	6	0	2	4	5	1	6	0
B M'gladbach	W	D	6	3	2	1	4	2	4	2
Schalke	W	D	6	3	2	1	5	1	6	0
E Frankfurt	W	D	5	2	2	1	2	3	1	3
Leverkusen	W	W	6	1	1	4	2	4	3	1
Augsburg	D	W	6	3	3	0	2	4	2	4
Hamburg	D	L	6	3	1	2	5	1	2	3
Mainz	W	D	6	2	1	3	1	3	3	3
Wolfsburg	D	L	6	3	2	1	3	3	4	2
Stuttgart			5	2	1	2	4	1	4	0
Hannover			5	4	1	0	3	2	3	2

Season	Division	Pos	P	W	D	L	F	A	GD	Pts
2016-17	Bundesliga	4	34	16	14	4	64	37	+27	62
2015-16	Bundesliga	15	34	9	10	15	39	54	-15	37
2014-15	Bundesliga	8	34	12	8	14	49	55	-6	44

Over/Under 53%/47% 9th   **Both score** 65%/35% 4th

LEVERKUSEN

BayArena · bayer04.de

	2016-17 H	2016-17 A	P	W	D	L	OV	UN	BS	CS
Bayern Munich	D	L	6	2	3	1	1	5	2	4
RB Leipzig	L	L	1	0	0	1	1	0	1	0
Dortmund	W	L	6	1	3	2	2	4	2	3
Hoffenheim	L	L	6	4	0	2	4	2	2	3
Cologne	D	D	4	1	1	2	4	0	4	0
Hertha	W	W	5	4	1	0	5	0	5	0
Freiburg	D	L	5	3	1	1	1	4	2	2
Werder Bremen	D	L	6	3	2	1	3	3	4	2
B M'gladbach	L	L	6	2	2	2	4	2	5	1
Schalke	L	W	6	2	1	3	4	3	2	2
E Frankfurt	W	L	5	3	1	1	3	2	2	2
Leverkusen										
Augsburg	D	W	6	4	2	0	3	3	4	2
Hamburg	W	L	6	5	1	0	5	1	3	3
Mainz	L	W	6	2	2	2	4	2	2	2
Wolfsburg	D	W	6	3	2	1	5	1	5	1
Stuttgart			5	4	1	0	5	0	4	1
Hannover			5	5	0	0	3	2	1	4

Season	Division	Pos	P	W	D	L	F	A	GD	Pts
2016-17	Bundesliga	12	34	11	8	15	53	55	-2	41
2015-16	Bundesliga	3	34	18	6	10	56	40	+16	60
2014-15	Bundesliga	4	34	17	10	7	62	37	+25	61

Over/Under 62%/38% 4th **Both score** 68%/32% 2nd

MAINZ

Opel Arena · mainz05.de

	2016-17 H	2016-17 A	P	W	D	L	OV	UN	BS	CS
Bayern Munich	L	D	6	1	0	5	5	1	3	0
RB Leipzig	L	L	1	0	0	1	1	0	1	0
Dortmund	D	L	6	1	1	4	3	3	4	1
Hoffenheim	D	L	6	2	3	1	5	1	3	2
Cologne	D	L	4	2	1	1	2	2	1	3
Hertha	W	L	5	1	2	2	1	4	2	2
Freiburg	W	L	5	3	2	0	3	2	3	2
Werder Bremen	L	W	6	1	1	4	4	2	4	1
B M'gladbach	L	L	6	1	2	3	4	2	3	2
Schalke	L	L	6	2	1	3	3	3	3	1
E Frankfurt	W	L	5	4	1	0	3	2	3	2
Leverkusen	L	W	6	3	0	3	4	2	4	2
Augsburg	W	W	6	5	0	1	3	3	2	3
Hamburg	W	D	6	2	2	2	4	2	4	2
Mainz										
Wolfsburg	D	D	6	2	4	0	0	6	3	3
Stuttgart			5	3	2	0	3	2	4	1
Hannover			5	3	2	0	2	3	2	3

Season	Division	Pos	P	W	D	L	F	A	GD	Pts
2016-17	Bundesliga	15	34	10	7	17	44	55	-11	37
2015-16	Bundesliga	6	34	14	8	12	46	42	+4	50
2014-15	Bundesliga	11	34	9	13	12	45	47	-2	40

Over/Under 59%/41% 7th **Both score** 56%/44% 7th

MONCHENGLADBACH

Borussia-Park · borussia.de

	2016-17 H	2016-17 A	P	W	D	L	OV	UN	BS	CS
Bayern Munich	L	L	6	2	1	3	3	3	3	1
RB Leipzig	L	D	1	0	0	1	1	0	1	0
Dortmund	L	L	6	2	2	2	3	3	5	1
Hoffenheim	D	L	6	3	2	1	5	1	6	0
Cologne	L	W	4	3	0	1	2	2	1	3
Hertha	W	L	5	4	1	0	3	2	1	4
Freiburg	W	L	5	3	2	0	1	4	1	4
Werder Bremen	W	W	6	5	1	0	5	1	5	1
B M'gladbach										
Schalke	W	L	6	5	0	1	5	1	4	1
E Frankfurt	D	D	5	3	1	1	3	2	2	3
Leverkusen	W	W	6	3	2	1	5	1	4	1
Augsburg	D	L	6	2	2	2	3	3	4	2
Hamburg	D	L	6	2	3	1	3	3	3	2
Mainz	W	W	6	4	1	1	2	4	3	3
Wolfsburg	L	D	6	2	1	3	3	3	3	3
Stuttgart			5	1	3	1	2	3	4	1
Hannover			5	5	0	0	3	2	2	3

Season	Division	Pos	P	W	D	L	F	A	GD	Pts
2016-17	Bundesliga	9	34	12	9	13	45	49	-4	45
2015-16	Bundesliga	4	34	17	4	13	67	50	+17	55
2014-15	Bundesliga	3	34	19	9	6	53	26	+27	66

Over/Under 53%/47% 9th **Both score** 56%/44% 7th

RB LEIPZIG

Red Bull Arena · dierotenbullen.com

	2016-17 H	2016-17 A	P	W	D	L	OV	UN	BS	CS
Bayern Munich	L	L	1	0	0	1	1	0	1	0
RB Leipzig										
Dortmund	W	L	1	1	0	0	0	1	0	1
Hoffenheim	W	D	1	1	0	0	1	0	1	0
Cologne	W	D	1	1	0	0	1	0	1	0
Hertha	W	W	1	1	0	0	0	1	0	1
Freiburg	W	W	2	1	1	0	1	1	1	1
Werder Bremen	W	L	1	1	0	0	0	1	0	1
B M'gladbach	D	W	1	0	1	0	0	1	1	0
Schalke	W	D	1	1	0	0	1	0	1	0
E Frankfurt	W	D	1	1	0	0	1	0	0	1
Leverkusen	W	W	1	1	0	0	0	1	0	1
Augsburg	W	D	1	1	0	0	1	0	1	0
Hamburg	L	W	1	0	0	1	1	0	0	0
Mainz	W	W	1	1	0	0	1	0	1	0
Wolfsburg	L	W	1	0	0	1	0	1	0	0
Stuttgart			-	-	-	-	-	-	-	-
Hannover			-	-	-	-	-	-	-	-

Season	Division	Pos	P	W	D	L	F	A	GD	Pts
2016-17	Bundesliga	2	34	20	7	7	66	39	+27	67
2015-16	2.Bundesliga	2	34	20	7	7	54	32	+22	67
2014-15	2.Bundesliga	5	34	13	11	10	39	31	+8	50

Over/Under 65%/35% 3rd **Both score** 53%/47% 12th

SCHALKE

Veltins-Arena — schalke04.de

	2016-17 H	A	P	W	D	L	OV	UN	BS	CS
Bayern Munich	L	D	6	0	1	5	2	4	2	0
RB Leipzig	D	L	1	0	1	0	0	1	1	0
Dortmund	D	D	6	2	2	2	5	1	6	0
Hoffenheim	D	L	6	5	1	0	4	2	3	3
Cologne	L	D	4	1	0	3	4	0	3	0
Hertha	W	L	5	5	0	0	2	3	1	4
Freiburg	D	L	5	2	2	1	2	3	3	2
Werder Bremen	W	L	6	4	1	1	5	1	5	1
B M'gladbach	W	L	6	4	1	1	2	4	2	3
Schalke										
E Frankfurt	L	L	5	2	2	1	1	4	2	2
Leverkusen	L	W	6	2	1	3	2	4	2	2
Augsburg	W	D	6	5	1	0	4	2	4	2
Hamburg	D	L	6	3	3	0	4	2	5	1
Mainz	W	W	6	4	2	0	4	2	3	3
Wolfsburg	W	W	6	6	0	0	6	0	3	3
Stuttgart			5	3	1	1	4	1	4	1
Hannover			5	5	0	0	3	2	2	3

Season	Division	Pos	P	W	D	L	F	A	GD	Pts
2016-17	Bundesliga	10	34	11	10	13	45	40	+5	43
2015-16	Bundesliga	5	34	15	7	12	51	49	+2	52
2014-15	Bundesliga	6	34	13	9	12	42	40	+2	48

Over/Under 41%/59% 17th Both score 56%/44% 7th

STUTTGART

Mercedes-Benz Arena — vfb.de

	2016-17 H	A	P	W	D	L	OV	UN	BS	CS
Bayern Munich			5	0	0	5	3	2	3	0
RB Leipzig			-	-	-	-	-	-	-	-
Dortmund			5	0	1	4	4	1	4	0
Hoffenheim			5	3	0	2	3	2	2	1
Cologne			3	0	1	2	2	1	2	0
Hertha			4	2	1	1	2	2	1	3
Freiburg			4	3	1	0	3	1	3	1
Werder Bremen			5	2	2	1	3	2	5	0
B M'gladbach			5	1	0	4	2	3	1	1
Schalke			5	3	0	2	4	1	2	1
E Frankfurt			4	2	1	1	3	1	4	0
Leverkusen			5	0	2	3	2	3	2	0
Augsburg			5	2	0	3	4	1	3	0
Hamburg			5	3	0	2	3	2	3	1
Mainz			5	2	1	2	4	1	4	1
Wolfsburg			5	2	0	3	4	1	3	0
Stuttgart										
Hannover	L	L	6	3	0	3	5	1	4	2

Season	Division	Pos	P	W	D	L	F	A	GD	Pts
2016-17	2.Bundesliga	1	34	21	6	7	63	37	+26	69
2015-16	Bundesliga	17	34	9	6	19	50	75	-25	33
2014-15	Bundesliga	14	34	9	9	16	42	60	-18	36

Over/Under 59%/41% 1st Both score 59%/41% 5th

WERDER BREMEN

Weserstadion — werder.de

	2016-17 H	A	P	W	D	L	OV	UN	BS	CS
Bayern Munich	L	L	6	0	0	6	4	2	2	0
RB Leipzig	W	L	1	1	0	0	1	0	0	1
Dortmund	L	L	6	1	0	5	5	1	4	0
Hoffenheim	L	D	6	1	4	1	3	3	6	0
Cologne	D	L	4	1	2	1	1	3	3	0
Hertha	W	W	5	4	1	0	2	3	2	3
Freiburg	L		5	1	2	2	3	2	4	1
Werder Bremen										
B M'gladbach	L	L	6	2	2	2	3	3	3	1
Schalke	W	L	6	1	1	4	4	2	2	1
E Frankfurt	L	D	5	2	1	2	2	3	2	2
Leverkusen	W	L	6	3	1	2	4	2	4	1
Augsburg	L	L	6	2	1	3	3	3	4	1
Hamburg	W	D	6	5	0	1	2	4	2	4
Mainz	L	W	6	1	2	3	4	2	4	1
Wolfsburg	W	W	6	3	0	3	6	0	5	0
Stuttgart			5	3	2	0	2	3	3	2
Hannover			5	4	1	0	4	1	3	2

Season	Division	Pos	P	W	D	L	F	A	GD	Pts
2016-17	Bundesliga	8	34	13	6	15	61	64	-3	45
2015-16	Bundesliga	13	34	10	8	16	50	65	-15	38
2014-15	Bundesliga	10	34	11	10	13	50	65	-15	43

Over/Under 76%/24% 1st Both score 76%/24% 1st

WOLFSBURG

Volkswagen Arena — vfl-wolfsburg.de

	2016-17 H	A	P	W	D	L	OV	UN	BS	CS
Bayern Munich	L	L	6	1	0	5	3	3	2	0
RB Leipzig	L	W	1	0	0	1	0	1	0	0
Dortmund	L	L	6	2	1	3	6	0	6	0
Hoffenheim	W	D	6	4	1	1	6	0	5	1
Cologne	D	L	4	2	2	0	1	3	2	2
Hertha	L	L	5	3	0	2	3	2	3	2
Freiburg	L	W	5	2	1	2	3	2	2	1
Werder Bremen	L	L	6	4	1	1	5	1	4	2
B M'gladbach	D	W	6	4	2	0	3	3	4	2
Schalke	L	L	6	3	1	2	4	2	3	2
E Frankfurt	W	W	5	3	1	1	3	2	3	1
Leverkusen	L	D	6	5	0	1	6	0	6	0
Augsburg	L	W	6	1	2	3	2	4	4	1
Hamburg	W	L	6	3	3	0	1	5	4	2
Mainz	D	D	6	2	3	1	3	3	2	3
Wolfsburg										
Stuttgart			5	5	0	0	3	2	3	2
Hannover			5	1	2	2	4	1	4	0

Season	Division	Pos	P	W	D	L	F	A	GD	Pts
2016-17	Bundesliga	16	34	10	7	17	34	52	-18	37
2015-16	Bundesliga	8	34	12	9	13	47	49	-2	45
2014-15	Bundesliga	2	34	20	9	5	73	38	+35	69

Over/Under 50%/50% 12th Both score 44%/56% 14th

GERMAN BUNDESLIGA

Bundesliga 2016-17

Pos	H	A		P	W	D	L	F	A	W	D	L	F	A	GD	Pts
					Home					**Away**						
1	1	1	Bayern Munich (CL)	34	13	4	0	55	9	12	3	2	34	13	67	82
2	4	2	RB Leipzig (CL)	34	12	2	3	35	16	8	5	4	31	23	27	67
3	2	4	Dortmund (CL)	34	13	4	0	41	12	5	6	6	31	28	32	64
4	3	3	Hoffenheim (CL)	34	11	6	0	35	14	5	8	4	29	23	27	62
5	6	10	Cologne (EL)	34	9	6	2	29	17	3	7	7	22	25	9	49
6	5	15	Hertha Berlin (EL)	34	12	1	4	28	19	3	3	11	15	28	-4	49
7	7	11	Freiburg (EL)	34	10	2	5	23	24	4	4	9	19	36	-18	48
8	13	6	Werder Bremen	34	8	1	8	28	24	5	5	7	33	40	-3	45
9	11	8	B M'gladbach	34	7	5	5	26	18	5	4	8	19	31	-4	45
10	8	13	Schalke	34	8	5	4	29	15	3	5	9	16	25	5	43
11	9	14	Frankfurt	34	7	7	3	24	18	4	2	11	12	25	-7	42
12	14	5	Leverkusen	34	5	6	6	27	28	6	2	9	26	27	-2	41
13	15	9	Augsburg	34	5	6	6	22	25	4	5	8	13	26	-16	38
14	10	17	Hamburg	34	8	4	5	21	25	2	4	11	12	36	-28	38
15	12	16	Mainz	34	7	4	6	30	26	3	3	11	14	29	-11	37
16	17	7	Wolfsburg*	34	5	3	9	15	25	5	4	8	19	27	-18	37
17	18	12	Ingolstadt (R)	34	4	5	8	21	30	4	3	10	15	27	-21	32
18	16	18	Darmstadt (R)	34	6	3	8	18	25	1	1	15	10	38	-35	25

*Wolfsburg avoided relegation by winning relegation playoff

Bundesliga results 2016-17

	Augsburg	Bayern Munich	Cologne	Darmstadt	Dortmund	E Frankfurt	Freiburg	Hamburg	Hertha Berlin	Hoffenheim	Ingolstadt	Leverkusen	Mainz	M'gladbach	RB Leipzig	Schalke	Werder Bremen	Wolfsburg
Augsburg		1-3	2-1	1-0	1-1	1-1	1-1	4-0	0-0	0-2	2-3	1-3	1-3	1-0	2-2	1-1	3-2	0-2
Bayern Munich	6-0		1-1	1-0	4-1	3-0	4-1	8-0	3-0	1-1	3-1	2-1	2-2	2-0	3-0	1-1	6-0	5-0
Cologne	0-0	0-3		2-0	1-1	1-0	3-0	3-0	4-2	1-1	2-1	1-1	2-0	2-3	1-1	1-1	4-3	1-0
Darmstadt	1-2	0-1	1-6		2-1	1-0	3-0	0-2	0-2	1-1	0-1	0-2	2-1	0-0	0-2	2-1	2-2	3-1
Dortmund	1-1	1-0	0-0	6-0		3-1	3-1	3-0	1-1	2-1	1-0	6-2	2-1	4-1	1-0	0-0	4-3	3-0
E Frankfurt	3-1	2-2	1-0	2-0	2-1		1-2	0-0	3-3	0-0	0-2	2-1	3-0	0-0	2-2	1-0	2-2	0-2
Freiburg	2-1	1-2	2-1	1-0	0-3	1-0		1-0	2-1	1-1	1-1	2-1	1-0	3-1	1-4	2-0	2-5	0-3
Hamburg	1-0	0-1	2-1	1-2	2-5	0-3	2-2		1-0	2-1	1-1	1-0	0-0	2-1	0-4	2-1	2-2	2-1
Hertha Berlin	2-0	1-1	2-1	2-0	2-1	2-0	2-1	2-0		1-3	1-0	2-6	2-1	3-0	1-4	2-0	0-1	1-0
Hoffenheim	0-0	1-0	4-0	2-0	2-2	1-0	2-1	2-2	1-0		5-2	1-0	4-0	5-3	2-2	2-1	1-1	0-0
Ingolstadt	0-2	0-2	2-2	3-2	3-3	0-2	1-2	3-1	0-2	1-2		1-1	2-1	0-2	1-0	1-1	2-4	1-1
Leverkusen	0-0	0-0	2-2	3-2	2-0	3-0	1-1	3-1	3-1	0-3	1-2		0-2	2-3	2-3	1-4	1-1	3-3
Mainz	2-0	1-3	0-0	2-1	1-1	4-2	4-2	3-1	1-0	4-4	2-0	2-3		1-2	2-3	0-1	0-2	1-1
M'gladbach	1-1	0-1	1-2	2-2	2-3	0-0	3-0	0-0	1-0	1-1	2-0	2-1	1-0		1-2	4-2	4-1	1-2
RB Leipzig	2-1	4-5	3-1	4-0	1-0	3-0	4-0	0-3	2-0	2-1	0-0	1-0	3-1	1-1		2-1	3-1	0-1
Schalke	3-0	0-2	1-3	3-1	1-1	0-1	1-1	1-1	2-0	1-1	1-0	3-0	4-0	1-1	3-1		4-1	
Werder Bremen	1-2	1-2	1-1	2-0	1-2	1-2	1-3	2-1	2-0	3-5	2-1	2-1	1-2	0-1	3-0	3-0		2-1
Wolfsburg	1-2	0-6	0-0	1-0	1-5	1-0	0-1	1-0	2-3	2-1	3-0	1-2	2-0	0-0	1-1	0-1	0-1	

Top scorers

	Team	Goals scored
P-E Aubameyang	Dortmund	31
R Lewandowski	Bayern	30
A Modeste	Cologne	25
T Werner	RB Leipzig	21
M Gomez	Wolfsburg	16

Over 2.5 goals top five

	H	A	%
W Bremen	13	13	76%
Freiburg	10	13	68%
RB Leipzig	11	11	65%
Dortmund, Hamburg, Leverkusen			62%

Both to score top seven

	H	A	%
W Bremen	12	14	76%
Dortmund	9	14	68%
Leverkusen	11	12	68%
Freiburg	10	12	65%
Hoffenheim	8	14	65%

ALAVES

Estadio Mendizorroza   deportivoalaves.com

	2016-17 H	A	Last six seasons at home P	W	D	L	OV	UN	BS	CS
Real Madrid	L	L	1	0	0	1	1	0	1	0
Barcelona	L	W	1	0	0	1	1	0	0	0
Atl Madrid	D	D	1	0	1	0	0	1	0	1
Sevilla	D	L	1	0	1	0	0	1	1	0
Villarreal	W	W	1	1	0	0	1	0	1	0
Sociedad	W	L	1	1	0	0	0	1	0	1
Ath Bilbao	W	D	1	1	0	0	0	1	0	1
Espanyol	L	L	1	0	0	1	0	1	0	0
Alaves										
Eibar	D	D	2	0	1	1	0	2	0	1
Malaga	D	W	1	0	1	0	0	1	1	0
Valencia	W	L	1	1	0	0	1	0	1	0
Celta	W	L	1	1	0	0	1	0	1	0
Las Palmas	D	D	3	0	3	0	0	3	3	0
Betis	W	W	2	1	0	1	1	1	1	1
Deportivo	D	W	2	0	2	0	0	2	1	1
Leganes	D	D	3	1	2	0	1	2	1	2
Levante			-	-	-	-	-	-	-	-
Girona			3	1	1	1	1	2	1	1
Getafe			-	-	-	-	-	-	-	-

Season	Division	Pos	P	W	D	L	F	A	GD	Pts
2016-17	Primera Liga	9	38	14	13	11	41	43	-2	55
2015-16	Liga Segunda	1	42	21	12	9	49	35	+14	75
2014-15	Liga Segunda	12	42	14	11	17	49	53	-4	53

Over/Under 42%/58% 17th   **Both score** 50%/50% 15th

ATH BILBAO

San Mames   athletic-club.net

	2016-17 H	A	Last six seasons at home P	W	D	L	OV	UN	BS	CS
Real Madrid	L	L	6	1	1	4	4	2	3	1
Barcelona	L	L	6	1	2	3	3	3	3	1
Atl Madrid	D	L	6	2	1	3	5	1	3	2
Sevilla	W	L	6	6	0	0	4	2	4	2
Villarreal	W	L	5	3	2	0	1	4	1	4
Sociedad	W	W	6	2	2	2	2	4	4	1
Ath Bilbao										
Espanyol	W	D	6	3	1	2	5	1	4	1
Alaves	D	L	1	0	1	0	0	1	0	1
Eibar	W	W	3	2	1	0	2	1	2	1
Malaga	W	L	6	3	3	0	2	4	1	5
Valencia	W	L	6	3	2	1	3	4	3	1
Celta	W	W	5	4	1	0	3	2	4	1
Las Palmas	W	L	2	1	1	0	2	0	2	0
Betis	W	L	5	3	0	2	5	0	5	0
Deportivo	W	W	4	2	2	0	2	2	4	0
Leganes	D	D	1	0	1	0	0	1	1	0
Levante			5	4	0	1	3	2	1	3
Girona			-	-	-	-	-	-	-	-
Getafe			5	3	1	1	3	2	2	3

Season	Division	Pos	P	W	D	L	F	A	GD	Pts
2016-17	Primera Liga	7	38	19	6	13	53	43	+10	63
2015-16	Primera Liga	5	38	18	8	12	58	45	+13	62
2014-15	Primera Liga	7	38	15	10	13	42	41	+1	55

Over/Under 58%/42% 9th   **Both score** 58%/42% 9th

ATL MADRID

Wanda Metropolitano   clubatleticodemadrid.com

	2016-17 H	A	Last six seasons at home P	W	D	L	OV	UN	BS	CS
Real Madrid	L	D	6	1	2	3	5	1	4	1
Barcelona	L	D	6	0	1	5	4	2	4	1
Atl Madrid										
Sevilla	W	L	6	3	3	0	3	3	2	4
Villarreal	L	L	5	2	1	2	1	4	0	3
Sociedad	W	L	6	4	1	1	2	4	1	4
Ath Bilbao	W	D	6	5	1	0	4	2	3	3
Espanyol	D	W	6	5	1	0	1	5	1	5
Alaves	D	D	1	0	1	0	0	1	1	0
Eibar	W	W	3	3	0	0	2	1	2	1
Malaga	W	W	6	5	1	0	4	2	5	1
Valencia	W	W	6	3	3	0	3	3	3	3
Celta	W	W	5	4	1	0	3	2	3	2
Las Palmas	W	W	2	2	0	0	2	0	2	0
Betis	W	D	5	4	0	1	2	3	1	3
Deportivo	W	D	4	4	0	0	2	2	0	4
Leganes	W	D	1	1	0	0	0	1	0	1
Levante			5	5	0	0	3	2	3	2
Girona			-	-	-	-	-	-	-	-
Getafe			5	5	0	0	2	3	0	5

Season	Division	Pos	P	W	D	L	F	A	GD	Pts
2016-17	Primera Liga	3	38	23	9	6	70	27	+43	78
2015-16	Primera Liga	3	38	28	4	6	63	18	+45	88
2014-15	Primera Liga	3	38	23	9	6	67	29	+38	78

Over/Under 42%/58% 17th   **Both score** 34%/66% 20th

BARCELONA

Camp Nou   fcbarcelona.cat

	2016-17 H	A	Last six seasons at home P	W	D	L	OV	UN	BS	CS
Real Madrid	D	W	6	2	2	2	5	1	6	0
Barcelona										
Atl Madrid	D	W	6	4	2	0	4	2	5	1
Sevilla	W	W	6	5	1	0	5	1	4	2
Villarreal	W	D	5	5	0	0	5	0	3	2
Sociedad	W	D	6	6	0	0	5	1	4	2
Ath Bilbao	W	W	6	6	0	0	4	2	2	4
Espanyol	W	W	6	6	0	0	5	1	2	4
Alaves	L	W	1	0	0	1	1	0	1	0
Eibar	W	W	3	3	0	0	3	0	2	1
Malaga	D	L	6	4	1	1	3	3	2	3
Valencia	W	W	6	4	0	2	4	2	4	2
Celta	W	L	5	4	0	1	4	1	2	2
Las Palmas	W	W	2	2	0	0	2	0	1	1
Betis	W	D	5	5	0	0	5	0	4	1
Deportivo	W	D	4	2	2	0	3	1	2	2
Leganes	W	W	1	1	0	0	1	0	1	0
Levante			5	5	0	0	4	1	1	4
Girona			-	-	-	-	-	-	-	-
Getafe			5	4	1	0	5	0	2	3

Season	Division	Pos	P	W	D	L	F	A	GD	Pts
2016-17	Primera Liga	2	38	28	6	4	116	37	+79	90
2015-16	Primera Liga	1	38	29	4	5	112	29	+83	91
2014-15	Primera Liga	1	38	30	4	4	110	21	+89	94

Over/Under 76%/24% 2nd   **Both score** 63%/37% 5th

BETIS

Benito Villamarin — realbetisbalompie.es

2016-17	H	A	Last six seasons at home P	W	D	L	OV	UN	BS	CS
Real Madrid	L	L	5	1	1	3	3	2	3	1
Barcelona	D	L	5	0	2	3	3	2	4	0
Atl Madrid	D	L	5	0	2	3	2	3	3	0
Sevilla	L	L	5	0	3	2	2	3	3	1
Villarreal	L	L	4	2	1	1	1	3	2	1
Sociedad	L	L	5	2	0	3	2	3	2	2
Ath Bilbao	W	L	5	2	1	2	2	3	3	1
Espanyol	L	L	5	2	1	2	1	4	2	2
Alaves	L	L	2	0	0	2	2	0	2	0
Eibar	W	L	2	1	0	1	1	1	0	1
Malaga	W	W	5	2	1	2	2	3	1	3
Valencia	D	W	5	4	1	0	2	3	2	3
Celta	D	W	4	1	2	1	2	2	3	1
Las Palmas	W	L	3	2	1	0	0	3	0	3
Betis										
Deportivo	D	D	3	0	2	1	1	2	2	1
Leganes	W	L	2	1	0	1	1	1	1	1
Levante			4	2	1	1	0	4	0	3
Girona			1	1	0	0	1	0	1	0
Getafe			4	2	2	0	1	3	2	2

Season	Division	Pos	P	W	D	L	F	A	GD	Pts
2016-17	Primera Liga	15	38	10	9	19	41	64	-23	39
2015-16	Primera Liga	10	38	11	12	15	34	52	-18	45
2014-15	Liga Segunda	1	42	25	9	8	73	40	+33	84

Over/Under 47%/53% 14th **Both score** 53%/47% 11th

CELTA VIGO

Balaidos — celtavigo.net

2016-17	H	A	Last six seasons at home P	W	D	L	OV	UN	BS	CS
Real Madrid	L	L	5	1	0	4	4	1	4	1
Barcelona	W	L	5	2	1	2	4	1	3	0
Atl Madrid	L	L	5	1	0	4	2	3	1	1
Sevilla	L	L	5	2	2	1	1	4	2	2
Villarreal	L	L	4	0	2	2	1	3	1	2
Sociedad	D	L	5	1	4	0	3	2	4	1
Ath Bilbao	L	L	5	0	2	3	2	3	2	1
Espanyol	D	W	5	3	2	0	3	2	3	2
Alaves	W	L	1	1	0	0	0	1	0	1
Eibar	L	L	3	1	0	2	1	2	1	0
Malaga	W	L	5	3	0	2	1	4	1	2
Valencia	W	L	5	2	1	2	3	2	4	0
Celta										
Las Palmas	W	D	3	1	1	1	3	0	3	0
Betis	L	D	4	1	1	2	1	3	2	0
Deportivo	W	W	5	2	2	1	3	2	5	0
Leganes	L	W	1	0	0	1	0	1	0	0
Levante			4	2	1	1	2	2	2	1
Girona			1	1	0	0	0	1	0	0
Getafe			4	2	2	0	2	2	3	1

Season	Division	Pos	P	W	D	L	F	A	GD	Pts
2016-17	Primera Liga	13	38	13	6	19	53	69	-16	45
2015-16	Primera Liga	6	38	17	9	12	51	59	-8	60
2014-15	Primera Liga	8	38	13	12	13	47	44	+3	51

Over/Under 68%/32% 3rd **Both score** 50%/50% 15th

DEPORTIVO LA CORUNA

Estadio Municipal de Riazor — canaldeportivo.com

2016-17	H	A	Last six seasons at home P	W	D	L	OV	UN	BS	CS
Real Madrid	L	L	4	0	0	4	3	1	3	0
Barcelona	W	L	4	1	0	3	4	0	2	0
Atl Madrid	D	L	4	0	3	1	1	3	3	1
Sevilla	L	L	4	0	1	3	2	2	3	0
Villarreal	D	D	3	0	1	2	1	2	2	1
Sociedad	W	L	4	1	2	1	1	3	1	2
Ath Bilbao	L	L	4	1	2	1	1	3	2	1
Espanyol	L	D	4	2	1	1	2	2	1	3
Alaves	L	D	2	1	0	1	1	1	1	0
Eibar	W	L	4	3	1	0	1	3	2	2
Malaga	W	L	4	2	1	1	1	3	1	2
Valencia	D	L	4	1	2	1	2	2	3	1
Celta	L	L	5	3	0	2	2	3	2	1
Las Palmas	W	L	4	2	0	2	4	0	3	1
Betis	D	D	3	0	2	1	2	1	3	0
Deportivo										
Leganes	L	L	1	0	0	1	1	0	1	0
Levante			3	2	0	1	1	2	1	1
Girona			2	1	1	0	1	1	1	1
Getafe			3	0	1	2	1	2	2	0

Season	Division	Pos	P	W	D	L	F	A	GD	Pts
2016-17	Primera Liga	16	38	8	12	18	43	61	-18	36
2015-16	Primera Liga	15	38	8	18	12	45	61	-16	42
2014-15	Primera Liga	16	38	7	14	17	35	60	-25	35

Over/Under 50%/50% 12th **Both score** 55%/45% 10th

EIBAR

Estadio Municipal de Ipurua — sdeibar.com

2016-17	H	A	Last six seasons at home P	W	D	L	OV	UN	BS	CS
Real Madrid	L	D	3	0	0	3	2	1	1	0
Barcelona	L	L	3	0	0	3	2	1	0	0
Atl Madrid	L	L	3	0	0	3	1	2	1	0
Sevilla	D	L	3	0	2	1	1	2	3	0
Villarreal	W	W	3	1	1	1	2	1	3	0
Sociedad	W	D	3	3	0	0	1	2	1	2
Ath Bilbao	L	L	3	1	0	2	0	3	0	1
Espanyol	D	D	3	1	1	1	1	2	2	0
Alaves	D	D	2	1	1	0	0	2	0	2
Eibar										
Malaga	W	L	3	2	0	1	2	1	1	2
Valencia	W	W	3	1	1	1	0	3	1	1
Celta	W	W	3	1	1	1	0	3	1	1
Las Palmas	W	L	3	2	0	1	1	2	1	1
Betis	W	L	2	1	1	0	1	1	2	0
Deportivo	W	L	4	2	1	1	2	2	3	0
Leganes	W	D	1	1	0	0	0	1	0	0
Levante			2	1	1	0	1	1	1	1
Girona			1	0	0	1	1	0	0	0
Getafe			2	2	0	0	2	0	2	0

Season	Division	Pos	P	W	D	L	F	A	GD	Pts
2016-17	Primera Liga	10	38	15	9	14	56	51	+5	54
2015-16	Primera Liga	14	38	11	10	17	49	61	-12	48
2014-15	Primera Liga	18	38	9	8	21	34	55	-21	35

Over/Under 50%/50% 12th **Both score** 53%/47% 11th

ESPANYOL

Cornella-El Prat   rcdespanyol.com

2016-17	H	A	Last six seasons at home P	W	D	L	OV	UN	BS	CS
Real Madrid	L	L	6	0	1	5	3	3	2	0
Barcelona	L	L	6	0	2	4	1	5	1	1
Atl Madrid	L	D	6	2	1	3	2	4	2	2
Sevilla	W	L	6	2	2	2	4	2	5	1
Villarreal	D	L	5	0	4	1	2	3	3	2
Sociedad	L	D	6	1	2	3	5	1	4	1
Ath Bilbao	D	L	6	4	2	0	4	2	4	2
Espanyol										
Alaves	W	W	1	1	0	0	0	1	0	1
Eibar	D	D	3	1	1	1	3	0	3	0
Malaga	D	W	6	1	4	1	3	3	3	3
Valencia	L	L	6	3	1	2	4	2	3	2
Celta	L	D	5	3	1	1	0	5	1	3
Las Palmas	W	D	2	2	0	0	1	1	1	1
Betis	W	W	5	3	1	1	2	3	1	3
Deportivo	D	W	4	2	2	0	0	4	1	3
Leganes	W	W	1	1	0	0	1	0	0	1
Levante			5	2	2	1	3	2	4	1
Girona			-	-	-	-	-	-	-	-
Getafe			5	3	0	2	0	5	0	3

Season	Division	Pos	P	W	D	L	F	A	GD	Pts
2016-17	Primera Liga	8	38	15	11	12	49	50	-1	56
2015-16	Primera Liga	13	38	12	7	19	40	74	-34	43
2014-15	Primera Liga	10	38	13	10	15	47	51	-4	49

Over/Under 47%/53% 14th   **Both score** 50%/50% 15th

GETAFE

Coliseum Alfonso Perez   getafecf.com

2016-17	H	A	Last six seasons at home P	W	D	L	OV	UN	BS	CS
Real Madrid			5	1	0	4	4	1	2	0
Barcelona			5	1	1	3	2	3	2	2
Atl Madrid			5	1	1	3	1	4	1	1
Sevilla			5	3	2	0	2	3	4	1
Villarreal			4	1	2	1	0	4	1	2
Sociedad			5	2	2	1	2	3	3	1
Ath Bilbao			5	1	1	3	1	4	1	2
Espanyol			5	2	2	1	2	3	3	1
Alaves			-	-	-	-	-	-	-	-
Eibar			2	0	2	0	0	2	2	0
Malaga			5	4	0	1	1	4	1	4
Valencia			5	1	1	3	3	2	2	0
Celta			4	3	0	1	2	2	2	1
Las Palmas			1	1	0	0	1	0	0	1
Betis			4	3	0	1	2	2	2	2
Deportivo			3	2	1	0	2	1	2	1
Leganes			-	-	-	-	-	-	-	-
Levante	W	D	6	3	1	2	1	5	1	3
Girona	L	L	1	0	0	1	0	1	0	0
Getafe										

Season	Division	Pos	P	W	D	L	F	A	GD	Pts
2016-17	Liga Segunda	3	42	18	14	10	55	43	+12	68
2015-16	Primera Liga	19	38	9	9	20	37	67	-30	36
2014-15	Primera Liga	15	38	10	7	21	33	64	-31	37

Over/Under 33%/67% 28th   **Both score** 45%/55% 20th

GIRONA

Estadi Municipal de Montilivi   gironafc.cat

2016-17	H	A	Last six seasons at home P	W	D	L	OV	UN	BS	CS
Real Madrid			-	-	-	-	-	-	-	-
Barcelona			-	-	-	-	-	-	-	-
Atl Madrid			-	-	-	-	-	-	-	-
Sevilla			-	-	-	-	-	-	-	-
Villarreal			1	1	0	0	0	1	0	1
Sociedad			-	-	-	-	-	-	-	-
Ath Bilbao			-	-	-	-	-	-	-	-
Espanyol			-	-	-	-	-	-	-	-
Alaves			3	2	1	0	1	2	1	2
Eibar			1	0	1	0	0	1	1	0
Malaga			-	-	-	-	-	-	-	-
Valencia			-	-	-	-	-	-	-	-
Celta			1	0	0	1	0	1	0	0
Las Palmas			4	2	0	2	3	1	2	1
Betis			1	0	0	1	1	0	1	0
Deportivo			2	2	0	0	1	1	1	1
Leganes			2	1	1	0	1	1	2	0
Levante	W	L	1	1	0	0	1	0	1	0
Girona										
Getafe	W	W	1	1	0	0	1	0	1	0

Season	Division	Pos	P	W	D	L	F	A	GD	Pts
2016-17	Liga Segunda	2	42	20	10	12	65	45	+20	70
2015-16	Liga Segunda	4	42	17	15	10	46	28	+18	66
2014-15	Liga Segunda	3	42	24	10	8	63	35	+28	82

Over/Under 52%/48% 2nd   **Both score** 55%/45% 6th

LAS PALMAS

Estadio Gran Canaria   udlaspalmas.es

2016-17	H	A	Last six seasons at home P	W	D	L	OV	UN	BS	CS
Real Madrid	D	D	2	0	1	1	2	0	2	0
Barcelona	L	L	2	0	2	0	2	0	2	0
Atl Madrid	L	L	2	0	0	2	2	0	0	0
Sevilla	L	L	2	1	0	1	0	2	0	1
Villarreal	W	L	3	1	2	0	1	2	1	2
Sociedad	L	L	2	1	0	1	0	2	0	1
Ath Bilbao	W	L	2	1	1	0	1	1	1	1
Espanyol	D	L	2	1	1	0	1	1	0	2
Alaves	D	D	3	1	1	1	1	2	2	0
Eibar	W	D	3	1	1	1	0	3	1	1
Malaga	W	L	2	1	1	0	2	0	1	1
Valencia	W	W	2	2	0	0	2	0	2	0
Celta	D	L	3	2	1	0	3	0	3	0
Las Palmas										
Betis	W	L	3	2	0	1	2	1	1	1
Deportivo	D	L	4	0	1	3	0	4	1	0
Leganes	D	L	2	1	1	0	0	2	1	1
Levante			1	0	1	0	0	1	0	1
Girona			4	4	0	0	3	1	3	1
Getafe			1	1	0	0	1	0	0	1

Season	Division	Pos	P	W	D	L	F	A	GD	Pts
2016-17	Primera Liga	14	38	10	9	19	53	74	-21	39
2015-16	Primera Liga	11	38	12	8	18	45	53	-8	44
2014-15	Liga Segunda	4	42	22	12	8	73	47	+26	78

Over/Under 61%/39% 7th   **Both score** 61%/39% 7th

LEGANES

Municipal de Butarque   deportivoleganes.com

	2016-17 H	A	Last six seasons at home P	W	D	L	OV	UN	BS	CS
Real Madrid	L	L	1	0	0	1	1	0	1	0
Barcelona	L	L	1	0	0	1	1	0	1	0
Atl Madrid	D	L	1	0	1	0	0	1	0	1
Sevilla	L	D	1	0	0	1	1	0	1	0
Villarreal	D	L	1	0	1	0	0	1	0	1
Sociedad	L	D	1	0	0	1	0	1	0	0
Ath Bilbao	D	D	1	0	1	0	0	1	0	1
Espanyol	L	L	1	0	0	1	0	1	0	0
Alaves	D	D	3	1	2	0	0	3	2	1
Eibar	D	L	1	0	1	0	0	1	1	0
Malaga	D	L	1	0	1	0	0	1	0	1
Valencia	L	L	1	0	0	1	1	0	1	0
Celta	L	W	1	0	0	1	0	1	0	0
Las Palmas	W	D	2	2	0	0	2	0	1	1
Betis	W	L	2	2	0	0	1	1	0	2
Deportivo	W	W	1	1	0	0	1	0	0	1
Leganes										
Levante			-	-	-	-	-	-	-	-
Girona			2	0	1	1	2	0	2	0
Getafe			-	-	-	-	-	-	-	-

Season	Division	Pos	P	W	D	L	F	A	GD	Pts
2016-17	Primera Liga	17	38	8	11	19	36	55	-19	35
2015-16	Liga Segunda	2	42	20	14	8	59	34	+25	74
2014-15	Liga Segunda	10	42	15	11	16	48	42	+6	56

Over/Under 42%/58% 17th   **Both score** 42%/58% 19th

LEVANTE

Ciutat de Valencia   levanteud.com

	2016-17 H	A	Last six seasons at home P	W	D	L	OV	UN	BS	CS
Real Madrid			5	1	0	4	4	1	3	1
Barcelona			5	0	1	4	3	2	2	0
Atl Madrid			5	3	2	0	2	3	3	2
Sevilla			5	2	2	1	4	2	3	
Villarreal			4	2	0	2	1	3	0	2
Sociedad			5	2	2	1	3	2	3	1
Ath Bilbao			5	2	1	2	4	1	3	1
Espanyol			5	4	1	0	5	0	4	1
Alaves			-	-	-	-	-	-	-	-
Eibar			2	1	1	0	2	0	2	0
Malaga			5	3	0	2	3	2	2	2
Valencia			5	4	0	1	1	4	1	3
Celta			4	0	0	4	1	3	1	0
Las Palmas			1	1	0	0	1	0	1	0
Betis			4	1	1	2	2	2	3	0
Deportivo			3	0	2	1	1	2	1	1
Leganes			-	-	-	-	-	-	-	-
Levante										
Girona	W	L	1	1	0	0	1	0	1	0
Getafe	D	L	6	1	4	1	2	4	3	3

Season	Division	Pos	P	W	D	L	F	A	GD	Pts
2016-17	Liga Segunda	1	42	25	9	8	57	32	+25	84
2015-16	Primera Liga	20	38	8	8	22	37	70	-33	32
2014-15	Primera Liga	14	38	9	10	19	34	67	-33	37

Over/Under 36%/64% 24th   **Both score** 43%/57% 22nd

MALAGA

La Rosaleda   malagacf.es

	2016-17 H	A	Last six seasons at home P	W	D	L	OV	UN	BS	CS
Real Madrid	L	L	6	1	1	4	3	3	3	0
Barcelona	W	D	6	1	1	4	3	3	3	2
Atl Madrid	L	L	6	1	3	2	1	5	1	3
Sevilla	W	L	6	3	2	1	4	2	4	2
Villarreal	L	D	5	2	1	2	1	4	2	1
Sociedad	L	D	6	1	2	3	2	4	4	0
Ath Bilbao	W	L	6	4	0	2	2	4	2	3
Espanyol	L	D	6	1	1	4	2	4	3	0
Alaves	L	L	1	0	0	1	1	0	1	0
Eibar	W	L	3	2	1	0	2	1	2	1
Malaga										
Valencia	W	D	6	4	1	1	2	4	1	5
Celta	W	L	5	3	1	1	2	3	1	3
Las Palmas	W	L	2	2	0	0	2	0	2	0
Betis	L	L	5	2	0	3	3	2	2	1
Deportivo	W	L	4	3	1	0	2	2	3	1
Leganes	W	D	1	1	0	0	1	0	0	1
Levante			5	4	1	0	2	3	2	3
Girona			-	-	-	-	-	-	-	-
Getafe			5	5	0	0	4	1	3	2

Season	Division	Pos	P	W	D	L	F	A	GD	Pts
2016-17	Primera Liga	11	38	12	10	16	49	55	-6	46
2015-16	Primera Liga	8	38	12	12	14	38	35	+3	48
2014-15	Primera Liga	9	38	14	8	16	42	48	-6	50

Over/Under 47%/53% 14th   **Both score** 53%/47% 11th

REAL MADRID

Santiago Bernabeu   realmadrid.com

	2016-17 H	A	Last six seasons at home P	W	D	L	OV	UN	BS	CS
Real Madrid										
Barcelona	L	D	6	2	0	4	6	0	5	0
Atl Madrid	D	W	6	2	1	3	2	4	3	1
Sevilla	W	L	6	6	0	0	6	0	4	2
Villarreal	D	W	5	3	2	0	3	2	3	2
Sociedad	W	W	6	6	0	0	6	0	5	1
Ath Bilbao	W	W	6	6	0	0	6	0	5	1
Espanyol	W	W	6	5	1	0	5	1	2	4
Alaves	W	W	1	1	0	0	1	0	0	1
Eibar	D	W	3	2	1	0	2	1	1	2
Malaga	W	W	6	4	2	0	3	3	4	2
Valencia	W	L	6	2	4	0	4	2	5	1
Celta	W	W	5	5	0	0	4	1	2	3
Las Palmas	D	D	2	1	1	0	2	0	2	0
Betis	W	W	5	5	0	0	5	0	4	1
Deportivo	W	W	4	4	0	0	3	1	2	2
Leganes	W	W	1	1	0	0	1	0	0	1
Levante			5	5	0	0	4	1	2	3
Girona			-	-	-	-	-	-	-	-
Getafe			5	5	0	0	5	0	4	1

Season	Division	Pos	P	W	D	L	F	A	GD	Pts
2016-17	Primera Liga	1	38	29	6	3	106	41	+65	93
2015-16	Primera Liga	2	38	28	6	4	110	34	+76	90
2014-15	Primera Liga	2	38	30	2	6	118	38	+80	92

Over/Under 82%/18% 1st   **Both score** 74%/26% 1st

SEVILLA

Ramón Sanchez Pizjuan — sevillafc.es

	2016-17 H	A	Last six seasons at home P	W	D	L	OV	UN	BS	CS
Real Madrid	W	L	6	4	0	2	5	1	5	1
Barcelona	L	L	6	1	1	4	5	1	5	0
Atl Madrid	W	L	6	1	2	3	2	4	2	2
Sevilla										
Villarreal	D	D	5	2	2	1	3	2	3	2
Sociedad	D	W	6	3	1	2	2	4	3	3
Ath Bilbao	W	L	6	4	1	1	2	4	3	3
Espanyol	W	L	6	5	1	0	4	2	3	3
Alaves	W	D	1	1	0	0	1	0	1	0
Eibar	W	D	3	2	1	0	0	3	0	3
Malaga	W	L	6	4	1	1	4	2	4	1
Valencia	W	D	6	4	2	0	2	4	3	3
Celta	W	W	5	3	0	2	3	2	3	1
Las Palmas	W	W	2	2	0	0	1	1	1	1
Betis	W	W	5	4	0	1	3	2	2	3
Deportivo	W	W	4	3	1	0	3	1	4	0
Leganes	D	W	1	0	1	0	0	1	1	0
Levante			5	1	3	1	2	3	4	1
Girona										
Getafe			5	5	0	0	4	1	1	4

Season	Division	Pos	P	W	D	L	F	A	GD	Pts
2016-17	Primera Liga	4	38	21	9	8	69	49	+20	72
2015-16	Primera Liga	7	38	14	10	14	51	50	+1	52
2014-15	Primera Liga	5	38	23	7	8	71	45	+26	76

Over/Under 61%/39% 7th   **Both score** 63%/37% 5th

SOCIEDAD

Anoeta — realsociedad.com

	2016-17 H	A	Last six seasons at home P	W	D	L	OV	UN	BS	CS
Real Madrid	L	L	6	1	1	4	4	2	2	0
Barcelona	D	L	6	4	2	0	3	3	4	2
Atl Madrid	W	L	6	2	0	4	3	3	2	1
Sevilla	L	D	6	4	1	1	3	3	3	2
Villarreal	L	L	5	0	2	3	1	4	2	1
Sociedad										
Ath Bilbao	L	L	6	2	2	2	1	5	2	3
Espanyol	D	W	6	2	2	2	4	3	2	
Alaves	W	L	1	1	0	0	1	0	0	1
Eibar	D	W	3	2	1	0	2	1	2	1
Malaga	D	W	6	2	3	1	3	3	4	1
Valencia	W	W	6	5	1	0	2	4	3	3
Celta	W	D	5	3	1	1	3	2	4	1
Las Palmas	W	W	2	1	0	1	1	1	1	0
Betis	W	W	5	3	2	0	3	2	4	1
Deportivo	W	L	4	1	3	0	1	3	3	1
Leganes	D	W	1	0	1	0	0	1	1	0
Levante			5	1	3	1	2	3	3	2
Girona										
Getafe			5	1	2	2	2	3	3	2

Season	Division	Pos	P	W	D	L	F	A	GD	Pts
2016-17	Primera Liga	6	38	19	7	12	59	53	+6	64
2015-16	Primera Liga	9	38	13	9	16	45	48	-3	48
2014-15	Primera Liga	12	38	11	13	14	44	51	-7	46

Over/Under 53%/47% 11th   **Both score** 53%/47% 11th

VALENCIA

Mestalla — valenciafc.com

	2016-17 H	A	Last six seasons at home P	W	D	L	OV	UN	BS	CS
Real Madrid	W	L	6	2	1	3	6	0	5	0
Barcelona	L	L	6	0	3	3	3	3	5	0
Atl Madrid	L	L	6	3	0	3	2	4	2	2
Sevilla	D	L	6	4	1	1	4	2	4	2
Villarreal	L	W	5	2	1	2	2	3	2	2
Sociedad	L	L	6	1	0	5	3	3	3	1
Ath Bilbao	W	L	6	2	3	1	2	4	3	2
Espanyol	W	W	6	5	1	0	6	0	6	0
Alaves	W	L	1	1	0	0	1	0	1	0
Eibar	L	L	3	2	0	1	3	0	1	1
Malaga	D	L	6	5	1	0	4	2	2	4
Valencia										
Celta	W	L	5	3	1	1	3	2	4	0
Las Palmas	L	L	2	0	1	1	1	1	2	0
Betis	L	D	5	3	1	1	4	1	1	4
Deportivo	W	W	4	2	2	0	2	2	2	2
Leganes	W	W	1	1	0	0	0	1	0	1
Levante			5	3	0	2	3	2	2	3
Girona			-	-	-	-	-	-	-	-
Getafe			5	3	1	1	4	1	4	1

Season	Division	Pos	P	W	D	L	F	A	GD	Pts
2016-17	Primera Liga	12	38	13	7	18	56	65	-9	46
2015-16	Primera Liga	12	38	11	11	16	46	48	-2	44
2014-15	Primera Liga	4	38	22	11	5	70	32	+38	77

Over/Under 68%/32% 3rd   **Both score** 68%/32% 2nd

VILLARREAL

El Madrigal — villarrealcf.es

	2016-17 H	A	Last six seasons at home P	W	D	L	OV	UN	BS	CS
Real Madrid	L	D	5	1	2	2	2	3	3	1
Barcelona	D	L	5	0	3	2	2	3	3	1
Atl Madrid	W	W	5	2	1	2	1	4	1	2
Sevilla	D	D	5	1	2	2	3	2	3	1
Villarreal										
Sociedad	W	W	5	3	2	0	3	2	3	2
Ath Bilbao	W	L	5	3	2	0	3	2	4	1
Espanyol	W	D	5	3	1	1	3	2	2	2
Alaves	L	L	1	0	0	1	0	1	0	0
Eibar	L	L	3	1	1	1	2	2	1	1
Malaga	D	W	5	3	2	0	2	3	4	1
Valencia	L	W	5	2	1	2	3	2	3	1
Celta	W	W	4	2	0	2	3	1	2	1
Las Palmas	W	L	3	1	1	1	2	2	2	0
Betis	W	W	4	2	2	0	0	4	1	3
Deportivo	D	D	3	1	1	1	1	2	0	2
Leganes	W	D	1	1	0	0	1	0	1	0
Levante			4	3	0	1	2	2	0	3
Girona			1	1	0	0	1	0	1	0
Getafe			4	2	0	2	2	2	2	1

Season	Division	Pos	P	W	D	L	F	A	GD	Pts
2016-17	Primera Liga	5	38	19	10	9	56	33	+23	67
2015-16	Primera Liga	4	38	18	10	10	44	35	+9	64
2014-15	Primera Liga	6	38	16	12	10	48	37	+11	60

Over/Under 42%/58% 17th   **Both score** 47%/53% 18th

La Liga 2016-17

Pos	H	A		P	W	D	L	F	A	W	D	L	F	A	GD	Pts
1	2	1	Real Madrid (CL)	38	14	4	1	48	20	15	2	2	58	21	65	93
2	1	2	Barcelona (CL)	38	15	3	1	64	17	13	3	3	52	20	79	90
3	4	3	Atl Madrid (CL)	38	14	2	3	40	14	9	7	3	30	13	43	78
4	3	8	Seville (CL)	38	14	4	1	39	16	7	5	7	30	33	20	72
5	6	4	Villarreal (EL)	38	11	4	4	35	18	8	6	5	21	15	23	67
6	7	5	Real Sociedad (EL)	38	10	5	4	30	24	9	2	8	29	29	6	64
7	5	10	Ath Bilbao (EL)	38	13	4	2	36	18	6	2	11	17	25	10	63
8	11	6	Espanyol	38	8	5	6	28	24	7	6	6	21	26	-1	56
9	13	7	Alaves	38	7	8	4	19	21	7	5	7	22	22	-2	55
10	9	9	Eibar	38	10	3	6	29	21	5	6	8	27	30	5	54
11	10	13	Malaga	38	10	2	7	32	25	2	8	9	17	30	-6	46
12	14	11	Valencia	38	8	4	7	32	32	5	3	11	24	33	-9	46
13	12	12	Celta Vigo	38	9	2	8	30	32	4	4	11	23	37	-16	45
14	8	19	Las Palmas	38	9	6	4	33	25	1	3	15	20	49	-21	39
15	16	15	Real Betis	38	6	7	6	22	24	4	2	13	19	40	-23	39
16	15	17	Deportivo	38	7	5	7	27	23	1	7	11	16	38	-18	36
17	17	14	Leganes	38	5	6	8	22	23	3	5	11	14	32	-19	35
18	18	16	Sporting Gijon (R)	38	5	4	10	26	38	2	6	11	16	34	-30	31
19	20	18	Osasuna (R)	38	2	7	10	23	39	2	3	14	17	55	-54	22
20	19	20	Granada (R)	38	4	4	11	17	32	0	4	15	13	50	-52	20

La Liga results 2016-17

	Alaves	Ath Bilbao	Atl Madrid	Barcelona	Betis	Celta Vigo	Deportivo	Eibar	Espanyol	Granada	Las Palmas	Leganes	Malaga	Osasuna	Real Madrid	Seville	Sociedad	Sporting Gijon	Valencia	Villarreal
Alaves		1-0	0-0	0-6	1-0	3-1	0-0	0-0	0-1	3-1	1-1	2-2	1-1	0-1	1-4	1-1	1-0	0-0	2-1	2-1
Ath Bilbao	0-0		2-2	0-1	2-1	2-1	2-1	3-1	2-0	3-1	5-1	1-1	1-0	1-1	1-2	3-1	3-2	2-1	2-1	1-0
Atl Madrid	1-1	3-1		1-2	1-0	3-2	1-0	1-0	0-0	7-1	1-0	2-0	4-2	3-0	0-3	3-1	1-0	5-0	3-0	0-1
Barcelona	1-2	3-0	1-1		6-2	5-0	4-0	4-2	4-1	1-0	5-0	2-1	0-0	7-1	1-1	3-0	3-2	6-1	4-2	4-1
Betis	1-4	1-0	1-1	1-1		3-3	0-0	2-0	0-1	2-2	2-0	2-0	1-0	2-0	1-6	1-2	2-3	0-0	0-0	0-1
Celta	1-0	0-3	0-4	4-3	0-1		4-1	0-2	2-2	3-1	3-1	0-1	3-1	3-0	1-0	0-3	2-2	2-1	2-1	0-1
Deportivo	0-1	1-1	1-1	2-1	1-1	0-1		2-1	1-2	0-0	3-0	1-2	2-0	2-0	2-6	2-3	5-1	2-1	1-1	0-0
Eibar	0-0	0-1	0-2	0-4	3-1	1-0	3-1		1-1	4-0	3-1	2-0	3-0	2-3	1-4	1-1	2-0	0-1	1-0	2-1
Espanyol	1-0	0-0	0-1	0-3	2-1	0-2	1-1	3-3		3-1	4-3	3-0	2-2	3-0	0-2	3-1	1-2	2-1	0-1	0-0
Granada	2-1	1-2	0-1	1-4	4-1	0-3	1-1	1-2	1-2		1-0	0-1	0-2	1-1	0-4	2-1	0-2	0-0	1-3	1-1
Las Palmas	1-1	3-1	0-5	1-4	4-1	3-3	1-1	1-0	0-0	5-1		1-1	1-0	5-2	2-2	0-1	0-1	1-0	3-1	1-0
Leganes	1-1	0-0	0-0	1-5	4-0	0-2	4-0	1-1	0-1	1-0	3-0		0-0	2-0	2-4	2-3	0-2	0-2	1-2	0-0
Malaga	1-2	2-1	0-2	2-0	1-2	3-0	4-3	2-1	0-1	1-1	2-1	4-0		1-1	0-2	4-2	0-2	3-2	2-0	0-2
Osasuna	0-1	1-2	0-3	0-3	1-2	0-0	2-2	1-1	1-2	2-1	2-2	2-1	1-1		1-3	3-4	0-2	2-2	3-3	1-4
Real Madrid	3-0	2-1	1-1	2-3	2-1	2-1	3-2	1-1	2-0	5-0	3-3	3-0	2-1	5-2		4-1	3-0	2-1	2-1	1-1
Seville	2-1	1-0	1-0	1-2	1-0	2-1	4-2	2-0	6-4	2-0	2-1	1-1	4-1	5-0	2-1		1-1	0-0	2-1	0-0
Sociedad	3-0	0-2	2-0	1-1	1-0	1-0	1-0	2-2	1-1	2-1	4-1	1-1	2-2	3-2	0-3	0-4		3-1	3-2	0-1
Sporting Gijon	2-4	2-1	1-4	0-5	2-2	1-1	0-1	2-3	1-1	3-1	1-0	2-1	0-1	3-1	2-3	1-1	1-3		1-2	1-3
Valencia	2-1	2-0	0-2	2-3	2-3	3-2	3-0	0-4	2-1	1-1	2-4	1-0	2-2	4-1	2-1	0-0	2-3	1-1		1-3
Villarreal	0-2	3-1	3-0	1-1	2-0	5-0	0-0	2-3	2-0	2-0	2-1	2-1	1-1	3-1	2-3	0-0	2-1	3-1	0-2	

Top scorers

	Team	Goals scored
L Messi	Barcelona	37
L Suarez	Barcelona	29
C Ronaldo	Real Madrid	25
I Aspas	Celta Vigo	19
A Griezmann	Atl Madrid	16
A Aduriz	Ath Bilbao	16

Over 2.5 goals

	H	A	%
Real Madrid	15	16	82%
Barcelona	15	14	76%
Celta	14	12	68%
Osasuna	14	12	68%
Valencia	13	13	68%
Sporting Gijon	13	11	63%

Both to score

	H	A	%
Real Madrid	14	14	74%
Sporting Gijon	15	11	68%
Valencia	13	13	68%
Osasuna	14	11	66%
Barcelona	12	12	63%
Seville	11	13	63%

AMIENS

Stade de la Licorne — amiensfootball.com

	2016-17 H	A	P	W	D	L	OV	UN	BS	CS
Monaco			1	0	0	1	1	0	1	0
Paris St-Germain			-	-	-	-	-	-	-	-
Nice			-	-	-	-	-	-	-	-
Lyon			-	-	-	-	-	-	-	-
Marseille			-	-	-	-	-	-	-	-
Bordeaux			-	-	-	-	-	-	-	-
Nantes			1	0	0	1	0	1	0	0
St Etienne			-	-	-	-	-	-	-	-
Rennes			-	-	-	-	-	-	-	-
Guingamp			1	0	1	0	0	1	0	1
Lille			-	-	-	-	-	-	-	-
Angers			1	1	0	0	0	1	0	1
Toulouse			-	-	-	-	-	-	-	-
Metz			1	0	1	0	0	1	1	0
Montpellier			-	-	-	-	-	-	-	-
Dijon			-	-	-	-	-	-	-	-
Caen			-	-	-	-	-	-	-	-
Strasbourg	W	L	1	1	0	0	1	0	1	0
Amiens										
Troyes	L	L	2	0	1	1	0	2	1	0

Season	Division	Pos	P	W	D	L	F	A	GD	Pts
2016-17	Ligue 2	2	38	19	9	10	56	38	+18	66
2015-16	National	3	34	14	13	7	44	35	+9	55
2014-15	National	11	34	10	11	13	45	48	-3	41

Over/Under 50%/50% 8th **Both score** 47%/53% 18th

ANGERS

Stade Raymond Kopa — angers-sco.fr

	2016-17 H	A	P	W	D	L	OV	UN	BS	CS
Monaco	L	L	4	1	0	3	3	1	2	1
Paris St-Germain	L	L	2	0	1	1	0	2	0	1
Nice	L	W	2	0	1	1	0	2	1	0
Lyon	L	L	2	0	0	2	2	0	1	0
Marseille	D	L	2	0	1	1	0	2	1	0
Bordeaux	D	W	2	0	2	0	0	2	2	0
Nantes	L	L	4	2	1	1	0	4	0	3
St Etienne	L	L	2	0	1	1	1	1	1	1
Rennes	D	D	2	0	1	1	0	2	0	1
Guingamp	W	L	4	2	1	1	2	2	1	3
Lille	W	W	2	2	0	0	0	2	0	2
Angers										
Toulouse	D	L	2	0	1	1	1	1	1	1
Metz	W	L	3	2	1	0	2	1	2	1
Montpellier	W	L	2	1	0	1	1	1	1	1
Dijon	W	L	4	2	2	0	2	2	2	2
Caen	W	W	4	2	1	1	2	2	3	1
Strasbourg			-	-	-	-	-	-	-	-
Amiens			1	0	1	0	0	1	0	1
Troyes			4	1	1	2	2	2	2	1

Season	Division	Pos	P	W	D	L	F	A	GD	Pts
2016-17	Ligue 1	12	38	13	7	18	40	49	-9	46
2015-16	Ligue 1	9	38	13	11	14	40	38	+2	50
2014-15	Ligue 2	3	38	18	10	10	47	30	+17	64

Over/Under 45%/55% 11th **Both score** 45%/55% 10th

BORDEAUX

Matmut Atlantique — girondins.com

	2016-17 H	A	P	W	D	L	OV	UN	BS	CS
Monaco	L	L	4	2	0	2	3	1	2	0
Paris St-Germain	L	L	6	1	2	3	2	4	3	0
Nice	D	L	6	0	4	2	2	4	4	2
Lyon	D	W	6	2	1	3	4	2	3	1
Marseille	D	D	6	3	3	0	1	5	4	2
Bordeaux										
Nantes	W	W	4	3	0	1	2	2	1	2
St Etienne	W	D	6	3	1	2	3	3	3	3
Rennes	D	D	6	4	2	0	3	3	3	3
Guingamp	W	D	4	3	1	0	2	2	2	2
Lille	L	W	6	3	2	1	0	6	2	3
Angers	L	D	2	0	0	2	1	1	1	0
Toulouse	W	L	6	4	1	1	1	5	2	3
Metz	W	W	2	1	1	0	1	1	1	0
Montpellier	W	L	6	4	2	0	4	2	4	2
Dijon	W	D	2	1	1	0	1	1	2	0
Caen	D	W	4	1	2	1	1	3	2	2
Strasbourg			-	-	-	-	-	-	-	-
Amiens			-	-	-	-	-	-	-	-
Troyes			2	1	1	0	0	2	0	2

Season	Division	Pos	P	W	D	L	F	A	GD	Pts
2016-17	Ligue 1	6	38	15	14	9	53	43	+10	59
2015-16	Ligue 1	11	38	12	14	12	50	57	-7	50
2014-15	Ligue 1	6	38	17	12	9	47	44	+3	63

Over/Under 45%/55% 11th **Both score** 50%/50% 7th

CAEN

Stade Michel d'Ornano — smcaen.fr

	2016-17 H	A	P	W	D	L	OV	UN	BS	CS
Monaco	L	L	4	1	1	2	4	0	1	1
Paris St-Germain	L	D	4	0	1	3	3	1	1	0
Nice	W	D	4	2	1	1	1	3	2	2
Lyon	W	L	4	3	0	1	3	1	1	2
Marseille	L	L	4	0	0	4	4	0	4	0
Bordeaux	L	D	4	2	0	2	2	2	1	2
Nantes	L	L	4	0	0	4	1	3	1	0
St Etienne	L	W	4	2	0	2	1	3	1	2
Rennes	L	L	4	1	0	3	0	4	0	1
Guingamp	D	W	4	1	1	2	2	2	3	0
Lille	L	L	4	0	0	4	2	2	2	0
Angers	L	L	4	1	2	1	1	3	2	2
Toulouse	W	W	4	3	0	1	0	4	0	3
Metz	W	D	3	1	1	1	2	2	0	2
Montpellier	L	L	4	1	1	2	2	2	3	0
Dijon	D	L	4	2	2	0	4	0	3	1
Caen										
Strasbourg			-	-	-	-	-	-	-	-
Amiens			-	-	-	-	-	-	-	-
Troyes			2	1	1	0	1	1	2	0

Season	Division	Pos	P	W	D	L	F	A	GD	Pts
2016-17	Ligue 1	17	38	10	7	21	36	65	-29	37
2015-16	Ligue 1	7	38	16	6	16	39	52	-13	54
2014-15	Ligue 1	13	38	12	10	16	54	55	-1	46

Over/Under 39%/61% 14th **Both score** 37%/63% 19th

DIJON

Stade Gaston Gerard   dfco.fr

	2016-17 H	A	P	W	D	L	OV	UN	BS	CS
Monaco	D	L	2	0	1	1	0	2	1	0
Paris St-Germain	L	L	2	0	0	2	2	0	2	0
Nice	L	L	2	1	0	1	1	1	0	1
Lyon	W	L	2	1	0	1	2	0	2	0
Marseille	L	D	2	0	0	2	2	0	2	0
Bordeaux	D	L	2	1	1	0	0	2	0	2
Nantes	L	L	2	1	0	1	1	1	0	0
St Etienne	L	D	2	0	0	2	1	1	1	0
Rennes	W	D	2	1	0	1	2	0	1	1
Guingamp	D	L	2	1	1	0	1	1	1	1
Lille	D	L	2	0	1	1	0	2	0	1
Angers	W	L	4	1	2	1	2	2	3	1
Toulouse	W	D	2	1	1	0	0	2	1	1
Metz	D	L	3	0	2	1	2	1	1	1
Montpellier	D	D	2	0	2	0	1	1	2	0
Dijon										
Caen	W	D	4	3	1	0	1	3	1	3
Strasbourg			-	-	-	-	-	-	-	-
Amiens			-	-	-	-	-	-	-	-
Troyes			2	1	0	1	1	1	1	0

Season	Division	Pos	P	W	D	L	F	A	GD	Pts
2016-17	Ligue 1	16	38	8	13	17	46	58	-12	37
2015-16	Ligue 2	2	38	20	10	8	62	36	+26	70
2014-15	Ligue 2	4	38	17	10	11	44	34	+10	61

Over/Under 50%/50% 7th   **Both score** 55%/45% 4th

GUINGAMP

Stade Municipal du Roudourou   eaguingamp.com

	2016-17 H	A	P	W	D	L	OV	UN	BS	CS
Monaco	L	D	6	2	1	3	4	2	3	2
Paris St-Germain	W	L	4	2	1	1	1	3	2	1
Nice	L	L	4	1	0	3	2	2	2	1
Lyon	W	W	4	1	0	3	2	2	2	0
Marseille	W	L	4	2	0	2	2	2	2	1
Bordeaux	D	L	4	1	1	2	2	2	3	0
Nantes	W	L	6	4	1	1	2	4	2	3
St Etienne	L	L	4	1	1	2	0	4	0	2
Rennes	D	L	4	1	1	2	0	4	1	1
Guingamp										
Lille	W	L	4	1	2	1	0	4	1	2
Angers	W	L	4	3	1	0	2	2	2	2
Toulouse	W	L	4	4	0	0	2	2	2	2
Metz	W	D	3	1	0	2	0	3	0	1
Montpellier	D	D	4	0	2	2	2	2	3	0
Dijon	W	D	2	2	0	0	1	1	0	2
Caen	L	D	4	2	1	1	3	1	2	1
Strasbourg			-	-	-	-	-	-	-	-
Amiens			1	0	1	0	0	1	1	0
Troyes			2	1	1	0	1	1	0	2

Season	Division	Pos	P	W	D	L	F	A	GD	Pts
2016-17	Ligue 1	10	38	14	8	16	46	53	-7	50
2015-16	Ligue 1	16	38	11	11	16	47	56	-9	44
2014-15	Ligue 1	10	38	15	4	19	41	55	-14	49

Over/Under 50%/50% 7th   **Both score** 47%/53% 8th

LILLE

Stade Pierre-Mauroy   losc.fr

	2016-17 H	A	P	W	D	L	OV	UN	BS	CS
Monaco	L	L	4	2	0	2	2	2	2	1
Paris St-Germain	L	L	6	1	1	4	3	3	4	0
Nice	L	D	6	0	3	3	2	4	3	1
Lyon	L	W	6	3	2	1	2	4	3	2
Marseille	D	L	6	2	2	2	3	3	3	2
Bordeaux	L	W	6	3	1	2	4	2	4	2
Nantes	W	D	4	2	1	1	1	3	0	3
St Etienne	D	L	6	3	3	0	1	5	3	3
Rennes	D	L	6	3	0	3	1	5	3	3
Guingamp	W	L	4	2	1	1	2	2	1	3
Lille										
Angers	L	L	2	0	1	1	1	1	1	1
Toulouse	L	D	6	5	0	1	3	3	2	4
Metz	L	L	2	0	1	1	0	2	0	1
Montpellier	W	W	6	4	1	1	2	4	2	3
Dijon	W	D	2	2	0	0	0	2	0	2
Caen	W	W	4	4	0	0	2	2	1	3
Strasbourg			-	-	-	-	-	-	-	-
Amiens			-	-	-	-	-	-	-	-
Troyes			2	0	1	1	1	1	2	0

Season	Division	Pos	P	W	D	L	F	A	GD	Pts
2016-17	Ligue 1	11	38	13	7	18	40	47	-7	46
2015-16	Ligue 1	5	38	15	15	8	39	27	+12	60
2014-15	Ligue 1	8	38	16	8	14	43	42	+1	56

Over/Under 45%/55% 11th   **Both score** 45%/55% 10th

LYON

Parc Olympique Lyonnais   olweb.fr

	2016-17 H	A	P	W	D	L	OV	UN	BS	CS
Monaco	L	W	4	2	0	2	4	0	4	0
Paris St-Germain	L	L	6	2	2	2	3	3	4	1
Nice	D	L	6	2	2	2	5	1	4	2
Lyon										
Marseille	W	D	6	3	3	0	2	4	3	3
Bordeaux	D	L	6	2	2	2	3	3	4	1
Nantes	W	W	4	4	0	0	2	2	2	2
St Etienne	W	L	6	3	2	1	3	3	3	3
Rennes	W	D	6	3	1	2	4	2	4	4
Guingamp	L	L	4	3	0	1	3	1	3	1
Lille	L	W	6	2	2	2	4	2	3	3
Angers	W	W	2	1	0	1	0	2	0	1
Toulouse	W	W	6	5	1	0	5	1	3	3
Metz	W	W	2	2	0	0	1	1	0	2
Montpellier	W	W	6	4	1	1	4	2	4	2
Dijon	W	L	2	2	0	0	2	0	2	0
Caen	W	L	4	3	0	1	3	1	2	2
Strasbourg			-	-	-	-	-	-	-	-
Amiens			-	-	-	-	-	-	-	-
Troyes			2	2	0	0	2	0	2	0

Season	Division	Pos	P	W	D	L	F	A	GD	Pts
2016-17	Ligue 1	4	38	21	4	13	77	48	+29	67
2015-16	Ligue 1	2	38	19	8	11	67	43	+24	65
2014-15	Ligue 1	2	38	22	9	7	72	33	+39	75

Over/Under 68%/32% 2nd   **Both score** 58%/42% 1st

MARSEILLE

Stade Velodrome — om.net

	2016-17 H	A	P	W	D	L	OV	UN	BS	CS
Monaco	L	L	4	1	1	2	4	0	4	0
Paris St-Germain	L	D	6	1	1	4	6	0	5	1
Nice	W	L	6	3	1	2	3	3	2	2
Lyon	D	L	6	1	4	1	3	3	4	2
Marseille										
Bordeaux	D	D	6	2	4	0	2	4	2	4
Nantes	W	L	4	2	1	1	1	3	2	1
St Etienne	W	D	6	4	2	0	3	3	3	3
Rennes	W	L	6	3	0	3	3	3	2	2
Guingamp	W	L	4	3	1	0	1	3	1	3
Lille	W	D	6	4	2	0	1	5	2	4
Angers	W		2	1	0	1	2	0	1	1
Toulouse	D	D	6	2	3	1	2	4	3	2
Metz	W		2	2	0	0	1	1	1	1
Montpellier	W	L	6	3	1	2	4	2	4	1
Dijon	D	W	2	0	1	1	1	1	2	0
Caen	W	W	4	1	1	2	1	3	2	1
Strasbourg			-	-	-	-	-	-	-	-
Amiens			-	-	-	-	-	-	-	-
Troyes			2	2	0	0	2	0	1	1

Season	Division	Pos	P	W	D	L	F	A	GD	Pts
2016-17	Ligue 1	5	38	17	11	10	57	41	+16	62
2015-16	Ligue 1	13	38	10	18	10	48	42	+6	48
2014-15	Ligue 1	4	38	21	6	11	76	42	+34	69

Over/Under 50%/50% 7th **Both score** 47%/53% 8th

METZ

Stade Saint-Symphorien — fcmetz.com

	2016-17 H	A	P	W	D	L	OV	UN	BS	CS
Monaco	L	L	3	0	0	3	1	2	0	0
Paris St-Germain	L	L	2	0	0	2	2	0	2	0
Nice	L	D	2	0	1	1	1	1	1	1
Lyon	L	L	2	1	0	1	2	0	1	0
Marseille	W	L	2	1	0	1	0	2	0	1
Bordeaux	L	L	2	0	1	1	1	1	0	1
Nantes	D	W	3	0	2	1	1	2	3	0
St Etienne	D	D	2	0	1	1	1	1	1	1
Rennes	D	L	2	0	2	0	0	2	1	1
Guingamp	D	L	3	0	1	2	2	1	2	0
Lille	W	W	2	1	0	1	2	0	2	0
Angers		L	3	2	1	0	0	3	1	2
Toulouse	D	W	2	1	1	0	1	1	2	0
Metz										
Montpellier	W	W	2	1	0	1	1	1	1	1
Dijon	W	D	3	2	0	1	2	1	2	1
Caen	D	L	3	2	1	0	3	0	3	0
Strasbourg			-	-	-	-	-	-	-	-
Amiens			1	1	0	0	0	1	0	1
Troyes			2	1	1	0	1	1	1	1

Season	Division	Pos	P	W	D	L	F	A	GD	Pts
2016-17	Ligue 1	14	38	11	10	17	39	72	-33	43
2015-16	Ligue 2	3	38	19	8	11	54	39	+15	65
2014-15	Ligue 1	19	38	7	9	22	31	61	-30	30

Over/Under 58%/42% 3rd **Both score** 39%/61% 17th

MONACO

Stade Louis II — asmonaco.com

	2016-17 H	A	P	W	D	L	OV	UN	BS	CS
Monaco										
Paris St-Germain	W	D	4	1	2	1	2	2	2	1
Nice	W	L	4	3	0	1	1	3	0	3
Lyon	L	W	4	1	2	1	2	2	3	1
Marseille	W	W	4	4	0	0	2	2	1	3
Bordeaux	W	W	4	1	2	1	2	2	3	1
Nantes	W	W	6	5	0	1	3	3	2	3
St Etienne	W	W	4	3	1	0	1	3	2	2
Rennes	W	W	4	2	2	0	1	3	2	2
Guingamp	D	W	6	3	3	0	3	3	4	2
Lille	W	W	4	1	3	0	1	3	2	2
Angers	W	W	4	2	1	1	3	1	3	1
Toulouse	W	L	4	3	0	1	3	1	2	2
Metz	W	W	3	2	0	1	1	2	0	2
Montpellier	W	W	4	3	1	0	2	2	2	2
Dijon	W	D	2	1	1	0	1	1	2	0
Caen	W	W	4	1	2	1	2	2	3	0
Strasbourg			-	-	-	-	-	-	-	-
Amiens			1	0	1	0	0	1	1	0
Troyes			2	1	0	1	1	1	1	0

Season	Division	Pos	P	W	D	L	F	A	GD	Pts
2016-17	Ligue 1	1	38	30	5	3	107	31	+76	95
2015-16	Ligue 1	3	38	17	14	7	57	50	+7	65
2014-15	Ligue 1	3	38	20	11	7	51	26	+25	71

Over/Under 82%/18% 1st **Both score** 53%/47% 5th

MONTPELLIER

Stade de la Mosson — mhscfoot.com

	2016-17 H	A	P	W	D	L	OV	UN	BS	CS
Monaco	L	L	4	0	1	3	2	2	3	0
Paris St-Germain	W	L	6	1	2	3	3	3	3	1
Nice	D	L	6	4	1	1	3	3	4	1
Lyon	L	L	6	2	0	4	4	2	4	1
Marseille	W	L	6	3	0	3	3	3	3	1
Bordeaux	W	L	6	3	1	2	1	5	1	3
Nantes	L	L	4	2	1	1	3	1	3	1
St Etienne	W	L	6	2	1	3	2	4	3	1
Rennes	D	L	6	3	3	0	1	5	1	5
Guingamp	D	D	4	2	2	0	2	2	4	0
Lille	L	L	6	2	1	3	3	3	1	3
Angers	L	L	2	1	0	1	0	2	0	1
Toulouse	L	L	6	3	2	1	1	5	3	2
Metz	L	L	2	1	0	1	0	2	0	1
Montpellier										
Dijon	D	D	2	1	1	0	1	1	2	0
Caen	W	W	4	3	0	1	3	1	2	2
Strasbourg			-	-	-	-	-	-	-	-
Amiens			-	-	-	-	-	-	-	-
Troyes			2	1	1	0	1	1	2	0

Season	Division	Pos	P	W	D	L	F	A	GD	Pts
2016-17	Ligue 1	15	38	10	9	19	48	66	-18	39
2015-16	Ligue 1	12	38	14	7	17	49	47	+2	49
2014-15	Ligue 1	7	38	16	8	14	46	39	+7	56

Over/Under 53%/47% 6th **Both score** 58%/42% 1st

FRENCH LIGUE 1

NANTES

Beaujoire-Louis Fonteneau fcnantes.com

	2016-17 H	2016-17 A	Last six seasons at home P	W	D	L	OV	UN	BS	CS
Monaco	L	L	6	1	2	3	1	5	1	2
Paris St-Germain	L	L	4	0	0	4	2	2	2	0
Nice	D	L	4	3	1	0	1	3	2	2
Lyon	L	L	4	0	2	2	2	2	2	1
Marseille	W	L	4	2	1	1	1	3	2	1
Bordeaux	L	L	4	1	2	1	2	2	2	1
Nantes										
St Etienne	D	D	4	1	2	1	2	2	2	2
Rennes	L	D	4	0	1	3	2	2	2	0
Guingamp	W	L	6	5	1	0	2	4	2	4
Lille	D	L	4	0	2	2	1	3	1	1
Angers	W	W	4	4	0	0	2	2	2	2
Toulouse	D	W	4	0	2	2	2	2	4	0
Metz	L	D	3	0	2	1	1	2	0	2
Montpellier	W	W	4	3	0	1	1	3	1	2
Dijon	W	W	2	2	0	0	1	1	1	1
Caen	W	W	4	2	0	2	3	1	3	1
Strasbourg			-	-	-	-	-	-	-	-
Amiens			1	1	0	0	1	0	0	1
Troyes			2	1	1	0	1	1	1	1

Season	Division	Pos	P	W	D	L	F	A	GD	Pts
2016-17	Ligue 1	7	38	14	9	15	40	54	-14	51
2015-16	Ligue 1	14	38	12	12	14	33	44	-11	48
2014-15	Ligue 1	14	38	11	12	15	29	40	-11	45

Over/Under 39%/61% 14th **Both score** 45%/55% 10th

NICE

Allianz Riviera ogcnice.com

	2016-17 H	2016-17 A	Last six seasons at home P	W	D	L	OV	UN	BS	CS
Monaco	W	L	4	1	0	3	3	1	1	1
Paris St-Germain	W	D	6	2	1	3	4	2	3	1
Nice										
Lyon	W	D	6	2	1	3	3	3	3	2
Marseille	W	L	6	3	2	1	2	4	4	1
Bordeaux	W	D	6	3	0	3	5	1	4	1
Nantes	W	D	4	1	2	1	2	2	2	2
St Etienne	W	W	6	2	2	2	0	6	1	3
Rennes	W	W	6	5	0	1	3	3	2	4
Guingamp	W	W	4	2	0	2	2	2	2	1
Lille	D	W	6	2	3	1	1	5	2	3
Angers	L	W	2	1	0	1	1	1	1	0
Toulouse	W	W	6	4	1	1	2	4	2	3
Metz	D	W	2	1	1	0	0	2	0	2
Montpellier	W	D	6	3	2	1	2	4	3	2
Dijon	W	W	2	1	1	0	1	1	2	0
Caen	D	L	4	2	2	0	2	2	3	1
Strasbourg			-	-	-	-	-	-	-	-
Amiens			-	-	-	-	-	-	-	-
Troyes			2	2	0	0	2	0	2	0

Season	Division	Pos	P	W	D	L	F	A	GD	Pts
2016-17	Ligue 1	3	38	22	12	4	63	36	+27	78
2015-16	Ligue 1	4	38	18	9	11	58	41	+17	63
2014-15	Ligue 1	11	38	13	9	16	44	53	-9	48

Over/Under 50%/50% 7th **Both score** 58%/42% 1st

PARIS SAINT-GERMAIN

Parc des Princes psg.fr

	2016-17 H	2016-17 A	Last six seasons at home P	W	D	L	OV	UN	BS	CS
Monaco	D	L	4	0	3	1	0	4	3	0
Paris St-Germain										
Nice	D	L	6	5	1	0	5	1	4	2
Lyon	W	W	6	5	1	0	3	3	3	3
Marseille	D	W	6	5	1	0	2	4	2	4
Bordeaux	W	W	6	3	3	0	2	4	2	4
Nantes	W	W	4	4	0	0	3	1	1	3
St Etienne	D	W	6	4	1	1	3	3	3	3
Rennes	W	W	6	4	0	2	5	1	2	4
Guingamp	W	L	4	4	0	0	3	1	0	4
Lille	W	W	6	3	3	0	3	3	3	3
Angers	W	W	2	2	0	0	1	1	1	1
Toulouse	D	L	6	5	1	0	3	3	2	4
Metz	W	W	2	2	0	0	2	0	1	1
Montpellier	W	L	6	3	3	0	2	4	1	5
Dijon	W	W	2	2	0	0	1	1	0	2
Caen	D	W	4	2	0	2	3	1	3	1
Strasbourg			-	-	-	-	-	-	-	-
Amiens			-	-	-	-	-	-	-	-
Troyes			2	2	0	0	2	0	1	1

Season	Division	Pos	P	W	D	L	F	A	GD	Pts
2016-17	Ligue 1	2	38	27	6	5	83	27	+56	87
2015-16	Ligue 1	1	38	30	6	2	102	19	+83	96
2014-15	Ligue 1	1	38	24	11	3	83	36	+47	83

Over/Under 58%/42% 3rd **Both score** 39%/61% 17th

RENNES

Roazhon Park staderennais.com

	2016-17 H	2016-17 A	Last six seasons at home P	W	D	L	OV	UN	BS	CS
Monaco	L	L	4	1	1	2	1	3	2	1
Paris St-Germain	L	L	6	0	2	4	1	5	3	0
Nice	D	L	6	2	2	2	5	1	4	1
Lyon	D	L	6	1	3	2	1	5	3	1
Marseille	W	L	6	1	3	2	3	3	5	0
Bordeaux	D	D	6	1	4	1	1	5	4	1
Nantes	D	W	4	1	2	1	2	2	3	1
St Etienne	W	D	6	2	3	1	2	4	3	2
Rennes										
Guingamp	W	D	4	2	0	2	1	3	0	2
Lille	W	D	6	3	3	0	0	6	2	4
Angers	D	D	2	1	1	0	0	2	1	1
Toulouse	W	D	6	3	0	3	3	3	2	2
Metz	W	D	2	2	0	0	0	2	0	2
Montpellier	W	D	6	3	1	2	3	3	2	2
Dijon	D	L	2	1	1	0	1	1	1	1
Caen	W	W	4	2	1	1	2	2	3	1
Strasbourg			-	-	-	-	-	-	-	-
Amiens			-	-	-	-	-	-	-	-
Troyes			2	0	1	1	1	1	2	0

Season	Division	Pos	P	W	D	L	F	A	GD	Pts
2016-17	Ligue 1	9	38	12	14	12	36	42	-6	50
2015-16	Ligue 1	8	38	13	13	12	52	54	-2	52
2014-15	Ligue 1	9	38	13	11	14	35	42	-7	50

Over/Under 26%/74% 20th **Both score** 45%/55% 10th

SAINT-ETIENNE

Stade Geoffroy-Guichard   asse.fr

	2016-17 H	A	Last six seasons at home P	W	D	L	OV	UN	BS	CS
Monaco	D	L	4	1	3	0	0	4	3	1
Paris St-Germain	L	D	6	0	2	4	3	3	2	0
Nice	L	L	6	2	1	3	4	2	3	2
Lyon	W	L	6	3	0	3	2	4	1	3
Marseille	D	L	6	1	4	1	1	5	2	3
Bordeaux	D	L	6	1	4	1	3	3	5	1
Nantes	D	D	4	3	1	0	0	4	1	3
St Etienne										
Rennes	D	L	6	2	4	0	1	5	2	4
Guingamp	W	W	4	4	0	0	2	2	1	3
Lille	W	D	6	3	0	3	3	3	3	2
Angers	W	W	2	2	0	0	1	1	1	1
Toulouse	D	W	6	0	4	2	2	4	3	2
Metz	D	D	2	1	1	0	1	1	1	1
Montpellier	W	L	6	5	1	0	3	3	3	3
Dijon	D	W	2	1	1	0	0	2	1	1
Caen	L	W	4	2	0	2	1	3	1	2
Strasbourg			-	-	-	-	-	-	-	-
Amiens			-	-	-	-	-	-	-	-
Troyes			2	2	0	0	0	2	0	2

Season	Division	Pos	P	W	D	L	F	A	GD	Pts
2016-17	Ligue 1	8	38	12	14	12	41	42	-1	50
2015-16	Ligue 1	6	38	17	7	14	42	37	+5	58
2014-15	Ligue 1	5	38	19	12	7	51	30	+21	69

Over/Under 37%/63% 18th   **Both score** 42%/58% 15th

STRASBOURG

Stade de la Meinau   rcstrasbourgalsace.fr

	2016-17 H	A	Last six seasons at home P	W	D	L	OV	UN	BS	CS
Monaco			-	-	-	-	-	-	-	-
Paris St-Germain			-	-	-	-	-	-	-	-
Nice			-	-	-	-	-	-	-	-
Lyon			-	-	-	-	-	-	-	-
Marseille			-	-	-	-	-	-	-	-
Bordeaux			-	-	-	-	-	-	-	-
Nantes			-	-	-	-	-	-	-	-
St Etienne			-	-	-	-	-	-	-	-
Rennes			-	-	-	-	-	-	-	-
Guingamp			-	-	-	-	-	-	-	-
Lille			-	-	-	-	-	-	-	-
Angers			-	-	-	-	-	-	-	-
Toulouse			-	-	-	-	-	-	-	-
Metz			-	-	-	-	-	-	-	-
Montpellier			-	-	-	-	-	-	-	-
Dijon			-	-	-	-	-	-	-	-
Caen			-	-	-	-	-	-	-	-
Strasbourg										
Amiens	W	L	1	1	0	0	0	1	0	1
Troyes	W	L	1	1	0	0	0	1	0	1

Season	Division	Pos	P	W	D	L	F	A	GD	Pts
2016-17	Ligue 2	1	38	19	10	9	63	47	+16	67
2015-16	National	1	34	15	13	6	35	19	+16	58
2014-15	National	4	34	19	8	7	50	29	+21	65

Over/Under 53%/47% 5th   **Both score** 61%/39% 4th

TOULOUSE

Stadium Municipal   tfc.info

	2016-17 H	A	Last six seasons at home P	W	D	L	OV	UN	BS	CS
Monaco	W	L	4	1	1	2	1	3	2	0
Paris St-Germain	W	D	6	1	1	4	3	3	3	1
Nice	D	L	6	2	2	2	2	4	3	3
Lyon	L	L	6	3	1	2	5	1	3	3
Marseille	D	D	6	0	4	2	1	5	3	2
Bordeaux	W	L	6	4	2	0	4	2	4	2
Nantes	L	D	4	0	3	1	0	4	2	1
St Etienne	L	D	6	2	2	2	3	3	3	1
Rennes	D	L	6	2	2	2	4	2	3	2
Guingamp	W	L	4	1	2	1	2	2	3	1
Lille	D	W	6	2	3	1	3	3	5	1
Angers	W	D	2	1	0	1	2	0	1	1
Toulouse										
Metz	L	D	2	1	0	1	2	0	1	1
Montpellier	W	W	6	3	2	1	0	6	2	3
Dijon	D	L	2	1	1	0	0	2	0	2
Caen	L	L	4	2	1	1	1	3	1	2
Strasbourg			-	-	-	-	-	-	-	-
Amiens			-	-	-	-	-	-	-	-
Troyes			2	1	1	0	1	1	1	1

Season	Division	Pos	P	W	D	L	F	A	GD	Pts
2016-17	Ligue 1	13	38	10	14	14	37	41	-4	44
2015-16	Ligue 1	17	38	9	13	16	45	55	-10	40
2014-15	Ligue 1	17	38	12	6	20	43	64	-21	42

Over/Under 39%/61% 14th   **Both score** 45%/55% 10th

TROYES

Stade de l'Aube   estac.fr

	2016-17 H	A	Last six seasons at home P	W	D	L	OV	UN	BS	CS
Monaco			2	0	2	0	0	2	1	1
Paris St-Germain			2	0	0	2	1	1	0	0
Nice			2	0	2	0	1	1	2	0
Lyon			2	0	0	2	1	1	1	0
Marseille			2	1	1	0	0	2	1	1
Bordeaux			2	1	0	1	1	1	1	1
Nantes			2	1	0	1	0	2	0	1
St Etienne			2	0	1	1	1	1	1	0
Rennes			2	0	0	2	0	2	0	0
Guingamp			2	0	1	1	0	2	1	0
Lille			2	0	2	0	0	2	2	0
Angers			4	2	1	1	3	1	3	0
Toulouse			2	0	0	2	1	1	0	0
Metz			2	1	0	1	0	2	0	1
Montpellier			2	0	2	0	0	2	1	1
Dijon			2	2	0	0	0	2	0	2
Caen			2	1	0	1	2	0	2	0
Strasbourg	W	L	1	1	0	0	1	0	0	1
Amiens	W	W	2	2	0	0	1	1	0	2
Troyes										

Season	Division	Pos	P	W	D	L	F	A	GD	Pts
2016-17	Ligue 2	3	38	19	9	10	59	43	+16	66
2015-16	Ligue 1	20	38	3	9	26	28	83	-55	18
2014-15	Ligue 2	1	38	24	6	8	61	24	+37	78

Over/Under 47%/53% 12th   **Both score** 55%/45% 9th

Ligue 1 2016-17

Pos	H	A		P	W	D	L	F	A	W	D	L	F	A	GD	Pts
						Home					Away					
1	1	1	Monaco (CL)	38	17	1	1	63	13	13	4	2	44	18	76	95
2	3	2	Paris St-G (CL)	38	13	6	0	42	7	14	0	5	41	20	56	87
3	2	3	Nice (CL)	38	14	4	1	39	16	8	8	3	24	20	27	78
4	6	4	Lyon (EL)	38	12	1	6	46	26	9	3	7	31	22	29	67
5	4	9	Marseille (EL)	38	13	4	2	33	13	4	7	8	24	28	16	62
6	8	5	Bordeaux (EL)	38	9	6	4	27	19	6	8	5	26	24	10	59
7	13	6	Nantes	38	8	4	7	19	24	6	5	8	21	30	-14	51
8	10	8	St-Etienne	38	7	9	3	24	18	5	5	9	17	24	-1	50
9	7	14	Rennes	38	10	6	3	26	15	2	8	9	10	27	-6	50
10	5	17	Guingamp	38	12	3	4	28	13	2	5	12	18	40	-7	50
11	18	7	Lille	38	7	3	9	24	24	6	4	9	16	23	-7	46
12	12	10	Angers	38	8	5	6	23	17	5	2	12	17	32	-9	46
13	9	13	Toulouse	38	8	6	5	28	18	2	8	9	9	23	-4	44
14	14	11	Metz	38	7	7	5	27	34	4	3	12	12	38	-33	43
15	11	19	Montpellier	38	8	5	6	28	22	2	4	13	20	44	-18	39
16	15	18	Dijon	38	7	6	6	27	21	1	7	11	19	37	-12	37
17	20	12	Caen	38	7	2	10	21	37	3	5	11	15	28	-29	37
18	16	16	Lorient (R)	38	7	4	8	25	29	3	2	14	19	41	-26	36
19	19	15	Nancy (R)	38	7	3	9	21	23	2	5	12	8	29	-23	35
20	17	20	Bastia (R)	38	5	9	5	17	14	3	1	15	12	40	-25	34

Ligue 1 results 2016-17

	Angers	Bastia	Bordeaux	Caen	Dijon	Guingamp	Lille	Lorient	Lyon	Marseille	Metz	Monaco	Montpellier	Nancy	Nantes	Nice	Paris St-G	Rennes	St Etienne	Toulouse
Angers		3-0	1-1	2-1	3-1	3-0	1-0	2-2	1-2	1-1	2-1	0-1	2-0	1-0	0-2	0-1	0-2	0-0	1-2	0-0
Bastia	1-2		1-1	1-1	0-0	1-0	0-1	2-0	0-0	1-2	2-0	1-1	1-1	0-0	2-2	1-1	0-1	1-0	0-0	2-1
Bordeaux	0-1	2-0		0-0	3-2	3-0	0-1	2-1	1-1	1-1	3-0	0-4	5-1	1-1	1-0	0-0	0-3	1-1	3-2	1-0
Caen	2-3	2-0	0-4		3-3	1-1	0-1	3-2	3-2	1-5	3-0	0-3	0-2	1-0	0-2	1-0	0-6	0-1	0-2	1-0
Dijon	3-2	1-2	0-0	2-0		3-3	0-0	1-0	4-2	1-2	0-0	1-1	3-3	2-0	0-1	0-1	1-3	3-0	0-1	2-0
Guingamp	1-0	5-0	1-1	0-1	4-0		1-0	1-0	2-1	2-1	1-0	1-2	1-1	1-0	2-0	0-1	2-1	1-1	0-2	2-1
Lille	1-2	2-1	2-3	4-2	1-0	3-0		0-1	0-1	0-0	0-2	1-4	2-1	1-0	3-0	1-2	0-1	1-1	1-1	1-2
Lorient	1-1	0-3	1-1	1-0	2-3	3-1	1-0		1-0	1-4	5-1	0-3	2-2	0-2	1-2	0-1	1-2	2-1	2-1	1-1
Lyon	2-0	2-1	1-3	2-0	4-2	1-3	1-2	1-4		3-1	5-0	1-2	5-1	4-0	3-2	3-3	1-2	1-0	2-0	4-0
Marseille	3-0	1-0	0-0	1-0	1-1	2-0	2-0	2-0	0-0		1-0	1-4	5-1	3-0	2-1	2-1	1-5	2-0	4-0	0-0
Metz	2-0	1-0	0-3	2-2	2-1	2-2	3-3	0-3	1-0	1-0		0-7	2-0	2-1	1-1	2-4	2-3	1-1	0-0	1-1
Monaco	2-1	5-0	2-1	2-1	2-1	2-2	4-0	4-0	1-3	4-0	5-0		6-2	6-0	4-0	3-0	3-1	3-0	2-0	3-1
Montpellier	1-0	2-1	4-0	3-2	1-1	1-1	0-3	2-0	1-3	3-1	0-1	1-2		0-0	2-3	1-1	3-0	1-1	2-1	0-1
Nancy	2-0	1-0	0-2	2-0	1-0	0-2	1-2	2-3	0-3	0-0	4-0	0-3	0-3		1-1	0-1	1-2	3-0	3-1	0-0
Nantes	2-1	1-0	0-1	1-0	3-1	4-1	0-0	1-0	0-6	3-2	0-3	0-1	1-0	0-2		1-1	0-2	1-2	0-0	1-1
Nice	0-2	1-1	2-1	2-2	2-1	3-1	1-1	2-1	2-0	3-2	0-0	4-0	2-1	3-1	4-1		3-1	1-0	1-0	3-0
Paris St-G	2-0	5-0	2-0	1-1	3-0	4-0	2-1	5-0	2-1	0-0	3-0	1-1	2-0	1-0	2-0	2-2		4-0	1-1	0-0
Rennes	1-1	1-2	1-1	2-0	1-1	1-0	2-0	1-0	1-1	3-2	1-0	2-3	1-0	2-0	1-1	2-2	0-1		2-0	1-0
St Etienne	2-1	1-0	2-2	0-1	1-1	1-0	3-1	4-0	2-0	0-0	2-2	1-1	3-1	0-0	1-1	0-1	0-5	1-1		0-0
Toulouse	4-0	4-1	4-1	0-1	0-0	2-1	1-1	3-2	1-2	0-0	1-2	3-1	1-0	1-1	0-1	1-1	2-0	0-0	0-3	

Bastia v Lyon abandoned due to crowd trouble with the score at 0-0. Lyon awarded the win

Top scorers

	Team	Goals scored
E Cavani	Paris SG	35
A Lacazette	Lyon	28
R Falcao	Monaco	21
B Gomis	Marseille	20
M Balotelli (Nice), K Mbappe (Monaco), I Santini (Caen), F Thauvin(Marseille)		15

Over 2.5 goals

	H	A	%
Monaco	18	13	82%
Lyon	15	11	68%
Lorient	11	11	58%
Metz	11	11	58%
Paris St-G	9	13	58%
Montpellier	10	10	53%

Both to score

	H	A	%
Lyon	12	10	58%
Montpellier	11	11	58%
Nice	12	10	58%
Dijon	8	13	55%
Lorient	12	8	53%
Monaco	9	11	53%

Uefa Association Coefficients 2016-17

Pos	Change	Country	12-13	13-14	14-15	15-16	16-17	Pts	Change
1	–	Spain	17.714	23	20.214	23.928	20.142	**104.998**	-0.715
2	–	Germany	17.928	14.714	15.857	16.428	14.571	**79.498**	-0.679
3	–	England	16.428	16.785	13.571	14.25	14.928	**75.962**	-0.322
4	–	Italy	14.416	14.166	19	11.5	14.25	**73.332**	2.893
5	1	France	11.75	8.5	10.916	11.083	14.416	**56.665**	3.916
6	1	Russia	9.75	10.416	9.666	11.5	9.2	**50.532**	-0.55
7	-2	Portugal	11.75	9.916	9.083	10.5	8.083	**49.332**	-3.75
8	–	Ukraine	9.5	7.833	10	9.8	5.5	**42.633**	-2.25
9	–	Belgium	6.5	6.4	9.6	7.4	12.5	**42.4**	2.4
10	1	Turkey	10.2	6.7	6	6.6	9.7	**39.2**	4.6
11	2	Czech Republic	8.5	8	3.875	7.3	5.5	**33.175**	0.25
12	–	Switzerland	8.375	7.2	6.9	5.3	4.3	**32.075**	-1.7
13	-3	Holland	4.214	5.916	6.083	5.75	9.1	**31.063**	-4.5
14	–	Greece	4.4	6.1	6.2	5.4	5.8	**27.9**	-1.8
15	1	Austria	2.25	7.8	4.125	3.8	7.375	**25.35**	0.25
16	1	Croatia	4.375	4.375	6.875	4.5	5.125	**25.25**	1.375
17	-2	Romania	6.8	6.875	5.125	2.25	3.3	**24.35**	-1.033
18	6	Denmark	3.3	3.8	2.9	5.5	8.5	**24**	5.4
19	1	Belarus	4.5	1.75	5.5	5.125	3	**19.875**	-0.125
20	-2	Poland	2.5	3.125	4.75	5.5	3.875	**19.75**	-2.75
21	–	Sweden	5.125	3.2	3.9	4.75	2.75	**19.725**	-0.15
22	1	Israel	3.25	5.75	1.375	2.25	6.75	**19.375**	0.75
23	2	Scotland	4.3	3.25	4	3	4.375	**18.925**	1.625
24	-5	Cyprus	4	2.75	3.3	3	5.5	**18.55**	-3.625
25	-3	Norway	4.9	2.6	2.2	7.25	1.375	**18.325**	-0.925
26	–	Azerbaijan	3	2.5	3.625	4.375	4.25	**17.75**	2.875
27	2	Bulgaria	0.75	5.625	4.25	1	4.25	**15.875**	2.75
28	-1	Serbia	3	2.5	2.75	4.25	2.875	**15.375**	0.75
29	-1	Kazakhstan	1.375	3.125	3.375	4.625	2.75	**15.25**	1.125
30	–	Slovenia	3.25	2.625	4	1	2.25	**13.125**	0
31	–	Slovakia	1.5	1.625	2.75	3.75	2.125	**11.75**	-0.25
32	–	Liechtenstein	0	1	2.5	5	2.5	**11**	0.5
33	–	Hungary	3	0.875	2.125	1.625	1.875	**9.5**	-0.375
34	–	Moldova	2.25	3.375	1.75	1.25	0.875	**9.5**	0.375
35	–	Iceland	1.25	2.5	2.5	1.125	1	**8.375**	-0.375
36	1	Finland	2	0.5	2.4	1	1.75	**7.65**	0.25
37	2	Albania	0.75	2	0.875	2.125	0.875	**6.625**	0
38	3	Ireland	1	0.25	2	0.7	2.625	**6.575**	1.125
39	-1	Bosnia-Hz	1.25	1.5	1.75	1.5	0.5	**6.5**	-0.625
40	-4	Georgia	1.5	1.875	1.25	0.625	1.125	**6.375**	-1.75
41	1	Latvia	1.25	1.625	0.25	1.625	1.375	**6.125**	0.75
42	-2	Macedonia	1.25	0.5	1.125	1.5	1.25	**5.625**	-0.375
43	4	Estonia	0.375	1	1.5	1	1.375	**5.25**	1
44	–	Montenegro	1.375	1.25	0.75	1	0.875	**5.25**	0.375
45	3	Armenia	0.875	1.125	0.375	1.625	1.125	**5.125**	1
46	-3	Luxembourg	1.375	1.5	0.5	0.75	0.75	**4.875**	-0.375
47	-1	Northern Ireland	1	0.875	1.375	0.75	0.5	**4.5**	0
48	-3	Lithuania	1.125	1.25	0.5	0.75	0.5	**4.125**	-0.5
49	1	Malta	0.875	0.875	0.125	0.875	1.25	**4**	0.417
50	1	Wales	0.5	0.75	0.125	1.5	1	**3.875**	0.375
51	-2	Faroe Islands	0.5	0.875	1.375	0.375	0.375	**3.5**	-0.125
52	–	Gibraltar	–	–	0.25	0.75	1.5	**2.5**	1.5
53	–	Andorra	0	0.333	0.5	0.166	0.166	**1.165**	0.166
54	–	San Marino	0	0.333	0	0	0	**0.333**	0
55	–	Kosovo	–	–	–	–	–	**0**	0

Uefa's country coefficients are calculated from performances of each FA's clubs in the last five Europa League and Champions League seasons. They are used to allocate places in Uefa's club competitions and determine seedings with the top 12 receiving at least one place in the Champions League group stage.

Two points are awarded for a win and one for a draw, and half that in qualifying matches. An extra point is awarded for every round from the last 16 of the Champions League and the quarter-finals of the Europa League. Four extra points are given for reaching the group stage of the Champions League and four more for the knockout rounds.

The country coefficient is the sum of the average points for each nation in each of the last five seasons. England's clubs have averaged 16.428, 16.785, 13.571, 14.25 and 14.928 over the last five campaigns – add them together and you get 75.962, England's country coefficient.

Russia

		P	W	D	L	F	A	GD	Pts
1	Spartak Moscow	30	22	3	5	46	27	19	69
2	CSKA Moscow	30	18	8	4	47	15	32	62
3	Zenit	30	18	7	5	50	19	31	61
4	Krasnodar	30	12	13	5	40	22	18	49
5	Terek Grozny	30	14	6	10	38	35	3	48
6	Rostov	30	13	9	8	36	18	18	48
7	Ufa	30	12	7	11	22	25	-3	43
8	Lokomotiv M.	30	10	12	8	39	27	12	42
9	Rubin Kazan	30	10	8	12	30	34	-4	38
10	Amkar Perm	30	8	11	11	25	29	-4	35
11	Ural	30	8	6	16	24	44	-20	30
12	Anzhi	30	7	9	14	24	38	-14	30
13	Orenburg	30	7	9	14	25	36	-11	30
14	Arsenal Tula	30	7	7	16	18	40	-22	28
15	Krylya Sovetov	30	6	10	14	31	39	-8	28
16	Tom Tomsk	30	3	5	22	17	64	-47	14

Portugal

		P	W	D	L	F	A	GD	Pts
1	Benfica	34	25	7	2	72	18	54	82
2	Porto	34	22	10	2	71	19	52	76
3	Sporting	34	21	7	6	68	36	32	70
4	V Guimaraes	34	18	8	8	50	39	11	62
5	Braga	34	15	9	10	53	36	15	54
6	Maritimo	34	13	11	10	34	32	2	50
7	Rio Ave	34	14	7	13	41	39	2	49
8	Feirense	34	14	6	14	31	45	-14	48
9	Boavista	34	10	13	11	33	36	-3	43
10	Estoril	34	10	8	16	36	42	-6	38
11	Chaves	34	8	14	12	35	42	-7	38
12	Vitoria Setubal	34	10	8	16	30	39	-9	38
13	Pacos Ferreira	34	8	12	14	32	45	-13	36
14	Belenenses	34	9	9	16	27	45	-18	36
15	Moreirense	34	8	9	17	33	48	-15	33
16	Tondela	34	8	8	18	29	52	-23	32
17	Arouca	34	9	5	20	33	57	-24	32
18	Nacional	34	4	9	21	22	58	-36	21

Ukraine

		P	W	D	L	F	A	GD	Pts
1	Shakhtar Don.	32	25	5	2	66	24	42	80
2	Dynamo Kyiv	32	21	4	7	69	33	36	67
3	Zorya	32	16	6	10	45	31	14	54
4	Olimpik Donetsk	32	11	11	10	33	44	-11	44
5	Oleksandria	32	10	10	12	41	43	-2	40
6	Chornomorets	32	10	8	14	25	37	-12	38
7	Vorskla	32	11	9	12	32	32	0	42
8	Stal Kamianske	32	11	8	13	27	31	-4	41
9	Zirka	32	9	7	16	29	43	-14	34
10	Karpaty Lviv*	32	9	9	14	35	41	-6	30
11	Dnipro*	31	8	13	10	31	37	-6	22
12	Volyn*	31	3	4	24	14	51	-37	7

Points deductions: Karpaty Lviv 6, Dnipro 15, Volyn 6

Belgium (Championship playoff)

		P	W	D	L	F	A	GD	Pts
1	Anderlecht	10	6	3	1	14	6	8	52
2	Club Brugge	10	4	3	3	16	14	2	45
3	Gent	10	4	4	2	16	11	5	41
4	KV Oostende	10	3	3	4	14	17	-3	37
5	Charleroi	10	2	4	4	10	13	-3	35
6	Zulte-Waregem	10	1	3	6	12	21	-9	33

Points from regular season are halved, rounded up and carried over into round-robin championship playoff

Turkey

		P	W	D	L	F	A	GD	Pts
1	Beşiktaş	34	23	8	3	73	30	43	77
2	Istanbul Basak.	34	21	10	3	63	28	35	73
3	Fenerbahce	34	18	10	6	60	32	28	64
4	Galatasaray	34	20	4	10	65	40	25	64
5	Antalyaspor	34	17	7	10	47	40	7	58
6	Trabzonspor	34	14	9	11	39	34	5	51
7	Akhisarspor	34	14	6	14	46	42	4	48
8	Genclerbirligi	34	12	10	12	33	34	-1	46
9	Konyaspor	34	11	10	13	40	45	-5	43
10	Kasimpasa	34	12	7	15	46	50	-4	43
11	Karabukspor	34	12	7	15	38	48	-10	43
12	Alanyaspor	34	12	4	18	54	65	-11	40
13	Osmanlispor	34	9	11	14	37	45	-8	38
14	Bursaspor	34	11	5	18	34	58	-24	38
15	Kayserispor	34	10	8	16	47	58	-11	38
16	Rizespor	34	10	6	18	44	53	-9	36
17	Gaziantepspor	34	7	5	22	30	65	-35	26
18	Adanaspor	34	6	7	21	33	62	-29	25

Czech Republic

		P	W	D	L	F	A	GD	Pts
1	Slavia Prague	30	20	9	1	65	22	43	69
2	Viktoria Plzen	30	20	7	3	47	21	26	67
3	Sparta Prague	30	16	9	5	47	26	21	57
4	Mlada Boleslav	30	13	10	7	47	37	10	49
5	Teplice	30	13	9	8	38	25	13	48
6	Zlin	30	11	8	11	34	35	-1	41
7	Dukla Prague	30	11	7	12	39	35	4	40
8	Jablonec	30	9	12	9	43	38	5	39
9	Slovan Liberec	30	10	9	11	31	28	3	39
10	Karvina	30	9	7	14	39	49	-10	34
11	Slovacko	30	6	14	10	29	38	-9	32
12	Zbrojovka Brno	30	6	14	10	32	45	-13	32
13	Bohemians	30	7	7	16	22	39	-17	28
14	Vysocina	30	6	9	15	26	47	-21	27
15	Hradec Kralove	30	8	3	19	29	51	-22	27
16	Pribram	30	6	4	20	29	61	-32	22

Switzerland

		P	W	D	L	F	A	GD	Pts
1	Basel	36	26	8	2	92	35	57	86
2	Young Boys	36	20	9	7	72	44	28	69
3	Lugano	36	15	8	13	52	61	-9	53
4	Sion	36	15	6	15	60	55	5	51
5	Luzern	36	14	8	14	62	66	-4	50
6	Thun	36	11	12	13	58	63	-5	45
7	St Gallen	36	11	8	17	43	57	-14	41
8	Grasshopper	36	10	8	18	47	61	-14	38
9	Lausanne	36	9	8	19	51	62	-11	35
10	Vaduz	36	7	9	20	45	78	-33	30

Holland (top ten)

		P	W	D	L	F	A	GD	Pts
1	Feyenoord	34	26	4	4	86	25	61	82
2	Ajax	34	25	6	3	79	23	56	81
3	PSV	34	22	10	2	68	23	45	76
4	Utrecht	34	18	8	8	54	38	16	62
5	Vitesse	34	15	6	13	51	40	11	51
6	AZ	34	12	13	9	56	52	4	49
7	Twente	34	12	9	13	48	50	-2	45
8	Groningen	34	10	13	11	55	51	4	43
9	Heerenveen	34	12	7	15	54	53	1	43
10	Heracles	34	12	7	15	53	55	-2	43

EUROPA LEAGUE

First qualifying round
Tuesday June 28, 2016
Kapaz .... (0) 0-0 (0) .... Dacia
Partizan Tirana (0) 0-0 (0) .....S. Bratislava
Rabotnicki....... (0) 1-1 (1) ... Buducnost P.
St Patrick's ...... (1) 1-0 (0) . Jeunesse Esch
Thursday June 30, 2016
AEK Larnaca .... (3) 3-0 (0) .... Folgore
AIK Solna .... (1) 2-0 (0) ....Bala Town
Aberdeen .... (0) 3-1 (0) .... Fola Esch
Admira Wacker (1) 1-0 (0)Spartak Myjava
Aktobe............. (1) 1-1 (1) ....MTK
Atlantas .... (0) 0-2 (0) .... HJK Helsinki
Balzan .... (0) 0-2 (1) .. Neftchi Baku
Banants .... (0) 0-1 (1)Omonia Nicosia
Beroe Stara ..... (0) 0-0 (0) Radnik Bijeljina
Bokelj .... (1) 1-1 (1) .. Vojvodina NS
Breidablik .... (1) 2-3 (3) .... Jelgava
College Europa (2) 2-0 (0)Pyunik Yerevan
Connah's Q.... (0) 0-0 (0) .... Stabaek
Cukaricki .... (0) 3-0 (0) .... Ordabasy
Differdange.... (1) 1-1 (0) .... Cliftonville
Dila............... (1) 1-0 (0) ...Shirak Gumri
Dinamo Minsk (1) 2-1 (0) .... Sp. Jurmala
Domzale .... (3) 3-1 (1) .... FC Lusitans
FC Zimbru .... (0) 0-1 (1) Chikhura Sach.
FK Trakai......... (0) 2-1 (1)..Nomme Kalju
Hearts............. (2) 2-1 (1) .... Tallinna FC
IFK Goth'burg . (3) 5-0 (0) ..... Llandudno
KR Reykjavik ... (1) 2-1 (1) ..... Glenavon
Kukesi............. (1) 1-1 (0) .. Rudar Pljevlja
La Fiorita .... (0) 0-5 (2) .... Debrecen
Levadia Tallinn (0) 1-1 (1) ....HB Torshavn
Linfield .... (0) 0-1 (0) .... Cork City
M. Tel Aviv ...... (2) 3-0 (0) .ND HIT Gorica
Midtjylland ..... (0) 1-0 (0) .....FK Suduva
NK Siroki Brijeg (1) 1-1 (1) ...... Birkirkara
NSI Runavik .... (0) 0-2 (1) .... Shakhtyor
Odd Grenland . (0) 2-0 (0) ..... Mariehamn
Qabala............ (3) 5-1 (0) .... Samtredia
Shamrock R..... (0) 0-2 (1) .... RoPS
Shkendija........ (1) 2-0 (0) .... Cracovia
Slavia Sofia ..... (0) 1-0 (0) Zaglebie Lubin
Sloboda Tuzla . (0) 0-0 (0) ..Beitar J'salem
Spartak Trnava (2) 3-0 (0) ...... Hibernians
Teuta .... (0) 0-1 (1) ..Kairat Almaty
UE Santa......... (0) 1-3 (1) ..Loko. Zagreb
Vaduz .... (2) 3-1 (0) . Sileks Kratovo
Valur............... (0) 1-4 (0) ....Brondby
Ventspils......... (2) 2-0 (0) ....Vikingur
Videoton......... (1) 3-0 (0) ...Olimpia Balti

Second legs
Tuesday July 5, 2016
Birkirkara .... (1) 2-0 (0)NK Siroki Brijeg
Birkirkara won 3-1 on agg
Chikhura Sach. (1) 2-3 (1) .... FC Zimbru
3-3 on agg, Zimbru won on away goals
Jeunesse Esch . (1) 2-1 (1) ...... St Patrick's
2-2 on agg, St Patrick's won on away goals

Wednesday July 6, 2016
Tallinna FC ...... (0) 2-4 (3) ....Hearts
Hearts won 6-3 on agg
Thursday July 7, 2016
Bala Town....... (0) 0-2 (2) ....AIK Solna
AIK won 4-0 on agg
Beitar J'salem.. (0) 1-0 (0) . Sloboda Tuzla
Beitar Jerusalem won 1-0 on agg
Brondby.......... (3) 6-0 (0) ....Valur
Brondy won 10-1 on agg
Buducnost P. .. (1) 1-0 (0) ......Rabotnicki
Buducnost won 2-1 on agg
Cliftonville ...... (1) 2-0 (0) .....Differdange
Cliftonville won 3-1 on agg
Cork City .... (0) 1-1 (0) .... Linfield
Cork City won 2-1 on agg
Cracovia .... (0) 1-2 (1) ....Shkendija
Shkendija won 4-1 on agg
Dacia .... (0) 0-1 (0) .... Kapaz
Kapaz won 1-0 on agg
Debrecen .... (1) 2-0 (0) .... La Fiorita
Debrecen won 7-0 on agg
FC Lusitans ..... (1) 1-2 (2) .... Domzale
Domzale won 5-2 on agg
FK Suduva....... (0) 0-1 (1) .... Midtjylland
Midtjylland won 2-0 on agg
Fola Esch .... (1) 1-0 (0) ....Aberdeen
Aberdeen won 3-2 on agg
Folgore Falciano(1)1-3 (0) ....AEK Larnaca
AEK Larnaca won 6-1 on agg
Glenavon .... (0) 0-6 (2) ... KR Reykjavik
KR Reykjavik won 8-1 on agg
HB Torshavn.... (0) 0-2 (0) Levadia Tallinn
Levadia Tallinn won 3-1 on agg
HJK Helsinki .... (1) 1-1 (0) .... Atlantas
HJK won 3-1 on agg
Hibernians ...... (0) 0-3 (1) Spartak Trnava
Spartak Trnava won 6-0 on agg
Jelgava .... (1) 2-2 (2) .... Breidablik
Jelgava won 5-4 on agg
Kairat Almaty.. (2) 5-0 (0) .... Teuta
Kairat won 6-0 on agg
Llandudno ...... (0) 1-2 (1) . IFK Goth'burg
IFK Gothenburg won 7-1 on agg
Loko. Zagreb... (2) 4-1 (0) ....UE Santa
Loko. Zagreb won 7-2 on agg
MTK................ (1) 2-0 (0) ....Aktobe
MTK won 3-1 on agg
Mariehamn..... (1) 1-1 (0) . Odd Grenland
Odd won 3-1 on agg
ND HIT Gorica. (0) 0-1 (1) ......M. Tel Aviv
Maccabi Tel-Aviv won 4-0 on agg
Neftchi Baku.... (1) 1-2 (0) .... Balzan
Neftchi Baku won 3-2 on agg
Nomme Kalju.. (4) 4-1 (1) ....FK Trakai
Nomme Kalju won 5-3 on agg
Olimpia Balti.... (2) 2-0 (0) ....Videoton
Videoton won 3-2 on agg
Omonia Nicosia(0) 4-1 (0) .... Banants
Omonia Nicosia won 5-1 on agg
Ordabasy .... (1) 3-3 (3) ....Cukaricki
Cukaricki won 6-3 on agg
Pyunik Yerevan(1) 2-1 (1)College Europa
College Europa won 3-2 on agg

Radnik Bijeljina(0) 0-2 (0).....Beroe Stara
Beroe Stara won 2-0 on agg
RoPS.............. (1) 1-1 (1).....Shamrock R
RoPS won 3-1 on agg
Rudar Pljevlja.. (0) 0-1 (0)............Kukesi
Kukesi won 2-1 on agg
Samtredia .... (1) 2-1 (1)............Qabala
Qabala won 6-3 on agg
Shakhtyor .... (2) 5-0 (0) .... NSI Runavik
Shakhtyor won 7-0 on agg
Shirak Gumri... (0) 1-0 (0)...............Dila
AET – 1-1 on agg, Shirak won 4-1 pens
Sileks Kratovo . (1) 1-2 (0) .... Vaduz
Vaduz won 5-2 on agg
Spartak Myjava(1) 2-3 (2)Admira Wacker
Admira Wacker won 4-3 on agg
Sp. Jurmala ..... (0) 0-2 (1) Dinamo Minsk
Dinamo Minsk won 4-1 on agg
Stabaek .... (0) 0-1 (1) .....Connah's Q
Connah's Quay won 1-0 on agg
Vikingur.......... (0) 0-2 (0)........Ventspils
Ventspils won 4-0 on agg
Vojvodina NS .. (2) 5-0 (0) .... Bokelj
Vojvodina won 6-1 on agg
Zaglebie Lubin (1) 3-0 (0).....Slavia Sofia
Zaglebie won 3-1 on agg

Second qualifying round
Thursday July 14, 2016
AIK Solna .... (1) 1-0 (0)College Europa
Aberdeen .... (0) 3-0 (0)........Ventspils
Admira Wacker(1) 1-0 (0)............. Kapaz
Austria Vienna (1) 1-0 (0)............Kukesi
Beitar J'salem.. (0) 1-0 (0)Omonia Nicosia
Beroe Stara ..... (0) 1-1 (1)... HJK Helsinki
Birkirkara .... (0) 0-0 (0)............Hearts
CSMS Iasi........ (2) 2-2 (0) ... Hajduk Split
Cliftonville ...... (1) 2-3 (0)...AEK Larnaca
Debrecen .... (1) 1-2 (1)..... Torpedo Zh
Dinamo Minsk (1) 1-1 (0)..... St Patrick's
FC Zimbru .... (1) 2-2 (1)... Osmanlispor
Genk................ (1) 2-0 (0)... Buducnost P.
Hacken .... (0) 1-1 (0)......Cork City
Hibernian........ (0) 0-1 (1)............Brondby
Ioannina .... (2) 3-0 (0). Odd Grenland
KR Reykjavik ... (0) 3-3 (2)..Grasshoppers
Kairat Almaty.. (1) 1-1 (0)...M. Tel Aviv
Levadia Tallinn (1) 3-1 (0)..Slavia Prague
M. Haifa .... (0) 1-1 (0)..Nomme Kalju
MTK................ (1) 1-2 (1)............Qabala
Midtjylland ..... (1) 3-0 (0)............. Vaduz
NK Maribor..... (0) 0-0 (0).....Levski Sofia
Neftchi Baku... (0) 0-0 (0).....Shkendija
Partizan .... (0) 0-0 (0) Zaglebie Lubin
Piast Gliwice ... (0) 0-3 (2) . IFK Goth'burg
RoPS............... (0) 1-1 (0)...Loko. Zagreb
S. Bratislava ... (0) 0-0 (0)............Jelgava
Shakhtyor .... (1) 1-1 (0).......Domzale
Shirak Gumri... (1) 1-1 (0) Spartak Trnava
SonderjyskE .... (1) 2-1 (1)...Stromsgodset
Videoton......... (2) 2-0 (0).........Cukaricki
Vojvodina NS .. (1) 1-0 (0).....Connah's Q

An all-too familiar scenario unfolded in Europa League qualifying with all three Scottish representatives crashing out before they even managed to reach the playoff round

Second legs
Wednesday July 20, 2016
Kapaz .... (0) 0-2 (1)Admira Wacker
Admira won 3-0 on agg
Thursday July 21, 2016
AEK Larnaca.... (1) 2-0 (0) ...... Cliftonville
AEK won 5-2 on agg
Brondby.......... (0) 0-1 (0) .... Hibernian
AET – 1-1 on agg, Brondby won 5-3 pens
Buducnost P.... (2) 2-0 (0) .... Genk
AET – 2-2 on agg, Genk won 4-2 pens
College Europa(0) 0-1 (0) .... AIK Solna
AIK won 2-0 on agg
Connah's Q..... (0) 1-2 (1) .. Vojvodina NS
Vojvodina won 3-1 on agg
Cork City......... (1) 1-0 (0) .... Hacken
Cork City won 2-1 on agg
Cukaricki......... (1) 1-1 (0) .... Videoton
Videoton won 3-1 on agg
Domzale .... (1) 2-1 (0) .... Shakhtyor
Domzale won 3-2 on agg
Grasshoppers.. (1) 2-1 (0) ... KR Reykjavik
Grasshoppers won 5-4 on agg
HJK Helsinki .... (1) 1-0 (0) ..... Beroe Stara
HJK won 2-1 on agg
Hajduk Split .... (1) 2-1 (1) .... CSMS Iasi
Hajduk Split won 4-3 on agg
Hearts............. (0) 1-2 (0) .... Birkirkara
Birkirkara won 2-1 on agg

IFK Goth'burg . (0) 0-0 (0) ... Piast Gliwice
IFK Gothenburg won 3-0 on agg
Jelgava .... (1) 3-0 (0) .... S. Bratislava
Jelgava won 3-0 on agg
Kukesi............. (0) 1-4 (1) Austria Vienna
Austria Vienna won 5-1 on agg
Levski Sofia..... (1) 1-1 (0) ..... NK Maribor
1-1 on agg, NK Maribor won on away goals
Loko. Zagreb... (1) 3-0 (0) .... RoPS
Loko. Zagreb won 4-1 on agg
M. Tel Aviv...... (1) 2-1 (0) .. Kairat Almaty
Maccabi Tel Aviv won 3-2 on agg
Nomme Kalju.. (0) 1-1 (1) .... M. Haifa
AET – 2-2 on agg, Nomme won 5-3 pens
Odd Grenland . (0) 3-1 (0) .... Ioannina
AET – 3-0 after 90, Ioannina won 4-3 on agg
Omonia Nicosia(2) 3-2 (2) ..Beitar J'salem
3-3 on agg, Beitar won on away goals
Osmanlispor ... (2) 5-0 (0) .... FC Zimbru
Osmanlispor won 7-2 on agg
Qabala........... (2) 2-0 (0) .... MTK
Qabala won 4-1 on agg
Shkendija......... (1) 1-0 (0) ... Neftchi Baku
Shkendija won 1-0 on agg
Slavia Prague.. (1) 2-0 (0) Levadia Tallinn
3-3 on agg, Slavia won on away goals
Spartak Trnava (0) 2-0 (0) ... Shirak Gumri
Spartak Trnava won 2-0 on agg
St Patrick's ...... (0) 0-1 (1) Dinamo Minsk
Dinamo Minsk won 2-1 on agg

Stromsgodset.. (2) 2-2 (0) .... SonderjyskE
SonderjyskE won 4-3 on agg
Torpedo Zh ..... (1) 1-0 (0) .... Debrecen
Torpedo Zhodin won 3-1 on agg
Vaduz .... (0) 2-2 (1) ..... Midtjylland
Midtjylland won 5-2 on agg
Ventspils .... (0) 0-1 (0) .... Aberdeen
Aberdeen won 4-0 on agg
Zaglebie Lubin (0) 0-0 (0) .... Partizan
AET – 0-0 on agg, Zaglebie won 4-3 on pens

Third qualifying round
Thursday July 28, 2016
AEK Larnaca.... (0) 1-1 (1)Spartak Moscow
AZ Alkmaar..... (1) 1-0 (0) .... Ioannina
Aberdeen........ (0) 1-1 (0) ..... NK Maribor
Admira Wacker (1) 1-2 (1) Slovan Liberec
Austria Vienna (0) 0-1 (0) Spartak Trnava
Birkirkara .... (0) 0-3 (1) .... Krasnodar
Domzale .... (1) 2-1 (1) .... West Ham
Genk............... (1) 1-0 (0) .... Cork City
Gent .... (2) 5-0 (0) .... Viitorul C
Grasshoppers.. (1) 2-1 (0) .. Ap Limassol
Heracles........... (0) 1-1 (0) .... Arouca
Hertha Berlin... (1) 1-0 (0) .... Brondby
IFK Goth'burg . (0) 1-2 (0) ... HJK Helsinki
Istanbul Buyuk.(0) 0-0 (0) .... Rijeka
Jelgava .... (0) 1-1 (1) .. Beitar J'salem
Lille .... (0) 1-1 (1) .... Qabala
Loko. Zagreb... (0) 0-0 (0) .... Poltava

Deja vu for West Ham who were again knocked out of Europa League qualifying by Romanian minnows Astra Giurgiu

Lucerne............(1) 1-1 (1).........Sassuolo
Oleksandria ....(0) 0-3 (0)....Hajduk Split
Osmanlispor ...(0) 1-0 (0)..Nomme Kalju
Panathinaikos .(0) 1-0 (0)........AIK Solna
Pandurii..........(1) 1-3 (1)......M. Tel Aviv
Shkendija........(0) 2-0 (0)Mlada Boleslav
Slavia Prague..(0) 0-0 (0)...........Rio Ave
St-Etienne.......(0) 0-0 (0)....AEK Athens
Torpedo Zh .....(0) 0-0 (0).. Rapid Vienna
Videoton.........(0) 0-1 (0).... Midtjylland
Vojvodina NS ..(1) 1-1 (0) Dinamo Minsk
Zaglebie Lubin (1) 1-2 (2)....SonderjyskE

Second legs
Wednesday August 3, 2016
Slovan Liberec (2) 2-0 (0)Admira Wacker
Slovan Liberec won 4-1 on agg

Thursday August 4, 2016
AEK Athens.....(0) 0-1 (1).......St-Etienne
St-Etienne won 1-0 on agg
AIK Solna........(0) 0-2 (0). Panathinaikos
Panathinaikos won 3-0 on agg
Ap Limassol ....(0) 3-3 (0)..Grasshoppers
AET – 2-1 after 90, Grasshopper won 5-4 on agg
Arouca............(0) 0-0 (0)..........Heracles
1-1 on agg, Arouca won on away goals
Beitar J'salem..(2) 3-0 (0)...........Jelgava
Beitar Jerusalem won 4-1 on agg
Brondby..........(2) 3-1 (1)...Hertha Berlin
Brondby won 3-2 on agg
Cork City........(0) 1-2 (2)..............Genk
Genk won 3-1 on agg
Dinamo Minsk (0) 0-2 (1).. Vojvodina NS
Vojvodina won 3-1 on agg
Krasnodar.......(3) 3-1 (0)........Birkirkara
Krasnodar won 6-1 on agg

HJK Helsinki ....(0) 0-2 (1). IFK Goth'burg
IFK Gothenburg won 3-2 on agg
Hajduk Split....(1) 3-1 (1)....Oleksandria
Hajduk Split won 6-1 on agg
Ioannina.........(1) 1-2 (2).....AZ Alkmaar
AZ Alkmaar won 3-1 on agg
M. Tel Aviv......(1) 2-1 (0)..........Pandurii
Maccabi Tel-Aviv won 5-2 on agg
Midtjylland .....(0) 1-1 (0).........Videoton
AET – 0-1 after 90, Midtjylland won 2-1 on agg
Mlada Boleslav(0) 1-0 (0)........Shkendija
Shkendija won 2-1 on agg
NK Maribor.....(0) 1-0 (0)........Aberdeen
NK Maribor won 2-1 on agg
Nomme Kalju.. (0) 0-2 (2) ... Osmanlispor
Osmanlispor won 3-0 on agg
Poltava ....(0) 2-3 (1)...Loko. Zagreb
Loko. Zagreb won 3-2 on agg
Qabala............(1) 1-0 (0)...............Lille
Qabala won 2-1 on agg
Rapid Vienna ..(2) 3-0 (0)..... Torpedo Zh
Rapid Vienna won 3-0 on agg
Rijeka ....(1) 2-2 (1)Istanbul Buyuk.
2-2 on agg, Istanbul won on away goals
Rio Ave...........(0) 1-1 (1)...Slavia Prague
1-1 on agg, Slavia won on away goals
Sassuolo ....(2) 3-0 (0)...........Lucerne
Sassuolo won 4-1 on agg
SonderjyskE ....(0) 1-1 (1) Zaglebie Lubin
SonderjyskE won 3-2 on agg
Spartak Moscow(0) 0-1 (0)....AEK Larnaca
AEK Larnaca won 2-1 on agg
Spartak Trnava (0) 0-1 (0) Austria Vienna
AET – 1-1 on agg, Vienna won 5-4 on pens
Viitorul C ....(0) 0-0 (0)...............Gent
Gent won 5-0 on agg
West Ham.......(2) 3-0 (0).........Domzale
West Ham won 4-2 on agg

Playoff round
Wednesday August 17, 2016
Beitar J'salem.. (1) 1-2 (2).......St-Etienne
Thursday August 18, 2016
AEK Larnaca....(0) 0-1 (1) Slovan Liberec
Arouca............(0) 0-1 (1).....Olympiakos
Astana............(0) 2-0 (0)... Bate Borisov
Astra Giurgiu ..(0) 1-1 (1).......West Ham
Austria Vienna (0) 2-1 (0)......Rosenborg
Dinamo Tbilisi. (0) 0-3 (1) PAOK Salonika
Dukla Trencin..(0) 0-4 (1).. Rapid Vienna
Krasnodar.......(3) 4-0 (0) Partizan Tirana
Fenerbahce.....(1) 3-0 (0)..Grasshoppers
Gent ....(1) 2-1 (1)........Shkendija
IFK Goth'burg .(0) 1-0 (0).....FK Qarabag
Istanbul Buyuk.(0) 1-2 (2).........Shakhtar
Loko. Zagreb...(0) 2-2 (1)...............Genk
M. Tel Aviv......(1) 2-1 (0)... Hajduk Split
Midtjylland .....(0) 0-1 (1)... Osmanlispor
Panathinaikos .(1) 3-0 (0)..........Brondby
Qabala............(3) 1-1 (1)....NK Maribor
Sassuolo ....(2) 3-0 (0) Crvena Zvezda
Slavia Prague..(0) 0-3 (0)......Anderlecht
SonderjyskE ....(0) 0-0 (0) . Sparta Prague
Vojvodina NS ..(0) 0-3 (2).....AZ Alkmaar

Second legs
Thursday August 25, 2016
AZ Alkmaar.....(0) 3-0 (0).. Vojvodina NS
AZ Alkmaar won 3-0 on agg
Anderlecht......(2) 3-0 (0).. Slavia Prague
Anderlecht won 6-0 on agg
Bate Borisov ...(1) 2-2 (0)............Astana
Astana won 4-2 on agg

Brondby..........(1) 1-1 (0) . Panathinaikos
Panathinaikos won 4-1 on agg
Crvena Zvezda (0) 1-1 (1) ....Sassuolo
Sassuolo won 4-1 on agg
FK Qarabag.....(2) 3-0 (0) . IFK Goth'burg
Qarabag won 3-1 on agg
Genk...............(1) 2-0 (0) ...Loko. Zagreb
Genk won 4-2 on agg
Grasshoppers..(0) 0-2 (0) .....Fenerbahce
Fenerbahce won 5-0 on agg
Hajduk Split...(1) 2-1 (0)......M. Tel Aviv
AET – 3-3 on agg, Tel Aviv won 4-3 pens
NK Maribor.....(0) 1-0 (0) ....Qabala
Qabala won 3-2 on agg
Olympiakos.....(0) 2-1 (0) ....Arouca
AET – 0-1 after 90, Olympiakos won 3-1 on agg
Osmanlispor ...(1) 2-0 (0) ..... Midtjylland
Osmanlispor won 3-0 on agg
PAOK Salonika (2) 2-0 (0) .Dinamo Tbilisi
PAOK Salonika won 5-0 on agg
Partizan Tirana (0) 0-0 (0) .... Krasnodar
Krasnodar won 4-0 on agg
Rapid Vienna ..(0) 0-2 (2) ..Dukla Trencin
Rapid Vienna won 4-2 on agg
Rosenborg ......(0) 1-2 (0) Austria Vienna
Austria Vienna won 4-2 on agg
Shakhtar ....(1) 2-0 (0)Istanbul Buyuk.
Shakhtar won 4-1 on agg
Shkendija.........(0) 0-4 (0) .... Gent
Gent won 6-1 on agg
Slovan Liberec (3) 3-0 (0) ....AEK Larnaca
Slovan Liberec won 4-0 on agg
Sparta Prague . (1) 3-2 (2) .... SonderjyskE
Sparta Prague won 3-2 on agg
St-Etienne ....(0) 0-0 (0) ..Beitar J'salem
St-Etienne won 2-1 on agg
West Ham.......(0) 0-1 (1) .. Astra Giurgiu
Astra Giurgiu won 2-1 on agg

Group A

	P	W	D	L	F	A	GD	Pts
Fenerbahce	6	4	1	1	8	6	2	13
Man Utd	6	4	0	2	12	4	8	12
Feyenoord	6	2	1	3	3	7	-4	7
Zorya	6	0	2	4	2	8	-6	2

Thursday September 15, 2016
Feyenoord ......(0) 1-0 (0) .... Man Utd
Zorya..............(0) 1-1 (0) .....Fenerbahce

Thursday September 29, 2016
Fenerbahce.....(1) 1-0 (0) ..... Feyenoord
Man Utd ....(0) 1-0 (0) ....Zorya

Thursday October 20, 2016
Feyenoord ......(0) 1-0 (0) ....Zorya
Man Utd ....(3) 4-1 (0) .....Fenerbahce

Thursday November 3, 2016
Fenerbahce.....(1) 2-1 (0) .... Man Utd
Zorya..............(1) 1-1 (1) ...... Feyenoord

Thursday November 24, 2016
Fenerbahce.....(0) 2-0 (0) ....Zorya
Man Utd ....(1) 4-0 (0) ..... Feyenoord

Thursday December 8, 2016
Feyenoord ......(0) 0-1 (1) .....Fenerbahce
Zorya..............(0) 0-2 (0) ...... Man Utd

Group B

	P	W	D	L	F	A	GD	Pts
Apoel	6	4	0	2	8	6	2	12
Olympiakos	6	2	2	2	7	6	1	8
Young Boys	6	2	2	2	7	4	3	8
Astana	6	1	2	3	5	11	-6	5

Thursday September 15, 2016
Apoel Nicosia . (0) 2-1 (1) ....Astana
Young Boys.....(0) 0-1 (1) .....Olympiakos

Thursday September 29, 2016
Astana............(0) 0-0 (0) .....Young Boys
Olympiakos.....(0) 0-1 (0) . Apoel Nicosia

Thursday October 20, 2016
Olympiakos.....(3) 4-1 (0) ....Astana
Young Boys.....(1) 3-1 (1) . Apoel Nicosia

Thursday November 3, 2016
Apoel Nicosia . (0) 1-0 (0) .....Young Boys
Astana............(1) 1-1 (1) .....Olympiakos

Thursday November 24, 2016
Astana............(0) 2-1 (1) . Apoel Nicosia
Olympiakos.....(0) 1-1 (0) .....Young Boys

Thursday December 8, 2016
Apoel Nicosia . (1) 2-0 (0) .....Olympiakos
Young Boys.....(0) 3-0 (0) ....Astana

Group C

	P	W	D	L	F	A	GD	Pts
St-Etienne	6	3	3	0	8	5	3	12
Anderlecht	6	3	2	1	16	8	8	11
Mainz	6	2	3	1	8	10	-2	9
Qabala	6	0	0	6	5	14	-9	0

Thursday September 15, 2016
Anderlecht ......(2) 3-1 (1) ....Qabala
Mainz ....(0) 1-1 (0) ......St-Etienne

Thursday September 29, 2016
Qabala.............(0) 2-3 (1) .... Mainz
St-Etienne ....(0) 1-1 (0) ......Anderlecht

Thursday October 20, 2016
Mainz ....(1) 1-1 (0) ......Anderlecht
St-Etienne ....(0) 1-0 (0) ....Qabala

Thursday November 3, 2016
Anderlecht ......(2) 6-1 (1) .... Mainz
Qabala.............(1) 1-2 (1) ......St-Etienne

Thursday November 24, 2016
Qabala.............(1) 1-3 (1) ......Anderlecht
St-Etienne ....(0) 0-0 (0) .... Mainz

Thursday December 8, 2016
Anderlecht ......(2) 2-3 (0) ......St-Etienne
Mainz ....(2) 2-0 (0) ....Qabala

Group D

	P	W	D	L	F	A	GD	Pts
Zenit	6	5	0	1	17	8	9	15
AZ Alkmaar	6	2	2	2	6	10	-4	8
M. Tel-Aviv	6	2	1	3	7	9	-2	7
Dundalk	6	1	1	4	5	8	-3	4

Thursday September 15, 2016
AZ Alkmaar.....(0) 1-1 (0) ....Dundalk
M. Tel Aviv......(1) 3-4 (0) ....Zenit

Thursday September 29, 2016
Dundalk...........(0) 1-0 (0) .....M. Tel Aviv
Zenit...............(1) 5-0 (0) .....AZ Alkmaar

Thursday October 20, 2016
AZ Alkmaar.....(0) 1-2 (1) ......M. Tel Aviv
Dundalk...........(0) 1-2 (0) ....Zenit

Thursday November 3, 2016
M. Tel Aviv......(0) 0-0 (0) .....AZ Alkmaar
Zenit...............(1) 2-1 (0) ....Dundalk

Thursday November 24, 2016
Dundalk...........(0) 0-1 (1) .....AZ Alkmaar
Zenit...............(1) 2-0 (0) .....M. Tel Aviv

Thursday December 8, 2016
AZ Alkmaar.....(2) 3-2 (0) ....Zenit
M. Tel Aviv......(2) 2-1 (1) ....Dundalk

Group E

	P	W	D	L	F	A	GD	Pts
Roma	6	3	3	0	16	7	9	12
Astra Giurgiu	6	2	2	2	7	10	-3	8
Viktoria Plzen	6	1	3	2	7	10	-3	6
Austria Vienna	6	1	2	3	11	14	-3	5

Thursday September 15, 2016
Astra Giurgiu .. (1) 2-3 (2) Austria Vienna
Viktoria Plzen..(1) 1-1 (1) ....Roma

Thursday September 29, 2016
Austria Vienna (0) 0-0 (0) ..Viktoria Plzen
Roma..............(2) 4-0 (0) . Astra Giurgiu

Thursday October 20, 2016
Roma..............(2) 3-3 (1) Austria Vienna
Viktoria Plzen..(0) 1-2 (1) . Astra Giurgiu

Thursday November 3, 2016
Astra Giurgiu .. (1) 1-1 (1) ..Viktoria Plzen
Austria Vienna (1) 2-4 (2) ....Roma

Thursday November 24, 2016
Austria Vienna (0) 1-2 (0) .. Astra Giurgiu
Roma..............(1) 4-1 (1) ..Viktoria Plzen

Thursday December 8, 2016
Astra Giurgiu .. (0) 0-0 (0) ....Roma
Viktoria Plzen..(1) 3-2 (2) Austria Vienna

Group F

	P	W	D	L	F	A	GD	Pts
Genk	6	4	0	2	13	9	4	12
Ath Bilbao	6	3	1	2	10	11	-1	10
Rapid Vienna	6	1	3	2	7	8	-1	6
Sassuolo	6	1	2	3	9	11	-2	5

Thursday September 15, 2016
Rapid Vienna ..(0) 3-2 (1) ....Genk
Sassuolo ....(0) 3-0 (0) ...... Ath Bilbao

Thursday September 29, 2016
Ath Bilbao ......(0) 1-0 (0) . Rapid Vienna
Genk...............(2) 3-1 (0) ....Sassuolo

Thursday October 20, 2016
Genk...............(1) 2-0 (0) ...... Ath Bilbao
Rapid Vienna ..(1) 1-1 (0) ....Sassuolo

Thursday November 3, 2016
Ath Bilbao ......(3) 5-3 (1) ....Genk
Sassuolo ....(2) 2-2 (0) .. Rapid Vienna

Thursday November 24, 2016
Ath Bilbao ......(1) 3-2 (1) ....Sassuolo
Genk...............(1) 1-0 (0) .. Rapid Vienna

Thursday December 8, 2016
Rapid Vienna ..(0) 1-1 (0) ...... Ath Bilbao

Friday December 9, 2016
Sassuolo ....(0) 0-2 (0) ....Genk

Group G

	P	W	D	L	F	A	GD	Pts
Ajax	6	4	2	0	11	6	5	14
Celta Vigo	6	2	3	1	10	7	3	9
St Liege	6	1	4	1	8	6	2	7
Panathinaikos	6	0	1	5	3	13	-10	1

Thursday September 15, 2016
Panathinaikos . (1) 1-2 (1) ....Ajax
St Liege...........(1) 1-1 (1) ......Celta Vigo
Thursday September 29, 2016
Ajax...............(1) 1-0 (0) ....St Liege
Celta Vigo.......(0) 2-0 (0) . Panathinaikos
Thursday October 20, 2016
Celta Vigo.......(2) 2-1 (1) ....Ajax
St Liege...........(1) 2-2 (2) . Panathinaikos
Thursday November 3, 2016
Ajax...............(1) 3-2 (0) ......Celta Vigo
Panathinaikos . (0) 0-3 (0) ....St Liege
Thursday November 24, 2016
Ajax...............(1) 2-0 (0) . Panathinaikos
Celta Vigo.......(1) 1-1 (0) ....St Liege
Thursday December 8, 2016
Panathinaikos . (0) 0-2 (1) ......Celta Vigo
St Liege...........(0) 1-1 (1) ....Ajax

Group H

	P	W	D	L	F	A	GD	Pts
Shakhtar	6	6	0	0	21	5	16	18
Gent	6	2	2	2	9	13	-4	8
Braga	6	1	3	2	9	11	-2	6
Konyaspor	6	0	1	5	2	12	-10	1

Thursday September 15, 2016
Braga..............(1) 1-1 (1) ....Gent
Konyaspor ......(0) 0-1 (0) ....Shakhtar
Thursday September 29, 2016
Gent ....(2) 2-0 (0) ......Konyaspor
Shakhtar ....(1) 2-0 (0) ....Braga
Thursday October 20, 2016
Konyaspor ......(1) 1-1 (0) ....Braga
Shakhtar ....(2) 5-0 (0) ....Gent
Thursday November 3, 2016
Braga..............(2) 3-1 (1) ......Konyaspor
Gent ....(1) 3-5 (3) ....Shakhtar
Thursday November 24, 2016
Gent ....(2) 2-2 (2) ....Braga
Shakhtar ....(2) 4-0 (0) ......Konyaspor
Thursday December 8, 2016
Braga..............(1) 2-4 (2) ....Shakhtar
Konyaspor ......(0) 0-1 (0) ....Gent

Group I

	P	W	D	L	F	A	GD	Pts
Schalke	6	5	0	1	9	3	6	15
Krasnodar	6	2	1	3	8	8	0	7
RB Salzburg	6	2	1	3	6	6	0	7
Nice	6	2	0	4	5	11	-6	6

Thursday September 15, 2016
RB Salzburg .... (0) 0-1 (1) ....Krasnodar
Nice...............(0) 0-1 (0) ....Schalke
Thursday September 29, 2016
Krasnodar.......(2) 5-2 (1) ....Nice
Schalke ....(1) 3-1 (0) .... RB Salzburg

Thursday October 20, 2016
Krasnodar......(0) 0-1 (1) ....Schalke
RB Salzburg .... (0) 0-1 (1) ....Nice
Thursday November 3, 2016
Nice...............(0) 0-2 (0) .... RB Salzburg
Schalke ....(2) 2-0 (0) ....Krasnodar
Thursday November 24, 2016
Krasnodar.......(0) 1-1 (1) .... RB Salzburg
Schalke ....(1) 2-0 (0) ....Nice
Thursday December 8, 2016
Nice...............(0) 2-1 (0) ....Krasnodar
RB Salzburg ....(1) 2-0 (0) ....Schalke

Group J

	P	W	D	L	F	A	GD	Pts
Fiorentina	6	4	1	1	15	6	9	13
PAOK Salonika	6	3	1	2	7	6	1	10
FK Qarabag	6	2	1	3	7	12	-5	7
Slovan Liberec	6	1	1	4	7	12	-5	4

Thursday September 15, 2016
FK Qarabag.....(1) 2-2 (1) Slovan Liberec
PAOK Salonika (0) 0-0 (0) ....Fiorentina
Thursday September 29, 2016
Fiorentina ....(3) 5-1 (0) ....FK Qarabag
Slovan Liberec (1) 1-2 (1) PAOK Salonika
Thursday October 20, 2016
FK Qarabag.....(0) 2-0 (0) PAOK Salonika
Slovan Liberec (0) 1-3 (2) ....Fiorentina
Thursday November 3, 2016
Fiorentina ....(2) 3-0 (0) Slovan Liberec
PAOK Salonika (0) 0-1 (0) .....FK Qarabag
Thursday November 24, 2016
Fiorentina ....(1) 2-3 (2) PAOK Salonika
Slovan Liberec (1) 3-0 (0) ....FK Qarabag
Thursday December 8, 2016
FK Qarabag.....(0) 1-2 (0) ....Fiorentina
PAOK Salonika (1) 2-0 (0) Slovan Liberec

Group K

	P	W	D	L	F	A	GD	Pts
Sparta Prague	6	4	0	2	8	6	2	12
H Be'er Sheva	6	2	2	2	6	6	0	8
Southampton	6	2	2	2	6	4	2	8
Inter	6	2	0	4	7	11	-4	6

Thursday September 15, 2016
Inter ....(0) 0-2 (0) . H Be'er Sheva
Southampton . . (2) 3-0 (0) . Sparta Prague
Thursday September 29, 2016
H Be'er Sheva . (0) 0-0 (0) ...Southampton
Sparta Prague . (2) 3-1 (0) ....Inter
Thursday October 20, 2016
H Be'er Sheva . (0) 0-1 (0) . Sparta Prague
Inter ....(0) 1-0 (0) ...Southampton
Thursday November 3, 2016
Southampton.. (0) 2-1 (1) ....Inter
Sparta Prague . (2) 2-0 (0) . H Be'er Sheva
Thursday November 24, 2016
H Be'er Sheva . (0) 3-2 (2) ....Inter
Sparta Prague . (1) 1-0 (0) ...Southampton
Thursday December 8, 2016
Inter ....(1) 2-1 (0) . Sparta Prague
Southampton.. (0) 1-1 (0) . H Be'er Sheva

Group L

	P	W	D	L	F	A	GD	Pts
Osmanlispor	6	3	1	2	10	7	3	10
Villarreal	6	2	3	1	9	8	1	9
FC Zurich	6	1	3	2	5	7	-2	6
Steaua	6	1	3	2	5	7	-2	6

Thursday September 15, 2016
Osmanlispor ... (0) 2-0 (0) ....Steaua
Villarreal ....(2) 2-1 (1) ....FC Zurich
Thursday September 29, 2016
FC Zurich ....(1) 2-1 (0) ... Osmanlispor
Steaua ....(1) 1-1 (1) ....Villarreal
Thursday October 20, 2016
Osmanlispor ... (2) 2-2 (1) ....Villarreal
Steaua ....(0) 1-1 (0) ....FC Zurich
Thursday November 3, 2016
FC Zurich ....(0) 0-0 (0) ....Steaua
Villarreal ....(0) 1-2 (1) ... Osmanlispor
Thursday November 24, 2016
FC Zurich ....(0) 1-1 (0) ....Villarreal
Steaua ....(0) 2-1 (1) ... Osmanlispor
Thursday December 8, 2016
Osmanlispor ... (0) 2-0 (0) ....FC Zurich
Villarreal ....(1) 2-1 (0) ....Steaua

Round of 32
Thursday February 16, 2017
AZ Alkmaar..... (0) 1-4 (2) ....Lyon
Anderlecht ..... (2) 2-0 (0) ....Zenit
Astra Giurgiu .. (1) 2-2 (1) ....Genk
Ath Bilbao ......(1) 3-2 (1) . Apoel Nicosia
Celta Vigo ....(0) 0-1 (1) ....Shakhtar
Krasnodar.......(1) 1-0 (0) .....Fenerbahce
Gent ....(0) 1-0 (0) ......Tottenham
H Be'er Sheva . (1) 1-3 (1) ....Besiktas
Legia Warsaw . (0) 0-0 (0) ....Ajax
Ludogorets .....(0) 1-2 (1)FC Copenhagen
Man Utd ....(1) 3-0 (0) ......St-Etienne
M'gladbach ....(0) 0-1 (1) ....Fiorentina
Olympiakos..... (0) 0-0 (0) ... Osmanlispor
PAOK Salonika (0) 0-3 (1) ....Schalke
R. Rostov ....(3) 4-0 (0) . Sparta Prague
Villarreal ....(0) 0-4 (1) ....Roma

Second legs
Wednesday February 22, 2017
Fenerbahce......(1) 1-1 (1) ....Krasnodar
    Krasnodar won 2-1 on agg
Schalke ....(1) 1-1 (1) PAOK Salonika
    Schalke won 4-1 on agg
St-Etienne ....(0) 0-1 (1) ....Man Utd
    Man Utd won 4-0 on agg
Thursday February 23, 2017
Ajax...............(0) 1-0 (0) . Legia Warsaw
    Ajax won 1-0 on agg
Apoel Nicosia . (0) 2-0 (0) ...... Ath Bilbao
    Apoel Nicosia won 4-3 on agg
Besiktas ....(1) 2-1 (0) . H Be'er Sheva
    Besiktas won 5-2 on agg
FC Copenhagen(0) 0-0 (0) ..... Ludogorets
    FC Copenhagen won 2-1 on agg
Fiorentina ....(2) 2-4 (1) .... M'gladbach
    M'gladbach won 4-3 on agg

Paul Pogba collects the Europa League trophy for Manchester United

Genk .... (0) 1-0 (0) .. Astra Giurgiu
Genk won 3-2 on agg
Lyon .... (4) 7-1 (1) ..... AZ Alkmaar
Lyon won 11-2 on agg
Osmanlispor ... (0) 0-3 (0) ..... Olympiakos
Roma .... (0) 0-1 (1) .... Villarreal
Roma won 4-1 on agg
Shakhtar .... (0) 0-2 (0) ...... Celta Vigo
AET – 0-1 after 90, Celta won 2-1 on agg
Sparta Prague . (0) 1-1 (1) .... R. Rostov
R. Rostov won 5-1 on agg
Tottenham ...... (1) 2-2 (1) .... Gent
Gent won 3-2 on agg
Zenit .... (1) 3-1 (0) ...... Anderlecht
3-3 on agg, Anderlecht won on away goals

Round of 16
Thursday March 9, 2017
Apoel Nicosia . (0) 0-1 (1) ...... Anderlecht
Celta Vigo .... (0) 2-1 (0) .... Krasnodar
FC Copenhagen (1) 2-1 (1) .... Ajax
Gent .... (1) 2-5 (4) .... Genk
Lyon .... (4) 4-2 (2) .... Roma
Olympiakos ..... (1) 1-1 (0) .... Besiktas
R. Rostov .... (0) 1-1 (1) .... Man Utd
Schalke .... (1) 1-1 (1) .... M'gladbach

Second legs
Thursday March 16, 2017
Ajax .... (2) 2-0 (0) FC Copenhagen
Ajax won 3-2 on agg
Anderlecht ...... (0) 1-0 (0) . Apoel Nicosia
Anderlecht won 2-0 on agg
Besiktas .... (2) 4-1 (1) ..... Olympiakos
Besiktas won 5-2 on agg
Krasnodar .... (0) 0-2 (0) .... Celta Vigo
Celta Vigo won 4-1 on agg
Genk .... (1) 1-1 (0) .... Gent
Genk won 6-3 on agg
Man Utd .... (0) 1-0 (0) .... R. Rostov
Man Utd won 2-1 on agg
M'gladbach .... (2) 2-2 (0) .... Schalke
3-3 on agg, Schalke won on away goals
Roma .... (1) 2-1 (1) .... Lyon
Lyon won 5-4 on agg

Quarter-finals
Thursday April 13, 2017
Ajax .... (1) 2-0 (0) .... Schalke
Anderlecht ...... (0) 1-1 (1) .... Man Utd
Celta Vigo .... (3) 3-2 (1) .... Genk
Lyon .... (0) 2-1 (1) .... Besiktas

Second legs
Thursday April 20, 2017
Besiktas .... (1) 2-1 (1) .... Lyon
AET – 3-3 on agg, Lyon won 7-6 on pens

Genk .... (0) 1-1 (0) .... Celta Vigo
Celta Vigo won 4-3 on agg
Man Utd .... (1) 2-1 (1) ...... Anderlecht
AET – 1-1 after 90, Man Utd won 3-2 on agg
Schalke .... (0) 3-2 (0) .... Ajax
AET – 2-0 after 90, Ajax won 4-3 on agg

Semi-finals
Wednesday May 3, 2017
Ajax .... (2) 4-1 (0) .... Lyon
Thursday May 4, 2017
Celta Vigo .... (0) 0-1 (0) .... Man Utd

Second legs
Thursday May 11, 2017
Lyon .... (2) 3-1 (1) .... Ajax
Ajax won 5-4 on agg
Man Utd .... (1) 1-1 (0) .... Celta Vigo
Man Utd won 2-1 on agg

Europa League final
Wednesday May 18, 2016
Ajax .... (0) 0-2 (1) .... Man Utd
POS 69/31 SH ON 3/4 SH OFF 7/1 CRN 5/2
SCORERS **Man Utd:** Pogba (18) Mkhitaryan (48)
CARDS **Ajax:** Veltman | Younes | Riedewald |
Man Utd: Mkhitaryan | Fellaini | Mata |

CHAMPIONS LEAGUE

First qualifying round
Tuesday June 28, 2016
FC Santa Coloma(0) 0-0 (0) .... Alashkert
Flora Tallinn .... (1) 2-1 (0) ... Lincoln Red I
The New Saints(2) 2-1 (1) .... Tre Penne
Valletta .... (0) 1-0 (0) .. B36 Torshavn

Second legs
Tuesday July 5, 2016
Alashkert .... (1) 3-0 (0)FC Santa Coloma
Alashkert won 3-0 on agg
B36 Torshavn .. (1) 2-1 (1) .... Valletta
2-2 on agg. Valletta won on away goals
Tre Penne........ (0) 0-3 (1)The New Saints
The New Saints won 5-1 on agg

Wednesday July 6, 2016
Lincoln Red I ... (1) 2-0 (0) .... Flora Tallinn
Lincoln Red Imps won 3-2 on agg

Second qualifying round
Tuesday July 12, 2016
Bate Borisov ... (1) 2-0 (0) .... SJK
Dinamo Tbilisi. (0) 2-0 (0) .... Alashkert
FK Qarabag..... (2) 2-0 (0)F91 Dudelange
H Be'er Sheva . (1) 3-2 (1) .... FC Sheriff
Lincoln Red I ... (0) 1-0 (0) .... Celtic
RB Salzburg .... (0) 1-0 (0) .... Dag Liepaja
The New Saints(0) 0-0 (0) . Apoel Nicosia

Valletta .... (1) 1-2 (0) Crvena Zvezda
Vardar Skopje . (0) 1-2 (2) ...... Din Zagreb
Zrinjski Mostar (0) 1-1 (0) . Legia Warsaw

Wednesday July 13, 2016
Crusaders .... (0) 0-3 (2)FC Copenhagen
Dundalk.......... (0) 1-1 (0) .. Hafnarfjordur
Ludogorets ..... (2) 2-0 (0) .. Mladost Pod.
O. Ljubljana ..... () 3-4 () ... Dukla Trencin
Partizan Tirana (0) 1-1 (0) .... Ferencvaros
Rosenborg ...... (0) 3-1 (0) ..... Norrkoping
Zalgiris Vilnius (0) 0-0 (0) .... Astana

Second legs
Tuesday July 19, 2016
Alashkert .... (0) 1-1 (1) . Dinamo Tbilisi
Dinamo Tbilisi won 3-1 on agg
Apoel Nicosia . (0) 3-0 (0)The New Saints
Apoel Nicosia won 3-0 on agg
Crvena Zvezda (1) 2-1 (1) .... Valletta
Crvena Zvezda won 4-2 on agg
Dag Liepaja .... (0) 0-2 (1) .... RB Salzburg
RB Salzburg won 3-0 on agg
FC Copenhagen(2) 6-0 (0) .... Crusaders
FC Copenhagen won 9-0 on agg
FC Sheriff........ (0) 0-0 (0) . H Be'er Sheva
Hapoel Be'er Sheva won 3-2 on agg
Legia Warsaw . (1) 2-0 (0) Zrinjski Mostar
Legia Warsaw won 3-1 on agg
Mladost Pod. .. (0) 0-3 (1) ..... Ludogorets
Ludogorets won 5-0 on agg
SJK.................. (1) 2-2 (2) ... Bate Borisov
Bate Borisov won 4-2 on agg

Wednesday July 20, 2016
Astana .... (1) 2-1 (0) Zalgiris Vilnius
Astana won 2-1 on agg
Celtic .... (3) 3-0 (0) .... Lincoln R I
Celtic won 3-1 on agg
Dinamo Zagreb(0) 3-2 (1) . Vardar Skopje
Dinamo Zagreb won 5-3 on agg
Dukla Trencin.. (2) 2-3 (2) .... O. Ljubljana
6-6 on agg. Trencin won on away goals
F91 Dudelange(0) 1-1 (0) ..... FK Qarabag
FK Qarabag won 3-1 on agg
Ferencvaros .... (1) 1-1 (1) Partizan Tirana
AET – 2-2 on agg, Partizan 3-1 on pens
Hafnarfjordur.. (1) 2-2 (0) .... Dundalk
3-3 on agg. Dundalk won on away goals
Norrkoping ..... (0) 3-2 (1) ...... Rosenborg
Rosenborg won 5-4 on agg

Third qualifying round
Tuesday July 26, 2016
Ajax............... (0) 1-1 (1) PAOK Salonika
Bate Borisov ... (0) 1-0 (0) .... Dundalk
Din Zagreb...... (2) 2-0 (0) . Dinamo Tbilisi
Ludogorets ..... (1) 2-2 (0) Crvena Zvezda
Partizan Tirana (0) 0-1 (0) .... RB Salzburg
Rostov .... (1) 2-2 (1) ...... Anderlecht
Shakhtar .... (1) 2-0 (0) .... Young Boys
Sparta Prague . (1) 1-1 (0) .... Steaua
Viktoria Plzen .. (0) 0-0 (0) .... FK Qarabag

Clockwise from top left: Celtic recovered from a first-leg defeat to Lincoln Red Imps to reach the group stage; Barcelona's stunning comeback against PSG will live long in the memory; Juve legend Gianluigi Buffon was again denied European glory; Dortmund's campaign was derailed by a disgraceful attack on their team bus

Wednesday July 27, 2016

Astana .... (1) 1-1 (0) .... Celtic
Astra Giurgiu .. (1) 1-1 (0) FC Copenhagen
Dukla Trencin .. (0) 0-1 (0) . Legia Warsaw
Fenerbahce ..... (1) 2-1 (1) .... Monaco
Olympiakos ..... (0) 0-0 (0) . H Be'er Sheva
Rosenborg ...... (2) 2-1 (0) . Apoel Nicosia

Second legs
Tuesday August 2, 2016

Apoel Nicosia . (0) 3-0 (0) ...... Rosenborg
Apoel won 4-2 on agg
Crvena Zvezda (1) 2-4 (2) ..... Ludogorets
AET – 2-2 after 90. Ludogorets won 6-4 on agg
Dinamo Tbilisi. (0) 0-1 (1) ...... Din Zagreb
Dinamo Zagreb won 3-0 on agg
Dundalk .... (1) 3-0 (0) ... Bate Borisov
Dundalk won 3-1 on agg
FK Qarabag ..... (1) 1-1 (0) .. Viktoria Plzen
1-1 on agg. Plzen won on away goals

Wednesday August 3, 2016

Anderlecht ...... (0) 0-2 (1) .... Rostov
Rostov won 4-2 on agg
Celtic .... (1) 2-1 (0) .... Astana
Celtic won 3-2 on agg

FC Copenhagen (3) 3-0 (0) .. Astra Giurgiu
FC Copenhagen won 4-1 on agg
H Be'er Sheva . (0) 1-0 (0) .....Olympiakos
Hapoel Be'er Sheva won 1-0 on agg
Legia Warsaw . (0) 0-0 (0) .. Dukla Trencin
Legia won 1-0 on agg
Monaco .... (2) 3-1 (0) .....Fenerbahce
Monaco won 4-3 on agg
PAOK Salonika (1) 1-2 (1) .... Ajax
Ajax won 3-2 on agg
RB Salzburg .... (0) 2-0 (0) Partizan Tirana
RB Salzburg won 3-0 on agg
Steaua .... (1) 2-0 (0) . Sparta Prague
Steaua won 3-1 on agg
Young Boys ..... (0) 2-0 (0) .... Shakhtar
AET – 2-0 after 90, 2 agg. Young Boys 4-2 pens

Playoff round
Tuesday August 16, 2016

Ajax .... (1) 1-1 (1) .... Rostov
Din Zagreb ...... (0) 1-1 (1) .... RB Salzburg
FC Copenhagen (1) 1-0 (0). Apoel Nicosia
Steaua .... (0) 0-5 (2) .... Man City
Young Boys ..... (0) 1-3 (1) .... M'gladbach

Wednesday August 17, 2016

Celtic .... (3) 5-2 (0). H Be'er Sheva
Dundalk .... (0) 0-2 (0) . Legia Warsaw
Ludogorets ..... (0) 2-0 (0) ..Viktoria Plzen
Porto .... (0) 1-1 (1) .... Roma
Villarreal .... (1) 1-2 (1) .... Monaco

Second legs
Tuesday August 23, 2016

H Be'er Sheva . (1) 2-0 (0) .... Celtic
Celtic won 5-4 on agg
Legia Warsaw . (0) 1-1 (1) .... Dundalk
Legia Warsaw won 3-1 on agg
Monaco .... (0) 1-0 (0) .... Villarreal
Monaco won 3-1 on agg
Roma .... (0) 0-3 (1) .... Porto
Porto won 4-1 on agg
Viktoria Plzen.. (1) 2-2 (1) ..... Ludogorets
Ludogorets won 4-2 on agg

Wednesday August 24, 2016

Apoel Nicosia . (0) 1-1 (0) FC Copenhagen
FC Copenhagen won 2-1 on agg
Man City .... (0) 1-0 (0) .... Steaua
Man City won 6-0 on agg
M'gladbach ..... (3) 6-1 (0) .....Young Boys
M'gladbach won 9-2 on agg
Rostov .... (1) 4-1 (0) .... Ajax
Rostov won 5-2 on agg
RB Salzburg .... (1) 1-2 (1) ...... Din Zagreb
AET – 1-1 after 90, Din Zagreb 3-2 on agg

Group A

	P	W	D	L	F	A	GD	Pts
Arsenal	6	4	2	0	18	6	12	14
Paris St-G	6	3	3	0	13	7	6	12
Ludogorets	6	0	3	3	6	15	-9	3
Basel	6	0	2	4	3	12	-9	2

Tuesday September 13, 2016
Basel ....(0) 1-1 (1)..... Ludogorets
Paris St-G.........(1) 1-1 (0)............. Arsenal
Wednesday September 28, 2016
Arsenal ....(2) 2-0 (0)............... Basel
Ludogorets .....(1) 1-3 (1)........ Paris St-G
Wednesday October 19, 2016
Arsenal ....(1) 6-0 (0)..... Ludogorets
Paris St-G.........(1) 3-0 (0)............... Basel
Tuesday November 1, 2016
Basel ....(0) 1-2 (1)........ Paris St-G
Ludogorets .....(2) 2-3 (2)........... Arsenal
Wednesday November 23, 2016
Arsenal ....(1) 2-2 (1).........Paris St-G
Ludogorets .....(0) 0-0 (0)............... Basel
Tuesday December 6, 2016
Basel ....(0) 1-4 (2)........... Arsenal
Paris St-G........(0) 2-2 (1)..... Ludogorets

Group B

	P	W	D	L	F	A	GD	Pts
Napoli	6	3	2	1	11	8	3	11
Benfica	6	2	2	2	10	10	0	8
Besiktas	6	1	4	1	9	14	-5	7
Dynamo Kiev	6	1	2	3	8	6	2	5

Tuesday September 13, 2016
Benfica ....(1) 1-1 (0)........... Besiktas
Dynamo Kiev ..(1) 1-2 (2)............. Napoli
Wednesday September 28, 2016
Besiktas ....(1) 1-1 (0).. Dynamo Kiev
Napoli ....(1) 4-2 (0)........... Benfica
Wednesday October 19, 2016
Dynamo Kiev ..(0) 0-2 (1)........... Benfica
Napoli ....(1) 2-3 (1)......... Besiktas
Tuesday November 1, 2016
Benfica ....(1) 1-0 (0).. Dynamo Kiev
Besiktas ....(0) 1-1 (0)............. Napoli
Wednesday November 23, 2016
Besiktas ....(0) 3-3 (3)........... Benfica
Napoli ....(0) 0-0 (0).. Dynamo Kiev
Tuesday December 6, 2016
Benfica ....(0) 1-2 (0)............. Napoli
Dynamo Kiev ..(4) 6-0 (0).......... Besiktas

Group C

	P	W	D	L	F	A	GD	Pts
Barcelona	6	5	0	1	20	4	16	15
Man City	6	2	3	1	12	10	2	9
B M'gladbach	6	1	2	3	5	12	-7	5
Celtic	6	0	3	3	5	16	-11	3

Tuesday September 13, 2016
Barcelona ....(2) 7-0 (0)............. Celtic
Wednesday September 14, 2016
Man City.........(2) 4-0 (0).... M'gladbach
Wednesday September 28, 2016
Celtic ....(2) 3-3 (3)......... Man City
M'gladbach .....(1) 1-2 (0)....... Barcelona

Wednesday October 19, 2016
Barcelona ....(1) 4-0 (0)......... Man City
Celtic ....(0) 0-2 (0).... M'gladbach
Tuesday November 1, 2016
Man City ....(1) 3-1 (1)....... Barcelona
M'gladbach ....(1) 1-1 (1)............... Celtic
Wednesday November 23, 2016
Celtic ....(0) 0-2 (1)...... Barcelona
M'gladbach ....(1) 1-1 (1).........Man City
Tuesday December 6, 2016
Barcelona ....(1) 4-0 (0).... M'gladbach
Man City.........(1) 1-1 (1)............. Celtic

Group D

	P	W	D	L	F	A	GD	Pts
Atl Madrid	6	5	0	1	7	2	5	15
B Munich	6	4	0	2	14	6	8	12
Rostov	6	1	2	3	6	12	-6	5
PSV	6	0	2	4	4	11	-7	2

Tuesday September 13, 2016
B Munich ....(2) 5-0 (0)............. Rostov
PSV Eindhoven (0) 0-1 (1)...... Atl Madrid
Wednesday September 28, 2016
Atl Madrid ......(1) 1-0 (0)........ B Munich
Rostov ....(2) 2-2 (2)PSV Eindhoven
Wednesday October 19, 2016
B Munich ....(2) 4-1 (1)PSV Eindhoven
Rostov ....(0) 0-1 (0)...... Atl Madrid

Tuesday November 1, 2016
Atl Madrid ......(1) 2-1 (1)............ Rostov
PSV Eindhoven (1) 1-2 (1)........ B Munich
Wednesday November 23, 2016
Atl Madrid ......(0) 2-0 (0)PSV Eindhoven
Rostov ....(1) 3-2 (1)........ B Munich
Tuesday December 6, 2016
B Munich ....(1) 1-0 (0)...... Atl Madrid
PSV Eindhoven (0) 0-0 (0)............. Rostov

Group E

	P	W	D	L	F	A	GD	Pts
Monaco	6	3	2	1	9	7	2	11
Leverkusen	6	2	4	0	8	4	4	10
Tottenham	6	2	1	3	6	6	0	7
CSKA Moscow	6	0	3	3	5	11	-6	3

Wednesday September 14, 2016
B Leverkusen ..(2) 2-2 (2) CSKA Moscow
Tottenham ......(1) 1-2 (2)........... Monaco
Tuesday September 27, 2016
CSKA Moscow (0) 0-1 (0)...... Tottenham
Monaco ....(0) 1-1 (0).. B Leverkusen
Tuesday October 18, 2016
B Leverkusen ..(0) 0-0 (0)...... Tottenham
CSKA Moscow (1) 1-1 (1).......... Monaco
Wednesday November 2, 2016
Monaco ....(3) 3-0 (0) CSKA Moscow
Tottenham ......(0) 0-1 (0).. B Leverkusen

Clockwise from main: Man City found a way to keep Barca quiet at the Etihad; even Leicester were pretty surprised how well Leicester performed; Arsenal took another last-16 hammering; while Spurs failed to make any kind of impression

Tuesday November 22, 2016
CSKA Moscow (0) 1-1 (1).. B Leverkusen
Monaco .... (0) 2-1 (0) ...... Tottenham
Wednesday December 7, 2016
B Leverkusen .. (1) 3-0 (0) .... Monaco
Tottenham ...... (2) 3-1 (1) CSKA Moscow

Group F

	P	W	D	L	F	A	GD	Pts
Dortmund	6	4	2	0	21	9	12	14
Real Madrid	6	3	3	0	16	10	6	12
Legia Warsaw	6	1	1	4	9	24	-15	4
Sporting	6	1	0	5	5	8	-3	3

Wednesday September 14, 2016
Legia Warsaw . (0) 0-6 (3) .... B Dortmund
Real Madrid .... (0) 2-1 (0) .... Sporting
Tuesday September 27, 2016
B Dortmund .... (1) 2-2 (1) .... Real Madrid
Sporting .... (2) 2-0 (0) . Legia Warsaw
Tuesday October 18, 2016
Real Madrid .... (3) 5-1 (1) . Legia Warsaw
Sporting .... (0) 1-2 (2) .... B Dortmund
Wednesday November 2, 2016
B Dortmund .... (1) 1-0 (0) .... Sporting
Legia Warsaw . (1) 3-3 (2) .... Real Madrid
Tuesday November 22, 2016
B Dortmund .... (5) 8-4 (2) . Legia Warsaw
Sporting .... (0) 1-2 (1) .... Real Madrid

Wednesday December 7, 2016
Legia Warsaw . (1) 1-0 (0) .... Sporting
Real Madrid .... (1) 2-2 (0) .... B Dortmund

Group G

	P	W	D	L	F	A	GD	Pts
Leicester	6	4	1	1	7	6	1	13
Porto	6	3	2	1	9	3	6	11
Copenhagen	6	2	3	1	7	2	5	9
Club Brugge	6	0	0	6	2	14	-12	0

Wednesday September 14, 2016
Club Brugge.... (0) 0-3 (2) .... Leicester
Porto .... (1) 1-1 (0) FC Copenhagen
Tuesday September 27, 2016
FC Copenhagen (0) 4-0 (0) .... Club Brugge
Leicester .... (1) 1-0 (0) .... Porto
Tuesday October 18, 2016
Club Brugge.... (1) 1-2 (0) .... Porto
Leicester .... (1) 1-0 (0) FC Copenhagen
Wednesday November 2, 2016
FC Copenhagen (0) 0-0 (0) .... Leicester
Porto .... (1) 1-0 (0) .... Club Brugge
Tuesday November 22, 2016
FC Copenhagen (0) 0-0 (0) .... Porto
Leicester .... (2) 2-1 (0) .... Club Brugge
Wednesday December 7, 2016
Club Brugge.... (0) 0-2 (2) FC Copenhagen
Porto .... (3) 5-0 (0) .... Leicester

Group H

	P	W	D	L	F	A	GD	Pts
Juventus	6	4	2	0	11	2	9	14
Seville	6	3	2	1	7	3	4	11
Lyon	6	2	2	2	5	3	2	8
Din Zagreb	6	0	0	6	0	15	-15	0

Wednesday September 14, 2016
Juventus .... (0) 0-0 (0) .... Seville
Lyon .... (1) 3-0 (0) ...... Din Zagreb
Tuesday September 27, 2016
Din Zagreb...... (0) 0-4 (2) .... Juventus
Seville .... (0) 1-0 (0) .... Lyon
Tuesday October 18, 2016
Din Zagreb...... (0) 0-1 (1) .... Seville
Lyon .... (0) 0-1 (0) .... Juventus
Wednesday November 2, 2016
Juventus .... (1) 1-1 (0) .... Lyon
Seville .... (1) 4-0 (0) ...... Din Zagreb
Tuesday November 22, 2016
Din Zagreb...... (0) 0-1 (0) .... Lyon
Seville .... (1) 1-3 (1) .... Juventus
Wednesday December 7, 2016
Juventus .... (0) 2-0 (0) ...... Din Zagreb
Lyon .... (0) 0-0 (0) .... Seville

Real Madrid's Marcelo better hold on tight to that trophy...

Round of 16

First legs

Tuesday February 14, 2017

Benfica .... (0) 1-0 (0) .... B Dortmund
Paris St-G. .... (2) 4-0 (0) .... Barcelona

Wednesday February 15, 2017

B Munich .... (1) 5-1 (1) .... Arsenal
Real Madrid .... (1) 3-1 (1) .... Napoli

Tuesday February 21, 2017

B Leverkusen .. (0) 2-4 (2) ...... Atl Madrid
Man City .... (1) 5-3 (2) .... Monaco

Wednesday February 22, 2017

Porto .... (0) 0-2 (0) .... Juventus
Seville .... (1) 2-1 (0) .... Leicester

Second legs

Tuesday March 7, 2017

Arsenal .... (1) 1-5 (0) .... B Munich
  Bayern Munich won 10-2 on agg
Napoli .... (1) 1-3 (0) .... Real Madrid
  Real Madrid won 6-2 on agg

Wednesday March 8, 2017

B Dortmund .... (1) 4-0 (0) .... Benfica
  B Dortmund won 4-1 on agg
Barcelona .... (2) 6-1 (0) .... Paris St-G.
  Barcelona won 6-5 on agg

Tuesday March 14, 2017

Juventus .... (1) 1-0 (0) .... Porto
  Juventus won 3-0 on agg
Leicester .... (1) 2-0 (0) .... Seville
  Leicester won 3-2 on agg

Wednesday March 15, 2017

Atl Madrid ...... (0) 0-0 (0) .. B Leverkusen
  Atl won 4-2 on agg
Monaco .... (2) 3-1 (0) .... Man City
  6-6 on agg – Monaco won on away goals

Quarter-finals

Tuesday April 11, 2017

Juventus .... (2) 3-0 (0) .... Barcelona

Wednesday April 12, 2017

Atl Madrid ..... (1) 1-0 (0) .... Leicester
B Dortmund .... (0) 2-3 (0) .... Monaco
B Munich .... (1) 1-2 (0) .... Real Madrid

Second legs

Tuesday April 18, 2017

Leicester .... (0) 1-1 (1) ...... Atl Madrid
  Atl Madrid won 2-1 on agg
Real Madrid .... (0) 4-2 (2) .... B Munich
  AET. 1-2 after 90 mins. Real won 6-3 on agg

Wednesday April 19, 2017

Barcelona .... (0) 0-0 (0) .... Juventus
  Juventus won 3-0 on agg

Monaco .... (2) 3-1 (0) .... B Dortmund
  Monaco won 6-3 on agg

Semi-finals

Tuesday May 2, 2017

Real Madrid .... (1) 3-0 (0) ...... Atl Madrid

Wednesday May 3, 2017

Monaco .... (0) 0-2 (1) .... Juventus

Second legs

Tuesday May 9, 2017

Juventus .... (2) 2-1 (0) .... Monaco
  Juventus won 4-1 on agg

Wednesday May 3, 2017

Atl Madrid ...... (2) 2-1 (1) .... Real Madrid
  Real Madrid won 4-2 on agg

Champions League final

Saturday June 3, 2017

Juventus .... (1) 1-4 (1) .... Real Madrid
POS 44/56 SH ON 4/5 SH OFF 1/6 CRN 1/1
SCORERS **Juventus:** Mandzukic (27)
Real Madrid: Ronaldo (20, 64) Casemiro (61)
Asensio (90)
CARDS **Juventus:** Dybala ▌ Alex Sandro ▌
Pjanic ▌ Cuadrado ▌▌
Real Madrid: Ramos ▌ Carvajal ▌ Kroos ▌
Asensio ▌

QUICK BETS

BET ON THE ACTION AS IT HAPPENS

New 5 min interval markets available on televised matches.

betfair EXCHANGE

WORLD CUP 2018 QUALIFYING

Uefa – 13 qualifiers

Comprised of nine round-robin home-and-away six-team groups. Group winners qualify for World Cup finals while eight best-ranked runners-up playoff for final four Uefa slots.

EUROPE

Sunday September 4, 2016
Czech Rep ...... (0) 0-0 (0) .... N Ireland
Denmark .... (1) 1-0 (0) ....Armenia
Kazakhstan .... (0) 2-2 (2) .... Poland
Lithuania .... (2) 2-2 (0) ....Slovenia
Malta .... (1) 1-5 (1).......... Scotland
Norway .... (0) 0-3 (2) ....Germany
Romania .... (0) 1-1 (0) ... Montenegro
San Marino .... (0) 0-1 (1).....Azerbaijan
Slovakia .... (0) 0-1 (0) ....England

Monday September 5, 2016
Albania .... (1) 2-1 (0) ... Macedonia
Croatia .... (1) 1-1 (1)............Turkey
Finland............ (1) 1-1 (0) ....Kosovo
Georgia........... (0) 1-2 (2) ....Austria
Israel .... (1) 1-3 (0) ....Italy
Serbia.............. (0) 2-2 (1)............Ireland
Spain............... (1) 8-0 (0) ..Liechtenstein
Ukraine .... (1) 1-1 (1)...........Iceland
Wales .... (2) 4-0 (0) ....Moldova

Tuesday September 6, 2016
Andorra........... (0) 0-1 (0) .... Latvia
Belarus............ (0) 0-0 (0) ....France
Bosnia-Hz....... (2) 5-0 (0) ....Estonia
Bulgaria .... (1) 4-3 (0) ... Luxembourg
Cyprus............ (0) 0-3 (1)........ Belgium
Faroe Islands..(0) 0-0 (0) ....Hungary
Gibraltar......... (1) 1-4 (4) ....Greece
Sweden .... (1) 1-1 (0) ....Holland
Switzerland.... (2) 2-0 (0) .... Portugal

Thursday October 6, 2016
Austria .... (1) 2-2 (2) .... Wales
Iceland .... (1) 3-2 (2) .... Finland
Ireland .... (0) 1-0 (0) .... Georgia
Italy................ (0) 1-1 (0) .... Spain
Kosovo .... (0) 0-6 (3) ....Croatia
Liechtenstein . (0) 0-2 (1)...........Albania
Macedonia..... (0) 1-2 (2) .... Israel
Moldova.......... (0) 0-3 (2) .... Serbia
Turkey .... (1) 2-2 (2) ....Ukraine

Friday October 7, 2016
Belgium........... (2) 4-0 (0) ..... Bosnia-Hz
Estonia .... (0) 4-0 (0) ....Gibraltar
France .... (3) 4-1 (1)..........Bulgaria
Greece............. (2) 2-0 (0) ....Cyprus
Holland .... (2) 4-1 (0) ....Belarus
Hungary.......... (0) 2-3 (0) ... Switzerland
Latvia.............. (0) 0-2 (1)...Faroe Islands
Luxembourg.... (0) 0-1 (0) ....Sweden
Portugal.......... (3) 6-0 (0) .... Andorra

Saturday October 8, 2016
Armenia........... (0) 0-5 (4) .... Romania
Azerbaijan....... (1) 1-0 (0) ....Norway
England........... (2) 2-0 (0) ....Malta
Germany .... (1) 3-0 (0) .....Czech Rep
Montenegro.... (1) 5-0 (0) ...Kazakhstan
N Ireland .... (1) 4-0 (0) .....San Marino
Poland............. (2) 3-2 (0) ....Denmark
Scotland.......... (0) 1-1 (0) ......Lithuania
Slovenia .... (0) 1-0 (0) ....Slovakia

Sunday October 9, 2016
Albania .... (0) 0-2 (0) .... Spain
Finland............ (0) 0-1 (1)...........Croatia
Iceland .... (2) 2-0 (0) ....Turkey
Israel .... (2) 2-1 (0) ..Liechtenstein
Macedonia..... (2) 2-3 (1)..............Italy
Moldova.......... (1) 1-3 (1)...........Ireland
Serbia.............. (3) 3-2 (1)...........Austria
Ukraine .... (1) 3-0 (0) ....Kosovo
Wales .... (1) 1-1 (0) .... Georgia

Monday October 10, 2016
Andorra........... (0) 1-2 (1)..... Switzerland
Belarus............ (0) 1-1 (0) ... Luxembourg
Bosnia-Hz....... (0) 2-0 (0) ....Cyprus
Estonia .... (0) 0-2 (1)...........Greece
Faroe Islands.. (0) 0-6 (3) .... Portugal
Gibraltar......... (0) 0-6 (3) .... Belgium
Holland .... (0) 0-1 (1)............France
Latvia.............. (0) 0-2 (1)...........Hungary
Sweden .... (2) 3-0 (0) ....Bulgaria

Tuesday October 11, 2016
Kazakhstan .... (0) 0-0 (0) .... Romania
Czech Rep ...... (0) 0-0 (0) ...Azerbaijan
Germany .... (2) 2-0 (0) ..... N Ireland
Norway .... (1) 4-1 (0) .....San Marino
Denmark .... (0) 0-1 (1)... Montenegro
Poland............. (0) 2-1 (0) ....Armenia;
Lithuania........ (0) 2-0 (0) ....Malta
Slovakia .... (1) 3-0 (0) .... Scotland
Slovenia .... (0) 0-0 (0) ....England

Friday November 11, 2016
Armenia........... (0) 3-2 (2) ... Montenegro
France .... (0) 2-1 (0) ....Sweden
Czech Rep ...... (1) 2-1 (0) ....Norway
N Ireland .... (2) 4-0 (0) ...Azerbaijan
San Marino .... (0) 0-8 (3) ....Germany
Denmark .... (2) 4-1 (1)....Kazakhstan
Romania .... (0) 0-3 (1)...........Poland
England........... (1) 3-0 (0) .... Scotland
Malta .... (0) 0-1 (0) ....Slovenia
Slovakia .... (3) 4-0 (0) ......Lithuania

Saturday November 12, 2016
Austria .... (0) 0-1 (0) ....Ireland
Georgia........... (1) 1-1 (0) ....Moldova
Croatia .... (1) 2-0 (0) ....Iceland
Wales .... (1) 1-1 (0) .... Serbia
Albania .... (0) 0-3 (1).............. Israel
Liechtenstein . (0) 0-4 (4) .... Italy
Spain............... (1) 4-0 (0) ... Macedonia
Ukraine .... (1) 1-0 (0) ....Finland
Turkey .... (0) 2-0 (0) ....Kosovo

Group A	P	W	D	L	F	A	GD	Pts
Sweden	6	4	1	1	12	4	8	13
France	6	4	1	1	11	5	6	13
Holland	6	3	1	2	13	6	7	10
Bulgaria	6	3	0	3	9	12	-3	9
Belarus	6	1	2	3	4	11	-7	5
Luxembourg	6	0	1	5	6	17	-11	1

Group B	P	W	D	L	F	A	GD	Pts
Switzerland	6	6	0	0	12	3	9	18
Portugal	6	5	0	1	22	3	19	15
Hungary	6	2	1	3	8	7	1	7
Faroe Islands	6	1	2	3	2	10	-8	5
Andorra	6	1	1	4	2	13	-11	4
Latvia	6	1	0	5	2	12	-10	3

Group C	P	W	D	L	F	A	GD	Pts
Germany	6	6	0	0	27	1	26	18
N Ireland	6	4	1	1	11	2	9	13
Czech Rep	6	2	3	1	9	5	4	9
Azerbaijan	6	2	1	3	3	9	-6	7
Norway	6	1	1	4	6	10	-4	4
San Marino	6	0	0	6	1	30	-29	0

Group D	P	W	D	L	F	A	GD	Pts
Serbia	6	3	3	0	13	7	6	12
Ireland	6	3	3	0	8	4	4	12
Wales	6	1	5	0	9	5	4	8
Austria	6	2	2	2	9	8	1	8
Georgia	6	0	3	3	6	10	-4	3
Moldova	6	0	2	4	4	15	-11	2

Group E	P	W	D	L	F	A	GD	Pts
Poland	6	5	1	0	15	7	8	16
Montenegro	6	3	1	2	14	7	7	10
Denmark	6	3	1	2	10	6	4	10
Romania	6	1	3	2	7	7	0	6
Armenia	6	2	0	4	7	14	-7	6
Kazakhstan	6	0	2	4	4	16	-12	2

Group F	P	W	D	L	F	A	GD	Pts
England	6	4	2	0	10	2	8	14
Slovakia	6	4	0	2	12	4	8	12
Slovenia	6	3	2	1	6	3	3	11
Scotland	6	2	2	2	9	10	-1	8
Lithuania	6	1	2	3	6	11	-5	5
Malta	6	0	0	6	2	15	-13	0

Group G	P	W	D	L	F	A	GD	Pts
Spain	6	5	1	0	21	3	18	16
Italy	6	5	1	0	18	4	14	16
Albania	6	3	0	3	7	8	-1	9
Israel	6	3	0	3	9	12	-3	9
Macedonia	6	1	0	5	8	13	-5	3
Liechtenstein	6	0	0	6	1	24	-23	0

Group H	P	W	D	L	F	A	GD	Pts
Belgium	6	5	1	0	24	2	22	16
Greece	6	3	3	0	10	3	7	12
Bosnia-Hz	6	3	2	1	13	5	8	11
Cyprus	6	2	1	3	5	9	-4	7
Estonia	6	1	1	4	5	17	-12	4
Gibraltar	6	0	0	6	3	24	-21	0

Group I	P	W	D	L	F	A	GD	Pts
Croatia	6	4	1	1	11	2	9	13
Iceland	6	4	1	1	9	6	3	13
Turkey	6	3	2	1	11	6	5	11
Ukraine	6	3	2	1	9	4	5	11
Finland	6	0	1	5	4	10	-6	1
Kosovo	6	0	1	5	3	18	-15	1

Sunday November 13, 2016
Bulgaria .... (1) 1-0 (0) .... Belarus
Luxembourg... (1) 1-3 (1)............Holland
Hungary......... (2) 4-0 (0) ....Andorra
Portugal........ (1) 4-1 (0) .... Latvia
Switzerland.... (1) 2-0 (0) .. Faroe Islands
Belgium.......... (3) 8-1 (1)........... Estonia
Greece............ (0) 1-1 (1)...... Bosnia-Hz
Cyprus............ (1) 3-1 (0) .... Gibraltar

Friday March 24, 2017
Austria .... (0) 2-0 (0) .... Moldova
Croatia .... (1) 1-0 (0) ....Ukraine
Georgia .... (1) 1-3 (1)............ Serbia
Ireland .... (0) 0-0 (0) .... Wales
Italy................ (1) 2-0 (0) ....Albania
Kosovo............ (0) 1-2 (2) ....Iceland
Liechtenstein . (0) 0-3 (1)...... Macedonia
Spain............... (2) 4-1 (0) .... Israel
Turkey............. (2) 2-0 (0) .... Finland

Saturday March 25, 2017
Andorra.......... (0) 0-0 (0) .. Faroe Islands
Belgium.......... (0) 1-1 (0) .... Greece
Bosnia-Hz....... (2) 5-0 (0) ....Gibraltar
Bulgaria .... (2) 2-0 (0) ....Holland
Cyprus............ (0) 0-0 (0) .... Estonia
Luxembourg.... (1) 1-3 (2) ....France
Portugal........ (2) 3-0 (0) ....Hungary
Sweden.......... (1) 4-0 (0) .... Belarus
Switzerland.... (0) 1-0 (0) .... Latvia

Sunday March 26, 2017
Armenia .... (0) 2-0 (0) .....Kazakhstan
Azerbaijan....... (1) 1-4 (3) ....Germany
England............ (1) 2-0 (0) .... Lithuania
Malta .... (1) 1-3 (2) ....Slovakia
Montenegro.... (0) 1-2 (1)............ Poland
N Ireland......... (2) 2-0 (0) ....Norway
Romania.......... (0) 0-0 (0) ....Denmark
San Marino ..... (0) 0-6 (5) ....Czech Rep
Scotland.......... (1) 1-0 (0) ....Slovenia

Friday June 9, 2017
Andorra.......... (1) 1-0 (0) ....Hungary
Belarus............ (1) 2-1 (0) ....Bulgaria
Bosnia-Hz....... (0) 0-0 (0) .... Greece
Estonia............ (0) 0-2 (1)........... Belgium
Faroe Islands.. (0) 0-2 (1)..... Switzerland
Gibraltar.......... (1) 1-2 (1)........... Cyprus
Holland .... (2) 5-0 (0) .. Luxembourg
Latvia............... (0) 0-3 (1) .... Portugal
Sweden............ (1) 2-1 (1)...........France

Saturday June 10, 2017
Azerbaijan...... (0) 0-1 (0) ... N Ireland
Germany......... (4) 7-0 (0) ...San Marino
Kazakhstan..... (0) 1-3 (1)........Denmark
Lithuania........ (0) 1-2 (1)..........Slovakia
Montenegro.... (2) 4-1 (0) ....Armenia
Norway............ (0) 1-1 (1).......Czech Rep
Poland............ (1) 3-1 (0) .... Romania
Scotland......... (2) 2-2 (0) ....England
Slovenia.......... (1) 2-0 (0) ....Malta

Sunday June 11, 2017
Finland............ (0) 1-2 (0) ....Ukraine
Iceland............ (0) 1-0 (0) ....Croatia
Ireland .... (0) 1-1 (1)...........Austria
Israel................ (0) 0-3 (2) ....Albania
Italy................. (1) 5-0 (0) ..Liechtenstein
Kosovo............ (1) 1-4 (2)...........Turkey
Macedonia..... (0) 1-2 (2) .... Spain
Moldova......... (2) 2-2 (0) ....Georgia
Serbia.............. (0) 1-1 (1)............. Wales

Remaining Uefa fixtures
Thursday August 31, 2017
Bulgaria v Sweden; France v Holland;
Luxembourg v Belarus; Hungary v
Latvia; Portugal v Faroe Islands; Swit-
zerland v Andorra; Cyprus v Bosnia-Hz;
Greece v Estonia; Belgium v Gibraltar

Friday September 1, 2017
Kazakhstan v Montenegro; Czech Rep
v Germany; Norway v Azerbaijan;
San Marino v N Ireland; Denmark v
Poland; Romania v Armenia; Lithuania
v Scotland; Malta v England; Slovakia
v Slovenia

Saturday September 2, 2017
Georgia v Ireland; Serbia v Moldova;
Albania v Liechtenstein;
Finland v Iceland; Wales v Austria;
Israel v Macedonia; Spain v Italy;
Ukraine v Turkey; Croatia v Kosovo

Sunday September 3, 2017
Belarus v Sweden; Holland v Bulgaria;
Faroe Islands v Andorra; Estonia v Cy-
prus; France v Luxembourg; Hungary v
Portugal; Latvia v Switzerland; Greece v
Belgium; Gibraltar v Bosnia-Hz

Monday September 4, 2017
Azerbaijan v San Marino; Armenia
v Denmark; Germany v Norway; N
Ireland v Czech Rep; Montenegro v
Romania; Poland v Kazakhstan; England
v Slovakia; Scotland v Malta; Slovenia
v Lithuania

Tuesday September 5, 2017
Austria v Georgia; Moldova v Wales;
Ireland v Serbia; Macedonia v Albania;
Italy v Israel; Liechtenstein v Spain;
Iceland v Ukraine; Turkey v Croatia;
Kosovo v Finland

Thursday October 5, 2017
Azerbaijan v Czech Rep; Armenia v Poland; N Ireland v Germany; San Marino
v Norway; Montenegro v Denmark;
Romania v Kazakhstan; England v
Slovenia; Malta v Lithuania; Scotland
v Slovakia

Friday October 6, 2017
Georgia v Wales; Austria v Serbia;
Ireland v Moldova; Italy v Macedonia;
Liechtenstein v Israel; Spain v Albania;
Croatia v Finland; Turkey v Iceland;
Kosovo v Ukraine

Saturday October 7, 2017
Sweden v Luxembourg; Faroe Islands v
Latvia; Bosnia-Hz v Belgium; Gibraltar v
Holland; Bulgaria v France; Andorra v
Portugal; Switzerland v Hungary;
Cyprus v Greece; Gibraltar v Estonia

Sunday October 8, 2017
Denmark v Romania; Kazakhstan v Armenia; Poland v Montenegro; Lithuania
v England; Slovakia v Malta; Slovenia v
Scotland; Czech Rep v San Marino; Germany v Azerbaijan; Norway v N Ireland

Monday October 9, 2017
Moldova v Austria; Serbia v Georgia;
Wales v Ireland; Albania v Italy; Mac-
edonia v Liechtenstein; Israel v Spain;
Finland v Turkey; Ukraine v Croatia;
Iceland v Kosovo

Tuesday October 10, 2017
France v Belarus; Luxembourg v Bulgar-
ia; Holland v Sweden; Hungary v Faroe
Islands; Latvia v Andorra; Portugal v
Switzerland; Belgium v Cyprus; Estonia
v Bosnia-Hz; Greece v Gibraltar

Uefa playoff round
First legs to be played November 9-11
with second legs on November 12-14

OFC qualifying – 0.5 teams
Round Three was home-and-away
round-robin format, with group
winners New Zealand and Solomon
Islands contesting playoff to determine
Oceania winner. Winner goes into
interconfederation playoff against fifth-
placed Conmebol representative, with
winner qualifying for World Cup finals.
Home and away interconfederation ties
to be played on November 6-14.

OCEANIA (ROUND THREE)

Group A

	P	W	D	L	F	A	GD	Pts
New Zealand	4	3	1	0	6	0	6	10
New Caledonia	4	1	2	1	4	5	-1	5
Fiji	4	0	1	3	2	8	-5	0

Group B

	P	W	D	L	F	A	GD	Pts
Solomon Isls	4	3	0	1	6	6	0	9
Tahiti	4	2	0	2	7	4	3	6
Pap New Guin	4	1	0	3	6	9	-3	3

Tuesday November 8, 2016
Tahiti.............. (0) 3-0 (0) .... Solomon I

Saturday November 12-15, 2016
New Zealand.. (1) 2-0 (0)New Caledonia
Solomon I....... (0) 1-0 (0) .... Tahiti
New Caledonia(0) 0-0 (0) .. New Zealand

Friday March 24, 2017
Fiji .... (0) 0-2 (0) .. New Zealand
P New Guinea (1) 1-3 (0) .... Tahiti

Tuesday March 28, 2017
New Zealand.. (1) 2-0 (0) ....Fiji
Tahiti............... (0) 1-2 (0) P New Guinea

Tuesday June 6-8, 2017
Fiji .... (0) 2-2 (0)New Caledonia
Soloman I....... (0) 3-2 (0) P New Guinea

Saturday June 10-12, 2017
New Caledonia(0) 2-1 (0) ....Fiji
P New Guinea (1) 1-2 (2) .... Solomon I

OFC playoff final
Friday September 1, 2017
New Zealand.... v Solomon Islands
Tuesday September 5, 2017
Solomon Islands v ..... New Zealand

Conmebol – 4.5 qualifiers

Straight ten-team home-and-away round-robin league comprised of all ten Conmebol representative. Top four South American sides qualify for World Cup finals. Fifth-place finisher qualifies for inter-confederation playoff against OFC winner, with home and away ties to be played on November 6-14.

Group A

	P	W	D	L	F	A	GD	Pts
Brazil	14	10	3	1	35	10	25	33
Colombia	14	7	3	4	18	15	3	24
Uruguay	14	7	2	5	26	17	9	23
Chile	14	7	2	5	24	19	5	23
Argentina	14	6	4	4	15	14	1	22
Ecuador	14	6	2	6	23	20	3	20
Peru	14	5	3	6	22	23	-1	18
Paraguay	14	5	3	6	13	21	-8	18
Bolivia	14	3	1	10	12	32	-20	10
Venezuela	14	1	3	10	17	34	-17	6

Thursday October 8, 2015
Argentina...... (0) 0-2 (0) .... Ecuador
Bolivia............ (0) 0-2 (1).........Uruguay
Chile............... (0) 2-0 (0) .... Brazil
Colombia .... (1) 2-0 (0) .... Peru
Venezuela ...... (0) 0-1 (0) .... Paraguay
Tuesday October 13, 2015
Brazil............. (2) 3-1 (0) ......Venezuela
Ecuador.......... (0) 2-0 (0) .... Bolivia
Paraguay......... (0) 0-0 (0) ...... Argentina
Peru .... (2) 3-4 (3) .... Chile
Uruguay .... (1) 3-0 (0) ....Colombia
Thursday November 12-13, 2015
Argentina...... (1) 1-1 (0) .... Brazil
Bolivia............ (3) 4-2 (1).......Venezuela
Chile............... (1) 1-1 (0) ....Colombia
Ecuador.......... (2) 2-1 (0) ....Uruguay
Peru .... (1) 1-0 (0) ...... Paraguay
Tuesday November 17-18, 2015
Brazil............. (1) 3-0 (0) .... Peru
Colombia .... (0) 0-1 (1)...... Argentina
Paraguay......... (0) 2-1 (0) .... Bolivia
Uruguay .... (1) 3-0 (0) .... Chile
Venezuela ...... (0) 1-3 (2) .... Ecuador
Thursday March 24-25, 2016
Bolivia............ (0) 2-3 (2) ......Colombia
Brazil............. (2) 2-2 (1)........Uruguay
Chile............... (1) 1-2 (2) ... Argentina
Ecuador.......... (1) 2-2 (1).......Paraguay
Peru .... (0) 2-2 (1).......Venezuela
Tuesday March 29, 2016
Argentina...... (2) 2-0 (0) .... Bolivia
Colombia .... (1) 3-1 (0) .... Ecuador
Paraguay......... (1) 2-2 (0) .... Brazil
Uruguay .... (0) 1-0 (0) .... Peru
Venezuela ...... (1) 1-4 (1)............... Chile
Thursday September 1, 2016
Argentina....... (1) 1-0 (0) ....Uruguay
Bolivia............ (1) 2-0 (0) .... Peru

Colombia .... (1) 2-0 (0) ......Venezuela
Ecuador........... (0) 0-3 (0) .... Brazil
Paraguay........ (2) 2-1 (1)............... Chile
Tuesday September 6, 2016
Brazil............. (1) 2-1 (1)........Colombia
Chile............... (0) 0-0 (0) .... Bolivia
Peru .... (1) 2-1 (1)......... Ecuador
Uruguay .... (3) 4-0 (0) ...... Paraguay
Venezuela ...... (1) 2-2 (0) ...... Argentina
Thursday October 6, 2016
Brazil............. (4) 5-0 (0) .... Bolivia
Ecuador.......... (2) 3-0 (0) .... Chile
Paraguay........ (0) 0-1 (0) ......Colombia
Peru .... (0) 2-2 (1)...... Argentina
Uruguay .... (1) 3-0 (0) ......Venezuela
Tuesday October 11, 2016
Argentina....... (0) 0-1 (1)......... Paraguay
Bolivia............ (2) 2-2 (0) .... Ecuador
Chile............... (1) 2-1 (0) .... Peru
Colombia .... (1) 2-2 (1).......Uruguay
Venezuela ...... (0) 0-2 (1)............. Brazil
Thursday November 10, 2016
Brazil............. (2) 3-0 (0) ...... Argentina
Colombia .... (0) 0-0 (0) .... Chile
Paraguay........ (1) 1-4 (0) .... Peru
Uruguay .... (2) 2-1 (1)......... Ecuador
Venezuela ...... (2) 5-0 (0) .... Bolivia
Tuesday November 15, 2016
Argentina....... (2) 3-0 (0) ......Colombia
Bolivia............ (0) 1-0 (0) ...... Paraguay
Chile............... (1) 3-1 (1).......Uruguay
Ecuador.......... (0) 3-0 (0) ......Venezuela
Peru .... (0) 0-2 (0) .... Brazil
Thursday March 23, 2017
Argentina....... (1) 1-0 (0) .... Chile
Colombia .... (1) 1-0 (0) .... Bolivia
Paraguay........ (1) 2-1 (0) .... Ecuador
Uruguay .... (1) 1-4 (1)............. Brazil
Venezuela ...... (2) 2-2 (0) .... Peru
Tuesday March 28, 2017
Bolivia............ (1) 2-0 (0) ...... Argentina
Brazil............. (1) 3-0 (0) ...... Paraguay
Chile............... (3) 3-1 (0) ......Venezuela
Ecuador.......... (0) 0-2 (2) ......Colombia
Peru .... (1) 2-1 (1).......Uruguay

Remaining Conmebol fixtures
Wednesday August 30, 2017
Chile v Paraguay; Brazil v Ecuador;
Venezuela v Colombia; Peru v Bolivia;
Uruguay v Argentina
Monday September 4, 2017
Colombia v Brazil; Paraguay v Uruguay;
Argentina v Venezuela; Ecuador v Peru;
Bolivia v Chile
Wednesday October 4, 2017
Colombia v Paraguay; Chile v Ecuador;
Argentina v Peru; Venezuela v Uruguay;
Bolivia v Brazil
Monday October 9, 2017
Paraguay v Venezuela; Brazil v Chile;
Ecuador v Argentina; Peru v Colombia;
Uruguay v Bolivia

Concacaf qualifying – 3.5 teams

Round five comprised of the top six teams from qualifying rounds one to four, making up a six-team home-and-away round-robin league. The top three Concacaf teams from round five qualify automatically for the World Cup finals. Fourth-place team goes into interconfederation playoff against the fifth-place AFC representative, with home and away ties to be played on November 6-14.

Round Five

	P	W	D	L	F	A	GD	Pts
Mexico	6	4	2	0	9	2	+7	14
Costa Rica	6	3	2	1	9	4	+5	11
USA	6	2	2	2	11	8	+3	8
Panama	6	1	4	1	4	4	0	7
Honduras	6	1	2	3	6	14	-8	5
Trinidad & T	6	1	0	5	3	10	-7	3

Friday November 11, 2016
Honduras .... (0) 0-1 (1)........... Panama
Trinidad & T ... (0) 0-2 (0) ...... Costa Rica
USA .... (0) 1-2 (1)............Mexico
Monday November 14, 2016
Costa Rica...... (1) 4-0 (0) ....USA
Honduras .... (2) 3-1 (0) ...Trinidad & T
Panama........... (0) 0-0 (0) ....Mexico
Thursday March 23, 2017
Mexico .... (2) 2-0 (0) ...... Costa Rica
Trinidad & T ... (1) 1-0 (0) .... Panama
USA .... (3) 6-0 (0) ....Honduras
Tuesday March 28, 2017
Panama........... (1) 1-1 (1)...............USA
Trinidad & T ... (0) 0-1 (0) ....Mexico
Honduras .... (1) 1-1 (0) ...... Costa Rica
Thursday June 8, 2017
Costa Rica...... (0) 0-0 (0) .... Panama
Mexico .... (1) 3-0 (0) ....Honduras
USA .... (2) 2-0 (0) .... Trinidad
Sunday June 11, 2017
Mexico .... (1) 1-1 (1)...............USA
Tuesday June 13, 2017
Costa Rica...... (2) 2-1 (1).......Trinidad & T
Panama........... (1) 2-2 (1).......Honduras

Remaining Concacaf fixtures
Thursday August 31, 2017
USA v Costa Rica; Mexico v Panama;
Trinidad & T v Honduras
Monday September 4, 2017
Honduras v USA; Costa Rica
v Mexico; Panama v Trinidad & T
Thursday October 5, 2017
Costa Rica v Honduras; USA v
Panama; Mexico v Trinidad & T
Monday October 9, 2017
Trinidad & T v USA; Honduras
v Mexico; Panama v Costa Rica

CAF qualifying – 5 teams

The 20 round two qualifiers are split into five four-team home-and-away round-robin groups. Five group winners qualify for the World Cup finals.

AFRICA (ROUND THREE)

Group A

	P	W	D	L	F	A	GD	Pts
Congo DR	2	2	0	0	6	1	5	6
Tunisia	2	2	0	0	3	0	3	6
Guinea	2	0	0	2	1	4	-3	0
Libya	2	0	0	2	0	5	-5	0

Group B

	P	W	D	L	F	A	GD	Pts
Nigeria	2	2	0	0	5	2	3	6
Cameroon	2	0	2	0	2	2	0	2
Zambia	2	0	1	1	2	3	-1	1
Algeria	2	0	1	1	2	4	-2	1

Group C

	P	W	D	L	F	A	GD	Pts
Ivory Coast	2	1	1	0	3	1	2	4
Gabon	2	0	2	0	0	0	0	2
Morocco	2	0	2	0	0	0	0	2
Mali	2	0	1	1	1	3	-2	1

Group D

	P	W	D	L	F	A	GD	Pts
Burkina Faso	2	1	1	0	3	1	2	4
South Africa	2	1	1	0	3	2	1	4
Senegal	2	1	0	1	3	2	1	3
Cape Verde	2	0	0	2	0	4	-4	0

Group E

	P	W	D	L	F	A	GD	Pts
Egypt	2	2	0	0	4	1	3	6
Uganda	2	1	1	0	1	0	1	4
Ghana	2	0	1	1	0	2	-2	1
Congo	2	0	0	2	1	3	-2	0

Friday October 7, 2016
Ghana .... (0) 0-0 (0) ....Uganda
Saturday October 8, 2016
Burkina Faso .. (0) 1-1 (1) ... South Africa
DR Congo...... (2) 4-0 (0) ....Libya
Gabon............. (0) 0-0 (0) ....Morocco
Ivory Coast..... (3) 3-1 (1) ....Mali
Senegal .... (1) 2-0 (0) .....Cape Verde
Sunday October 9, 2016
Algeria............. (1) 1-1 (1)........Cameroon
Congo .... (1) 1-2 (1)...............Egypt
Tunisia............. (2) 2-0 (0) ....Guinea
Zambia............. (0) 1-2 (2) ....Nigeria
Friday November 11, 2016
Libya .... (0) 0-1 (0) ....Tunisia
Saturday November 12, 2016
Cameroon ...... (1) 1-1 (1)...........Zambia
Cape Verde .... (0) 0-2 (2) ...Burkina Faso
Nigeria .... (2) 3-1 (0) ....Algeria
Mali................. (0) 0-0 (0) ....Gabon
Morocco.......... (0) 0-0 (0) .....Ivory Coast
South Africa ... (2) 2-1 (0) .... Senegal
Uganda .... (1) 1-0 (0) ....Congo
Sunday November 13, 2016
Egypt.............. (1) 2-0 (0) ....Ghana
Guinea .... (1) 1-2 (0) ... DR Congo

Remaining CAF fixtures

Sunday August 27, 2017
Tunisia v DR Congo; Guinea v Libya;
Nigeria v Cameroon; Zambia v Algeria;
Gabon v Ivory Coast; Morocco v Mali;
Senegal v Burkina Faso; Cape Verde v
South Africa; Ghana v Congo;
Uganda v Egypt

Friday September 1, 2017
DR Congo v Tunisia; Libya v Guinea;
Algeria v Zambia; Cameroon v Nigeria;
Ivory Coast v Gabon; Mali v Morocco;
Burkina Faso v Senegal; South Africa v
Cape Verde; Egypt v Uganda;
Congo v Ghana

Sunday October 1, 2017
Guinea v Tunisia; Libya v DR Congo;
Nigeria v Zambia; Cameroon v Algeria;
Mali v Ivory Coast; Morocco v Gabon;
South Africa v Burkina Faso;
Cape Verde v Senegal; Egypt v Congo;
Uganda v Ghana

Sunday November 5, 2017
DR Congo v Guinea; Tunisia v Libya;
Zambia v Cameroon; Algeria v Nigeria;
Ivory Coast v Morocco; Gabon v Mali;
Senegal v South Africa; Burkina Faso v
Cape Verde; Congo v Uganda;
Ghana v Egypt

AFC qualifying – 4.5 teams

Round Three splits 12 qualifiers into two six-team round-robin home-and-away groups. Top two in each group qualify for the World Cup finals. The two third-place teams playoff against each other in in Round Four, with the winner qualifying for an intercontinental playoff against Concacaf's fourth-place finisher.

ASIA (ROUND THREE)

Group A

	P	W	D	L	F	A	GD	Pts
Iran	8	6	2	0	8	0	+8	20
South Korea	8	4	1	3	11	10	+1	13
Uzbekistan	8	4	0	4	6	6	0	12
Syria	8	2	3	3	4	5	-1	9
Qatar	8	2	1	5	6	10	-4	7
China PR	8	1	3	4	5	9	-4	6

Group B

	P	W	D	L	F	A	GD	Pts
Japan	8	5	2	1	15	6	+9	17
Saudi Arabia	8	5	1	2	15	8	7	16
Australia	8	4	4	0	14	8	6	16
UAE	8	3	1	4	8	11	-3	10
Iraq	8	1	2	5	8	11	-3	5
Thailand	8	0	2	6	4	20	-16	2

Thursday September 1, 2016
Australia .... (0) 2-0 (0) ....Iraq
Iran .... (0) 2-0 (0) ....Qatar
Japan .... (1) 1-2 (1)................. UAE
Saudi Arabia .. (0) 1-0 (0) .... Thailand
South Korea ... (1) 3-2 (0) ....China
Uzbekistan ..... (0) 1-0 (0) .... Syria

Tuesday September 6, 2016
China.............. (0) 0-0 (0) ....Iran
Iraq .... (1) 1-2 (0) ...Saudi Arabia
Qatar.............. (0) 0-1 (0) ..... Uzbekistan
Syria .... (0) 0-0 (0) ....South Korea
Thailand......... (0) 0-2 (1)..............Japan
UAE .... (0) 0-1 (0) ....Australia

Thursday October 6, 2016
China.............. (0) 0-1 (0) .... Syria
Japan .... (1) 2-1 (0) ....Iraq
Saudi Arabia .. (1) 2-2 (1).........Australia
South Korea ... (1) 3-2 (2) ....Qatar
UAE .... (1) 3-1 (0) .... Thailand
Uzbekistan ..... (0) 0-1 (1) ....Iran

Tuesday October 11, 2016
Australia .... (0) 1-1 (1)..............Japan
Iran .... (1) 1-0 (0) ....South Korea
Iraq .... (2) 4-0 (0) .... Thailand
Qatar.............. (1) 1-0 (0) .... Syria
Saudi Arabia .. (0) 3-0 (0) .... UAE
Uzbekistan ..... (0) 2-0 (0) ....China

Tuesday November 15, 2016
China.............. (0) 0-0 (0) ....Qatar
Japan .... (1) 2-1 (0) ...Saudi Arabia
South Korea ... (0) 2-1 (1)...... Uzbekistan
Syria .... (0) 0-0 (0) ....Iran
Thailand......... (1) 2-2 (1).........Australia
UAE .... (1) 2-0 (0) ....Iraq

Thursday March 23, 2017
China.............. (1) 1-0 (0) ....South Korea
Iraq .... (0) 1-1 (1) ....Australia
Qatar.............. (0) 0-1 (0) ....Iran
Syria .... (1) 1-0 (0) ..... Uzbekistan
Thailand......... (0) 0-3 (1)...Saudi Arabia
UAE .... (0) 2-0 (0) ....Japan

Tuesday March 28, 2017
Australia .... (1) 2-0 (0) .... UAE
Iran .... (0) 1-0 (0) ....China
Japan .... (2) 4-0 (0) .... Thailand
Saudi Arabia .. (0) 1-0 (0) ....Iraq
South Korea ... (1) 1-0 (0) .... Syria
Uzbekistan ..... (0) 1-0 (0) ....Qatar

Wednesday June 7, 2017
Australia .... (2) 3-2 (2) ...Saudi Arabia

Monday June 12, 2017
Iran .... (1) 2-0 (0) ..... Uzbekistan

Tuesday June 13, 2017
Iraq .... (0) 1-1 (1)..............Japan
Qatar.............. (1) 3-2 (2) ...South Korea
Syria .... (1) 2-2 (0) ....China
Thailand......... (0) 1-1 (0) .... UAE

Remaining AFC fixtures

Wednesday August 30, 2017
Syria v Qatar; China v Uzbekistan;
South Korea v Iran; Thailand v Iraq;
UAE v Saudi Arabia; Japan v Australia

Monday September 4, 2017
Qatar v China; Iran v Syria; Uzbekistan
v South Korea; Iraq v UAE; Australia v
Thailand; Saudi Arabia v Japan

AFC playoff round

Asia's third-place teams playoff home and away on October 5 and 10

To the right of each fixture are results for the corresponding league match in each of the last six seasons. The most recent result – 2016-17 – is on the right. The results cover matches in the Premier League, Championship, League One, League Two, National League, Scottish Premiership, Scottish Championship, Scottish League One and Scottish League Two.

Where Scottish clubs have met more than once at the same venue in the same season, results are separated by an oblique stroke with the most recent to the right. The Scottish Premiership will split into top- and bottom-six sections later in the season. These fixtures cover the period until the split.

Please note that TV coverage and postponements will cause alterations to the fixture list.

	2011-12	2012-13	2013-14	2014-15	2015-16	2016-17
Friday August 4, 2017						
Championship						
Sunderland v Derby	-	-	-	-	-	-
Saturday August 5, 2017						
Championship						
Aston Villa v Hull	-	-	3-1	2-1	-	-
Bristol City v Barnsley	2-0	5-3	-	2-2	-	3-2
Burton v Cardiff	-	-	-	-	-	2-0
Fulham v Norwich	2-1	5-0	1-0	1-0	-	2-2
Ipswich v Birmingham	1-1	3-1	1-0	4-2	1-1	1-1
Nottm Forest v Millwall	3-1	1-4	1-2	0-1	-	-
Preston v Sheffield Wed	0-2	-	-	-	1-0	1-1
QPR v Reading	-	1-1	1-3	-	1-1	1-1
Sheffield United v Brentford	2-0	2-2	0-0	-	-	-
Wolves v Middlesbrough	-	3-2	-	2-0	1-3	-
League One						
Bradford v Blackpool	-	-	-	-	1-0	-
Bury v Walsall	2-1	1-1	-	-	2-3	3-3
Charlton v Bristol Rovers	-	-	-	-	-	4-1
Doncaster v Gillingham	-	-	-	1-2	2-2	-
Fleetwood Town v Rotherham	-	1-1	-	-	-	-
MK Dons v Wigan	-	-	-	-	-	-
Oldham v Oxford	-	-	-	-	-	2-1
Peterborough v Plymouth	-	-	-	-	-	-
Portsmouth v Rochdale	-	-	3-0	-	-	-
Scunthorpe v AFC Wimbledon	-	-	0-0	-	-	1-2
Shrewsbury v Northampton	1-1	-	-	1-2	-	2-4
Southend v Blackburn	-	-	-	-	-	-
League Two						
Accrington v Colchester	-	-	-	-	-	2-1
Carlisle v Swindon	-	2-2	1-0	-	-	-
Chesterfield v Grimsby	-	-	-	-	-	-
Coventry v Notts County	-	1-2	3-0	0-1	-	-
Crawley Town v Port Vale	3-2	-	0-3	1-2	-	-
Crewe v Mansfield	-	-	-	-	-	1-1
Exeter v Cambridge U	-	-	-	2-2	1-0	1-2
Forest Green v Barnet	-	-	1-2	1-2	-	-
Luton v Yeovil	-	-	-	-	1-1	1-1
Morecambe v Cheltenham	3-1	0-0	0-1	0-0	-	1-2
Stevenage v Newport County	-	-	-	2-1	2-1	3-1
Wycombe v Lincoln	-	-	-	-	-	-
National League						
Bromley v Eastleigh	-	-	1-2	-	2-2	0-5
Dag & Red v Barrow	-	-	-	-	-	1-4
FC Halifax v Aldershot	-	-	-	-	-	-
Fylde v Boreham Wood	-	-	-	-	-	-

Results cover matches from Premier League to National League and Scottish Premiership to Scottish League Two

	2011-12	2012-13	2013-14	2014-15	2015-16	2016-17
Guiseley v Ebbsfleet	-	-	-	-	-	-
Hartlepool v Dover	-	-	-	-	-	-
Maidstone v Maidenhead	-	-	-	-	1-2	-
Solihull Moors v Chester	-	-	-	-	-	3-2
Sutton United v Leyton Orient	-	-	-	-	-	-
Torquay v Tranmere	-	-	-	-	0-1	0-0
Woking v Gateshead	-	2-1	1-2	3-0	1-1	3-0
Wrexham v Macclesfield	-	0-0	1-0	2-2	2-3	0-3
Scottish Premiership						
Aberdeen v Hamilton	-	-	-	3-0	1-0/3-0	2-1
Celtic v Hearts	1-0/5-0	1-0/4-1	2-0	-	0-0/3-1	4-0/2-0
Dundee v Ross County	1-2/1-1	0-1/0-2	-	1-1	3-3/5-2	0-0/1-1
Hibernian v Partick	-	-	1-1/1-1	-	-	-
Kilmarnock v St Johnstone	1-2/0-0	1-2	0-0/1-2	0-1	2-1/3-0	0-1
Scottish Championship						
Dumbarton v Morton	-	1-5/0-3	3-1/2-0	-	1-2/0-0	0-2/1-0
Inverness CT v Dundee United	2-3	4-0/0-0/1-2	1-1/1-1	1-0/2-1/3-0	2-2/2-3	-
Livingston v Dunfermline	-	2-1/2-2	-	-	-	-
Queen of Sth v Brechin	-	1-0/2-1	-	-	-	-
St Mirren v Falkirk	-	-	-	-	2-3/0-0	1-1/1-2
Scottish League One						
Albion v Ayr	-	2-0/1-3	-	-	3-0/1-3	-
Alloa v Raith	-	-	1-0/0-1	0-1/0-0	0-1/1-1	-
Arbroath v Queens Park	-	-	-	1-2/1-1	1-2/0-1	-
Forfar v Airdrieonians	3-2/2-3	-	3-3/1-1	1-1/2-0	2-3/0-2	-
Stranraer v East Fife	-	2-6/3-1	2-0/2-0	-	-	1-1/2-1
Scottish League Two						
Annan v Peterhead	2-0/0-3	2-1/0-0	2-0/2-1	-	-	-
Berwick v Clyde	0-2/3-0	2-1/3-3	0-1/3-0	4-0/0-0	0-5/3-0	1-1/4-3
Edinburgh City v Montrose	-	-	-	-	-	0-1/1-1
Elgin v Cowdenbeath	-	-	-	-	-	3-1/0-0
Stenhousemuir v Stirling	4-0/4-0	-	-	4-5/1-2	-	-

Sunday August 6, 2017

Championship

	2011-12	2012-13	2013-14	2014-15	2015-16	2016-17
Bolton v Leeds	-	2-2	0-1	1-1	1-1	-

Scottish Premiership

	2011-12	2012-13	2013-14	2014-15	2015-16	2016-17
Motherwell v Rangers	0-3/1-2	-	-	-	-	0-2

Tuesday August 8, 2017

National League

	2011-12	2012-13	2013-14	2014-15	2015-16	2016-17
Aldershot v Torquay	0-1	1-0	-	2-0	0-0	1-1
Barrow v FC Halifax	-	-	-	-	-	1-
Boreham Wood v Dag & Red	-	-	-	-	-	1-3
Chester v Fylde	-	-	-	-	-	-
Dover v Bromley	-	-	0-2	-	2-3	1-0
Eastleigh v Sutton United	-	-	-	-	-	2-1
Ebbsfleet v Maidstone	-	-	-	-	0-1	-
Gateshead v Guiseley	-	-	-	-	3-0	1-1
Leyton Orient v Solihull Moors	-	-	-	-	-	-
Macclesfield v Hartlepool	-	-	-	-	-	-
Maidenhead v Wrexham	-	-	-	-	-	-
Tranmere v Woking	-	-	-	-	1-0	3-1

Friday August 11, 2017

Premier League

	2011-12	2012-13	2013-14	2014-15	2015-16	2016-17
Arsenal v Leicester	-	-	-	2-1	2-1	1-0

Scottish Premiership

	2011-12	2012-13	2013-14	2014-15	2015-16	2016-17
Partick v Celtic	-	-	1-2/1-5	0-3	0-2/1-2	1-4/0-5

Results cover matches from Premier League to National League and Scottish Premiership to Scottish League Two

Saturday August 12, 2017

Premier League

	2011-12	2012-13	2013-14	2014-15	2015-16	2016-17
Brighton v Man City	-	-	-	-	-	-
Chelsea v Burnley	-	-	-	1-1	-	3-0
Crystal Palace v Huddersfield	-	1-1	-	-	-	-
Everton v Stoke	0-1	1-0	4-0	0-1	3-4	1-0
Southampton v Swansea	-	1-1	2-0	0-1	3-1	1-0
Watford v Liverpool	-	-	-	-	3-0	0-1
West Brom v Bournemouth	-	-	-	-	1-2	2-1

Championship

	2011-12	2012-13	2013-14	2014-15	2015-16	2016-17
Barnsley v Ipswich	3-5	1-1	2-2	-	-	1-1
Birmingham v Bristol City	2-2	2-0	-	-	4-2	1-0
Brentford v Nottm Forest	-	-	-	2-2	2-1	1-0
Cardiff v Aston Villa	-	-	0-0	-	-	1-0
Derby v Wolves	-	0-0	-	5-0	4-2	3-1
Hull v Burton	-	-	-	-	-	-
Leeds v Preston	-	-	-	-	1-0	3-0
Middlesbrough v Sheffield United	-	-	-	-	-	-
Millwall v Bolton	-	2-1	1-1	0-1	-	0-2
Norwich v Sunderland	2-1	2-1	2-0	-	0-3	-
Reading v Fulham	-	3-3	-	3-0	2-2	1-0
Sheffield Wed v QPR	-	-	3-0	-	1-1	1-0

League One

	2011-12	2012-13	2013-14	2014-15	2015-16	2016-17
AFC Wimbledon v Shrewsbury	3-1	-	-	2-2	-	1-1
Blackburn v Doncaster	-	-	1-0	-	-	-
Blackpool v MK Dons	-	-	-	-	-	1-2
Bristol Rovers v Peterborough	-	-	-	-	-	-
Gillingham v Bradford	0-0	3-1	0-1	1-0	3-0	1-1
Northampton v Fleetwood Town	-	3-1	1-0	-	-	1-1
Oxford v Portsmouth	-	-	0-0	0-1	1-1	-
Plymouth v Charlton	-	-	-	-	-	-
Rochdale v Scunthorpe	1-0	-	0-4	3-1	2-1	3-2
Rotherham v Southend	0-4	0-3	-	-	-	-
Walsall v Oldham	0-1	3-1	1-0	2-0	1-1	2-0
Wigan v Bury	-	-	-	-	3-0	-

League Two

	2011-12	2012-13	2013-14	2014-15	2015-16	2016-17
Barnet v Luton	-	-	1-2	-	2-1	0-1
Cambridge U v Carlisle	-	-	-	5-0	0-0	2-2
Cheltenham v Crawley Town	3-1	-	-	-	-	2-1
Colchester v Stevenage	1-6	1-0	4-0	-	-	4-0
Grimsby v Coventry	-	-	-	-	-	-
Lincoln v Morecambe	-	-	-	-	-	-
Mansfield v Forest Green	1-0	1-0	-	-	-	-
Newport County v Crewe	-	-	-	-	-	1-1
Notts County v Chesterfield	1-0	-	-	0-1	-	-
Port Vale v Wycombe	-	4-1	-	-	-	-
Swindon v Exeter	-	-	-	-	1-0	-
Yeovil v Accrington	-	-	-	-	-	1-1

National League

	2011-12	2012-13	2013-14	2014-15	2015-16	2016-17
Aldershot v Guiseley	-	-	-	-	1-0	1-0
Barrow v Woking	-	2-0	-	-	2-1	2-2
Boreham Wood v Solihull Moors	-	-	-	-	-	0-0
Chester v FC Halifax	-	-	-	2-0	2-1	1-1
Dover v Wrexham	-	-	-	-	-	0-1
Eastleigh v Dag & Red	-	-	-	-	-	-
Ebbsfleet v Fylde	-	-	-	-	-	-
Gateshead v Torquay	-	-	-	3-1	1-2	0-0
Leyton Orient v Maidstone	-	-	-	-	-	-
Macclesfield v Bromley	-	-	-	-	2-0	1-2
Maidenhead v Hartlepool	-	-	-	-	-	-
Tranmere v Sutton United	-	-	-	-	-	3-2

Results cover matches from Premier League to National League and Scottish Premiership to Scottish League Two

	2011-12	2012-13	2013-14	2014-15	2015-16	2016-17
Scottish Premiership						
Hamilton v Dundee	1-6/3-1	-	0-3/1-1	2-1	1-1/2-1	0-1/4-0
Hearts v Kilmarnock	0-1	1-3/0-3	0-4/5-0		1-1/1-0	4-0
Rangers v Hibernian	1-0/4-0		-	1-3/0-2	1-0/4-2	-
Ross County v Aberdeen	-	2-1	1-0/1-1	0-1	2-0/2-3	2-1
St Johnstone v Motherwell	0-3	1-3/2-0	2-0/3-0	2-1	2-1/2-1	1-1
Scottish Championship						
Brechin v Livingston	-	-	-	-	-	0-3/0-2
Dundee United v Queen of Sth	-					1-1/3-3
Dunfermline v Inverness CT	3-3/1-1	-	-	-	-	-
Falkirk v Dumbarton		3-4/1-3	1-2/2-0	1-1/3-3	2-1/1-0	1-0/2-2
Morton v St Mirren	-	-	-	-	0-0/0-1	3-1/1-4
Scottish League One						
Airdrieonians v Arbroath	3-3/2-0		2-1/2-0	-	-	-
Ayr v Forfar	-	2-3/2-1	2-0/2-3	2-0/1-0	2-2/2-1	-
East Fife v Alloa		0-1/2-1	-	-		2-2/0-0
Queens Park v Albion	-	-	1-1/4-0	0-1/0-1	-	2-1/2-0
Raith v Stranraer	-	-	-	-	-	-
Scottish League Two						
Clyde v Annan	0-0/1-1	2-1/2-3	2-1/0-3	1-1/1-0	4-2/2-1	2-3/2-1
Cowdenbeath v Edinburgh City	-	-	-	-	-	2-0/1-2
Montrose v Stenhousemuir	-	-	-	-	-	-
Peterhead v Elgin	1-3/3-0	1-1/0-1	2-2/2-1	-	-	-
Stirling v Berwick	-	6-3/1-0	3-1/2-1	-	1-3/2-1	0-0/2-2

Sunday August 13, 2017

Premier League						
Man United v West Ham	-	1-0	3-1	2-1	0-0	1-1
Newcastle v Tottenham	2-2	2-1	0-4	1-3	5-1	-

Tuesday August 15, 2017

Championship						
Barnsley v Nottm Forest	1-1	1-4	1-0	-	-	2-5
Birmingham v Bolton	-	2-1	1-2	0-1	1-0	-
Brentford v Bristol City	-	-	3-1	-	1-1	2-0
Cardiff v Sheffield United	-	-	-	-	-	-
Derby v Preston	-	-	-	-	0-0	1-1
Hull v Wolves	-	2-1	-	-	2-1	-
Leeds v Fulham	-	-	-	0-1	1-1	1-1
Middlesbrough v Burton	-	-	-	-	-	-
Millwall v Ipswich	4-1	0-0	1-0	1-3	-	-
Norwich v QPR	2-1	1-1	-	-	-	4-0
Reading v Aston Villa	-	1-2	-	-	-	1-2
Sheffield Wed v Sunderland	-	-	-	-	-	-

National League						
Bromley v Leyton Orient	-	-	-	-	-	-
Dag & Red v Ebbsfleet	-	-	-	-	-	-
FC Halifax v Dover	-	-	-	-	-	-
Fylde v Maidenhead	-	-	-	-	-	-
Guiseley v Tranmere	-	-	-	-	2-2	1-2
Hartlepool v Chester	-	-	-	-	-	-
Maidstone v Aldershot	-	-	-	-	-	0-2
Solihull Moors v Barrow	-	-	0-2	3-4	-	2-4
Sutton United v Macclesfield	-	-	-	-	-	2-0
Torquay v Boreham Wood	-	-	-	-	1-2	0-1
Woking v Eastleigh	-	-	-	1-1	2-1	3-3
Wrexham v Gateshead	2-1	1-1	3-2	0-3	4-0	0-2

Friday August 18, 2017

Championship						
Burton v Birmingham	-	-	-	-	-	2-0

Results cover matches from Premier League to National League and Scottish Premiership to Scottish League Two

Saturday August 19, 2017

Premier League

	2011-12	2012-13	2013-14	2014-15	2015-16	2016-17
Bournemouth v Watford	-	-	1-1	2-0	1-1	2-2
Burnley v West Brom	-	-	-	2-2	-	2-2
Leicester v Brighton	1-0	1-0	1-4	-	-	-
Liverpool v Crystal Palace	-	-	3-1	1-3	1-2	1-2
Southampton v West Ham	1-0	1-1	0-0	0-0	1-0	1-3
Stoke v Arsenal	1-1	0-0	1-0	3-2	0-0	1-4
Swansea v Man United	0-1	1-1	1-4	2-1	2-1	1-3

Championship

	2011-12	2012-13	2013-14	2014-15	2015-16	2016-17
Aston Villa v Norwich	3-2	1-1	4-1	-	2-0	2-0
Bolton v Derby	-	2-0	2-2	0-2	0-0	-
Bristol City v Millwall	1-0	1-1	-	-	-	-
Fulham v Sheffield Wed	-	-	-	4-0	0-1	1-1
Ipswich v Brentford	-	-	-	1-1	1-3	1-1
Nottm Forest v Middlesbrough	2-0	0-0	2-2	2-1	1-2	-
Preston v Reading	-	-	-	-	1-0	3-0
QPR v Hull	-	-	-	0-1	1-2	-
Sheffield United v Barnsley	-	-	-	0-1	0-0	-
Sunderland v Leeds	-	-	-	-	-	-
Wolves v Cardiff	-	1-2	-	1-0	1-3	3-1

League One

	2011-12	2012-13	2013-14	2014-15	2015-16	2016-17
Bradford v Blackburn	-	-	-	-	-	-
Bury v Bristol Rovers	-	-	2-1	-	-	3-0
Charlton v Northampton	-	-	-	-	-	1-1
Doncaster v Blackpool	1-3	-	1-3	-	0-1	0-1
Fleetwood Town v AFC Wimbledon	-	1-1	0-0	-	-	0-0
MK Dons v Gillingham	-	-	0-1	4-2	-	3-2
Oldham v Wigan	-	-	-	-	1-1	-
Peterborough v Rotherham	-	-	0-1	-	-	-
Portsmouth v Walsall	-	1-2	-	-	-	-
Scunthorpe v Oxford	-	-	1-0	-	-	1-1
Shrewsbury v Rochdale	-	-	-	-	2-0	1-0
Southend v Plymouth	2-0	0-2	1-0	0-0	-	-

League Two

	2011-12	2012-13	2013-14	2014-15	2015-16	2016-17
Accrington v Mansfield	-	-	1-1	2-1	1-0	1-1
Carlisle v Cheltenham	-	-	-	1-0	-	1-1
Chesterfield v Port Vale	-	2-2	-	3-0	4-2	1-0
Coventry v Newport County	-	-	-	-	-	-
Crawley Town v Cambridge U	-	-	-	-	1-0	1-3
Crewe v Barnet	3-1	-	-	-	-	4-1
Exeter v Lincoln	-	-	-	-	-	-
Forest Green v Yeovil	-	-	-	-	-	-
Luton v Colchester	-	-	-	-	-	0-1
Morecambe v Swindon	0-1	-	-	-	-	-
Stevenage v Grimsby	-	-	-	-	-	2-0
Wycombe v Notts County	3-4	-	-	-	2-2	0-1

National League

	2011-12	2012-13	2013-14	2014-15	2015-16	2016-17
Boreham Wood v Aldershot	-	-	-	-	0-1	1-1
Bromley v Hartlepool	-	-	-	-	-	-
Chester v Sutton United	-	-	-	-	-	4-0
Dover v Barrow	-	-	-	-	3-1	3-1
Eastleigh v Tranmere	-	-	-	-	0-1	0-2
Fylde v Dag & Red	-	-	-	-	-	-
Gateshead v Macclesfield	-	2-2	2-2	2-1	0-3	1-1
Guiseley v Torquay	-	-	-	-	4-3	2-0
Maidenhead v Ebbsfleet	-	-	1-0	0-4	0-0	1-2
Maidstone v Wrexham	-	-	-	-	-	2-2
Solihull Moors v FC Halifax	-	-	-	-	-	-
Woking v Leyton Orient	-	-	-	-	-	-

Results cover matches from Premier League to National League and Scottish Premiership to Scottish League Two

	2011-12	2012-13	2013-14	2014-15	2015-16	2016-17
Scottish Premiership						
Aberdeen v Dundee	-	2-0/1-0	-	3-3	2-0/1-0	3-0
Hibernian v Hamilton	-	-	-	-	-	-
Kilmarnock v Celtic	3-3/0-6	1-3	2-5/0-3	0-2	2-2/0-1	0-1
Motherwell v Ross County	-	3-2/2-0	3-1/2-1	2-2/1-1	1-1/1-2	4-1/0-1
Rangers v Hearts	1-1/1-2	-	-	1-2/2-1	-	2-0/2-1
St Johnstone v Partick	-	-	1-1/1-1	2-0	1-2/1-2	1-2/1-0
Scottish Championship						
Dundee United v Brechin	-	-	-	-	-	-
Dunfermline v Falkirk	-	0-1/0-2	-	-	-	1-1/1-2
Inverness CT v Morton	-	-	-	-	-	-
Livingston v St Mirren	-	-	-	-	0-1/2-3	-
Queen of Sth v Dumbarton	-	-	1-2/3-1	3-0/2-1	1-0/6-0	1-2/1-2
Scottish League One						
Albion v Airdrieonians	7-2/0-1	-	-	-	1-3/1-2	1-2/3-4
Alloa v Queens Park	1-0/4-0	-	-	-	-	1-1/2-2
Arbroath v East Fife	3-0/2-2	2-0/1-0	2-2/2-1	0-2/1-1	1-1/0-1	-
Raith v Forfar	-	-	-	-	-	-
Stranraer v Ayr	-	2-0/0-1	1-1/4-0	3-1/1-0	1-2/1-0	-
Scottish League Two						
Berwick v Annan	0-1/1-3	3-1/0-2	4-2/1-4	2-0/2-2	0-2/3-2	2-0/4-1
Elgin v Clyde	0-3/1-1	2-1/4-2	1-0/3-1	1-0/2-0	1-1/1-0	0-2/4-1
Montrose v Cowdenbeath	-	-	-	-	-	1-2/2-1
Stenhousemuir v Peterhead	-	-	-	1-2/2-1	4-3/1-4	2-2/3-1
Stirling v Edinburgh City	-	-	-	-	-	1-1/1-0

Sunday August 20, 2017

Premier League						
Huddersfield v Newcastle	-	-	-	-	-	1-3
Tottenham v Chelsea	1-1	2-4	1-1	5-3	0-0	2-0

Monday August 21, 2017

Premier League						
Man City v Everton	2-0	1-1	3-1	1-0	0-0	1-1

Friday August 25, 2017

Championship						
Bristol City v Aston Villa	-	-	-	-	-	3-1

Saturday August 26, 2017

Premier League						
Bournemouth v Man City	-	-	-	-	0-4	0-2
Chelsea v Everton	3-1	2-1	1-0	1-0	3-3	5-0
Crystal Palace v Swansea	-	-	0-2	1-0	0-0	1-2
Huddersfield v Southampton	-	-	-	-	-	-
Man United v Leicester	-	-	-	3-1	1-1	4-1
Newcastle v West Ham	-	0-1	0-0	2-0	2-1	-
Tottenham v Burnley	-	-	-	2-1	-	2-1
Watford v Brighton	1-0	0-1	2-0	1-1	-	-
Championship						
Barnsley v Sunderland	-	-	-	-	-	-
Birmingham v Reading	2-0	-	1-2	6-1	2-1	0-1
Brentford v Wolves	-	-	0-3	4-0	3-0	1-2
Burton v Sheffield Wed	-	-	-	-	-	3-1
Cardiff v QPR	-	-	-	-	0-0	0-2
Hull v Bolton	-	3-1	-	-	1-0	-
Ipswich v Fulham	-	-	-	2-1	1-1	0-2
Middlesbrough v Preston	-	-	-	-	1-0	-
Millwall v Norwich	-	-	-	1-4	-	-
Nottm Forest v Leeds	0-4	4-2	2-1	1-1	1-1	3-1
Sheffield United v Derby	-	-	-	-	-	-

Results cover matches from Premier League to National League and Scottish Premiership to Scottish League Two

	2011-12	2012-13	2013-14	2014-15	2015-16	2016-17
League One						
AFC Wimbledon v Doncaster	-	-	-	-	-	-
Blackburn v MK Dons	-	-	-	-	3-2	-
Blackpool v Oldham	-	-	-	-	0-0	-
Bristol Rovers v Fleetwood Town	-	0-0	1-3	-	-	2-1
Gillingham v Southend	1-2	1-0	-	-	1-1	2-1
Northampton v Peterborough	-	-	-	-	-	0-1
Oxford v Shrewsbury	2-0	-	-	0-2	-	2-0
Plymouth v Scunthorpe	-	-	0-2	-	-	-
Rochdale v Bury	3-0	-	1-0	-	3-0	2-0
Rotherham v Charlton	-	-	-	1-1	1-4	-
Walsall v Bradford	-	-	0-2	0-0	2-1	1-1
Wigan v Portsmouth	-	-	-	-	-	-
League Two						
Barnet v Stevenage	-	-	-	-	3-2	1-2
Cambridge U v Morecambe	-	-	-	1-2	7-0	1-2
Cheltenham v Exeter	-	3-0	1-0	1-2	-	1-3
Colchester v Forest Green	-	-	-	-	-	-
Grimsby v Wycombe	-	-	-	-	-	1-2
Lincoln v Carlisle	-	-	-	-	-	-
Mansfield v Luton	1-1	2-2	-	1-0	0-2	1-1
Newport County v Chesterfield	-	-	3-2	-	-	-
Notts County v Accrington	-	-	-	-	1-1	0-2
Port Vale v Crewe	1-1	-	1-3	0-1	3-0	-
Swindon v Crawley Town	3-0	3-0	1-1	1-2	-	-
Yeovil v Coventry	-	1-1	-	0-0	-	-
National League						
Aldershot v Chester	-	-	2-0	0-1	3-1	0-0
Barrow v Maidenhead	-	-	-	-	-	-
Dag & Red v Bromley	-	-	-	-	-	2-1
Ebbsfleet v Gateshead	0-1	3-1	-	-	-	-
FC Halifax v Guiseley	-	-	-	-	-	-
Hartlepool v Fylde	-	-	-	-	-	-
Leyton Orient v Eastleigh	-	-	-	-	-	-
Macclesfield v Dover	-	-	-	1-0	0-0	2-1
Sutton United v Maidstone	-	-	-	-	-	2-2
Torquay v Solihull Moors	-	-	-	-	-	3-0
Tranmere v Boreham Wood	-	-	-	-	0-2	2-1
Wrexham v Woking	-	3-1	2-0	1-2	1-3	2-1
Scottish Premiership						
Celtic v St Johnstone	0-1/2-0/1-0	1-1/4-0	2-1/3-0	0-1	3-1/3-1	1-0/4-1
Hearts v Motherwell	2-0/0-1	1-0/1-2	0-1	-	2-0/6-0	3-0
Kilmarnock v Hamilton	-	-	-	1-0/2-3	1-2/0-1	0-0
Partick v Aberdeen	-	-	0-3/3-1	0-1	0-2/1-2	1-2/0-6
Scottish Championship						
Brechin v Inverness CT	-	-	-	-	-	-
Dumbarton v Dunfermline	-	0-2/0-1	-	-	-	2-2/0-2
Falkirk v Queen of Sth	1-0/3-0	-	2-1/1-0	1-1/1-1	0-0/3-1	2-2/2-2
Morton v Livingston	2-1/1-3	2-2/2-1	1-5/2-0	-	1-0/2-1	-
St Mirren v Dundee United	2-2	0-1/0-0	4-1	0-3/1-1	-	0-2/3-2
Scottish League One						
Airdrieonians v Alloa	-	-	-	-	-	2-1/0-1
Ayr v Arbroath	-	2-0/0-1	2-0/2-1	-	-	-
East Fife v Raith	-	-	-	-	-	-
Forfar v Albion	0-2/4-0	4-2/4-2	-	-	4-0/1-0	-
Queens Park v Stranraer	2-0/3-2	-	-	-	-	0-2/0-1

Results cover matches from Premier League to National League and Scottish Premiership to Scottish League Two

	2011-12	2012-13	2013-14	2014-15	2015-16	2016-17
Scottish League Two						
Annan v Montrose	2-1/1-2	2-1/1-1	2-1/1-0	2-2/4-3	3-2/3-3	2-3/5-1
Clyde v Stenhousemuir	-	-	-	-	-	-
Cowdenbeath v Berwick						0-2/0-1
Edinburgh City v Elgin						1-2/3-0
Peterhead v Stirling	-	2-2/0-0	3-1/0-4	1-1/2-1	-	-
Sunday August 27, 2017						
Premier League						
Liverpool v Arsenal	1-2	0-2	5-1	2-2	3-3	3-1
West Brom v Stoke	0-1	0-1	1-2	1-0	2-1	1-0
Scottish Premiership						
Dundee v Hibernian	-	3-1	-	-	-	-
Ross County v Rangers	-	-	-	-	-	1-1
Monday August 28, 2017						
National League						
Boreham Wood v Wrexham	-	-	-	-	0-1	0-1
Bromley v Sutton United	-	-	-	-	-	1-0
Chester v Macclesfield	-	-	2-1	1-0	0-2	2-3
Dover v Ebbsfleet	-	-	2-1	-	-	-
Eastleigh v Aldershot	-	-	-	1-0	1-1	1-1
Fylde v Barrow	-	-	-	-	-	-
Gateshead v FC Halifax	-	-	-	-	-	-
Guiseley v Hartlepool	-	-	-	-	-	-
Maidenhead v Leyton Orient	-	-	-	-	-	-
Maidstone v Dag & Red	-	-	-	-	-	0-1
Solihull Moors v Tranmere	-	-	-	-	-	0-3
Woking v Torquay	-	-	-	3-2	2-2	3-1
Saturday September 2, 2017						
League One						
Blackpool v AFC Wimbledon	-	-	-	-	-	-
Bradford v Bristol Rovers	2-2	4-1	-	-	-	1-1
Bury v Scunthorpe	0-0	2-1	2-2	-	1-2	1-2
Doncaster v Peterborough	1-1	-	-	0-2	1-2	-
Gillingham v Shrewsbury	0-1	-	1-1	-	2-3	1-1
MK Dons v Oxford	-	-	-	-	-	0-0
Oldham v Charlton	0-1	-	-	-	-	1-0
Southend v Rochdale	-	3-1	1-1	-	2-2	2-1
Walsall v Plymouth	-	-	-	-	-	-
Wigan v Northampton	-	-	-	-	-	-
League Two						
Cambridge U v Colchester	-	-	-	-	-	1-1
Carlisle v Mansfield	-	-	-	2-1	1-2	5-2
Cheltenham v Stevenage	-	-	-	0-1	0-0	0-0
Chesterfield v Coventry	-	-	-	2-3	1-1	1-0
Crawley Town v Yeovil	-	0-1	-	2-0	0-1	2-0
Exeter v Newport County	-	-	0-2	2-0	1-1	0-1
Grimsby v Crewe	-	-	-	-	-	0-2
Lincoln v Luton	1-1	1-2	0-0	-	-	-
Morecambe v Accrington	1-2	0-0	1-2	1-1	1-0	1-2
Port Vale v Notts County	-	-	2-1	0-2	-	-
Swindon v Barnet	4-0	-	-	-	-	-
Wycombe v Forest Green	-	-	-	-	-	-
National League						
Aldershot v Solihull Moors	-	-	-	-	-	2-0
Barrow v Boreham Wood	-	-	-	-	0-0	1-1
Dag & Red v Gateshead	-	-	-	-	-	0-5
Ebbsfleet v Eastleigh	-	-	3-1	-	-	-

Results cover matches from Premier League to National League and Scottish Premiership to Scottish League Two

	2011-12	2012-13	2013-14	2014-15	2015-16	2016-17
FC Halifax v Fylde	-	-	-	-	-	-
Hartlepool v Maidstone	-	-	-	-	-	-
Leyton Orient v Guiseley	-	-	-	-	-	-
Macclesfield v Woking	-	0-0	3-2	2-1	2-1	3-1
Sutton United v Maidenhead	-	-	-	-	-	-
Torquay v Chester	-	-	-	0-1	2-0	0-1
Tranmere v Dover	-	-	-	-	0-1	1-0
Wrexham v Bromley	-	-	-	-	2-0	2-1

Sunday September 3, 2017

League One

	2011-12	2012-13	2013-14	2014-15	2015-16	2016-17
Blackburn v Fleetwood Town	-	-	-	-	-	-
Portsmouth v Rotherham	-	-	-	-	-	-

Friday September 8, 2017

Championship

	2011-12	2012-13	2013-14	2014-15	2015-16	2016-17
Derby v Hull	0-2	1-2	-	-	4-0	-

Saturday September 9, 2017

Premier League

	2011-12	2012-13	2013-14	2014-15	2015-16	2016-17
Arsenal v Bournemouth	-	-	-	-	2-0	3-1
Brighton v West Brom	-	-	-	-	-	-
Everton v Tottenham	1-0	2-1	0-0	0-1	1-1	1-1
Leicester v Chelsea	-	-	-	1-3	2-1	0-3
Man City v Liverpool	3-0	2-2	2-1	3-1	1-4	1-1
Southampton v Watford	4-0	-	-	-	2-0	1-1
Stoke v Man United	1-1	0-2	2-1	1-1	2-0	1-1

Championship

	2011-12	2012-13	2013-14	2014-15	2015-16	2016-17
Aston Villa v Brentford	-	-	-	-	-	1-1
Bolton v Middlesbrough	-	2-1	2-2	1-2	1-2	-
Fulham v Cardiff	-	-	1-2	1-1	2-1	2-2
Leeds v Burton	-	-	-	-	-	2-0
Norwich v Birmingham	-	-	-	2-2	-	2-0
Preston v Barnsley	-	-	-	1-0	-	1-2
QPR v Ipswich	-	-	1-0	-	1-0	2-1
Reading v Bristol City	1-0	-	-	-	1-0	2-1
Sheffield Wed v Nottm Forest	-	0-1	0-1	0-1	1-0	2-1
Sunderland v Sheffield United	-	-	-	-	-	-
Wolves v Millwall	-	0-1	-	4-2	-	-

League One

	2011-12	2012-13	2013-14	2014-15	2015-16	2016-17
AFC Wimbledon v Portsmouth	-	-	4-0	1-0	0-1	-
Bristol Rovers v Walsall	-	-	-	-	-	1-1
Charlton v Southend	-	-	-	-	-	2-1
Fleetwood Town v Oldham	-	-	-	0-2	1-1	1-0
Northampton v Doncaster	-	-	-	-	-	-
Oxford v Gillingham	0-0	0-0	-	-	-	1-0
Peterborough v Bradford	-	-	2-1	2-0	0-4	0-1
Plymouth v MK Dons	-	-	-	-	-	-
Rochdale v Blackburn	-	-	-	-	-	-
Rotherham v Bury	-	-	-	-	-	-
Scunthorpe v Blackpool	-	-	-	-	0-1	-
Shrewsbury v Wigan	-	-	-	-	1-5	-

League Two

	2011-12	2012-13	2013-14	2014-15	2015-16	2016-17
Accrington v Carlisle	-	-	-	3-1	1-1	1-1
Barnet v Cambridge U	-	-	2-2	-	0-0	0-1
Colchester v Crawley Town	-	1-1	1-1	2-3	-	2-3
Coventry v Port Vale	-	-	2-2	2-3	1-0	2-1
Crewe v Chesterfield	-	-	-	0-0	1-2	-
Forest Green v Exeter	-	-	-	-	-	-
Luton v Swindon	-	-	-	-	-	-

Results cover matches from Premier League to National League and Scottish Premiership to Scottish League Two

	2011-12	2012-13	2013-14	2014-15	2015-16	2016-17
Mansfield v Grimsby	2-1	2-0	-	-	-	0-1
Newport County v Wycombe	-	-	2-0	0-2	1-0	0-1
Notts County v Morecambe	-	-	-	-	2-2	1-2
Stevenage v Lincoln	-	-	-	-	-	-
Yeovil v Cheltenham	-	-	-	-	-	4-2
National League						
Aldershot v Dover	-	-	-	3-1	1-1	1-0
Boreham Wood v Leyton Orient	-	-	-	-	-	-
Chester v Ebbsfleet	-	-	-	-	-	-
FC Halifax v Maidenhead	-	-	-	-	-	-
Fylde v Bromley	-	-	-	-	-	-
Guiseley v Eastleigh	-	-	-	-	1-4	1-1
Hartlepool v Dag & Red	-	-	2-1	0-2	3-1	-
Maidstone v Woking	-	-	-	-	-	0-3
Solihull Moors v Macclesfield	-	-	-	-	-	2-3
Sutton United v Gateshead	-	-	-	-	-	3-0
Torquay v Wrexham	-	-	-	2-1	0-1	1-1
Tranmere v Barrow	-	-	-	-	0-1	2-0
Scottish Premiership						
Hamilton v Celtic	-	-	-	0-2	1-2/1-1	0-3
Hearts v Aberdeen	3-0/3-0	2-0	2-1/1-1	-	1-3/2-1	0-1/1-2
Motherwell v Kilmarnock	0-0	2-2	2-1/1-2	1-1/3-1	1-0/0-2	0-0/3-1
Rangers v Dundee	-	-	-	-	-	1-0
Ross County v Partick	2-2/3-0	-	1-3/1-1	1-0/1-2	1-0/1-0	1-3
St Johnstone v Hibernian	3-1	0-1	1-2/2-0	-	-	-
Scottish Championship						
Brechin v Falkirk	-	-	-	-	-	-
Dundee United v Dumbarton	-	-	-	-	-	2-1/2-2
Livingston v Queen of Sth	2-2/2-2	-	3-3/1-2	2-2/1-0	0-1/0-2	-
Morton v Dunfermline	-	4-2/0-1	-	2-1/2-0	-	2-1/0-1
St Mirren v Inverness CT	1-2/0-1	2-2/2-1	0-0	0-1/1-2	-	-
Scottish League One						
Alloa v Forfar	-	2-1/1-0	-	-	-	-
Arbroath v Albion	6-2/6-1	2-1/2-1	-	1-0/0-2	-	-
East Fife v Queens Park	-	-	-	2-2/0-0	0-2/1-1	1-2/0-0
Raith v Ayr	0-1/2-2	-	-	-	-	1-1/2-1
Stranraer v Airdrieonians	-	-	3-1/1-1	1-0/1-0	1-3/4-0	1-2/2-1
Scottish League Two						
Edinburgh City v Berwick	-	-	-	-	-	1-2/2-2
Elgin v Annan	3-0/1-2	2-2/3-1	2-3/2-3	0-0/4-5	3-2/2-2	0-2/3-2
Peterhead v Montrose	2-3/2-1	2-0/0-1	3-0/4-0	-	-	-
Stenhousemuir v Cowdenbeath	3-1/0-2	-	-	-	4-2/2-3	-
Stirling v Clyde	-	0-1/2-0	1-1/4-1	-	0-1/1-2	1-1/3-0

Sunday September 10, 2017

Premier League

	2011-12	2012-13	2013-14	2014-15	2015-16	2016-17
Burnley v Crystal Palace	1-1	1-0	-	2-3	-	3-2
Swansea v Newcastle	0-2	1-0	3-0	2-2	2-0	-

Monday September 11, 2017

Premier League

	2011-12	2012-13	2013-14	2014-15	2015-16	2016-17
West Ham v Huddersfield	-	-	-	-	-	-

Tuesday September 12, 2017

Championship

	2011-12	2012-13	2013-14	2014-15	2015-16	2016-17
Aston Villa v Middlesbrough	-	-	-	-	-	-
Bolton v Sheffield United	-	-	-	-	-	1-0
Derby v Ipswich	0-0	0-1	4-4	1-1	0-1	0-1
Fulham v Hull	-	-	2-2	-	0-1	-

Results cover matches from Premier League to National League and Scottish Premiership to Scottish League Two

	2011-12	2012-13	2013-14	2014-15	2015-16	2016-17
Leeds v Birmingham	1-4	0-1	4-0	1-1	0-2	1-2
Norwich v Burton	-	-	-	-	-	3-1
Preston v Cardiff	-	-	-	-	0-0	3-0
QPR v Millwall	-	-	1-1	-	-	-
Reading v Barnsley	1-2	-	1-3	-	-	0-0
Sheffield Wed v Brentford	0-0	-	-	1-0	4-0	1-2
Sunderland v Nottm Forest	-	-	-	-	-	-
Wolves v Bristol City	-	2-1	3-1	-	2-1	3-2

League One						
AFC Wimbledon v Gillingham	3-1	0-1	-	-	-	2-0
Bristol Rovers v Oldham	-	-	-	-	-	1-0
Charlton v Wigan	-	-	0-0	2-1	-	-
Fleetwood Town v Bury	-	-	2-1	-	2-0	0-0
Northampton v Portsmouth	-	-	0-1	1-0	1-2	-
Oxford v Bradford	1-1	0-2	-	-	-	1-0
Peterborough v MK Dons	-	-	2-1	3-2	-	0-4
Plymouth v Blackpool	-	-	-	-	-	0-3
Rochdale v Doncaster	-	-	-	1-3	2-2	-
Rotherham v Walsall	-	-	1-1	-	-	-
Scunthorpe v Blackburn	-	-	-	-	-	-
Shrewsbury v Southend	2-1	-	-	1-1	1-2	1-0

League Two						
Accrington v Grimsby	-	-	-	-	-	1-1
Barnet v Exeter	-	1-2	-	-	2-0	1-4
Colchester v Chesterfield	1-2	-	-	2-1	1-1	-
Coventry v Carlisle	-	1-2	1-2	-	-	-
Crewe v Cambridge U	-	-	-	-	-	1-2
Forest Green v Lincoln	0-2	3-0	4-1	3-3	3-1	2-3
Luton v Port Vale	-	-	-	-	-	-
Mansfield v Wycombe	-	-	2-2	0-0	0-2	1-1
Newport County v Cheltenham	-	-	0-1	1-1	-	2-2
Notts County v Swindon	-	1-0	2-0	0-3	-	-
Stevenage v Crawley Town	-	1-2	2-0	-	0-1	2-1
Yeovil v Morecambe	-	-	-	-	2-4	0-1

National League						
Barrow v Guiseley	-	-	1-0	1-0	1-1	3-0
Bromley v Torquay	-	-	-	-	0-2	1-0
Dag & Red v Sutton United	-	-	-	-	-	2-2
Dover v Boreham Wood	-	-	-	-	2-1	1-4
Eastleigh v Maidstone	-	-	-	-	-	3-0
Ebbsfleet v Aldershot	-	-	-	-	-	-
Gateshead v Chester	-	-	3-2	2-1	1-0	3-0
Leyton Orient v FC Halifax	-	-	-	-	-	-
Macclesfield v Fylde	-	-	-	-	-	-
Maidenhead v Tranmere	-	-	-	-	-	2-1
Woking v Solihull Moors	-	-	-	-	-	-
Wrexham v Hartlepool	-	-	-	-	-	-

Friday September 15, 2017

Premier League						
Bournemouth v Brighton	-	-	1-1	3-2	-	-

Saturday September 16, 2017

Premier League						
Crystal Palace v Southampton	0-2	-	0-1	1-3	1-0	3-0
Huddersfield v Leicester	-	0-2	0-2	-	-	-
Liverpool v Burnley	-	-	-	2-0	-	2-1
Newcastle v Stoke	3-0	2-1	5-1	1-1	0-0	-
Tottenham v Swansea	3-1	1-0	1-0	3-2	2-1	5-0
Watford v Man City	-	-	-	-	1-2	0-5
West Brom v West Ham	-	0-0	1-0	1-2	0-3	4-2

Results cover matches from Premier League to National League and Scottish Premiership to Scottish League Two

	2011-12	2012-13	2013-14	2014-15	2015-16	2016-17
Championship						
Barnsley v Aston Villa	-	-	-	-	-	1-1
Birmingham v Preston	-	-	-	-	2-2	2-2
Brentford v Reading	-	-	-	3-1	1-3	4-1
Bristol City v Derby	1-1	0-2	-	-	2-3	1-1
Burton v Fulham	-	-	-	-	-	0-2
Cardiff v Sheffield Wed	-	1-0	-	2-1	2-2	1-1
Hull v Sunderland	-	-	1-0	1-1	-	0-2
Ipswich v Bolton	-	1-0	1-0	1-0	2-0	-
Middlesbrough v QPR	-	-	1-3	-	1-0	-
Millwall v Leeds	0-1	1-0	2-0	2-0	-	-
Nottm Forest v Wolves	-	3-1	-	1-2	1-1	0-2
Sheffield United v Norwich	-	-	-	-	-	-
League One						
Blackburn v AFC Wimbledon	-	-	-	-	-	-
Blackpool v Oxford	-	-	-	-	-	-
Bradford v Rotherham	2-3	0-2	0-1	-	-	-
Bury v Plymouth	-	-	4-0	2-1	-	-
Doncaster v Scunthorpe	-	4-0	-	5-2	0-1	-
Gillingham v Charlton	-	-	-	-	-	1-1
MK Dons v Rochdale	3-1	-	-	2-2	-	2-2
Oldham v Shrewsbury	-	1-0	1-2	-	1-1	2-3
Portsmouth v Fleetwood Town	-	-	0-1	-	-	-
Southend v Northampton	2-2	1-2	2-0	2-0	-	2-2
Walsall v Peterborough	-	-	2-0	0-0	2-0	2-0
Wigan v Bristol Rovers	-	-	-	-	-	-
League Two						
Cambridge U v Coventry	-	-	-	-	-	-
Carlisle v Barnet	-	-	-	-	3-2	1-1
Cheltenham v Colchester	-	-	-	-	-	0-3
Chesterfield v Accrington	-	4-3	1-0	-	-	-
Crawley Town v Notts County	-	0-0	1-0	2-0	0-1	1-3
Exeter v Crewe	-	-	-	-	-	4-0
Grimsby v Yeovil	-	-	-	-	-	4-2
Lincoln v Mansfield	1-1	0-1	-	-	-	-
Morecambe v Newport County	-	-	4-1	3-2	1-2	0-1
Port Vale v Forest Green	-	-	-	-	-	-
Swindon v Stevenage	-	3-0	1-0	-	-	-
Wycombe v Luton	-	-	-	1-1	0-1	1-1
National League						
Barrow v Torquay	-	-	-	-	4-0	0-0
Bromley v Solihull Moors	-	-	-	-	-	0-1
Dag & Red v FC Halifax	-	-	-	-	-	-
Dover v Chester	-	-	-	2-0	0-0	3-1
Eastleigh v Fylde	-	-	-	-	-	-
Ebbsfleet v Tranmere	-	-	-	-	-	-
Gateshead v Aldershot	-	-	0-0	1-1	3-2	1-1
Leyton Orient v Hartlepool	1-1	1-0	-	-	0-2	2-1
Macclesfield v Maidstone	-	-	-	-	-	3-0
Maidenhead v Boreham Wood	-	-	-	-	-	-
Woking v Sutton United	-	-	-	-	-	2-1
Wrexham v Guiseley	-	-	-	-	3-3	3-1
Scottish Premiership						
Aberdeen v Kilmarnock	2-2/0-0	0-2/1-0	2-1/2-1	1-0	2-0/2-1	5-1
Celtic v Ross County	-	4-0	2-1/1-1	0-0	2-0/2-0/1-1	2-0
Dundee v St Johnstone	-	1-3/2-2	-	1-1/0-2	2-1/2-0	3-0
Hamilton v Hearts	-	-	-	-	3-2/0-0	3-3
Hibernian v Motherwell	0-1/1-1	2-3	0-1/3-3	-	-	-
Partick v Rangers	-	-	-	-	-	1-2/1-2

Results cover matches from Premier League to National League and Scottish Premiership to Scottish League Two

	2011-12	2012-13	2013-14	2014-15	2015-16	2016-17
Scottish Championship						
Dumbarton v Brechin	1-0/4-2	-	-	-	-	-
Dunfermline v St Mirren	0-0/1-1	-	-	-	-	4-3/1-1
Falkirk v Dundee United	-	-	-	-	-	3-1/3-0
Inverness CT v Livingston	-	-	-	-	-	-
Queen of Sth v Morton	4-1/2-1	-	2-0/3-0	-	2-2/1-0	0-5/3-0
Scottish League One						
Airdrieonians v East Fife	1-3/2-0	-	1-3/2-1	-	-	1-1/2-2
Albion v Stranraer	-	2-1/2-3	-	-	0-2/0-1	3-2/3-0
Ayr v Alloa	-	0-0/0-2	-	-	-	-
Forfar v Arbroath	1-1/2-4	1-1/2-4	1-1/0-2	-	-	0-1/1-1
Queens Park v Raith	-	-	-	-	-	-
Scottish League Two						
Annan v Stenhousemuir	-	-	-	-	-	-
Berwick v Elgin	1-1/3-3	0-0/2-1	2-3/2-3	1-1/0-2	2-3/2-0	2-4/0-1
Clyde v Edinburgh City	-	-	-	-	-	0-0/3-1
Cowdenbeath v Peterhead	-	-	-	-	2-2/2-3	-
Montrose v Stirling	-	3-2/2-2	1-2/0-0	-	1-3/1-1	2-2/1-3

Sunday September 17, 2017

Premier League						
Chelsea v Arsenal	3-5	2-1	6-0	2-0	2-0	3-1
Man United v Everton	4-4	2-0	0-1	2-1	1-0	1-1

Saturday September 23, 2017

Premier League						
Burnley v Huddersfield	-	0-1	3-2	-	2-1	-
Everton v Bournemouth	-	-	-	-	2-1	6-3
Leicester v Liverpool	-	-	-	1-3	2-0	3-1
Man City v Crystal Palace	-	-	1-0	3-0	4-0	5-0
Southampton v Man United	-	2-3	1-1	1-2	2-3	0-0
Stoke v Chelsea	0-0	0-4	3-2	0-2	1-0	1-2
Swansea v Watford	-	-	-	-	1-0	0-0
West Ham v Tottenham	-	2-3	2-0	0-1	1-0	1-0
Championship						
Aston Villa v Nottm Forest	-	-	-	-	-	2-2
Bolton v Brentford	-	-	-	3-1	1-1	-
Derby v Birmingham	2-1	3-2	1-1	2-2	0-3	1-0
Fulham v Middlesbrough	-	-	-	4-3	0-2	-
Leeds v Ipswich	3-1	2-0	1-1	2-1	0-1	1-0
Norwich v Bristol City	-	-	-	-	-	1-0
Preston v Millwall	-	-	-	-	-	-
QPR v Burton	-	-	-	-	-	1-2
Reading v Hull	0-1	-	-	-	1-2	-
Sheffield Wed v Sheffield United	1-0	-	-	-	-	-
Sunderland v Cardiff	-	-	4-0	-	-	-
Wolves v Barnsley	-	3-1	-	-	-	0-4
League One						
AFC Wimbledon v MK Dons	-	-	-	-	-	2-0
Bristol Rovers v Blackpool	-	-	-	-	-	-
Charlton v Bury	1-1	-	-	-	-	0-1
Fleetwood Town v Southend	-	0-0	1-1	-	1-1	1-1
Northampton v Bradford	1-3	0-1	-	-	-	1-2
Oxford v Walsall	-	-	-	-	-	0-0
Peterborough v Wigan	-	-	-	-	2-3	-
Plymouth v Doncaster	-	-	-	-	-	2-0
Rochdale v Gillingham	-	1-1	-	1-1	1-1	4-1
Rotherham v Oldham	-	-	3-2	-	-	-
Scunthorpe v Portsmouth	-	2-1	5-1	-	-	-
Shrewsbury v Blackburn	-	-	-	-	-	-

Results cover matches from Premier League to National League and Scottish Premiership to Scottish League Two

	2011-12	2012-13	2013-14	2014-15	2015-16	2016-17
League Two						
Accrington v Cheltenham	0-1	2-2	0-1	1-1	-	1-1
Barnet v Crawley Town	1-2	-	-	-	4-2	2-2
Colchester v Wycombe	1-1	-	-	-	-	1-0
Coventry v Exeter	-	-	-	-	-	-
Crewe v Carlisle	-	1-0	2-1	-	-	1-1
Forest Green v Swindon	-	-	-	-	-	-
Luton v Chesterfield	-	-	-	-	-	-
Mansfield v Cambridge U	1-2	3-1	-	0-0	0-0	0-0
Newport County v Grimsby	0-0	0-0	-	-	-	0-0
Notts County v Lincoln	-	-	-	-	-	-
Stevenage v Morecambe	-	-	-	1-1	4-3	0-1
Yeovil v Port Vale	-	-	-	1-2	-	-
National League						
Aldershot v Leyton Orient	-	-	-	-	-	-
Boreham Wood v Ebbsfleet	-	-	-	-	-	-
Chester v Maidenhead	-	-	-	-	-	-
FC Halifax v Bromley	-	-	-	-	-	-
Fylde v Woking	-	-	-	-	-	-
Guiseley v Dover	-	-	-	-	0-1	0-4
Hartlepool v Eastleigh	-	-	-	-	-	-
Maidstone v Gateshead	-	-	-	-	-	0-2
Solihull Moors v Dag & Red	-	-	-	-	-	2-5
Sutton United v Barrow	-	-	-	-	-	0-0
Torquay v Macclesfield	3-0	-	-	1-1	1-0	1-1
Tranmere v Wrexham	-	-	-	-	1-2	2-0
Scottish Premiership						
Hearts v Partick	-	-	0-2/2-4	-	3-0/1-0	1-1/2-2
Kilmarnock v Dundee	-	0-0/1-2	-	1-3	0-4/0-0	2-0/0-1
Motherwell v Aberdeen	1-0/1-0	4-1	1-3/2-2	0-2	1-2/2-1	1-3
Rangers v Celtic	4-2/3-2	-	-	-	-	1-2/1-5
Ross County v Hibernian	-	3-2/1-0	0-2/1-0	-	-	-
St Johnstone v Hamilton	-	-	-	0-1	4-1/0-0	3-0
Scottish Championship						
Brechin v Dunfermline	-	-	1-1/3-2	1-1/3-0	1-6/1-2	-
Dumbarton v Inverness CT	-	-	-	-	-	-
Dundee United v Morton	-	-	-	-	-	2-1/1-1
Falkirk v Livingston	4-3/2-5	1-2/2-0	4-1/1-1	0-0/2-0	2-0/1-2	-
St Mirren v Queen of Sth	-	-	-	-	1-0/2-1	1-3/0-3
Scottish League One						
Alloa v Albion	-	5-1/4-1	-	-	-	0-0/1-1
East Fife v Forfar	4-3/4-0	3-0/1-2	1-3/2-1	-	-	-
Queens Park v Ayr	-	-	-	-	-	-
Raith v Airdrieonians	-	2-0/2-0	-	-	-	-
Stranraer v Arbroath	-	1-1/2-0	3-2/1-1	-	-	-
Scottish League Two						
Clyde v Cowdenbeath	-	-	-	-	-	5-3/0-2
Edinburgh City v Peterhead	-	-	-	-	-	-
Elgin v Montrose	3-1/2-1	6-1/3-2	3-3/2-3	0-1/4-0	2-0/1-1	4-1/1-1
Stenhousemuir v Berwick	-	-	-	-	-	-
Stirling v Annan	-	5-1/2-1	0-2/1-1	-	1-0/2-1	3-1/1-0

Sunday September 24, 2017

Premier League						
Brighton v Newcastle	-	-	-	-	-	1-2

Monday September 25, 2017

Premier League						
Arsenal v West Brom	3-0	2-0	1-0	4-1	2-0	1-0

Results cover matches from Premier League to National League and Scottish Premiership to Scottish League Two

Tuesday September 26, 2017

Championship

	2011-12	2012-13	2013-14	2014-15	2015-16	2016-17
Barnsley v QPR	-	-	2-3	-	-	3-2
Birmingham v Sheffield Wed	-	0-0	4-1	0-2	1-2	2-1
Brentford v Derby	-	-	-	2-1	1-3	4-0
Bristol City v Bolton	-	1-2	-	-	6-0	-
Burton v Aston Villa	-	-	-	-	-	1-1
Cardiff v Leeds	1-1	2-1	-	3-1	0-2	0-2
Hull v Preston	-	-	-	-	2-0	-
Ipswich v Sunderland	-	-	-	-	-	-
Middlesbrough v Norwich	-	-	-	4-0	-	-
Millwall v Reading	1-2	-	0-3	0-0	-	-
Nottm Forest v Fulham	-	-	-	5-3	3-0	1-1
Sheffield United v Wolves	-	-	0-2	-	-	-

League One

	2011-12	2012-13	2013-14	2014-15	2015-16	2016-17
Blackburn v Rotherham	-	-	-	2-1	1-0	4-2
Blackpool v Rochdale	-	-	-	-	0-2	-
Bradford v Fleetwood Town	-	1-0	-	2-2	2-1	2-1
Bury v Oxford	-	-	1-1	0-1	-	2-3
Doncaster v Shrewsbury	-	1-0	-	-	0-1	-
Gillingham v Scunthorpe	-	-	-	0-3	2-1	3-2
MK Dons v Northampton	-	-	-	-	-	5-3
Oldham v Peterborough	-	-	5-4	1-1	1-5	2-0
Portsmouth v Bristol Rovers	-	-	3-2	-	3-1	-
Southend v AFC Wimbledon	2-0	1-3	0-1	0-1	-	3-0
Walsall v Charlton	1-1	-	-	-	-	1-2
Wigan v Plymouth	-	-	-	-	-	-

League Two

	2011-12	2012-13	2013-14	2014-15	2015-16	2016-17
Cambridge U v Forest Green	1-1	0-0	2-1	-	-	-
Carlisle v Stevenage	1-0	2-1	0-0	3-0	1-0	1-1
Cheltenham v Mansfield	-	-	1-2	1-1	-	0-0
Chesterfield v Yeovil	2-2	-	-	0-0	-	-
Crawley Town v Newport County	-	-	-	-	2-0	3-1
Exeter v Notts County	1-1	-	-	-	1-1	0-2
Grimsby v Colchester	-	-	-	-	-	1-0
Lincoln v Barnet	-	-	3-3	4-1	-	-
Morecambe v Luton	-	-	-	3-0	1-3	0-2
Port Vale v Accrington	4-1	3-0	-	-	-	-
Swindon v Coventry	-	2-2	2-1	1-1	2-2	1-0
Wycombe v Crewe	-	-	-	-	-	5-1

Saturday September 30, 2017

Premier League

	2011-12	2012-13	2013-14	2014-15	2015-16	2016-17
Bournemouth v Leicester	-	-	0-1	-	1-1	1-0
Chelsea v Man City	2-1	0-0	2-1	1-1	0-3	2-1
Huddersfield v Tottenham	-	-	-	-	-	-
Man United v Crystal Palace	-	-	2-0	1-0	2-0	2-0
Stoke v Southampton	-	3-3	1-1	2-1	1-2	0-0
West Brom v Watford	-	-	-	-	0-1	3-1
West Ham v Swansea	-	1-0	2-0	3-1	1-4	1-0

Championship

	2011-12	2012-13	2013-14	2014-15	2015-16	2016-17
Aston Villa v Bolton	1-2	-	-	-	-	-
Burton v Wolves	-	-	-	-	-	2-1
Cardiff v Derby	2-0	1-1	-	0-2	2-1	0-2
Hull v Birmingham	2-1	5-2	-	-	2-0	-
Ipswich v Bristol City	3-0	1-1	-	-	2-2	2-1
Middlesbrough v Brentford	-	-	-	4-0	3-1	-
Millwall v Barnsley	0-0	1-2	1-0	-	2-3	-

Results cover matches from Premier League to National League and Scottish Premiership to Scottish League Two

	2011-12	2012-13	2013-14	2014-15	2015-16	2016-17
Nottm Forest v Sheffield United	-	-	-	-	-	-
Preston v Sunderland	-	-	-	-	-	-
QPR v Fulham	0-1	2-1	-	-	1-3	1-1
Reading v Norwich	-	0-0	-	2-1	-	3-1
Sheffield Wed v Leeds	-	1-1	6-0	1-2	2-0	0-2
League One						
AFC Wimbledon v Rochdale	-	1-2	0-3	-	-	3-1
Blackburn v Gillingham	-	-	-	-	-	-
Bradford v Doncaster	-	-	-	1-2	2-1	-
Bristol Rovers v Plymouth	2-3	2-1	2-1	-	1-1	-
Bury v MK Dons	0-0	1-4	-	-	-	0-0
Fleetwood Town v Charlton	-	-	-	-	-	2-2
Peterborough v Oxford	-	-	-	-	-	1-2
Portsmouth v Oldham	-	0-1	-	-	-	-
Rotherham v Northampton	1-1	3-1	-	-	-	-
Shrewsbury v Scunthorpe	-	0-1	-	-	2-2	0-1
Southend v Blackpool	-	-	-	-	1-0	-
Wigan v Walsall	-	-	-	-	0-0	-
League Two						
Chesterfield v Cheltenham	-	4-1	2-0	-	-	-
Coventry v Crewe	-	1-2	2-2	1-3	3-2	-
Crawley Town v Carlisle	-	1-1	0-0	-	0-1	3-3
Exeter v Morecambe	-	0-3	1-1	1-1	1-1	3-1
Forest Green v Accrington	-	-	-	-	-	-
Grimsby v Lincoln	3-1	1-1	1-1	1-3	2-0	-
Luton v Newport County	2-0	2-2	-	3-0	1-1	2-1
Mansfield v Notts County	-	-	-	-	5-0	3-1
Stevenage v Port Vale	-	-	1-1	-	-	-
Swindon v Cambridge U	-	-	-	-	-	-
Wycombe v Barnet	-	0-0	-	-	1-1	0-2
Yeovil v Colchester	3-2	3-1	-	0-1	-	2-1
National League						
Barrow v Maidstone	-	-	-	-	-	3-0
Bromley v Tranmere	-	-	-	-	0-1	0-2
Dag & Red v Torquay	1-1	2-2	0-1	-	-	0-1
Dover v Solihull Moors	-	-	-	-	-	0-0
Eastleigh v Chester	-	-	-	3-2	1-0	0-3
Ebbsfleet v FC Halifax	-	-	-	-	-	-
Gateshead v Boreham Wood	-	-	-	-	2-1	1-1
Leyton Orient v Fylde	-	-	-	-	-	-
Macclesfield v Aldershot	0-1	-	1-1	0-0	0-2	0-2
Maidenhead v Guiseley	-	-	-	-	-	-
Woking v Hartlepool	-	-	-	-	-	-
Wrexham v Sutton United	-	-	-	-	-	1-0
Scottish Premiership						
Aberdeen v St Johnstone	0-0/0-0	2-0	0-0/1-0/1-1	2-0/0-1	1-5/1-1	0-0/0-2
Celtic v Hibernian	0-0	2-2/3-0	1-0	-	-	-
Dundee v Hearts	-	1-0/1-0	-	-	1-2/0-1	3-2
Hamilton v Rangers	-	-	-	-	-	1-2
Kilmarnock v Ross County	-	3-0	2-0/2-2	0-3/1-2	0-4/0-2	3-2/1-2
Motherwell v Partick	-	-	1-0/4-3	1-0/0-0	2-1/3-1	2-0
Scottish Championship						
Dunfermline v Dundee United	1-4	-	-	-	-	1-3/1-1
Inverness CT v Queen of Sth	-	-	-	-	-	-
Livingston v Dumbarton	-	5-0/2-3	1-3/1-2	1-2/1-2	1-1/2-0	-
Morton v Falkirk	3-2/0-0	1-2/2-0	0-2/1-1	-	1-1/0-1	1-1/2-2
St Mirren v Brechin	-	-	-	-	-	-

Results cover matches from Premier League to National League and Scottish Premiership to Scottish League Two

	2011-12	2012-13	2013-14	2014-15	2015-16	2016-17
Scottish League One						
Airdrieonians v Queens Park	-	-	-	-	-	4-1/3-2
Albion v Raith	-	-	-	-	-	-
Arbroath v Alloa	-	1-2/0-1	-	-	-	-
Ayr v East Fife	-	2-3/2-1	2-0/4-1	-	-	-
Forfar v Stranraer	-	4-0/3-1	1-2/1-0	1-1/1-0	1-2/1-1	-
Scottish League Two						
Annan v Cowdenbeath	-	-	-	-	-	2-0/1-0
Montrose v Clyde	4-0/5-0	2-3/1-1	0-2/0-2	0-3/0-1	2-0/2-1	2-1/1-1
Peterhead v Berwick	1-0/1-2	1-0/1-1	1-1/3-0	-	-	-
Stenhousemuir v Edinburgh City	-	-	-	-	-	-
Stirling v Elgin	-	1-4/1-1	1-1/2-2	-	3-1/0-0	0-4/1-0
Sunday October 1, 2017						
Premier League						
Arsenal v Brighton	-	-	-	-	-	-
Everton v Burnley	-	-	-	1-0	-	3-1
Newcastle v Liverpool	2-0	0-6	2-2	1-0	2-0	-
Tuesday October 3, 2017						
National League						
Aldershot v Dag & Red	1-1	1-0	-	-	-	3-1
Boreham Wood v Eastleigh	-	-	-	-	1-1	0-1
Chester v Woking	-	-	0-2	2-3	1-2	2-3
FC Halifax v Wrexham	-	-	-	-	-	-
Fylde v Gateshead	-	-	-	-	-	-
Guiseley v Macclesfield	-	-	-	-	0-3	1-2
Hartlepool v Barrow	-	-	-	-	-	-
Maidstone v Bromley	-	-	-	-	-	0-2
Solihull Moors v Ebbsfleet	-	-	-	-	-	-
Sutton United v Dover	-	-	-	-	-	0-6
Torquay v Maidenhead	-	-	-	-	-	-
Tranmere v Leyton Orient	2-0	3-1	0-4	-	-	-
Saturday October 7, 2017						
League One						
Blackpool v Blackburn	-	2-0	2-2	1-2	-	-
Charlton v Peterborough	-	2-0	-	-	-	0-2
Doncaster v Southend	-	-	-	-	0-0	-
Gillingham v Portsmouth	-	-	-	-	-	-
MK Dons v Bradford	-	-	2-3	1-2	-	1-2
Northampton v Bristol Rovers	3-2	1-0	0-0	-	2-2	2-3
Oldham v Bury	0-2	1-2	-	-	0-1	0-0
Oxford v AFC Wimbledon	1-0	3-2	2-1	0-0	1-0	1-3
Plymouth v Fleetwood Town	-	2-1	0-2	-	-	-
Rochdale v Rotherham	-	1-2	-	-	-	-
Scunthorpe v Wigan	-	-	-	-	1-1	-
Walsall v Shrewsbury	-	3-1	1-0	-	2-1	3-2
League Two						
Accrington v Luton	-	-	-	2-2	1-1	1-4
Barnet v Coventry	-	-	-	-	-	-
Cambridge U v Wycombe	-	-	-	0-1	1-0	1-2
Carlisle v Exeter	4-1	-	-	1-3	1-0	3-2
Cheltenham v Swindon	1-0	-	-	-	-	-
Colchester v Mansfield	-	-	-	-	-	2-0
Crewe v Stevenage	-	1-2	0-3	-	-	1-2
Lincoln v Chesterfield	-	-	-	-	-	-
Morecambe v Crawley Town	6-0	-	-	-	3-1	2-3
Newport County v Yeovil	-	-	-	-	0-0	1-0
Notts County v Forest Green	-	-	-	-	-	-
Port Vale v Grimsby	-	-	-	-	-	-

Results cover matches from Premier League to National League and Scottish Premiership to Scottish League Two

	2011-12	2012-13	2013-14	2014-15	2015-16	2016-17
National League						
Barrow v Leyton Orient	-	-	-	-	-	-
Boreham Wood v FC Halifax	-	-	-	-	-	-
Gateshead v Bromley	-	-	-	-	3-1	0-2
Macclesfield v Ebbsfleet	-	1-2	-	-	-	-
Maidenhead v Aldershot	-	-	-	-	-	-
Maidstone v Guiseley	-	-	-	-	-	1-1
Solihull Moors v Hartlepool	-	-	-	-	-	-
Sutton United v Fylde	-	-	-	-	-	-
Torquay v Dover	-	-	-	2-0	2-3	2-1
Tranmere v Chester	-	-	-	-	2-0	2-2
Woking v Dag & Red	-	-	-	-	-	1-3
Wrexham v Eastleigh	-	-	-	3-0	2-3	0-0

Saturday October 14, 2017

	2011-12	2012-13	2013-14	2014-15	2015-16	2016-17
Premier League						
Brighton v Everton	-	-	-	-	-	-
Burnley v West Ham	2-2	-	-	1-3	-	1-2
Crystal Palace v Chelsea	-	-	1-0	1-2	0-3	0-1
Leicester v West Brom	-	-	-	0-1	2-2	1-2
Liverpool v Man United	1-1	1-2	1-0	1-2	0-1	0-0
Man City v Stoke	3-0	3-0	1-0	0-1	4-0	0-0
Southampton v Newcastle	-	2-0	4-0	4-0	3-1	-
Swansea v Huddersfield	-	-	-	-	-	-
Tottenham v Bournemouth	-	-	-	-	3-0	4-0
Watford v Arsenal	-	-	-	-	0-3	1-3
Championship						
Barnsley v Middlesbrough	1-3	1-0	3-2	-	-	-
Birmingham v Cardiff	1-1	0-1	-	0-0	1-0	0-0
Bolton v Sheffield Wed	-	0-1	1-1	0-0	0-0	-
Brentford v Millwall	-	-	-	2-2	-	-
Bristol City v Burton	-	-	-	-	-	0-0
Derby v Nottm Forest	1-0	1-1	5-0	1-2	1-0	3-0
Fulham v Preston	-	-	-	-	1-1	3-1
Leeds v Reading	0-1	-	2-4	0-0	3-2	2-0
Norwich v Hull	-	-	1-0	-	-	-
Sheffield United v Ipswich	-	-	-	-	-	-
Sunderland v QPR	3-1	0-0	-	0-2	-	-
Wolves v Aston Villa	2-3	-	-	-	-	1-0
League One						
Bristol Rovers v Oxford	0-0	0-2	1-1	-	0-1	2-1
Bury v Bradford	-	-	-	-	0-0	0-2
Charlton v Doncaster	-	-	2-0	-	-	-
Fleetwood Town v Rochdale	-	0-3	0-0	1-0	1-1	0-0
Northampton v AFC Wimbledon	1-0	2-0	2-2	2-0	1-1	0-0
Oldham v Blackburn	-	-	-	-	-	-
Peterborough v Gillingham	-	-	2-0	1-2	1-1	1-1
Plymouth v Shrewsbury	1-0	-	-	1-0	-	-
Portsmouth v MK Dons	-	1-1	-	-	-	-
Rotherham v Scunthorpe	-	-	-	-	-	-
Walsall v Blackpool	-	-	-	-	1-1	-
Wigan v Southend	-	-	-	-	4-1	-
League Two						
Accrington v Coventry	-	-	-	-	-	-
Chesterfield v Morecambe	-	1-1	1-0	-	-	-
Colchester v Carlisle	1-1	2-0	1-1	-	-	4-1
Forest Green v Newport County	1-1	1-2	-	-	-	-
Grimsby v Crawley Town	-	-	-	-	-	1-1

Results cover matches from Premier League to National League and Scottish Premiership to Scottish League Two

	2011-12	2012-13	2013-14	2014-15	2015-16	2016-17
Lincoln v Cambridge U	0-1	0-0	1-0	-	-	-
Luton v Stevenage	-	-	-	2-0	0-1	0-2
Mansfield v Swindon	-	-	-	-	-	-
Notts County v Barnet	-	-	-	-	4-2	1-0
Port Vale v Cheltenham	1-2	3-2	-	-	-	-
Wycombe v Exeter	3-1	0-1	1-1	2-1	1-0	1-0
Yeovil v Crewe	-	1-0	-	1-1	-	3-0
Scottish Premiership						
Celtic v Dundee	-	2-0/5-0	-	2-1/5-0	6-0/0-0	2-1
Hamilton v Motherwell	-	-	-	5-0/2-0	1-0/0-1	1-1/0-1
Hibernian v Aberdeen	0-0/0-0	0-1/0-0	0-2/0-2	-	-	-
Partick v Kilmarnock	-	-	1-1/1-1	1-1/1-4	2-2/0-0	0-0
Ross County v Hearts	-	2-2	2-1/1-2	-	1-2/0-3	2-2
St Johnstone v Rangers	0-2/1-2/0-4	-	-	-	-	1-1/1-2
Scottish Championship						
Brechin v Morton	-	-	-	3-1/1-1	-	-
Dumbarton v St Mirren	-	-	-	-	1-0/2-1	1-1/2-2
Falkirk v Inverness CT	-	-	-	-	-	-
Livingston v Dundee United	-	-	-	-	-	-
Queen of Sth v Dunfermline	-	-	-	-	-	2-2/0-1
Scottish League One						
Ayr v Airdrieonians	-	-	2-2/3-0	2-3/0-1	3-0/0-3	-
East Fife v Albion	2-0/1-2	1-2/2-0	-	0-0/1-0	-	2-2/2-0
Queens Park v Forfar	-	-	-	-	-	-
Raith v Arbroath	-	-	-	-	-	-
Stranraer v Alloa	2-3/0-4	3-2/1-2	-	-	-	2-5/1-2
Tuesday October 17, 2017						
League One						
AFC Wimbledon v Rotherham	1-2	0-1	-	-	-	-
Blackburn v Plymouth	-	-	-	-	-	-
Blackpool v Bury	-	-	-	-	1-1	-
Bradford v Oldham	-	-	2-3	2-0	1-0	1-1
Doncaster v Portsmouth	3-4	1-1	-	-	-	3-1
Gillingham v Wigan	-	-	-	-	2-0	-
MK Dons v Walsall	0-1	2-4	1-0	0-3	-	1-1
Oxford v Charlton	-	-	-	-	-	1-1
Rochdale v Northampton	-	0-0	3-2	-	-	1-1
Scunthorpe v Fleetwood Town	-	-	0-0	0-2	1-0	0-2
Shrewsbury v Bristol Rovers	1-0	-	-	-	-	2-0
Southend v Peterborough	-	-	-	-	2-1	1-1
League Two						
Barnet v Mansfield	-	-	-	-	1-3	0-2
Cambridge U v Yeovil	-	-	-	-	3-0	1-0
Carlisle v Wycombe	2-2	-	-	2-3	1-1	1-0
Cheltenham v Grimsby	-	-	-	-	3-1	2-1
Coventry v Forest Green	-	-	-	-	-	-
Crawley Town v Chesterfield	-	-	-	1-1	-	-
Crewe v Notts County	-	1-2	1-3	0-3	-	2-2
Exeter v Luton	-	-	-	1-1	2-3	0-0
Morecambe v Port Vale	0-0	1-3	-	-	-	-
Newport County v Colchester	-	-	-	-	-	1-1
Stevenage v Accrington	-	-	-	2-1	1-1	0-3
Swindon v Lincoln	-	-	-	-	-	-
Saturday October 21, 2017						
Premier League						
Chelsea v Watford	-	-	-	-	2-2	4-3
Everton v Arsenal	0-1	1-1	3-0	2-2	0-2	2-1
Huddersfield v Man United	-	-	-	-	-	-

Results cover matches from Premier League to National League and Scottish Premiership to Scottish League Two

	2011-12	2012-13	2013-14	2014-15	2015-16	2016-17
Man City v Burnley	-	-	-	2-2	-	2-1
Newcastle v Crystal Palace	-	-	1-0	3-3	1-0	-
Southampton v West Brom	-	0-3	1-0	0-0	3-0	1-2
Stoke v Bournemouth	-	-	-	-	2-1	0-1
Swansea v Leicester	-	-	-	2-0	0-3	2-0
Tottenham v Liverpool	4-0	2-1	0-5	0-3	0-0	1-1
West Ham v Brighton	6-0	-	-	-	-	-
Championship						
Aston Villa v Fulham	1-0	1-1	1-2	-	-	1-0
Barnsley v Hull	2-1	2-0	-	-	-	-
Bolton v QPR	2-1	-	0-1	-	1-1	-
Brentford v Sunderland	-	-	-	-	-	-
Bristol City v Leeds	0-3	2-3	-	-	2-2	1-0
Derby v Sheffield Wed	-	2-2	3-0	3-2	1-1	2-0
Ipswich v Norwich	-	-	-	0-1	-	1-1
Middlesbrough v Cardiff	0-2	2-1	-	2-1	3-1	-
Millwall v Birmingham	0-6	3-3	2-3	1-3	-	-
Nottm Forest v Burton	-	-	-	-	-	4-3
Sheffield United v Reading	-	-	-	-	-	-
Wolves v Preston	-	-	2-0	-	1-2	1-0
League One						
AFC Wimbledon v Plymouth	1-2	1-1	1-1	0-0	0-2	-
Blackburn v Portsmouth	-	-	-	-	-	-
Blackpool v Wigan	-	-	1-0	1-3	0-4	-
Bradford v Charlton	-	-	-	-	-	0-0
Doncaster v Walsall	-	1-2	-	0-2	1-2	-
Gillingham v Northampton	4-3	2-0	-	-	-	2-1
MK Dons v Oldham	5-0	2-0	2-1	7-0	-	1-0
Oxford v Rotherham	2-1	0-4	-	-	-	-
Rochdale v Bristol Rovers	-	2-1	2-0	-	-	0-0
Scunthorpe v Peterborough	-	-	-	2-0	0-4	1-1
Shrewsbury v Fleetwood Town	-	-	-	-	1-1	0-1
Southend v Bury	-	-	0-0	1-1	4-1	1-0
League Two						
Barnet v Yeovil	-	-	-	-	3-4	2-2
Cambridge U v Chesterfield	-	-	-	-	-	-
Carlisle v Notts County	0-3	0-4	2-1	-	3-0	1-2
Cheltenham v Lincoln	-	-	-	-	3-1	-
Coventry v Colchester	-	2-2	2-0	1-0	0-1	-
Crawley Town v Luton	-	-	-	-	2-1	2-0
Crewe v Accrington	2-0	-	-	-	-	0-1
Exeter v Port Vale	-	0-2	-	-	-	-
Morecambe v Grimsby	-	-	-	-	-	1-0
Newport County v Mansfield	1-0	2-0	1-1	0-1	1-0	2-3
Stevenage v Forest Green	-	-	-	-	-	-
Swindon v Wycombe	-	-	-	-	-	-
National League						
Aldershot v Tranmere	-	-	-	-	0-0	3-1
Bromley v Woking	-	-	-	-	2-1	2-1
Chester v Boreham Wood	-	-	-	-	2-2	0-2
Dag & Red v Wrexham	-	-	-	-	-	3-0
Dover v Maidenhead	-	-	2-0	-	-	-
Eastleigh v Gateshead	-	-	-	2-2	1-2	1-1
Ebbsfleet v Barrow	1-2	2-4	-	-	-	-
FC Halifax v Torquay	-	-	-	-	-	-
Fylde v Maidstone	-	-	-	-	-	-
Guiseley v Solihull Moors	-	-	0-3	3-0	-	1-1
Hartlepool v Sutton United	-	-	-	-	-	-
Leyton Orient v Macclesfield	-	-	-	-	-	-

Results cover matches from Premier League to National League and Scottish Premiership to Scottish League Two

	2011-12	2012-13	2013-14	2014-15	2015-16	2016-17
Scottish Premiership						
Hearts v St Johnstone	1-2/2-0	2-0/2-0	0-2	-	4-3/0-3/2-2	2-2
Kilmarnock v Hibernian	4-1/1-3	1-1/1-3	1-2/1-1	-	-	-
Motherwell v Celtic	1-2/0-3	0-2/2-1/3-1	0-5/3-3	0-1	0-1/1-2	3-4
Partick v Dundee	0-1/0-0	-	-	1-1	0-1/2-4/1-2	2-0
Rangers v Aberdeen	2-0/1-1	-	-	-	-	2-1/1-2
Ross County v Hamilton	1-0/5-1	-	-	0-1/2-1	2-0/2-1	1-1/3-2
Scottish Championship						
Brechin v Queen of Sth	-	0-3/0-6	-	-	-	-
Dundee United v Inverness CT	3-1/3-0	4-4	0-1/2-1	1-1	1-1/0-2	-
Dunfermline v Livingston	-	4-0/0-1	-	-	-	-
Falkirk v St Mirren	-	-	-	-	3-0/3-2	3-1/2-2
Morton v Dumbarton	-	3-0/0-3	2-0/3-0	-	0-0/2-0	1-1/2-1
Scottish League One						
Albion v Queens Park	-	-	2-1/1-0	1-0/2-1	-	2-0/1-1
Alloa v East Fife	-	1-1/1-1	-	-	-	2-1/3-0
Arbroath v Airdrieonians	3-1/2-2	-	3-2/0-1	-	-	-
Forfar v Ayr	-	2-1/2-1	0-1/4-2	2-0/1-3	2-2/3-1	-
Stranraer v Raith	-	-	-	-	-	-
Scottish League Two						
Berwick v Montrose	1-2/2-2	1-4/4-0	1-1/5-0	2-2/3-3	2-1/1-0	1-2/0-1
Clyde v Peterhead	2-0/0-1	0-2/2-0	1-3/0-2	-	-	-
Cowdenbeath v Stirling	2-0/4-1	-	-	-	-	0-2/0-2
Edinburgh City v Annan	-	-	-	-	-	1-0/2-0
Elgin v Stenhousemuir	-	-	-	-	-	-

Tuesday October 24, 2017

	2011-12	2012-13	2013-14	2014-15	2015-16	2016-17
National League						
Aldershot v Sutton United	-	-	-	-	-	2-0
Bromley v Maidenhead	-	-	6-1	4-2	-	-
Chester v Barrow	-	-	-	-	1-2	1-2
Dag & Red v Macclesfield	2-0	-	-	-	-	1-1
Dover v Woking	-	-	-	2-1	2-0	3-1
Eastleigh v Solihull Moors	-	-	-	-	-	2-0
Ebbsfleet v Torquay	-	-	-	-	-	-
FC Halifax v Maidstone	-	-	-	-	-	-
Fylde v Wrexham	-	-	-	-	-	-
Guiseley v Boreham Wood	-	-	-	-	1-1	3-1
Hartlepool v Tranmere	0-2	0-2	-	0-0	-	-
Leyton Orient v Gateshead	-	-	-	-	-	-

Wednesday October 25, 2017

	2011-12	2012-13	2013-14	2014-15	2015-16	2016-17
Scottish Premiership						
Aberdeen v Celtic	0-1/1-1	0-2	0-2/2-1	1-2/0-1	2-1/2-1	0-1/1-3
Dundee v Motherwell	-	1-2/0-3	-	4-1	2-1/2-2	2-0
Hamilton v Partick	1-0/2-2	1-0/0-2	-	3-3/1-1	0-0/1-2	1-1
Hibernian v Hearts	1-3	1-1/0-0	2-1/1-2	1-1/2-0	-	-
Rangers v Kilmarnock	2-0/0-1	-	-	-	-	3-0
St Johnstone v Ross County	-	1-1/2-2	4-0/0-1	2-1	1-1/1-1	2-4

Saturday October 28, 2017

	2011-12	2012-13	2013-14	2014-15	2015-16	2016-17
Premier League						
Arsenal v Swansea	1-0	0-2	2-2	0-1	1-2	3-2
Bournemouth v Chelsea	-	-	-	-	1-4	1-3
Brighton v Southampton	3-0	-	-	-	-	-
Burnley v Newcastle	-	-	-	1-1	-	-
Crystal Palace v West Ham	2-2	-	1-0	1-3	1-3	0-1
Leicester v Everton	-	-	-	2-2	3-1	0-2
Liverpool v Huddersfield	-	-	-	-	-	-
Man United v Tottenham	3-0	2-3	1-2	3-0	1-0	1-0
Watford v Stoke	-	-	-	-	1-2	0-1
West Brom v Man City	0-0	1-2	2-3	1-3	0-3	0-4

Results cover matches from Premier League to National League and Scottish Premiership to Scottish League Two

	2011-12	2012-13	2013-14	2014-15	2015-16	2016-17
Championship						
Birmingham v Aston Villa	-	-	-	-	-	1-1
Burton v Ipswich	-	-	-	-	-	1-2
Cardiff v Millwall	0-0	1-0	-	0-0	-	-
Fulham v Bolton	2-0	-	-	4-0	1-0	-
Hull v Nottm Forest	2-1	1-2	-	-	1-1	-
Leeds v Sheffield United	-	-	-	-	-	-
Norwich v Derby	-	-	-	1-1	-	3-0
Preston v Brentford	1-3	1-1	0-3	-	1-3	4-2
QPR v Wolves	1-2	-	-	-	1-1	1-2
Reading v Middlesbrough	0-0	-	2-0	0-0	2-0	-
Sheffield Wed v Barnsley	-	2-1	1-0	-	-	2-0
Sunderland v Bristol City	-	-	-	-	-	-
League One						
Bristol Rovers v MK Dons	-	-	-	-	-	0-0
Bury v Doncaster	-	2-0	-	-	1-0	-
Charlton v AFC Wimbledon	-	-	-	-	-	1-2
Fleetwood Town v Oxford	-	3-0	1-1	-	-	2-0
Northampton v Blackpool	-	-	-	-	-	-
Oldham v Scunthorpe	1-2	1-1	-	3-2	2-4	2-0
Peterborough v Shrewsbury	-	-	1-0	-	1-1	2-1
Plymouth v Rochdale	-	3-1	1-0	-	-	-
Portsmouth v Bradford	-	-	-	-	-	-
Rotherham v Gillingham	3-0	1-2	4-1	-	-	-
Walsall v Southend	-	-	-	-	1-0	0-0
Wigan v Blackburn	3-3	-	2-1	1-1	-	3-0
League Two						
Accrington v Barnet	0-3	3-2	-	-	2-2	1-0
Chesterfield v Carlisle	4-1	-	-	-	-	-
Colchester v Crewe	-	1-2	1-2	2-3	2-3	4-0
Forest Green v Morecambe	-	-	-	-	-	-
Grimsby v Cambridge U	2-1	0-1	0-1	-	-	2-1
Lincoln v Crawley Town	-	-	-	-	-	-
Luton v Coventry	-	-	-	-	-	-
Mansfield v Exeter	-	-	0-0	2-3	0-2	1-2
Notts County v Newport County	-	-	-	-	4-3	0-3
Port Vale v Swindon	0-2	-	2-3	0-1	1-0	3-2
Wycombe v Cheltenham	-	1-1	1-2	2-1	-	3-3
Yeovil v Stevenage	0-6	1-3	-	-	2-2	1-1
National League						
Barrow v Aldershot	-	-	-	-	1-3	1-0
Boreham Wood v Bromley	-	-	-	-	2-3	0-0
Gateshead v Dover	-	-	-	1-2	2-3	4-2
Macclesfield v Eastleigh	-	-	-	2-0	1-2	0-1
Maidenhead v Dag & Red	-	-	-	-	-	-
Maidstone v Chester	-	-	-	-	-	4-2
Solihull Moors v Fylde	-	-	-	-	-	-
Sutton United v Ebbsfleet	-	-	-	-	-	-
Torquay v Hartlepool	-	-	0-0	-	-	-
Tranmere v FC Halifax	-	-	-	-	-	-
Woking v Guiseley	-	-	-	-	0-1	0-0
Wrexham v Leyton Orient	-	-	-	-	-	-
Scottish Premiership						
Aberdeen v Ross County	-	0-0/0-1	1-0	3-0/4-0	3-1/0-4	4-0/1-0
Celtic v Kilmarnock	2-1	0-2/4-1	4-0	2-0/4-1	0-0	6-1/3-1
Dundee v Hamilton	0-1/2-2	-	0-0/1-0	2-0/1-1	4-0/0-1	1-1/0-2
Hearts v Rangers	0-2/0-3	-	-	2-0/2-2	-	2-0/4-1
Motherwell v Hibernian	4-3	0-4/4-1	1-0	-	-	-
Partick v St Johnstone	-	-	0-1	0-0/3-0	2-0	0-2/0-1

Results cover matches from Premier League to National League and Scottish Premiership to Scottish League Two

	2011-12	2012-13	2013-14	2014-15	2015-16	2016-17
Scottish Championship						
Dumbarton v Dundee United	-	-	-	-	-	1-0/1-0
Inverness CT v Dunfermline	1-1/0-0	-	-	-	-	-
Livingston v Brechin	-	-	-	-	-	2-1/3-0
Queen of Sth v Falkirk	1-5/0-0	-	2-0/1-2	3-0/1-0	2-2/2-2	2-0/0-2
St Mirren v Morton	-	-	-	-	1-1/3-1	1-1/1-1
Scottish League One						
Airdrieonians v Albion	4-0/1-0	-	-	-	1-1/1-1	0-2/1-2
Ayr v Stranraer	-	2-1/2-1	3-6/5-0	0-2/0-2	3-1/2-1	-
East Fife v Arbroath	2-2/1-3	2-1/0-1	2-1/1-0	1-5/2-0	0-1/2-1	-
Forfar v Raith	-	-	-	-	-	-
Queens Park v Alloa	1-3/1-2	-	-	-	-	1-2/0-2
Scottish League Two						
Berwick v Cowdenbeath	-	-	-	-	-	1-1/1-3
Clyde v Elgin	1-2/0-2	2-2/1-1	2-1/4-0	2-1/0-2	4-2/1-0	2-1/3-2
Montrose v Edinburgh City	-	-	-	-	-	0-1/3-0
Peterhead v Annan	2-3/3-2	2-0/2-0	2-2/3-1	-	-	-
Stirling v Stenhousemuir	2-2/3-1	-	-	0-4/3-2	-	-
Tuesday October 31, 2017						
Championship						
Birmingham v Brentford	-	-	-	1-0	2-1	1-3
Burton v Barnsley	-	-	-	-	0-0	0-0
Cardiff v Ipswich	2-2	0-0	-	3-1	1-0	3-1
Fulham v Bristol City	-	-	-	-	1-2	0-4
Hull v Middlesbrough	2-1	1-0	-	-	3-0	4-2
Leeds v Derby	0-2	1-2	1-1	2-0	2-2	1-0
Norwich v Wolves	2-1	-	-	2-0	-	3-1
Preston v Aston Villa	-	-	-	-	-	2-0
QPR v Sheffield United	-	-	-	-	-	-
Reading v Nottm Forest	1-0	-	1-1	0-3	2-1	2-0
Sheffield Wed v Millwall	-	3-2	2-2	1-1	-	-
Sunderland v Bolton	2-2	-	-	-	-	-
Saturday November 4, 2017						
Premier League						
Chelsea v Man United	3-3	2-3	3-1	1-0	1-1	4-0
Everton v Watford	-	-	-	-	2-2	1-0
Huddersfield v West Brom	-	-	-	-	-	-
Man City v Arsenal	1-0	1-1	6-3	0-2	2-2	2-1
Newcastle v Bournemouth	-	-	-	-	1-3	-
Southampton v Burnley	2-0	-	-	2-0	-	3-1
Stoke v Leicester	-	-	-	0-1	2-2	2-2
Swansea v Brighton	-	-	-	-	-	-
Tottenham v Crystal Palace	-	-	2-0	0-0	1-0	1-0
West Ham v Liverpool	-	2-3	1-2	3-1	2-0	0-4
Championship						
Aston Villa v Sheffield Wed	-	-	-	-	-	2-0
Barnsley v Birmingham	1-3	1-2	0-3	-	-	2-2
Bolton v Norwich	1-2	-	-	1-2	-	-
Brentford v Leeds	-	-	-	2-0	1-1	2-0
Bristol City v Cardiff	1-2	4-2	-	-	0-2	2-3
Derby v Reading	0-1	-	1-3	0-3	1-1	3-2
Ipswich v Preston	-	-	-	-	1-1	1-0
Middlesbrough v Sunderland	-	-	-	-	-	1-0
Millwall v Burton	-	-	-	-	2-0	-
Nottm Forest v QPR	-	-	2-0	-	0-0	1-1
Sheffield United v Hull	-	-	-	-	-	-
Wolves v Fulham	2-0	-	-	3-0	3-2	4-4

Results cover matches from Premier League to National League and Scottish Premiership to Scottish League Two

Scottish Premiership						
Hamilton v Aberdeen	-	-	-	3-0/0-3	1-1	1-0/1-0
Hibernian v Dundee	-	3-0/1-1/1-0	-	-	-	-
Kilmarnock v Hearts	0-0/1-1	1-0/0-1	2-0/4-2	-	2-2	2-0/0-0
Rangers v Partick	-	-	-	-	-	2-0/2-0
Ross County v Motherwell	-	0-0/3-0	1-2	1-2/3-2	3-0/1-3	1-1/1-2
St Johnstone v Celtic	0-2	2-1/1-1	0-1/3-3	0-3/1-2/0-0	0-3/2-1	2-4/2-5
Scottish Championship						
Brechin v Dumbarton	3-3/2-2	-	-	-	-	-
Dundee United v St Mirren	1-1/0-0	3-4	4-0/3-2	3-0	-	2-1/3-2
Falkirk v Dunfermline	-	2-2/1-0	-	-	-	2-1/2-0
Livingston v Inverness CT	-	-	-	-	-	-
Morton v Queen of Sth	2-2/2-2	-	0-2/1-1	-	2-0/3-2	1-0/1-0
Scottish League One						
Albion v Forfar	1-0/2-2	2-3/1-2	-	-	1-1/3-2	-
Alloa v Airdrieonians	-	-	-	-	-	1-2/2-1
Arbroath v Ayr	-	4-2/1-4	0-3/2-3	-	-	-
Raith v East Fife	-	-	-	-	-	-
Stranraer v Queens Park	2-3/2-3	-	-	-	-	0-2/1-1
Scottish League Two						
Annan v Berwick	2-2/1-1	3-2/2-2	3-2/4-0	2-0/4-2	1-0/1-0	3-1/2-1
Cowdenbeath v Montrose	-	-	-	-	-	2-0/0-2
Edinburgh City v Stirling	-	-	-	-	-	2-0/1-0
Elgin v Peterhead	6-1/1-2	2-0/0-3	2-4/2-3	-	-	-
Stenhousemuir v Clyde	-	-	-	-	-	-

Saturday November 11, 2017

	2011-12	2012-13	2013-14	2014-15	2015-16	2016-17
League One						
AFC Wimbledon v Peterborough	-	-	-	-	-	0-0
Blackburn v Walsall	-	-	-	-	-	-
Blackpool v Portsmouth	1-1	-	-	-	-	3-1
Bradford v Plymouth	1-1	1-0	-	-	-	-
Doncaster v Rotherham	-	-	-	-	-	-
Gillingham v Bury	-	-	-	-	3-1	2-1
MK Dons v Fleetwood Town	-	-	-	2-1	-	0-1
Oxford v Northampton	2-0	2-1	2-0	1-1	0-1	0-1
Rochdale v Wigan	-	-	-	-	0-2	-
Scunthorpe v Bristol Rovers	-	-	1-1	-	-	3-1
Shrewsbury v Charlton	-	-	-	-	-	4-3
Southend v Oldham	-	-	-	-	0-1	3-0
League Two						
Barnet v Colchester	-	-	-	-	-	1-1
Cambridge U v Accrington	-	-	-	2-2	2-3	2-1
Carlisle v Yeovil	3-2	3-3	-	-	3-2	2-1
Cheltenham v Luton	-	-	-	1-1	-	1-1
Coventry v Mansfield	-	-	-	-	-	-
Crawley Town v Forest Green	-	-	-	-	-	-
Crewe v Lincoln	-	-	-	-	-	-
Exeter v Grimsby	-	-	-	-	-	0-0
Morecambe v Wycombe	-	0-1	1-1	1-3	0-1	1-1
Newport County v Port Vale	-	-	-	-	-	-
Stevenage v Notts County	0-2	2-0	0-1	-	0-2	3-0
Swindon v Chesterfield	-	-	-	3-1	1-0	0-1
National League						
Aldershot v Fylde	-	-	-	-	-	-
Barrow v Macclesfield	-	1-0	-	-	1-1	1-1
Boreham Wood v Hartlepool	-	-	-	-	-	-

Results cover matches from Premier League to National League and Scottish Premiership to Scottish League Two

	2011-12	2012-13	2013-14	2014-15	2015-16	2016-17
Chester v Wrexham	-	-	0-0	2-1	3-2	1-1
Dover v Eastleigh	-	-	1-2	2-1	1-2	3-0
Ebbsfleet v Leyton Orient	-	-	-	-	-	-
FC Halifax v Woking	-	-	-	-	-	-
Guiseley v Bromley	-	-	-	-	2-0	1-4
Maidenhead v Gateshead	-	-	-	-	-	-
Solihull Moors v Sutton United	-	-	-	-	-	3-0
Torquay v Maidstone	-	-	-	-	-	2-3
Tranmere v Dag & Red	-	-	-	2-3	-	0-2

Scottish Championship						
Dumbarton v Queen of Sth	-	-	0-1/0-3	0-4/0-0	0-2/4-2	0-0/1-2
Dundee United v Falkirk	-	-	-	-	-	1-0/1-1
Dunfermline v Morton	-	2-2/1-4	-	1-2/0-4	-	2-1/3-1
Inverness CT v Brechin	-	-	-	-	-	-
St Mirren v Livingston	-	-	-	-	1-1/1-4	-

Scottish League One						
Airdrieonians v Stranraer	-	-	3-2/1-1	3-3/1-1	0-1/1-1	1-0/1-2
Albion v Alloa	-	0-3/1-5	-	-	-	0-4/1-1
Ayr v Raith	2-1/1-1	-	-	-	-	0-2/1-0
Forfar v East Fife	3-2/1-4	3-2/3-2	2-0/1-2	-	-	-
Queens Park v Arbroath	-	-	-	0-2/2-1	1-0/2-1	-

Scottish League Two						
Berwick v Edinburgh City	-	-	-	-	-	1-3/3-2
Clyde v Stirling	-	2-1/1-2	2-1/1-0	-	0-1/3-1	1-1/2-3
Cowdenbeath v Elgin	-	-	-	-	-	0-1/1-1
Montrose v Annan	2-3/1-1	0-0/5-1	0-2/2-1	2-0/2-1	1-1/0-5	2-2/2-3
Peterhead v Stenhousemuir	-	-	-	1-0/2-0	2-2/4-1	0-2/0-1

Saturday November 18, 2017						
Premier League						
Arsenal v Tottenham	5-2	5-2	1-0	1-1	1-1	1-1
Bournemouth v Huddersfield	2-0	-	2-1	1-1	-	-
Brighton v Stoke	-	-	-	-	-	-
Burnley v Swansea	-	-	-	0-1	-	0-1
Crystal Palace v Everton	-	-	0-0	0-1	0-0	0-1
Leicester v Man City	-	-	-	0-1	0-0	4-2
Liverpool v Southampton	-	1-0	0-1	2-1	1-1	0-0
Man United v Newcastle	1-1	4-3	0-1	3-1	0-0	-
Watford v West Ham	0-4	-	-	-	2-0	1-1
West Brom v Chelsea	1-0	2-1	1-1	3-0	2-3	0-1

Championship						
Birmingham v Nottm Forest	1-2	2-1	0-0	2-1	0-1	0-0
Burton v Sheffield United	-	-	-	-	0-0	-
Cardiff v Brentford	-	-	-	2-3	3-2	2-1
Fulham v Derby	-	-	-	2-0	1-1	2-2
Hull v Ipswich	2-2	2-1	-	-	3-0	-
Leeds v Middlesbrough	0-1	2-1	2-1	1-0	0-0	-
Norwich v Barnsley	-	-	-	-	-	2-0
Preston v Bolton	-	-	-	-	0-0	-
QPR v Aston Villa	1-1	1-1	-	2-0	-	0-1
Reading v Wolves	-	-	-	3-3	0-0	2-1
Sheffield Wed v Bristol City	-	2-3	-	-	2-0	3-2
Sunderland v Millwall	-	-	-	-	-	-

League One						
Bristol Rovers v AFC Wimbledon	1-0	1-0	3-0	-	3-1	2-0
Bury v Blackburn	-	-	-	-	-	-
Charlton v MK Dons	2-1	-	-	-	0-0	0-2

Results cover matches from Premier League to National League and Scottish Premiership to Scottish League Two

	2011-12	2012-13	2013-14	2014-15	2015-16	2016-17
Fleetwood Town v Doncaster	-	-	-	3-1	0-0	-
Northampton v Scunthorpe	-	-	1-1	-	-	1-2
Oldham v Rochdale	2-0	-	-	3-0	2-3	1-1
Peterborough v Blackpool	3-1	1-4	-	-	5-1	-
Plymouth v Oxford	1-1	0-1	0-2	1-2	2-2	-
Portsmouth v Southend	-	-	1-2	1-2	-	-
Rotherham v Shrewsbury	1-1	-	2-2	-	-	-
Walsall v Gillingham	-	-	1-1	1-1	3-2	1-2
Wigan v Bradford	-	-	-	-	1-0	-
League Two						
Accrington v Newport County	-	-	3-3	0-2	2-2	1-3
Chesterfield v Exeter	0-2	4-0	1-1	-	-	-
Colchester v Morecambe	-	-	-	-	-	2-2
Forest Green v Crewe	-	-	-	-	-	-
Grimsby v Carlisle	-	-	-	-	-	2-2
Lincoln v Coventry	-	-	-	-	-	-
Luton v Cambridge U	0-1	3-2	0-0	3-2	0-0	2-0
Mansfield v Stevenage	-	-	-	1-0	2-1	1-2
Notts County v Cheltenham	-	-	-	-	-	2-1
Port Vale v Barnet	1-2	3-0	-	-	-	-
Wycombe v Crawley Town	-	-	-	-	2-0	1-2
Yeovil v Swindon	-	0-2	-	1-1	-	-
National League						
Bromley v Chester	-	-	-	-	3-0	0-1
Dag & Red v Guiseley	-	-	-	-	-	1-2
Eastleigh v Barrow	-	-	-	-	3-1	2-0
Fylde v Torquay	-	-	-	-	-	-
Gateshead v Tranmere	-	-	-	-	1-4	0-1
Hartlepool v Aldershot	-	-	-	-	-	-
Leyton Orient v Dover	-	-	-	-	-	-
Macclesfield v Boreham Wood	-	-	-	-	0-0	0-2
Maidstone v Solihull Moors	-	-	-	-	-	2-4
Sutton United v FC Halifax	-	-	-	-	-	-
Woking v Maidenhead	-	-	-	-	-	-
Wrexham v Ebbsfleet	1-0	4-1	-	-	-	-
Scottish Premiership						
Aberdeen v Motherwell	1-2	3-3/0-0	0-1/0-1	1-0/2-1	1-1/4-1	7-2/1-0
Dundee v Kilmarnock	-	0-0/2-3	-	1-1/1-0	1-2/1-1	1-1/1-1
Hibernian v St Johnstone	3-2/2-3	2-0/1-3	0-0	-	-	-
Partick v Hearts	-	-	1-1/2-4	-	0-4	1-2/2-0
Rangers v Hamilton	-	-	-	-	-	1-1/4-0
Ross County v Celtic	-	1-1/3-2/1-1	1-4	0-5/0-1	1-4	0-4/2-2

Tuesday November 21, 2017

Championship						
Aston Villa v Sunderland	0-0	6-1	0-0	0-0	2-2	-
Barnsley v Cardiff	0-1	1-2	-	-	-	0-0
Bolton v Reading	-	-	1-1	1-1	0-1	-
Brentford v Burton	-	-	-	-	-	2-1
Bristol City v Preston	-	-	1-1	0-1	1-2	1-2
Derby v QPR	-	-	1-0	-	1-0	1-0
Ipswich v Sheffield Wed	-	0-3	2-1	2-1	2-1	0-1
Middlesbrough v Birmingham	3-1	0-1	3-1	2-0	0-0	-
Millwall v Hull	2-0	0-1	-	-	-	-
Nottm Forest v Norwich	-	-	-	2-1	-	1-2
Sheffield United v Fulham	-	-	-	-	-	-
Wolves v Leeds	-	2-2	-	4-3	2-3	0-1

Results cover matches from Premier League to National League and Scottish Premiership to Scottish League Two

	2011-12	2012-13	2013-14	2014-15	2015-16	2016-17
League One						
Blackpool v Gillingham	-	-	-	-	1-0	-
Bradford v Scunthorpe	-	-	-	1-1	1-0	0-0
Bristol Rovers v Rotherham	5-2	1-2	-	-	-	-
Bury v Shrewsbury	-	2-2	-	1-0	2-2	2-1
Charlton v Rochdale	1-1	-	-	-	-	0-1
MK Dons v Southend	-	-	-	-	-	0-3
Oldham v AFC Wimbledon	-	-	-	-	-	0-0
Oxford v Blackburn	-	-	-	-	-	-
Peterborough v Portsmouth	0-3	-	-	-	-	-
Plymouth v Northampton	4-1	3-2	1-0	2-0	1-2	-
Walsall v Fleetwood Town	-	-	-	1-0	3-1	0-1
Wigan v Doncaster	-	-	2-2	-	0-0	-
League Two						
Accrington v Wycombe	-	0-2	1-1	1-1	1-1	2-2
Cheltenham v Cambridge U	-	-	-	3-1	-	0-1
Chesterfield v Forest Green	-	-	-	-	-	-
Colchester v Lincoln	-	-	-	-	-	-
Crawley Town v Exeter	-	-	-	-	0-2	1-2
Grimsby v Swindon	-	-	-	-	-	-
Luton v Carlisle	-	-	-	1-0	3-4	1-1
Morecambe v Crewe	1-2	-	-	-	-	0-0
Newport County v Barnet	-	-	-	-	0-3	2-2
Port Vale v Mansfield	-	-	-	-	-	-
Stevenage v Coventry	-	1-3	0-1	-	-	-
Yeovil v Notts County	1-0	0-0	-	1-1	1-0	2-0
National League						
Bromley v Aldershot	-	-	-	-	1-3	2-2
Dag & Red v Dover	-	-	-	-	-	2-0
Eastleigh v Maidenhead	-	-	3-2	-	-	-
Fylde v Guiseley	-	-	-	-	-	-
Gateshead v Barrow	2-0	0-1	-	-	1-1	4-1
Hartlepool v FC Halifax	-	-	-	-	-	-
Leyton Orient v Chester	-	-	-	-	-	-
Macclesfield v Tranmere	-	-	-	-	1-2	4-2
Maidstone v Boreham Wood	-	-	-	-	-	1-0
Sutton United v Torquay	-	-	-	-	-	2-0
Woking v Ebbsfleet	-	1-0	-	-	-	-
Wrexham v Solihull Moors	-	-	-	-	-	1-0

Saturday November 25, 2017

	2011-12	2012-13	2013-14	2014-15	2015-16	2016-17
Premier League						
Burnley v Arsenal	-	-	-	0-1	-	0-1
Crystal Palace v Stoke	-	-	1-0	1-1	2-1	4-1
Huddersfield v Man City	-	-	-	-	-	-
Liverpool v Chelsea	4-1	2-2	0-2	1-2	1-1	1-1
Man United v Brighton	-	-	-	-	-	-
Newcastle v Watford	-	-	-	-	1-2	-
Southampton v Everton	-	0-0	2-0	3-0	0-3	1-0
Swansea v Bournemouth	-	-	-	-	2-2	0-3
Tottenham v West Brom	1-0	1-1	1-1	0-1	1-1	4-0
West Ham v Leicester	3-2	-	-	2-0	1-2	2-3
Championship						
Aston Villa v Ipswich	-	-	-	-	-	0-1
Barnsley v Leeds	4-1	2-0	0-1	-	-	3-2
Burton v Sunderland	-	-	-	-	-	-
Fulham v Millwall	-	-	-	0-1	-	-
Hull v Bristol City	3-0	0-0	-	-	4-0	-
Middlesbrough v Derby	2-0	2-2	1-0	2-0	2-0	-
Norwich v Preston	-	-	-	-	-	0-1

Results cover matches from Premier League to National League and Scottish Premiership to Scottish League Two

| --- | --- | --- | --- | --- | --- | --- |
Nottm Forest v Cardiff	0-1	3-1	-	1-2	1-2	1-2
QPR v Brentford	-	-	-	-	3-0	0-2
Reading v Sheffield Wed	-	-	0-2	2-0	1-1	2-1
Sheffield United v Birmingham	-	-	-	-	-	-
Wolves v Bolton	2-3	2-2	-	1-0	2-2	-

League One

	2011-12	2012-13	2013-14	2014-15	2015-16	2016-17
AFC Wimbledon v Walsall	-	-	-	-	-	1-0
Blackburn v Bristol Rovers	-	-	-	-	-	-
Doncaster v MK Dons	-	0-0	-	0-0	-	-
Fleetwood Town v Blackpool	-	-	-	-	0-0	-
Gillingham v Oldham	-	-	0-1	3-2	3-3	1-2
Northampton v Bury	-	-	0-3	2-3	-	3-2
Portsmouth v Plymouth	-	-	3-3	2-1	1-2	1-1
Rochdale v Peterborough	-	-	-	0-1	2-0	2-3
Rotherham v Wigan	-	-	-	1-2	-	3-2
Scunthorpe v Charlton	1-1	-	-	-	-	0-0
Shrewsbury v Bradford	1-0	-	2-1	-	1-1	1-0
Southend v Oxford	2-1	1-0	3-0	1-1	-	2-1

League Two

	2011-12	2012-13	2013-14	2014-15	2015-16	2016-17
Barnet v Grimsby	-	-	2-1	1-3	-	3-1
Cambridge U v Stevenage	-	-	-	1-1	1-0	0-0
Carlisle v Morecambe	-	-	-	1-1	2-3	1-1
Coventry v Crawley Town	-	3-1	2-2	2-2	-	-
Crewe v Luton	-	-	-	-	-	1-2
Exeter v Accrington	-	2-0	0-1	1-2	2-1	0-2
Forest Green v Cheltenham	-	-	-	-	2-2	-
Lincoln v Port Vale	-	-	-	-	-	-
Mansfield v Chesterfield	-	-	0-0	-	-	-
Notts County v Colchester	4-1	3-1	2-0	2-1	-	3-1
Swindon v Newport County	-	-	-	-	-	-
Wycombe v Yeovil	2-3	-	-	-	0-0	1-1

National League

	2011-12	2012-13	2013-14	2014-15	2015-16	2016-17
Aldershot v Wrexham	-	-	2-0	1-1	0-1	2-0
Barrow v Bromley	-	-	-	-	1-1	1-1
Boreham Wood v Woking	-	-	-	-	1-1	2-1
Chester v Dag & Red	-	-	-	-	-	3-0
Dover v Fylde	-	-	-	-	-	-
Ebbsfleet v Hartlepool	-	-	-	-	-	-
FC Halifax v Eastleigh	-	-	-	-	-	-
Guiseley v Sutton United	-	-	-	-	-	2-1
Maidenhead v Macclesfield	-	-	-	-	-	-
Solihull Moors v Gateshead	-	-	-	-	-	0-2
Torquay v Leyton Orient	-	-	-	-	-	-
Tranmere v Maidstone	-	-	-	-	-	2-1

Scottish Premiership

	2011-12	2012-13	2013-14	2014-15	2015-16	2016-17
Celtic v Partick	-	-	1-0	1-0/2-0	1-0	1-0/1-1
Dundee v Rangers	-	-	-	-	-	1-2/2-1
Hamilton v Hibernian	-	-	-	-	-	-
Hearts v Ross County	-	2-2/4-2	2-2/2-0	-	2-0/1-1	0-0/0-1
Kilmarnock v Aberdeen	2-0/1-1	1-3/1-1	0-1	0-2/1-2	0-4	0-4/1-2
Motherwell v St Johnstone	0-3/3-2/5-1	1-1/3-2	4-0/2-1	0-1/1-1	2-0/1-2	1-2/1-2

Scottish Championship

	2011-12	2012-13	2013-14	2014-15	2015-16	2016-17
Brechin v Dundee United	-	-	-	-	-	-
Dunfermline v Dumbarton	-	4-0/3-4	-	-	-	4-3/5-1
Falkirk v Morton	1-0/0-2	0-1/4-1	3-1/1-1	-	1-0/1-0	1-1/0-1
Inverness CT v St Mirren	2-1/0-0	2-2	3-0/2-2	1-0	-	-
Queen of Sth v Livingston	0-2/0-4	-	2-2/2-0	1-1/3-1	1-4/3-1	-

Results cover matches from Premier League to National League and Scottish Premiership to Scottish League Two

	2011-12	2012-13	2013-14	2014-15	2015-16	2016-17
Scottish League One						
Alloa v Ayr	-	1-0/2-2	-	-	-	-
Arbroath v Forfar	4-1/0-1	1-1/3-1	3-0/2-3	-	-	2-0/0-1
East Fife v Airdrieonians	2-0/2-0	-	1-0/0-0	-	-	0-1/0-4
Raith v Queens Park	-	-	-	-	-	-
Stranraer v Albion	-	1-1/3-2	-	-	0-1/0-0	3-2/3-0
Scottish League Two						
Annan v Clyde	1-0/1-0	1-3/0-1	1-2/0-1	2-1/0-1	2-3/3-3	3-2/1-0
Edinburgh City v Cowdenbeath	-	-	-	-	-	1-1/1-1
Elgin v Berwick	4-1/4-0	3-1/1-2	2-0/1-3	2-1/3-3	4-1/1-0	6-0/2-2
Stenhousemuir v Montrose	-	-	-	-	-	-
Stirling v Peterhead	-	1-0/0-1	2-0/1-2	2-3/2-1	-	-

Tuesday November 28, 2017

Premier League						
Arsenal v Huddersfield	-	-	-	-	-	-
Bournemouth v Burnley	-	-	1-1	-	-	2-1
Brighton v Crystal Palace	1-3	3-0	-	-	-	-
Leicester v Tottenham	-	-	-	1-2	1-1	1-6
Watford v Man United	-	-	-	-	1-2	3-1
West Brom v Newcastle	1-3	1-1	1-0	0-2	1-0	-

Wednesday November 29, 2017

Premier League						
Chelsea v Swansea	4-1	2-0	1-0	4-2	2-2	3-1
Everton v West Ham	-	2-0	1-0	2-1	2-3	2-0
Man City v Southampton	-	3-2	4-1	2-0	3-1	1-1
Stoke v Liverpool	1-0	3-1	3-5	6-1	0-1	1-2

Saturday December 2, 2017

Premier League						
Arsenal v Man United	1-2	1-1	0-0	1-2	3-0	2-0
Bournemouth v Southampton	-	-	-	-	2-0	1-3
Brighton v Liverpool	-	-	-	-	-	-
Chelsea v Newcastle	0-2	2-0	3-0	2-0	5-1	-
Everton v Huddersfield	-	-	-	-	-	-
Leicester v Burnley	0-0	2-1	1-1	2-2	-	3-0
Man City v West Ham	-	2-1	2-0	2-0	1-2	3-1
Stoke v Swansea	2-0	2-0	1-1	2-1	2-2	3-1
Watford v Tottenham	-	-	-	-	1-2	1-4
West Brom v Crystal Palace	-	-	2-0	2-2	3-2	0-2

Championship						
Birmingham v Wolves	-	2-3	-	2-1	0-2	1-3
Bolton v Barnsley	-	1-1	1-0	-	-	-
Brentford v Fulham	-	-	-	2-1	3-0	0-2
Bristol City v Middlesbrough	0-1	2-0	-	-	1-0	-
Cardiff v Norwich	-	-	2-1	2-4	-	0-1
Derby v Burton	-	-	-	-	-	0-0
Ipswich v Nottm Forest	1-3	3-1	1-1	2-1	1-0	0-2
Leeds v Aston Villa	-	-	-	-	-	2-0
Millwall v Sheffield United	-	-	-	-	1-0	2-1
Preston v QPR	-	-	-	-	1-1	2-1
Sheffield Wed v Hull	-	0-1	-	-	1-1	-
Sunderland v Reading	-	3-0	-	-	-	-

National League						
Bromley v Dover	-	-	0-4	-	1-1	0-2
Dag & Red v Boreham Wood	-	-	-	-	-	0-2
FC Halifax v Barrow	-	-	-	-	-	-
Fylde v Chester	-	-	-	-	-	-
Guiseley v Gateshead	-	-	-	-	0-2	1-1

Results cover matches from Premier League to National League and Scottish Premiership to Scottish League Two

	2011-12	2012-13	2013-14	2014-15	2015-16	2016-17
Hartlepool v Macclesfield	-	-	-	-	-	-
Maidstone v Ebbsfleet	-	-	-	-	0-2	-
Solihull Moors v Leyton Orient	-	-	-	-	-	-
Sutton United v Eastleigh	-	-	-	-	-	1-1
Torquay v Aldershot	1-0	4-3	-	1-1	0-2	0-0
Woking v Tranmere	-	-	-	-	4-1	0-3
Wrexham v Maidenhead	-	-	-	-	-	-

Scottish Premiership						
Aberdeen v Rangers	1-2	-	-	-	-	2-1/0-3
Celtic v Motherwell	4-0/1-0	1-0	2-0/3-0	1-1/4-0	1-2/7-0	2-0/2-0
Hearts v Hamilton	-	-	-	-	2-0	3-1/4-0
Partick v Hibernian	-	-	0-1/3-1	-	-	-
Ross County v Dundee	1-1/3-0	1-1	-	2-1/1-0	5-2	1-3/2-1
St Johnstone v Kilmarnock	2-0	2-1/2-0	3-1	1-2/0-0	2-1	0-1/0-2

Scottish Championship						
Dundee United v Dunfermline	0-1/3-0	-	-	-	-	1-0/1-0
Livingston v Falkirk	1-1/1-2	2-1/1-2	0-3/0-1	0-1/2-1	1-2/1-1	-
Morton v Brechin	-	-	-	2-2/0-2	-	-
Queen of Sth v Inverness CT	-	-	-	-	-	-
St Mirren v Dumbarton	-	-	-	-	1-2/1-0	0-1/1-1

Scottish League One						
Airdrieonians v Forfar	4-4/3-0	-	0-2/5-1	1-2/3-1	0-1/1-1	-
Arbroath v Stranraer	-	2-1/1-0	1-2/4-2	-	-	-
Ayr v Albion	-	2-1/5-2	-	-	1-0/0-1	-
Queens Park v East Fife	-	-	-	3-0/1-0	0-2/3-0	1-0/2-2
Raith v Alloa	-	-	4-2/1-1	1-1/2-1	3-0/0-1	-

Scottish League Two						
Annan v Elgin	1-1/1-1	2-0/2-2	2-1/2-0	3-3/2-3	1-1/4-2	1-0/1-0
Berwick v Stirling	-	4-1/1-0	1-1/4-0	-	1-2/1-0	3-2/0-1
Clyde v Montrose	1-0/1-2	1-2/1-0	0-3/1-1	1-2/2-0	3-1/3-3	2-1/1-2
Cowdenbeath v Stenhousemuir	2-0/0-0	-	-	-	2-2/1-3	-
Peterhead v Edinburgh City	-	-	-	-	-	-

Saturday December 9, 2017

Premier League						
Burnley v Watford	2-2	1-1	0-0	-	-	2-0
Crystal Palace v Bournemouth	-	-	-	-	1-2	1-1
Huddersfield v Brighton	-	1-2	1-1	1-1	1-1	3-1
Liverpool v Everton	3-0	0-0	4-0	1-1	4-0	3-1
Man United v Man City	1-6	1-2	0-3	4-2	0-0	1-2
Newcastle v Leicester	-	-	-	1-0	0-3	-
Southampton v Arsenal	-	1-1	2-2	2-0	4-0	0-2
Swansea v West Brom	3-0	3-1	1-2	3-0	1-0	2-1
Tottenham v Stoke	1-1	0-0	3-0	1-2	2-2	4-0
West Ham v Chelsea	-	3-1	0-3	0-1	2-1	1-2

Championship						
Aston Villa v Millwall	-	-	-	-	-	-
Barnsley v Derby	3-2	1-1	1-2	-	-	2-0
Burton v Preston	-	-	-	-	-	0-1
Fulham v Birmingham	-	-	-	1-1	2-5	0-1
Hull v Brentford	-	-	-	-	2-0	-
Middlesbrough v Ipswich	0-0	2-0	2-0	4-1	0-0	-
Norwich v Sheffield Wed	-	-	-	2-0	-	0-0
Nottm Forest v Bolton	-	1-1	3-0	4-1	3-0	-
QPR v Leeds	-	-	1-1	-	1-0	3-0
Reading v Cardiff	1-2	-	-	1-1	1-1	2-1
Sheffield United v Bristol City	-	-	3-0	1-2	-	-
Wolves v Sunderland	2-1	-	-	-	-	-

Results cover matches from Premier League to National League and Scottish Premiership to Scottish League Two

	2011-12	2012-13	2013-14	2014-15	2015-16	2016-17
League One						
Blackpool v Rotherham	-	-	-	1-1	-	-
Bradford v Rochdale	-	2-4	-	1-2	2-2	4-0
Bristol Rovers v Southend	1-0	2-3	0-0	-	-	2-0
Bury v AFC Wimbledon	-	-	1-1	2-0	-	1-2
Charlton v Portsmouth	-	-	-	-	-	-
MK Dons v Shrewsbury	-	2-3	3-2	-	-	2-1
Oldham v Northampton	-	-	-	-	-	0-0
Oxford v Doncaster	-	-	-	-	-	-
Peterborough v Blackburn	-	1-4	-	-	-	-
Plymouth v Gillingham	0-1	2-2	-	-	-	-
Walsall v Scunthorpe	2-2	1-4	-	1-4	0-0	1-4
Wigan v Fleetwood Town	-	-	-	-	2-1	-
League Two						
Accrington v Swindon	0-2	-	-	-	-	-
Cheltenham v Crewe	0-1	-	-	-	-	2-0
Chesterfield v Barnet	-	0-1	-	-	-	-
Colchester v Exeter	2-0	-	-	-	-	2-3
Crawley Town v Mansfield	-	-	-	-	0-1	2-2
Grimsby v Forest Green	2-1	1-0	3-1	2-1	1-1	-
Luton v Notts County	-	-	-	-	0-2	2-1
Morecambe v Coventry	-	-	-	-	-	-
Newport County v Carlisle	-	-	-	2-1	1-0	2-0
Port Vale v Cambridge U	-	-	-	-	-	-
Stevenage v Wycombe	1-1	-	-	1-3	2-1	3-0
Yeovil v Lincoln	-	-	-	-	-	-
National League						
Aldershot v FC Halifax	-	-	-	-	-	-
Barrow v Dag & Red	-	-	-	-	-	2-1
Boreham Wood v Fylde	-	-	-	-	-	-
Chester v Solihull Moors	-	-	-	-	-	0-3
Dover v Hartlepool	-	-	-	-	-	-
Eastleigh v Bromley	-	-	2-1	-	2-0	2-1
Ebbsfleet v Guiseley	-	-	-	-	-	-
Gateshead v Woking	-	2-1	0-2	0-0	1-5	2-1
Leyton Orient v Sutton United	-	-	-	-	-	-
Macclesfield v Wrexham	-	2-0	3-2	2-2	0-0	3-0
Maidenhead v Maidstone	-	-	-	-	0-2	-
Tranmere v Torquay	-	-	-	-	2-1	2-1
Scottish Premiership						
Dundee v Aberdeen	-	1-3/1-1	-	2-3/1-1/1-1	0-2	1-3/0-7
Hamilton v St Johnstone	-	-	-	1-0/1-1	2-4	1-1/1-0
Hibernian v Celtic	0-2/0-5	1-0	1-1/0-4	-	-	-
Kilmarnock v Partick	-	-	2-1/1-2	3-0/2-2	2-5/0-2	2-2/1-1
Motherwell v Hearts	1-0/3-0	0-0	2-1/4-1	-	2-2/1-0	1-3/0-3
Rangers v Ross County	-	-	-	-	-	0-0/1-1
Scottish Championship						
Brechin v St Mirren	-	-	-	-	-	-
Dumbarton v Livingston	-	3-4/0-3	1-2/2-2	1-0/1-5	2-1/1-0	-
Dunfermline v Queen of Sth	-	-	-	-	-	0-1/1-1
Inverness CT v Falkirk	-	-	-	-	-	-
Morton v Dundee United	-	-	-	-	-	0-0/1-1
Scottish League One						
Airdrieonians v Raith	-	0-0/1-2	-	-	-	-
Albion v Arbroath	1-0/1-1	4-0/0-1	-	2-1/1-1	-	-
Ayr v Queens Park	-	-	-	-	-	-
East Fife v Stranraer	-	0-1/1-1	1-2/1-1	-	-	2-0/0-0
Forfar v Alloa	-	2-3/0-1	-	-	-	-

Results cover matches from Premier League to National League and Scottish Premiership to Scottish League Two

	2011-12	2012-13	2013-14	2014-15	2015-16	2016-17
Scottish League Two						
Elgin v Edinburgh City	-	-	-	-	-	3-0/3-1
Montrose v Berwick	3-5/1-1	3-1/1-3	1-1/0-0	2-1/0-2	4-1/1-0	0-0/2-1
Peterhead v Clyde	0-0/1-1	1-0/3-0	1-1/2-0	-	-	-
Stenhousemuir v Annan	-	-	-	-	-	-
Stirling v Cowdenbeath	1-1/0-2	-	-	-	-	1-2/0-3
Tuesday December 12, 2017						
Premier League						
Burnley v Stoke	-	-	-	0-0	-	1-0
Crystal Palace v Watford	4-0	2-3	-	-	1-2	1-0
Huddersfield v Chelsea	-	-	-	-	-	-
Man United v Bournemouth	-	-	-	-	3-1	1-1
Swansea v Man City	1-0	0-0	2-3	2-4	1-1	1-3
West Ham v Arsenal	-	1-3	1-3	1-2	3-3	1-5
Wednesday December 13, 2017						
Premier League						
Liverpool v West Brom	0-1	0-2	4-1	2-1	2-2	2-1
Newcastle v Everton	2-1	1-2	0-3	3-2	0-1	-
Southampton v Leicester	0-2	-	-	2-0	2-2	3-0
Tottenham v Brighton	-	-	-	-	-	-
Scottish Premiership						
Celtic v Hamilton	-	-	-	0-1/4-0	8-1	1-0/2-0
Hearts v Dundee	-	0-1/1-0	-	-	1-1	2-0/1-0
Hibernian v Rangers	0-2	-	-	4-0/0-2	2-1/3-2	-
Partick v Motherwell	-	-	1-5	3-1/2-0	1-0	1-1/1-0
Ross County v Kilmarnock	-	0-0/0-1	1-2/2-1	1-2/2-1	3-2	2-0/1-2
St Johnstone v Aberdeen	1-2	1-2/3-1	0-2	1-0/1-1	3-4/3-0	0-0/1-2
Saturday December 16, 2017						
Premier League						
Arsenal v Newcastle	2-1	7-3	3-0	4-1	1-0	-
Bournemouth v Liverpool	-	-	-	-	1-2	4-3
Brighton v Burnley	0-1	1-0	2-0	-	2-2	-
Chelsea v Southampton	-	2-2	3-1	1-1	1-3	4-2
Everton v Swansea	1-0	0-0	3-2	0-0	1-2	1-1
Leicester v Crystal Palace	3-0	1-2	-	0-1	1-0	3-1
Man City v Tottenham	3-2	2-1	6-0	4-1	1-2	2-2
Stoke v West Ham	-	0-1	3-1	2-2	2-1	0-0
Watford v Huddersfield	-	4-0	1-4	4-2	-	-
West Brom v Man United	1-2	5-5	0-3	2-2	1-0	0-2
Championship						
Birmingham v QPR	-	-	0-2	-	2-1	1-4
Bolton v Burton	-	-	-	-	-	-
Brentford v Barnsley	-	-	-	-	-	0-2
Bristol City v Nottm Forest	0-0	2-0	-	-	2-0	2-1
Cardiff v Hull	0-3	2-1	0-4	-	0-2	-
Derby v Aston Villa	-	-	-	-	-	0-0
Ipswich v Reading	2-3	-	2-0	0-1	2-1	2-2
Leeds v Norwich	-	-	-	0-2	-	3-3
Millwall v Middlesbrough	1-3	3-1	0-2	1-5	-	-
Preston v Sheffield United	2-4	0-1	0-0	1-1	-	-
Sheffield Wed v Wolves	-	0-0	-	0-1	4-1	0-0
Sunderland v Fulham	0-0	2-2	0-1	-	-	-
League One						
AFC Wimbledon v Wigan	-	-	-	-	-	-
Blackburn v Charlton	-	1-2	0-1	2-0	3-0	-
Doncaster v Oldham	-	1-0	-	0-2	1-1	-
Fleetwood Town v Peterborough	-	-	-	1-1	2-0	2-0

Results cover matches from Premier League to National League and Scottish Premiership to Scottish League Two

	2011-12	2012-13	2013-14	2014-15	2015-16	2016-17
Gillingham v Bristol Rovers	4-1	4-0	-	-	-	3-1
Northampton v Walsall	-	-	-	-	-	2-0
Portsmouth v Bury	-	2-0	1-0	0-1	-	-
Rochdale v Oxford	-	2-0	3-0	-	-	0-4
Rotherham v Plymouth	1-0	1-0	-	-	-	-
Scunthorpe v MK Dons	0-3	0-3	-	1-1	-	2-1
Shrewsbury v Blackpool	-	-	-	-	2-0	-
Southend v Bradford	0-1	2-2	-	-	0-1	3-0
League Two						
Barnet v Morecambe	0-2	4-1	-	-	0-0	2-2
Cambridge U v Newport County	1-1	0-0	-	4-0	3-0	3-2
Carlisle v Port Vale	-	-	0-1	-	-	-
Coventry v Cheltenham	-	-	-	-	-	-
Crewe v Crawley Town	1-1	2-0	1-0	0-0	-	0-2
Exeter v Stevenage	1-1	-	-	0-0	3-3	1-1
Forest Green v Luton	3-0	1-2	0-0	-	-	-
Lincoln v Accrington	-	-	-	-	-	-
Mansfield v Yeovil	-	-	-	-	0-1	1-0
Notts County v Grimsby	-	-	-	-	-	2-2
Swindon v Colchester	-	0-1	0-0	2-2	1-2	-
Wycombe v Chesterfield	3-2	2-1	1-0	-	-	-
Scottish Premiership						
Aberdeen v Hibernian	1-0/1-2	2-1/0-0	1-0	-	-	-
Dundee v Partick	0-1/0-3	-	-	1-1/1-0	1-1	0-2/0-1
Hamilton v Ross County	5-1/0-2	-	-	4-0/2-2	1-3	1-0/1-1
Hearts v Celtic	2-0/0-4	0-4	1-3/0-2	-	2-2/1-3	1-2/0-5
Kilmarnock v Motherwell	0-0/2-0	1-2/2-0	0-2	2-0/1-2	0-1	1-2/1-2
Rangers v St Johnstone	0-0	-	-	-	-	1-1/3-2
Scottish Championship						
Falkirk v Brechin	-	-	-	-	-	-
Inverness CT v Dumbarton	-	-	-	-	-	-
Livingston v Morton	1-1/0-0	2-2/0-2	2-2/0-1	-	2-4/0-0	-
Queen of Sth v Dundee United	-	-	-	-	-	1-4/4-2
St Mirren v Dunfermline	2-1/4-4	-	-	-	-	0-1/0-0
Scottish League One						
Alloa v Arbroath	-	2-3/0-1	-	-	-	-
East Fife v Ayr	-	2-3/3-3	1-4/0-5	-	-	-
Queens Park v Airdrieonians	-	-	-	-	-	1-3/2-1
Raith v Albion	-	-	-	-	-	-
Stranraer v Forfar	-	4-1/0-3	0-4/3-1	1-1/4-2	0-0/1-0	-
Scottish League Two						
Annan v Stirling	-	5-2/0-1	4-4/1-2	-	1-1/2-2	3-2/4-1
Berwick v Peterhead	2-1/0-1	1-1/0-2	1-3/1-2	-	-	-
Cowdenbeath v Clyde	-	-	-	-	-	1-0/1-0
Edinburgh City v Stenhousemuir	-	-	-	-	-	-
Montrose v Elgin	3-0/2-3	2-2/4-1	3-3/0-3	2-3/2-1	2-0/3-1	0-5/0-3

Saturday December 23, 2017

Premier League						
Arsenal v Liverpool	0-2	2-2	2-0	4-1	0-0	3-4
Brighton v Watford	2-2	1-3	1-1	0-2	-	-
Burnley v Tottenham	-	-	-	0-0	-	0-2
Everton v Chelsea	2-0	1-2	1-0	3-6	3-1	0-3
Leicester v Man United	-	-	-	5-3	1-1	0-3
Man City v Bournemouth	-	-	-	-	5-1	4-0
Southampton v Huddersfield	-	-	-	-	-	-
Stoke v West Brom	1-2	0-0	0-0	2-0	0-1	1-1
Swansea v Crystal Palace	-	-	1-1	1-1	1-1	5-4
West Ham v Newcastle	-	0-0	1-3	1-0	2-0	-

Results cover matches from Premier League to National League and Scottish Premiership to Scottish League Two

	2011-12	2012-13	2013-14	2014-15	2015-16	2016-17
Championship						
Aston Villa v Sheffield United	-	-	-	-	-	-
Bolton v Cardiff	-	2-1	-	3-0	2-3	-
Derby v Millwall	3-0	1-0	0-1	0-0	-	-
Fulham v Barnsley	-	-	-	-	-	2-0
Leeds v Hull	4-1	2-3	-	-	2-1	-
Norwich v Brentford	-	-	-	1-2	-	5-0
Preston v Nottm Forest	-	-	-	-	1-0	1-1
QPR v Bristol City	-	-	-	-	1-0	1-0
Reading v Burton	-	-	-	-	-	3-0
Sheffield Wed v Middlesbrough	-	2-0	1-0	2-0	1-3	-
Sunderland v Birmingham	-	-	-	-	-	-
Wolves v Ipswich	-	0-2	-	1-1	0-0	0-0
League One						
AFC Wimbledon v Bradford	3-1	2-1	-	-	-	2-3
Bristol Rovers v Doncaster	-	-	-	-	-	-
Charlton v Blackpool	-	2-1	0-0	2-2	-	-
Fleetwood Town v Gillingham	-	2-2	-	1-0	2-1	2-1
Northampton v Blackburn	-	-	-	-	-	-
Oxford v Wigan	-	-	-	-	-	-
Peterborough v Bury	-	-	-	-	2-3	3-1
Plymouth v Oldham	-	-	-	-	-	-
Rochdale v Walsall	3-3	-	-	4-0	1-2	4-0
Rotherham v MK Dons	-	-	2-2	-	1-4	-
Scunthorpe v Southend	-	-	2-2	-	1-0	4-0
Shrewsbury v Portsmouth	-	3-2	-	2-1	-	-
League Two						
Accrington v Crawley Town	0-1	-	-	-	4-1	1-0
Barnet v Cheltenham	2-2	0-0	-	-	-	3-1
Colchester v Port Vale	-	-	1-0	1-2	2-1	-
Coventry v Wycombe	-	-	-	-	-	-
Crewe v Swindon	2-0	2-1	1-1	0-0	1-3	-
Forest Green v Carlisle	-	-	-	-	-	-
Luton v Grimsby	1-1	1-1	0-0	-	-	1-2
Mansfield v Morecambe	-	-	1-2	1-0	2-1	0-1
Newport County v Lincoln	1-0	2-1	-	-	-	-
Notts County v Cambridge U	-	-	-	-	1-2	0-1
Stevenage v Chesterfield	2-2	-	-	-	-	-
Yeovil v Exeter	2-2	-	-	-	0-2	0-0
National League						
Bromley v Macclesfield	-	-	-	-	1-0	0-1
Dag & Red v Eastleigh	-	-	-	-	-	4-0
FC Halifax v Chester	-	-	-	-	-	-
Fylde v Ebbsfleet	-	-	-	-	-	-
Guiseley v Aldershot	-	-	-	-	0-4	1-0
Hartlepool v Maidenhead	-	-	-	-	-	-
Maidstone v Leyton Orient	-	-	-	-	-	-
Solihull Moors v Boreham Wood	-	-	-	-	-	1-1
Sutton United v Tranmere	-	-	-	-	-	1-0
Torquay v Gateshead	-	-	-	2-2	0-2	3-1
Woking v Barrow	-	3-1	-	-	2-2	1-1
Wrexham v Dover	-	-	-	1-1	0-1	0-0
Scottish Premiership						
Celtic v Aberdeen	2-1	1-0/4-3	3-1/5-2	2-1/4-0	3-1/3-2	4-1/1-0
Hibernian v Ross County	-	0-1	0-0/2-1	-	-	-
Kilmarnock v Rangers	1-0	-	-	-	-	1-1/0-0
Motherwell v Dundee	-	1-1	-	1-3/0-1	3-1	0-0/1-5/2-3
Partick v Hamilton	1-1/2-0	4-0/1-0	-	1-2/5-0	1-1/2-2	2-2/2-0
St Johnstone v Hearts	2-0/2-1	2-2	1-0/3-3	-	0-0	1-0/1-0/1-0

Results cover matches from Premier League to National League and Scottish Premiership to Scottish League Two

	2011-12	2012-13	2013-14	2014-15	2015-16	2016-17
Scottish Championship						
Dumbarton v Falkirk	-	0-2/0-2	1-1/2-1	0-3/1-0	0-5/1-1	2-1/0-1
Dundee United v Livingston	-	-	-	-	-	-
Dunfermline v Brechin	-	-	3-1/2-1	0-0/0-1	3-1/3-1	-
Morton v Inverness CT	-	-	-	-	-	-
Queen of Sth v St Mirren	-	-	-	-	0-2/1-0	2-3/0-2
Scottish League One						
Airdrieonians v Ayr	-	-	0-1/3-0	3-0/2-0	1-2/0-1	-
Albion v East Fife	0-3/1-1	0-3/1-1	-	2-0/2-3	-	1-0/0-1
Alloa v Stranraer	1-0/3-1	3-0/4-1	-	-	-	2-2/1-0
Arbroath v Raith	-	-	-	-	-	-
Forfar v Queens Park	-	-	-	-	-	-
Scottish League Two						
Annan v Edinburgh City	-	-	-	-	-	1-1/1-0
Clyde v Berwick	1-4/2-2	2-1/2-1	1-0/3-3	3-3/0-3	1-1/2-1	3-2/1-1
Peterhead v Cowdenbeath	-	-	-	-	7-0/0-1	-
Stenhousemuir v Elgin	-	-	-	-	-	-
Stirling v Montrose	-	1-3/3-1	3-1/2-2	-	1-0/7-0	2-0/1-2

Tuesday December 26, 2017

	2011-12	2012-13	2013-14	2014-15	2015-16	2016-17
Premier League						
Bournemouth v West Ham	-	-	-	-	1-3	3-2
Chelsea v Brighton	-	-	-	-	-	-
Crystal Palace v Arsenal	-	-	0-2	1-2	1-2	3-0
Huddersfield v Stoke	-	-	-	-	-	-
Liverpool v Swansea	0-0	5-0	4-3	4-1	1-0	2-3
Man United v Burnley	-	-	-	3-1	-	0-0
Newcastle v Man City	0-2	1-3	0-2	0-2	1-1	-
Tottenham v Southampton	-	1-0	3-2	1-0	1-2	2-1
Watford v Leicester	3-2	2-1	0-3	-	0-1	2-1
West Brom v Everton	0-1	2-0	1-1	0-2	2-3	1-2
Championship						
Barnsley v Preston	-	-	-	1-1	-	0-0
Birmingham v Norwich	-	-	-	0-0	-	3-0
Brentford v Aston Villa	-	-	-	-	-	3-0
Bristol City v Reading	2-3	-	-	-	0-2	2-3
Burton v Leeds	-	-	-	-	-	2-1
Cardiff v Fulham	-	-	3-1	1-0	1-1	2-2
Hull v Derby	0-1	2-1	-	-	0-2	-
Ipswich v QPR	-	-	1-3	-	2-1	3-0
Middlesbrough v Bolton	-	2-1	1-0	1-0	3-0	-
Millwall v Wolves	-	0-2	1-0	3-3	-	-
Nottm Forest v Sheffield Wed	-	1-0	3-3	0-2	0-3	1-2
Sheffield United v Sunderland	-	-	-	-	-	-
League One						
Blackburn v Rochdale	-	-	-	-	-	-
Blackpool v Scunthorpe	-	-	-	-	5-0	-
Bradford v Peterborough	-	-	1-0	0-1	0-2	1-0
Bury v Rotherham	-	-	-	-	-	-
Doncaster v Northampton	-	-	-	-	-	-
Gillingham v Oxford	1-0	0-1	-	-	-	0-1
MK Dons v Plymouth	-	-	-	-	-	-
Oldham v Fleetwood Town	-	-	-	1-0	1-0	2-0
Portsmouth v AFC Wimbledon	-	-	1-0	0-2	0-0	-
Southend v Charlton	-	-	-	-	-	1-1
Walsall v Bristol Rovers	-	-	-	-	-	3-1
Wigan v Shrewsbury	-	-	-	-	1-0	-

Results cover matches from Premier League to National League and Scottish Premiership to Scottish League Two

	2011-12	2012-13	2013-14	2014-15	2015-16	2016-17
League Two						
Cambridge U v Barnet	-	-	1-1	-	2-1	1-1
Carlisle v Accrington	-	-	-	1-0	2-0	1-1
Cheltenham v Yeovil	-	-	-	-	-	2-0
Chesterfield v Crewe	-	-	-	1-0	3-1	-
Crawley Town v Colchester	-	3-0	1-0	0-0	-	1-1
Exeter v Forest Green	-	-	-	-	-	-
Grimsby v Mansfield	0-0	4-1	-	-	-	3-0
Lincoln v Stevenage	-	-	-	-	-	-
Morecambe v Notts County	-	-	-	-	4-1	4-1
Port Vale v Coventry	-	-	3-2	0-2	1-1	0-2
Swindon v Luton	-	-	-	-	-	-
Wycombe v Newport County	-	-	0-1	1-2	0-2	2-1
National League						
Aldershot v Woking	-	-	2-1	0-1	0-1	4-0
Barrow v Wrexham	3-1	0-1	-	-	2-0	1-1
Boreham Wood v Sutton United	-	-	-	-	-	1-0
Chester v Guiseley	-	-	-	-	1-1	2-0
Dover v Maidstone	-	-	-	-	-	1-1
Eastleigh v Torquay	-	-	-	1-2	3-2	3-0
Ebbsfleet v Bromley	-	-	1-3	0-1	-	-
Gateshead v Hartlepool	-	-	-	-	-	-
Leyton Orient v Dag & Red	-	-	-	-	3-2	-
Macclesfield v FC Halifax	-	-	-	-	-	-
Maidenhead v Solihull Moors	-	-	-	-	-	-
Tranmere v Fylde	-	-	-	-	-	-

Wednesday December 27, 2017

	2011-12	2012-13	2013-14	2014-15	2015-16	2016-17
Scottish Premiership						
Aberdeen v Partick	-	-	4-0	2-0/0-0	0-0	2-1/2-0
Dundee v Celtic	-	0-2	-	1-1/1-2	0-0	0-1/1-2
Hamilton v Kilmarnock	-	-	-	0-0/0-0	0-1/0-4	1-2/1-1/0-2
Hearts v Hibernian	2-0/2-0	0-0/1-2	1-0/2-0	2-1/1-1	-	-
Rangers v Motherwell	3-0/0-0	-	-	-	-	2-1/1-1
Ross County v St Johnstone	-	1-2/1-0	1-0	1-2/1-0	2-3/0-1	0-2/1-2

Saturday December 30, 2017

	2011-12	2012-13	2013-14	2014-15	2015-16	2016-17
Premier League						
Bournemouth v Everton	-	-	-	-	3-3	1-0
Chelsea v Stoke	1-0	1-0	3-0	2-1	1-1	4-2
Crystal Palace v Man City	-	-	0-2	2-1	0-1	1-2
Huddersfield v Burnley	-	2-0	2-1	-	1-3	-
Liverpool v Leicester	-	-	-	2-2	1-0	4-1
Man United v Southampton	-	2-1	1-1	0-1	0-1	2-0
Newcastle v Brighton	-	-	-	-	-	2-0
Tottenham v West Ham	-	3-1	0-3	2-2	4-1	3-2
Watford v Swansea	-	-	-	-	1-0	1-0
West Brom v Arsenal	2-3	1-2	1-1	0-1	2-1	3-1
Championship						
Barnsley v Reading	0-4	-	1-1	-	-	1-2
Birmingham v Leeds	1-0	1-0	1-3	1-1	1-2	1-3
Brentford v Sheffield Wed	1-2	-	-	0-0	1-2	1-1
Bristol City v Wolves	-	1-4	1-2	-	1-0	3-1
Burton v Norwich	-	-	-	-	-	2-1
Cardiff v Preston	-	-	-	-	2-1	2-0
Hull v Fulham	-	-	6-0	-	2-1	-
Ipswich v Derby	1-0	1-2	2-1	0-1	0-1	0-3
Middlesbrough v Aston Villa	-	-	-	-	-	-
Millwall v QPR	-	-	2-2	-	-	-
Nottm Forest v Sunderland	-	-	-	-	-	-
Sheffield United v Bolton	-	-	-	-	-	2-0

Results cover matches from Premier League to National League and Scottish Premiership to Scottish League Two

	2011-12	2012-13	2013-14	2014-15	2015-16	2016-17
League One						
Blackburn v Scunthorpe	-	-	-	-	-	-
Blackpool v Plymouth	-	-	-	-	-	0-1
Bradford v Oxford	2-1	1-2	-	-	-	1-0
Bury v Fleetwood Town	-	-	2-2	-	3-4	0-0
Doncaster v Rochdale	-	-	-	1-1	0-2	-
Gillingham v AFC Wimbledon	3-4	2-2	-	-	-	2-2
MK Dons v Peterborough	-	-	0-2	3-0	-	0-2
Oldham v Bristol Rovers	-	-	-	-	-	0-2
Portsmouth v Northampton	-	-	0-0	2-0	1-2	-
Southend v Shrewsbury	3-0	-	-	1-0	0-1	1-1
Walsall v Rotherham	-	-	1-1	-	-	-
Wigan v Charlton	-	-	2-1	0-3	-	-
League Two						
Cambridge U v Crewe	-	-	-	-	-	2-1
Carlisle v Coventry	-	1-0	0-4	-	-	-
Cheltenham v Newport County	-	-	0-0	0-1	-	1-1
Chesterfield v Colchester	0-1	-	-	6-0	3-3	-
Crawley Town v Stevenage	-	1-1	1-1	-	2-1	1-2
Exeter v Barnet	-	2-2	-	-	1-1	2-1
Grimsby v Accrington	-	-	-	-	-	2-0
Lincoln v Forest Green	1-1	1-2	2-1	1-2	0-1	3-1
Morecambe v Yeovil	-	-	-	-	2-1	1-3
Port Vale v Luton	-	-	-	-	-	-
Swindon v Notts County	-	0-0	2-0	3-0	-	-
Wycombe v Mansfield	-	-	0-1	2-1	1-0	0-1
National League						
Aldershot v Maidstone	-	-	-	-	-	1-0
Barrow v Solihull Moors	-	-	0-2	1-3	-	2-1
Boreham Wood v Torquay	-	-	-	-	0-1	2-0
Chester v Hartlepool	-	-	-	-	-	-
Dover v FC Halifax	-	-	-	-	-	-
Eastleigh v Woking	-	-	-	2-2	2-1	0-1
Ebbsfleet v Dag & Red	-	-	-	-	-	-
Gateshead v Wrexham	1-4	0-1	0-3	3-1	2-1	2-2
Leyton Orient v Bromley	-	-	-	-	-	-
Macclesfield v Sutton United	-	-	-	-	-	0-0
Maidenhead v Fylde	-	-	-	-	-	-
Tranmere v Guiseley	-	-	-	-	2-1	1-0
Scottish Premiership						
Aberdeen v Hearts	0-0	0-0/2-0/1-1	1-3	-	1-0/0-1	0-0/2-0
Celtic v Rangers	1-0/3-0	-	-	-	-	5-1/1-1
Hibernian v Kilmarnock	1-1/0-1	2-1/2-2	3-0/0-1	-	-	-
Motherwell v Hamilton	-	-	-	0-4/4-0	3-3	4-2/0-0
Partick v Ross County	0-1/0-1	-	3-3/2-3	4-0/1-3	1-0	1-1/2-1
St Johnstone v Dundee	-	1-0	-	0-1/1-0	1-1	2-1/2-0
Scottish Championship						
Brechin v Inverness CT	-	-	-	-	-	-
Dumbarton v Morton	-	1-5/0-3	3-1/2-0	-	1-2/0-0	0-2/1-0
Falkirk v Queen of Sth	1-0/3-0	-	2-1/1-0	1-1/1-1	0-0/3-1	2-2/2-2
Livingston v Dunfermline	-	2-1/2-2	-	-	-	-
St Mirren v Dundee United	2-2	0-1/0-0	4-1	0-3/1-1	-	0-2/3-2
Scottish League One						
Airdrieonians v Alloa	-	-	-	-	-	2-1/0-1
Arbroath v East Fife	3-0/2-2	2-0/1-0	2-2/2-1	0-2/1-1	1-1/0-1	-
Ayr v Forfar	-	2-3/2-1	2-0/2-3	2-0/1-0	2-2/2-1	-
Queens Park v Albion	-	-	1-1/4-0	0-1/0-1	-	2-1/2-0
Raith v Stranraer	-	-	-	-	-	-

Results cover matches from Premier League to National League and Scottish Premiership to Scottish League Two

	2011-12	2012-13	2013-14	2014-15	2015-16	2016-17
Scottish League Two						
Berwick v Stenhousemuir	-	-	-	-	-	-
Cowdenbeath v Annan	-	-	-	-	-	2-2/0-1
Edinburgh City v Clyde	-	-	-	-	-	0-1/0-0
Elgin v Stirling	-	3-1/1-2	4-0/2-3	-	1-0/2-1	2-3/2-2
Montrose v Peterhead	2-1/1-3	2-0/0-6	2-1/2-3	-	-	-

Monday January 1, 2018

	2011-12	2012-13	2013-14	2014-15	2015-16	2016-17
Premier League						
Arsenal v Chelsea	0-0	1-2	0-0	0-0	0-1	3-0
Brighton v Bournemouth	-	-	1-1	0-2	-	-
Burnley v Liverpool	-	-	-	0-1	-	2-0
Everton v Man United	0-1	1-0	2-0	3-0	0-3	1-1
Leicester v Huddersfield	-	6-1	2-1	-	-	-
Man City v Watford	-	-	-	-	2-0	2-0
Southampton v Crystal Palace	2-0	-	2-0	1-0	4-1	3-1
Stoke v Newcastle	1-3	2-1	1-0	1-0	1-0	-
Swansea v Tottenham	1-1	1-2	1-3	1-2	2-2	1-3
West Ham v West Brom	-	3-1	3-3	1-1	1-1	2-2
Championship						
Aston Villa v Bristol City	-	-	-	-	-	2-0
Bolton v Hull	-	4-1	-	-	1-0	-
Derby v Sheffield United	-	-	-	-	-	-
Fulham v Ipswich	-	-	-	1-2	1-2	3-1
Leeds v Nottm Forest	3-7	2-1	0-2	0-0	0-1	2-0
Norwich v Millwall	-	-	-	6-1	-	-
Preston v Middlesbrough	-	-	-	-	0-0	-
QPR v Cardiff	-	-	-	-	2-2	2-1
Reading v Birmingham	1-0	-	2-0	0-1	0-2	0-0
Sheffield Wed v Burton	-	-	-	-	-	1-1
Sunderland v Barnsley	-	-	-	-	-	-
Wolves v Brentford	-	-	0-0	2-1	0-2	3-1
League One						
AFC Wimbledon v Southend	1-4	0-4	0-1	0-0	-	0-2
Bristol Rovers v Portsmouth	-	-	2-0	-	1-2	-
Charlton v Gillingham	-	-	-	-	-	3-0
Fleetwood Town v Bradford	-	2-2	-	0-2	1-1	2-1
Northampton v Wigan	-	-	-	-	-	-
Oxford v MK Dons	-	-	-	-	-	1-0
Peterborough v Doncaster	1-2	-	-	0-0	4-0	-
Plymouth v Walsall	-	-	-	-	-	-
Rochdale v Blackpool	-	-	-	-	3-0	-
Rotherham v Blackburn	-	-	-	2-0	0-1	1-1
Scunthorpe v Bury	1-3	1-2	2-2	-	2-1	3-2
Shrewsbury v Oldham	-	1-0	1-2	-	0-1	1-0
League Two						
Accrington v Morecambe	1-1	2-0	5-1	2-1	2-2	2-3
Barnet v Swindon	0-2	-	-	-	-	-
Colchester v Cambridge U	-	-	-	-	-	2-0
Coventry v Chesterfield	-	-	-	0-0	1-0	2-0
Crewe v Grimsby	-	-	-	-	-	5-0
Forest Green v Wycombe	-	-	-	-	-	-
Luton v Lincoln	1-0	3-0	3-2	-	-	-
Mansfield v Carlisle	-	-	-	3-2	1-1	2-0
Newport County v Exeter	-	-	1-1	2-2	1-1	1-4
Notts County v Port Vale	-	-	4-2	0-1	-	-
Stevenage v Cheltenham	-	-	-	5-1	-	2-1
Yeovil v Crawley Town	-	2-2	-	2-1	2-1	5-0

Results cover matches from Premier League to National League and Scottish Premiership to Scottish League Two

National League

	2011-12	2012-13	2013-14	2014-15	2015-16	2016-17
Bromley v Ebbsfleet	-	-	0-0	1-2	-	-
Dag & Red v Leyton Orient	-	-	-	-	1-3	-
FC Halifax v Macclesfield	-	-	-	-	-	-
Fylde v Tranmere	-	-	-	-	-	-
Guiseley v Chester	-	-	-	-	3-3	1-1
Hartlepool v Gateshead	-	-	-	-	-	-
Maidstone v Dover	-	-	-	-	-	1-4
Solihull Moors v Maidenhead	-	-	-	-	-	-
Sutton United v Boreham Wood	-	-	-	-	-	1-0
Torquay v Eastleigh	-	-	-	2-0	0-1	2-3
Woking v Aldershot	-	-	1-2	1-2	2-1	1-2
Wrexham v Barrow	2-0	3-0	-	-	4-1	2-2

Tuesday January 2, 2018

Scottish Championship

	2011-12	2012-13	2013-14	2014-15	2015-16	2016-17
Dundee United v Brechin	-	-	-	-	-	-
Dunfermline v Falkirk	-	0-1/0-2	-	-	-	1-1/1-2
Inverness CT v Livingston	-	-	-	-	-	-
Morton v St Mirren	-	-	-	-	0-0/0-1	3-1/1-4
Queen of Sth v Dumbarton	-	-	1-2/3-1	3-0/2-1	1-0/6-0	1-2/1-2

Scottish League One

	2011-12	2012-13	2013-14	2014-15	2015-16	2016-17
Albion v Airdrieonians	7-2/0-1	-	-	-	1-3/1-2	1-2/3-4
Alloa v Queens Park	1-0/4-0	-	-	-	-	1-1/2-2
East Fife v Raith	-	-	-	-	-	-
Forfar v Arbroath	1-1/2-4	1-1/2-4	1-1/0-2	-	-	0-1/1-1
Stranraer v Ayr	-	2-0/0-1	1-1/4-0	3-1/1-0	1-2/1-0	-

Scottish League Two

	2011-12	2012-13	2013-14	2014-15	2015-16	2016-17
Clyde v Annan	0-0/1-1	2-1/2-3	2-1/0-3	1-1/1-0	4-2/2-1	2-3/2-1
Edinburgh City v Berwick	-	-	-	-	-	1-2/2-2
Montrose v Cowdenbeath	-	-	-	-	-	1-2/2-1
Peterhead v Elgin	1-3/3-0	1-1/0-1	2-2/2-1	-	-	-
Stenhousemuir v Stirling	4-0/4-0	-	-	4-5/1-2	-	-

Saturday January 6, 2018

League One

	2011-12	2012-13	2013-14	2014-15	2015-16	2016-17
AFC Wimbledon v Blackburn	-	-	-	-	-	-
Bristol Rovers v Wigan	-	-	-	-	-	-
Charlton v Oldham	1-1	-	-	-	-	1-1
Fleetwood Town v Portsmouth	-	-	3-1	-	-	-
Northampton v Southend	2-5	3-3	2-1	1-1	-	4-0
Oxford v Blackpool	-	-	-	-	-	-
Peterborough v Walsall	-	-	0-0	0-0	1-1	1-1
Plymouth v Bury	-	-	2-1	0-2	-	-
Rochdale v MK Dons	1-2	-	-	2-3	-	0-1
Rotherham v Bradford	3-0	4-0	0-0	-	-	-
Scunthorpe v Doncaster	-	2-3	-	1-2	2-0	-
Shrewsbury v Gillingham	2-0	-	2-0	-	2-2	2-3

League Two

	2011-12	2012-13	2013-14	2014-15	2015-16	2016-17
Accrington v Chesterfield	-	1-0	3-1	-	-	-
Barnet v Carlisle	-	-	-	-	0-0	0-1
Colchester v Cheltenham	-	-	-	-	-	2-0
Coventry v Cambridge U	-	-	-	-	-	-
Crewe v Exeter	-	-	-	-	-	2-0
Forest Green v Port Vale	-	-	-	-	-	-
Luton v Wycombe	-	-	-	2-3	0-2	4-1
Mansfield v Lincoln	2-1	0-0	-	-	-	-
Newport County v Morecambe	-	-	2-3	0-1	1-2	1-1
Notts County v Crawley Town	-	1-1	1-0	5-3	4-1	2-1
Stevenage v Swindon	-	0-4	2-0	-	-	-
Yeovil v Grimsby	-	-	-	-	-	0-0

Results cover matches from Premier League to National League and Scottish Premiership to Scottish League Two

	2011-12	2012-13	2013-14	2014-15	2015-16	2016-17
National League						
Barrow v Tranmere	-	-	-	-	3-4	2-1
Bromley v Fylde	-	-	-	-	-	-
Dag & Red v Hartlepool	-	-	0-2	2-0	0-1	-
Dover v Aldershot	-	-	-	3-0	5-2	1-2
Eastleigh v Guiseley	-	-	-	-	1-1	2-1
Ebbsfleet v Chester	-	-	-	-	-	-
Gateshead v Sutton United	-	-	-	-	-	1-0
Leyton Orient v Boreham Wood	-	-	-	-	-	-
Macclesfield v Solihull Moors	-	-	-	-	-	1-3
Maidenhead v FC Halifax	-	-	-	-	-	-
Woking v Maidstone	-	-	-	-	-	2-4
Wrexham v Torquay	-	-	-	0-0	3-1	1-1
Scottish Championship						
Brechin v Morton	-	-	-	3-1/1-1	-	-
Dumbarton v Dunfermline	-	0-2/0-1	-	-	-	2-2/0-2
Falkirk v Dundee United	-	-	-	-	-	3-1/3-0
Livingston v Queen of Sth	2-2/2-2	-	3-3/1-2	2-2/1-0	0-1/0-2	-
St Mirren v Inverness CT	1-2/0-1	2-2/2-1	0-0	0-1/1-2	-	-
Scottish League One						
Airdrieonians v East Fife	1-3/2-0	-	1-3/2-1	-	-	1-1/2-2
Alloa v Albion	-	5-1/4-1	-	-	-	0-0/1-1
Ayr v Arbroath	-	2-0/0-1	2-0/2-1	-	-	-
Queens Park v Stranraer	2-0/3-2	-	-	-	-	0-2/0-1
Raith v Forfar	-	-	-	-	-	-
Scottish League Two						
Annan v Montrose	2-1/1-2	2-1/1-1	2-1/1-0	2-2/4-3	3-2/3-3	2-3/5-1
Cowdenbeath v Edinburgh City	-	-	-	-	-	2-0/1-2
Elgin v Clyde	0-3/1-1	2-1/4-2	1-0/3-1	1-0/2-0	1-1/1-0	0-2/4-1
Stenhousemuir v Peterhead	-	-	-	1-2/2-1	4-3/1-4	2-2/3-1
Stirling v Berwick	-	6-3/1-0	3-1/2-1	-	1-3/2-1	0-0/2-2
Saturday January 13, 2018						
Premier League						
Bournemouth v Arsenal	-	-	-	-	0-2	3-3
Chelsea v Leicester	-	-	-	2-0	1-1	3-0
Crystal Palace v Burnley	2-0	4-3	-	0-0	-	0-2
Huddersfield v West Ham	-	-	-	-	-	-
Liverpool v Man City	1-1	2-2	3-2	2-1	3-0	1-0
Man United v Stoke	2-0	4-2	3-2	2-1	3-0	1-1
Newcastle v Swansea	0-0	1-2	1-2	2-3	3-0	-
Tottenham v Everton	2-0	2-2	1-0	2-1	0-0	3-2
Watford v Southampton	0-3	-	-	-	0-0	3-4
West Brom v Brighton	-	-	-	-	-	-
Championship						
Barnsley v Wolves	-	2-1	-	-	-	1-3
Birmingham v Derby	2-2	3-1	3-3	0-4	1-1	1-2
Brentford v Bolton	-	-	-	2-2	3-1	-
Bristol City v Norwich	-	-	-	-	-	1-1
Burton v QPR	-	-	-	-	-	1-1
Cardiff v Sunderland	-	-	2-2	-	-	-
Hull v Reading	1-0	-	-	-	2-1	-
Ipswich v Leeds	2-1	3-0	1-2	4-1	2-1	1-1
Middlesbrough v Fulham	-	-	-	2-0	0-0	-
Millwall v Preston	-	-	-	-	-	-
Nottm Forest v Aston Villa	-	-	-	-	-	2-1
Sheffield United v Sheffield Wed	2-2	-	-	-	-	-

Results cover matches from Premier League to National League and Scottish Premiership to Scottish League Two

	2011-12	2012-13	2013-14	2014-15	2015-16	2016-17
League One						
Blackburn v Shrewsbury	-	-	-	-	-	-
Blackpool v Bristol Rovers	-	-	-	-	-	-
Bradford v Northampton	2-1	1-0	-	-	-	1-0
Bury v Charlton	1-2	-	-	-	-	2-0
Doncaster v Plymouth	-	-	-	-	-	0-1
Gillingham v Rochdale	-	1-2	-	1-0	2-0	3-0
MK Dons v AFC Wimbledon	-	-	-	-	-	1-0
Oldham v Rotherham	-	-	0-2	-	-	-
Portsmouth v Scunthorpe	-	2-1	1-2	-	-	-
Southend v Fleetwood Town	-	1-1	2-0	-	2-2	0-2
Walsall v Oxford	-	-	-	-	-	1-1
Wigan v Peterborough	-	-	-	-	1-1	-
League Two						
Cambridge U v Mansfield	1-2	4-1	-	3-1	1-1	1-3
Carlisle v Crewe	-	0-0	2-1	-	-	0-2
Cheltenham v Accrington	4-1	0-3	1-2	2-1	-	3-0
Chesterfield v Luton	-	-	-	-	-	-
Crawley Town v Barnet	1-0	-	-	-	0-3	1-1
Exeter v Coventry	-	-	-	-	-	-
Grimsby v Newport County	2-2	3-0	-	-	-	1-0
Lincoln v Notts County	-	-	-	-	-	-
Morecambe v Stevenage	-	-	-	0-0	1-4	0-2
Port Vale v Yeovil	-	-	-	4-1	-	-
Swindon v Forest Green	-	-	-	-	-	-
Wycombe v Colchester	0-0	-	-	-	-	0-2
Scottish Championship						
Brechin v Livingston	-	-	-	-	-	0-3/0-2
Dumbarton v St Mirren	-	-	-	-	1-0/2-1	1-1/2-2
Dunfermline v Dundee United	1-4	-	-	-	-	1-3/1-1
Inverness CT v Queen of Sth	-	-	-	-	-	-
Morton v Falkirk	3-2/0-0	1-2/2-0	0-2/1-1	-	1-1/0-1	1-1/2-2
Scottish League One						
Arbroath v Queens Park	-	-	-	1-2/1-1	1-2/0-1	-
East Fife v Alloa	-	0-1/2-1	-	-	-	2-2/0-0
Forfar v Albion	0-2/4-0	4-2/4-2	-	-	4-0/1-0	-
Raith v Ayr	0-1/2-2	-	-	-	-	1-1/2-1
Stranraer v Airdrieonians	-	-	3-1/1-1	1-0/1-0	1-3/4-0	1-2/2-1
Scottish League Two						
Berwick v Annan	0-1/1-3	3-1/0-2	4-2/1-4	2-0/2-2	0-2/3-2	2-0/4-1
Clyde v Stenhousemuir	-	-	-	-	-	-
Edinburgh City v Montrose	-	-	-	-	-	0-1/1-1
Elgin v Cowdenbeath	-	-	-	-	-	3-1/0-0
Peterhead v Stirling	-	2-2/0-0	3-1/0-4	1-1/2-1	-	-
Saturday January 20, 2018						
Premier League						
Arsenal v Crystal Palace	-	-	2-0	2-1	1-1	2-0
Brighton v Chelsea	-	-	-	-	-	-
Burnley v Man United	-	-	-	0-0	-	0-2
Everton v West Brom	2-0	2-1	0-0	0-0	0-1	3-0
Leicester v Watford	2-0	1-2	2-2	-	2-1	3-0
Man City v Newcastle	3-1	4-0	4-0	5-0	6-1	-
Southampton v Tottenham	-	1-2	2-3	2-2	0-2	1-4
Stoke v Huddersfield	-	-	-	-	-	-
Swansea v Liverpool	1-0	0-0	2-2	0-1	3-1	1-2
West Ham v Bournemouth	-	-	-	-	3-4	1-0

Results cover matches from Premier League to National League and Scottish Premiership to Scottish League Two

	2011-12	2012-13	2013-14	2014-15	2015-16	2016-17
Championship						
Aston Villa v Barnsley	-	-	-	-	-	1-3
Bolton v Ipswich	-	1-2	1-1	0-0	2-2	-
Derby v Bristol City	2-1	3-0	-	-	4-0	3-3
Fulham v Burton	-	-	-	-	-	1-1
Leeds v Millwall	2-0	1-0	2-1	1-0	-	-
Norwich v Sheffield United	-	-	-	-	-	-
Preston v Birmingham	-	-	-	-	1-1	2-1
QPR v Middlesbrough	-	-	2-0	-	2-3	-
Reading v Brentford	-	-	-	0-2	1-2	3-2
Sheffield Wed v Cardiff	-	0-2	-	1-1	3-0	1-0
Sunderland v Hull	-	-	0-2	1-3	-	3-0
Wolves v Nottm Forest	-	1-2	-	0-3	1-1	1-0
League One						
AFC Wimbledon v Blackpool	-	-	-	-	-	-
Bristol Rovers v Bradford	2-1	3-3	-	-	-	1-1
Charlton v Walsall	1-0	-	-	-	-	1-1
Fleetwood Town v Blackburn	-	-	-	-	-	-
Northampton v MK Dons	-	-	-	-	-	3-2
Oxford v Bury	-	-	2-1	2-1	-	5-1
Peterborough v Oldham	-	-	2-1	2-2	1-2	1-1
Plymouth v Wigan	-	-	-	-	-	-
Rochdale v Southend	-	4-2	0-3	-	4-1	3-0
Rotherham v Portsmouth	-	-	-	-	-	-
Scunthorpe v Gillingham	-	-	-	2-1	0-0	5-0
Shrewsbury v Doncaster	-	1-2	-	-	1-2	-
League Two						
Accrington v Port Vale	2-2	2-0	-	-	-	-
Barnet v Lincoln	-	-	1-1	1-2	-	-
Colchester v Grimsby	-	-	-	-	-	3-2
Coventry v Swindon	-	1-2	1-2	0-3	0-0	1-3
Crewe v Wycombe	-	-	-	-	-	2-1
Forest Green v Cambridge U	2-1	1-1	3-2	-	-	-
Luton v Morecambe	-	-	-	2-3	1-0	3-1
Mansfield v Cheltenham	-	-	0-2	1-1	-	1-1
Newport County v Crawley Town	-	-	-	-	0-3	1-0
Notts County v Exeter	2-1	-	-	-	1-4	2-2
Stevenage v Carlisle	1-0	1-1	1-3	1-0	0-1	1-2
Yeovil v Chesterfield	3-2	-	-	2-3	-	-
National League						
Aldershot v Ebbsfleet	-	-	-	-	-	-
Boreham Wood v Dover	-	-	-	-	3-0	5-0
Chester v Gateshead	-	-	1-1	1-0	4-2	1-2
FC Halifax v Leyton Orient	-	-	-	-	-	-
Fylde v Macclesfield	-	-	-	-	-	-
Guiseley v Barrow	-	-	2-1	2-3	3-1	1-0
Hartlepool v Wrexham	-	-	-	-	-	-
Maidstone v Eastleigh	-	-	-	-	-	2-1
Solihull Moors v Woking	-	-	-	-	-	2-2
Sutton United v Dag & Red	-	-	-	-	-	1-0
Torquay v Bromley	-	-	-	-	3-7	1-0
Tranmere v Maidenhead	-	-	-	-	-	-
Scottish League Two						
Annan v Peterhead	2-0/0-3	2-1/0-0	2-0/2-1	-	-	-
Berwick v Elgin	1-1/3-3	0-0/2-1	2-3/2-3	1-1/0-2	2-3/2-0	2-4/0-1
Montrose v Clyde	4-0/5-0	2-3/1-1	0-2/0-2	0-3/0-1	2-0/2-1	2-1/1-1
Stenhousemuir v Cowdenbeath	3-1/0-2	-	-	-	4-2/2-3	-
Stirling v Edinburgh City	-	-	-	-	-	1-1/1-0

Results cover matches from Premier League to National League and Scottish Premiership to Scottish League Two

Wednesday January 24, 2018
Scottish Premiership

	2011-12	2012-13	2013-14	2014-15	2015-16	2016-17
Dundee v Hibernian	-	3-1	-	-	-	-
Hamilton v Hearts	-	-	-	-	3-2/0-0	3-3
Kilmarnock v St Johnstone	1-2/0-0	1-2	0-0/1-2	0-1	2-1/3-0	0-1
Motherwell v Ross County	-	3-2/2-0	3-1/2-1	2-2/1-1	1-1/1-2	4-1/0-1
Partick v Celtic	-	-	1-2/1-5	0-3	0-2/1-2	1-4/0-5
Rangers v Aberdeen	2-0/1-1	-	-	-	-	2-1/1-2

Saturday January 27, 2018
Championship

	2011-12	2012-13	2013-14	2014-15	2015-16	2016-17
Barnsley v Fulham	-	-	-	-	-	2-4
Birmingham v Sunderland	-	-	-	-	-	-
Brentford v Norwich	-	-	-	0-3	-	0-0
Bristol City v QPR	-	-	-	-	1-1	2-1
Burton v Reading	-	-	-	-	-	2-4
Cardiff v Bolton	-	1-1	-	0-3	2-1	-
Hull v Leeds	0-0	2-0	-	-	2-2	-
Ipswich v Wolves	-	0-2	-	2-1	2-2	0-0
Middlesbrough v Sheffield Wed	-	3-1	1-1	2-3	1-0	-
Millwall v Derby	0-0	2-1	1-5	3-3	-	-
Nottm Forest v Preston	-	-	-	-	1-0	1-1
Sheffield United v Aston Villa	-	-	-	-	-	-

League One

	2011-12	2012-13	2013-14	2014-15	2015-16	2016-17
Blackburn v Northampton	-	-	-	-	-	-
Blackpool v Charlton	-	0-2	0-3	0-3	-	-
Bradford v AFC Wimbledon	1-2	5-1	-	-	-	3-0
Bury v Peterborough	-	-	-	-	3-1	5-1
Doncaster v Bristol Rovers	-	-	-	-	-	-
Gillingham v Fleetwood Town	-	2-2	-	0-1	5-1	2-3
MK Dons v Rotherham	-	-	3-2	-	0-4	-
Oldham v Plymouth	-	-	-	-	-	-
Portsmouth v Shrewsbury	-	3-1	-	0-2	-	-
Southend v Scunthorpe	-	-	0-1	-	2-1	3-1
Walsall v Rochdale	0-0	-	-	3-2	0-3	0-2
Wigan v Oxford	-	-	-	-	-	-

League Two

	2011-12	2012-13	2013-14	2014-15	2015-16	2016-17
Cambridge U v Notts County	-	-	-	-	3-1	4-0
Carlisle v Forest Green	-	-	-	-	-	-
Cheltenham v Barnet	2-0	1-0	-	-	-	1-2
Chesterfield v Stevenage	1-1	-	-	-	-	-
Crawley Town v Accrington	1-1	-	-	-	0-3	0-0
Exeter v Yeovil	1-1	-	-	-	3-2	3-3
Grimsby v Luton	0-1	4-1	1-2	-	-	1-1
Lincoln v Newport County	2-0	2-4	-	-	-	-
Morecambe v Mansfield	-	-	0-1	2-1	1-2	1-3
Port Vale v Colchester	-	-	2-0	1-2	2-0	-
Swindon v Crewe	3-0	4-1	5-0	2-0	4-3	-
Wycombe v Coventry	-	-	-	-	-	-

National League

	2011-12	2012-13	2013-14	2014-15	2015-16	2016-17
Barrow v Sutton United	-	-	-	-	-	0-0
Bromley v FC Halifax	-	-	-	-	-	-
Dag & Red v Solihull Moors	-	-	-	-	-	4-4
Dover v Guiseley	-	-	-	-	0-0	2-0
Eastleigh v Hartlepool	-	-	-	-	-	-
Ebbsfleet v Boreham Wood	-	-	-	-	-	-
Gateshead v Maidstone	-	-	-	-	-	1-2
Leyton Orient v Aldershot	-	-	-	-	-	-
Macclesfield v Torquay	1-2	-	-	1-0	1-2	2-0
Maidenhead v Chester	-	-	-	-	-	-
Woking v Fylde	-	-	-	-	-	-
Wrexham v Tranmere	-	-	-	-	2-2	0-1

Results cover matches from Premier League to National League and Scottish Premiership to Scottish League Two

	2011-12	2012-13	2013-14	2014-15	2015-16	2016-17
Scottish Premiership						
Aberdeen v Kilmarnock	2-2/0-0	0-2/1-0	2-1/2-1	1-0	2-0/2-1	5-1
Celtic v Hibernian	0-0	2-2/3-0	1-0	-	-	-
Hamilton v Dundee	1-6/3-1	-	0-3/1-1	2-1	1-1/2-1	0-1/4-0
Hearts v Motherwell	2-0/0-1	1-0/1-2	0-1	-	2-0/6-0	3-0
Ross County v Rangers	-	-	-	-	-	1-1
St Johnstone v Partick	-	-	1-1/1-1	2-0	1-2/1-2	1-2/1-0
Scottish Championship						
Dundee United v Morton	-	-	-	-	-	2-1/1-1
Dunfermline v St Mirren	0-0/1-1	-	-	-	-	4-3/1-1
Falkirk v Inverness CT	-	-	-	-	-	-
Livingston v Dumbarton	-	5-0/2-3	1-3/1-2	1-2/1-2	1-1/2-0	-
Queen of Sth v Brechin	-	1-0/2-1	-	-	-	-
Scottish League One						
Airdrieonians v Arbroath	3-3/2-0	-	2-1/2-0	-	-	-
Albion v Stranraer	-	2-1/2-3	-	-	0-2/0-1	3-2/3-0
Alloa v Raith	-	-	1-0/0-1	0-1/0-0	0-1/1-1	-
East Fife v Forfar	4-3/4-0	3-0/1-2	1-3/2-1	-	-	-
Queens Park v Ayr	-	-	-	-	-	-
Scottish League Two						
Clyde v Peterhead	2-0/0-1	0-2/2-0	1-3/0-2	-	-	-
Cowdenbeath v Berwick	-	-	-	-	-	0-2/0-1
Edinburgh City v Annan	-	-	-	-	-	1-0/2-0
Elgin v Stenhousemuir	-	-	-	-	-	-
Montrose v Stirling	-	3-2/2-2	1-2/0-0	-	1-3/1-1	2-2/1-3

Tuesday January 30, 2018

	2011-12	2012-13	2013-14	2014-15	2015-16	2016-17
Premier League						
Huddersfield v Liverpool	-	-	-	-	-	-
Swansea v Arsenal	3-2	0-2	1-2	2-1	0-3	0-4
West Ham v Crystal Palace	0-0	-	0-1	1-3	2-2	3-0

Wednesday January 31, 2018

	2011-12	2012-13	2013-14	2014-15	2015-16	2016-17
Premier League						
Chelsea v Bournemouth	-	-	-	-	0-1	3-0
Everton v Leicester	-	-	-	2-2	2-3	4-2
Man City v West Brom	4-0	1-0	3-1	3-0	2-1	3-1
Newcastle v Burnley	-	-	-	3-3	-	-
Southampton v Brighton	3-0	-	-	-	-	-
Stoke v Watford	-	-	-	-	0-2	2-0
Tottenham v Man United	1-3	1-1	2-2	0-0	3-0	2-1
Scottish Premiership						
Celtic v Hearts	1-0/5-0	1-0/4-1	2-0	-	0-0/3-1	4-0/2-0
Hibernian v Motherwell	0-1/1-1	2-3	0-1/3-3	-	-	-
Kilmarnock v Dundee	-	0-0/1-2	-	1-3	0-4/0-0	2-0/0-1
Partick v Rangers	-	-	-	-	-	1-2/1-2
Ross County v Aberdeen	-	2-1	1-0/1-1	0-1	2-0/2-3	2-1
St Johnstone v Hamilton	-	-	-	0-1	4-1/0-0	3-0

Saturday February 3, 2018

	2011-12	2012-13	2013-14	2014-15	2015-16	2016-17
Premier League						
Arsenal v Everton	1-0	0-0	1-1	2-0	2-1	3-1
Bournemouth v Stoke	-	-	-	-	1-3	2-2
Brighton v West Ham	0-1	-	-	-	-	-
Burnley v Man City	-	-	-	1-0	-	1-2
Crystal Palace v Newcastle	-	-	0-3	1-1	5-1	-
Leicester v Swansea	-	-	-	2-0	4-0	2-1
Liverpool v Tottenham	0-0	3-2	4-0	3-2	1-1	2-0
Man United v Huddersfield	-	-	-	-	-	-
Watford v Chelsea	-	-	-	-	0-0	1-2
West Brom v Southampton	-	2-0	0-1	1-0	0-0	0-1

Results cover matches from Premier League to National League and Scottish Premiership to Scottish League Two

	2011-12	2012-13	2013-14	2014-15	2015-16	2016-17
Championship						
Aston Villa v Burton	-	-	-	-	-	2-1
Bolton v Bristol City	-	3-2	-	-	0-0	-
Derby v Brentford	-	-	-	1-1	2-0	0-0
Fulham v Nottm Forest	-	-	-	3-2	1-3	3-2
Leeds v Cardiff	1-1	0-1	-	1-2	1-0	0-2
Norwich v Middlesbrough	-	-	-	0-1	-	-
Preston v Hull	-	-	-	-	1-0	-
QPR v Barnsley	-	-	2-0	-	-	2-1
Reading v Millwall	2-2	-	1-1	3-2	-	-
Sheffield Wed v Birmingham	-	3-2	4-1	0-0	3-0	3-0
Sunderland v Ipswich	-	-	-	-	-	-
Wolves v Sheffield United	-	-	2-0	-	-	-
League One						
Bristol Rovers v Shrewsbury	1-0	-	-	-	-	2-0
Bury v Blackpool	-	-	-	-	4-3	-
Charlton v Oxford	-	-	-	-	-	0-1
Fleetwood Town v Scunthorpe	-	-	0-1	2-2	2-1	2-2
Northampton v Rochdale	-	3-1	0-3	-	-	2-3
Oldham v Bradford	-	-	1-1	2-1	1-2	1-2
Peterborough v Southend	-	-	-	-	0-0	1-4
Plymouth v Blackburn	-	-	-	-	-	-
Portsmouth v Doncaster	3-1	0-1	-	-	-	1-2
Rotherham v AFC Wimbledon	1-0	1-0	-	-	-	-
Walsall v MK Dons	0-2	1-0	0-3	1-1	-	1-4
Wigan v Gillingham	-	-	-	-	3-2	-
League Two						
Accrington v Stevenage	-	-	-	2-2	0-0	0-1
Chesterfield v Crawley Town	-	-	-	3-0	-	-
Colchester v Newport County	-	-	-	-	-	0-0
Forest Green v Coventry	-	-	-	-	-	-
Grimsby v Cheltenham	-	-	-	-	0-1	0-1
Lincoln v Swindon	-	-	-	-	-	-
Luton v Exeter	-	-	-	2-3	4-1	1-1
Mansfield v Barnet	-	-	-	-	1-1	0-1
Notts County v Crewe	-	1-1	4-0	2-1	-	1-1
Port Vale v Morecambe	0-4	0-1	-	-	-	-
Wycombe v Carlisle	1-1	-	-	3-1	1-1	1-2
Yeovil v Cambridge U	-	-	-	-	2-3	1-1
National League						
Aldershot v Gateshead	-	-	1-2	1-2	1-2	3-0
Boreham Wood v Maidenhead	-	-	-	-	-	-
Chester v Dover	-	-	-	3-1	1-1	5-0
FC Halifax v Dag & Red	-	-	-	-	-	-
Fylde v Eastleigh	-	-	-	-	-	-
Guiseley v Wrexham	-	-	-	-	3-1	2-3
Hartlepool v Leyton Orient	2-1	2-1	-	-	3-1	1-3
Maidstone v Macclesfield	-	-	-	-	-	2-1
Solihull Moors v Bromley	-	-	-	-	-	1-0
Sutton United v Woking	-	-	-	-	-	4-1
Torquay v Barrow	-	-	-	-	2-2	1-1
Tranmere v Ebbsfleet	-	-	-	-	-	-
Scottish Premiership						
Aberdeen v Hamilton	-	-	-	3-0	1-0/3-0	2-1
Dundee v Ross County	1-2/1-1	0-1/0-2	-	1-1	3-3/5-2	0-0/1-1
Hearts v St Johnstone	1-2/2-0	2-0/2-0	0-2	-	4-3/0-3/2-2	2-2
Kilmarnock v Celtic	3-3/0-6	1-3	2-5/0-3	0-2	2-2/0-1	0-1
Motherwell v Partick	-	-	1-0/4-3	1-0/0-0	2-1/3-1	2-0
Rangers v Hibernian	1-0/4-0	-	-	1-3/0-2	1-0/4-2	-

Results cover matches from Premier League to National League and Scottish Premiership to Scottish League Two

	2011-12	2012-13	2013-14	2014-15	2015-16	2016-17
Scottish Championship						
Dumbarton v Brechin	1-0/4-2	-	-	-	-	-
Falkirk v Livingston	4-3/2-5	1-2/2-0	4-1/1-1	0-0/2-0	2-0/1-2	-
Inverness CT v Dundee United	2-3	4-0/0-0/1-2	1-1/1-1	1-0/2-1/3-0	2-2/2-3	-
Morton v Dunfermline	-	4-2/0-1	-	2-1/2-0	-	2-1/0-1
St Mirren v Queen of Sth	-	-	-	-	1-0/2-1	1-3/0-3
Scottish League One						
Arbroath v Albion	6-2/6-1	2-1/2-1	-	1-0/0-2	-	-
Ayr v Alloa	-	0-0/0-2	-	-	-	-
Forfar v Airdrieonians	3-2/2-3	-	3-3/1-1	1-1/2-0	2-3/0-2	-
Queens Park v Raith	-	-	-	-	-	-
Stranraer v East Fife	-	2-6/3-1	2-0/2-0	-	-	1-1/2-1
Scottish League Two						
Annan v Cowdenbeath	-	-	-	-	-	2-0/1-0
Clyde v Edinburgh City	-	-	-	-	-	0-0/3-1
Peterhead v Montrose	2-3/2-1	2-0/0-1	3-0/4-0	-	-	-
Stenhousemuir v Berwick	-	-	-	-	-	-
Stirling v Elgin	-	1-4/1-1	1-1/2-2	-	3-1/0-0	0-4/1-0

Saturday February 10, 2018

	2011-12	2012-13	2013-14	2014-15	2015-16	2016-17
Premier League						
Chelsea v West Brom	2-1	1-0	2-2	2-0	2-2	1-0
Everton v Crystal Palace	-	-	2-3	2-3	1-1	1-1
Huddersfield v Bournemouth	0-1	-	5-1	0-4	-	-
Man City v Leicester	-	-	-	2-0	1-3	2-1
Newcastle v Man United	3-0	0-3	0-4	0-1	3-3	-
Southampton v Liverpool	-	3-1	0-3	0-2	3-2	0-0
Stoke v Brighton	-	-	-	-	-	-
Swansea v Burnley	-	-	-	1-0	-	3-2
Tottenham v Arsenal	2-1	2-1	0-1	2-1	2-2	2-0
West Ham v Watford	1-1	-	-	-	3-1	2-4
Championship						
Aston Villa v Birmingham	-	-	-	-	-	1-0
Barnsley v Sheffield Wed	-	0-1	1-1	-	-	1-1
Bolton v Fulham	0-3	-	-	3-1	2-2	-
Brentford v Preston	1-3	1-0	1-0	-	2-1	5-0
Bristol City v Sunderland	-	-	-	-	-	-
Derby v Norwich	-	-	-	2-2	-	1-0
Ipswich v Burton	-	-	-	-	-	2-0
Middlesbrough v Reading	0-2	-	3-0	0-1	2-1	-
Millwall v Cardiff	0-0	0-2	-	1-0	-	-
Nottm Forest v Hull	0-1	1-2	-	-	0-1	-
Sheffield United v Leeds	-	-	-	-	-	-
Wolves v QPR	0-3	-	-	-	2-3	1-2
League One						
AFC Wimbledon v Northampton	0-3	1-1	0-2	2-2	1-1	0-1
Blackburn v Oldham	-	-	-	-	-	-
Blackpool v Walsall	-	-	-	-	0-4	-
Bradford v Bury	-	-	-	-	2-1	1-1
Doncaster v Charlton	-	-	3-0	-	-	-
Gillingham v Peterborough	-	-	2-2	2-1	2-1	0-1
MK Dons v Portsmouth	-	2-2	-	-	-	-
Oxford v Bristol Rovers	3-0	0-2	0-1	-	1-2	0-2
Rochdale v Fleetwood Town	-	0-0	1-2	0-2	1-0	2-1
Scunthorpe v Rotherham	-	-	-	-	-	-
Shrewsbury v Plymouth	1-1	-	-	0-2	-	-
Southend v Wigan	-	-	-	-	0-0	-

Results cover matches from Premier League to National League and Scottish Premiership to Scottish League Two

	2011-12	2012-13	2013-14	2014-15	2015-16	2016-17
League Two						
Barnet v Notts County	-	-	-	-	3-1	3-2
Cambridge U v Lincoln	2-0	2-1	1-0	-	-	-
Carlisle v Colchester	1-0	0-2	2-4	-	-	2-0
Cheltenham v Port Vale	2-0	1-1	-	-	-	-
Coventry v Accrington	-	-	-	-	-	-
Crawley Town v Grimsby	-	-	-	-	-	3-2
Crewe v Yeovil	-	0-1	-	1-0	-	0-1
Exeter v Wycombe	1-3	3-2	0-1	2-1	0-2	4-2
Morecambe v Chesterfield	-	2-0	4-3	-	-	-
Newport County v Forest Green	0-0	0-5	-	-	-	-
Stevenage v Luton	-	-	-	1-2	0-0	2-1
Swindon v Mansfield	-	-	-	-	-	-
National League						
Barrow v Hartlepool	-	-	-	-	-	-
Bromley v Maidstone	-	-	-	-	-	2-0
Dag & Red v Aldershot	2-5	0-0	-	-	-	1-0
Dover v Sutton United	-	-	-	-	-	3-1
Eastleigh v Boreham Wood	-	-	-	-	1-0	2-2
Ebbsfleet v Solihull Moors	-	-	-	-	-	-
Gateshead v Fylde	-	-	-	-	-	-
Leyton Orient v Tranmere	0-1	2-1	2-0	-	-	-
Macclesfield v Guiseley	-	-	-	-	1-0	1-2
Maidenhead v Torquay	-	-	-	-	-	-
Woking v Chester	-	-	0-1	1-0	5-2	3-1
Wrexham v FC Halifax	-	-	-	-	-	-
Scottish League One						
Albion v Ayr	-	2-0/1-3	-	-	3-0/1-3	-
Alloa v Forfar	-	2-1/1-0	-	-	-	-
East Fife v Queens Park	-	-	-	2-2/0-0	0-2/1-1	1-2/0-0
Raith v Airdrieonians	-	2-0/2-0	-	-	-	-
Stranraer v Arbroath	-	1-1/2-0	3-2/1-1	-	-	-
Scottish League Two						
Berwick v Clyde	0-2/3-0	2-1/3-3	0-1/3-0	4-0/0-0	0-5/3-0	1-1/4-3
Cowdenbeath v Stirling	2-0/4-1	-	-	-	-	0-2/0-2
Edinburgh City v Peterhead	-	-	-	-	-	-
Elgin v Annan	3-0/1-2	2-2/3-1	2-3/2-3	0-0/4-5	3-2/2-2	0-2/3-2
Montrose v Stenhousemuir	-	-	-	-	-	-

Tuesday February 13, 2018

	2011-12	2012-13	2013-14	2014-15	2015-16	2016-17
League One						
Bristol Rovers v Rochdale	-	2-1	1-2	-	-	2-2
Bury v Southend	-	-	1-1	0-1	3-2	1-4
Charlton v Bradford	-	-	-	-	-	1-1
Fleetwood Town v Shrewsbury	-	-	-	-	0-0	3-0
Northampton v Gillingham	1-1	1-2	-	-	-	0-0
Oldham v MK Dons	2-1	3-1	1-2	1-3	-	0-2
Peterborough v Scunthorpe	-	-	-	1-2	0-2	0-2
Plymouth v AFC Wimbledon	0-2	1-2	1-2	1-1	1-2	-
Portsmouth v Blackburn	-	-	-	-	-	-
Rotherham v Oxford	1-0	3-1	-	-	-	-
Walsall v Doncaster	-	0-3	-	3-0	2-0	-
Wigan v Blackpool	-	-	0-2	1-0	0-1	-
League Two						
Accrington v Crewe	0-2	-	-	-	-	3-2
Chesterfield v Cambridge U	-	-	-	-	-	-
Colchester v Coventry	-	1-3	2-1	0-1	1-3	-
Forest Green v Stevenage	-	-	-	-	-	-
Grimsby v Morecambe	-	-	-	-	-	2-0
Lincoln v Cheltenham	-	-	-	-	1-1	-

Results cover matches from Premier League to National League and Scottish Premiership to Scottish League Two

	2011-12	2012-13	2013-14	2014-15	2015-16	2016-17
Luton v Crawley Town	-	-	-	-	0-1	2-1
Mansfield v Newport County	5-0	3-4	2-1	1-0	3-0	2-1
Notts County v Carlisle	2-0	1-0	4-1	-	0-5	2-3
Port Vale v Exeter	-	0-2	-	-	-	-
Wycombe v Swindon	-	-	-	-	-	-
Yeovil v Barnet	-	-	-	-	2-2	0-1

Saturday February 17, 2018

Championship

	2011-12	2012-13	2013-14	2014-15	2015-16	2016-17
Birmingham v Millwall	3-0	1-1	4-0	0-1	-	-
Burton v Nottm Forest	-	-	-	-	-	1-0
Cardiff v Middlesbrough	2-3	1-0	-	0-1	1-0	-
Fulham v Aston Villa	0-0	1-0	2-0	-	-	3-1
Hull v Barnsley	3-1	1-0	-	-	-	-
Leeds v Bristol City	2-1	1-0	-	-	1-0	2-1
Norwich v Ipswich	-	-	-	2-0	-	1-1
Preston v Wolves	-	-	0-0	-	1-1	0-0
QPR v Bolton	0-4	-	2-1	-	4-3	-
Reading v Sheffield United	-	-	-	-	-	-
Sheffield Wed v Derby	-	2-2	0-1	0-0	0-0	2-1
Sunderland v Brentford	-	-	-	-	-	-

League One

	2011-12	2012-13	2013-14	2014-15	2015-16	2016-17
AFC Wimbledon v Bristol Rovers	2-3	3-1	0-0	-	0-0	0-1
Blackburn v Bury	-	-	-	-	-	-
Blackpool v Peterborough	2-1	0-1	-	-	2-0	-
Bradford v Wigan	-	-	-	-	1-1	-
Doncaster v Fleetwood Town	-	-	-	0-0	2-0	-
Gillingham v Walsall	-	-	2-2	0-0	1-2	1-1
MK Dons v Charlton	1-1	-	-	-	1-0	0-1
Oxford v Plymouth	5-1	2-1	2-3	0-0	1-0	-
Rochdale v Oldham	3-2	-	-	0-3	0-0	1-0
Scunthorpe v Northampton	-	-	1-1	-	-	1-1
Shrewsbury v Rotherham	3-1	-	0-3	-	-	-
Southend v Portsmouth	-	-	2-1	2-0	-	-

League Two

	2011-12	2012-13	2013-14	2014-15	2015-16	2016-17
Barnet v Accrington	0-0	1-1	-	-	1-2	2-0
Cambridge U v Grimsby	0-1	0-0	1-2	-	-	0-1
Carlisle v Chesterfield	2-1	-	-	-	-	-
Cheltenham v Wycombe	-	4-0	1-1	1-4	-	0-1
Coventry v Luton	-	-	-	-	-	-
Crawley Town v Lincoln	-	-	-	-	-	-
Crewe v Colchester	-	3-2	0-0	0-3	1-1	2-0
Exeter v Mansfield	-	-	0-1	1-2	2-3	2-0
Morecambe v Forest Green	-	-	-	-	-	-
Newport County v Notts County	-	-	-	-	0-1	2-1
Stevenage v Yeovil	0-0	0-2	-	-	0-0	2-2
Swindon v Port Vale	5-0	-	5-2	1-0	2-2	1-0

National League

	2011-12	2012-13	2013-14	2014-15	2015-16	2016-17
Aldershot v Macclesfield	1-2	-	1-0	0-1	0-3	1-2
Boreham Wood v Gateshead	-	-	-	-	2-3	0-4
Chester v Eastleigh	-	-	-	0-1	1-0	0-1
FC Halifax v Ebbsfleet	-	-	-	-	-	-
Fylde v Leyton Orient	-	-	-	-	-	-
Guiseley v Maidenhead	-	-	-	-	-	-
Hartlepool v Woking	-	-	-	-	-	-
Maidstone v Barrow	-	-	-	-	-	2-1
Solihull Moors v Dover	-	-	-	-	-	2-3
Sutton United v Wrexham	-	-	-	-	-	1-0
Torquay v Dag & Red	1-0	2-1	0-1	-	-	1-0
Tranmere v Bromley	-	-	-	-	4-0	2-2

Results cover matches from Premier League to National League and Scottish Premiership to Scottish League Two

	2011-12	2012-13	2013-14	2014-15	2015-16	2016-17
Scottish Premiership						
Celtic v St Johnstone	0-1/2-0/1-0	1-1/4-0	2-1/3-0	0-1	3-1/3-1	1-0/4-1
Hamilton v Rangers	-	-	-	-	-	1-2
Hibernian v Aberdeen	0-0/0-0	0-1/0-0	0-2/0-2	-	-	-
Motherwell v Kilmarnock	0-0	2-2	2-1/1-2	1-1/3-1	1-0/0-2	0-0/3-1
Partick v Dundee	0-1/0-0	-	-	1-1	0-1/2-4/1-2	2-0
Ross County v Hearts	-	2-2	2-1/1-2	-	1-2/0-3	2-2
Scottish Championship						
Brechin v Falkirk	-	-	-	-	-	-
Dundee United v Dumbarton	-	-	-	-	-	2-1/2-2
Dunfermline v Inverness CT	3-3/1-1	-	-	-	-	-
Livingston v St Mirren	-	-	-	-	0-1/2-3	-
Queen of Sth v Morton	4-1/2-1	-	2-0/3-0	-	2-2/1-0	0-5/3-0
Scottish League One						
Airdrieonians v Queens Park	-	-	-	-	-	4-1/3-2
Albion v Raith	-	-	-	-	-	-
Arbroath v Alloa	-	1-2/0-1	-	-	-	-
Ayr v East Fife	-	2-3/2-1	2-0/4-1	-	-	-
Forfar v Stranraer	-	4-0/3-1	1-2/1-0	1-1/1-0	1-2/1-1	-
Scottish League Two						
Clyde v Cowdenbeath	-	-	-	-	-	5-3/0-2
Elgin v Montrose	3-1/2-1	6-1/3-2	3-3/2-3	0-1/4-0	2-0/1-1	4-1/1-1
Peterhead v Berwick	1-0/1-2	1-0/1-1	1-1/3-0	-	-	-
Stenhousemuir v Edinburgh City	-	-	-	-	-	-
Stirling v Annan	-	5-1/2-1	0-2/1-1	-	1-0/2-1	3-1/1-0
Tuesday February 20, 2018						
Championship						
Aston Villa v Preston	-	-	-	-	-	2-2
Barnsley v Burton	-	-	-	-	1-0	1-1
Bolton v Sunderland	0-2	-	-	-	-	-
Brentford v Birmingham	-	-	-	1-1	0-2	1-2
Bristol City v Fulham	-	-	-	-	1-4	0-2
Derby v Leeds	1-0	3-1	3-1	2-0	1-2	1-0
Ipswich v Cardiff	3-0	1-2	-	3-1	0-0	1-1
Middlesbrough v Hull	1-0	2-0	-	-	1-0	1-0
Millwall v Sheffield Wed	-	1-2	1-1	1-3	-	-
Nottm Forest v Reading	1-0	-	2-3	4-0	3-1	3-2
Sheffield United v QPR	-	-	-	-	-	-
Wolves v Norwich	2-2	-	-	1-0	-	1-2
National League						
Aldershot v Bromley	-	-	-	-	1-1	4-0
Barrow v Gateshead	1-2	0-2	-	-	0-0	0-0
Boreham Wood v Maidstone	-	-	-	-	-	0-1
Chester v Leyton Orient	-	-	-	-	-	-
Dover v Dag & Red	-	-	-	-	-	1-2
Ebbsfleet v Woking	-	2-2	-	-	-	-
FC Halifax v Hartlepool	-	-	-	-	-	-
Guiseley v Fylde	-	-	-	-	-	-
Maidenhead v Eastleigh	-	-	1-3	-	-	-
Solihull Moors v Wrexham	-	-	-	-	-	0-1
Torquay v Sutton United	-	-	-	-	-	2-3
Tranmere v Macclesfield	-	-	-	-	0-1	1-0
Saturday February 24, 2018						
Premier League						
Arsenal v Man City	1-0	0-2	1-1	2-2	2-1	2-2
Bournemouth v Newcastle	-	-	-	-	0-1	-
Brighton v Swansea	-	-	-	-	-	-

Results cover matches from Premier League to National League and Scottish Premiership to Scottish League Two

	2011-12	2012-13	2013-14	2014-15	2015-16	2016-17
Burnley v Southampton	1-1	-	-	1-0	-	1-0
Crystal Palace v Tottenham	-	-	0-1	2-1	1-3	0-1
Leicester v Stoke	-	-	-	0-1	3-0	2-0
Liverpool v West Ham	-	0-0	4-1	2-0	0-3	2-2
Man United v Chelsea	3-1	0-1	0-0	1-1	0-0	2-0
Watford v Everton	-	-	-	-	1-1	3-2
West Brom v Huddersfield	-	-	-	-	-	-
Championship						
Birmingham v Barnsley	1-1	0-5	1-1	-	-	0-3
Burton v Millwall	-	-	-	-	2-1	-
Cardiff v Bristol City	3-1	2-1	-	-	0-0	2-1
Fulham v Wolves	5-0	-	-	0-1	0-3	1-3
Hull v Sheffield United	-	-	-	-	-	-
Leeds v Brentford	-	-	-	0-1	1-1	1-0
Norwich v Bolton	2-0	-	-	2-1	-	-
Preston v Ipswich	-	-	-	-	1-2	1-1
QPR v Nottm Forest	-	-	5-2	-	1-2	2-0
Reading v Derby	2-2	-	0-0	0-3	0-1	1-1
Sheffield Wed v Aston Villa	-	-	-	-	-	1-0
Sunderland v Middlesbrough	-	-	-	-	-	1-2
League One						
Bristol Rovers v Scunthorpe	-	-	0-0	-	-	1-1
Bury v Gillingham	-	-	-	-	0-1	1-2
Charlton v Shrewsbury	-	-	-	-	-	3-0
Fleetwood Town v MK Dons	-	-	-	0-3	-	1-4
Northampton v Oxford	2-1	1-0	3-1	1-3	1-0	0-0
Oldham v Southend	-	-	-	-	2-5	0-2
Peterborough v AFC Wimbledon	-	-	-	-	-	0-1
Plymouth v Bradford	1-0	0-0	-	-	-	-
Portsmouth v Blackpool	1-0	-	-	-	-	2-0
Rotherham v Doncaster	-	-	-	-	-	-
Walsall v Blackburn	-	-	-	-	-	-
Wigan v Rochdale	-	-	-	-	1-0	-
League Two						
Accrington v Cambridge U	-	-	-	2-1	1-1	2-0
Chesterfield v Swindon	-	-	-	0-3	0-4	3-1
Colchester v Barnet	-	-	-	-	-	2-1
Forest Green v Crawley Town	-	-	-	-	-	-
Grimsby v Exeter	-	-	-	-	-	0-3
Lincoln v Crewe	-	-	-	-	-	-
Luton v Cheltenham	-	-	-	1-0	-	2-3
Mansfield v Coventry	-	-	-	-	-	-
Notts County v Stevenage	1-0	1-2	0-1	-	1-0	1-1
Port Vale v Newport County	-	-	-	-	-	-
Wycombe v Morecambe	-	2-2	1-0	0-1	0-2	2-0
Yeovil v Carlisle	0-3	1-3	-	-	0-0	0-2
National League						
Bromley v Barrow	-	-	-	-	5-0	4-1
Dag & Red v Chester	-	-	-	-	-	3-2
Eastleigh v FC Halifax	-	-	-	-	-	-
Fylde v Dover	-	-	-	-	-	-
Gateshead v Solihull Moors	-	-	-	-	-	0-0
Hartlepool v Ebbsfleet	-	-	-	-	-	-
Leyton Orient v Torquay	-	-	-	-	-	-
Macclesfield v Maidenhead	-	-	-	-	-	-
Maidstone v Tranmere	-	-	-	-	-	0-1
Sutton United v Guiseley	-	-	-	-	-	1-0
Woking v Boreham Wood	-	-	-	-	0-0	0-0
Wrexham v Aldershot	-	-	2-1	3-1	3-0	0-2

Results cover matches from Premier League to National League and Scottish Premiership to Scottish League Two

	2011-12	2012-13	2013-14	2014-15	2015-16	2016-17

Scottish Premiership

	2011-12	2012-13	2013-14	2014-15	2015-16	2016-17
Aberdeen v Celtic	0-1/1-1	0-2	0-2/2-1	1-2/0-1	2-1/2-1	0-1/1-3
Dundee v Motherwell	-	1-2/0-3	-	4-1	2-1/2-2	2-0
Hamilton v Partick	1-0/2-2	1-0/0-2	-	3-3/1-1	0-0/1-2	1-1
Kilmarnock v Hibernian	4-1/1-3	1-1/1-3	1-2/1-1	-	-	-
Rangers v Hearts	1-1/1-2	-	-	1-2/2-1	-	2-0/2-1
St Johnstone v Ross County	-	1-1/2-2	4-0/0-1	2-1	1-1/1-1	2-4

Scottish Championship

	2011-12	2012-13	2013-14	2014-15	2015-16	2016-17
Falkirk v Dumbarton	-	3-4/1-3	1-2/2-0	1-1/3-3	2-1/1-0	1-0/2-2
Inverness CT v Morton	-	-	-	-	-	-
Livingston v Dundee United	-	-	-	-	-	-
Queen of Sth v Dunfermline	-	-	-	-	-	2-2/0-1
St Mirren v Brechin	-	-	-	-	-	-

Scottish League One

	2011-12	2012-13	2013-14	2014-15	2015-16	2016-17
Ayr v Airdrieonians	-	-	2-2/3-0	2-3/0-1	3-0/0-3	-
East Fife v Albion	2-0/1-2	1-2/2-0	-	0-0/1-0	-	2-2/2-0
Queens Park v Forfar	-	-	-	-	-	-
Raith v Arbroath	-	-	-	-	-	-
Stranraer v Alloa	2-3/0-4	3-2/1-2	-	-	-	2-5/1-2

Scottish League Two

	2011-12	2012-13	2013-14	2014-15	2015-16	2016-17
Annan v Stenhousemuir	-	-	-	-	-	-
Berwick v Montrose	1-2/2-2	1-4/4-0	1-1/5-0	2-2/3-3	2-1/1-0	1-2/0-1
Cowdenbeath v Peterhead	-	-	-	-	2-2/2-3	-
Edinburgh City v Elgin	-	-	-	-	-	1-2/3-0
Stirling v Clyde	-	0-1/2-0	1-1/4-1	-	0-1/1-2	1-1/3-0

Tuesday February 27, 2018

Scottish Championship

	2011-12	2012-13	2013-14	2014-15	2015-16	2016-17
Brechin v Dunfermline	-	-	1-1/3-2	1-1/3-0	1-6/1-2	-
Dumbarton v Inverness CT	-	-	-	-	-	1-1/3-3
Dundee United v Queen of Sth	-	-	-	-	-	-
Morton v Livingston	2-1/1-3	2-2/2-1	1-5/2-0	-	1-0/2-1	-
St Mirren v Falkirk	-	-	-	-	2-3/0-0	1-1/1-2

Wednesday February 28, 2018

Scottish Premiership

	2011-12	2012-13	2013-14	2014-15	2015-16	2016-17
Celtic v Dundee	-	2-0/5-0	-	2-1/5-0	6-0/0-0	2-1
Hearts v Kilmarnock	0-1	1-3/0-3	0-4/5-0	-	1-1/1-0	4-0
Hibernian v Hamilton	-	-	-	-	-	-
Motherwell v Aberdeen	1-0/1-0	4-1	1-3/2-2	0-2	1-2/2-1	1-3
Ross County v Partick	2-2/3-0	-	1-3/1-1	1-0/1-2	1-0/1-0	1-3
St Johnstone v Rangers	0-2/1-2/0-4	-	-	-	-	1-1/1-2

Saturday March 3, 2018

Premier League

	2011-12	2012-13	2013-14	2014-15	2015-16	2016-17
Brighton v Arsenal	-	-	-	-	-	-
Burnley v Everton	-	-	-	1-3	-	2-1
Crystal Palace v Man United	-	-	0-2	1-2	0-0	1-2
Leicester v Bournemouth	-	-	2-1	-	0-0	1-1
Liverpool v Newcastle	3-1	1-1	2-1	2-0	2-2	-
Man City v Chelsea	2-1	2-0	0-1	1-1	3-0	1-3
Southampton v Stoke	-	1-1	2-2	1-0	0-1	0-1
Swansea v West Ham	-	3-0	0-0	1-1	0-0	1-4
Tottenham v Huddersfield	-	-	-	-	-	-
Watford v West Brom	-	-	-	-	0-0	2-0

Championship

	2011-12	2012-13	2013-14	2014-15	2015-16	2016-17
Aston Villa v QPR	2-2	3-2	-	3-3	-	1-0
Barnsley v Norwich	-	-	-	-	-	2-1
Bolton v Preston	-	-	-	-	1-2	-
Brentford v Cardiff	-	-	-	1-2	2-1	2-2

Results cover matches from Premier League to National League and Scottish Premiership to Scottish League Two

	2011-12	2012-13	2013-14	2014-15	2015-16	2016-17
Bristol City v Sheffield Wed	-	1-1	-	-	4-1	2-2
Derby v Fulham	-	-	-	5-1	2-0	4-2
Ipswich v Hull	0-1	1-2	-	-	0-1	-
Middlesbrough v Leeds	0-2	1-0	0-0	0-1	3-0	-
Millwall v Sunderland	-	-	-	-	-	-
Nottm Forest v Birmingham	1-3	2-2	1-0	1-3	1-1	3-1
Sheffield United v Burton	-	-	-	-	0-1	-
Wolves v Reading	-	-	-	1-2	1-0	2-0

League One

	2011-12	2012-13	2013-14	2014-15	2015-16	2016-17
AFC Wimbledon v Charlton	-	-	-	-	-	1-1
Blackburn v Wigan	0-1	-	4-3	3-1	-	1-0
Blackpool v Northampton	-	-	-	-	-	-
Bradford v Portsmouth	-	-	-	-	-	-
Doncaster v Bury	-	2-1	-	-	1-1	-
Gillingham v Rotherham	0-0	1-0	3-4	-	-	-
MK Dons v Bristol Rovers	-	-	-	-	-	3-3
Oxford v Fleetwood Town	-	1-2	0-2	-	-	1-3
Rochdale v Plymouth	-	1-0	3-0	-	-	-
Scunthorpe v Oldham	1-2	2-2	-	0-1	1-1	1-0
Shrewsbury v Peterborough	-	-	2-4	-	3-4	1-1
Southend v Walsall	-	-	-	-	0-2	3-2

League Two

	2011-12	2012-13	2013-14	2014-15	2015-16	2016-17
Barnet v Port Vale	1-3	0-0	-	-	-	-
Cambridge U v Luton	1-1	2-2	1-1	0-1	1-3	0-3
Carlisle v Grimsby	-	-	-	-	-	1-3
Cheltenham v Notts County	-	-	-	-	-	2-3
Coventry v Lincoln	-	-	-	-	-	-
Crawley Town v Wycombe	-	-	-	-	0-0	1-0
Crewe v Forest Green	-	-	-	-	-	-
Exeter v Chesterfield	2-1	0-1	0-2	-	-	-
Morecambe v Colchester	-	-	-	-	-	1-1
Newport County v Accrington	-	-	4-1	1-1	0-2	1-0
Stevenage v Mansfield	-	-	-	3-0	0-2	0-1
Swindon v Yeovil	-	4-1	-	0-1	-	-

National League

	2011-12	2012-13	2013-14	2014-15	2015-16	2016-17
Aldershot v Hartlepool	-	-	-	-	-	-
Barrow v Eastleigh	-	-	-	-	1-0	4-0
Boreham Wood v Macclesfield	-	-	-	-	0-0	2-4
Chester v Bromley	-	-	-	-	1-1	1-1
Dover v Leyton Orient	-	-	-	-	-	-
Ebbsfleet v Wrexham	0-5	1-1	-	-	-	-
FC Halifax v Sutton United	-	-	-	-	-	-
Guiseley v Dag & Red	-	-	-	-	-	0-2
Maidenhead v Woking	-	-	-	-	-	-
Solihull Moors v Maidstone	-	-	-	-	-	2-0
Torquay v Fylde	-	-	-	-	-	-
Tranmere v Gateshead	-	-	-	-	3-1	0-1

Scottish Championship

	2011-12	2012-13	2013-14	2014-15	2015-16	2016-17
Dundee United v St Mirren	1-1/0-0	3-4	4-0/3-2	3-0	-	2-1/3-2
Dunfermline v Livingston	-	4-0/0-1	-	-	-	-
Inverness CT v Brechin	-	-	-	-	-	-
Morton v Dumbarton	-	3-0/0-3	2-0/3-0	-	0-0/2-0	1-1/2-1
Queen of Sth v Falkirk	1-5/0-0	-	2-0/1-2	3-0/1-0	2-2/2-2	2-0/0-2

Scottish League One

	2011-12	2012-13	2013-14	2014-15	2015-16	2016-17
Airdrieonians v Stranraer	-	-	3-2/1-1	3-3/1-1	0-1/1-1	1-0/1-2
Albion v Queens Park	-	-	2-1/1-0	1-0/2-1	-	2-0/1-1
Alloa v East Fife	-	1-1/1-1	-	-	-	2-1/3-0
Arbroath v Ayr	-	4-2/1-4	0-3/2-3	-	-	-
Forfar v Raith	-	-	-	-	-	-

Results cover matches from Premier League to National League and Scottish Premiership to Scottish League Two

	2011-12	2012-13	2013-14	2014-15	2015-16	2016-17

Scottish League Two

	2011-12	2012-13	2013-14	2014-15	2015-16	2016-17
Berwick v Stirling	-	4-1/1-0	1-1/4-0	-	1-2/1-0	3-2/0-1
Clyde v Elgin	1-2/0-2	2-2/1-1	2-1/4-0	2-1/0-2	4-2/1-0	2-1/3-2
Edinburgh City v Cowdenbeath	-	-	-	-	-	1-1/1-1
Montrose v Annan	2-3/1-1	0-0/5-1	0-2/2-1	2-0/2-1	1-1/0-5	2-2/2-3
Peterhead v Stenhousemuir	-	-	-	1-0/2-0	2-2/4-1	0-2/0-1

Tuesday March 6, 2018

Championship

	2011-12	2012-13	2013-14	2014-15	2015-16	2016-17
Birmingham v Middlesbrough	3-0	3-2	2-2	1-1	2-2	-
Burton v Brentford	-	-	-	-	-	3-5
Cardiff v Barnsley	5-3	1-1	-	-	-	3-4
Fulham v Sheffield United	-	-	-	-	-	-
Hull v Millwall	2-0	4-1	-	-	-	-
Leeds v Wolves	-	1-0	-	1-2	2-1	0-1
Norwich v Nottm Forest	-	-	-	3-1	-	5-1
Preston v Bristol City	-	-	1-0	1-1	1-1	5-0
QPR v Derby	-	-	2-1	-	2-0	0-1
Reading v Bolton	-	-	7-1	0-0	2-1	-
Sheffield Wed v Ipswich	-	1-1	1-1	1-1	1-1	1-2
Sunderland v Aston Villa	2-2	0-1	0-1	0-4	3-1	-

Saturday March 10, 2018

Premier League

	2011-12	2012-13	2013-14	2014-15	2015-16	2016-17
Arsenal v Watford	-	-	-	-	4-0	1-2
Bournemouth v Tottenham	-	-	-	-	1-5	0-0
Chelsea v Crystal Palace	-	-	2-1	1-0	1-2	1-2
Everton v Brighton	-	-	-	-	-	-
Huddersfield v Swansea	-	-	-	-	-	-
Man United v Liverpool	2-1	2-1	0-3	3-0	3-1	1-1
Newcastle v Southampton	-	4-2	1-1	1-2	2-2	-
Stoke v Man City	1-1	1-1	0-0	1-4	2-0	1-4
West Brom v Leicester	-	-	-	2-3	2-3	0-1
West Ham v Burnley	1-2	-	-	1-0	-	1-0

Championship

	2011-12	2012-13	2013-14	2014-15	2015-16	2016-17
Aston Villa v Wolves	0-0	-	-	-	-	1-1
Burton v Bristol City	-	-	-	-	-	1-2
Cardiff v Birmingham	1-0	2-1	-	2-0	1-1	1-1
Hull v Norwich	-	-	1-0	-	-	-
Ipswich v Sheffield United	-	-	-	-	-	-
Middlesbrough v Barnsley	2-0	2-3	3-1	-	-	-
Millwall v Brentford	-	-	-	2-3	-	-
Nottm Forest v Derby	1-2	0-1	1-0	1-1	1-0	2-2
Preston v Fulham	-	-	-	-	1-2	1-2
QPR v Sunderland	2-3	3-1	-	1-0	-	-
Reading v Leeds	2-0	-	1-0	0-2	0-0	1-0
Sheffield Wed v Bolton	-	1-2	1-3	1-2	3-2	-

League One

	2011-12	2012-13	2013-14	2014-15	2015-16	2016-17
AFC Wimbledon v Oxford	0-2	0-3	0-2	0-0	1-2	2-1
Blackburn v Blackpool	-	1-1	2-0	1-1	-	-
Bradford v MK Dons	-	-	1-0	2-1	-	2-2
Bristol Rovers v Northampton	2-1	3-1	1-0	-	0-1	5-0
Bury v Oldham	0-0	0-1	-	-	1-1	0-1
Fleetwood Town v Plymouth	-	3-0	0-4	-	-	-
Peterborough v Charlton	-	2-2	-	-	-	2-0
Portsmouth v Gillingham	-	-	-	-	-	-
Rotherham v Rochdale	-	2-3	-	-	-	-
Shrewsbury v Walsall	-	1-0	0-1	-	1-3	1-1
Southend v Doncaster	-	-	-	-	0-3	-
Wigan v Scunthorpe	-	-	-	-	3-0	-

Results cover matches from Premier League to National League and Scottish Premiership to Scottish League Two

	2011-12	2012-13	2013-14	2014-15	2015-16	2016-17
League Two						
Chesterfield v Lincoln	-	-	-	-	-	-
Coventry v Barnet	-	-	-	-	-	-
Crawley Town v Morecambe	1-1	-	-	-	1-1	1-3
Exeter v Carlisle	0-0	-	-	2-0	2-2	2-3
Forest Green v Notts County	-	-	-	-	-	-
Grimsby v Port Vale	-	-	-	-	-	-
Luton v Accrington	-	-	-	2-0	0-2	1-0
Mansfield v Colchester	-	-	-	-	-	0-0
Stevenage v Crewe	-	2-2	1-0	-	-	1-2
Swindon v Cheltenham	1-0	-	-	-	-	-
Wycombe v Cambridge U	-	-	-	1-0	1-0	1-0
Yeovil v Newport County	-	-	-	-	1-0	1-0
National League						
Bromley v Guiseley	-	-	-	-	2-0	1-1
Dag & Red v Tranmere	-	-	-	0-1	-	0-0
Eastleigh v Dover	-	-	1-0	0-1	2-5	2-4
Fylde v Aldershot	-	-	-	-	-	-
Gateshead v Maidenhead	-	-	-	-	-	-
Hartlepool v Boreham Wood	-	-	-	-	-	-
Leyton Orient v Ebbsfleet	-	-	-	-	-	-
Macclesfield v Barrow	-	2-0	-	-	1-2	0-1
Maidstone v Torquay	-	-	-	-	-	2-1
Sutton United v Solihull Moors	-	-	-	-	-	1-3
Woking v FC Halifax	-	-	-	-	-	-
Wrexham v Chester	-	-	0-2	1-0	3-0	0-0
Scottish Premiership						
Dundee v St Johnstone	-	1-3/2-2	-	1-1/0-2	2-1/2-0	3-0
Hamilton v Motherwell	-	-	-	5-0/2-0	1-0/0-1	1-1/0-1
Hibernian v Hearts	1-3	1-1/0-0	2-1/1-2	1-1/2-0	-	-
Kilmarnock v Ross County	-	3-0	2-0/2-2	0-3/1-2	0-4/0-2	3-2/1-2
Partick v Aberdeen	-	-	0-3/3-1	0-1	0-2/1-2	1-2/0-6
Rangers v Celtic	4-2/3-2	-	-	-	-	1-2/1-5
Scottish Championship						
Brechin v Dundee United	-	-	-	-	-	-
Dumbarton v Queen of Sth	-	-	0-1/0-3	0-4/0-0	0-2/4-2	0-0/1-2
Falkirk v Morton	1-0/0-2	0-1/4-1	3-1/1-1	-	1-0/1-0	1-1/0-1
Livingston v Inverness CT	-	-	-	-	-	-
St Mirren v Dunfermline	2-1/4-4	-	-	-	-	0-1/0-0
Scottish League One						
Arbroath v Forfar	4-1/0-1	1-1/3-1	3-0/2-3	-	-	2-0/0-1
Ayr v Raith	2-1/1-1	-	-	-	-	0-2/1-0
East Fife v Airdrieonians	2-0/2-0	-	1-0/0-0	-	-	0-1/0-4
Queens Park v Alloa	1-3/1-2	-	-	-	-	1-2/0-2
Stranraer v Albion	-	1-1/3-2	-	-	0-1/0-0	3-2/3-0
Scottish League Two						
Annan v Edinburgh City	-	-	-	-	-	1-1/1-0
Cowdenbeath v Montrose	-	-	-	-	-	2-0/0-2
Elgin v Berwick	4-1/4-0	3-1/1-2	2-0/1-3	2-1/3-3	4-1/1-0	6-0/2-2
Stenhousemuir v Clyde	-	-	-	-	-	-
Stirling v Peterhead	-	1-0/0-1	2-0/1-2	2-3/2-1	-	-
Saturday March 17, 2018						
Premier League						
Bournemouth v West Brom	-	-	-	-	1-1	1-0
Burnley v Chelsea	-	-	-	1-3	-	1-1
Huddersfield v Crystal Palace	-	1-0	-	-	-	-
Leicester v Arsenal	-	-	-	1-1	2-5	0-0

Results cover matches from Premier League to National League and Scottish Premiership to Scottish League Two

	2011-12	2012-13	2013-14	2014-15	2015-16	2016-17
Liverpool v Watford	-	-	-	-	2-0	6-1
Man City v Brighton	-	-	-	-	-	-
Stoke v Everton	1-1	1-1	1-1	2-0	0-3	1-1
Swansea v Southampton	-	0-0	0-1	0-1	0-1	2-1
Tottenham v Newcastle	5-0	2-1	0-1	1-2	1-2	-
West Ham v Man United	-	2-2	0-2	1-1	3-2	0-2
Championship						
Barnsley v Millwall	1-3	2-0	1-0	-	2-1	-
Birmingham v Hull	0-0	2-3	-	-	1-0	-
Bolton v Aston Villa	1-2	-	-	-	-	-
Brentford v Middlesbrough	-	-	-	0-1	0-1	-
Bristol City v Ipswich	0-3	2-1	-	-	2-1	2-0
Derby v Cardiff	0-3	1-1	-	2-2	2-0	3-4
Fulham v QPR	6-0	3-2	-	-	4-0	1-2
Leeds v Sheffield Wed	-	2-1	1-1	1-1	1-1	1-0
Norwich v Reading	-	2-1	-	1-2	-	7-1
Sheffield United v Nottm Forest	-	-	-	-	-	-
Sunderland v Preston	-	-	-	-	-	-
Wolves v Burton	-	-	-	-	-	1-1
League One						
Blackpool v Southend	-	-	-	-	2-0	-
Charlton v Fleetwood Town	-	-	-	-	-	1-1
Doncaster v Bradford	-	-	-	0-3	0-1	-
Gillingham v Blackburn	-	-	-	-	-	-
MK Dons v Bury	2-1	1-1	-	-	-	1-3
Northampton v Rotherham	1-1	2-1	-	-	-	-
Oldham v Portsmouth	-	1-0	-	-	-	-
Oxford v Peterborough	-	-	-	-	-	2-1
Plymouth v Bristol Rovers	1-1	1-1	1-0	-	1-1	-
Rochdale v AFC Wimbledon	-	0-1	1-2	-	-	1-1
Scunthorpe v Shrewsbury	-	0-0	-	-	2-1	0-1
Walsall v Wigan	-	-	-	-	1-2	-
League Two						
Accrington v Forest Green	-	-	-	-	-	-
Barnet v Wycombe	-	1-0	-	-	0-2	0-2
Cambridge U v Swindon	-	-	-	-	-	-
Carlisle v Crawley Town	-	0-2	1-1	-	3-1	3-1
Cheltenham v Chesterfield	-	1-0	1-4	-	-	-
Colchester v Yeovil	2-2	2-0	-	2-0	-	2-0
Crewe v Coventry	-	1-0	1-2	2-1	0-5	-
Lincoln v Grimsby	1-2	1-4	0-2	3-2	1-1	-
Morecambe v Exeter	-	0-3	2-0	0-2	1-1	0-3
Newport County v Luton	0-1	5-2	-	1-0	3-0	1-1
Notts County v Mansfield	-	-	-	-	0-2	0-0
Port Vale v Stevenage	-	-	2-2	-	-	-
National League						
Boreham Wood v Tranmere	-	-	-	-	0-0	0-1
Bromley v Dag & Red	-	-	-	-	-	1-3
Chester v Aldershot	-	-	1-1	1-0	8-2	2-0
Dover v Macclesfield	-	-	-	0-1	2-1	2-2
Eastleigh v Leyton Orient	-	-	-	-	-	-
Fylde v Hartlepool	-	-	-	-	-	-
Gateshead v Ebbsfleet	2-3	2-0	-	-	-	-
Guiseley v FC Halifax	-	-	-	-	-	-
Maidenhead v Barrow	-	-	-	-	-	-
Maidstone v Sutton United	-	-	-	-	-	1-1
Solihull Moors v Torquay	-	-	-	-	-	0-1
Woking v Wrexham	-	2-0	2-1	1-1	0-1	2-0

Results cover matches from Premier League to National League and Scottish Premiership to Scottish League Two

	2011-12	2012-13	2013-14	2014-15	2015-16	2016-17
Scottish Premiership						
Aberdeen v Dundee	-	2-0/1-0	-	3-3	2-0/1-0	3-0
Hearts v Partick	-	-	0-2/2-4	-	3-0/1-0	1-1/2-2
Motherwell v Celtic	1-2/0-3	0-2/2-1/3-1	0-5/3-3	0-1	0-1/1-2	3-4
Rangers v Kilmarnock	2-0/0-1	-	-	-	-	3-0
Ross County v Hamilton	1-0/5-1	-	-	0-1/2-1	2-0/2-1	1-1/3-2
St Johnstone v Hibernian	3-1	0-1	1-2/2-0	-	-	-
Scottish Championship						
Brechin v Dumbarton	3-3/2-2	-	-	-	-	-
Dundee United v Inverness CT	3-1/3-0	4-4	0-1/2-1	1-1	1-1/0-2	-
Dunfermline v Morton	-	2-2/1-4	-	1-2/0-4	-	2-1/3-1
Livingston v Falkirk	1-1/1-2	2-1/1-2	0-3/0-1	0-1/2-1	1-2/1-1	-
Queen of Sth v St Mirren	-	-	-	-	0-2/1-0	2-3/0-2
Scottish League One						
Albion v Arbroath	1-0/1-1	4-0/0-1	-	2-1/1-1	-	-
Alloa v Airdrieonians	-	-	-	-	-	1-2/2-1
Forfar v Ayr	-	2-1/2-1	0-1/4-2	2-0/1-3	2-2/3-1	-
Raith v East Fife	-	-	-	-	-	-
Stranraer v Queens Park	2-3/2-3	-	-	-	-	0-2/1-1
Scottish League Two						
Annan v Clyde	1-0/1-0	1-3/0-1	1-2/0-1	2-1/0-1	2-3/3-3	3-2/1-0
Berwick v Stenhousemuir	-	-	-	-	-	-
Cowdenbeath v Elgin	-	-	-	-	-	0-1/1-1
Edinburgh City v Stirling	-	-	-	-	-	2-0/1-0
Montrose v Peterhead	2-1/1-3	2-0/0-6	2-1/2-3	-	-	-
Saturday March 24, 2018						
League One						
Bradford v Gillingham	2-2	0-1	1-1	1-1	1-2	2-2
Bury v Wigan	-	-	-	-	2-2	-
Charlton v Plymouth	-	-	-	-	-	-
Doncaster v Blackburn	-	-	2-0	-	-	-
Fleetwood Town v Northampton	-	1-0	2-0	-	-	3-0
MK Dons v Blackpool	-	-	-	-	-	-
Oldham v Walsall	2-1	1-1	0-1	2-1	1-0	0-0
Peterborough v Bristol Rovers	-	-	-	-	-	4-2
Portsmouth v Oxford	-	-	1-4	0-0	0-1	-
Scunthorpe v Rochdale	1-0	-	3-0	2-1	1-1	2-1
Shrewsbury v AFC Wimbledon	0-0	-	-	2-0	-	2-1
Southend v Rotherham	0-2	1-1	-	-	-	-
League Two						
Accrington v Yeovil	-	-	-	-	2-1	1-1
Carlisle v Cambridge U	-	-	-	0-1	4-4	0-3
Chesterfield v Notts County	1-3	-	-	1-1	-	-
Coventry v Grimsby	-	-	-	-	-	-
Crawley Town v Cheltenham	4-2	-	-	-	-	0-0
Crewe v Newport County	-	-	-	-	-	1-2
Exeter v Swindon	-	-	-	-	-	-
Forest Green v Mansfield	1-1	1-2	-	-	-	-
Luton v Barnet	-	-	2-1	-	2-0	3-1
Morecambe v Lincoln	-	-	-	-	-	-
Stevenage v Colchester	0-0	0-2	2-3	-	-	2-4
Wycombe v Port Vale	-	1-1	-	-	-	-
National League						
Aldershot v Boreham Wood	-	-	-	-	1-2	2-0
Barrow v Dover	-	-	-	-	2-1	2-3
Dag & Red v Fylde	-	-	-	-	-	-
Ebbsfleet v Maidenhead	-	-	1-1	1-0	3-1	2-3

Results cover matches from Premier League to National League and Scottish Premiership to Scottish League Two

	2011-12	2012-13	2013-14	2014-15	2015-16	2016-17
FC Halifax v Solihull Moors	-	-	-	-	-	-
Hartlepool v Bromley	-	-	-	-	-	-
Leyton Orient v Woking	-	-	-	-	-	-
Macclesfield v Gateshead	-	0-4	0-2	1-1	1-0	1-1
Sutton United v Chester	-	-	-	-	-	5-2
Torquay v Guiseley	-	-	-	-	1-1	1-2
Tranmere v Eastleigh	-	-	-	-	1-2	2-1
Wrexham v Maidstone	-	-	-	-	-	1-3

Scottish Championship

	2011-12	2012-13	2013-14	2014-15	2015-16	2016-17
Dundee United v Dunfermline	0-1/3-0	-	-	-	-	1-0/1-0
Inverness CT v Falkirk	-	-	-	-	-	-
Morton v Brechin	-	-	-	2-2/0-2	-	-
Queen of Sth v Livingston	0-2/0-4	-	2-2/2-0	1-1/3-1	1-4/3-1	-
St Mirren v Dumbarton	-	-	-	-	1-2/1-0	0-1/1-1

Scottish League One

	2011-12	2012-13	2013-14	2014-15	2015-16	2016-17
Airdrieonians v Raith	-	0-0/1-2	-	-	-	-
Albion v Alloa	-	0-3/1-5	-	-	-	0-4/1-1
Arbroath v Stranraer	-	2-1/1-0	1-2/4-2	-	-	-
Ayr v Queens Park	-	-	-	-	-	-
Forfar v East Fife	3-2/1-4	3-2/3-2	2-0/1-2	-	-	-

Scottish League Two

	2011-12	2012-13	2013-14	2014-15	2015-16	2016-17
Berwick v Edinburgh City	-	-	-	-	-	1-3/3-2
Clyde v Montrose	1-0/1-2	1-2/1-0	0-3/1-1	1-2/2-0	3-1/3-3	2-1/1-2
Peterhead v Annan	2-3/3-2	2-0/2-0	2-2/3-1	-	-	-
Stenhousemuir v Elgin	-	-	-	-	-	-
Stirling v Cowdenbeath	1-1/0-2	-	-	-	-	1-2/0-3

Friday March 30, 2018

National League

	2011-12	2012-13	2013-14	2014-15	2015-16	2016-17
Boreham Wood v Barrow	-	-	-	-	0-2	1-1
Bromley v Wrexham	-	-	-	-	3-1	4-3
Chester v Torquay	-	-	-	0-2	4-1	1-0
Dover v Tranmere	-	-	-	-	0-0	1-4
Eastleigh v Ebbsfleet	-	-	3-1	-	-	-
Fylde v FC Halifax	-	-	-	-	-	-
Gateshead v Dag & Red	-	-	-	-	-	1-0
Guiseley v Leyton Orient	-	-	-	-	-	-
Maidenhead v Sutton United	-	-	-	-	-	-
Maidstone v Hartlepool	-	-	-	-	-	-
Solihull Moors v Aldershot	-	-	-	-	-	0-2
Woking v Macclesfield	-	5-4	3-2	0-0	2-5	1-0

Saturday March 31, 2018

Premier League

	2011-12	2012-13	2013-14	2014-15	2015-16	2016-17
Arsenal v Stoke	3-1	1-0	3-1	3-0	2-0	3-1
Brighton v Leicester	1-0	1-1	3-1	-	-	-
Chelsea v Tottenham	0-0	2-2	4-0	3-0	2-2	2-1
Crystal Palace v Liverpool	-	-	3-3	3-1	1-2	2-4
Everton v Man City	1-0	2-0	2-3	1-1	0-2	4-0
Man United v Swansea	2-0	2-1	2-0	1-2	2-1	1-1
Newcastle v Huddersfield	-	-	-	-	-	1-2
Watford v Bournemouth	-	-	6-1	1-1	0-0	2-2
West Brom v Burnley	-	-	-	4-0	-	4-0
West Ham v Southampton	1-1	4-1	3-1	1-3	2-1	0-3

Championship

	2011-12	2012-13	2013-14	2014-15	2015-16	2016-17
Barnsley v Bristol City	1-2	1-0	-	2-2	-	2-2
Birmingham v Ipswich	2-1	0-1	1-1	2-2	3-0	2-1
Brentford v Sheffield United	0-2	2-0	3-1	-	-	-
Cardiff v Burton	-	-	-	-	-	1-0
Derby v Sunderland	-	-	-	-	-	-

Results cover matches from Premier League to National League and Scottish Premiership to Scottish League Two

	2011-12	2012-13	2013-14	2014-15	2015-16	2016-17
Hull v Aston Villa	-	-	0-0	2-0	-	-
Leeds v Bolton	-	1-0	1-5	1-0	2-1	-
Middlesbrough v Wolves	-	2-0	-	2-1	2-1	-
Millwall v Nottm Forest	2-0	0-1	2-2	0-0	-	-
Norwich v Fulham	1-1	0-0	1-2	4-2	-	1-3
Reading v QPR	-	0-0	1-1	-	0-1	0-1
Sheffield Wed v Preston	2-0	-	-	-	3-1	2-1
League One						
AFC Wimbledon v Fleetwood Town	-	2-1	2-0	-	-	2-2
Blackburn v Bradford	-	-	-	-	-	-
Blackpool v Doncaster	2-1	-	1-1	-	0-2	4-2
Bristol Rovers v Bury	-	-	1-1	-	-	4-2
Gillingham v MK Dons	-	-	3-2	4-2	-	1-0
Northampton v Charlton	-	-	-	-	-	2-1
Oxford v Scunthorpe	-	-	0-2	-	-	2-1
Plymouth v Southend	2-2	1-1	1-1	2-0	-	-
Rochdale v Shrewsbury	-	-	-	-	3-2	2-1
Rotherham v Peterborough	-	-	0-1	-	-	-
Walsall v Portsmouth	-	2-0	-	-	-	-
Wigan v Oldham	-	-	-	-	0-0	-
League Two						
Barnet v Crewe	2-0	-	-	-	-	0-0
Cambridge U v Crawley Town	-	-	-	-	0-3	2-0
Cheltenham v Carlisle	-	-	-	0-0	-	1-0
Colchester v Luton	-	-	-	-	-	2-1
Grimsby v Stevenage	-	-	-	-	-	5-2
Lincoln v Exeter	-	-	-	-	-	-
Mansfield v Accrington	-	-	2-3	0-1	2-3	4-4
Newport County v Coventry	-	-	-	-	-	-
Notts County v Wycombe	1-1	-	-	-	0-0	0-2
Port Vale v Chesterfield	-	0-2	-	1-2	3-2	1-0
Swindon v Morecambe	3-0	-	-	-	-	-
Yeovil v Forest Green	-	-	-	-	-	-
Scottish Premiership						
Aberdeen v St Johnstone	0-0/0-0	2-0	0-0/1-0/1-1	2-0/0-1	1-5/1-1	0-0/0-2
Celtic v Ross County	-	4-0	2-1/1-1	0-0	2-0/2-0/1-1	2-0
Dundee v Hearts	-	1-0/1-0	-	-	1-2/0-1	3-2
Hibernian v Partick	-	-	1-1/1-1	-	-	-
Kilmarnock v Hamilton	-	-	-	1-0/2-3	1-2/0-1	0-0
Motherwell v Rangers	0-3/1-2	-	-	-	-	0-2
Scottish Championship						
Dumbarton v Livingston	-	3-4/0-3	1-2/2-2	1-0/1-5	2-1/1-0	-
Dunfermline v Queen of Sth	-	-	-	-	-	0-1/1-1
Falkirk v Brechin	-	-	-	-	-	-
Inverness CT v St Mirren	2-1/0-0	2-2	3-0/2-2	1-0	-	-
Morton v Dundee United	-	-	-	-	-	0-0/1-1
Scottish League One						
Alloa v Arbroath	-	2-3/0-1	-	-	-	-
East Fife v Ayr	-	2-3/3-3	1-4/0-5	-	-	-
Queens Park v Airdrieonians	-	-	-	-	-	1-3/2-1
Raith v Albion	-	-	-	-	-	-
Stranraer v Forfar	-	4-1/0-3	0-4/3-1	1-1/4-2	0-0/1-0	-
Scottish League Two						
Annan v Berwick	2-2/1-1	3-2/2-2	3-2/4-0	2-0/4-2	1-0/1-0	3-1/2-1
Cowdenbeath v Stenhousemuir	2-0/0-0	-	-	-	2-2/1-3	-
Elgin v Stirling	-	3-1/1-2	4-0/2-3	-	1-0/2-1	2-3/2-2
Montrose v Edinburgh City	-	-	-	-	-	0-1/3-0
Peterhead v Clyde	0-0/1-1	1-0/3-0	1-1/2-0	-	-	-

Results cover matches from Premier League to National League and Scottish Premiership to Scottish League Two

	2011-12	2012-13	2013-14	2014-15	2015-16	2016-17

Monday April 2, 2018

Championship

	2011-12	2012-13	2013-14	2014-15	2015-16	2016-17
Aston Villa v Reading	-	1-0	-	-	-	1-3
Bolton v Birmingham	-	3-1	2-2	0-1	0-1	-
Bristol City v Brentford	-	-	1-2	-	2-4	0-1
Burton v Middlesbrough	-	-	-	-	-	-
Fulham v Leeds	-	-	-	0-3	1-1	1-1
Ipswich v Millwall	0-3	3-0	3-0	2-0	-	-
Nottm Forest v Barnsley	0-0	0-0	3-2	-	-	0-1
Preston v Derby	-	-	-	-	1-2	0-1
QPR v Norwich	1-2	0-0	-	-	-	2-1
Sheffield United v Cardiff	-	-	-	-	-	-
Sunderland v Sheffield Wed	-	-	-	-	-	-
Wolves v Hull	-	1-0	-	-	1-1	-

League One

	2011-12	2012-13	2013-14	2014-15	2015-16	2016-17
Bradford v Walsall	-	-	0-2	1-1	4-0	1-0
Bury v Rochdale	2-4	-	0-0	-	0-0	0-1
Charlton v Rotherham	-	-	-	1-1	1-1	-
Doncaster v AFC Wimbledon	-	-	-	-	-	-
Fleetwood Town v Bristol Rovers	-	0-3	3-1	-	-	3-1
MK Dons v Blackburn	-	-	-	-	3-0	-
Oldham v Blackpool	-	-	-	-	1-0	-
Peterborough v Northampton	-	-	-	-	-	3-0
Portsmouth v Wigan	-	-	-	-	-	-
Scunthorpe v Plymouth	-	-	1-0	-	-	-
Shrewsbury v Oxford	2-2	-	-	2-0	-	2-0
Southend v Gillingham	1-0	0-1	-	-	1-1	1-3

League Two

	2011-12	2012-13	2013-14	2014-15	2015-16	2016-17
Accrington v Notts County	-	-	-	-	3-2	2-0
Carlisle v Lincoln	-	-	-	-	-	-
Chesterfield v Newport County	-	-	1-1	-	-	-
Coventry v Yeovil	-	0-1	-	2-1	-	-
Crawley Town v Swindon	0-3	1-1	0-0	1-0	-	-
Crewe v Port Vale	1-1	-	1-2	2-1	0-0	-
Exeter v Cheltenham	-	0-1	1-1	1-0	-	3-0
Forest Green v Colchester	-	-	-	-	-	-
Luton v Mansfield	0-0	2-3	-	3-0	1-0	1-1
Morecambe v Cambridge U	-	-	-	0-2	2-4	2-0
Stevenage v Barnet	-	-	-	-	0-0	1-0
Wycombe v Grimsby	-	-	-	-	-	2-1

National League

	2011-12	2012-13	2013-14	2014-15	2015-16	2016-17
Aldershot v Eastleigh	-	-	-	0-2	1-2	0-1
Barrow v Fylde	-	-	-	-	-	-
Dag & Red v Maidstone	-	-	-	-	-	0-2
Ebbsfleet v Dover	-	-	0-2	-	-	-
FC Halifax v Gateshead	-	-	-	-	-	-
Hartlepool v Guiseley	-	-	-	-	-	-
Leyton Orient v Maidenhead	-	-	-	-	-	-
Macclesfield v Chester	-	-	3-2	3-1	1-2	0-0
Sutton United v Bromley	-	-	-	-	-	2-0
Torquay v Woking	-	-	-	1-0	0-1	1-2
Tranmere v Solihull Moors	-	-	-	-	-	9-0
Wrexham v Boreham Wood	-	-	-	-	1-0	2-1

Saturday April 7, 2018

Premier League

	2011-12	2012-13	2013-14	2014-15	2015-16	2016-17
Arsenal v Southampton	-	6-1	2-0	1-0	0-0	2-1
Bournemouth v Crystal Palace	-	-	-	-	0-0	0-2
Brighton v Huddersfield	-	4-1	0-0	0-0	2-1	1-0

Results cover matches from Premier League to National League and Scottish Premiership to Scottish League Two

	2011-12	2012-13	2013-14	2014-15	2015-16	2016-17
Chelsea v West Ham	-	2-0	0-0	2-0	2-2	2-1
Everton v Liverpool	0-2	2-2	3-3	0-0	1-1	0-1
Leicester v Newcastle	-	-	-	3-0	1-0	-
Man City v Man United	1-0	2-3	4-1	1-0	0-1	0-0
Stoke v Tottenham	2-1	1-2	0-1	3-0	0-4	0-4
Watford v Burnley	3-2	3-3	1-1	-	-	2-1
West Brom v Swansea	1-2	2-1	0-2	2-0	1-1	3-1
Championship						
Barnsley v Sheffield United	-	-	-	0-2	1-1	-
Birmingham v Burton	-	-	-	-	-	0-2
Brentford v Ipswich	-	-	-	2-4	2-2	2-0
Cardiff v Wolves	-	3-1	-	0-1	2-0	2-1
Derby v Bolton	-	1-1	0-0	4-1	4-1	-
Hull v QPR	-	-	-	2-1	1-1	-
Leeds v Sunderland	-	-	-	-	-	-
Middlesbrough v Nottm Forest	2-1	1-0	1-1	3-0	0-1	-
Millwall v Bristol City	1-2	2-1	-	-	-	-
Norwich v Aston Villa	2-0	1-2	0-1	-	2-0	1-0
Reading v Preston	-	-	-	-	1-2	1-0
Sheffield Wed v Fulham	-	-	-	1-1	3-2	1-2
League One						
AFC Wimbledon v Scunthorpe	-	-	3-2	-	-	1-2
Blackburn v Southend	-	-	-	-	-	-
Blackpool v Bradford	-	-	-	-	0-1	-
Bristol Rovers v Charlton	-	-	-	-	-	1-5
Gillingham v Doncaster	-	-	-	1-1	1-0	-
Northampton v Shrewsbury	2-7	-	-	1-1	-	1-1
Oxford v Oldham	-	-	-	-	-	1-1
Plymouth v Peterborough	-	-	-	-	-	-
Rochdale v Portsmouth	-	-	3-0	-	-	-
Rotherham v Fleetwood Town	-	2-1	-	-	-	-
Walsall v Bury	2-4	1-1	-	-	0-1	3-3
Wigan v MK Dons	-	-	-	-	-	-
League Two						
Barnet v Forest Green	-	-	2-1	1-3	-	-
Cambridge U v Exeter	-	-	-	1-2	0-1	1-0
Cheltenham v Morecambe	1-2	2-0	3-0	1-1	-	3-1
Colchester v Accrington	-	-	-	-	-	1-2
Grimsby v Chesterfield	-	-	-	-	-	-
Lincoln v Wycombe	-	-	-	-	-	-
Mansfield v Crewe	-	-	-	-	-	3-0
Newport County v Stevenage	-	-	-	2-0	2-2	0-2
Notts County v Coventry	-	2-2	3-0	0-0	-	-
Port Vale v Crawley Town	2-2	-	2-1	2-3	-	-
Swindon v Carlisle	-	4-0	3-1	-	-	-
Yeovil v Luton	-	-	-	-	3-2	0-4
National League						
Aldershot v Maidenhead	-	-	-	-	-	-
Bromley v Gateshead	-	-	-	-	3-0	3-2
Chester v Tranmere	-	-	-	-	0-1	2-3
Dag & Red v Woking	-	-	-	-	-	1-1
Dover v Torquay	-	-	-	2-2	5-0	1-2
Eastleigh v Wrexham	-	-	-	2-2	1-1	1-1
Ebbsfleet v Macclesfield	-	0-4	-	-	-	-
FC Halifax v Boreham Wood	-	-	-	-	-	-
Fylde v Sutton United	-	-	-	-	-	-
Guiseley v Maidstone	-	-	-	-	-	2-1
Hartlepool v Solihull Moors	-	-	-	-	-	-
Leyton Orient v Barrow	-	-	-	-	-	-

Results cover matches from Premier League to National League and Scottish Premiership to Scottish League Two

	2011-12	2012-13	2013-14	2014-15	2015-16	2016-17
Scottish Premiership						
Hamilton v Celtic	-	-	-	0-2	1-2/1-1	0-3
Hearts v Aberdeen	3-0/3-0	2-0	2-1/1-1	-	1-3/2-1	0-1/1-2
Partick v Kilmarnock	-	-	1-1/1-1	1-1/1-4	2-2/0-0	0-0
Rangers v Dundee	-	-	-	-	-	1-0
Ross County v Hibernian	-	3-2/1-0	0-2/1-0	-	-	-
St Johnstone v Motherwell	0-3	1-3/2-0	2-0/3-0	2-1	2-1/2-1	1-1
Scottish Championship						
Brechin v St Mirren	-	-	-	-	-	-
Dumbarton v Dundee United	-	-	-	-	-	1-0/1-0
Falkirk v Dunfermline	-	2-2/1-0	-	-	-	2-1/2-0
Livingston v Morton	1-1/0-0	2-2/0-2	2-2/0-1	-	2-4/0-0	-
Queen of Sth v Inverness CT	-	-	-	-	-	-
Scottish League One						
Airdrieonians v Ayr	-	-	0-1/3-0	3-0/2-0	1-2/0-1	-
Albion v Forfar	1-0/2-2	2-3/1-2	-	-	1-1/3-2	-
Alloa v Stranraer	1-0/3-1	3-0/4-1	-	-	-	2-2/1-0
Arbroath v Raith	-	-	-	-	-	-
Queens Park v East Fife	-	-	-	3-0/1-0	0-2/3-0	1-0/2-2
Scottish League Two						
Annan v Elgin	1-1/1-1	2-0/2-2	2-1/2-0	3-3/2-3	1-1/4-2	1-0/1-0
Berwick v Peterhead	2-1/0-1	1-1/0-2	1-3/1-2	-	-	-
Cowdenbeath v Clyde	-	-	-	-	-	1-0/1-0
Edinburgh City v Stenhousemuir	-	-	-	-	-	-
Stirling v Montrose	-	1-3/3-1	3-1/2-2	-	1-0/7-0	2-0/1-2

Tuesday April 10, 2018

	2011-12	2012-13	2013-14	2014-15	2015-16	2016-17
Championship						
Aston Villa v Cardiff	-	-	2-0	-	-	3-1
Bolton v Millwall	-	1-1	3-1	2-0	-	2-0
Bristol City v Birmingham	0-2	0-1	-	-	0-0	0-1
Burton v Hull	-	-	-	-	-	-
Fulham v Reading	-	2-4	-	2-1	4-2	5-0
Ipswich v Barnsley	1-0	1-1	1-1	-	-	4-2
Nottm Forest v Brentford	-	-	-	1-3	0-3	2-3
Preston v Leeds	-	-	-	-	1-1	1-4
QPR v Sheffield Wed	-	-	2-1	-	0-0	1-2
Sheffield United v Middlesbrough	-	-	-	-	-	-
Sunderland v Norwich	3-0	1-1	0-0	-	1-3	-
Wolves v Derby	-	1-1	-	2-0	2-1	2-3

Saturday April 14, 2018

	2011-12	2012-13	2013-14	2014-15	2015-16	2016-17
Premier League						
Burnley v Leicester	1-3	0-1	0-2	0-1	-	1-0
Crystal Palace v Brighton	1-1	3-0	-	-	-	-
Huddersfield v Watford	-	2-3	1-2	3-1	-	-
Liverpool v Bournemouth	-	-	-	-	1-0	2-2
Man United v West Brom	2-0	2-0	1-2	0-1	2-0	0-0
Newcastle v Arsenal	0-0	0-1	0-1	1-2	0-1	-
Southampton v Chelsea	-	2-1	0-3	1-1	1-2	0-2
Swansea v Everton	0-2	0-3	1-2	1-1	0-0	1-0
Tottenham v Man City	1-5	3-1	1-5	0-1	4-1	2-0
West Ham v Stoke	-	1-1	0-1	1-1	0-0	1-1
Championship						
Aston Villa v Leeds	-	-	-	-	-	1-1
Barnsley v Bolton	-	2-3	0-1	-	-	-
Burton v Derby	-	-	-	-	-	1-0
Fulham v Brentford	-	-	-	1-4	2-2	1-1
Hull v Sheffield Wed	-	1-3	-	-	0-0	-

Results cover matches from Premier League to National League and Scottish Premiership to Scottish League Two

	2011-12	2012-13	2013-14	2014-15	2015-16	2016-17
Middlesbrough v Bristol City	1-1	1-3	-	-	0-1	-
Norwich v Cardiff	-	-	0-0	3-2	-	3-2
Nottm Forest v Ipswich	3-2	1-0	0-0	2-2	1-1	3-0
QPR v Preston	-	-	-	-	0-0	0-2
Reading v Sunderland	-	2-1	-	-	-	-
Sheffield United v Millwall	-	-	-	-	1-2	2-0
Wolves v Birmingham	-	1-0	-	0-0	0-0	1-2
League One						
Blackpool v Fleetwood Town	-	-	-	-	1-0	-
Bradford v Shrewsbury	3-1	-	2-1	-	1-1	2-0
Bristol Rovers v Blackburn	-	-	-	-	-	-
Bury v Northampton	-	-	1-1	2-1	-	3-0
Charlton v Scunthorpe	2-2	-	-	-	-	2-1
MK Dons v Doncaster	-	3-0	-	3-0	-	-
Oldham v Gillingham	-	-	1-0	0-0	2-1	1-0
Oxford v Southend	0-2	2-0	0-2	2-3	-	0-2
Peterborough v Rochdale	-	-	-	2-1	1-2	3-1
Plymouth v Portsmouth	-	-	1-1	3-0	1-2	2-2
Walsall v AFC Wimbledon	-	-	-	-	-	3-1
Wigan v Rotherham	-	-	-	1-2	-	3-2
League Two						
Accrington v Exeter	-	0-3	2-3	2-3	4-2	1-2
Cheltenham v Forest Green	-	-	-	-	1-1	-
Chesterfield v Mansfield	-	-	0-1	-	-	-
Colchester v Notts County	4-2	0-2	0-4	0-1	-	2-1
Crawley Town v Coventry	-	2-0	3-2	1-2	-	-
Grimsby v Barnet	-	-	2-1	3-1	-	2-2
Luton v Crewe	-	-	-	-	-	1-1
Morecambe v Carlisle	-	-	-	0-1	1-2	0-3
Newport County v Swindon	-	-	-	-	-	-
Port Vale v Lincoln	-	-	-	-	-	-
Stevenage v Cambridge U	-	-	-	3-2	2-0	1-2
Yeovil v Wycombe	1-0	-	-	-	0-1	1-0
National League						
Barrow v Ebbsfleet	1-1	1-1	-	-	-	-
Boreham Wood v Chester	-	-	-	-	0-0	1-1
Gateshead v Eastleigh	-	-	-	2-3	2-1	2-2
Macclesfield v Leyton Orient	-	-	-	-	-	-
Maidenhead v Dover	-	-	1-2	-	-	-
Maidstone v Fylde	-	-	-	-	-	-
Solihull Moors v Guiseley	-	-	0-3	0-1	-	3-2
Sutton United v Hartlepool	-	-	-	-	-	-
Torquay v FC Halifax	-	-	-	-	-	-
Tranmere v Aldershot	-	-	-	-	3-1	2-2
Woking v Bromley	-	-	-	-	2-0	2-1
Wrexham v Dag & Red	-	-	-	-	-	0-1
Scottish Championship						
Dundee United v Falkirk	-	-	-	-	-	1-0/1-1
Dunfermline v Brechin	-	-	3-1/2-1	0-0/0-1	3-1/3-1	-
Inverness CT v Dumbarton	-	-	-	-	-	-
Morton v Queen of Sth	2-2/2-2	-	0-2/1-1	-	2-0/3-2	1-0/1-0
St Mirren v Livingston	-	-	-	-	1-1/1-4	-
Scottish League One						
Airdrieonians v Albion	4-0/1-0	-	-	-	1-1/1-1	0-2/1-2
Ayr v Stranraer	-	2-1/2-1	3-6/5-0	0-2/0-2	3-1/2-1	-
East Fife v Arbroath	2-2/1-3	2-1/0-1	2-1/1-0	1-5/2-0	0-1/2-1	-
Forfar v Alloa	-	2-3/0-1	-	-	-	-
Raith v Queens Park	-	-	-	-	-	-

Results cover matches from Premier League to National League and Scottish Premiership to Scottish League Two

	2011-12	2012-13	2013-14	2014-15	2015-16	2016-17
Scottish League Two						
Clyde v Stirling	-	2-1/1-2	2-1/1-0	-	0-1/3-1	1-1/2-3
Elgin v Edinburgh City	-	-	-	-	-	3-0/3-1
Montrose v Berwick	3-5/1-1	3-1/1-3	1-1/0-0	2-1/0-2	4-1/1-0	0-0/2-1
Peterhead v Cowdenbeath	-	-	-	-	7-0/0-1	-
Stenhousemuir v Annan	-	-	-	-	-	-

Saturday April 21, 2018

	2011-12	2012-13	2013-14	2014-15	2015-16	2016-17
Premier League						
Arsenal v West Ham	-	5-1	3-1	3-0	0-2	3-0
Bournemouth v Man United	-	-	-	-	2-1	1-3
Brighton v Tottenham	-	-	-	-	-	-
Chelsea v Huddersfield	-	-	-	-	-	-
Everton v Newcastle	3-1	2-2	3-2	3-0	3-0	-
Leicester v Southampton	3-2	-	-	2-0	1-0	0-0
Man City v Swansea	4-0	1-0	3-0	2-1	2-1	2-1
Stoke v Burnley	-	-	-	1-2	-	2-0
Watford v Crystal Palace	0-2	2-2	-	-	0-1	1-1
West Brom v Liverpool	0-2	3-0	1-1	0-0	1-1	0-1
Championship						
Birmingham v Sheffield United	-	-	-	-	-	-
Bolton v Wolves	1-1	2-0	-	2-2	2-1	-
Brentford v QPR	-	-	-	-	1-0	3-1
Bristol City v Hull	1-1	1-2	-	-	1-1	-
Cardiff v Nottm Forest	1-0	3-0	-	2-1	1-1	1-0
Derby v Middlesbrough	0-1	3-1	2-1	0-1	1-1	-
Ipswich v Aston Villa	-	-	-	-	-	0-0
Leeds v Barnsley	1-2	1-0	0-0	-	-	2-1
Millwall v Fulham	-	-	-	0-0	-	-
Preston v Norwich	-	-	-	-	-	1-3
Sheffield Wed v Reading	-	-	5-2	1-0	1-1	0-2
Sunderland v Burton	-	-	-	-	-	-
League One						
AFC Wimbledon v Oldham	-	-	-	-	-	0-0
Blackburn v Peterborough	-	2-3	-	-	-	-
Doncaster v Oxford	-	-	-	-	-	-
Fleetwood Town v Wigan	-	-	-	-	1-3	-
Gillingham v Blackpool	-	-	-	-	2-1	-
Northampton v Plymouth	0-0	1-0	0-2	2-3	0-2	-
Portsmouth v Charlton	-	-	-	-	-	-
Rochdale v Bradford	-	0-0	-	0-2	1-3	1-1
Rotherham v Bristol Rovers	0-1	1-3	-	-	-	-
Scunthorpe v Walsall	0-1	1-1	-	2-1	0-1	0-0
Shrewsbury v Bury	-	0-0	-	5-0	2-0	2-1
Southend v MK Dons	-	-	-	-	-	1-2
League Two						
Barnet v Newport County	-	-	-	-	2-0	0-0
Cambridge U v Cheltenham	-	-	-	1-2	-	3-1
Carlisle v Luton	-	-	-	0-1	1-2	0-0
Coventry v Stevenage	-	1-2	1-0	-	-	-
Crewe v Morecambe	0-1	-	-	-	-	2-1
Exeter v Crawley Town	-	-	-	-	2-2	0-1
Forest Green v Chesterfield	-	-	-	-	-	-
Lincoln v Colchester	-	-	-	-	-	-
Mansfield v Port Vale	-	-	-	-	-	-
Notts County v Yeovil	3-1	1-2	-	1-2	2-0	0-0
Swindon v Grimsby	-	-	-	-	-	-
Wycombe v Accrington	-	0-1	0-0	2-2	0-1	1-1

Results cover matches from Premier League to National League and Scottish Premiership to Scottish League Two

	2011-12	2012-13	2013-14	2014-15	2015-16	2016-17
National League						
Aldershot v Barrow	-	-	-	-	0-1	2-2
Bromley v Boreham Wood	-	-	-	-	1-2	1-0
Chester v Maidstone	-	-	-	-	-	1-3
Dag & Red v Maidenhead	-	-	-	-	-	-
Dover v Gateshead	-	-	-	1-0	4-0	2-0
Eastleigh v Macclesfield	-	-	-	4-0	1-0	0-1
Ebbsfleet v Sutton United	-	-	-	-	-	-
FC Halifax v Tranmere	-	-	-	-	-	-
Fylde v Solihull Moors	-	-	-	-	-	-
Guiseley v Woking	-	-	-	-	4-4	1-1
Hartlepool v Torquay	-	-	3-0	-	-	-
Leyton Orient v Wrexham	-	-	-	-	-	-
Scottish Championship						
Dumbarton v Falkirk	-	0-2/0-2	1-1/2-1	0-3/1-0	0-5/1-1	2-1/0-1
Inverness CT v Dunfermline	1-1/0-0	-	-	-	-	-
Livingston v Brechin	-	-	-	-	-	2-1/3-0
Queen of Sth v Dundee United	-	-	-	-	-	1-4/4-2
St Mirren v Morton	-	-	-	-	1-1/3-1	1-1/1-1
Scottish League One						
Albion v East Fife	0-3/1-1	0-3/1-1	-	2-0/2-3	-	1-0/0-1
Alloa v Ayr	-	1-0/2-2	-	-	-	-
Arbroath v Airdrieonians	3-1/2-2	-	3-2/0-1	-	-	-
Forfar v Queens Park	-	-	-	-	-	-
Stranraer v Raith	-	-	-	-	-	-
Scottish League Two						
Annan v Stirling	-	5-2/0-1	4-4/1-2	-	1-1/2-2	3-2/4-1
Berwick v Cowdenbeath	-	-	-	-	-	1-1/1-3
Edinburgh City v Clyde	-	-	-	-	-	0-1/0-0
Elgin v Peterhead	6-1/1-2	2-0/0-3	2-4/2-3	-	-	-
Stenhousemuir v Montrose	-	-	-	-	-	-
Saturday April 28, 2018						
Premier League						
Burnley v Brighton	1-0	1-3	0-0	-	1-1	-
Crystal Palace v Leicester	1-2	2-2	-	2-0	0-1	2-2
Huddersfield v Everton	-	-	-	-	-	-
Liverpool v Stoke	0-0	0-0	1-0	1-0	4-1	4-1
Man United v Arsenal	8-2	2-1	1-0	1-1	3-2	1-1
Newcastle v West Brom	2-3	2-1	2-1	1-1	1-0	-
Southampton v Bournemouth	-	-	-	-	2-0	0-0
Swansea v Chelsea	1-1	1-1	0-1	0-5	1-0	2-2
Tottenham v Watford	-	-	-	-	1-0	4-0
West Ham v Man City	-	0-0	1-3	2-1	2-2	0-4
Championship						
Aston Villa v Derby	-	-	-	-	-	1-0
Barnsley v Brentford	-	-	-	-	-	1-1
Burton v Bolton	-	-	-	-	-	-
Fulham v Sunderland	2-1	1-3	1-4	-	-	-
Hull v Cardiff	2-1	2-2	1-1	-	2-0	-
Middlesbrough v Millwall	1-1	1-2	1-2	3-0	-	-
Norwich v Leeds	-	-	-	1-1	-	2-3
Nottm Forest v Bristol City	0-1	1-0	-	-	1-2	1-0
QPR v Birmingham	-	-	1-0	-	2-0	1-1
Reading v Ipswich	-	-	2-1	1-0	5-1	2-1
Sheffield United v Preston	2-1	0-0	0-1	2-1	-	-
Wolves v Sheffield Wed	-	1-0	-	3-0	2-1	0-2

Results cover matches from Premier League to National League and Scottish Premiership to Scottish League Two

	2011-12	2012-13	2013-14	2014-15	2015-16	2016-17
League One						
Blackpool v Shrewsbury	-	-	-	-	2-3	-
Bradford v Southend	2-0	2-2	-	-	2-0	1-1
Bristol Rovers v Gillingham	2-2	0-2	-	-	-	2-1
Bury v Portsmouth	-	2-0	4-4	3-0	-	-
Charlton v Blackburn	-	1-1	1-3	1-3	1-1	-
MK Dons v Scunthorpe	0-0	0-1	-	2-0	-	0-1
Oldham v Doncaster	-	1-2	-	2-2	1-2	-
Oxford v Rochdale	-	3-0	1-1	-	-	1-0
Peterborough v Fleetwood Town	-	-	-	1-0	2-1	1-2
Plymouth v Rotherham	1-4	0-1	-	-	-	-
Walsall v Northampton	-	-	-	-	-	2-1
Wigan v AFC Wimbledon	-	-	-	-	-	-
League Two						
Accrington v Lincoln	-	-	-	-	-	-
Cheltenham v Coventry	-	-	-	-	-	-
Chesterfield v Wycombe	4-0	3-1	2-0	-	-	-
Colchester v Swindon	-	0-1	1-2	1-1	1-4	-
Crawley Town v Crewe	1-1	2-0	1-2	1-1	-	0-3
Grimsby v Notts County	-	-	-	-	-	2-0
Luton v Forest Green	1-1	1-1	4-1	-	-	-
Morecambe v Barnet	0-1	4-1	-	-	4-2	0-1
Newport County v Cambridge U	0-1	6-2	-	1-1	0-1	1-2
Port Vale v Carlisle	-	-	2-1	-	-	-
Stevenage v Exeter	0-0	-	-	1-0	0-2	0-2
Yeovil v Mansfield	-	-	-	-	0-1	0-0
National League						
Barrow v Chester	-	-	-	-	3-2	3-2
Boreham Wood v Guiseley	-	-	-	-	1-0	0-0
Gateshead v Leyton Orient	-	-	-	-	-	-
Macclesfield v Dag & Red	0-1	-	-	-	-	1-4
Maidenhead v Bromley	-	-	0-1	4-4	-	-
Maidstone v FC Halifax	-	-	-	-	-	-
Solihull Moors v Eastleigh	-	-	-	-	-	2-0
Sutton United v Aldershot	-	-	-	-	-	2-0
Torquay v Ebbsfleet	-	-	-	-	-	-
Tranmere v Hartlepool	1-1	0-1	-	1-1	-	1-0
Woking v Dover	-	-	-	6-1	0-1	-
Wrexham v Fylde	-	-	-	-	-	-
Scottish Championship						
Brechin v Queen of Sth	-	0-3/0-6	-	-	-	-
Dundee United v Livingston	-	-	-	-	-	4-3/5-1
Dunfermline v Dumbarton	-	4-0/3-4	-	-	-	3-1/2-2
Falkirk v St Mirren	-	-	-	-	3-0/3-2	3-1/2-2
Morton v Inverness CT	-	-	-	-	-	-
Scottish League One						
Airdrieonians v Forfar	4-4/3-0	-	0-2/5-1	1-2/3-1	0-1/1-1	-
Ayr v Albion	-	2-1/5-2	-	-	1-0/0-1	-
East Fife v Stranraer	-	0-1/1-1	1-2/1-1	-	-	2-0/0-0
Queens Park v Arbroath	-	-	-	0-2/2-1	1-0/2-1	-
Raith v Alloa	-	-	4-2/1-1	1-1/2-1	3-0/0-1	-
Scottish League Two						
Clyde v Berwick	1-4/2-2	2-1/2-1	1-0/3-3	3-3/0-3	1-1/2-1	3-2/1-1
Cowdenbeath v Annan	-	-	-	-	-	2-2/0-1
Montrose v Elgin	3-0/2-3	2-2/4-1	3-3/0-3	2-3/2-1	2-0/3-1	0-5/0-3
Peterhead v Edinburgh City	-	-	-	-	-	-
Stirling v Stenhousemuir	2-2/3-1	-	-	0-4/3-2	-	-
Saturday May 5, 2018						
Premier League						
Arsenal v Burnley	-	-	-	3-0	-	2-1
Bournemouth v Swansea	-	-	-	-	3-2	2-0

Results cover matches from Premier League to National League and Scottish Premiership to Scottish League Two

	2011-12	2012-13	2013-14	2014-15	2015-16	2016-17
Brighton v Man United	-	-	-	-	-	-
Chelsea v Liverpool	1-2	1-1	2-1	1-1	1-3	1-2
Everton v Southampton	-	3-1	2-1	1-0	1-1	3-0
Leicester v West Ham	1-2	-	-	2-1	2-2	1-0
Man City v Huddersfield	-	-	-	-	-	-
Stoke v Crystal Palace	-	-	2-1	1-2	1-2	1-0
Watford v Newcastle	-	-	-	-	2-1	-
West Brom v Tottenham	1-3	0-1	3-3	0-3	1-1	1-1

League One

	2011-12	2012-13	2013-14	2014-15	2015-16	2016-17
AFC Wimbledon v Bury	-	-	0-1	3-2	-	5-1
Blackburn v Oxford	-	-	-	-	-	-
Doncaster v Wigan	-	-	3-0	-	3-1	-
Fleetwood Town v Walsall	-	-	-	0-1	0-1	2-1
Gillingham v Plymouth	3-0	2-1	-	-	-	-
Northampton v Oldham	-	-	-	-	-	1-2
Portsmouth v Peterborough	2-3	-	-	-	-	-
Rochdale v Charlton	2-3	-	-	-	-	3-3
Rotherham v Blackpool	-	-	-	1-1	-	-
Scunthorpe v Bradford	-	-	-	1-1	0-2	3-2
Shrewsbury v MK Dons	-	2-2	0-0	-	-	0-1
Southend v Bristol Rovers	1-1	0-0	1-1	-	-	1-1

League Two

	2011-12	2012-13	2013-14	2014-15	2015-16	2016-17
Barnet v Chesterfield	-	0-2	-	-	-	-
Cambridge U v Port Vale	-	-	-	-	-	-
Carlisle v Newport County	-	-	-	2-3	0-1	2-1
Coventry v Morecambe	-	-	-	-	-	-
Crewe v Cheltenham	1-0	-	-	-	-	0-0
Exeter v Colchester	1-1	-	-	-	-	3-0
Forest Green v Grimsby	0-1	0-1	2-1	2-1	0-1	-
Lincoln v Yeovil	-	-	-	-	-	-
Mansfield v Crawley Town	-	-	-	-	4-0	3-1
Notts County v Luton	-	-	-	-	3-2	0-0
Swindon v Accrington	2-0	-	-	-	-	-
Wycombe v Stevenage	0-1	-	-	2-2	1-0	1-0

Sunday May 6, 2018

Championship

	2011-12	2012-13	2013-14	2014-15	2015-16	2016-17
Birmingham v Fulham	-	-	-	1-2	1-1	1-0
Bolton v Nottm Forest	-	2-2	1-1	2-2	1-1	-
Brentford v Hull	-	-	-	-	0-2	-
Bristol City v Sheffield United	-	-	0-1	1-3	-	-
Cardiff v Reading	3-1	-	-	2-1	2-0	0-1
Derby v Barnsley	1-1	2-0	2-1	-	-	2-1
Ipswich v Middlesbrough	1-1	4-0	3-1	2-0	0-2	-
Leeds v QPR	-	-	0-1	-	1-1	0-0
Millwall v Aston Villa	-	-	-	-	-	-
Preston v Burton	-	-	-	-	-	1-1
Sheffield Wed v Norwich	-	-	-	0-0	-	5-1
Sunderland v Wolves	0-0	-	-	-	-	-

Sunday May 13, 2018

Premier League

	2011-12	2012-13	2013-14	2014-15	2015-16	2016-17
Burnley v Bournemouth	-	-	1-1	-	-	3-2
Crystal Palace v West Brom	-	-	3-1	0-2	2-0	0-1
Huddersfield v Arsenal	-	-	-	-	-	-
Liverpool v Brighton	-	-	-	-	-	-
Man United v Watford	-	-	-	-	1-0	2-0
Newcastle v Chelsea	0-3	3-2	2-0	2-1	2-2	-
Southampton v Man City	-	3-1	1-1	0-3	4-2	0-3
Swansea v Stoke	2-0	3-1	3-3	2-0	0-1	2-0
Tottenham v Leicester	-	-	-	4-3	0-1	1-1
West Ham v Everton	-	1-2	2-3	1-2	1-1	0-0

Results cover matches from Premier League to National League and Scottish Premiership to Scottish League Two

Premier League

Champions	Chelsea
Champions League	Tottenham
	Manchester City
	Liverpool
	Manchester United
Europa League	Arsenal
	Everton
Relegated	Hull
	Middlesbrough
	Sunderland

Championship

Champions	Newcastle
Promoted	Brighton
Playoff winners	Huddersfield
Relegated	Blackburn
	Wigan
	Rotherham

League One

Champions	Sheffield United
Promoted	Bolton
Playoff winners	Millwall
Relegated	Port Vale
	Swindon
	Coventry
	Chesterfield

League Two

Champions	Portsmouth
Promoted	Plymouth
	Doncaster
Playoff winners	Blackpool
Relegated	Hartlepool
	Leyton Orient

National League

Champions	Lincoln
Playoff winners	Forest Green
Relegated	York
	Braintree
	Southport
	North Ferriby

National League North

Champions	Fylde
Playoff winners	Halifax
Relegated	Worcester
	Stalybridge Celtic
	Altrincham

National League South

Champions	Maidenhead
Playoff winners	Ebbsfleet
Relegated	Gosport
	Bishop's Stortford
	Margate

Community Shield

Winners	Manchester United
Beaten finalists	Leicester

FA Cup

Winners	Arsenal
Beaten finalists	Chelsea

League Cup

Winners	Manchester United
Beaten finalists	Southampton

Football League Trophy

Winners	Coventry
Beaten finalists	Oxford United

FA Trophy

Winners	York
Beaten finalists	Macclesfield

Alexis Sanchez's Arsenal toasted FA Cup glory

Celtic captured a memorable treble

Scottish Premiership	
Champions	Celtic
Europa League	Aberdeen
	Rangers
	St Johnstone
Relegated	Inverness

Scottish Championship	
Champions	Hibernian
Relegated	Raith Rovers
	Ayr

Scottish League One	
Champions	Livingston
Promoted	Brechin
Relegated	Peterhead
	Stenhousemuir

Scottish League Two	
Champions	Arbroath
Promoted	Forfar

Scottish Cup	
Winners	Celtic
Beaten finalists	Aberdeen

Scottish League Cup	
Winners	Celtic
Beaten finalists	Aberdeen

Scottish Challenge Cup	
Winners	Dundee United
Beaten finalists	St Mirren

Champions League	
Winners	Real Madrid
Beaten finalists	Juventus

Europa League	
Winners	Manchester United
Beaten finalists	Ajax

Uefa Super Cup	
Winners	Real Madrid
Beaten finalists	Seville

Fifa Club World Cup	
Winners	Real Madrid
Beaten finalists	Kashima Antlers

Middlesbrough backers were counting some big losses in 2016-17

Premier League

Crystal Palace ...... +12.60	Hull .... -1.95
Chelsea.............. +11.78	Arsenal .... -2.26
Watford .... +8.37	Man City .... -3.52
Swansea................ +6.84	Bournemouth.......... -5.43
Tottenham .... +6.64	Leicester .... -5.87
Burnley .... +5.05	Man Utd .... -6.42
Liverpool .... +1.40	Sunderland .... -9.70
Everton .... +0.24	Stoke ....-11.17
West Ham.............. -0.01	Southampton........ -12.86
West Brom............. -0.23	Middlesbrough ...... -26.07

Championship

Reading............... +25.87	QPR .... +0.35
Huddersfield .... +15.93	Cardiff .... +0.05
Leeds.................. +14.02	Ipswich.................. -2.15
Brighton .... +9.99	Burton .... -2.45
Sheff Wed............. +8.57	Norwich .... -5.21
Fulham .... +8.24	Birmingham............ -5.40
Newcastle............ +7.83	Nottm Forest........... -5.84
Barnsley................ +6.00	Bristol City .... -6.18
Brentford .... +5.12	Derby .... -6.89
Preston .... +1.83	Aston Villa .... -12.03
Wolves .... +1.01	Wigan .... -15.14
Blackburn .... +0.79	Rotherham............. -27.80

All profit & loss figures calculated to a £1 level stake at best bookmakers' odds published in the Racing Post on match day

League One

Fleetwood .... +19.14	Bristol Rovers........... -5.43
Southend............. +13.65	Bradford .... -5.53
Bolton.................. +12.72	MK Dons.................. -5.96
Scunthorpe .... +7.84	AFC Wimbledon....... -6.76
Sheff Utd .... +7.54	Oldham .... -7.16
Oxford Utd............ +6.72	Port Vale .... -9.38
Shrewsbury .... +2.65	Gillingham.............. -9.68
Walsall .... -0.27	Bury .... -9.80
Rochdale .... -1.47	Charlton .... -9.89
Peterborough.......... -1.70	Northampton.......... -10.58
Swindon .... -4.30	Chesterfield .... -14.43
Millwall .... -4.83	Coventry............... -20.66

League Two

Plymouth .... +18.62	Portsmouth............ +0.91
Stevenage........... +14.99	Accrington .... -0.57
Exeter .... +11.96	Blackpool................ -0.97
Morecambe .... +10.10	Luton...................... -1.22
Notts County .... +5.67	Mansfield .... -2.36
Grimsby................ +4.72	Barnet..................... -3.63
Doncaster .... +3.90	Newport County ...... -4.65
Colchester............. +3.18	Carlisle .... -5.28
Crewe .... +2.40	Hartlepool .... -6.52
Cambridge Utd ...... +2.04	Cheltenham .... -13.33
Wycombe .... +1.61	Yeovil .... -13.69
Crawley .... +0.94	Leyton Orient......... -15.15

National League

North Ferriby .... +31.40	Forest Green .... +0.23
Lincoln................ +14.19	Solihull Moors .... -0.76
Dagenham & R .... +13.64	Guiseley................... -1.13
Aldershot .... +10.67	Boreham Wood........ -3.03
Bromley .... +8.65	Southport .... -3.57
Tranmere .... +6.36	Braintree................ -4.01
Maidstone .... +5.65	Woking................... -4.05
Dover .... +5.19	Wrexham................ -7.03
Gateshead .... +4.79	Chester.................. -7.49
Barrow .... +3.51	Sutton Utd .... -11.07
Torquay .... +1.66	Eastleigh.............. -14.91
Macclesfield.......... +1.25	York...................... -19.69

Scottish Premiership

St Johnstone .... +9.63	Ross County............ -4.73
Celtic .... +7.62	Motherwell............. -9.05
Aberdeen.............. +4.72	Hamilton.............. -10.80
Kilmarnock............ -0.93	Partick................. -11.18
Rangers .... -3.09	Hearts.................. -14.46
Dundee.................. -4.38	Inverness CT .... -19.37

Scottish Championship

Dumbarton .... +0.15	Hibernian............... -5.44
Falkirk.................. -0.14	Dunfermline........... -5.93
Morton .... -1.62	Dundee Utd .... -8.30
Ayr .... -4.90	Queen of Sth.......... -8.87
St Mirren .... -5.35	Raith..................... -8.96

Scottish League One

Livingston........... +13.42	East Fife................ +1.75
Airdrieonians .... +8.61	Alloa...................... -0.65
Brechin .... +7.02	Albion................... -1.70
Stenhousemuir...... +6.63	Peterhead .... -5.28
Queen's Park......... +4.63	Stranraer................ -7.83

Scottish League Two

Annan .... +17.06	Stirling.................. +1.22
Montrose............ +12.78	Berwick.................. -7.40
Arbroath .... +8.19	Elgin City............... -8.42
Edinburgh City....... +3.60	Cowdenbeath........ -11.20
Forfar .... +1.36	Clyde .... -14.63

SOCCERBASE.COM

Italian Serie A

Atalanta .... +16.91	Sassuolo .... -1.33
Roma.................... +9.48	Fiorentina .... -3.13
Sampdoria .... +6.59	Palermo .... -3.60
Chievo .... +4.16	Crotone .... -3.74
Cagliari .... +4.07	Empoli .... -3.83
Napoli .... +3.51	Udinese .... -5.68
Juventus .... +3.24	Genoa .... -9.71
Lazio .... +1.29	Bologna .... -10.00
Inter .... -0.14	Torino .... -11.54
Milan..................... -0.73	Pescara .... -25.75

Spanish Primera Liga

Alaves .... +50.41	Malaga................... -2.87
Villarreal .... +12.04	Atletico Madrid........ -3.58
Real Sociedad .... +6.96	Valencia................. -4.78
Seville.................. +4.30	Real Betis............... -7.47
Eibar.................... +2.83	Deportivo .... -9.35
Espanyol .... +1.65	Las Palmas .... -13.48
Real Madrid........... +1.64	Leganes .... -15.37
Barcelona .... -0.69	Sporting Gijon ...... -16.95
Athletic Bilbao .... -1.12	Osasuna .... -18.40
Celta Vigo............... -1.55	Granada .... -24.13

German Bundesliga

Werder Bremen.... +10.72	B M'gladbach .... -4.15
RB Leipzig........... +10.71	Wolfsburg............... -4.21
Hoffenheim.......... +10.56	B Dortmund .... -5.08
Freiburg .... +9.57	Cologne .... -5.87
Hertha Berlin .... +5.41	Ingolstadt .... -6.76
Darmstadt .... +4.45	Augsburg................ -7.29
E Frankfurt............ +0.46	Bayer Leverkusen.... -7.58
Hamburg .... -0.65	Mainz .... -9.42
Bayern Munich .... -1.68	Schalke .... -9.67

French Ligue 1

Nice.................... +20.06	Paris St-Germain ...... -1.29
Monaco .... +17.86	Marseille................ -5.52
Metz...................... +7.64	Caen...................... -6.12
Guingamp .... +5.50	St-Etienne .... -6.73
Lyon .... +2.21	Toulouse .... -7.42
Angers.................. +1.53	Rennes .... -7.76
Nantes.................. +1.25	Montpellier............. -9.42
Lorient .... +0.25	Bastia .... -9.84
Lille .... -0.13	Nancy .... -14.23
Bordeaux................ -0.67	Dijon .... -15.00

Multiple bets

Selections	2	3	4	5	6	7
Doubles	1	3	6	10	15	21
Trebles		1	4	10	20	35
Fourfolds			1	5	15	35
Fivefolds				1	6	21
Sixfolds					1	7
Sevenfolds						1
Full cover	3	7	15	31	63	127

Patent (3 selections, 7 bets) 3 singles, 3 doubles, 1 treble
Trixie (3 selections, 4 bets) 3 doubles, 1 treble

Yankee (4 selections, 11 bets) 6 doubles, 4 trebles, 1 four-fold
Lucky 15 (4 selections, 15 bets) 4 singles,

6 doubles, 4 trebles, 1 four-fold
Canadian (5 selections, 26 bets) 10 doubles, 10 trebles, 5 four-folds, 1 five-fold
Lucky 31 (5 selections, 31 bets) 5 singles, 10 doubles, 10 trebles, 5 four-folds, 1 five-fold
Heinz (6 selections, 57 bets) 15 doubles, 20 trebles, 15 four-folds, 6 five-folds, 1 six-fold

Lucky 63 (6 selections, 63 bets) 6 singles, 15 doubles, 20 trebles, 15 four-folds, 6 five-folds, 1 six-fold
Super Heinz (7 selections, 120 bets) 21 doubles, 35 trebles, 35 four-folds, 21 five-folds, 7 six-folds, 1 seven-fold
Goliath (8 selections, 247 bets) 28 doubles, 56 trebles, 70 four-folds, 56 five-folds, 28 six-folds, 8 seven-folds, 1 eight-fold

INDEX OF TEAMS